HUMAN COMMUNICATION

HUMAN COMMUNICATION

The Basic Course

EIGHTH EDITION

Joseph A. DeVito

Hunter College of the City University of New York

LONGMAN

An imprint of Addison Wesley Longman, Inc.

New York • Reading, Massachusetts • Menlo Park, California • Harlow, England
Don Mills, Ontario • Sydney • Mexico City • Madrid • Amsterdam

Editor-in-Chief: Priscilla McGeehon
Acquisitions Editor: Michael Greer
Development Director: Lisa Pinto
Marketing Manager: Megan Galvin
Supplements Editor: Mark Toews
Full Service Production Manager: Eric Jorgensen
Project Coordination, Text Design, and Electronic Page Makeup: Electronic Publishing Services Inc., NYC
Cover Design Manager: Nancy Danahy
Cover Designer: Kay Petronio
Cover Illustration: Jerry Nelson/Illustration Works, Inc.
Photo Researcher: Julie Tesser
Senior Print Buyer: Hugh Crawford
Printer and Binder: World Color Versailles Book Services
Cover Printer: The Lehigh Press, Inc.

Library of Congress Cataloging-in-Publication Data

DeVito, Joseph A.
    Human Communication : the basic course / Joseph A. DeVito. -- 8th ed.
        p.   cm.
    Includes bibliographical references and index.
    ISBN 0-321-04420-7
    1. Communication.   I. Title.
  P90.D485   2000
  302.2--dc21   99-19728
                                                 CIP

Please visit our website at http://www.awlonline.com

ISBN 0-321-04420-7

12345678910—WCV—02010099

CONTENTS IN BRIEF

CONTENTS IN DETAIL

SPECIALIZED CONTENTS

BUILDING COMMUNICATION SKILLS

UNDERSTANDING THEORY AND RESEARCH

MEDIA WATCH

SELF-TESTS

SELF-TESTS (continued)

PREFACE

It's a real pleasure to write a preface to a book that is now in its eighth edition. *Human Communication: The Basic Course* is designed for the introductory college course that surveys the broad field of communication. It covers classic approaches and new developments; it covers research and theory and now, in this edition, gives coordinate attention to significant communication skills.

The book is addressed to students who have little or no prior background in communication. For those students who will take this course as their only communication course, it will provide a thorough foundation in the theory, research, and skills of this essential liberal art. For those who will take additional and advanced courses or who are beginning their majors in communication, it will provide the essential foundation for more advanced and specialized study.

MAJOR FEATURES OF HUMAN COMMUNICATION

The eighth edition, revised in light of comments from a large number of instructors, builds on the successful features of previous editions but represents a major revision. Consequently, the major features of the text (especially those new to this edition) and how they are presented, need to be explained.

Comprehensive Coverage of Human Communication

The eighth edition of Human Communication offers comprehensive coverage of the fundamentals of human communication, including perception, listening, self, and verbal and nonverbal messages [Chapters 1-8]; interpersonal communication [Chapters 9-11]; small group communication, including interviewing [Chapters 12-14], and public speaking [Chapters 15-19]. Because we have combined and consolidated some material, the number of units has been reduced from 23 in the previous edition to 19 in this eighth edition.

Balance of Theory/Research and Skills

The eighth edition gives coordinate emphasis to research and theory, on the one hand, and practical communication skills, on the other. To this end, "Understanding Theory and Research" boxes appear throughout the text and highlight just a small sampling of the many theories and research findings in communication. These boxes provide an introductory explanation of how we know what we know about communication, how researchers go about expanding our knowledge of communication in all its forms, and some of the interesting theories and research findings. In addition, theories and research are discussed throughout the text. Ideally, theory and research, only introduced in this text, will be continued and expanded in depth and breadth by more advanced and more specialized communication courses and texts. A complete list of these "Understanding Theory and Research" boxes appears in the Specialized Table of Contents on page xii.

Similarly, "Building Communication Skills" boxes appear throughout the text and identify and provide practice in some of the more important skills in human communication. In addition, skills implications are discussed throughout. A complete list of these "Building Communication Skills" boxes appears in the Specialized Table of Contents on page xi.

Thorough Coverage of Public Speaking

In this eighth edition, five full units (instead of the previous edition's three units) are devoted to public speaking. The first three of these units cover the essential ten-steps for preparing and presenting a public speech.

Unit 15, "Public Speaking Topics, Audiences, and Research," introduces the study of public speaking, its nature, benefits, and historical roots, and the first three steps for speech preparation:

1. select your topic and purpose
2. analyze your audience
3. research your topic

Unit 16, "Supporting and Organizing Your Speech," covers four steps:

4. formulate your thesis and major propositions
5. support your major propositions
6. organize your speech
7. construct your conclusion, introduction, and transitions

Unit 17, "Style and Delivery," covers the remaining three steps:

8. word your speech
9. rehearse your speech
10. present your speech

The next two units (Units 18 and 19) cover informative and persuasive speeches respectively—the types of speeches and the strategies for informing and persuading an audience.

Inclusion of Cultural Issues

This edition—as did the previous edition—reflects the growing importance of culture and intercultural interactions in all forms of human communication. There are few communications that are not influenced by culture in some way. Thus, a cultural consciousness is essential in any text in communication. In this eighth edition, this cultural consciousness and coverage is seen in several ways.

1. First, a cultural perspective is established in Unit 1 where the nature of culture and the aim of a cultural perspective are explained.
2. Second, an entire unit (Unit 6, "Culture") more fully explains the nature of culture and some of the ways in which cultures differ from one another and the influences these differences have on communication.
3. Third, cultural issues are integrated throughout the text. Here are major examples:
   - Unit 1 discusses the relevance of culture and the aim of the cultural perspective presented in this text, the cultural context of communication, and the relationship of culture to competence.
   - Unit 2 considers the role of culture in the principles of adjustment and communication accommodation.
   - Unit 3 considers cultural variations in implicit personality theory and the role of culture in uncertainty.
   - Unit 4 considers a variety of cultural and gender differences in listening.
   - Unit 5 considers the role of culture in developing self-concept and its influence in self-disclosure.
   - Unit 6 is devoted entirely to culture and focuses on the connection between culture and communication, the ways in which cultures differ (collective and individual, high and low context, power distance, and masculine and feminine), and the nature of intercultural communication.
   - Unit 7 looks at cultural and gender rules in verbal messages, for example, directness and politeness; sexist, heterosexist, and racist language, and the cultural identifiers people prefer.
   - Unit 8 looks at the cultural influences on each of the major types of nonverbal communication.
   - Unit 9 examines the cultural influences on conversational rules and the nature of cultural sensitivity as a general conversational skill.
   - Unit 10 looks at cultural influences on interpersonal relationship rules and the cultural bias in relationship research.
   - Unit 11 discusses cultural and gender differences on interpersonal conflict and the importance of face-saving in different cultures.
   - Unit 12 looks at the cultural customs and differences in interviewing styles and preferences.
   - Unit 13 examines the small group as a culture and looks at the role of norms in small group communication.
   - Unit 14 looks at small group membership and leadership in cultural perspective.
   - Unit 15 covers cultural sensitivity and speech topics, cultural factors in audience analysis, and sacred and secular cultures.
   - Unit 16 discusses cultural considerations in organization (high and low context cultures), cultural sensitivity in presentation aids, and culture shock (in sample outlines and in the illustration of a PowerPoint Speech).
   - Unit 17 covers the role of culture in emotional display.
   - Unit 18 discusses the cultural implications of the knowledge gap hypothesis.
   - Unit 19 explains some of the cultural differences in persuasive strategies.

Coverage of Mass Media

The coverage of mass media continues to be presented in "Media Watch" boxes that interject important concepts from and about the media. Sixteen "Media Watch" boxes are presented throughout the text. These boxes integrate mass media with the other areas of communication and sensitize the reader to the ever-present, ever-influential media. They also connect the concepts of interpersonal, small group, and public speaking with the concepts and theories of the media. These "Media Watch" boxes cover these three major areas:

Media theories:
uses and gratifications theory (Unit 2); cultivation theory (Unit 3): cultural imperialism (Unit 6); spiral of silence (Unit 9); agenda-setting theory (Unit 14); the knowledge gap hypothesis (Unit 18)

Central concepts:
media ethics (Unit 1); outing (Unit 5); gatekeepers (Unit 13); reversing the process of media influence (Unit 17); media credibility (Unit 19)

Types and forms of media:
talk radio (Unit 4); human communication in cyberspace (Unit 7); legible clothing (Unit 8); parasocial relationships (Unit 10); the television talk show (Unit 12)

Integration of Technology

A special goal of this revision was to integrate the new technologies into human communication. This was done in a number of ways. First, there are numerous sections throughout the text that cover communication via computer, for example:

- politeness (netiquette) on the net is discussed in Unit 7, "Verbal Messages."
- online relationships are discussed in Unit 10, "Interpersonal Relationships."
- online conflicts are discussed in Unit 11, "Conflict."
- the web's value and how to use it in seeking employment and in preparing for interviews is covered in Unit 12, "Interviewing."
- Listservs and IRC groups as small groups are discussed in Unit 13, "Small Groups."
- how to conduct research using email, newsgroups, and the web and how to evaluate In-

ternet (and CD ROM) material is presented in detail in Unit 15, "Public Speaking Topics, Audiences, and Research." In addition, Internet sources are integrated along side print sources throughout the discussion of research materials.

- a thorough discussion of computer assisted presentations in public speaking is presented in Unit 16, "Supporting and Organizing Your Speech." Here the values of computer assisted presentations are discussed along with suggesting for preparing slides and for presenting them to an audience. In addition, a complete Slide Show Speech (prepared in PowerPoint) is presented as an example.

A second major way in which the new technologies are integrated is in the website exercises, "Going Online," that appear throughout the text. These pages will introduce students to websites helpful in learning about and mastering the skills of human communication. Some of these websites are largely academic—for example, the websites of the National Communication Association and The International Listening Association—and will help in illustrating the breadth and depth of the study of human communication. Others more playfully introduce a different perspective on human communication—for example, a website that writes love letters, will prove useful in examining the theories of interpersonal relationships.

Integrated Coverage of Ethical Issues

In this edition, ethical issues are woven into the discussions throughout the text. Among the most important discussions are the following:

- Unit 1, "Preliminaries to Human Communication," introduces ethics as an essential element in the communication process and discusses ethics and individual choice. Also, a media watch box discusses media ethics.
- Unit 4, "Listening," considers the ethical responsibilities of the listener.
- Unit 7, "Verbal Messages," includes a discussion of how language can be used unethically, particularly in lying and in gossiping.
- Unit 13, "Small Groups," includes the National Communication Association's "Credo for Free and Responsible Use of Electronic Communication Networks" which serves as a

useful reminder that even in using the most sophisticated technologies ethical considerations are still crucial.

- Unit 15, "Public Speaking Topics, Audiences, and Research," which introduces public speaking, discusses general ethical issues in public speaking, plagiarism, and the ethical responsibility to benefit the audience.
- Unit 17, "Style and Delivery," discusses when speech is unethical and offers an exercise exploring responding to audience questions both strategically and ethically.
- Unit 19, "The Persuasive Speech," discusses persuasive strategies and ethics (identifying eight unethical persuasive techniques), the ethics of emotional appeals, and the ethics of credibility appeals.

Interactive Pedagogy

As in previous editions, *Human Communication* continues to emphasize new and useful pedagogical aids, especially those that are interactive, to help the student better understand the theory and research and to effectively build and polish the skills of human communication.

- **Self-Tests.** These popular interactive self-tests, called "Test Yourself," have been increased to 28 in this edition. These self-tests are designed to help personalize the material and they appear throughout the text. Fourteen of these are research-based instruments and fourteen serve a more purely pedagogical function of introducing the material covered in the unit.
- **Critical thinking questions.** These questions, appearing at the end of each unit, now focus more clearly on the central concepts and skills of the unit. These questions will prove useful for expanding upon, evaluating, and applying the concepts, theories, and research findings discussed in the text.
- **Key terms and glossary.** A list of key terms is provided at the end of each unit to facilitate reviewing the major terms and concepts discussed in the unit. Each term is followed by the page number on which the term is introduced. In addition, a thorough glossary at the end of the book provides brief definitions of the significant concepts and skills in the study of human communication.

- **Unit openers.** The major topics covered in the unit and the learning goals that the reader should be able to achieve are identified in the unit opening grids.
- **Summary statements.** At the end of each unit appears a list of summary propositions that review the essential concepts and principles covered in the unit.

SUPPLEMENTARY MATERIALS

The ancillary package for the eighth edition of *Human Communication* includes the following instructional resources:

Resources for Instructors

Instructor's Manual/ Test Bank with Transparency Masters

The Instructor's Manual includes chapter objectives, chapter outlines, a wealth of thought-provoking discussion questions, a section devoted to active learning ideas, and a set of transparency masters. The Test Bank contains hundreds of challenging and thoroughly revised multiple-choice, true-false, and short answer questions along with an answer key. The questions closely follow the text chapters and are cross-referenced with corresponding page numbers.

Computerized Test Generator

The printed Test Bank is also available electronically through our computerized testing system, TestGen-EQ 2.0. This fully networkable test generating software is now available on CD-rom. TestGen-EQ's friendly graphical interface enables instructors to view, edit, and add questions, transfer questions to tests, and print tests in a variety of fonts and forms. Search and sort features allow instructors to locate questions quickly and arrange them in a preferred order. Six question formats are available, including short-answer, true-false, multiple choice, essay, matching, and bimodal.

PowerPoint Slides

New to this edition, the transparency masters will now be available as PowerPoint presentation slides on CD-rom.

Overhead Transparency Package

A set of 75, four-color acetate transparencies is available to adopters. The set includes graphs, charts, and tables from the text.

Teaching Public Speaking

This introduction to teaching the public speaking course offers suggestions for everything from lecturing to designing classroom assignments to incorporating cultural diversity into lesson plans. Essential for graduate teaching assistants and first-time instructors, it will also provide new insight to the more experienced professor. An extensive bibliography and a listing of media resources is also included.

Great Ideas for Teaching Speech (GIFTS)

This unique supplement offers instructors a myriad of creative ideas for enlivening their public speaking course. All of the assignments found in GIFTS have been successfully employed by experienced public speaking instructors in their classrooms.

ESL Guide for Public Speaking

The ESL Guide for Public Speaking provides strategies and resources for instructors teaching in a bilingual or multi-lingual classroom. It also includes suggestions for further reading and a listing of related Web sites.

Longman's Communication Video Library

A large selection of videos is available to users. The videos cover such topics as effective listening, interpersonal relationships, interviewing, small group communication, and public speaking. We also offer a variety of accompanying printed video guides. Please contact your local sales representative for more information on titles and availability.

Resources for Students

The Speech Writer's Workshop and Brainstorms CD-ROM

A virtual handbook for public speaking, this exciting public speaking software is now available on CD-ROM. The software includes five separate features: 1) a *speech handbook* with tips for researching and preparing speeches plus information about grammar, usage, and syntax; 2) a *speech workshop* which guides students through the speech writing process while displaying a series of questions at each stage; 3) a *topics dictionary* which gives students hundreds of ideas for speeches—all divided into sub-categories to help students with outlining and organization; 4) a *citation database* that formats bibliographic entries in MLA or APA style; and 5) Brainstorms: How to Think More Creatively About Communication . . . or about anything else.

Study Wizard CD-ROM

This computerized student tutorial program, now available on CD-ROM, helps students review and master key concepts in the text. Using chapter and topic summaries, practice tests questions, and a comprehensive glossary, the software supplements the text by allowing students to explore new topics and test their understanding of terms and ideas already presented in the reading assignments. Students receive immediate feedback on test questions in the form of answer explanations and page references to the text. In addition, the program allows students to print chapter outlines, difficult vocabulary, missed test questions, or a diagnostic report, which includes suggestions for further study.

Student Guide to PowerPoint

Designed to introduce students to PowerPoint, this student guide explains how to use the program as a tool for planning, organizing, and delivering oral presentations. The supplement covers all of the requisite skills for mastering PowerPoint including outlining, designing and modifying slides, using graphics and animations, and presenting a slide show.

Studying Communication

This booklet introduces students to the field of communication and to the way in which research in the discipline is conducted. The booklet also offers students a variety of practical suggestions for how to get the most out of their study of communication including how to read a textbook, how to take a test, and how to write a paper for a communication course.

Brainstorms

This unique booklet integrates creative thinking into the communication course. *Brainstorms* explores the creative thinking process (its nature, values, characteristics, and stages) and its relationship to communication. It also provides 19 specific tools for thinking more creatively about communication (or anything else). The discussion of each tool includes its purposes, techniques, and an exercise to get started. Creative thinking sidebars and relevant quotations add to the interactive pedagogy.

http://www.awlonline.com/devito

This new website is an online study guide, providing valuable resources for both students and instructors using *Human Communication*, Eighth Edition. Students will find interactive practice tests, annotated research links, scenarios, and internet activites. Instructors will have access to complete text and supplement information, suggestions for classroom activities, and a Syllabus Builder tool that allows them to put their course on the web.

ACKNOWLEDGMENTS

It is a pleasure to thank the many people who have had an influence on the writing and production of this book. My major debt is to those colleagues who reviewed the manuscript for this edition and the previous editions and have given freely of their insights, suggestions, criticisms, time, and energy. To those who reviewed previous editions and to whose insights I return repeatedly, I am most grateful. Thank you:

Donald E. Baker, North Carolina Agricultural and Technical State University; Steven A. Beebe, Southwest Texas State University; Ernest G. Bormann, University of Minnesota; Bernard Brommel, Northeastern Illinois University; Edward Brown, Abilene Christian University; Michael Bruner, University of North Texas; Marcia L. Dewhurst, Ohio State University; Robert Dixon, St. Louis Community College at Meramac; Joseph R. Dominick, University of Georgia; Dennis Doyle, Central College; Kenneth D. Frandsen, University of New Mexico; Fran Franklin, University of Arkansas; Angela Gruppas, St. Louis Community College at Meramec; Michael Hecht, Pennsylvania State University; Mary Hinchcliff-Pelias, Southern Illinois University; Ted Hindemarsh, Brigham Young University; David D. Hudson, Golden West College; Fred Jandt, California State University at San Bernardino; Stephen Johnson, Freed-Hardeman College; Robert Kastenbaum, Arizona State University; Albert M. Katz, University of Wisconsin, Superior; Kathleen Kendall, State University of New York, Albany; Elaine Klein, Westchester Community College; Edward Lee Lamoureux, Bradley University; Larry Z. Leslie, University of South Florida; Joel Litvin, Bridgewater State College; Lisa Merrill, Hofstra University; Dreama Moon, Arizona State University; Don B. Morlan, University of Dayton; Jon F. Nussbaum, University of Oklahoma; Jerry S. Phillips, Trinity Valley Com-

munity College; Dorman Picklesimer, Jr., Boston College; George Ray, Cleveland State University; Mark V. Redmond, Iowa State University; Armeda C. Reitzel, Humboldt State University; Henry L. Roubicek, The University of Houston—Downtown; Thomas Ruddick, Edison State College; Robert M. Shuter, Marquette University; Gail Sorenson, California State University at Fresno; Don W. Stacks, University of Miami; James S. Taylor, Houston Baptist University; Gretchen Aggertt Weber, Indiana State University; Doris Werkman, Portland Community College; Robert Worthington, New Mexico State University; and Christopher Zahn, Cleveland State University.

To those who reviewed the seventh edition and the manuscript for this edition and shared many and valuable insights, I am most appreciative. Thank you:

Cynthia L. Allan, Dakota State University (SD)

Dru C. Bookout, Richland College (TX)

Michael S. Bruner, University of North Texas

Barbara L. Clinton, Highline Community College (WA)

Robert A. Cole, Southern Illinois University at Carbondale

Michael Dreher, Bethel College (MN)

Ted C. Hindmarsh, Brigham Young University (UT)

Elizabeth Lindsey, New Mexico State University Main Campus

Jerry S. Phillips, Trinity Valley Community College (TX)

I also wish to thank the many people at Longman and Electronic Publishing Services Inc. who together contributed their time and talents to make this book both attractive and functional. Thank you to Brooks Ellis, Project Editor; Nancy Crochiere, Development Editor; Priscilla McGeehon, Editor-in-Chief; Lisa Pinto, Development Manager; Mark Toews, Supplement Editor; and Eric Jorgensen, Full Service Production Manager.

Joseph A. DeVito

UNIT 1
Preliminaries To Human Communication

UNIT CONTENTS

Types of Human Communication

Culture and Human Communication

Elements of Human Communication

UNIT GOALS

After completing this unit, you should be able to

identify the major types of human communication

explain the nature of culture and its relevance to human communication

define *communication* and its elements: *communication context, sources-receivers, encoding-decoding, competence, messages, channel, feedback, feedforward, noise, communication effect,* and *ethics*

Of all the knowledge and skills you have, those concerning communication are among the most important and useful. Communication will always play a crucial part in your personal and professional lives and its mastery and competence will influence how effectively you live these lives.

TYPES OF HUMAN COMMUNICATION

Human communication is a vast field and ranges from talking to yourself to mass communication in which you talk to millions. Let's look at some of these areas more closely.

In **intrapersonal communication** you talk with yourself. You learn about and evaluate yourself, persuade yourself of this or that, reason about possible decisions to make, and rehearse the messages you intend to send to others.

Through **interpersonal communication** you interact with others, learn about them and about yourself, and reveal yourself to others. Whether with new acquaintances, old friends, lovers, or family members, it's through interpersonal communication that you establish, maintain, sometimes destroy (and sometimes repair) your personal relationships.

In **small group communication** you interact with others, solving problems, developing new ideas, and sharing knowledge and experiences. From the employment interview to the executive board meeting, from the informal social group having coffee to the formal meeting discussing issues of international concern, your work and social life are lived largely in small groups.

Through **public communication**, others inform and persuade you. And you in turn inform and persuade others—to do, to buy, or to think in a particular way, or to change an attitude, opinion, or value.

Through **mass communication** you are entertained, informed, and persuaded by the media—movies, television, radio, newspapers, and books. Also, through your viewing habits and buying patterns, you in turn influence the media's form and content.

With the exception of intrapersonal communication, all other forms of communication may be **intercultural,** in which you communicate with members from other cultures, that is, people who follow different customs, roles, and rules. Through intercultural communication, you come to understand new ways of thinking and new ways of behaving and begin to see the tremendous variety in human thought and experience.

This book, then, is about these types of communication and about your personal communication. Its major goal is to explain the concepts and principles, the theory and research central to these varied areas of human communication. Another goal is to provide the foundation and direction for learning the skills of human communication and for increasing your own communication competency. The relevance of these skills is seen throughout the communication spectrum; it's the difference between

- the self-confident and the self-conscious speaker
- the person who is hired and the one who is passed over
- the couple who argue constructively and the couple who argue by hurting each other and eventually destroying their relationship
- the group member who is too self-focused to listen openly and contribute to the group's goals and the member who helps accomplish the group's task *and* satisfy the interpersonal needs of the members
- the public speaker who lacks credibility and persuasive appeal and the speaker audiences believe and follow
- the uncritical consumer of media who is influenced without awareness and the critical, watchful consumer who uses media constructively

The areas of human communication, some common purposes of each area, and some theory- and skills-related concerns are summarized in Table 1.1. This table will give you a broad overview of the field of human communication and will preview the entire text.

Communication is an enormous field and for many of you this is your first academic exposure to it. It will take a great deal of time and effort to even begin mastering the theories and principles of human communication. Fortunately, the energy that you'll put into this book and this course will be more than repaid by the knowledge you'll gain and the skills you'll acquire and improve.

Your beliefs about communication influence how you communicate (as both sender and receiver) and how you approach the study of communication. So,

TABLE 1.1   **Human Communication**

This table identifies and arranges the forms of communication in terms of the number of persons involved, from one (in intrapersonal communication) to thousands and millions (in mass communication). It also previews (in general) the progression of topics in this book.

	Areas of Human Communication	Some Common Purposes	Some Theory-related Concerns	Some Skills-related Concerns
	Intrapersonal: communication with oneself	To think, reason, analyze, reflect	How does one's self-concept develop? How does one's self-concept influence communication? How can problem-solving and analyzing abilities be improved and taught? What is the relationship between personality and communication?	Enhancing self-esteem, increasing self-awareness, improving problem-solving and analyzing abilities, increasing self-control, reducing stress, managing interpersonal conflict
	Interpersonal: communication between two persons	To discover, relate, influence, play, help	What is interpersonal effectiveness? Why do people develop relationships? What holds friends, lovers, and families together? What tears them apart? How can relationships be repaired?	Increasing effectiveness in one-to-one communication, developing and maintaining effective relationships (friendship, love, family), improving conflict resolution abilities
	Small group: communication within a small group of persons	To share information, generate ideas, solve problems, help	What makes a leader? What type of leadership works best? What roles do members serve in groups? What do groups do well and what do they fail to do well? How can groups be made more effective?	Increasing effectiveness as a group member, improving leadership abilities, using groups to achieve specific purposes (for example, solving problems, generating ideas)
	Public: communication of speaker with audience	To inform, persuade, entertain	What kinds of organizational structure work best in informative and persuasive speaking? How can audiences be most effectively analyzed and adapted to? How can ideas be best developed for communication to an audience?	Communicating information more effectively; increasing persuasive abilities; developing, organizing, styling, and delivering messages with greater effectiveness
	Mass: communication addressed to an extremely large audience, mediated by audio and/or visual means	To entertain, persuade, and inform	What functions do the media serve? How do the media influence us? How can we influence the media? In what ways is information censored by the media for the public? How does advertising work?	Improving our ability to use the media to greater effectiveness, increasing our ability to control the media, avoiding being taken in by advertisements and tabloid journalism

before launching into the content of human communication, try examining these beliefs by taking the following self-test: "What Do You Believe About Communication?"

 SELF-TEST

What Do You Believe About Communication?

Respond to each of the following statements with TRUE if you believe the statement is usually true and FALSE if you believe the statement is usually false.

_____ 1. Good communicators are born, not made.

_____ 2. The more a couple communicates, the better their relationship will be.

_____ 3. Unlike effective speaking, effective listening can't be taught.

_____ 4. Opening lines such as "How are you?" or "Fine weather today" or "Have you got a light?" serve no really useful communication purpose.

_____ 5. When two people are in a close relationship for a long period of time, one should not have to communicate his or her needs and wants; the other person should know what these are.

_____ 6. When verbal and nonverbal messages contradict each other, people believe the verbal message.

_____ 7. Complete openness should be the goal of any meaningful interpersonal relationship.

_____ 8. When there is interpersonal conflict, each person should aim to win even at the expense of the other person.

_____ 9. Like good communicators, leaders are born, not made.

_____ 10 Fear of speaking in public is detrimental and must be eliminated.

As you may have figured out, all 10 statements are false. As you read this text, you'll discover not only why these beliefs are false but also the trouble you can get into when you assume they're true. Briefly,

here are some of the reasons why each of the statements is generally false:

1. Effective communication is a learned skill; although some people are born brighter or more extroverted, all can improve their abilities and become more effective communicators.
2. If you practice bad habits, you're more likely to grow less effective than more effective; consequently, it's important to learn and follow the principles of effectiveness.
3. Like speaking, listening is a learned skill and can be improved as you'll discover when you read Unit 4.
4. Actually, these "openers" serve an important social function; they literally open the channels of communication and pave the way for what is to follow.
5. This assumption is at the heart of many interpersonal difficulties—people aren't mind readers and to assume that they are merely sets up barriers to open and honest communication.
6. Whether you believe the verbal or the nonverbal messages depends on the total communication context, but generally research does find that people are more likely to believe the nonverbal messages.
7. This is generally not an effective strategy, although you may feel that we're ethically obligated to be totally honest.
8. Interpersonal conflict does not have to involve a winner and a loser; both people can win as demonstrated in Unit 11.
9. Leadership, like communication and listening, is a learned skill that you'll develop as you learn the principles of human communication and those unique to group leadership (Units 13 and 14).
10. Most speakers are nervous; managing, not eliminating, the fear, will enable you to become effective regardless of your current level of fear. ✔

CULTURE AND HUMAN COMMUNICATION

Culture refers to the beliefs, ways of behaving, and artifacts of a group that are transmitted through communication and learning rather than through genes. Gender is considered a cultural variable largely because cultures teach boys and girls different attitudes, beliefs, values, and ways of communicating and relating to one another. So, you act like a man or a woman in part because of what your culture has taught you about how men and women should act. This does not, of course, deny that biological differences also play a role in the differences between male and female behavior. In fact, recent research continues to uncover biological roots of behaviors we once thought were entirely learned, like happiness and shyness, for example (McCroskey 1997).

Because your communication is heavily influenced by the culture in which you were raised, culture is given a prominent place in this text. In this section we explain the relevance of culture to communication and the aims and benefits of a cultural perspective.

A walk through any large city, many small towns, and through just about any college campus will convince you that the United States is largely a collection of lots of different cultures (see Figure 1.1). These cultures coexist somewhat separately but also with each one influencing each other. This coexistence has led some researchers to refer to these cultures as co-cultures (Shuter 1990, Samovar & Porter 1995; Jandt 1999). Here are a few random facts to further support the importance of culture generally and of intercultural communication in particular (*Time*, December 2, 1993, p. 14):

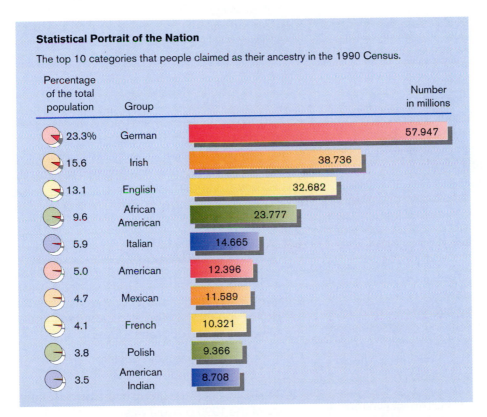

Statistical Portrait of the Nation

The top 10 categories that people claimed as their ancestry in the 1990 Census.

Percentage of the total population	Group	Number in millions
23.3%	German	57.947
15.6	Irish	38.736
13.1	English	32.682
9.6	African American	23.777
5.9	Italian	14.665
5.0	American	12.396
4.7	Mexican	11.589
4.1	French	10.321
3.8	Polish	9.366
3.5	American Indian	8.708

Figure 1.1 **Ancestry of U.S. residents.** With immigration patterns changing so rapidly, the portrait illustrated here is likely to look very different in the coming years. For example, by the year 2030, it is predicted that the U.S. population will be 73.6% white, 12% African American, 10.2% Hispanic, and 3.3% Asian American. By the year 2050 it is predicted that the percentages will be: 52.8% white, 24.5% Hispanic, 13.6% African American, and 8.2% Asian American (figures projected by the Census Bureau and reported in *New York Times*, March 14, 1996, p. A16). To what factors might you attribute these projections? What will your own state, city, or town look like in 2030? In 2050?

UNDERSTANDING
Theory and Research

WHAT'S A THEORY?

Throughout this unit and throughout this book you'll encounter a wide variety of theories. A theory is a generalization that explains how something works—for example, gravity, blood clotting, interpersonal attraction, or communication. In academic writing, the term is usually reserved for a well-established system of knowledge about how something works or how things are related.

Some of the theories you'll encounter try to explain how communication in general operates (for example, a theory that explains how people accommodate their speaking style to their listeners or one that views communication as a process whereby speaker and listener influence each other simultaneously). Other theories focus on more specific areas (for example, how communication works when relationships deteriorate, how friends self-disclose, how problem-solving groups communicate, how speakers influence audiences, and how the media affect people).

As you can see from these examples, and as you'll see throughout the text, almost every theory in communication has some practical implications.

- Over 30 million people in the United States speak languages other than English in their homes.
- In the school systems of areas such as New York; Fairfax County, Virginia; Chicago; and Los Angeles over 100 languages are spoken.
- Over 50% of the residents of such cities as Miami and Hialeah in Florida, Union City in New Jersey, and Huntington Park and Monterey Park in California are foreign born.
- The foreign-born population of the United States totaled almost 20 million in 1990, which represents approximately 8% of the total U.S. population; a 1997 update reports it as 25.8 million or 9.7 percent of the population (Schmidley & Alvarado 1997).
- Thirty percent of the U.S. Nobel prize-winners (since 1901) were foreign born.

We're also living in a time of striking changes in gender roles. Many men, for example, are doing a great deal more in the home, like housekeeping chores and caring for their children. More obvious perhaps is that many women are becoming much more visible in fields once occupied exclusively by men—politics, law enforcement, the military, and the clergy are just some examples. And, of course, women are increasingly entering the corporate executive ranks; the glass ceiling may not have disappeared, but it is cracked.

You may wish to continue this cultural awareness experience by taking the accompanying self-test, "What's Your Cultural Awareness?"

SELF-TEST

What's Your Cultural Awareness?

Complete each of the following statements with the choice you think is correct. If you don't know the answer, make an educated guess.

1. The major language of education in India is
   (a) English, (b) Hindi, (c) Urdu

2. The major ancestral group in the United States (as of the 1990 census) was
   (a) German, (b) Irish, (c) Mexican

3. The largest number of Africans are
   (a) Christians, (b) Muslims, (c) tribal religionists

4. The nation with the highest literacy rate (100%) is
   (a) Cuba, (b) Kyrgyzstan, (c) United States

5. The nation holding the most U.S. patents granted to residents of areas outside the United States and its territories is
   (a) France, (b) Germany, (c) Japan

6. The country with the longest expectation of life at birth is
   (a) Canada (b) Japan (c) Sweden

7. Based on projected census figures for 2020, the country with the largest population will be (we're purposely omitting China—that would be too easy)
   (a) India, (b) Indonesia, (c) United States

8. The nation whose per capita annual income is less than $1000 is
   (a) Nigeria, (b) Pakistan, (c) Philippines

9. The state with the largest number of native Americans (defined by the U.S. Department of Commerce, Bureau of the Census, as American Indian, Eskimo, and Aleut) is
   (a) Arizona, (b) California, (c) Oklahoma

10. The divorce rate is highest in
    (a) Japan, (b) Sweden, (c) United States

This test was designed to get you thinking about what you think about the world and different cultures. The answers (all, except item 6, are from current Almanacs are as follows:

1. English.
2. The answers are given in Figure 1.1.
3. The largest number of Africans are Christian (327,204,000), with Muslims (278,250,800) and tribal religionists (70,588,000) the next largest groups.
4. Of the nations listed in this question, only Kyrgyzstan has a literacy rate of 100% (along with Armenia, Australia, and Andorra). Cuba has a literacy rate of 99% (along with North Korea, Denmark, the Czech Republic, Ireland, and Barbados). The literacy rate for the United States is 97%. These figures contrast sharply with nations that have literacy rates below 50%, for example, Iran, Bangladesh, Senegal, Uganda, and Afghanistan.
5. Japan holds the largest number of patents, Germany is second, and France is third.
6. Japan has the longest life span, Canada is second, and Sweden is third (*Newsweek*, December 28, 1998–January 4, 1999, p. 71).

7. China will be first with a projected population of 1,424,725,000. India will rank a close second with a projected population of 1,320,746,000. The United States will be a distant third with 323,113,000, Indonesia will be fourth with 276,474,000, and Pakistan will be fifth with 275,100,000. By 2100, it is predicted, India will have the world's largest population.
8. All three nations listed have per capita annual incomes of less than $1000.
9. The three states listed have the greatest Native American population. Oklahoma ranks first with 252,420, California second with 242,164, and Arizona third with 203,527. The three states with the fewest are Vermont (1696), Delaware (2019), and New Hampshire (2134).
10. The divorce rate is highest in the United States (4.7 per 1000 population), Sweden has 2.22 per 1000, and Japan has 1.27 per 1000.

Did these questions and their answers surprise you in any way? For example, are you surprised that the United States is not in the top three in terms of life span? Are you surprised at the religions of Africa? Are you surprised that the divorce rate in the United States is twice as high as it is in Sweden? Can you trace any of these surprises to stereotypes you might have of certain countries?   ✔

The Relevance of Culture

There are lots of reasons for the cultural emphasis you'll find in this book. Most obviously, perhaps, are the vast demographic changes taking place throughout the United States. Whereas at one time, the United States was largely a country populated by Europeans, it's now a country greatly influenced by the enormous number of new citizens from Latin and South America, Africa, and Asia. And the same is true to an even greater extent on college and university campuses throughout the United States. With these changes have come different customs and the need to understand and adapt to new ways of looking at communication.

As a people we've become increasingly sensitive to cultural differences. American society has moved from an assimilationist perspective (people should leave their native culture behind and adapt to their new culture) to one that values cultural

How important is intercultural communication to you? Will its importance change for you in the next 5 or 10 years?

diversity (people should retain their native cultural ways). And, with some notable exceptions—hate speech, racism, sexism, homophobia, and classism come quickly to mind—we're more concerned with saying the right thing and ultimately with developing a society where all cultures can coexist and enrich each other. At the same time, the ability to interact effectively with members of other cultures often translates into financial gain and increased employment opportunities and advancement prospects.

Today, most countries are economically dependent on each other. Our economic lives depend on our ability to communicate effectively across different cultures.

Similarly, our political well-being depends in great part on that of other cultures. Political unrest in any part of the world—South Africa, Eastern Europe, and the Middle East, to take a few examples—affects our own security. Intercultural communication and understanding seem now more crucial than ever.

The rapid spread of communication technology has brought foreign and sometimes very different cultures right into your living rooms. News from foreign countries is commonplace. You see nightly—in vivid color—what is going on in remote countries. Technology has made intercultural communication easy, practical, and inevitable. Daily the media bombard you with evidence of racial tensions, religious disagreements, sexual bias, and, in general, the problems caused when intercultural communication fails. And, of course, the Internet has made intercultural communication as easy as writing a note on your computer. You can now just as easily communicate by e-mail with someone in Europe or Asia, for example, as you can with someone in another city or state.

Still another reason is that communication competence is specific to a given culture; what proves effective in one culture may prove ineffective in another. For example, in the United States corporate executives get down to business during the first several minutes of a meeting. In Japan, business executives interact socially for an extended period and try to find out something about each other. Thus, the communication principle influenced by U.S. culture would advise participants to get down to the meeting's agenda during the first five minutes. The principle influenced by Japanese culture would advise participants to avoid dealing with business until everyone has socialized sufficiently and feels well enough acquainted to begin negotiations. Neither principle is right and neither is

UNDERSTANDING
Theory and Research

WHAT'S RESEARCH?

Usually on the basis of some theory and its predictions—though sometimes from a simple desire to answer a question—research is conducted. Communication research is a systematic search for information about communication, the very information that is discussed throughout this text—information about perception and listening, verbal and nonverbal messages, interpersonal interactions, small group encounters, and public speaking situations.

Some research is designed **to explore** what exists, for example, What do people say after making a mistake or getting caught in a lie (Herzog 1996)? Other research is designed **to describe** the properties of some communication behavior, for example, What are the types of excuses? Still other research aims **to predict** what will happen in different situations, for example, What types of excuses will work best in a business relationship?

Research findings bearing on these questions give us useful generalizations about communication and help clarify how communication works and how we might use it more effectively.

---

wrong. Each is effective within its own culture and ineffective outside its own culture.

The Aim of a Cultural Perspective

Because culture permeates all forms of communication, it is necessary to understand its influences if you are to understand how communication works and master its skills. As illustrated throughout this text, culture influences communications of all types (Moon 1996). It influences what you say to yourself and how you talk with friends, lovers, and family in everyday conversation. It influences how you interact in groups and how much importance you place on the group versus the individual. It influences the topics you talk about and the strategies you use in communicating information or in persuading. And it influences how you use the media and in the credibility you attribute to them.

A cultural emphasis helps distinguish what is universal (true for all people) from what is relative (true for people in one culture and not true for people in other cultures) (Matsumoto 1994). The principles for communicating information and for changing listeners' attitudes, for example, will vary from one culture to another. If you are to understand communication, then you need to know how its principles vary and how the principles must be qualified and adjusted on the basis of cultural differences.

And of course this cultural understanding is needed to communicate effectively in a wide variety of intercultural situations. Success in communication—on your job and in your social life—will depend on your ability to communicate effectively with persons who are culturally different from yourself.

This emphasis on culture does not imply that you should accept all cultural practices or that all cultural practices are equal (Hatfield & Rapson 1996). For example, cock fighting, fox hunting, and bull fighting are parts of the culture of some Latin American countries, England, and Spain, but you need not find these activities acceptable or equal to a cultural practice in which animals are treated kindly. Further, a cultural emphasis does not imply that you have to accept or follow even the practices of your own culture. For example, even if the majority in your culture find cock fighting acceptable, you need not agree with or follow the practice. Similarly, you can reject your culture's values and beliefs, its religion or political system, or its attitudes toward the homeless, the handicapped, or the culturally different. Of course, going against your culture's traditions and values is often very difficult. But, it is important to realize that culture *influences* you, it does not *determine* your values or behavior. Often, for example, personality factors (your degree of assertiveness, extroversion, or optimism, for example) will prove more influential than culture (Hatfield & Rapson 1996).

As demonstrated throughout this text, cultural differences exist throughout the communication spectrum—from the way you use eye contact to the way you develop or dissolve a relationship (Chang & Holt 1996). But, these should not blind you to the great number of similarities existing among even the most widely separated cultures. Close interpersonal relationships, for example, are common in all cultures though they may be entered into for very different reasons by members of different cultures. Further, when reading about these differences, remember that these are usually matters of degree. Thus, most cultures value honesty, but not all value it to the same degree. The advances in media and technology and the widespread use of the Internet, for example, are influencing cultures and cultural change and are perhaps homogenizing the different cultures, lessening the differences and increasing the similarities. They are also Americanizing the different cultures because the dominant values and customs evidenced in the media and on the Internet are in large part American, a product of America's current dominance in both media and technology.

ELEMENTS OF HUMAN COMMUNICATION

Communication refers to the act, by one or more persons, of sending and receiving messages that are distorted by noise, occur within a context, have some effect, and provide some opportunity for feedback. Figure 1.2 illustrates the elements present in all communication acts, regardless of whether it's intrapersonal, interpersonal, small group, public speaking, or mass communication.

Communication Context

All communication takes place in a context that has at least four dimensions: physical, cultural, social-psychological, and temporal. The **physical context** is the tangible or concrete environment in which communication takes place—the room or hallway or park. This physical context exerts some influence on the content (what you say) as well as the form (how you say it) of your messages.

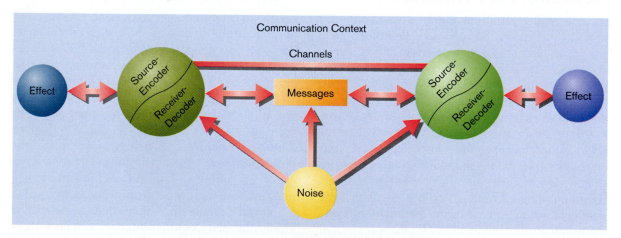

Figure 1.2   **The elements of human communication.**   This is a simplified view of the essentials of human communication and their relationship to each other. Messages (including feedforward and feedback) are sent simultaneously through a variety of channels from one encoder-decoder to another. The communication process takes place in a context (physical, cultural, social-psychological, and temporal) and is subjected to interference by noise (physical, psychological, and semantic). The interaction of messages with the encoder-decoder leads to some effect.

BUILDING
Communication Skills

HOW DO CULTURAL BELIEFS INFLUENCE YOU?

Review the following cultural maxims. Select any one that seems especially interesting and identify: the meaning of the maxim; the cultural value(s) it embodies and speaks to; your evaluation of the maxim, for example, its usefulness or value; and how it has influenced you in some specific communication situation.

A penny saved is a penny earned.
Blood is thicker than water.
Don't put off until tomorrow what you can do today.
If you've got it, flaunt it./Blow your own horn.
Nothing succeeds like success.
Real men don't cry.
Stick with your own kind.
Tell it like it is.
Time is money.
Tomorrow will take care of itself.

The **cultural context** refers to the communicators' rules and norms, beliefs and attitudes that are transmitted from one generation to another. For example, in some cultures it's considered polite to talk to strangers; in others, it's something to avoid. In some cultures, direct eye contact between child and adult signifies directness and honesty; in others it signifies defiance and lack of respect.

The **social-psychological context** includes, for example, the status relationships among the participants, the roles and the games that people play, and the cultural rules of the society in which they're communicating. It also includes the friendliness or unfriendliness, formality or informality, and seriousness or humorousness of the situation. Communication that would be permitted at a graduation party may not be considered appropriate in a hospital.

The **temporal (or time) context** includes the time of day as well as the time in history in which the communication takes place. For many people, the morning is not a time for communication. For others, the morning is ideal. Historical context is no less important because the appropriateness and impact of messages depend, in part, on the time in which they're uttered. Consider, for example, how messages on racial, sexual, or religious attitudes and values would be differently framed and responded to in different times in history.

Even more important is how a particular message fits into the temporal sequence of communication events. For example, consider the varied meanings a "simple" compliment paid to a friend would have depending on whether you said it immediately after your friend paid you a compliment, immediately before you asked your friend for a favor, or during an argument.

These four dimensions of context interact with one another. For example, arriving late for an appointment (temporal context) will be interpreted differently in different cultures (cultural context). Sometimes, arriving late might lead to changes in the social-psychological context, perhaps creating tension and unfriendliness, which in turn may lead to changes in the physical context, for example, choosing a less intimate restaurant for your lunch meeting.

Sources-Receivers

The hyphenated term sources-receivers emphasizes that each person involved in communication is both a source (or speaker) and a receiver (or listener). You send messages when you speak, write, gesture, or smile. You receive messages in listening, reading, smelling, and so on. As you send messages, however, you're also receiving messages. You're receiving your own messages (you hear yourself, you feel your own

How many dimensions of context (physical, temporal, social-psychological, and cultural) can you identify as potentially influencing the interaction shown in this photo? In what specific ways might these dimensions influence the communications taking place?

movements, you see many of your own gestures) and you're receiving the messages of the other person—visually, aurally, or even through touch or smell. You look at anyone you speak to for responses—approval, understanding, sympathy, agreement, and so on. As you decipher these nonverbal signals, you're performing receiving functions.

Source-Receiver Encoding-Decoding

In communication the act of producing messages—for example, speaking or writing—is called **encoding**. By putting your ideas into sound waves or on paper you're putting these ideas into a code, hence encoding. The act of receiving messages—for example, listening or reading—is called **decoding**. By translating sound waves or words on paper into ideas you take them out of code, hence decoding. Thus, speakers or writers as called **encoders**, and listeners or readers are called **decoders**.

Like source-receiver, the hyphenated term encoding-decoding emphasizes that you perform these functions simultaneously. As you speak (encoding), you're also deciphering the responses of the listener (decoding).

Source-Receiver Communicative Competence

Communicative competence refers to a person's knowledge of the social aspects of communication (Rubin 1982, 1985; Spitzberg & Cupach 1989). It includes such knowledge as the role the context plays in influencing the content and form of communication messages—for example, the knowledge that in certain contexts and with certain listeners one topic is appropriate and another is not. Knowledge about the rules of nonverbal behavior, for example, the appropriateness of touching, vocal volume, and physical closeness, is also part of communicative competence.

You learn communicative competence by observing others, by trial and error, and by explicit instruction (for example, as in this course and this text). One of the major goals of this text and this course is to spell out the nature of communicative competence and to increase your own competence. By increasing your competence, you'll have available a broader range of options in your communication activities. The process is comparable to learning vocabulary: the more vocabulary you know, the more ways you have for expressing yourself.

Messages and Channels

Communication messages take many forms. You send and receive messages through any one or any combination of sensory organs. Although you may customarily think of messages as being verbal (oral or written), you also communicate nonverbally. For example, the clothes you wear, the way you walk, shake hands, cock your head, comb your hair, sit,

Going Online

NCA Web site

This is the home page of the National Communication Association, the largest professional organization for people interested in communication. NCA is extremely broad in scope and has divisions and activities focusing on all the areas of human communication covered in this text. What can you learn about human communication from this Web site? You may wish to locate the Web sites of the professional organizations in your own major. What benefits might you derive from these Web sites?

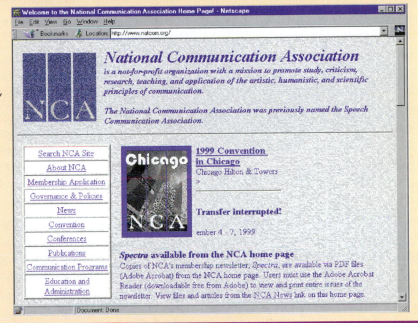

and smile all communicate messages. Everything about you communicates.

The communication channel is the medium through which the message passes. Communication rarely takes place over only one channel; you may use two, three, or four different channels simultaneously. For example, in face-to-face interactions you speak and listen (vocal channel), but you also gesture and receive these signals visually (visual channel). In addition you emit and detect odors (olfactory channel). Often you touch another person, and this too communicates (tactile channel).

Two special types of messages need to be explained more fully; these are feedback (the messages you send that are reactions to other messages) and feedforward (the messages you send as preface to your "main" messages).

Feedback Messages

Throughout the listening process, a listener gives a speaker feedback—messages sent back to the speaker reacting to what is said (Clement & Frandsen, 1976). Feedback tells the speaker what effect he or she is having on the listener(s). On the basis of this feedback, the speaker may adjust the messages by strengthening, deemphasizing, or changing the content or form of the messages. These adjustments then serve as feedback to the receiver who, in response, readjusts his or her feedback messages. The process is a circular one, with one person's feedback serving as the stimulus for the other person's feedback, just as any message serves as the stimulus for another person's message.

In the diagram of the universals of communication (Figure 1.2), the arrows from source-receiver to effect and from one source-receiver to the other source-receiver go in both directions to illustrate the notion of feedback. When you speak to another person you also hear yourself. That is, you get feedback from your own messages; you hear what you say, you feel the way you move, you see what you write.

In addition to this self-feedback, you get feedback from others, which can take many forms. A frown or a smile, a yea or a nay, a pat on the back or a punch in the mouth are all types of feedback.

Feedback can be looked upon in terms of five important dimensions: positive-negative, person focused-message focused, immediate-delayed; low monitoring-high monitoring, and critical-supportive. To use feedback effectively, then, you need to make educated choices along these dimensions (Figure 1.3).

Positive-Negative. Positive feedback (applause, smiles, and head nods signifying approval) tells the

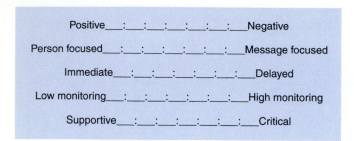

Figure 1.3 **Five dimensions of feedback.**   Close relationships seem to involve feedback existing toward the left side of the figure—strongly positive, person-focused, immediate, low in monitoring, and supportive. Acquaintance relationships seem to involve feedback somewhere in the middle of these scales. And relationships with those you dislike seem to involve feedback close to the right side of the scales—negative, message-focused, delayed, highly monitored, and critical. Do you think this is a generally accurate description of feedback in relationships?

speaker that the message is being well-received and that he or she should continue speaking in the same general mode. Negative feedback (boos, frowns, puzzled looks, and gestures signifying disapproval) tells the speaker that something is wrong and that some adjustment needs to be made.

Person-Focused and Message-Focused.   Feedback may center on the person ("You're sweet," "You've a great smile") or on the message ("Can you repeat that phone number?" "Your argument is a good one"). Especially in giving criticism (as in public speaking) it is important to make clear that your feedback relates to, say, the organization of the speech and not to the speaker himself or herself.

Immediate-Delayed.   In interpersonal situations, feedback is most often sent immediately after the message is received. In other communication situations, however, the feedback may be delayed. Instructor evaluation questionnaires completed at the end of the course provide feedback long after the class began. When you applaud or ask questions of the public speaker, the feedback is less delayed. In interview situations, the feedback may come weeks afterwards. In media situations, some feedback comes immediately through, for example, Nielsen ratings, while other feedback comes much later through viewing and buying patterns.

Low Monitoring-High Monitoring.   Feedback varies from the spontaneous and totally honest reaction (low-monitored feedback) to the carefully constructed response designed to serve a specific purpose (high-monitored feedback). In most interpersonal situations you probably give feedback spontaneously; you allow your responses to show without any monitoring. At other times, however, you may be more guarded as when your boss asks you how you like your job or when your grandfather asks what you think of his new motorcycle outfit.

Supportive-Critical.   Supportive feedback confirms the person and what that person says; it occurs when, for example, you console another, when you encourage the other to talk, or when you affirm the person's self-definition. Critical feedback, on the other hand, is evaluative. When you give critical feedback you judge another's performance as in, for example, evaluating a speech or coaching someone learning a new skill.

These categories are not exclusive. Feedback does not have to be either critical or supportive; it can be both. Thus, in teaching someone how to become a more effective interviewer, you might critically evaluate a specific interview but you might also express support for the effort. Similarly, you might respond to a friend's question immediately and then after a day or two elaborate on your response. Each feedback opportunity will, then, present you with choices along at least these five dimensions.

Feedforward Messages

Feedforward is information you provide before sending your primary messages (Richards 1951), revealing something about the messages to come. Feedforward includes such diverse examples as the preface or the table of contents to a book, the opening paragraph of a chapter, movie previews, magazine covers, and introductions in public speeches.

BUILDING
Communication Skills

HOW DO YOU GIVE FEEDBACK?

How would you give feedback (positive or negative? person-focused or message focused? immediate or delayed? low monitoring or high monitoring? supportive or critical?) in these varied situations? Write one or two sentences of feedback for each of these situations:

A friend—who you like but don't have romantic feelings for—asks you for a date.
Your instructor asks you to evaluate the course.
An interviewer asks if you want a credit card.
A homeless person smiles at you on the street.
A colleague at work tells a homophobic joke.

Feedforward messages are examples of meta-messages—messages that communicate about other messages. Such information may be verbal ("Wait until you hear this one") or nonverbal (a prolonged pause or hands motioning for silence to signal that an important message is about to be spoken). Or, as is most often the case, it's some combination of verbal and nonverbal signals. Feedforward may refer to the content of the message to follow ("I'll tell you exactly what they said to each other") or to the form ("I won't spare you the gory details"). Feedforward has four major functions: (1) to open the channels of communication, (2) to preview the message, (3) to altercast, and (4) to disclaim.

To Open the Channels of Communication. **Phatic communion** refers to messages that open the channels of communication rather than communicate information (Malinowski 1923; Lu 1998). Phatic communion is a perfect example of feedforward. It's information that tells us that the normal, expected, and accepted rules of interaction will be in effect. It tells us another person is willing to communicate. The infamous "opening line" ("Have you got a match?" or "Haven't we met before?") is a clear example of phatic communion. When such phatic messages don't precede an initial interaction, you sense that something is wrong and may conclude that the speaker lacks the basic skills of communication.

To Preview Future Messages. Feedforward messages frequently preview other messages. Feedforward may, for example, preview the content ("I'm afraid I have bad news for you"), the importance ("Listen to this before you make a move"), the form or style ("I'll be brief"), and the positive or negative quality of subsequent messages ("You're not going to like this, but here's what I heard").

To Altercast. Feedforward is often used to place the receiver in a specific role and to request that the receiver respond to you in terms of this assumed role. This process, known as **altercasting**, asks the receiver to approach your message from a particular role or even as someone else (McLaughlin 1984; Weinstein & Deutschberger 1963; Johnson 1993). For example, you might ask a friend, "As an advertising executive, what do you think of corrective advertising?" This question casts your friend into the role of advertising executive (rather than parent, Democrat, or Baptist, for example). It asks your friend to answer from a particular perspective.

To Disclaim. The disclaimer is a statement that aims to ensure that your message will be understood and will not reflect negatively on you. Disclaimers try to persuade the listener to hear your message as you wish it to be heard rather than through some assumption that might reflect negatively on you (Hewitt & Stokes 1975). For example, to insure that people listen to you fairly you might disclaim any thought that you're sexist and say, for example, "I'm no sexist, but . . . ." The disclaimer is discussed in greater detail in Unit 13.

Noise

Noise prevents a receiver from getting the message a source is sending. Noise may be physical (others talking loudly, cars honking, illegible handwriting, "garbage" on your computer screen), physiological (hearing or visual impairment, articulation disorders), psychological (preconceived ideas, wandering thoughts), or semantic (misunderstood meanings). Technically, noise is anything that distorts the message, anything that prevents the receiver from receiving the message.

A useful concept in understanding noise and its importance in communication is "signal-to-noise ratio." Signal refers to information that you'd find useful and noise refers to information that is useless (to you). So, for example, a mailing list or newsgroup that contained lots of useful information would be high on signal and low on noise; one that contained lots of useless information would be high on noise and low on signal.

Since messages may be visual as well as spoken, noise too may be visual. Thus, the sunglasses that prevent someone from seeing the nonverbal messages from your eyes would be considered noise, as would blurred type on a printed page. Table 1.2 identifies these four types of noise in more detail.

All communications contain noise. Noise cannot be totally eliminated, but its effects can be reduced. Making your language more precise, sharpening your skills for sending and receiving nonverbal messages, and improving your listening and feedback skills are some ways to combat the influence of noise.

Communication Effects

Communication always has some effect on one or more persons involved in the communication act. For every communication act, there is some consequence. For example, you may gain knowledge or learn how to analyze, synthesize, or evaluate something. These are intellectual or cognitive effects. Or you may acquire or change your attitudes, beliefs, emotions, and feelings. These are affective effects. You may even learn new bodily movements, such as throwing a ball or painting a picture, as well as

TABLE 1.2   Four Types of Noise

One of the most important skills in communication is to recognize the types of noise and to develop ways to combat them. Consider, for example, what kinds of noise occur in the classroom? What kinds of noise occur in your family communications? What kinds occur at work? What can you do to combat these kinds of noise?

Types of Noise	Definition	Example
Physical	Interference that is external to both speaker and listener, it interferes with the physical transmission of the signal or message	Screeching of passing cars, hum of computer, sunglasses
Physiological	Physical barriers within the speaker or listener	Visual impairments, hearing loss, articulation problems, memory loss
Psychological	Cognitive or mental interference	Biases and prejudices in senders and receivers, closed-mindedness, inaccurate expectations, extreme emotionalism (anger, hate, love, grief)
Semantic	Speaker and listener assigning different meanings	People speaking different languages, use of jargon or overly complex terms not understood by listener, dialectical differences in meaning

MEDIA WATCH

MEDIA ETHICS

As noted in the text, ethics is relevant to all forms of communication; the media are no exception. Because of its tremendous influence, media ethics is important to everyone who listens to the radio, watches television, or reads a newspaper (Elliott 1993). Here are just a few questions that raise ethical issues relevant to the media. They are presented here to stimulate you to think about these important topics and to watch the media more closely.

What do you think of checkbook journalism? Is it ethical for a news organization to pay someone for a story? For example, is it ethical to pay a juror from, say, the O.J. Simpson trial or from the President Clinton Grand Jury to reveal what went on at the trial or hearing? Can such payments lead people to distort the accuracy with which they present the events?

At what point, if any, does hate speech fall outside protection by the first amendment? Does a person have the right to say anything? And, if not, what (specifically) should people be prevented from saying?

Should anonymous speech (for example, writing and distributing social action pamphlets without any name attached) be granted the same protection as speech that identifies the author? Recently, the Supreme Court upheld the protection of anonymous speech (*New York Times* April 24, 1995, A16). Do you agree?

What about sex, nudity, and violence? Should the media be allowed greater freedom? Should the regulations governing such portrayals be made more stringent? And what standard should be used in making decisions about what is "too sexual," "too much nudity," and "too violent?" What do you think of the V-chip that locks out programs rated as violent? Would you support an S-chip or an N-chip that locks out programs containing sex or nudity?

What do you think of Shield laws—laws protecting reporters from revealing their sources if they promised anonymity in order to secure the information? What do you think of gag rules—rules prohibiting reporters from revealing certain information? What types of information, if any, should be covered by gag rules?

An advertising campaign for the Italian clothing conglomerate, Benetton, features scenes evoking extremely strong feelings. Scenes include a human body with "H.I.V. Positive" stamped on it and small Latin American children working in a stone quarry. A recent decision by a German court ruled the ads illegal. A French court fined Benetton $32,000 for the H.I.V. ad (Nash 1995). Do you think the decisions of these courts were fair? Were the ads "a provocative exploitation of suffering" as the French court ruled? Or were they designed to stimulate awareness and highlight social problems as Benetton argues? Do you think these decisions violate Benetton's (or any person's or company's) freedom of expression?

The next Media Watch appears on page 32.

---

appropriate verbal and nonverbal behaviors. These are psychomotor effects.

Ethics

Because communication has consequences, it also involves questions of ethics, of right and wrong (Bok 1978; Jaksa & Pritchard 1994). For example, while it may be effective to exaggerate or even lie in selling a product or in getting elected, it would not be ethical to do so.

The ethical dimension of communication is complicated because ethics is so interwoven with one's personal philosophy of life and the culture in which one is raised that it is difficult to propose guidelines for everyone. Nevertheless, ethical considerations need to be considered as integral to any communication act. The decisions you make concerning communication must be guided by what you consider right as well as what you consider effective.

SUMMARY

In this unit we introduced human communication, explained its major types and its relationship to culture, and defined its major elements and processes.

1. Communication refers to the act, by one or more persons, of sending and receiving messages that are distorted by noise, occur within a context, have some effect (and some ethical dimension), and provide some opportunity for feedback.

2. The major types of human communication are intrapersonal, interpersonal, small group, public, mass, and intercultural communication.

3. Culture refers to the collection of beliefs, attitudes, values, and ways of behavior shared by a group of people and passed down from one generation to another through communication rather than through genes.

4. All communication is influenced by culture; hence, an understanding of the role of culture is essential for understanding communication and for mastering its skills.

5. The universals of communication—the elements present in every communication act—are: context, source-receiver, message, channel, noise (physical, social-psychological, and semantic), sending or encoding processes, receiving or decoding processes, feedback and feedforward, effect, and ethics.

6. The communication context has at least four dimensions: physical, cultural, social-psychological, and temporal.

7. Communicative competence refers to knowledge of the elements and rules of communication, which vary from one culture to another.

8. Communication messages may be of varied forms and may be sent and received through any combination of sensory organs. The communication channel is the medium through which the messages are sent.

9. Feedback refers to messages or information that is sent back to the source. It may come from the source itself or from the receiver and may be indexed along such dimensions as positive and negative, person-focused and message-focused, immediate and delayed, low-monitored and high-monitored, and supportive and critical.

10. Feedforward refers to messages that preface other messages and may be used to open the channels of communication, to preview future messages, to disclaim, and to altercast.

11. Noise is anything that distorts the message; it's present to some degree in every communication transaction.

12. Communication always has an effect. Effects may be cognitive, affective, or psychomotor.

13. Communication ethics refers to the rightness or wrongness—the morality—of a communication transaction and is an integral part of every communication transaction.

KEY TERMS

intrapersonal communication (p. 2)

interpersonal communication (p. 2)

small group communication (p. 2)

public communication (p. 2)

mass communication (p. 2)

intercultural communication (p. 2)

culture (p. 4)

assimilationist position (p. 7)

communication context (p. 10)

sources-receivers (p. 11)

encoders-decoders (p. 12)

encoding-decoding (p. 12)

communication competence (p. 12)

message (p. 12)

channel (p. 12)

feedback (p. 13)

feedforward (p. 14)

altercasting (p. 15)

phatic communion (p. 15)

disclaimer (p. 15)

noise (p. 16)

communication effects (p. 16)

ethics (p. 17)

THINKING CRITICALLY ABOUT
Preliminaries to Human Communication

1. Do your college courses integrate a multicultural perspective? How is this reflected in your textbooks? What would be the ideal multicultural curriculum for your college? Is this also reflected in the media, for example, in newspapers, magazines, and television? Are your local media more or less "culturally integrated" than the national media?

2. What kinds of feedforward can you find in this textbook? What specific functions do these feedforwards serve?

3. Do you agree that using e-mail and whispering in Internet Relay Chat groups (IRCs) are similar to interpersonal conversation, that IRCs are similar to small groups, and that newsgroups are similar to public speaking? What other similarities can you identify? What differences can you identify?

4. What noted personality would you nominate for the "Communication Competence Hall of Fame"?

5. Some researchers (for example, Beier 1974) argue that the impulse to communicate two different feelings (for example, "I love you" and "I don't love you") creates messages in which the nonverbal contradicts the verbal message. Do you think this idea has validity? What other explanations might you offer to account for contradictory messages?

6. How would you go about finding answers to such questions as these:
   • Are instructors who accurately read student feedback better liked than instructors who can't read feedback as accurately? Is there a relationship between the ability to read feedback and the ability to communicate information or to motivate or persuade an audience?
   • Is knowledge about communication related to the ability to communicate effectively? That is, are those who know more about communication more effective communicators than those who know less?
   • Do people who watch more television feel less positive about themselves than do those who watch less television?
   • Do sunglasses influence the effectiveness of a speaker's interpersonal, small group, and public communication?

UNIT 2

Principles Of Communication

UNIT CONTENTS

UNIT GOALS

After completing this unit, you should be able to

explain the packaged nature of communication and double-bind messages

explain interpersonal communication as a transaction

explain the principle of adjustment in communication

distinguish between content and relationship dimensions of communication

define *punctuation*

distinguish between symmetrical and complementary transactions

explain the inevitability and irreversibility of communication

explain the five major purposes communication serves

The previous unit defined communication and explained some of its components and characteristics. This unit continues to explain the nature of communication by presenting eight principles. These principles are essential to understanding communication in all its forms and functions. However, these principles also have very practical implications. They provide insight into such day-to-day issues as:

- Why do disagreements so often center on trivial matters and yet seem so difficult to resolve?
- Why can you never know exactly what another person is thinking or feeling?
- How does power work in communication?
- Why might you and others see issues in extremely different, even opposite ways?

COMMUNICATION IS A PACKAGE OF SIGNALS

Communication behaviors, whether they involve verbal messages, gestures, or some combination thereof, usually occur in "packages" (Pittenger, Hockett, & Danehy 1960). Usually, verbal and nonverbal behaviors reinforce or support each other. All parts of a message system normally work together to communicate a particular meaning. You don't express fear with words while the rest of your body is relaxed. You don't express anger through your posture while your face smiles. Your entire body works together—verbally and nonverbally—to express your thoughts and feelings.

In any form of communication, whether interpersonal, small group, public speaking, or mass media, you probably pay little attention to its packaged nature. It goes unnoticed. But when there's an incongruity—when the weak handshake belies the verbal greeting, when the nervous posture belies the focused stare, when the constant preening belies the expressions of being comfortable and at ease—you take notice. Invariably you begin to question the credibility, the sincerity, and the honesty of the individual.

Often contradictory messages are sent over a period of time. Note, for example, that in the following interaction the employee is being given two directives—use initiative and don't use initiative. Regardless of what he or she does, rejection will follow.

EMPLOYER: You've got to learn to take more initiative. You never seem to take charge, to take control.

EMPLOYEE: [Takes the initiative, makes decisions.]

EMPLOYER: You've got to learn to follow the chain of command and not do things just because you want to.

EMPLOYEE: [Goes back to old ways, not taking any initiative.]

EMPLOYER: Well, I told you. We expect more initiative from you.

Contradictory messages are particularly damaging when children are involved. Children can neither escape from such situations nor communicate about the communications. They can't talk about the lack of correspondence between one set of messages and another set. Children can't ask their parents, for example, why their parents don't hold them or hug them when they say they love them.

These contradictory messages may be the result of the desire to communicate two different emotions or feelings. For example, you may like a person and want to communicate a positive feeling, but you may also feel resentment toward this person and want to communicate a negative feeling as well. The result is that you communicate both feelings; for example, you say that you're happy to see the person but your facial expression and body posture communicate your negative feelings (Beier 1974). In this example, and in many similar cases, the socially acceptable message is usually communicated verbally while the less socially acceptable message is communicated nonverbally.

COMMUNICATION IS TRANSACTIONAL

Communication is transactional (Barnlund 1970; Watzlawick 1977, 1978; Watzlawick, Beavin, & Jackson 1967; Wilmot 1987). One implication of viewing communication as transactional is that each person is seen as both speaker and listener, as simultaneously sending and receiving messages. Figure 2.1 illustrates this transactional view and compares it with earlier views of communication that may still influence the way you see communication.

"Transactional" also means that communication is an ever-changing process. It's an ongoing activity; all the elements of communication are in a state of constant change. You're constantly changing, the people

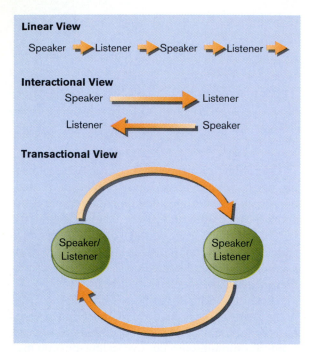

Linear View

Speaker → Listener → Speaker → Listener →

Interactional View

Speaker → Listener

Listener ← Speaker

Transactional View

Speaker/Listener   Speaker/Listener

Figure 2.1 **The transactional view of communication.** The top figure represents a linear view of communication, in which the speaker speaks and the listener listens. The middle figure represents an interactional view, in which speaker and listener take turns speaking and listening; A speaks while B listens, and then B speaks while A listens. The bottom figure represents a transactional view, in which each person serves simultaneously as speaker and listener; at the same time that you send messages, you're also receiving messages from your own communications and also from the messages of the other person(s).

with whom you're communicating are changing, and your environment is changing. Nothing in communication ever remains static.

In any transactional process, each element relates integrally to every other element. The elements of communication are interdependent (never independent). Each exists in relation to the others. For example, there can be no source without a receiver. There can be no message without a source. There can be no feedback without a receiver. Because of this interdependence, a change in any one element of the process produces changes in the other elements. For example, you're talking with a group of your friends when your mother enters the group. This change in "audi-

ence" will lead to other changes. Perhaps you or your friends will adjust what you're saying or how you say it. The new situation may also influence how often certain people talk, and so on. Regardless of what change is introduced, other changes will be produced as a result.

Each person in a communication transaction acts and reacts on the basis of the present situation. But, this present situation, your immediate context, is influenced by your history, past experiences, attitudes, cultural beliefs, self-image, future expectations, emotions, and a host of related issues. One implication of this is that actions and reactions in communication are determined not only by what is said, but also by the way each person interprets what is said. Your responses to a movie, for example, don't depend solely on the words and pictures in the film but also on your previous experiences, present emotions, knowledge, physical well being, and other factors.

Another implication is that two people listening to the same message will often derive two very different meanings. Although the words and symbols are the same, each person interprets them differently.

COMMUNICATION IS A PROCESS OF ADJUSTMENT

Communication may take place only to the extent that the communicators use the same system of signals (Pittenger, Hockett, & Danehy 1960). You will not be able to communicate with another person to the extent that your language systems differ. In reality, however, no two persons use identical signal systems, so this principle is relevant to all forms of communication. Parents and children, for example, not only have largely different vocabularies but also have different meanings for the terms they do share. Different cultures, even when they use a common language, often have greatly different nonverbal communication systems. To the extent that these systems differ, meaningful and effective communication will not take place.

Part of the art of communication is identifying the other person's signals, learning how they're used, and understanding what they mean. Those in close relationships will realize that learning the other person's signals takes a great deal of time and often a great deal of patience. If you want to understand what another person means (by a smile, by saying "I

BUILDING
Communication Skills

HOW DO YOU RESPOND TO CONTRADICTORY MESSAGES?

Compose responses to each of these statements that, let's assume, seem contradictory or that somehow don't ring true on the basis of what you know about the person.

- Even if I do fail the course, so what? I don't need it for graduation.

- I called three people. They all have something to do on Saturday night. I guess I'll just curl up with a good book or a good movie. It'll be better than a lousy date anyway.
- My parents are getting divorced after twenty years of marriage. My mother and father are both dating other people now so everything is going okay.
- My youngest child is going to need special treatments if he's going to walk again. The doctors are going to decide today on what kind of treatment. But all will end well in this, the best of all possible worlds.

love you," by arguing about trivia, by self-deprecating comments), rather than simply acknowledging what the other person says or does, you have to learn that person's system of signals.

This principle is especially important in intercultural communication, largely because people from different cultures use different signals and sometimes the same signals to signify quite different things. Focused eye contact means honesty and openness in much of the United States. But that same behavior may signify arrogance or disrespect in Japan and in many Hispanic cultures if, say, engaged in by a youngster with someone significantly older.

Communication Accommodation

An interesting theory largely revolving around adjustment is communication accommodation theory. This theory holds that speakers will adjust to or accommodate to the speaking style of their listeners to gain, for example, social approval and greater communication efficiency (Giles, Mulac, Bradac, & Johnson 1987). For example, when two people have a similar speech rate, they seem to be more attracted to each other than to those with dissimilar rates (Buller, LePoire, Aune, & Eloy 1992). Speech rate similarity has also been associated with greater immediacy, sociability, and intimacy (Buller & Aune

How does the principle of adjustment relate to communication between parents and children? Communication between students and teachers? Communication between members of different races or religions?

1992). Also, the speaker who uses language intensity similar to that of listeners is judged to have greater credibility than the speaker who used intensity different from that of listeners (Aune & Kikuchi 1993). Still another study found that roommates who had similar communication attitudes (both were high in communication competence and willingness to communicate and low in verbal aggressiveness) were highest in roommate liking and satisfaction (Martin & Anderson 1995).

As illustrated throughout this text, communication characteristics are influenced greatly by culture (Albert & Nelson 1993). Thus, the communication similarities that lead to attraction and more positive perceptions are likely to be present in *intra*cultural communication but absent in many *inter*cultural encounters. This may present an important (but not insurmountable) obstacle to intercultural communication.

COMMUNICATION INVOLVES CONTENT AND RELATIONSHIP DIMENSIONS

Communications, to a certain extent at least, refer to the real world, to something external to both speaker and listener. At the same time, however, communications also refer to the relationships between the parties (Watzlawick, Beavin, & Jackson 1967).

For example, an employer may say to a worker, "See me after the meeting." This simple message has a content aspect and a relational aspect. The content aspect refers to the behavioral responses expected—namely, that the worker see the employer after the meeting. The relational aspect tells how the communication is to be dealt with. Even the use of the simple command says that there's a status difference between the two parties: the employer can command the worker. This is perhaps seen most clearly when you imagine the worker giving this command to the employer; it appears awkward and out of place because it violates the expected communications between employer and worker.

In any communication situation the content dimension may stay the same but the relationship aspect may vary. Or, the relationship aspect may be the same while the content is different. For example, the employer could say to the worker either "You had better see me after the meeting" or "May I please see you after the meeting?" In each case the content is essentially the same; that is, the message

UNDERSTANDING
Theory and Research

WHAT'S THE USE OF THEORIES?

In reading about theories, you may well ask yourself, "Why should I learn this? Of what value is this material to me?" Here are a few answers to these very legitimate questions.

Communication theories help you understand the way communication works. Theories provide general principles that help you understand an enormous number of specific events—how and why these events occur and how they're related to each other. As one communication theorist puts it, "A good theory synthesizes the data, fo-

cuses our attention on what's crucial, and helps us ignore that which makes little difference" (Griffin 1991, p. 4).

Communication theories also help you predict future events. The theories summarize what's been found and can therefore offer useful and generally reasonable predictions for events that you've never encountered. For example, based on the theories of persuasion, you would be able to predict whether strong, medium, or weak appeals to fear would be more effective in persuading an audience. Or, based on the theories of conflict resolution, you would be able to predict which strategies will prove more effective in resolving the differences.

being communicated about the behaviors expected is the same in both cases. But the relationship dimension is very different. In the first it signifies a definite superior-inferior relationship and even a put-down of the worker. In the second, the employer signals a more equal relationship and shows respect for the worker.

Similarly, at times the content may be different but the relationship essentially the same. For example, a teenager might say to his or her parents, "May I go away this weekend?" and "May I use the car tonight?" The content of the two messages is clearly very different. The relationship dimension, however, is essentially the same. It's clearly a superior-inferior relationship in which permission to do certain things must be secured.

Ignoring Relationship Dimensions

Problems may arise when the distinction between the content and relationship levels of communication is ignored. Consider a couple arguing over the fact that Pat made plans to study during the weekend with friends without first asking Chris if that would be all right. Probably both would have agreed that to study over the weekend was the right choice to make. Thus the argument is not at all related to the content level. The argument centers on the relationship level. Chris expected to be consulted about plans for the weekend. Pat, in not doing so, rejected this definition of the relationship.

Let me give you a personal example. My mother came to stay for a week at a summer place I had. On the first day she swept the kitchen floor six times, though I had repeatedly told her that it did not need sweeping since I would be tracking in dirt and mud from outside—all her effort would be wasted. But she persisted in sweeping, saying that the floor was dirty and should be swept. On the content level, we were talking about the value of sweeping the kitchen floor. But on the relationship level we were talking about something quite different. We were each saying, "This is my house." When I realized this (though only after considerable argument), I stopped complaining about the relative usefulness of sweeping a floor that did not need sweeping and she stopped sweeping it.

Consider the following interchange:

DIALOGUE	COMMENTARY
PAUL: I'm going bowling tomorrow. The guys at the plant are starting a team.	He focuses on the content and ignores any relational implications of the message.
JUDY: Why can't we ever do anything together?	She responds primarily on a relational level and ignores the content implications of the message, and expresses her displeasure at being ignored in his decision.
PAUL: We can do something together anytime; tomorrow's the day they're organizing the team.	Again, he focuses almost exclusively on the content.

This example reflects research findings that show that men focus more on content messages, whereas women focus more on relationship messages (Pearson, West, & Turner 1995). Once we recognize this gender difference, we may be able to develop increased sensitivity to the opposite sex.

Recognizing Relationship Dimensions

Here's essentially the same situation but with the added sensitivity to relationship messages:

DIALOGUE	COMMENTARY
PAUL: The guys at the plant are organizing a bowling team. I'd sure like to be on the team. Do you mind if I go to the organizational meeting tomorrow?	Although he focuses on content, he shows awareness of the relational dimensions by asking if this would be a problem. He also shows this in expressing his desire rather than his decision to attend this meeting.
JUDY: That sounds great, but I'd really like to	She focuses on the relational dimension but also acknowledges his content orientation.

DIALOGUE	COMMENTARY
do something together tomorrow.	Note too that she does not respond as if she has to defend herself or her emphasis on relational aspects.
PAUL: How about your meeting me at Luigi's for dinner after the organizational meeting?	He responds to the relational aspect without abandoning his desire to join the bowling team—and seeks to incorporate it into his communications. He attempts to negotiate a solution that will meet both Judy's and his needs and desires.
JUDY: That sounds great. I'm dying for spaghetti and meatballs.	She responds to both messages, approving of both his joining the team and their dinner date.

Arguments over the content dimension are relatively easy to resolve. You may look something up in a book or ask someone what actually took place. Arguments on the relationship level, however, are much more difficult to resolve, in part because you (like me in the example of my mother) may not recognize that the argument is in fact a relationship one.

COMMUNICATION SEQUENCES ARE PUNCTUATED

Communicating events are continuous transactions. There's no clear-cut beginning or ending. As a participant in or an observer of the communication act, you divide up this continuous, circular process into causes and effects, or stimuli and responses. That is, you segment this continuous stream of communication into smaller pieces. You label some of these pieces causes or stimuli and others effects or responses.

Consider an example: The students are apathetic; the teacher does not prepare for classes. Figure 2.2(a) illustrates the sequence of events in which there's no absolute beginning and no absolute end. Each action (the students' apathy and the teacher's lack of preparation) stimulates the other. But there's no initial stimulus. Each of the events may be regarded as a stimulus and each as

a response, but there's no way to determine which is which.

Consider how the teacher might divide up this continuous transaction. Figure 2.2(b) illustrates the teacher's perception of this situation. From this point of view, the teacher sees the students' apathy as the stimulus for his or her lack of preparation, and the lack of preparation as the response to the students' apathy. In Figure 2.2(c) we see how the students might divide up the transaction. The students might see this "same" sequence of events as beginning with the teacher's lack of preparation as the stimulus (or cause) and their own apathy as the response (or effect).

This tendency to divide up the various communication transactions in sequences of stimuli and responses is referred to as punctuation (Watzlawick, Beavin, & Jackson 1967). People punctuate the continuous sequences of events into stimuli and responses for ease of understanding and remembering. And, as the example of the students and teacher illustrates, people punctuate communication in ways that allow them to look good and that are consistent with their own self-image.

If communication is to be effective, if you're to understand what another person means from his or her point of view, then you have to see the sequence of events as punctuated by the other person. Further, you have to recognize that your punctuation does not reflect what exists in reality. Rather, it reflects your own unique but fallible perception.

COMMUNICATION INVOLVES SYMMETRICAL AND COMPLEMENTARY TRANSACTIONS

Relationships can be described as either symmetrical or complementary (Watzlawick, Beavin, & Jackson 1967). In a **symmetrical relationship** the two individuals mirror each other's behavior. The behavior of one person is reflected in the behavior of the other. If one member nags, the other member responds in kind. If one member expresses jealousy, the other member expresses jealousy. If one member is passive, the other member is passive. The relationship is one of equality, with the emphasis on minimizing the differences between the two individuals.

Note, however, the problems that can arise in this type of relationship. Consider the situation of a

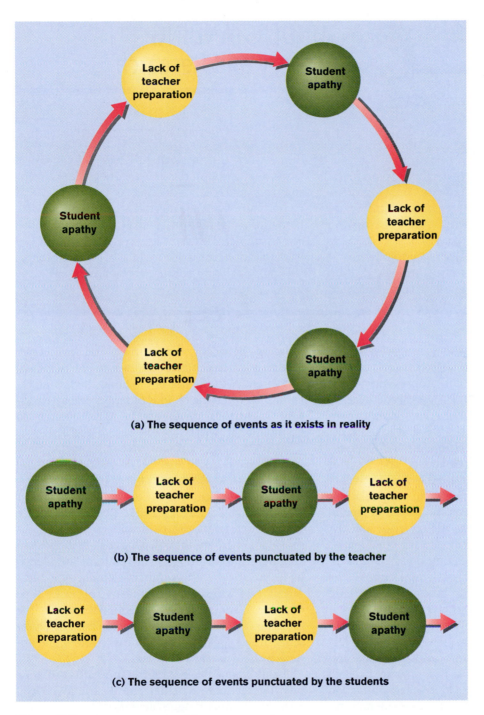

(a) The sequence of events as it exists in reality

(b) The sequence of events punctuated by the teacher

(c) The sequence of events punctuated by the students

Figure 2.2 **The Sequence of Events**   Try using this three-part figure, discussed in the text, to explain what might go on when Pat complains about Chris's nagging and Chris complains about Pat's avoidance and silence.

UNDERSTANDING
Theory and Research

DO THEORIES REVEAL TRUTH?

Despite their many values, theories don't reveal truth in any absolute sense. Rather, theories reveal some degree of accuracy, some degree of truth. In the natural sciences such as physics and chemistry, theories are extremely high in accuracy. If you mix two parts of hydrogen to one part of oxygen, you'll get water—every time you do it. In the social and behavioral sciences such as communication, sociology, and psychology, the theories are far less accurate in describing the way things work and in predicting how things will work. One communication theorist offers this summary guidance: "So because a theory does not reveal truth, does not mean that it fails to communicate a kind of truth. An insight or useful way of classifying or explaining events is a kind of truth. Just don't make the mistake of believing too hard in one theory because every theory has its limits" (Littlejohn 1996, p. 361).

husband and wife, both of whom are aggressive. The aggressiveness of the husband fosters aggressiveness in the wife; the anger of the wife arouses anger in the husband. As this escalates, the aggressiveness can no longer be contained, and the relationship is consumed by aggression.

In a **complementary relationship** the two individuals engage in different behaviors. The behavior of one serves as the stimulus for the complementary behavior of the other. In complementary relationships the differences between the parties are maximized. One partner acts as the superior and the other the inferior, one passive and the other active, one strong and the other weak. At times cultures establish such relationships—as, for example, the complementary relationship between teacher and student or between employer and employee.

Early marriages are likely to be complementary relationships where each person tries to complete himself or herself. When these couples separate and form new relationships, these new ones are likely to be symmetrical and involve a kind of reconfirmation of their own identity (Prosky 1992). Generally, research finds that complementary couples have a lower marital adjustment level than do symmetrical couples (Main & Oliver 1988; Holden 1991).

A problem in complementary relationships familiar to many college students is one created by extreme rigidity. Whereas the complementary relationship between a nurturing and protective mother and a dependent child was at one time vital and essential to the life of the child, that same relationship when the child is older becomes a handicap to further development. The change so essential to growth is not allowed to occur.

An interesting perspective on complementary and symmetrical relationships can be gained by looking at the ways in which these patterns combine to exert control in a relationship (Rogers-Millar & Millar 1979; Millar & Rogers 1987; Rogers & Farace 1975). Such relationships may occur in interpersonal, small group, interviewing, or organizational communication settings. Nine patterns are identified; three deal with symmetry (similar type messages), two with complementarity (opposite type messages), and four with transitional (neither the same nor opposite type messages). Table 2.1 presents these types of relationships to show one approach to research in this area.

Think about these patterns in relation to your own interactions, whether among friends, loved ones, family, or colleagues at work:

- How rigid or flexible are these patterns? For example, do you and your friends or colleagues share control and submission or does one of you exercise control and the other respond with submission?

TABLE 2.1   Relationship types

This classification is based on the research of Rogers-Millar & Millar 1979; Millar & Rogers 1987; and Rogers & Farace 1975. Do you find this classification helpful for understanding relationships?

Relationship Type	Example
In competitive symmetry each person tries to exert control over the other (symbolized by an upward arrow, ↑). Each communicates one-up messages (messages that attempt to control the behaviors of the other person):	Pat: Do it now. ↑ Chris: I'll do it when I'm good and ready; otherwise, do it yourself. ↑
In submissive symmetry each person communicates submission (symbolized by a downward arrow ↓); both messages are one-down (messages that indicate submission to what the other person wants):	Pat: What do you want for dinner? ↓ Chris: Whatever you'd like is fine with me. ↓
In neutralized symmetry each person communicates similarly but neither competitively, one-up, nor submissively, one-down (symbolized by a horizontal arrow →):	Pat: Jackie needs new shoes. → Chris: And a new jacket. →
In complementarity one person communicates the desire to control (one-up) and the other person communicates submission (one-down).	Pat: Here, honey, do it this way. ↑ Chris: Oh, that's great; you're so clever. ↓
In another type of complementarity—the reverse of the above—the submissive message (one-down) comes first and is followed by a controlling (one-up) message:	Pat: I need suggestions for managing this new team of recruits. ↓ Chris: Oh, that's easy; I've managed similar groups for years. ↑

Transition patterns are those that don't involve stating the opposite of the previous message; they don't respond to a competitive message with submission, nor to a submissive message with a competitive one. There are four possible transition patterns:

• A competitive message (one-up) is responded to without either another competitive message or a submissive message:	Pat: I want to go to the movies. ↑ Chris: There surely are a lot of choices this weekend. →
• A submissive message (one-down) is responded to without either another submissive message or a competitive message:	Pat: I'm just helpless with tools. ↓ Chris: Lots of people have difficulty using a router. →
• A transition message (one-across) is responded to with a competitive (one-up) message:	Pat: We can do it in lots of ways. → Chris: Well, here's the right way. ↑
• A transition message (one-across) is responded to with a submissive (one-down) message:	Pat: We can do it in lots of ways. → Chris: However you do it is fine. ↓

- Can you identify a relationship you have that makes use of one major pattern? What part do you play? Are you comfortable with this pattern?
- Can you identify a general pattern that you use in many or most of your interpersonal relationships? In most of your work relationships?

How satisfied are you with your customary patterns of expression?
- Can you identify relationships you have that began with one pattern of communication and over the years have shifted to another pattern? What happened?

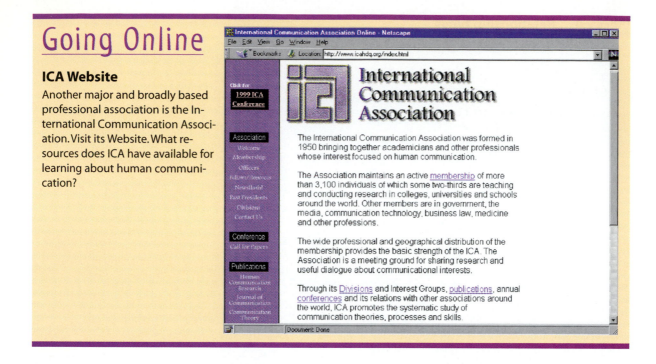

Going Online

ICA Website

Another major and broadly based professional association is the International Communication Association. Visit its Website. What resources does ICA have available for learning about human communication?

COMMUNICATION IS INEVITABLE, IRREVERSIBLE, AND UNREPEATABLE

Communication is a process that is inevitable, irreversible, and unrepeatable. Communication messages are always being sent (or almost always), can't be reversed or uncommunicated, and are always unique and one time occurrences. Let's look at these qualities in more detail.

Inevitability

In many instances communication takes place even though one of the individuals does not think he or she is communicating or does not want to communicate. Consider, for example, the student sitting in the back of the room with an expressionless face, perhaps staring out the window. Although the student might claim not to be communicating with the teacher, the teacher may derive any one of a variety of messages from this behavior. Perhaps the teacher assumes that the student lacks interest, is bored, or is worried about something. In any event, the teacher is receiving messages even though the student may not intend to communicate. In an interactional situation, you can't avoid communicating

(Watzlawick, Beavin, & Jackson 1967); communication is inevitable. This is not to say that all behavior is communication. For example, if the student looked out the window and the teacher failed to notice this, no communication would have taken place.

Further, when you're in an interactional situation you can't avoid responding to the messages of others. For example, if you notice someone winking at you, you must respond in some way. Even if you don't respond actively or openly, that lack of response is itself a response, and it communicates. Again, if you don't notice the winking, then obviously communication has not occurred.

Irreversibility

Notice that you can only reverse the processes of some systems. For example, you can turn water into ice and then the ice back into water. And you can repeat this reversal process as many times as you wish. Other systems, however, are irreversible. You can turn grapes into wine but you can't turn the wine back into grapes—the process can go in only one direction. Communication is such an irreversible process. Once you say something, once you press the send key on your e-mail, you can't uncommunicate it. You can of course try to reduce the

Do the symmetrical and complementary patterns of your relationships have anything to do with the degree of satisfaction you experience? For example, do you derive greater satisfaction from an interaction that relies on one pattern than you do with an interaction that relies on another pattern?

effects of your message by saying, for example, "I really didn't mean what I said" or "I was so angry I couldn't think straight." But regardless of how you try to negate or reduce the effects of your message, the message itself, once it has been sent and received, can't be reversed.

In face-to-face communication, the actual signals (the movements in the air) are evanescent; they fade almost as they're uttered. Some written messages, especially computer-mediated messages, such as those sent through e-mail, are unerasable. E-mails that are sent among employees in a large corporation, for example, are often stored on disk or tape. Currently, much litigation is proceeding by using as evidence racist or sexist e-mails that senders thought were erased, but weren't.

Because of irreversibility (and unerasability), be careful not to say things you may be sorry for later. Especially in conflict situations, when tempers run high, avoid saying things you may later wish to withdraw. Commitment messages—the "I love you" messages and their variants—also need to be monitored. Messages that could be interpreted as sexist, racist, or homophobic, which you thought were private, might later be retrieved by others and create all sorts of problems for you and your organization. In group and public communication situations, when messages are received by many people, it's especially crucial to recognize the irreversibility.

Unrepeatability

The reason for communication being unrepeatable is simple: everyone and everything is constantly changing. As a result, you can never recapture the exact same situation, frame of mind, or relationship dynamics that defined a previous communication act. For example, you can never repeat meeting someone for the first time, making a first impression in an interview, or resolving a specific group problem.

You can, of course, try again as when you say, "I'm sorry I came off so forward, can we try again?" But even after you say this you have not erased the initial impression. Instead you try to counteract this initial and perhaps negative impression by going through the motions again.

COMMUNICATION IS MULTI-PURPOSEFUL

Purposes need not be conscious nor must individuals agree about their purposes for communicating. Purposes may be conscious or unconscious, recognizable or unrecognizable. Further, although communication technologies are changing rapidly and drastically—we send electronic mail, work at computer terminals, and telecommute, for example—the purposes of communication are likely to remain essentially the same

MEDIA WATCH

USES AND GRATIFICATION THEORY

In much the same way that you enter relationships to serve some specific purpose, you also use the media to serve specific purposes. Wilbur Schramm, in his *Men, Women, Messages, and Media* (1982) proposes this formula: promise of reward/effort required = probability of selection.

Under the promise of reward, Schramm includes both immediate and delayed rewards. Rewards satisfy the needs of the audience. That is, you watch a particular television program because it satisfies your need for information or entertainment. The effort required for attending to mass communications depends on the availability of the media and the ease with which we may use them. Effort also includes the expense involved. For example, there's less effort required—less expense, less time lost—in watching television than in going to a movie. There's less effort in going to a movie than in going to a play. When we divide the effort required into the promise of reward, we obtain the probability of selection of a particular mass communication medium.

This approach to media has come to be referred to as the uses and gratifications approach. We can understand people's interaction with the media by the uses they get from the media and the gratifications they derive.

Four general gratifications are identified in the research (Dominick 1994): (1) learning something—finding out what the new tax laws will involve or how movie reviewers rate the new film you want to see; (2) diversion—allowing you to escape your worries, stimulating you, or perhaps allowing you to release emotional energy; (3) affiliation—going to the movies together, talking about the developments on "Days of Our Lives," or developing parasocial relationships (see Media Watch box in Unit 12); and (4) withdrawal—escaping from worries, responsibilities, and other people.

According to uses and gratifications theory, the audience members actively and consciously link themselves to certain media to gain gratification. The media are seen in this approach as competing with other sources (largely interpersonal) to serve the needs of the audience.

Can you use this theory of uses and gratifications to explain your conversational behavior? What uses does conversation serve for you? What gratifications do you derive from your conversations? Do you gravitate toward those conversations that will give you immediate gratification? Delayed gratification?

The next Media Watch appears on page 45.

---

throughout the electronic revolution and whatever revolutions follow (Arnold & Bowers 1984; Naisbitt 1984). Five general purposes or motives of communication can be identified: to discover, to relate, to help, to persuade, and to play.

These purposes of communication can also be looked at from at least two other perspectives. First, purposes may be seen as motives for engaging in communication. That is, you engage in communication to satisfy your need for knowledge or to form relationships. Second, these purposes may be viewed in terms of the results you want to achieve. That is, you engage in interpersonal communication to increase your knowledge of yourself and others or to

exert influence or power other others. Communication is usually motivated by a combination of factors and has a combination of results or effects. Any communication act serves a unique combination of purposes, is motivated by a unique combination of factors, and can produce a unique combination of results (Figure 2.3).

To Discover

One of the major purposes of communication concerns personal discovery. When you communicate with another person, you learn about yourself as well as about the other person. In fact, your self-perceptions result largely from what you've learned

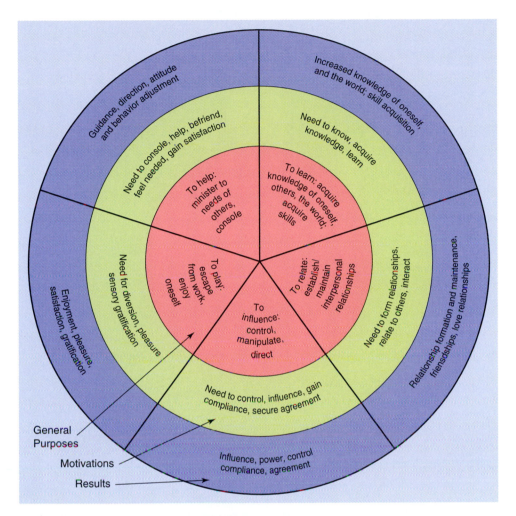

Figure 2.3 The multi-purposeful nature of human communication.   The innermost circle contains the general purposes. The middle circle contains the motivations. The outer circle contains the results that you might hope to achieve by engaging in communication. A similar typology of purposes comes from research on motives for communicating. In a series of studies, Rubin and her colleagues (Rubin & Martin 1998; Rubin, Fernandez-Collado, & Hernandez-Sampieri 1992; Rubin & Martin 1994; Rubin, Perse, & Barbato 1988; Rubin & Rubin 1992; Graham 1994; and Graham, Barbato, & Perse 1993) have identified six primary motives for communication: pleasure, affection, inclusion, escape, relaxation, and control. How do these compare to the five purposes discussed here?

about yourself from others during communications, especially your interpersonal encounters.

Much as communication gives you a better understanding of yourself and the person with whom you're communicating, it also helps you discover the external world—the world of objects, events, and other people. Today, you rely heavily on the various

communications media for information about entertainment, sports, war, economic developments, health and dietary concerns, and new products to buy. Much of what you acquire from the media interacts with what you learn from your interpersonal interactions. You get information from the media, discuss it with other people, and ultimately learn or

BUILDING
Communication Skills

WHAT'S HAPPENING?

How would you use the principles discussed in this unit to describe (not to solve) what is happening in each of the following situations? Realize that these scenarios are extremely brief and are written only as exercises to stimulate you to think more concretely about the principles. Note, too, that the objective is not to select the one correct principle (each scenario can probably be described with several principles), but to provide an opportunity to think about the principles in reference to specific situations.

- A couple, together for twenty years, argues constantly about the seemingly most insignificant things—who takes the dog out, who does the shopping, who decides where to go to dinner, and so on. It's gotten to the point where they rarely have a day without argument; both are considering separating.
- In teaching communication skills, Professor Jones frequently asks students to role play effective and ineffective communication patterns and offers criticism after each session. Although most students respond well to this instructional technique, Mariz has difficulty and has frequently left the class in tears.

- Pat has sought the assistance of a family therapist. The problem is simple: whatever Pat says, Chris says the opposite. If Pat wants to eat Chinese, Chris wants to eat Italian; if Pat wants Italian, Chris wants Chinese. And on and on. The problem is made worse by the fact that Chris has to win; Pat's wishes are invariably dismissed.
- In the heat of a big argument, Harry said he didn't want to ever see Peggy's family again: "They don't like me and I don't like them." Peggy reciprocated and said she felt the same way about his family. Now, weeks later, there remains a great deal of tension between them, especially when they find themselves with one or both families.
- Grace and Tom, senior executives at a large advertising agency, are engaged to be married. Recently, Grace made a presentation that was not received positively by the other members of the team. Grace feels that Tom—in not defending her proposal—created a negative attitude and actually encouraged others to reject her ideas. Tom says that he felt he could not defend her proposal because others would have felt his defense was motivated by their relationship and not by an objective evaluation of her proposal. So, he felt it was best to say nothing.

internalize the material as a result of the interaction between these two sources.

To Relate

One of our strongest motivations is to establish and maintain close relationships with others. The vast majority of people want to feel loved and liked, and in turn want to love and like others. You probably spend much of your communication time and energy establishing and maintaining social relationships. You communicate with your close friends in school, at work, and probably on the phone. You

talk with your parents, children, and brothers and sisters. You interact with your relational partner. All told, this takes a great deal of your time and attests to the importance of this purpose of communication.

Of course, you may also use communication to distance yourself from others, to argue and fight with friends and romantic partners, and even to dissolve relationships.

To Help

Therapists, counselors, teachers, parents, and friends are just a few categories of those who often—though not always—communicate to help. As is the case with therapists and counselors, entire professions are built around this communication function. But, there are few professions that don't make at least some significant use of this helping function. You also use this function when you constructively criticize, express empathy, work with a group to solve a problem, or listen attentively and supportively to a public speaker.

To Persuade

The mass media exist largely to persuade us to change our attitudes and behaviors. The media survive on advertisers' money, which is directed at getting us to buy a variety of items and services. Right now you probably spend much more time as consumers than originators of these mass-media messages. But in the not too distant future you'll no doubt be originating messages. You may work on a newspaper or edit a magazine, or work in an ad agency, television station, or a variety of other communication-related fields.

A great deal of your time is also spent in interpersonal persuasion, as both sources and receivers.

In your everyday interpersonal encounters you try to change the attitudes and behaviors of others. You try to get them to vote a particular way, try a new diet, buy a particular item, see a movie, read a book, take a specific course, believe that something is true or false, value or devalue some idea, and so on. The list is endless. Few of your interpersonal communications, in fact, don't seek to change attitudes or behaviors.

To Play

You probably also spend a great deal of your communication behavior on play. As viewed here, communication as play includes motives of pleasure, escape, and relaxation (Barbato & Perse 1992; Rubin, Perse, & Barbato 1988). For example, you often listen to comedians as well as friends largely because it's fun, enjoyable, and exciting. You tell jokes, say clever things, and relate interesting stories largely for the pleasure it gives to you and your listeners. Similarly, you may communicate because it relaxes you, allowing you to get away from pressures and responsibilities.

SUMMARY

In this unit we looked at some of the principles of human communication, principles that explain what communication is and how it works in a wide variety of situations and contexts.

1. Communication is normally a package of signals, each reinforcing the other. Opposing communication signals from the same source result in contradictory messages.
2. The double-bind, a special kind of contradictory message, may be created when contradictory messages are sent simultaneously.
3. Communication is a transactional process in which each person simultaneously sends and receives messages.
4. Communication is a process of adjustment and takes place only to the extent that the communicators use the same system of signals.

5. Communication involves both content dimensions and relationship dimensions.
6. Communication sequences are punctuated for processing. Different people divide up the communication sequence into stimuli and responses differently.
7. Communication involves symmetrical and complementary transactions.
8. In any interactional situation, communication is inevitable; you can't avoid communicating nor can you not respond to communication.
9. Communication is irreversible. You can't uncommunicate.
10. Communication is unrepeatable. You can't duplicate a previous communication act.
11. Communication is multi-purposeful and can be used to discover, relate, help, persuade, and play.

KEY TERMS

packaging (p. 21)

transaction (p. 21)

adjustment (p. 22)

content messages (p. 24)

relationship messages (p. 24)

punctuation (p. 26)

symmetrical relationships (p. 26)

complementary relationships (p. 26)

inevitability (p. 30)

irreversibility (p. 30)

unrepeatability (p. 31)

multi-purposeful (p. 31)

THINKING CRITICALLY ABOUT
the Principles of Human Communication

1. A good illustration of double-bind messages is that which takes place between a therapist and a client with disabilities; each seems to send contradictory messages that create "double-binds" for each other (Esten & Wilmot 1993). The client communicates both the desire to focus on the disability but also the desire to disregard it. What does the therapist do? If the therapist focuses on the disability, it's in violation of the client's desire to ignore it, and if the therapist ignores it, it's in violation of the client's desire to concentrate on it. Regardless of how the therapist responds, it's in violation of one of the client's preferences. What guidelines would you offer the therapist or the client, based on your understanding of contradictory messages?

2. Do you accommodate to the communication styles of those with whom you interact? Do teachers and students or lawyers and witnesses or doctors and patients accommodate to each other's communication style? In what direction is there likely to be greater accommodation? For example, is the teacher or the student more likely to accommodate the other?

3. Some researchers (for example, Beier 1974) argue that the impulse to communicate two different feelings (for example, "I love you" and "I don't love you") creates messages in which the nonverbal contradicts the verbal message. Do you think this idea has validity? What other explanations might you offer to account for contradictory messages?

4. Will the new communication technologies (for example, electronic mail, working at computer terminals, and telecommuting) change the basic purposes of communication identified here?

5. With very good intentions, you tell your partner "I guess you'll just never learn how to dress." To your surprise your partner becomes extremely offended. Although you know you can't take the statement back (communication really is irreversible), you want to lessen its negative tone and its effect on your partner. What do you say?

6. How would you go about finding answers to questions such as these?
   a. Is there a gender difference in the ability to appreciate the punctuation of another person?
   b. Does relative status influence who accommodates whom?
   c. Does the higher adjustment evidenced by symmetrical couples (over complementary couples) hold for all age groups? Does it hold for homosexual as it seems to hold for heterosexual relationships?
   d. What is the most effective way to "take back" an unkind or culturally insensitive remark?

UNIT 3
Perception

UNIT CONTENTS

UNIT GOALS

After completing this unit, you should be able to

define *perception* and explain the three stages in the perception process

explain how the following processes influence perception: implicit personality theory, the self-fulfilling prophecy, perceptual accentuation, primacy and recency, consistency, stereotyping, and attribution

explain the strategies for making perceptions more accurate

Perception is the process by which you become aware of the many stimuli impinging on your senses. Perception influences what stimuli or messages you take in and what meanings you give them once they reach awareness. Perception influences the way you see people, the evaluations you make of them and of their behaviors. Perception is therefore central to the study of communication in all its forms and functions. Here we look at (1) the process of perception, identifying its three main stages; (2) the processes that influence perception; and (3) how you can make your perceptions more accurate.

THE PERCEPTION PROCESS

Perception is complex. There's no one-to-one relationship between the messages that occur "out there" in the world—in the vibrations of the air and in the black marks on paper—and the messages that eventually get to your brain. What occurs "out there" may differ greatly from what reaches your conscious mind. Examining how and why these messages differ is crucial to understanding communication. We can illustrate how perception works by explaining the three steps involved in the process. These stages are not discrete and separate; in reality they're continuous and blend into and overlap one another (Figure 3.1).

Sensory Stimulation Occurs

At this first stage the sense organs are stimulated. You hear a recording. You see someone you haven't seen for years. You smell perfume on the person next to you. You taste a slice of pizza. You feel a sweaty palm as you shake hands.

Even when you have the sensory ability to perceive stimuli, you don't always do so. For example, when you're daydreaming in class, you don't hear what the teacher is saying until your own name is called. Then you wake up. You know you heard your name, but you don't know why. This is a clear example of perceiving what is meaningful to you and not perceiving what is not meaningful.

Sensory Stimulation Is Organized

At the second stage, the sensory stimulations are organized according to various principles. One of the more frequently used principles is that of **proximity**:

people or messages that are physically close to one another are perceived together, or as a unit. For example, you probably perceive people you often see together as a unit (such as a couple). Similarly, you perceive messages uttered one immediately after the other as a unit and assume that they're in some way related to each other.

Another such principle is **closure**: you perceive as closed, or complete, a figure or message that is in reality unclosed or incomplete. For example, you see a broken circle as a circle even though part of it is missing. You would even perceive a series of dots or dashes arranged in a circular pattern as a circle. Similarly, you fill in the fragmented messages you hear with those parts that seem logically to complete the messages.

You use the principle of **contrast** when you note that some items (people or messages, for example) don't belong together; they're too different from each other to be part of the same perceptual organization. So, for example, in a conversation or a public speech listeners will focus their attention on changes in intensity or rate since these contrast with the rest of the message.

Proximity, closure, and contrast are just three of the many organizing principles. In thinking about these principles, remember that whatever you perceive you also organize into a pattern that is meaningful to you. It is not a pattern that is necessarily true or logical in any objective sense.

Sensory Stimulation Is Interpreted-Evaluated

The third step in the perceptual process is interpretation-evaluation. This term is hyphenated to emphasize that its two parts cannot be separated. This third step is a subjective process involving evaluations on the part of the perceiver. Your interpretations-evaluations are not based solely on the external stimulus. Like communication, perception is a transactional process (Unit 2) and as a result is greatly influenced by your past experiences, needs, wants, value systems, beliefs about the way things are or should be, physical or emotional states at the time, expectations, and so on.

It should be clear from even this very incomplete list of influences that there's much room for individual interpretation of a given stimulus and hence disagreements. Although we may all be exposed to the same message, the way each person interprets-evaluates it

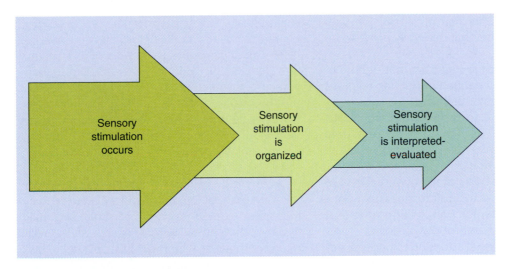

Figure 3.1 **The perception process.** The three arrows are designed to illustrate that the stages of perception overlap one another. Also, as the process goes from sensory stimulation to interpretation and evaluation, the focus narrows; for example, you organize *part of* what you sensed and you interpret and evaluate *part of* what you organized.

will differ. The interpretation-evaluation will also differ for the same person from one time to another. The sound of a popular rock group may be heard by one person as terrible noise and by another as great music. The sight of someone you've not seen for years may bring joy to you and anxiety to someone else. The smell of perfume may be pleasant to one person and repulsive to another. A sweaty palm may be perceived by one person to show nervousness and by another to show excitement.

PROCESSES INFLUENCING PERCEPTION

Between the occurrence of the stimulus (the uttering of the message, presence of the person, a smile or wink of the eye) and the evaluation or interpretation of that stimulation, perception is influenced by a number of significant psychological processes. Before reading about these processes, take the following self-test to analyze your own customary ways of perceiving others. Regardless of what form of communication you're engaged in—interpersonal, small group, public speaking, or mass communication—the ways in which you perceive the people involved

will influence your communications and your communication effectiveness.

 **SELF-TEST**

How Accurate Are You at People Perception?

Respond to each of the following statements with TRUE if the statement is usually accurate in describing your behavior. Respond with FALSE if the statement is usually inaccurate in describing your behavior. (Of course, when you take a test like this, you can often figure out the "right" answers and give these rather than really think about your own behaviors. Try to resist this very natural tendency to give the socially acceptable responses in this test as well as in similar tests throughout this text.)

_____ 1. I base most of my impressions of people on the first few minutes of our meeting.

_____ 2. When I know some things about another person I fill in what I don't know.

_____ 3. I make predictions about people's behaviors that generally prove to be true.

_____ 4. I have clear ideas of what people of different national, racial, and religious groups are really like.

_____ 5. I reserve making judgments about people until I learn a great deal about them and see them in a variety of situations.

_____ 6. On the basis of my observations of people, I formulate guesses about them (which I am willing to revise) rather than firm conclusions.

_____ 7. I pay special attention to people's behaviors that might contradict my initial impressions.

_____ 8. I delay formulating conclusions about people until I have lots of evidence.

_____ 9. I avoid making assumptions about what is going on in someone else's head on the basis of their behaviors.

_____ 10. I recognize that people are different, and I don't assume that everyone else is like me.

This brief perception test was designed to raise questions we will consider in this unit and not to provide a specific "perception score." The first four questions represent distortions of some common processes influencing perception. Ideally you would have responded FALSE to these four questions. Questions 5–10 represent guidelines for increasing accuracy in perceptions. Ideally you would have responded with TRUE to these six questions. ✔

Here we discuss seven major processes that influence your perception of others (Cook 1971; Rubin 1973; Rubin & McNeil 1985): implicit personality theory, the self-fulfilling prophecy, perceptual accentuation, primacy-recency, consistency, stereotyping, and attribution. Each of these processes also contains potential barriers to accurate perception that can significantly distort your perceptions and your interpersonal interactions.

Implicit Personality Theory

Each person has a subconscious or **implicit personality theory**, an implicit system of rules that says which characteristics of an individual go with other characteristics. The widely documented "halo effect" is a function of the implicit personality theory. If you believe an individual has a number of positive qualities (for example, is kind, generous, and friendly), you make the inference that she or he also has other positive qualities (for example, is supportive or empathic). The "reverse halo effect" operates in a similar way. If you know a person has a number of negative qualities, you're likely to infer that the person also has other negative qualities.

As might be expected, the implicit personality theories that people hold differ from culture to culture, group to group, and even person to person. For example, the Chinese have a concept, *shi gu,* which refers to "someone who is worldly, devoted to his or her family, socially skillful, and somewhat reserved" (Aronson, Wilson, & Akea 1994, p. 190). This concept is not easily encoded in English as you can tell by trying to find a general concept that covers this type of person. In English, on the other hand, we have a concept of the "artistic type," a generalization that is absent in Chinese. Thus, although it's easy for speakers of English or Chinese to refer to specific concepts—such as socially skilled or creative—each language creates its own generalized categories. In Chinese the qualities that make up *shi gu* are more easily seen as going together than they might be for an English speaker; they're part of the implicit personality theory of more Chinese than English speakers.

Similarly, consider the different personality theories that "graduate students" and "blue collar high school dropouts" might have for "college students." Likewise, an individual may have had great experiences with doctors and so may have a very positive personality theory of doctors, whereas another person may have had negative experiences with doctors and might have developed a very negative personality theory.

Potential Barriers with Implicit Personality Theories

Two serious barriers may occur when you use implicit personality theories. Your tendency to develop personality theories and to perceive individuals as confirming your theory can lead you to perceive qualities in an individual that your "theory" tells you should be present when they actually are not. For example, you may see "goodwill" in the "charitable" acts of a friend when a tax deduction may be the real motive. Conversely you may see "tax deduction" as the motive of the enemy when altruism might have been the motive. Because you more easily remember information that is consistent with your implicit theories than you would inconsistent information, you're unlikely to revise or modify your theories even when you come upon contradictory evidence (Cohen 1983).

Implicit personality theories can also lead you to ignore or distort qualities or characteristics that don't conform to your theory. You may ignore (simply not see) negative qualities in your friends that you would easily see in your enemies.

The Self-Fulfilling Prophecy

A **self-fulfilling prophecy** occurs when you make a prediction or formulate a belief that comes true because you made the prediction and acted on it as if it were true (Insel & Jacobson 1975; Merton 1957). There are four basic steps in the self-fulfilling prophecy:

1. You make a prediction or formulate a belief about a person or a situation. *You predict that Pat is awkward in interpersonal situations.*
2. You act toward that person or situation as if that prediction or belief were true. *You act toward Pat as if Pat were awkward.*
3. Because you act as if the belief were true, it becomes true. *Because of the way you act toward Pat, Pat becomes tense and manifests awkwardness.*
4. You observe your effect on the person or the resulting situation, and what you see strengthens your beliefs. *You observe Pat's awkwardness, and this reinforces your belief that Pat is in fact awkward.*

If you expect people to act in a certain way or if you make a prediction about the characteristics of a situation, your predictions will frequently come true because of the self-fulfilling prophecy. Consider, for example, people who enter a group situation convinced that the other members will dislike them. Almost invariably they're proved right, perhaps because they act in a way that encourages people to respond negatively. Such people fulfill their own prophecies.

Potential Barriers with the Self-Fulfilling Prophecy

The self-fulfilling prophecy may create two potential barriers. Your tendency to fulfill your own prophecies can lead you to influence another's behavior so it confirms your prophecy. Thus, if students believe

UNDERSTANDING
Theory and Research

WHAT'S YOUR PERSONALITY THEORY?

Think about your own use of implicit personality theories to fill in missing parts about a person and if you, make mistakes. Consider, for example, the following brief statements. Note the word in parentheses that you think best completes each sentence:

- Juan is energetic, eager, and (intelligent, unintelligent).
- Mary is bold, defiant, and (extroverted, introverted).
- Joe is bright, lively, and (thin, fat).
- Kadisha is attractive, intelligent, and (likable, unlikable).
- Susan is cheerful, positive, and (attractive, unattractive).
- Daryl is handsome, tall, and (flabby, muscular).

Certain choices in this list seem right and others seem wrong. What makes some seem right is your implicit personality theory, the system of rules that tells you which characteristics go with other characteristics. Most people's theories tell them that a person who is energetic and eager is also intelligent. Of course, there's no logical reason why an unintelligent person could not be energetic and eager. Or is there?

that Professor Crawford is a boring teacher and so they pay no attention and give no feedback, they may actually be creating a boring lecturer.

The self-fulfilling prophecy also distorts your perception by influencing you to see what you predicted rather than what is really there. For example, it can lead you to see yourself as a failure because you've made this prediction rather than because of any actual setbacks. It may lead you to see someone's behavior as creative because you have made this prediction and are expecting this person to act creatively.

Perceptual Accentuation

"Any port in a storm" is a phrase that appears in various guises throughout your communications. To the would-be actor, any part is better than no part at all. Spinach may taste horrible, but when you're starving, it can taste as good as pepperoni pizza. And so it goes.

This process, called **perceptual accentuation**, can lead you to see what you expect to see and what you want to see. You probably see people you like as being better looking and smarter than people you don't like. The obvious counter-argument to this is that you actually prefer good-looking and smart people and therefore seek them out. But perhaps that is not the entire story.

In a study reported by Zick Rubin (1973), male undergraduates participated in what they thought were two separate and unrelated studies that were actually two parts of a single experiment. In the first part, each subject read a passage. Half the subjects read an arousing sexual seduction scene. The other half read about sea gulls and herring gulls. In the second part of the experiment, subjects were asked to rate a female student on the basis of her photograph and a self-description. As predicted, the subjects who read the arousing scene rated the woman as significantly more attractive than did the other group. Further, the subjects who expected to go on a blind date with this woman rated her as more sexually receptive than did the subjects who were told that they had been assigned to date someone else. How can we account for such findings?

Although this experiment was a particularly dramatic demonstration of perceptual accentuation, this same general process occurs frequently. The thirsty person sees a mirage of water; the nicotine-deprived person sees a mirage of cigarettes and smoke.

Potential Barriers with Perceptual Accentuation

Perceptual accentuation can create a variety of barriers. Your tendency to perceive what you want or need can lead you to distort your perceptions of reality; to make you see what you need or want to see rather than what is really there. At the same time it can lead you to fail to perceive what you don't want to perceive. For example, people frequently perceive politeness and friendliness from a salesperson as demonstrating personal liking for them, not as a persuasive strategy. Similarly, you may not perceive that you're about to fail your chemistry course because you focus on what you want to perceive.

Accentuation can influence you to filter out or distort information that might damage or threaten your self image (for example, criticism of your writing or speaking) and thus make self-improvement extremely difficult.

It can also lead you to perceive in others the negative characteristics or qualities you have, a defense mechanism psychoanalysts refer to as projection.

In addition, accentuation can influence you to perceive and remember positive qualities better than negative ones (called the Pollyanna effect), and thus distort perceptions of others. In one study, for example, students who liked and who disliked Madonna viewed her video "Open Your Heart." Those who liked Madonna saw it as the story of a dancer and her son. Those who disliked Madonna saw it as the story of sexual attraction between a young boy and an older woman (Brown & Schulze 1990).

Primacy-Recency

Consider the following situation: You took a course in which half the classes were extremely dull and half were extremely exciting. It's now the end of the semester and you're reflecting on the course and the instructor. Would your evaluation be more favorable if the dull classes came during the first half of the semester and the exciting classes during the second half or if the order were reversed? Consider similar situations in other contexts. For example, would you evaluate a job more favorably if your initial experiences were positive or if your most recent experiences were positive? Do you evaluate a friend on the basis of your early or your most recent experiences? If what comes first exerts the most influence, the

UNDERSTANDING
Theory and Research

ARE YOU A PYGMALION?

A widely known example of the self-fulfilling prophecy is the Pygmalion effect (Rosenthal & Jacobson 1992). The effect is named after Pygmalion, the sculptor of Greek mythology. Pygmalion created a statue of a beautiful woman, whom he fell in love with. Venus, the goddess of love, rewarded Pygmalion by making the statue come to life as a real woman, Galatea. George Bernard Shaw used this idea for his play Pygmalion, the story of a poor and poorly-educated London flower merchant who is taught "proper speech" and enters society's upper class. The musical *My Fair Lady* was in turn based on Shaw's play.

In one research study, teachers were told that certain pupils were expected to do exceptionally well, that they were late bloomers. And although the experimenters actually selected the students' names at random, the students whose names were selected actually did perform at a higher level than the other students. Like the poor flower merchant, these students became what their teachers thought they were. The expectations of the teacher may have generated extra attention to the students and this perhaps positively affected their performance.

Have you ever observed the Pygmalion effect on others or perhaps on yourself? What kind of evidence would you want before accepting this theory?

---

result is a **primacy effect**. If what comes last (or is the most recent) exerts the most influence, the result is a **recency effect**.

In an early study on the effects of primacy-recency in interpersonal perception, a list of adjectives describing a person was read to a group of students (Asch 1946). Not surprisingly, the order in which the adjectives were read influenced the students' perceptions of the person. A person described as "intelligent, industrious, impulsive, critical, stubborn, and envious" was evaluated more positively than a person described as "envious, stubborn, critical, impulsive, industrious, and intelligent." The implication here is that you use early information to provide yourself with a general idea of what a person is like. You use later information to make more specific this general idea. The obvious practical implication of primacy-recency is that the first impression you make—interpersonally, in small groups, or in public speaking—is likely to be the most important. Through this first impression, people will filter additional information to formulate a picture of who they perceive you to be.

Potential Barriers with Primacy-Recency

Primacy-recency may lead to two major types of barriers. Your tendency to give greater weight to early information and to interpret later information in light of these early impressions can lead you to form a "total" picture of an individual on the basis of initial impressions that may not be typical or accurate. For example, you might form an image of someone as socially ill at ease. If this impression was based on watching this person at a stressful job interview, it's likely to be wrong. But, because of primacy you may fail to see accurately the later comfortable behavior.

Primacy may lead you to discount or distort later perceptions to avoid disrupting your initial impressions. For instance, you may fail to see signs of deceit in someone who made a good first impression because of the tendency to avoid disrupting or revising initial impressions.

Consistency

People have a strong tendency to maintain balance or **consistency** among perceptions. Consistency represents people's need to maintain balance among their attitudes. You expect certain things to go together and other things not to go together.

Consider your own attitudes in terms of consistency by responding to the following sentences; note the word in parentheses that you feel best represents your attitudes.

1. I expect a person I like to (like, dislike) me.
2. I expect a person I dislike to (like, dislike) me.
3. I expect my friend to (like, dislike) my friend.
4. I expect my friend to (like, dislike) my enemy.
5. I expect my enemy to (like, dislike) my friend.
6. I expect my enemy to (like, dislike) my enemy.

According to most consistency theories, your expectations would be as follows: You would expect a person you liked to like you (1) and a person you disliked to dislike you (2). You would expect a friend to like a friend (3) and to dislike an enemy (4). You would expect your enemy to dislike your friend (5) and to like your other enemy (6). All these expectations are intuitively satisfying. Or are they?

Further, you expect someone you like to have characteristics you like or admire. And you'd expect your enemies not to possess characteristics you liked or admired. Conversely, you'd expect persons you liked to lack unpleasant characteristics and persons you dislike to have unpleasant characteristics.

Potential Barriers with Consistency

Consistency can create three major barriers. Your tendency to see consistency in an individual can lead you to ignore or distort your perceptions of behaviors that are inconsistent with your picture of the whole person. For example, you may misinterpret Karla's unhappiness because your image of Karla is "happy, controlled, and contented."

Your desire for consistency may lead you to perceive specific behaviors as emanating from positive qualities in the people you like and from negative qualities in the people you dislike. You therefore fail to see the positive qualities in the people you dislike and the negative qualities in the people you like.

Stereotyping

A frequently used shortcut in perception is **stereotyping**. Originally stereotype was a printing term that referred to the plate that printed the same image over and over. A sociological or psychological stereotype is a fixed impression of a group of people.

Everyone has attitudinal stereotypes—of national groups, religious groups, racial groups, or perhaps of criminals, prostitutes, teachers, or plumbers. Consider, for example, if you have any stereotypes of, say, bodybuilders, the opposite sex, a racial group different from your own, members of a religion very different from your own, hard drug users, or college professors. Very likely you have stereotypes of several or perhaps all of these groups.

If you have these fixed impressions, you might, upon meeting a member of a particular group, see that person primarily as a member of that group. Initially, this may provide you with some helpful orientation. It creates problems when you apply to that person all the characteristics you assign to members of that group without examining this unique individual. If you meet a politician, for example, you may have a host of characteristics for politicians that you can readily apply to this person. To complicate matters further, you may see in this person's behavior the manifestation of various characteristics that you would not see if you did not know that this person was a politician. Although we often think of stereotypes as negative ("They're lazy, dirty, and only interested in getting high"), they may also be positive ("They're smart, hardworking, and extremely loyal"). Whether negative or positive, stereotypes distort your ability to perceive other people accurately. They prevent you from seeing an individual as an individual rather than as a member of a group.

Consider, however, another kind of stereotype: You're driving along a dark road and are stopped at a stop sign. A car pulls up beside you and three teenagers jump out and rap on your window. There may be a variety of reasons for this: they need help, they want to ask directions, they want to tell you that your trunk opened, or they may be in the process of carjacking. Your self-protective stereotype may help you decide on "carjacking" and may lead you to pull away and into the safety of a busy service station. In doing that, of course, you may have escaped being carjacked or you may have failed to help those who may have needed your help.

Potential Barriers with Stereotyping

Stereotyping can lead to two major barriers. The tendency to group people into classes and to respond to individuals primarily as members of that class can lead you to perceive someone as having

MEDIA WATCH

CULTIVATION THEORY

An interesting perspective on perception—how what you see influences what you think—is provided by cultivation theory. According to cultivation theory, the media, especially television, are the primary means by which you learn about your society and your culture (Gerbner, Gross, Morgan, & Signorielli 1980). It's through your exposure to television (and other media) that you learn about the world, its people, its values, and its customs.

Cultivation theory argues that heavy television viewers form an image of reality that is inconsistent with the facts (Potter 1986; Potter & Chang 1990). For example, heavy viewers see their chances of being a victim of a crime to be 1 in 10. In reality the ratio is 1 in 50. The difference, according to cultivation theorists, is due to the fact that television presents crime to be significantly higher than it really is. That is, crime is highlighted on television dramas as well as in news reports. Rarely does television devote attention to the absence of crime.

Heavy viewers also think that 20 percent of the world's population lives in the United States. In reality it's only 6 percent. Heavy viewers believe that the percentage of workers in managerial or professional jobs is 25 percent. In reality it's 5 percent.

Heavy viewers in the United States are more likely to believe that "hard work yields rewards" and that "good wins over evil" than are light viewers. Heavy sports program viewers were more likely to believe in the value of hard work and good conduct. And heavy soap opera viewers are more likely believe that "luck is important" and that "the strong survive" than are light viewers (Potter 1990). Television viewing has also been found to be related to attitudes and beliefs about which gender should do which household chores (Signorielli & Lears 1992). In Argentina, on the other hand, television viewing is related to antidemocratic attitudes (Morgan & Shanahan 1991).

What do you think of this theory? Do you think it's a valid explanation of at least one aspect of the media's influence? How would you go about testing it? For example, how would you go about testing whether teenagers who watch lots of television violence are more apt to engage in violence than teenagers who watch significantly less television violence? Do heavy television viewers have a greater expectation that they will experience violence?

The next Media Watch appears on page 61.

---

those qualities (usually negative) that you believe characterize the group to which he or she belongs (for example, all Venusians are lazy). Then, you will fail to appreciate the multifaceted nature of all people and all groups.

Stereotyping can also lead you to ignore the unique characteristics of an individual and therefore fail to benefit from the special contributions each can bring to an encounter.

Attribution

Attribution is a process through which you try to discover why people do what they do and even why you do what you do (Fiske & Taylor 1984; Jones & Davis 1965; Kelley 1979). One way we try to answer this question (in part) is to ask if the person acts this way because of who the person is (personality) or because of the situation. That is, your task is to determine whether the cause of the behavior is internal (due to who the person really is) or external (due to extenuating circumstances).

Internal behaviors are caused by the person's personality or some enduring trait. In this case you might hold the person responsible for his or her behaviors, and you would judge the behavior and the person in light of this responsibility. External behaviors, on the other hand, are caused by a situational factor. In this case you might not hold the person responsible for his or her behaviors.

Consider an example. A teacher has given ten students F's on a cultural anthropology examination. In

How do you feel about the people in this photo? Are your feelings generally positive or negative? Did you have to think about it? Some research claims that you really didn't have to think about this before assigning these people or any perception a positive or negative value. This research argues that all perceptions have a positive or negative value attached to them and that these evaluations are most often automatic and involve no conscious thought. Immediately upon perceiving a person, idea, or thing, a positive or negative value is attached (*New York Times,* August 8, 1995, C1, C10). What do you think of this viewpoint? One bit of evidence against this position would be the ability to identify three or four or five things, ideas, or people about which you feel *completely* neutral. Can you do it?

an attempt to discover what this behavior (assignment of the ten F's) reveals about the teacher, you have to determine whether the teacher was responsible for the behavior (the behavior was internally caused) or not (the behavior was externally caused). If you discover that a faculty committee made up the examination and that the committee set the standards for passing or failing, you could not attribute any particular motives to the teacher. You would have to conclude that the behavior was externally caused. In this case, it was caused by the department committee in conjunction with each student's performance on the examination.

On the other hand, assume that this teacher made up the examination and set the standards for passing and failing. Now you would be more apt to attribute the ten F's to internal causes. You would be strengthened in your belief that something within this teacher (some personality trait, for example) led to this behavior if you discovered that (1) no other teacher gave nearly as many F's, (2) this particular teacher frequently gave F's in cultural anthropology, (3) this teacher frequently gave F's in other courses as well, and (4) this teacher was free to give grades other than F. These four bits of added information would lead you to conclude that something in this teacher motivated the behavior. Each of these new items of information represents one of the principles you use in making causal judgments, or attributions: consensus, consistency, distinctiveness, and controllability.

Consensus

When you focus on the principle of consensus, you ask, "Do other people behave the same way as the person on whom I am focusing?" That is, does this person act in accordance with the general consensus? If the answer is no, you're more likely to attribute the behavior to some internal cause. In the previous example, you were strengthened in your belief that the teacher's behavior had an internal cause when you learned that other teachers did not follow this behavior—there was low consensus.

Consistency

When you focus on consistency you ask whether a person repeatedly behaves the same way in similar situations. If the answer is yes, there's high consistency, and you're likely to attribute the behavior to internal motivation. The fact that the teacher frequently gives F's in cultural anthropology leads you to attribute the cause to the teacher rather than to outside sources.

Distinctiveness

When you focus on the principle of distinctiveness, you ask if this person acts in similar ways in different situations. If the answer is yes, you're likely to conclude the behavior has an internal cause. Low distinctiveness indicates that this person acts in similar ways in different situations; it indicates that this situation is not distinctive.

Consider the alternative: Assume that this teacher gave all high grades and no failures in all other courses (that is, that the cultural anthropology class situation was distinctive). Then you would probably conclude that the motivation for the failures was external to the teacher and was unique to this class.

Controllability

Controllability refers to the degree to which you think a person was in control of his or her behavior. Let's say, for example, that you invited your friend Desmond to dinner for seven o'clock and he arrives at nine. Consider how you would respond to the reasons he might give you for his lateness:

> Reason No. 1: Oh, I got to watching this old movie and I wanted to see the end.

> Reason No. 2: On my way here I witnessed a robbery and felt I had to report it. At the police station the phones were all tied up.

> Reason No. 3: I got in a car accident and was taken to the hospital.

Assuming you would believe all three explanations, you would attribute very different motives to Desmond's behavior. With Reasons 1 and 2, you would conclude that Desmond was in control of his behavior; with Reason 3, you would conclude that Desmond was not in control of his behavior. Further, you would probably respond negatively to Reason 1 (Desmond was selfish and inconsiderate) and positively to Reason 2 (Desmond did his duty as a responsible citizen). Because Desmond was not in control of his behavior in Reason 3, you would probably not attribute either positive or negative motivation to Desmond's behavior. Instead you would probably feel sorry that he had an accident on the way to your house.

Consider your own tendency to make similar judgments based on controllability in a variety of situations. How would you respond to such situations as the following:

- Doris fails her midterm history exam.
- Sidney's car is repossessed because he failed to make the payments.
- Margie is 150 pounds overweight and is complaining that she feels awful.
- Thomas's wife has just filed for divorce and he is feeling depressed.

Very probably you'd be sympathetic to each of these people if you felt they were not in control of what happened—for example, if the examination was unfair, if Sidney lost his job because of employee discrimination, if Margie has a glandular problem, and if Thomas's wife is leaving him for a wealthy drug dealer. On the other hand, you might blame these people for their problems if you felt that they were in control of the situation—for example, if Doris partied instead of studied, if Sidney gambled his payments away, if Margie ate nothing but junk food and refused to exercise, and if Thomas had been repeatedly unfaithful and his wife finally gave up trying to change him.

Low consensus, high consistency, low distinctiveness, and high controllability lead to an attribution of internal causes. As a result you praise or blame the person for his or her behaviors. High consensus, low consistency, high distinctiveness, and low controllability lead to an attribution of external causes. As a result you might consider this person lucky or unlucky.

Potential Barriers with Attribution

Of course, the obvious problem is that we can only make guesses about another person's behaviors. Can we really know if Doris deserved to pass or fail the history exam? Can we really know if Sidney deserved to have his car repossessed? When you realize that such judgments are often based on guesses, you'll be more apt to seek further information before acting as if they were facts.

The Self-Serving Bias.   The **self-serving bias** is another perceptual barrier and is generally designed to preserve or raise our own self-esteem. When you evaluate your own behaviors by taking credit for the positive and denying responsibility for the negative, you're committing the self-serving bias. You're more likely to attribute your own negative behaviors to uncontrollable factors. For example, you're more likely to attribute getting a D on an exam to the difficulty of the test rather than to your failure to prepare adequately for it. And you're more likely to attribute your positive behaviors to controllable factors, to your own strength or intelligence or personality. For example, after getting an A on an exam, you're more likely to attribute it to your ability or hard work (Bernstein, Stephan, & Davis 1979).

Can you explain, with the concept of controllability, the attitudes that many people have about the homeless?

Sometimes we construct defensive attributions where we try to explain behavior in ways that make us seem less vulnerable. One way we do this is with unrealistic optimism, the belief that good things are more likely to happen to us than to others. For example, most people think that they will ultimately experience more good things and fewer bad things than their peers (Aronson, Wilson, & Akert 1994). A similar belief is the just world hypothesis, the belief that bad things will happen only to bad people. Since we're good people, we reason, good things will happen to us. Of course, in our mindful state we know that good things often happen to bad people and that bad things often happen to good people.

The Fundamental Attribution Error.   Perhaps the major difficulty in making accurate attributions is the **fundamental attribution error**: the tendency to conclude that people do what they do because that's the kind of people they are, not because of the situation they are in. When Pat is late for an appointment, we're more likely to conclude that Pat is inconsiderate or irresponsible rather than attribute the lateness to the bus breaking down or to a traffic accident. When we commit the fundamental attribution error we overvalue the contribution of internal factors and undervalue the influence of external factors.

When we explain our own behavior we also favor internal explanations, although not to as great an extent as we do when explaining the behaviors of others. In one study, managers who evaluated their own and the performance of their subordinates, used more internal explanations when evaluating the behavior of their subordinates than they did in evaluating their own (Martin & Klimoski 1990). One reason for giving greater weight to external factors in explaining our own behavior than we do in explaining the behavior of others is that we know the situation surrounding our own behavior. We know, for example, what's going on in our love life and we know our financial condition and so we naturally see the influence of these factors. But we rarely know as much about others and so we're more likely to give less weight to the external factors in their cases.

This fundamental attribution error is at least in part culturally influenced. For example, in the United States people are more likely to explain behavior by saying that people did what they did because of who they are. But when Hindus in India were asked to explain why their friends behaved as they did, they gave greater weight to external factors than did Americans in the United States (Miller 1984; Aronson 1994). Further, Americans have little hesitation in offering causal explanations of a person's behavior ("Pat did this because . . .").

BUILDING Communication Skills

HOW DO YOU MAKE ATTRIBUTIONS?

Consider how you would explain the following cases in terms of attribution theory. Do you think the individual's behavior was due to internal causes (for example, personality characteristics or various personal motives) or external causes (for example, the particular situation, the demands of others who might be in positions of authority, or the behaviors of others)? The behavior in question appears in italics.

1. *Mita's performance in the race was disappointing.* For the last few days she had to tend to her sick grandfather and got too little sleep.
2. *Peter just quit his job.* No one else that you know who has had this same job has ever quit.
3. *Karla just failed her chemistry test.* A number of other students (in fact, some 40 percent of the class) also failed the test. Karla has never failed a chemistry test before and, in fact, has never failed any other test in her life.

4. *Russell took the schoolchildren to the zoo.* Russell works for the board of education in a small town, and taking the students on trips is one of his major functions. All people previously on the job have taken the students to the zoo. Russell has never taken any other children to the zoo.
5. *Donna received A's on all her speeches.* In fact, everyone in the class got A's. This was the first A that Donna has ever received in public speaking and in fact the first A she has ever received in any course.

What information contained in the brief behavior descriptions enabled you to make judgments concerning (1) consensus, (2) consistency, (3) distinctiveness, and (4) controllability? What combination of these principles would lead you to conclude that the behavior was internally motivated? What combination would lead you to conclude that the behavior was externally motivated?

Hindus, on the other hand, are generally reluctant to explain a person's behavior in causal terms (Matsumoto 1994).

Overattribution. Another problem is **overattribution**—attributing everything a person does to one or two obvious characteristics. For example, attributing a person's behavior to alcoholic parents or to being born blind or into great wealth. And so we say, Sally has difficulty forming meaningful relationships because she grew up in a home of alcoholics, Alex overeats because he's blind, and Shandra is irresponsible because she never had to work for her money. Most behaviors and personality characteristics are the product of a wide variety of factors; it's almost always a mistake to select one factor and attribute everything to it.

You may find it interesting to review the accompanying box "What Do You Do When You Meet a Blind Person?" with these seven perceptual processes in mind (see p. 50). Specifically, how are your perceptions of blind and sighted people influenced by these perceptual processes? What types of barriers intrude on communication between blind and sighted persons?

CRITICAL PERCEPTION: MAKING PERCEPTIONS MORE ACCURATE

Successful communication depends largely on the accuracy of your perception. As a preface, realize that in addition to your perception of another's behaviors (verbal or nonverbal), you can also perceive what you think another person is feeling or thinking

WHAT DO YOU DO WHEN YOU MEET A BLIND PERSON

Give a Blind Person the Same Respect and Consideration You Would Give Someone Sighted

On the Street:
Ask if assistance would be helpful. Sometimes a blind person prefers to proceed unaided. If the person wants your help, offer your elbow. You should walk a half-step ahead so that your body movements will indicate when to change direction, stop and start, and step up or down at curbside.

Giving Directions:
Verbal directions should have the blind person as the reference point. Example: "You are facing Lexington Avenue and you will have to cross it as you continue east on 59th Street."

Handling Money:
When giving out bills, indicate the denomination of each so that the blind person can identify it and put it away. Coins are identified by touch.

Safety:
Half-open doors are a hazard to everyone, particularly to a blind person. Keep doors closed or wide open.

Dining Out:
Guide blind people to the table by offering your arm. Then place their hand on the chair back so they can seat themselves. Read the menu aloud and encourage the waiter to speak directly to the blind person rather than to you. Describe placement of food, using an imaginary clock face (e.g., vegetables are at 2 o'clock, salad plate is at 11 o'clock).

Traveling:
Just as a sighted person enjoys hearing a tour guide describe unfamiliar scenery, a blind person likes to hear about indoor and outdoor sights.

Guide Dogs:
These are working animals, not pets. Do not distract a guide dog by petting it or by seeking its attention.

Remember:
Talk with a blind person as you would with a sighted one, in a normal tone. You may use such expressions as "See you later" and "Did you see that?"

If you enter a room in which a blind person is alone, announce your presence by speaking or introducing yourself. In a group, address blind people by name if they are expected to reply. Excuse yourself when you are leaving.

Always ask before trying to help. Grabbing an arm or pushing is dangerous and discourteous. When you accompany blind people, offer to describe the surroundings.

(Source: From "What Do You Do When You Meet a Blind Person?", Reprinted by permission of The Lighthouse Inc. New York, NY)

(Laing, Phillipson, & Lee 1966; Littlejohn 1996). You can, for example, perceive Pat kissing Chris. This is a simple, relatively direct perception of some behavior. But you can also sense (or perceive)—on the basis of the kiss—that Pat loves Chris. Notice the difference: you've observed the kiss but have not observed the love. (Of course, you could continue in this vein and, from your conclusion that Pat loves Chris, conclude that Pat no longer loves Terry. That is, you can always formulate a conclusion on the basis of a previous conclusion. The process is unending.)

The important point to see here is that when your perceptions are based on something observable (here, the kiss), you have a greater chance of being accurate when you describe this kiss or even when you interpret and evaluate it. As you move further away from your actual observation, however, your chances of being accurate decrease—when, for example, you try to describe or evaluate

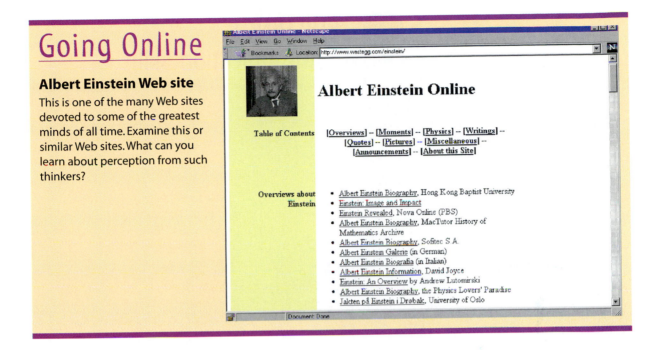

Going Online

Albert Einstein Web site

This is one of the many Web sites devoted to some of the greatest minds of all time. Examine this or similar Web sites. What can you learn about perception from such thinkers?

the love. Generally, when you draw conclusions on the basis of what you think someone is thinking as a result of the behavior, you have a greater chance of making errors than when you stick to conclusions about what you observe yourself.

We have already identified the potential barriers that can arise with each of the perceptual processes, for example, the self-serving bias and the fundamental attribution error, and the numerous potential problems in each of the seven perceptual processes. There are, however, additional suggestions we want to offer.

Become Aware of Your Perceptions

In addition to using the strategies of uncertainty reduction and perception checking and to being culturally sensitive, become aware of your perceptions. Subject your perceptions to logical analysis and critical thinking. Here are a few suggestions:

- Recognize your own role in perception. Your emotional and physiological state will influence the meaning you give to your perceptions. The sight of raw clams may be physically upsetting when you have a stomachache but mouthwatering when you're hungry.
- Avoid early conclusions. On the basis of your observations of behaviors, formulate hypotheses to test against additional information and evidence rather than drawing conclusions you then look to confirm. Delay formulating conclusions until you've had a chance to process a wide variety of cues.
- Avoid the one-cue conclusion. Look for a variety of cues pointing in the same direction. The more cues pointing to the same conclusion, the more likely your conclusion will be correct. Be especially alert to contradictory cues, ones that refute your initial hypotheses. It's relatively easy to perceive cues that confirm your hypotheses but more difficult to acknowledge contradictory evidence. At the same time, seek validation from others. Do others see things in the same way you do? If not, ask yourself if your perceptions may be in some way distorted.
- Beware of your own biases. Know when your perceptual evaluations are unduly influenced by your own biases: for example, perceiving only the positive in people you like and only the negative in people you don't like.

Check Your Perceptions

Perception checking is another way to reduce uncertainty and to make your perceptions more accurate.

BUILDING
Communication Skills

HOW DO YOU TAKE ANOTHER'S PERSPECTIVE?

Taking the perspective of the other person and looking at the world using this perspective, this point of view, rather than your own is crucial in achieving mutual understanding. For each of the specific behaviors listed below, identify specific circumstances that would lead to a *positive perception* and specific circumstances that might lead to a *negative perception*. The first one is done for you.

1. Giving a beggar in the street a 20-dollar bill.

   Positive perception: Grace once had to beg to get money for food. She now shares all she has with those who live as she once did.

   Negative perception: Grace is a first-class snob. She just wanted to impress her friends, to show them that she has so much money she can afford to give 20 dollars to a total stranger.

2. Ignoring a homeless person who asks for money.
3. A middle-aged man walking down the street with his arms around a teenage girl.
4. A mother refusing to admit her teenage son back into her house.

Often, in perceiving a person, you may assume a specific set of circumstances and on this basis evaluate specific behaviors as positive or negative. Also, you may evaluate the very same specific behavior positively or negatively depending on the circumstances that you infer are related to the behavior. Clearly, if you're to understand the perspective of another person, you need to understand the reasons for their behaviors and need to resist defining circumstances from your own perspective.

In its most basic form, perception checking consists of two steps:

1. Describe what you see or hear, recognizing that even descriptions are not really objective but are heavily influenced by who you are, your emotional state, and so on. At the same time, you may wish to describe what you think is happening. Again, try to do this as descriptively (not evaluatively) as you can. Sometimes you may wish to offer several possibilities.
   - You've called me from work a lot this week. You seem concerned that everything is all right at home.
   - You haven't talked with me all week.
   - You say that my work is fine but I haven't been given the same responsibilities that other editorial assistants have.

2. Ask the other person for confirmation. Do be careful that your request for confirmation does not sound as though you already know the answer. So avoid phrasing your questions defensively. Avoid saying, for example, "You really don't want to go out, do you? I knew you didn't when you turned on that lousy television." Instead, ask for confirmation in as supportive a way as possible:
   - Would you rather watch TV?
   - Are you worried about me or the kids?
   - Are you pleased with my work? Is there anything I can do to improve my job performance?

As these examples illustrate, the goal of perception checking is not to prove that your initial perception is correct but to explore further the thoughts and feelings of the other person. With this simple technique, you lessen your chances of misinterpreting another's feelings. At the same time, you give the other person an opportunity to elaborate on his or her thoughts and feelings.

Reduce Uncertainty

We all have a tendency to reduce uncertainty, a process that enables us to achieve greater accuracy in perception. In large part we learned about uncertainty and how to deal with it from our culture.

Culture and Uncertainty

People from different cultures differ greatly in their attitudes toward uncertainty and how to deal with it. These attitudes and ways of dealing with uncertainty have consequences for perceptual accuracy.

People in some cultures do little to avoid uncertainty and have little anxiety about not knowing what will happen next. Singapore, Jamaica, Denmark, Sweden, Hong Kong, and Ireland are examples. Uncertainty to them is a normal part of life and is accepted as it comes. Members of these cultures don't feel threatened by unknown situations. Other cultures do much to avoid uncertainty and have a great deal of anxiety about not knowing what will happen next; uncertainty is seen as threatening and something that must be counteracted. Greece, Portugal, Guatamala, Uruguay, Belgium, El Salvador, and Japan are examples.

Because weak uncertainty avoidance cultures have great tolerance for ambiguity and uncertainty, they minimize the rules governing communication and relationships (Hofstede 1997; Lustig & Koester 1999). People who don't follow the same rules as the cultural majority are readily tolerated. Different approaches and perspectives may even be encouraged in cultures with weak uncertainty avoidance. Strong uncertainty avoidance cultures create very clear-cut rules for communication. It's considered unacceptable for people to break these rules.

Students from weak uncertainty avoidance cultures appreciate freedom in education and prefer vague assignments without specific timetables. These students will want to be rewarded for creativity and will easily accept the teacher's (sometimes) lack of knowledge. Students from strong uncertainty avoidance cultures prefer highly structured experiences where there's very little ambiguity—specific objectives, detailed instructions, and definite timetables. These students expect to be judged on the basis of the right answers and expect the teacher to have all the answers all the time (Hofstede 1997).

Strategies for Reducing Uncertainty

Communication involves a gradual process of reducing uncertainty about each other (Berger & Bradac 1982). A variety of strategies can help reduce uncertainty. Observing another person while he or she is engaged in an active task, preferably interacting with others in more informal social situations, will often reveal a great deal about the person because people are less apt to monitor their behaviors and more likely to reveal their true selves in informal situations.

You can also manipulate the situation in such a way that you observe the person in more specific and more revealing contexts. Employment interviews, theatrical auditions, and student teaching are some of the ways in which the situation can be manipulated to observe how the person might act and react and hence to reduce uncertainty about the person.

New members of Internet chat groups usually lurk before joining the group discussion. Lurking, reading the exchanges between the other group members without saying anything yourself, will help you learn about the people in the group and about the group itself.

Another way to reduce uncertainty is to collect information about the person through asking others. You might inquire of a colleague if a third person finds you interesting and might like to have dinner with you.

And of course you can interact with the individual. For example, you can ask questions: "Do you enjoy sports?" "What did you think of that computer science course?" "What would you do if you got fired?" You also gain knowledge about another person by disclosing information about yourself. Your self-disclosure can create a relaxed environment that encourages subsequent disclosures from the person about whom you wish to learn more.

You probably use these strategies all the time to learn about people. Unfortunately, many people feel that they know someone well enough after only observing the person from a distance or from rumors. A combination of information—including and especially your own interactions—is most successful at reducing uncertainty.

Be Culturally Sensitive

You can increase your accuracy in perception by recognizing and being sensitive to cultural differences, especially those concerning values, attitudes, and be-liefs. You can easily see and accept different hair-styles, clothing, and foods. In basic values and beliefs, however, you may assume that down deep we're really all alike. We aren't. When you assume similarities and ignore differences, you may not per-ceive a situation accurately. Take a simple example. An American invites a Filipino coworker to dinner. The Filipino politely refuses. The American is hurt and feels that the Filipino does not want to be friendly. The Filipino is hurt and concludes that the invitation was not extended sincerely. Here, it seems, both the American and the Filipino assume that their customs for inviting people to dinner are the same

when, in fact, they aren't. A Filipino expects to be in-vited several times before accepting a dinner invita-tion. When an invitation is given only once it's viewed as insincere.

Within every cultural group there are wide and important differences. As all Americans are not alike, neither are all Indonesians, Greeks, Mexicans, and so on. When we make assumptions that all people of a certain culture are alike, we're thinking in stereotypes.

Recognizing differences between another culture and your own and recognizing differences among members of a particular culture will help you per-ceive the situation more accurately.

SUMMARY

In this unit we reviewed the process of perception, the processes influencing perception, and the principles for mak-ing perception more accurate.

1. Perception refers to the process by which you become aware of the many stimuli impinging on your senses.
2. The process of perception consists of three stages: sen-sory stimulation occurs; sensory stimulation is orga-nized; and sensory stimulation is interpreted-evaluated.
3. The following processes influence perception: (1) im-plicit personality theory, (2) self-fulfilling prophecy, (3) perceptual accentuation, (4) primacy-recency, (5) con-sistency, (6) stereotyping, and (7) attribution.
4. Implicit personality theory refers to the private person-ality theory that individuals hold and that influence how they perceive other people.
5. The self-fulfilling prophecy occurs when you make a pre-diction or formulate a belief that comes true because you've made the prediction and acted on it as if it were true.
6. Perceptual accentuation leads you to see what you ex-pect and what you want to see.
7. Primacy-recency refers to the relative influence of stim-uli as a result of the order in which you perceive them.

If what occurs first exerts the greatest influence, you're influenced by the primacy effect. If what occurs last ex-erts the greatest influence, you're experiencing a recency effect.

8. Consistency refers to the tendency to perceive that which enables you to achieve psychological balance or comfort among various attitude objects and the con-nections between and among them.
9. Stereotyping is the tendency to develop and maintain fixed, unchanging perceptions of groups of people and to use these perceptions to evaluate individual members of these groups, ignoring their individual, unique char-acteristics.
10. Attribution is the process by which you try to under-stand your own and others' behaviors and the motiva-tions for these behaviors. In this process you utilize four types of data: consensus, consistency, distinctiveness, and controllability.
11. Accuracy in perception can be increased by becoming aware of your perceptions, checking your perceptions, reducing uncertainty, and becoming aware of cultural differences and influences on perception.

KEY TERMS

perception (p. 38)

implicit personality theory (p. 40)

self-fulfilling prophecy (p. 41)

primacy recency (p. 42)

perceptional accentuation (p. 42)

consistency (pp. 43, 46)

stereotyping (p. 44)

attribution (p. 45)

consensus (p. 46)

distinctiveness (p. 46)

controllability (p. 47)

self-serving bias (p. 47)

fundamental attribution error (p. 48)

overattribution (p. 49)

uncertainty avoidance (p. 53)

THINKING CRITICALLY ABOUT
Perception

1. It has been argued that the self-fulfilling prophecy may be used in organizations to stimulate higher performance (Eden 1992; Field 1989). For example, managers could be given the belief that workers can perform at extremely high levels; managers would then act as if this were true and thus promote this high level behavior in the workers. How might it be used in the college classroom? How might it be used in parenting? Would you consider this behavior ethical?

2. For the next several days, record all examples of people perception, instances in which you drew a conclusion about another person. Try to classify these in terms of the processes identified in this chapter, for example, implicit personality theory, stereotyping, attribution. Record also the specific context in which they occurred. After you've identified the various processes, share your findings in groups of five or six or with the entire class. As always, only disclose what you wish to disclose. What processes do you use most frequently? Do these processes lead to any barriers to accurate perception?

3. In a study of stereotypes on British television it was found that gender stereotypes hadn't changed much over the last 10 years and that these were comparable to those found on North American television (Furnham and Bitar 1993). Other research suggests that these stereotypes have changed and that television depictions of men and women are erasing the stereotypes (Vernon, Williams, Phillips, & Wilson 1990). Do you find gender stereotypes on television? How many can you identify?

4. How would you use perception checking in such situations as these: (a) your friend says he wants to drop out of college; (b) your cousin hasn't called you in several months though you have called her at least six times; (c) another student seems totally detached from everything that happens in class?

5. How would you go about finding answers to such questions as these:
   a. Are there gender differences in accuracy of perception? Are there age differences?
   b. Are men or women more likely to use the self-serving bias in perceiving others?
   c. Do all cultures use essentially the same perceptual processes (implicit personality theory, self-fulfilling prophecy, and so on) in making judgments about others?
   d. Does a primacy effect operate in college students' perceptions of instructors? Does a recency effect operate in college instructors' perceptions of students?

UNIT 4
Listening

UNIT CONTENTS

UNIT GOALS

After completing this unit, you should be able to

define *listening* and explain the five processes involved in listening

explain the relevance of culture and gender to listening

define and distinguish between participatory and passive, empathic and objective, nonjudgmental and judgmental, surface and deep, and active and inactive listening

There can be little doubt that we all listen a great deal. Upon awakening you listen to the radio. On the way to school you listen to friends, people around you, screeching cars, singing birds, or falling rain. In school you listen to the teacher, to other students, and sometimes even to yourself. You listen to friends at lunch and return to class to listen to more teachers. You arrive home and again listen to family and friends. Perhaps you listen to CDs, radio, or television. All in all, you listen for a good part of your waking day.

Before reading about this area of human communication, examine your own listening habits and tendencies by taking the accompanying self-test, "How Good a Listener Are You?"

✔ SELF-TEST

How Good a Listener Are You?

Respond to each question with the following scale:

1 = always; 2 = frequently; 3 = sometimes; 4 = seldom; and 5 = never

_____ 1. I listen by participating; I interject comments throughout the conversation.

_____ 2. I listen to what the speaker is saying and feeling; I try to feel what the speaker feels.

_____ 3. I listen without judging the speaker.

_____ 4. I listen to the literal meanings that a speaker communicates; I don't look too deeply into hidden meanings.

_____ 5. I listen passively; I generally remain silent and take in what the other person is saying.

_____ 6. I listen objectively; I focus on the logic of the ideas rather than on the emotional meaning of the message.

_____ 7. I listen critically, evaluating the speaker and what the speaker is saying.

_____ 8. I look for the hidden meanings; the meanings that are revealed by subtle verbal or nonverbal cues.

These statements focus on the ways of listening discussed in this chapter. All ways are appropriate at times and all ways are inappropriate at times. It depends. So, the only responses that are really inappropriate are "always" and "never." Effective listening is listening that is appropriate to the specific communication situation. Review these statements and try to identify situations in which each statement would be appropriate and situations in which each statement would be inappropriate. ✔

If we measured importance by the time we spend on an activity, then listening would be our most important communication activity. A glance at Figure 4.1, which diagrams the results of three studies, should illustrate this point. Figure 4.1(a) shows the percentage of time spent in four activities during the everyday lives of adults from a wide variety of occupations (Rankin 1929). Figure 4.1(b) reflects the results from a similar study of adults as well as high school and college students done more recently (Werner 1975). The results from a study on the communication activities of college students (Barker, Edwards, Gaines, Gladney, & Holley 1980) are shown in Figure 4.1(c). These studies as well as others demonstrate that listening occupies more time than any other communication activity (Steil, Barker, & Watson 1983; Wolvin & Coakley 1982).

Another way to appreciate the importance of listening is to consider its many benefits. Table 4.1 presents five of these benefits.

THE PROCESS OF LISTENING

The process of listening can be described as a series of five steps: receiving, understanding, remembering, evaluating, and responding. The process is visualized in Figure 4.2. Note that the listening process is a circular one. The responses of Person A serve as the stimuli for Person B, whose responses in turn serve as the stimuli for Person A, and so on. As will become clear in the discussion of the five steps that follow, listening is not a process of transferring an idea from the mind of a speaker to the mind of a listener. Rather, it is a process of speaker and listener working together to achieve a common understanding.

In reviewing these five stages, keep in mind that listening, like speaking, comes with ethical responsibilities. Two particular responsibilities should be mentioned here. First, there is the responsibility to give the speaker an **honest hearing**, without prejudices or preconceptions. Avoid prejudging the speaker before listening to what he or she has to say.

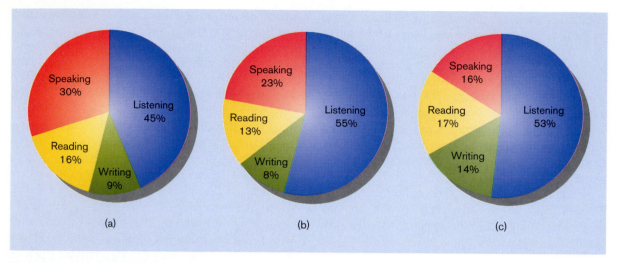

Figure 4.1   **Amount of time spent listening.**   How would a pie chart of your communication activities look for a typical school day? For a typical nonschool day?

At the same time, try to empathize with the speaker; try to understand emotionally as well as intellectually what the speaker means. Then, you can accept or reject the speaker's ideas on the basis of what is said rather than on the basis of some bias or incomplete understanding.

A second responsibility is to give the speaker open and honest feedback. The speaker has the right to expect honest responses just as the listener has the right to expect honesty from the speaker. Much as a listener has a right to expect an active speaker, the speaker has a right to expect a listener who will actively deal with, rather than just passively hear, the message.

Receiving

Unlike listening, hearing begins and ends with this first stage of receiving. Hearing is something that just happens when you open your ears or when you get within earshot of some auditory stimuli. Listening, on the other hand, is quite different.

Listening begins (but does not end) with receiving messages the speaker sends. Here you receive both the verbal and the nonverbal messages—the words as well as the gestures, facial expressions, variations in volume and rate, and lots more as you'll discover when we discuss mes-

sages in more detail in Units 7 and 8. For improved reception:

- focus attention on the speaker's verbal and nonverbal messages, on what is said and on what is not said
- look for both feedback to previous messages as well as feedforward (Unit 1), which can reveal how the speaker would like his or her message viewed
- avoid distractions in the environment and focus attention on the speaker rather than on what you'll say next
- maintain your role as listener and avoid interrupting the speaker until he or she is finished

Understanding

Understanding is the stage at which you learn what the speaker means. This understanding must take into consideration both the thoughts that are expressed as well as the emotional tone that accompanies these thoughts—the urgency or the joy or sorrow expressed in the message. For improved understanding:

- relate new information to what you already know
- see the speaker's messages from the speaker's point of view; avoid judging the message until

TABLE 4.1   The benefits of effective listening

This table identifies some of the benefits you can derive from effective listening. As you read the table, try to visualize the benefits as they might accrue to you from interpersonal, small group, and public communication.

Effective listening will result in increasing your ability to	Because you will	For example,
learn: to acquire knowledge of others, the world, and yourself, so as to avoid problems and make more reasonable decisions	profit from the insights of others and acquire information relevant to decisions you'll be called upon to make in business or in personal life	listening to Peter about his travels to Cuba will help you learn more about Peter and about life in another country listening to the difficulties of your sales staff may help you offer more pertinent sales training
relate, to gain social acceptance and popularity	find that people come to like those who are attentive and supportive	others will increase their liking of you once they see your genuine concern for them, communicated through attentive and supportive listening
influence the attitudes and behaviors of others	find that people are more likely to respect and follow those they feel have listened to and understood them	workers are more likely to follow your advice once they feel you've really listened to their insights and concerns
play	know when to suspend critical and evaluative thinking and when to simply engage in passive and accepting listening	listening to the anecdotes of coworkers will allow you to gain a more comfortable balance between the world of work and the world of play
help others	hear more, empathize more, and come to understand others more deeply	listening to your child's complaints about her teacher will increase your ability to help your child cope with school and her teacher

you've fully understood it—as the speaker intended it
- ask questions to clarify or to secure additional details or examples if necessary
- rephrase (paraphrase) the speaker's ideas in your own words

Remembering

Messages that you receive and understand need to be retained for at least some period of time. In some small group and public-speaking situations you can augment your memory by taking notes or by tape-recording the messages. In most interpersonal communication situations, however, such note taking would be considered inappropriate, although you often do write down a phone number, an appointment, or directions. Memory can be improved by:

- identifying the central ideas in a message and the major support advanced for them
- summarizing the message in a more easily retained form but being careful not to ignore crucial details or qualifications

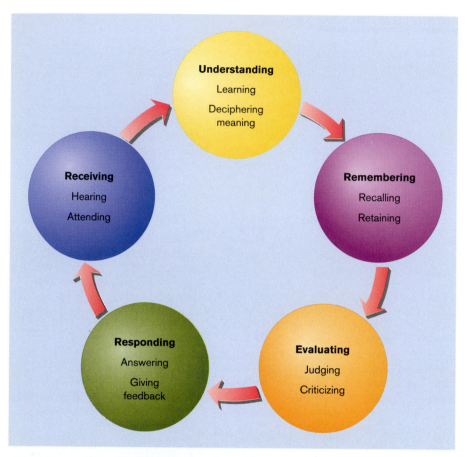

Figure 4.2 **A five-stage model of listening.** Of course, at each stage there will be lapses. Thus, for example, at the receiving stage, a listener receives part of the message and because of noise and perhaps other reasons fails to receive other parts. Similarly, at the stage of understanding, a listener understands part of the message and because of the inability to share another's meanings exactly (see Unit 7 for more on this) fails to understand other parts. The same is true for remembering, evaluating, and responding. This model draws on a variety of previous models that listening researchers have developed (for example, Alessandra 1986; Barker 1990; Brownell 1987; Steil, Barker, & Watson 1983).

• repeating names and key concepts to yourself or, if appropriate, aloud

Evaluating

Evaluating consists of judging the messages in some way. At times you may try to evaluate the speaker's underlying intent. Often this evaluation process goes on without much conscious thought. For example, Elaine tells you that she is up for a promotion and is really excited about it. You may then try to judge her intention. Does she want you to use your influence

with the company president? Is she preoccupied with her accomplishment and so tells everyone about it? Is she looking for a pat on the back? Generally, if you know the person well, you'll be able to identify the intention and therefore be able to respond appropriately.

In other situations, the evaluation is more in the nature of critical analysis. For example, in listening to proposals advanced in a business meeting, you would at this stage evaluate them. Is there evidence to show that these proposals are practical and will increase productivity? Is there contradictory evidence?

MEDIA WATCH

TALK RADIO

One of the most popular television shows today is *Frasier*, a situation comedy based on the life of a radio talk show psychiatrist. And we all remember that it was through talk radio that Tom Hanks and Meg Ryan got together in *Sleepless in Seattle*. Media researchers Cameron Armstrong and Alan Rubin (1989, p. 84) note that talk radio enables listeners to "communicate with the outside world, get quick answers to questions, express opinions, and simply talk to other people. In short, talk radio allows for interpersonal communication." By placing a call, anxiety and loneliness are lessened and psychological and physical security are increased (Armstrong & Rubin 1989).

Armstrong and Rubin find seven motives in listening to talk radio. Generally, they find that people listen for relaxation, exciting entertainment, convenience, voyeurism or escape, useful information, passing the time, and companionship. These motives are not unlike those found for face-to-face interpersonal communication (Rubin, Perse, & Barbato 1988).

Talk radio is a kind of substitute for interpersonal, face-to-face interaction and is similar to communicating via computer. In both talk radio and computer communication, there's significantly less ego involvement and much less potential threat to self-esteem. Both systems allow for a greater amount of anonymity (and hence psychological security and protection) than does face-to-face interaction. And yet, they provide many of the same rewards as does interpersonal face-to-face communication (Hofstetter and Gianos 1997).

Talk radio may also be an extremely persuasive medium. After the bombing of a federal building in Oklahoma City in April 1995, much criticism and defense was heard about talk radio. President Clinton criticized the extremists on talk radio for inciting and nourishing an antigovernment sentiment and connected the bombing to "right-wing hate radio" (*Newsweek* May 8, 1995, p. 44). Talk radio hosts such as Rush Limbaugh and G. Gordon Liddy rushed to the defense of talk radio and the right to criticize the government, arguing that the bombing had nothing to do with talk radio (*Newsweek* May 8, 1995, p. 39). Howard Halpern, president of the American Academy of Psychotherapists, writing to *The New York Times* (May 5, 1995, p. A30), argued that extremist talk is dangerous because it cuts the empathic bond of the listener with those who are attacked; it shows the members of the attacked group to be different and deserving of hate. By doing so, it allows and may even encourage physical attacks and mass violence, argues Halpern. Talk radio has also been found to be associated with political cynicism and the attitude that government is often unnresponsive to the needs of the people (Hollander 1996).

Talk radio provides avenues for minority points of view in a way similar to cable television. Some would argue that this is essential because the large media—the networks, national magazines, and major newspapers—will not cover such perspectives because these major media are focused on echoing the majority point of view.

Do you listen to talk radio? If so, what purposes does it serve for you? How persuasive is talk radio compared with, say, interpersonal interaction with college friends? Compared with network reporting?

The next Media Watch appears on page 85.

Are there alternative proposals that would be more practical and more productive?

In evaluating, try to

- resist evaluation until you fully understand the speaker's point of view
- assume that the speaker is a person of goodwill and give the speaker the benefit of any doubt by asking for clarification on issues that you feel you must object to (are there any other reasons for accepting this new proposal?)

UNDERSTANDING Theory and Research

WHAT DO YOU REMEMBER?

When you remember a message, do you remember it as it was spoken, or do you remember what you think you heard? The common sense theory, of course, claims that you remember what was said. But before accepting this simple explanation, try to memorize the list of twelve words presented below (Glucksberg & Danks 1975). Don't worry about the order of the words; only the number remembered counts. Take about 20 seconds to memorize as many words as possible. Then close the book and write down as many words as you can remember.

Word List

bed	comfort	night
rest	sound	eat
dream	awake	slumber
wake	tired	snore

Don't read any further until you've tried to memorize and reproduce the list of words.

If you're like my students, you not only remembered a good number of the words on the list but you also "remembered" at least one word that was not on the list: sleep. Most people recall the word sleep being on the list—but, as you can see, it wasn't. What happens is that you don't simply *reproduce* the list but you *reconstruct* it. In this case you gave the list meaning, and part of that meaning included the word "sleep." Memory for speech, then, is not reproductive; you don't simply reproduce in your memory what the speaker said. Rather, memory is reconstructive; you actually reconstruct the messages you hear into a system that seems to make sense to you. You do this with all types of messages; you reconstruct the messages you hear into meaningful wholes and in the process often remember distorted versions of what was said.

- distinguish facts from inferences (see Unit 5), opinions, and personal interpretations by the speaker
- identify any biases, self-interests, or prejudices that may lead the speaker to slant unfairly what is presented

Responding

Responding occurs in two phases: (1) responses you make while the speaker is talking and (2) responses you make after the speaker has stopped talking. These responses are feedback—information that you send back to the speaker and which tells the speaker how you feel and think about his or her messages. Responses made while the speaker is talking should be supportive and should acknowledge that you're listening to the speaker. These include what nonverbal researchers call **backchanneling cues**, such as "I see," "yes," "uh-huh," and similar signals that let the speaker know that you're attending to the message.

Responses made after the speaker has stopped talking are generally more elaborate and might include expressing empathy ("I know how you must feel"), asking for clarification ("Do you mean that this new health plan is to replace the old one or will it just be a supplement?"), challenging ("I think your evidence is weak here"), and agreeing ("You're absolutely right on this, and I'll support your proposal when it comes up for a vote"). In responding, try to

- be supportive of the speaker throughout the speaker's talk by using and varying backchanneling cues; using only one backchanneling cue—for example, saying "uh-huh" throughout may make it appear that you're not really listening
- express support for the speaker in your final responses
- be honest; the speaker has a right to expect honest responses, even if these express anger or disagreement

Going Online

ILA Website

This is the home page of the International Listening Association's Web site. What can you learn about listening from this Web site?

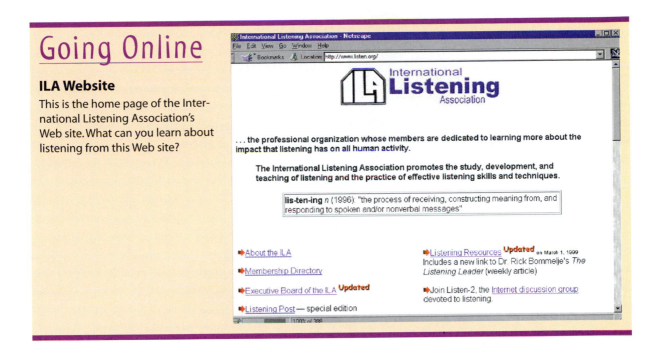

- state your thoughts and feelings as your own; use I-messages (for example, say "I think the new proposal will entail greater expense than you outlined" rather than "Everyone will object to the plan for costing too much.")

LISTENING, CULTURE, AND GENDER

Listening is difficult, in part, because of the inevitable differences in the communication systems between speaker and listener. Because each person has had a unique set of experiences, each person's communication and meaning system is going to be different from each other person's. When speaker and listener come from different cultures or are of different genders, the differences and their effects are naturally so much greater. Let's look first at culture.

Listening and Culture

The culture in which you were raised will influence your listening in a variety of ways. Here we look at some of these: language and speech, nonverbal behavioral differences, feedback, and credibility.

Language and Speech

Even when speaker and listener speak the same language, they speak it with different meanings and different accents. No two speakers speak exactly the same language. Every speaker speaks an **idiolect**, a unique variation of the language (King & DiMichael 1992). Speakers of the same language will, at the very least, have different meanings for the same terms because they have had different experiences.

Speakers and listeners who have different native languages and who may have learned English as a second language will have even greater differences in meaning. Translations are never precise and never fully capture the meaning in the other language. If your meaning for "house" was learned in a culture in which everyone lived in their own house with lots of land around it, then communicating with someone whose meaning was learned in a neighborhood of high-rise tenements is going to be difficult. Although you'll each hear the same word, the meanings you'll each develop will be drastically different. In adjusting your listening—especially when in an intercultural setting—understand that the speaker's meanings may be very different from yours even though you each know the same language.

Still another aspect of speech is that of accents. In many classrooms throughout the country, there will be a wide range of accents. Those whose native language is a tonal one such as Chinese (where differences in pitch signal important meaning differences) may speak English with variations in pitch that may seem puzzling to others. Those whose native language is Japanese may have trouble distinguishing "l" from "r" since Japanese does not

BUILDING Communication Skills

HOW CAN YOU REDUCE LISTENING BARRIERS?

Visualize yourself ready to talk with the following people on the topics noted. What barriers to listening (from any stage: receiving, understanding, remembering, evaluating, and responding) might arise in each encounter? What would you do to prevent these barriers from interfering with effective listening?

1. Elizabeth Taylor on the need to contribute to AIDS research.
2. Gloria Steinem on the contemporary women's movement.
3. President Bill Clinton on the role of the military in defending the world.
4. Spike Lee on race relations.
5. A catholic priest on the need to remain a virgin until marriage.
6. A person with AIDS on the need for lower drug prices.
7. A lesbian mother on current adoption laws.
8. Oprah Winfrey on the mistakes of modern psychology.
9. A homeless person on the need to use public spaces.
10. An Iranian couple on the need to return to fundamentalist values.

In thinking about these situations, consider, for example, how would your initial expectations influence your listening? How would your assessment of the person's credibility (even before he or she talk began to talk) affect how you listen? Will you begin listening with a positive, a negative, or a neutral attitude? How might these attitudes influence your listening?

---

include this distinction. The native language acts as a filter and influences the accent given to the second language.

Nonverbal Behavioral Differences

Speakers from different cultures have different display rules, cultural rules that govern which nonverbal behaviors are appropriate and which are inappropriate in a public setting. As you listen to another person, you also "listen" to their nonverbals. If these are drastically different from what you expect on the basis of the verbal message, they may be seen as a kind of noise or interference or they may be seen as contradictory messages. Also, different cultures may give very different meanings to the same nonverbal gesture; the thumb and forefinger forming a circle means "okay" in most of the United States, but it means "money" in Japan, "zero" in some Mediterranean countries, and "I'll kill you" in Tunisia.

Feedback

Members of some cultures give very direct and very honest feedback. Speakers from these cultures—the United States is a good example—expect the feedback to be an honest reflection of what their listeners are feeling. In other cultures—Japan and Korea are good examples—it's more important to be positive than to be truthful, and so they may respond with positive feedback (say, in commenting on a business colleague's proposal) even though they don't feel it. Listen to feedback, as you would all messages, with a full recognition that various cultures view feedback very differently.

Credibility

What makes a speaker credible or believable will vary from one culture to another. In some cultures, people would claim that competence is the most important factor in, say, choosing a teacher for their preschool children. In other cultures, the most important factor might be the goodness or morality of the teacher. Similarly, members of different cultures may perceive the credibility of the various media very differently. For example, members of a repressive society in which the government controls television news may come to attribute little credibility to such broadcasts. After all, this person might reason, television news is simply what the government wants you to know. This may be hard to understand or even recognize by someone raised in the United States, for example, where the media are free of such political control.

Listening and Gender

Deborah Tannen opens her chapter on listening in her best selling *You Just Don't Understand: Women and Men in Conversation* with several anecdotes illustrating that when men and women talk, men lecture and women listen. The lecturer is positioned as the superior, as the teacher, the expert. The listener is positioned as the inferior, as the student, the nonexpert.

Women, according to Tannen, seek to build rapport and establish a closer relationship, and so use listening to achieve these ends. For example, women use more listening cues (interjecting *yeah, uh-uh,* nodding in agreement, and smiling, for example) that let the other person known they're paying attention and are interested. Men not only use fewer listening cues but interrupt more and will often change the topic to one they know more about or one that is less relational or people-oriented or one that is more factual, for example, sports statistics, economic developments, or political problems. Men, research shows, play up their expertise, emphasize it, and use it in dominating the conversation. Women play down their expertise.

Now, you might be tempted to conclude from this that women play fair in conversation and that men don't; for example, men consistently seek to put themselves in a position superior to the woman. But, that may be too simple an explanation. Research shows, however, that men communicate this way not only with women but with other men as well. Men are not showing disrespect for their female conversational partners but are simply communicating as they normally do. Women, too, communicate as they do not only with men but also with other women.

Tannen argues that the goal of a man in conversation is to be accorded respect, and so he seeks to display his knowledge and expertise even if he has to change the topic to one he knows a great deal about. Women, on the other hand, seek to be liked and so they express agreement, rarely interrupt a man to take their turn as speaker, and give lots of cues (verbally and nonverbally) to indicate that they are listening.

There's no evidence to show that these differences represent any negative motives on the part of men to prove themselves superior or of women to ingratiate themselves. Rather, these differences in listening are largely the result of the way in which men and women have been socialized. Can men and women change these habitual ways of listening (and speaking)?

Do you find it easier to listen to and understand members of your own culture than members of other cultures? What specific elements of communication make such listening easier or more difficult?

LISTENING EFFECTIVELY

Because you listen for different reasons and toward different ends, the principles you follow in listening effectively should vary from one situation to another. Here we identify five dimensions of listening and illustrate the appropriateness of different listening modes for different communication situations.

Participatory and Passive Listening

The key to effective listening is to participate. Perhaps the best preparation for participatory listening is to act like one who is participating (physically and mentally) in the communication act. This may seem trivial and redundant. In practice, however, it may be the most abused rule of effective listening. Students often, for example, put their feet up on a nearby desk, nod their head to the side, and expect to listen effectively. It just will not happen this way. To see why, recall how your body reacts to important news. Almost immediately you assume an upright posture, turn toward the speaker, focus your eyes on the speaker, and remain relatively still and quiet. You do this reflexively because this is how you listen most effectively. This is not to say that you should be tense and uncomfortable when listening, but your body should reflect your active mind.

Even more important than this physical alertness is mental alertness. As a listener, participate in the communication interaction as an equal partner with the speaker, as one who is emotionally and intellectually ready to engage in the mutual sharing of meaning.

Passive listening, however, is not without merit. Passive listening—listening without talking and without directing the speaker in any nonverbal way—is a powerful means for communicating acceptance. Passive listening allows the speaker to develop his or her thoughts and ideas in the presence of another person who accepts but does not evaluate, who supports but does not intrude. By listening passively, you provide a supportive and receptive environment. Once that has been established, you may wish to participate in a more active way, verbally and nonverbally.

Another form of passive listening is just to sit back, relax, and let the auditory stimulation massage you without exerting any significant energy or effort and especially without your directing the stimuli in any way. Listening to music for pure enjoyment (rather than as a music critic) is perhaps the best example.

In regulating participatory and passive listening, keep the following guidelines in mind:

- Work at listening. Listening is hard work, so be prepared to participate actively. Avoid "the entertainment syndrome": the expectation that a speaker will entertain you (Floyd 1985). Avoid daydreaming, the natural tendency to let your mind wander.
- Combat sources of noise as much as possible. Remove distractions or other interferences (newspapers, magazines, stereos), so your listening task will have less competition.
- Because you can process information more quickly than a speaker can speak, there's often time left over. Use this time to summarize the speaker's thoughts, formulate questions, and draw connections between what you've heard and what you already know.
- Assume there's value in what the speaker is saying. Resist assuming that what you have to say is more valuable than the speaker's remarks.

Empathic and Objective Listening

If you're to understand what a person means and what a person is feeling, you need to listen with some degree of empathy (Rogers 1970; Rogers & Farson 1981). To empathize with others is to feel with them, to see the world as they see it, to feel what they feel. Only when you achieve this can you understand another person's meaning fully. Empathic listening is a means for both increasing understanding and for relationship enhancement (Barrett & Godfrey 1988; Snyder 1992).

There's no fast method for achieving empathy. Further, and unlike the Empath on "Star Trek," you can't feel what another person is feeling in any complete sense. But it's something we can approach with hard work. It's important, for example, that a student see the teacher's point of view through the eyes of the teacher. And it's equally important for the teacher to see the student's point of view from the student's perspective. Popular students might understand intellectually the reasons why an unpopular student might feel depressed. But that will not enable them to understand the feelings of depression emotionally. To accomplish that, they must put themselves in the position of the unpopular student, to role-play a bit and begin to feel that student's feelings and think that student's thoughts.

Although for most communication situations, empathic listening is the preferred mode of responding, there are times when you need to go beyond it to measure the meanings and feelings against some objective reality. It's important to listen to Peter tell you how the entire world hates him and to understand how Peter feels and why he feels this way. But then you need to look a bit more objectively at Peter and perhaps see the paranoia or the self-hatred. Sometimes you have to put your empathic responses aside and listen with objectivity and detachment.

In adjusting your empathic and objective listening focus, keep the following recommendations in mind:

- Punctuate from the speaker's point of view. If you're to understand the speaker's perspective, you must see the sequence of events as the speaker does and ascertain how this can influence what the speaker says and does.
- Engage in dialogue, not monologue. View the speaker as an equal. Try to eliminate any physical or psychological barriers to equality to encourage openness and empathy (for example, step from behind the large desk separating you from your employees). Avoid interrupting the speaker—a sign that what you have to say is more important.
- Seek to understand both thoughts and feelings. Don't consider your listening task finished until you've understood what the speaker is feeling as well as thinking.
- Avoid "offensive listening," the tendency to listen to bits and pieces of information that will enable you to attack the speaker or find fault with something the speaker has said.
- Strive especially to be objective when listening to friends or foes. Your attitudes may lead you to distort messages—to block out positive messages about a foe and negative messages about a friend. Guard against "expectancy hearing," when you fail to hear what the speaker is really saying and instead hear what you expect.

Think about some typical situations. How would you respond with empathy to each of these comments? Assume that all four people are your peers.

STEPHEN: I just can't seem to get my act together. Everything just falls apart as soon as I get involved.

PAT: I never felt so alone in my life. Chris left last night and said it was all over. We were together for three years and now—after a 10-minute argument—everything is lost.

MARIA: I just got $20,000 from my aunt's estate. She left it to me! Twenty thousand! Now, I can get that car and buy some new clothes.

LIN: I just can't bear the thought of going into work today. I'm really fed up with the company. They treat us all like idiots.

Nonjudgmental and Critical Listening

Effective listening includes both nonjudgmental and critical responses. You need to listen nonjudgmentally—with an open mind with a view toward understanding. However, you also need to listen critically with a view toward making some kind of evaluation or judgment. Clearly, you should first listen for understanding and suspend judgment. Only after you've fully understood the relevant messages should you evaluate or judge. Granted, listening with an open mind is extremely difficult. It's not easy, for example, to listen to arguments against some cherished belief or to criticisms of something you value. Further, you need to listen fairly, despite the red flag of an out-of-place expression or a hostile remark. Listening often stops when such a remark is made. Admittedly, to continue listening with an open mind is difficult. Yet it's particularly important in such situations that you do continue.

If meaningful communication is to take place, however, you need to supplement open-minded listening with critical listening. Listening with an open mind will help you understand the messages better. Listening with a critical mind will help you analyze that understanding and to evaluate the messages. As an intelligent and educated citizen, it's your responsibility to evaluate critically what you hear. This is especially true in the college environment. It's easy simply to listen to a teacher and take down what is said. Yet, it's perhaps even more important to evaluate and critically analyze what you hear. Contrary to what most students believe, most teachers appreciate the responses of critical listeners. They demonstrate that someone is listening and stimulate further examination of ideas. In adjusting your nonjudgmental and critical listening, focus on the following guidelines:

- Keep an open mind. Avoid prejudging. Delay your judgments until you fully understand the intention and the content the speaker is communicating. Avoid both positive and negative evaluation until you have a reasonably complete understanding.
- Avoid filtering out difficult messages. Avoid oversimplification—the tendency to eliminate details and to simplify complex messages so they're easier to remember. Avoid filtering out undesirable messages. None of us wants to hear that something we believe in is untrue, that people we care for are unkind, or that ideals we hold are self-destructive. Yet, it's important that educated people reexamine their beliefs by listening to these messages.
- Recognize your own biases. These may interfere with accurate listening and cause you to distort message reception through the process of assimilation—the tendency to integrate and interpret what you hear or think you hear with your own biases, prejudices, and expectations. For example, are your ethnic, national, or religious biases preventing you from appreciating a speaker's point of view?
- Avoid uncritical listening when you need to make evaluations and judgments. Recognize and combat the normal tendency to sharpen—a process in which one or two aspects of the message become highlighted, emphasized, and perhaps embellished. Often the concepts that are frequently sharpened are incidental remarks that somehow stand out from all the other messages.

Surface and Depth Listening

In Shakespeare's Julius Caesar, Marc Antony, in giving the funeral oration for Caesar, says: "I come to bury Caesar, not to praise him. / The evil that men do lives after them; / The good is oft interred with their bones." And later: "For Brutus is an honourable man; / So are they all, all honourable men." But Antony, as we know, did come to praise Caesar and to convince the crowd that Brutus was not an honorable man.

In most messages there's an obvious meaning that we can derive from a literal reading of the words and sentences. But there's often another level of meaning. Sometimes, as in Julius Caesar, it's the opposite of the literal meaning. At other times it seems totally unrelated. In reality, few messages have only one level of meaning. Most messages function on two or three levels at the same time. Consider some frequently heard messages: Carol asks you how you like her new haircut. On one level, the meaning is clear: Do you like the haircut? Do you like the painting? But there seems another level, perhaps a more important level: Carol is asking you to say something positive about her appearance. In the same way, the parent who complains about working hard at the office or in the home may in reality be asking for some expression of appreciation. The child who talks about the unfairness of the other children in the playground may be asking for affection and love, for some expression of caring. To appreciate these other meanings you need to engage in depth listening.

In listening, you have to be particularly sensitive to different levels of meaning. If you respond only to the surface-level communication (the literal meaning), you miss the opportunity to make meaningful contact with the other person's feelings and real needs. If you say to the parent, "You're always complaining. I bet you really love working so hard," you fail to respond to this call for understanding and appreciation.

In regulating your surface and depth listening, consider the following guidelines:

- Focus on both verbal and nonverbal messages. Recognize both consistent and inconsistent "packages" of messages and use these as guides for drawing inferences about the speaker's meaning. Ask questions when in doubt. Listen also to what is omitted. Remember that speakers communicate by what they leave out as well as by what they include. Listen, therefore, for omissions that may give you a clue to the speaker's meanings.
- Listen for both content and relational messages. The student who constantly challenges the teacher is on one level communicating disagreement over content. However, on another level—the relationship level—the student may be voicing objections to the instructor's authority or authoritarianism. To deal effectively with

the student, the instructor must listen and respond to both types of messages.

- Make special note of statements that refer back to the speaker. Remember that people inevitably talk about themselves. Whatever a person says is, in part, a function of who that person is. Listening for the different levels of meaning means attending to those personal, self-reference messages.

- Don't disregard the literal meaning of interpersonal messages in trying to uncover the more hidden meanings. Balance your listening between surface and the underlying meanings. Respond to the various levels of meaning in the messages of others as you would like others to respond to yours—sensitively but not obsessively, readily but not overambitiously.

Active and Inactive Listening

Consider the following exchange:

SPEAKER: I can't believe I have to redo this entire budget report. I really worked hard on this project and now I have to do it all over again.

LISTENER 1: That's not so bad; most people find they have to redo their first reports. That's the norm here.

LISTENER 2: So what? You don't intend to stay at this job. Anyway, you're getting paid by the hour, so what do you care?

LISTENER 3: You should be pleased that all you have to do is a simple rewrite. Peggy and Michael both had to completely redo their entire projects.

LISTENER 4: You have to rewrite that report you've worked on for the last three weeks? You sound really angry and frustrated.

All four listeners are probably trying to make the speaker feel better. But they go about it in very different ways and, we can be sure, with very different results. Listeners 1 and 2 try to lessen the significance of the rewrite. This well-intended response is extremely common but does little to promote meaningful communication and understanding. Listener 3 tries to give the situation a positive spin. With these responses, however, all three listeners are also suggesting that the speaker should not be feeling the way he or she does. They're also saying the speaker's

feelings are not legitimate and should be replaced with more logical feelings.

Listener 4's response, however, is different from the others. Listener 4 uses active listening. Active listening, which owes its development to Thomas Gordon (1975) who made it a cornerstone of his P-E-T (Parent-Effectiveness-Training) technique, is a process of sending back to the speaker what you as a listener think the speaker meant—both in content and in feelings. Active listening, then, is not merely repeating the speaker's exact words, but rather putting together into some meaningful whole your understanding of the speaker's total message.

Active listening serves several important functions. First, it helps you as a listener check your understanding of what the speaker said and, more important, what he or she meant. Reflecting back perceived meanings to the speaker gives the speaker an opportunity to offer clarification. In this way, future messages will have a better chance of being relevant.

Second, through active listening you let the speaker know that you acknowledge and accept his or her feelings. In the sample responses given, the first three listeners challenged the speaker's feelings. The active listener (Listener 4), who reflected back to the speaker what he or she thought was said, accepted what the speaker was feeling. In addition to accepting the speaker's feelings, Listener 4 also explicitly identified them: "You sound angry and frustrated," allowing the speaker an opportunity to correct the listener.

Third, active listening stimulates the speaker to explore feelings and thoughts. Listener 4's response encourages the speaker to elaborate on his or her feelings. This exploration also helps the speaker to deal with his or her feelings through this opportunity to talk them through.

Three simple techniques may prove useful in learning the process of active listening: paraphrase the speaker's meaning, express understanding, and ask questions.

- Paraphrase the speaker's meaning. Stating in your own words what you think the speaker means and feels helps ensure understanding and also shows interest in the speaker. Further, it demonstrates that you're listening to both thoughts and feelings. Paraphrasing gives the speaker a chance to extend what was originally

Active listening is not always to be preferred. There are times when you don't want to listen actively, for example, when you know the person is lying or being abusive. In these cases you may decide to listen critically or even end the interaction. In what cases would you decide against listening actively?

said. Thus, when Listener 4 echoes the speaker's thought, the speaker may elaborate on why rewriting the budget report meant so much. Perhaps the speaker fears that his or her other reports will be challenged or that this now means a much-anticipated promotion will not be forthcoming. In your paraphrase, be especially careful not to lead the speaker in the direction you think he or she should go. Paraphrases should be objective descriptions.

Be careful that you don't overdo paraphrase; only a very small percentage of statements need paraphrasing. Paraphrase when you feel there's a chance for misunderstanding or when you want to express support for the other person and keep the conversation going.

• Express understanding of the speaker's feelings. In addition to paraphrasing the content, echo the feelings the speaker expressed or implied ("You must have felt horrible"). This expression of feelings will help you further check your perception of the speaker's feelings. This will also allow the speaker to see his or her feelings more objectively. This is especially helpful when the speaker feels angry, hurt, or depressed.

When you echo the speaker's feelings, you also offer the speaker a chance to elaborate.

Most of us hold back our feelings until we're certain they (and, by extension, we) will be accepted. When we feel acceptance, we feel free to go into more detail. Active listening gives the speaker this important opportunity. In echoing feelings, be careful not to over- or understate the speaker's feelings; try to be as accurate as you can.

• Ask questions. Asking questions ensures your own understanding of the speaker's thoughts and feelings and secures additional information ("How did you feel when you read your job appraisal report?"). Your questions should provide just enough stimulation and support for the speaker to feel he or she can elaborate on these thoughts and feelings. These questions will further confirm your interest and concern for the speaker. Be careful, however, not to pry into unrelated areas or challenge the speaker in any way.

Although these types of listening—participatory and passive, empathic and objective, nonjudgmental and judgmental, surface and depth, and active and inactive listening—are easy to define and distinguish in a textbook, it's not always easy to choose the appropriate listening style for any given communication situation.

BUILDING Communication Skills

HOW CAN PARAPHRASING ENSURE UNDERSTANDING?

For each of the messages presented below, write a paraphrase that you think would be appropriate. After you complete the paraphrases, ask another person if he or she would accept them as objective restatements of thoughts and feelings. Rework the paraphrases until the other person agrees that they're accurate. A sample paraphrase is provided for Number 1.

1. I can't deal with my parents' constant fighting. I've seen it for the last 10 years and I really can't stand it anymore.
   Paraphrase: You have trouble dealing with their fighting. You seem really upset by this last fight.
2. I got a C on that paper. That's the worst grade I've ever received. I just can't believe that I got a C. This is my major. What am I going to do?

3. I can't understand why I didn't get that promotion. I was here longer and did better work than Thompson. Even my two supervisors said I was the next in line for the promotion. And now it looks like another one won't come along for at least a year.
4. That rotten, inconsiderate pig just up and left. He never even said goodbye. We were together for six months and after one small argument he leaves without a word. And he even took my bathrobe—that expensive one he bought for my last birthday.
5. I'm just not sure what to do. I really love Karen. She's the sweetest kid I've ever known. I mean she'd do anything for me. But, she really wants to get married. I do, too, and yet I don't want to make such a commitment. I mean that's a long-term thing. And, much as I hate to admit it, I don't want the responsibility of a wife, a family, a house. I really don't need that kind of pressure.

SUMMARY

In this unit we discussed the process of listening, the principles of effective listening, and a special kind of listening known as active listening.

1. Effective listening yields a wide variety of benefits in more effective learning, relating, influencing, playing, and helping.
2. Listening is a five-part process that begins with receiving and continues through understanding, remembering, evaluating, and responding.
3. Receiving consists of hearing the verbal signals and seeing the nonverbal signals.
4. Understanding involves learning what the speaker means, not merely what the words mean.
5. Remembering involves retaining the received message, a process that involves considerable reconstruction.
6. Evaluating consists in judging the messages you receive.
7. Responding involves giving feedback while the speaker is speaking and taking your turn at speaking after the speaker has finished.
8. Listening is influenced by a wide range of cultural factors such as language and speech, nonverbal behaviors, credibility, and feedback differences.
9. Effective listening involves adjusting our behaviors on the basis of at least five dimensions: participatory and passive listening, empathic and objective listening, nonjudgmental and critical listening, surface and depth listening, and active and inactive listening.
10. Participatory and passive listening refers to the degree to which the listener actively contributes to the communication act.

11. Empathic and objective listening refers to the degree to which the listener focuses on feeling what the speaker is feeling versus understanding the objective message.

12. Nonjudgmental and critical listening refers to the degree to which the listener evaluates what is said.

13. Surface and depth listening refers to the extent to which the listener focuses on the obvious or literal meanings versus the less obvious or hidden meanings.

14. Active and inactive listening refers to the extent to which the listener reflects back and expresses support for the speaker.

KEY TERMS

listening (p. 57)

receiving (p. 58)

understanding (p. 58)

remembering (p. 59)

evaluating (p. 59)

responding (p. 62)

empathic and objective listening (p. 66)

participatory and passive listening (p. 66)

nonjudgmental and critical listening (p. 67)

surface and depth listening (p. 68)

active and inactive listening (p. 69)

paraphrase (p. 68)

 ## THINKING CRITICALLY ABOUT
Listening

1. Using the five dimensions of listening effectiveness, how would you describe yourself as a listener when listening in class? When listening to your best friend? When listening to a romantic partner? When listening to parents? When listening to superiors at work?

2. What would be an appropriate active listening response for each of these situations?
   - Your friend Phil has just broken up a love affair and is telling you about it. "I can't seem to get Chris out of my mind," he says. "All I do is daydream about what we used to do and all the fun we used to have."
   - A young nephew tells you that he can't talk with his parents. No matter how hard he tries, they just don't listen. "I tried to tell them that I can't play baseball and I don't want to play baseball," he confides. "But they ignore me and tell me that all I need is practice."
   - Your mother has been having a difficult time at work. She was recently passed up for a promotion and received one of the lowest merit raises given in the company. "I'm not sure what I did wrong," she tells you. "I do my work, mind my own business, don't take my sick days like everyone else. How could they give that promotion to Helen who's only been with the company for two years? Maybe I should just quit."

3. Would you find it difficult to listen to friends who were complaining that the insurance premium on their Rolls Royce was going up? Why? Would you find it difficult to listen to friends complain that their rent was going up and that they feared becoming homeless? Why?

4. What type(s) of listening you would use in each of the following situations? What types of listening would be obviously inappropriate in each situation?
   - Your steady dating partner for the last five years tells you that spells of depression are becoming more frequent and more long lasting.
   - Your history instructor is giving a lecture on the contribution of the Ancient Greeks to modern civilization.
   - Your five-year-old daughter says she wants to become a nurse.
   - A salesperson tells you of the benefits of a new computer.
   - A gossip columnist details the secret lives of the stars.
   - The television advertiser explains the benefits of the new Volvo.

5. How would you go about finding answers to such questions as these:
   - Are women and men equally effective as listeners?
   - Can empathic listening be taught?
   - What kinds of listening make health professional-patient communication more effective? More personally satisfying?
   - What attitudes do business executives have toward listening and its importance in the workplace?

The Self In Communication

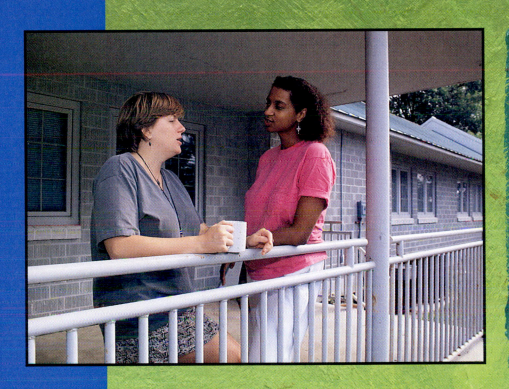

UNIT CONTENTS

UNIT GOALS

After completing this unit, you should be able to

define *self-concept* and explain how it develops

define *self-awareness* and explain how it may be increased

define *self-esteem* and explain the ways to raise it

define *self-disclosure* and explain the factors influencing it and its rewards and dangers

Of all the components of the communication act, the most important is the self. Who you are and how you perceive yourself and others influence your communications and your responses to the communications of others. In this unit, we explore four aspects of the self: self-concept, self-awareness, self-esteem, and self-disclosure—the process of revealing yourself to others.

SELF-CONCEPT

Your self-concept is your image of who you are. It's how you perceive yourself: your feelings and thoughts about your strengths and weaknesses and your abilities and limitations. Self-concept develops from the image that others have of you and reveal to you; the comparisons you make between yourself and others; your cultural experiences in the realms of race, ethnicity, gender, and gender roles; and your evaluation of your own thoughts and behaviors (Figure 5.1).

Other's Images of You

If you wished to see the way your hair looked, you would probably look in a mirror. But, what would you do if you wanted to see how friendly or how assertive you were? According to the concept of the *looking-glass self* (Cooley 1922), you would look at the image of yourself that others reveal to you through their behaviors and especially through the way they treat you and react to you.

Of course, you would not look to just anyone. Rather, you would look to those who are most significant in your life—to your *significant others*. As a child you would look to your parents and then to your elementary school teachers, for example. As an adult you might look to your friends and romantic partners. If these significant others think highly of you, you'll see a positive self-image reflected in their behaviors; if they think little of you, you'll see a more negative image.

Comparisons with Others

Another way you develop your self-concept is to compare yourself with others, to engage in what is

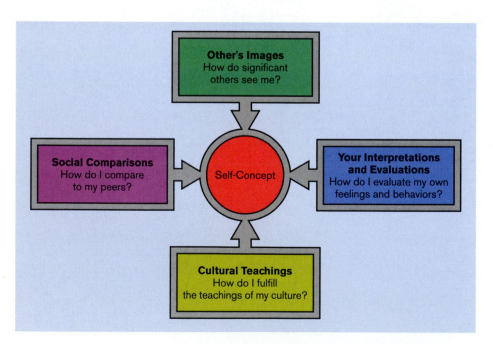

Figure 5.1 **The Sources of Self-Concept**   This diagram depicts the four sources of self-concept, the four contributors to how you see yourself. As you read about self-concept, consider the influence of each factor throughout your life. Which factor influenced you most as a preteen? Which influences you the most now? Which will influence you the most 25 or 30 years from now?

called **social comparisons** (Festinger 1954). Again, you don't choose just anyone. Rather, when you want to gain insight into who you are and how effective or competent you are, you look to your peers, generally to those who are distinctly similar to you (Miller, Turnbull, & McFarland 1988) or to those who have approximately the same ability as you do (Foody & Crundall 1993). For example, after an examination you probably want to know how you performed relative to the other students in your class. This gives you a clearer idea as to how effectively you performed. If you play on a baseball team, it's important to know your batting average in comparison with the batting average of others on the team. Absolute scores on the exam or of your batting average may be helpful in telling you something about your performance, but you gain a different perspective when you see your score in comparison with those of your peers.

Cultural Teachings

Through your parents, teachers, and the media, your culture instills in you a variety of beliefs, values, and attitudes—about success (how you define it and how you should achieve it); the relevance of a person's religion, race, or nationality; and the ethical principles you should follow in business and in your personal life. These teachings provide benchmarks against which you can measure yourself. For example, your success in achieving what your culture defines as success will contribute to a positive self-concept. Your failure to achieve what your culture teaches (for example, not being married by the time you're 30) will contribute to a negative self-concept.

When you demonstrate the qualities that your culture (or your organization) teaches, you'll see yourself as a cultural success and will be rewarded by other members of the culture (or organization). Seeing yourself as culturally successful and being rewarded by others will contribute positively to your self-concept. When you fail to demonstrate such qualities, you're more likely to see yourself as a cultural failure and to be punished by other members of the culture, contributing to a more negative self-concept.

Your Own Interpretations and Evaluations

You also react to your own behavior; you interpret it and evaluate it. These interpretations and evalua-

tions contribute to your self-concept. For example, let's say you believe that lying is wrong. If you lie, you'll probably evaluate this behavior in terms of your internalized beliefs about lying and will react negatively to your own behavior. You might, for example, experience guilt as a result of your behavior contradicting your beliefs. On the other hand, let's say that you pulled someone out of a burning building at great personal risk. You would probably evaluate this behavior positively; you would feel good about this behavior and, as a result, about yourself.

The more you understand why you view yourself as you do, the better you'll understand who you are. You can gain additional insight into yourself by looking more closely at self-awareness and especially at the Johari model of the self.

SELF-AWARENESS

If you listed some of the qualities you wanted to have, self-awareness would surely rank high. Self-awareness is eminently practical: the more you understand yourself, the more you'll be able to control your thoughts and behaviors.

The Four Selves

Figure 5.2 explains self-awareness by the **Johari Window** (Luft 1969, 1984). The window is broken up into four basic areas or quadrants, each of which contains a somewhat different self. Let's assume that this window and the four selves represent you.

The Open Self

The **open self** represents all the information, behaviors, attitudes, feelings, desires, motivations, ideas, and so on that you know about yourself and that others also know. The information included here might vary from your name, skin color, and sex to your age, political and religious affiliations, and job title. Your open self will vary in size depending on the individuals with whom you're dealing. Some people probably make you feel comfortable and support you. To them, you open yourself wide. To others you may prefer to leave most of yourself closed.

The size of the open self also varies from person to person. Some people tend to reveal their innermost desires and feelings. Others prefer to remain silent about both significant and insignificant details.

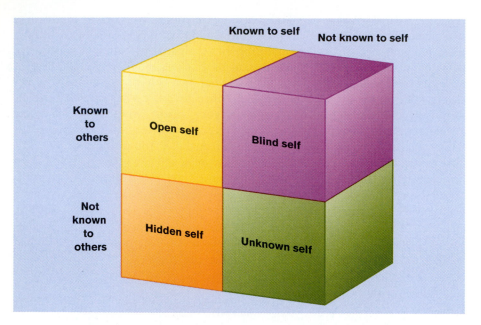

Figure 5.2 **The Johari Window.** Note that a change in any one of the quadrants produces changes in the other quadrants. Visualize the size of the entire window being constant, and the size of each quadrant being variable—sometimes small, sometimes large. As you communicate with others, information is moved from one quadrant to another. So, for example, if you reveal a secret, you shrink the hidden self and enlarge the open self. These several selves, then, are not separate and distinct from each other. Rather, each depends on the others. From *Group Process: An Introduction to Group Dynamics*, Third Edition by Joseph Luft. Copyright © 1984, 1970, 1963 by Joseph Luft. Reprinted by permission of Mayfield Publishing Company.

Most of us, however, open ourselves to some people about some things at some times.

The Blind Self

The **blind self** represents information about yourself that others know but you don't. This may vary from relatively insignificant habits—using the expression "you know," rubbing your nose when you get angry, or having a peculiar body odor—to something as significant as defense mechanisms, fight strategies, or repressed experiences.

Communication depends in great part on both parties having the same basic information about the other. Where blind areas exist, communication will be difficult. Yet blind areas will always exist for each of us. Although we may be able to shrink our blind areas, we can never eliminate them.

The Unknown Self

The **unknown self** represents those parts of yourself about which neither you nor others know. This is the information that is buried in your unconscious or that has somehow escaped notice.

You gain insight into the unknown self from a number of different sources. Sometimes this area is revealed through temporary changes brought about by drug experiences, special experimental conditions such as hypnosis or sensory deprivation, or various projective tests or dreams. The exploration of the unknown self through open, honest, and empathic interaction with trusted and trusting others—parents, friends, counselors, children, lovers—is an effective way of gaining insight.

The Hidden Self

The **hidden self** contains all that you know of yourself but keep hidden from others. This area includes all your successfully kept secrets about yourself and others. At the extremes, there are the overdisclosers and the underdisclosers. The overdisclosers tell all, keeping nothing hidden about themselves or others. They will tell you their family history, sexual problems, financial status, goals, failures and successes, and just about everything else. The underdisclosers tell nothing. They will talk about you but not about themselves.

Most of us fall somewhere between these two extremes. We keep certain things hidden and we disclose other things. We disclose to some people and we don't disclose to others. We are, in effect, selective disclosers.

Growing in Self-Awareness

Embedded in the foregoing discussion are suggestions on how to increase your own self-awareness. Some of these may now be made explicit.

Dialogue with Yourself

No one knows you better than you do. The problem is that we seldom if ever ask ourselves about ourselves. It can be interesting and revealing.

Consider what you know by taking the "Who Am I?" test (Bugental and Zelen, 1950). Head a piece of paper "Who Am I?" and write 10, 15, or 20 times, "I am . . ." Then complete each of the sentences. Try not to give only positive or socially acceptable responses; respond with what comes to mind first. On another piece of paper, divided into two columns, head one column "Strengths" or "Virtues" and the other column "Weaknesses" or "Vices." Fill in each column as quickly as possible.

Remember too that you're constantly changing. Consequently, your self-perceptions and goals also change, often in drastic ways. Update them at regular and frequent intervals.

Listen

You can learn about yourself from seeing yourself as others do. Conveniently, others are constantly giving you the very feedback you need to increase self-awareness. In every interpersonal interaction, people comment on you in some way—on what you do, what you say, how you look. Sometimes these comments are explicit: "You really look washed-out today." Most often they're only implicit, such as a stare or averted eyes. Often they're "hidden" in the way others look, what they talk about, and the focus of their interest.

Reduce Your Blind Self

Actively seek information to reduce your blind self. People will reveal such information when you encourage them. Use some of the situations that arise every day to gain self-information: "Do you think I came down too hard on the instructor today?" " Do you think I was assertive enough when I asked for the raise?" Don't, of course, seek this information constantly—your friends would quickly find others with whom to interact. But you can make use of some situations—perhaps those in which you're particularly unsure of what to do or how you appear—to reduce your blind self and increase self-awareness.

See Your Different Selves

To each of your friends and relatives, you're a somewhat different person. Yet you're really all of these. Try to see yourself as do the people with whom you interact. For starters, visualize how you're seen by your mother, your father, your teacher, your best friend, the stranger you sat next to on the bus, your employer, and your neighbor's child. Because you are, in fact, a composite of all of these views, it's important that you see yourself through the eyes of many people.

Increase Your Open Self

Self-awareness generally increases when you increase your open self. When you reveal yourself to others, you learn about yourself at the same time. You bring into clearer focus what you may have buried within. As you discuss yourself, you may see connections that you had previously missed. In receiving feedback from others, you gain still more insight.

Further, by increasing your open self, you increase the likelihood that a meaningful and intimate dialogue will develop. It's through such interactions that you best get to know yourself.

SELF-ESTEEM

Personal **self-esteem** refers to the way you feel about yourself. How much do you like yourself? How valuable a person do you think you are? How competent do you think you are? The answers to these questions reflect the value you place on yourself; they're a measure of your self-esteem.

There's also group self-esteem, which refers to your evaluation of your being a member of a particular racial or ethnic group (Porter & Washington 1993). Personal self-esteem is influenced by your group self-esteem. If you view your racial or ethnic group membership negatively, then its especially difficult to develop high positive self-esteem. Conversely, if you view your membership positively, then you are more likely to have high positive self-esteem.

Pride in one's group (racial, ethnic, religious, or gender, for example) and a supportive community contribute to group self-esteem and consequently to personal self-esteem.

The major reason that self-esteem is so important is simply that success breeds success. When you feel good about yourself—about who you are and what you are capable of doing—you perform more effectively. When you think like a success, you're more likely to act like a success. When you think you're a failure, you're more likely to act like a failure. Increasing your self-esteem will help you function more effectively in school, in your interpersonal relationships, and in your career.

Do realize that there are significant cultural differences in the way we're taught to view ourselves (Gudykunst & Ting-Toomey 1988). For example, in the United States, Australia, and Western Europe people are encouraged to be independent. Members of these cultures are taught to get ahead, to compete, to win, to achieve their goals, to realize their unique potential, to stand out from the crowd. In many Asian and African cultures, on the other hand, people are taught to value an interdependent self. Members of these cultures are taught to get along, to help others, and to not disagree, stand out, or be conspicuous. Although self-esteem depends largely on achieving your goals, your culture seems to select the specific goals.

Attack Your Self-Destructive Beliefs

Self-destructive beliefs are those things that you believe damage your self-esteem and prevent you from building meaningful and productive relationships. They may be about yourself ("I'm not creative," "I'm boring"), your world ("The world is an unhappy place," "People are out to get me"), and your relationships ("All the good people are already

BUILDING
Communication Skills

HOW DO YOU ATTACK SELF-DEFEATING DRIVERS?

Another approach to unrealistic beliefs is to focus on what Pamela Butler (1981) calls "drivers," beliefs that may motivate you to act in ways that are self-defeating. Consider the following drivers:

• The drive to **be perfect** impels you to try to perform at unrealistically high levels at work, school, and home; anything short of perfection is unacceptable.
• The drive to **be strong** tells you that weakness and any of the more vulnerable emotions like sadness, compassion, or loneliness are wrong.
• The drive to **please others** leads you to seek approval from others; you assume that if you gain the approval of others, then you're a worthy and deserving person, and if others disapprove of you, then you're worthless and undeserving.
• The drive to **hurry up** compels you to do things quickly, to do more than can be reasonably expected in any given amount of time.
• The drive to **try hard** makes you take on more responsibilities than any one person can be expected to handle.

Because these drivers set unrealistically high standards, they make it impossible for you to accomplish the very things you feel are essential for approval by others and by yourself. Recognizing that you may have internalized such drivers is the first step to eliminating them. The second step involves recognizing that these drivers are in fact unrealistic and self-defeating. Substituting realistic and self-affirming beliefs for these self-defeating drivers is the third step. How would you rephrase each of these five drivers into realistic and productive beliefs?

Television talk show hosts, especially Oprah Winfrey, generally emphasize the importance of self-esteem. Do you feel self-esteem is important to your own personal and professional success?

in relationships," "If I ever fall in love, I know I'll be hurt"). Identifying these beliefs will help you examine them critically and see that they're both illogical and self-defeating. A useful way to view self-destructive beliefs is given in the Building Communication Skills box entitled, "How Do You Attack Self-Defeating Drivers?"

Engage in Self-affirmation
Remind yourself of your successes from time to time. Focus on your good deeds, strengths, and positive qualities. Also, look carefully at the good relationships you have with friends and relatives. Concentrate on your potential, not your limitations (Brody 1991).

Seek Out Nurturing People
Seek out positive people who are optimistic and make you feel good about yourself. Avoid those who find fault with just about everything. Seek to build a network of supportive others (Brody 1991). At the same time, however, realize that you do not have to be loved by everyone. Many people believe that everyone should love them. This belief traps you into thinking you must always please others so they will like you.

Work on Projects That Will Result in Success
Success builds self-esteem. Each success makes achieving the next one a little easier. Remember that the failure of a project is not the failure of you as a person; failure is something that happens, not something inside you. Everyone faces defeat somewhere along the line. The attitude that distinguishes failures from successes is that successful people know how to deal with setbacks. Further, one defeat does not mean you'll fail the next time. Put failure in perspective, and don't make it an excuse for not trying again.

SELF-DISCLOSURE
When you reveal information from your hidden self, you're engaging in self-disclosure (Jourard 1968, 1971a, b). In this section we look at self-disclosure from a number of vantage points: the nature of self-disclosure, the factors influencing self-disclosure, the rewards and dangers of self-disclosure, and some guidelines to consider before self-disclosing. But before reading about these rewards and dangers, explore your own feelings about how willing you are to self-disclose by taking the following self-test.

SELF-TEST

How Willing to Self-Disclose Are You?

Respond to each of the following statements by indicating the likelihood of your disclosing such information to, for instance, other members of this class. Use the following scale: 1 = would definitely self-disclose; 2 = would probably self-disclose; 3 = don't know; 4 = would probably not self-disclose; 5 = would definitely not self-disclose

_____ 1. My religious beliefs.
_____ 2. My attitudes toward other religions, nationalities, and races.
_____ 3. My economic status.
_____ 4. My parents' attitudes toward other religions, races, and nationalities.
_____ 5. My feelings about my parents.
_____ 6. My sexual fantasies.
_____ 7. My ideal mate.
_____ 8. My drinking and/or drug-taking behavior.
_____ 9. My unfulfilled desires.
_____ 10. My feelings about the people in this group.

Would the results of this questionnaire have differed if the target audience of these disclosures was your parents? A stranger you would probably never see again? A best friend or lover? A teacher or counselor? If you have the opportunity, compare your responses with others. Is there much agreement among people in their willingness to self-disclose? Are there gender differences? Are there cultural differences? ✔

The Nature of Self-Disclosure

Self-disclosure is communication in which you reveal information about yourself. Because self-disclosure is a type of communication, it includes not only overt statements but also, for example, slips of the tongue and unconscious nonverbal signals. It varies from whispering a secret to a best friend to making a public confession on the Jerry Springer show.

As the term implies, self-disclosure concerns you—your thoughts, feelings, and behaviors. It might also, however, refer to your intimates since information about them usually has some impact on yourself. Thus, self-disclosure could refer to your own actions or the actions of, say, your parents or children, since these have a direct relationship to who you are.

Although by definition self-disclosure may be any information about the self, it's most often used to

UNDERSTANDING
Theory and Research

WHAT'S THE VALUE OF SELF-ESTEEM?

Anecdotal evidence strongly favors the importance of self-esteem. Popular books and magazine articles regularly provide us with ways to raise our self-esteem. The assumption is that positive self-esteem makes a person more productive and ultimately more successful. And success, in turn, raises a person's self-esteem. But,

the scientific evidence on that connection is not conclusive. For example, many people who have extremely low self-esteem have become quite successful in all fields. And, a surprisingly large number of criminals and delinquents are found to have extremely high self-esteem (Johnson 1998). How would you go about studying the relationship between self-esteem and personal refer to information that you normally keep hidden rather than simply information that you have not previously revealed.

Factors Influencing Self-Disclosure

Self-disclosure occurs more readily under certain circumstances than others. Here, we identify several factors influencing self-disclosure.

Group Size

Self-disclosure occurs more in small groups than in large groups. Dyads (groups of two people) are the most hospitable setting for self-disclosure. With one listener, you can attend carefully to the person's responses. On the basis of this support or lack of support, you can monitor the disclosures, continuing if the situation is supportive and stopping if it's not.

Liking

People tend to disclose to people they like or love, and not to disclose to people they dislike (Derlega, Winstead, Wong, & Greenspan 1987). This is not surprising, since people you like (and who probably like you) will be supportive and positive. Not only do you disclose to those you like, you probably also come to like those to whom you disclose (Berg & Archer, 1983). You probably also disclose more to those you trust (Wheeless & Grotz 1977; Petronio, 1991).

Receiver Relationship

At times self-disclosure is more likely to occur in temporary than permanent relationships—for example, between strangers on a train or plane, a kind of "in-flight intimacy" (McGill 1985). In this situation, two people establish an intimate self-disclosing relationship during some brief travel period, knowing that they will never see each other again.

When you self-disclose you generally expose some weakness or make yourself vulnerable in some way and so it's not surprising to find that intimate self-disclosures are less likely to occur in competitive rather than in noncompetitive relationships (Busse & Birk 1993).

You're also more likely to disclose to in-group members rather than to members of groups of which you're not a member. For example, people from the same race are more likely to disclose more to other members of the race than to members of another race and people with disabilities are more likely to disclose to others with disabilities than to those without disabilities (Stephan, Stephan, Wenzel, & Cornelius 1991).

Age

The opportunity for self-disclosure also seems greater when you talk with those who are approximately your own age (Collins & Gould 1994). For example, young women self-disclosed more to same-aged partners than to those significantly older than them. Older women disclosed more about the past than did the younger women. Also, the level of the

Do you find, as research says, that men self-disclose less than women? Are there situations in which men disclose more? Do men and women differ in the types of disclosures they make? An interesting twist on the general finding that women self-disclose more than men is the finding that among married couples, both husbands and wives self-disclosed equally, but wives reported that they made more emotional disclosures than did their husbands (Shimanoff 1985). Do you think this would also hold for dating couples?

UNDERSTANDING
Theory and Research

DO YOU DO WHAT THE OTHER PERSON DOES?

Generally, self-disclosure is reciprocal. In any interaction, it's more likely to occur if the other person has previously done so. This is the **dyadic effect**—what one person in a dyad does, the other does in response. The dyadic effect in self-disclosure takes a kind of spiral form with each self-disclosure prompting an additional self-disclosure by the other per-son, which in turn prompts still more self-disclosure, and so on. It's interesting to note that disclosures made in response to the disclosures of others are generally more intimate than those that are not the result of the dyadic effect (Berg & Archer 1983).

This dyadic effect is not universal across all cultures. For example, while Americans are likely to follow the dyadic effect and reciprocate with explicit, verbal self-disclosure, Koreans aren't (Won-Doornink 1985).

disclosure's intimacy seems to be more similar in similar age dyads than in differing age dyads. Not surprisingly, older people are more likely to engage in painful self-disclosures (talk of illness and loneli-ness, for example) than are younger people (Coup-land, Coupland, Giles, Henwood, et al. 1988).

Competence

Competent communicators self-disclose more than less competent ones. "It may very well be," note James McCroskey and Lawrence Wheeless (1976), "that people who are more competent also perceive themselves to be more competent, and thus have the self-confidence necessary to take more chances with self-disclosure. Or, even more likely, competent people may simply have more positive things to disclose about themselves than less competent people."

Personality

Highly sociable and extroverted people self-disclose more than those who are less sociable and more in-troverted. Sometimes, anxiety increases self-disclos-ing and at other times it reduces it to a minimum. People who are apprehensive about talking in gen-eral also self-disclose less than do those who are more comfortable in oral communication. People with high self-esteem are more likely to engage in self-disclosure than are those low in self-esteem (Dolgin, Meyer, & Schwartz 1991).

Topics

If you're like the people studied by researchers, you're more likely to disclose about some topics than others. For example, you're more likely to self-disclose infor-mation about your job or hobbies than about your sex life or financial situation (Jourard, 1968, 1971a). You would also disclose favorable information more read-ily than unfavorable information. Generally, the more personal and the more negative the topic, the less likely you are to self-disclose (Nakanishi 1986). Fur-ther, you're more likely to disclose information that reflects positively on the other person than informa-tion that reflects negatively (Shimanoff 1985).

Culture

Different cultures view self-disclosure differently. Peo-ple in the United States, for example, disclose more than do those in Great Britain, Germany, Japan, or Puerto Rico (Gudykunst 1983). And among the Kabre of Togo, secrecy is a major part of their everyday in-teraction (Piot 1993). American students also disclose more than do students from nine different Middle East countries (Jourard 1971). Similarly, American stu-dents self-disclose more on a variety of controversial issues and also self-disclose more to different types of people than do Chinese students (Chen 1992).

However, there are also important similarities across cultures. For example, people from Great Britain, Ger-many, the United States, and Puerto Rico are all more apt to disclose personal information—hobbies, interests, attitudes, and opinions on politics and religion—than information on finances, sex, personality, and interpersonal relationships (Jourard 1971a, 1971b). Similarly, one study showed self-disclosure patterns between American males to be virtually identical to the patterns between Korean males (Won-Doornink 1991).

Gender

Generally, men disclose less than do women (Naifeh & Smith 1984; Rosenfeld 1979) except in initial heterosexual encounters, in which men disclose more (Derlega, Winstead, Wong, & Hunter 1985). Research shows that sex role rather than biological gender accounts for the differences in self-disclosure (Pearson 1980; Shaffer, Pegalis, & Carnell 1992). In one study, "masculine women" self-disclosed to a lesser extent than did women who scored low on masculinity scales (Pearson 1980). Further, "feminine men" self-disclosed to a greater extent than did men who scored low on femininity scales.

The major reason both men and women give for avoiding self-disclosure is the fear of projecting an unfavorable image. In addition, men fear appearing inconsistent, losing control over the other person, and threatening the relationship. Women fear revealing information that may be used against them, giving others the impression that they're emotionally disturbed, or hurting their relationships (Rosenfeld 1979).

Thinking Critically about Self-Disclosure

Because self-disclosure and its effects can be so significant, think critically before deciding to disclose or not disclose. Specifically, weigh the rewards and dangers carefully. Also, think about the way you'll disclose and respond to the disclosures of others. In reading these topics, recall our earlier model of communication and the importance of culture (Unit 1). Not all societies and cultures view self-disclosure in the same way. In some cultures, disclosing one's inner feelings is considered a weakness. Among Anglo-Saxon Americans, for example, it would be considered "out of place" if a man cried at a happy occasion like a wedding. That same behavior would go unnoticed in some Latin cultures. Similarly, in Japan it's considered undesirable to reveal personal information, whereas in the United States it's considered desirable and is even expected (Barnlund 1989; Hall 1984).

The potential rewards and dangers of self-disclosure as well as any suggested guidelines, then, must be examined in terms of the specific culture and its rules. As with many such cultural rules, following them brings approval and violating them brings disapproval.

Also, remember that self-disclosure, like any communication, is irreversible (see Unit 2). Regardless of how many times you may try to qualify a self-disclosure or "take it back," once something is said it can't be withdrawn. Nor can you erase the conclusions and inferences listeners have made on the basis of your disclosures.

The Rewards of Self-Disclosure

One reason why self-disclosure is so significant is that its rewards are great. Self-disclosure may bring self-knowledge, increase your ability to cope, improve communication, and increase relationship depth.

When you self-disclose you gain a new perspective on yourself and a deeper **understanding of your own behavior**. In therapy, for example, often the insight comes while the client is self-disclosing. He or she may recognize some previously unknown facet of behavior or relationship. Through self-disclosure, then, you may also come to understand yourself more thoroughly.

Self-disclosure often enhances your **coping abilities** and may help you deal with your problems, especially guilt. One of the great fears many people have is that they will not be accepted because of some deep, dark secret, because of something they have done, or because of some feeling or attitude they have. By self-disclosing such feelings and receiving support rather than rejection, you may become better able to deal with any such guilt and perhaps reduce or even eliminate it (Pennebaker 1991).

Even self-acceptance is difficult without self-disclosure. If you accept yourself, in part at least through the eyes of others, then it becomes essential that you give others the opportunity to know and to respond to the "real" you. Through self-disclosure and subsequent support, you put yourself in a better position to receive positive responses to who you really are, stripped of the facade that the failure to self-disclose erects.

Self-disclosure may help to **improve communication**. You understand the messages of others largely to the extent that you understand the senders of those messages. You can understand what someone says better if you know that individual well. You can tell what certain nuances mean, when the person is serious and when joking, and when the person is being sarcastic out of fear and when out of resentment. Self-disclosure is an essential condition for getting to know another individual, for the process of adjustment considered in Unit 2.

Self-disclosure is often helpful for **establishing a meaningful relationship** between two people. Research has found, for example, that marital satisfaction is higher for couples who are middle to high self-disclosers; satisfaction is significantly less in low disclosing relationships (Rosenfeld & Bowen, 1991). Without self-disclosure, relationships of any meaningful depth seem difficult if not impossible. By self-disclosing, you tell others that you trust them, respect them, and care enough about them and your relationship to reveal yourself to them. This in turn leads the other individual to self-disclose (the dyadic effect) and forms at least the start of a meaningful relationship, one that is honest and open and goes beyond surface trivialities.

The Dangers of Self-Disclosure

In March 1995 television talk show host Jenny Jones did a show on self-disclosing your secret crushes. One panelist, Scott Amedure, disclosed his crush on another man, Jonathan Schmitz. Three days after the taping of the show—a show that was never aired—Scott Amedure was shot in his home. The police arrested Schmitz and charged him with murder (*New York Times*, March 19, 1995, Section 4, p. 16). Although this is an extreme demonstration of the dangers of self-disclosure, there are many risks to self-disclosing, such as personal and social rejection, material loss, and intrapersonal difficulties (Bochner 1984).

Although you usually self-disclose to someone whose responses you feel will be supportive, your disclosures may lead to **personal or social rejection**. Parents, normally the most supportive of all interpersonal relations, have frequently rejected children who self-disclosed their homosexuality, their plans to marry someone of a different religion, their decision to avoid the draft, their belief in a certain faith, or their HIV+ status. Your best friends and your closest intimates may reject you for similar self-disclosures.

Sometimes, self-disclosures result in **material losses**. Politicians who disclose inappropriate relationships with staff members may later find that their own political party no longer supports them and that voters are unwilling to vote for them. Teachers who disclose former or present drug-taking behavior or cohabitation with one of their students may find themselves being denied tenure, forced to teach undesirable schedules, and eventually becoming victims of "budget cuts." In the corporate world,

self-disclosures of alcoholism or drug addiction are often met with dismissal, demotion, or transfer.

When other people's reactions are not as predicted, **intrapersonal difficulties** may result. When you're rejected instead of supported, when your parents say that you disgust them instead of hugging you, and when your friends ignore you at school rather than seeking you out as before, you're in line for some intrapersonal difficulties. No one likes to be rejected, and those with fragile egos might well consider what damage such rejection could bring.

Guidelines for Self-Disclosing

Each person has to make her or his own decisions concerning self-disclosure. Each decision will be based on numerous variables, many of which we considered in the previous discussion. The following guidelines will help you raise the right questions before making what must be your decision.

Consider the motivation for self-disclosure. Effective self-disclosure is motivated by a concern for the relationship, for the others involved, and for yourself. Some people self-disclose out of a desire to hurt the listener. For example, a daughter who tells her parents that they hindered rather than helped her emotional development may be disclosing out of a desire to hurt and punish rather than to improve the relationship. Nor, of course, should self-disclosure be used to punish yourself (perhaps because of some guilt feeling or unresolved conflict).

Consider the appropriateness of self-disclosure. Effective self-disclosure should be appropriate to the context and to the relationship between speaker and listener. Before making any significant self-disclosure, ask yourself if the context is right. Could you arrange a better time and place? Is this self-disclosure appropriate to the relationship? Generally, the more intimate the disclosures, the closer the relationship should be. It's probably best to resist intimate disclosures with nonintimates and casual acquaintances, or in the early stages of a relationship. This suggestion applies especially to intimate negative disclosures, for example, financial or sexual difficulties or a history of drug dependency.

Consider the disclosures of the other person. During your disclosures, give the other person a chance to reciprocate with his or her own disclosures. If the other person does not also self-disclose, then reassess your own decision to open up. The lack of reciprocity may be a signal that this person— at this time and in this context—does not welcome

MEDIA WATCH

OUTING

Self-disclosure, as already noted, is a process by which you reveal to others information about yourself. Although at times you may be forced to self-disclose, we normally think of it as a voluntary process in which you control the amount of information you reveal to others about yourself. There is, however, another side to self-disclosure and that occurs when someone else reveals your hidden self, when someone else takes information from your hidden self and makes it public. Although this third-party disclosure can concern any aspect of one's hidden self, the media have made a special case out of revealing a person's affectional orientation; the process is called "outing."

Outing as a media process began in a relatively obscure gay magazine (*Outweek*). An article, "The Secret Gay Life of Malcolm Forbes," made public Forbes's homosexuality; it "outed" him (Gross 1991, Johansson and Percy 1994).

On March 3, 1995, the *Wall Street Journal* ran a front page story on Jann Wenner, the multimillionaire owner and publisher of *Rolling Stone, Us, Men's Journal,* and *Family Life*. The story was basically a financial one and focused on the possible effects Wenner's marital breakup would have on his media empire. The headline read: "Jann Wenner's Rift with Wife Shakes Up His Publishing Empire." Somewhat casually noted in the article—without Wenner's permission and against his wishes (Rotello 1995)—was the fact that the new person in Wenner's life was a man. This article, although not the first to discuss Wenner's gay relationship—the *New York Post, Advertising Age,* and *Newsweek* (*Newsweek*, March 20, 1995, p. 58) had run similar stories—has been singled out because of the prestige of the *Wall Street Journal* and because of the many issues this type of forced disclosure raises.

Many saw this as an invasion of privacy; Wenner's private life is his own and it's up to him if he wishes to reveal details of his private life. Others saw this as not only appropriate but the only way to deal fairly with gay relationships.

A few weeks later and across the Atlantic, the Church of England's third highest ranking cleric, the Bishop of London, David Hope, was pressured by gay and lesbian groups to announce his homosexuality (*New York Times,* March 19, 1995, p. 10). The Bishop called a news conference and condemned the tactics as "seriously intimidatory or worse."

These two cases are especially interesting in terms of self-disclosure and raise the issue of the legitimacy of outing (Gross 1991; Signorile 1993). In the first case, if Wenner were dating a woman, the media would have mentioned it, but few would have raised the privacy issue because he is a public figure and this divorce is a relevant issue that will likely impact on his financial empire. If the media reports on only extramarital heterosexual relationships, is it not at the same time saying that homosexual relationships are illegitimate and that they're not to be spoken of openly?

The David Hope case is different. Here, the Bishop wishes not to discuss his sexuality; he says that it's "ambiguous" and that he is celibate (*New York Times,* March 19, 1995, p. 10). Gay organizations in England, however, contend that he is a policy maker in the Church of England and that by outing him they're preventing him from taking a negative stand against homosexuality as the Church of England has done in the past. The outing serves the purpose of silencing or weakening any potential antihomosexual stand. It may be noted that at a subsequent meeting, the bishops of the Church of England, who represent 70 million members, issued a condemnation of homophobia and asked that the church reconsider its generally negative position on lesbian and gay relationships (Morales 1995).

Outing raises an interesting perspective on self-disclosure and the issues discussed here are just a small part of the subject. Further, the concept of outing might legitimately be extended to refer to revealing other hidden information—for example, an athlete's prison record or drug habit, a movie star's ill health or alcoholism, or a politician's friends or financial dealings. How do you feel about outing? If you were the editor of a newspaper, what would be your policy on outing? What guidelines should the media follow in dealing with issues that individuals wish to keep private? At what point does a person lose the right to be considered a private citizen and to privacy?

The next Media Watch appears on page 101.

BUILDING
Communication Skills

HOW DO YOU DECIDE ABOUT SELF-DISCLOSURE?

Should you self-disclose or not? Here are several instances of impending self-disclosure. For each, indicate whether or not you think the self-disclosure would be appropriate and why. In making your decision, consider each of the guidelines identified in this chapter.

1. Cathy has fallen in love with another man and wants to end her relationship with Tom, a coworker. She wants to call Tom on the phone, break the engagement, and disclose her new relationship.
2. Gregory plagiarized a term paper in anthropology. He's sorry, especially since the plagiarized paper only earned a grade of C+. He wants to disclose to his instructor and redo the paper.
3. A mother of two teenage children (one boy, one girl) has been feeling guilty for the past year over a romantic affair she had with her brother-in-law while her husband was in prison. The mother has been divorced for the last few months. She wants to disclose this affair and her guilt to her children.
4. Shandra is 27 years old and has been living in a romantic relationship with another woman for the past several years. Shandra wants to tell her parents, with whom she has been very close throughout her life, but can't seem to get up the courage. She decides to tell them in a long letter.
5. Roberto, a college sophomore, has just discovered he is HIV+. He wants to tell his parents and his best friends but fears their rejection. In his Mexican American culture, information like this is rarely disclosed, especially by men. His major advisor at school seems sensitive and empathic, and he wonders if he should tell this instructor. He wants the support of his friends and family and yet doesn't want them to reject him or treat him differently.

your disclosures. So disclose gradually and in small increments. When disclosures are made too rapidly and all at once, the normal reciprocity cannot operate. Further, you lose the ability to retreat if the responses are not positive enough.

Consider the possible burdens self-disclosure might entail. Carefully weigh any problems you may run into as a result of a disclosure. Can you afford to lose your job if you disclose your previous prison record? Are you willing to risk losing a relationship if you disclose previous relationship infidelities? Ask yourself whether you're making unreasonable demands on the listener. Parents often place unreasonable burdens on their children by self-disclosing marital problems, addictions, or self-doubts that children are too young or too emotionally involved to accept. Often such disclosures don't make the relationship a better one but instead add tension and friction. Sometimes the motivation is to ease one's own guilt without considering the burden this places on the other person.

Guidelines for Responding to Self-Disclosures

When someone discloses to you, it's usually a sign of trust and affection. In serving this most important receiver function, keep the following points in mind.

Use effective and active listening skills. In Unit 4 we identified the skills of effective listening. These are especially important when listening to self-disclosures. Listen actively, listen for different levels of meaning, listen with empathy, and listen with an open mind. Paraphrase the speaker so that you can be sure you understand both the thoughts and the feelings communicated. Express understanding of the speaker's feelings to allow her or him the opportunity to see these more objectively and through the eyes of another individual. Ask questions to ensure your own understanding and to signal your interest and attention.

Support and reinforce the discloser. Express support for the person during and after the disclosures.

Going Online

Self Improvement Online Web site.

This is the home page of the Self-Improvement Online Web site. Visit some Web sites related to this unit. What can you add to what was discussed here?

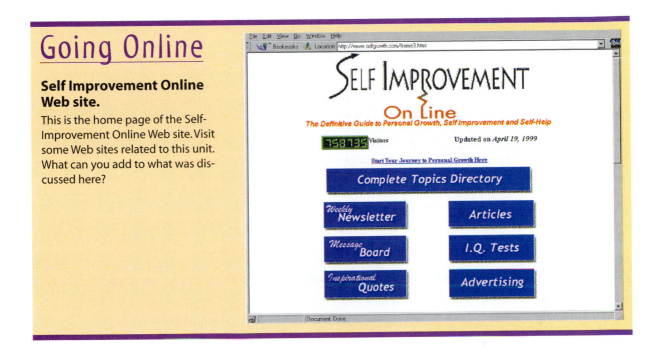

Refrain from evaluation during the disclosures; don't say, "You shouldn't have done that" or "Did you really cheat that often?" Concentrate on understanding and empathizing with the person. Allow the speaker to set her or his own pace; don't rush the person with the too frequent "So how did it all end?" type of response. Make your supportiveness clear through your verbal and nonverbal responses. For example, consider maintaining eye contact, leaning toward the speaker, asking relevant questions, and echoing the speaker's thoughts and feelings.

Maintain confidentiality. When a person confides in you, it's because she or he wants you to know these feelings and thoughts. If the discloser wishes others to share these details, then it's up to her or him to reveal them. If you tell others about these confidences, be prepared for all sorts of neg-

ative effects. Such indiscretion will likely inhibit future disclosures from this individual to anyone in general and to you in particular, and your relationship will probably suffer. Those to whom you reveal these disclosures will likely feel that since you've betrayed a confidence once, you'll do so again, perhaps with their own personal details. A general climate of distrust is easily established. But most important, betraying a confidence debases what should be a significant and meaningful interpersonal experience.

Don't use the disclosures as weapons. Many self-disclosures expose vulnerability or weakness. If you later turn around and use these against the person—called "hitting below the belt"—you betray that person's confidence and trust. The relationship is sure to suffer and may never fully recover.

SUMMARY

In this unit we looked at several aspects of the self: self-concept, self-awareness, self-esteem, and self-disclosure.

1. Self-concept refers to the image you have of yourself. It's developed from the image others have of you and reveal, the comparisons you make between yourself and others, and the way you evaluate your own thoughts and behaviors.
2. In the Johari Window model of the self, there are four major areas: the open self, the blind self, the hidden self, and the unknown self.
3. To increase self-awareness, ask yourself about yourself, listen to others to see yourself as others do, actively seek information from others about yourself, see yourself from different perspectives, and increase your open self.
4. Self-esteem refers to the way you feel about yourself, the value you place on yourself, and the positive-negative evaluation you make of yourself. It may be increased by attacking your self-destructive beliefs, engaging in self-affirmation, seeking out nurturing people, working on

projects that will result in success, and recognizing that you don't have to be loved by everyone.

5. Self-disclosure refers to a form of communication in which information about the self (usually information that is normally kept hidden) is communicated to another person.

6. Self-disclosure is more likely to occur when the potential discloser is with one other person, when the discloser likes or loves the listener, when the two people are approximately the same age, when the listener also discloses, when the discloser feels competent, when the discloser is highly sociable and extroverted, and when the topic of disclosure is fairly impersonal and positive.

7. The rewards of self-disclosure include increased self-knowledge, a better ability to cope with difficult situa-tions and guilt, more efficient communication, and a better chance for a meaningful relationship.

8. The dangers of self-disclosure include personal and so-cial rejection, material loss, and intrapersonal difficulties.

9. Before self-disclosing, consider the motivation and ap-propriateness of the self-disclosure, the opportunity available for open and honest responses, the disclo-sures of the other person, and the possible burdens that your self-disclosure might impose on you and your listeners.

10. When listening to disclosures, practice the skills of ef-fective and active listening, support and reinforce the discloser, keep the disclosures confidential, and don't use the disclosures as weapons against the person.

KEY TERMS

self-concept (p. 74)

looking-glass self (p. 74)

social comparison processes (p. 75)

Johari Window (p. 75)

self-awareness (p. 75)

unknown self (p. 76)

self-esteem (p. 77)

self-destructive beliefs (p. 78)

self-affirmation (p. 79)

self-disclosure (p. 79)

dyadic effect (p. 82)

outing (p. 85)

THINKING CRITICALLY ABOUT
the Self in Communication

1. Do you operate with the uniqueness bias when you compare yourself to others? Do you see advantages and disadvantages to this bias?

2. Have you self-disclosed more in close relationships, in casual relationships, or in temporary acquaintanceships? What accounts for these differences?

3. As a parent would you share with your children your fi-nancial and personal worries? The answer, it seems, would depend at least in part on your socioeconomic status and on whether you're a single parent or one of two parents (McLoyd & Wilson 1992). Research finds that members of middle-class two-parent families are re-luctant to share financial problems with their children, preferring to shelter them from some of life's harsher re-alities. Low-income single mothers, however, feel that sharing this with their children will protect them be-cause they will know how difficult life is and what they're up against. The researchers argue that this prac-tice of disclosing such problems actually creates prob-lems for the child such as aggressiveness, difficulties in concentrating on learning in school, and anxiety disor-ders. What would your general advice be to parents about disclosing such matters?

4. What do you think of people self-disclosing publicly on, say, a television talk show? Would you go on such a show? What topics would you be willing to discuss? What topics would you be unwilling to discuss?

5. How would you go about finding answers to such ques-tions as these?
   a. Under what circumstances do people compare them-selves with those of less ability and under what cir-cumstances do people compare themselves with those of greater ability?
   b. Is intelligence related to self-awareness? To self-esteem?
   c. Do men and women differ in the topics of their self-disclosures when talking with each other? When talk-ing with same sex others? Do same sex and opposite sex couples self-disclose similarly?
   d. Does the physical context influence the amount and type of self-disclosure that takes place between two strangers meeting for the first time?

Culture And Communication

UNIT GOALS

After completing this unit, you should be able to

define *culture, enculturation*, and *acculturation*

distinguish between collectivist and individualistic orientation, low- and high-context cultures, high- and low-power distances, and masculine and feminine cultures

define *intercultural communication* and explain the general principles for increasing effectiveness in intercultural communication

In this unit we look in depth at a topic we've already introduced: culture. Here, we examine the nature of culture and its relationship to communication, the ways in which cultures differ, and the nature of and guidelines for effective intercultural communication.

CULTURE AND COMMUNICATION

Culture (introduced briefly in Unit 1) refers to the relatively specialized lifestyle of a group of people—consisting of their values, beliefs, artifacts, ways of behaving, and ways of communicating. Included in "culture" would be all that members of a social group have produced and developed—their language, modes of thinking, art, laws, and religion.

Culture is passed on from one generation to the next through communication, not through genes. Thus, culture does not refer to color of skin or shape of eyes since these are passed on through genes, not communication. Culture does refer to beliefs in a supreme being, to attitudes toward success and happiness, and to the values placed on friendship, love, family, or money since these are transmitted not by genes but by communication.

Culture is not synonymous with race or nationality. However, members of a particular race or country are often taught similar beliefs, attitudes, and values. And this similarity makes it possible to speak of "Hispanic culture" or "African American culture." But we need to recognize that within any large culture—especially a culture based on race or nationality—there will be enormous differences. The Kansas farmer and the Wall Street executive may both be, say, German American, but they may differ widely in their attitudes and beliefs and in their general lifestyle. In some ways the Kansas farmer may be closer in attitudes and values to the Chinese farmer than to the executive. Further, the fact that you're born into a particular race and nationality does not mean that you have to adopt their dominant attitudes or ways of behaving.

Culture is transmitted from one generation to another through **enculturation**, the process by which you learn the culture into which you're born (your native culture). Parents, peer groups, schools, religious institutions, and government agencies are the main teachers of culture.

A different process of learning culture is **acculturation**, the process by which you learn the rules and norms of a culture different from your native culture. Through acculturation, your original or native culture is modified through direct contact with or exposure to a new and different culture. For example, when immigrants settle in the United States (the host culture), their own culture becomes influenced by the host culture. Gradually, the values, ways of behaving, and beliefs of the host culture become more and more a part of the immigrants' culture. At the same time, of course, the host culture changes too as it interacts with the immigrants' culture. Generally, however, the culture of the immigrant changes more. The reasons for this are that the host country's members far outnumber the immigrant group and the media are largely dominated by and reflect the values and customs of the host culture.

The acceptance of the new culture depends on a number of factors (Kim 1988). Immigrants who come from cultures similar to the host culture will become acculturated more easily. Similarly, those who are younger and better educated become acculturated more quickly than do the older and less well-educated. Personality factors also play a part. Persons who are risk takers and open-minded, for example, have greater acculturation potential. Also, persons who are familiar with the host culture prior to immigration—whether through interpersonal contact or media exposure—will be acculturated more readily.

Before exploring further the role of culture in communication, consider your own cultural values and beliefs by taking the accompanying self-test. This test illustrates how your own cultural values and beliefs may influence your interpersonal, small group, and public communications, in the messages you send and in the messages you listen to.

HOW CULTURES DIFFER

There are at least four major ways in which cultures differ that are especially important for communication. Following Hofstede (1997), Gudykunst (1991), and Hall and Hall (1987) we discuss collectivism and individualism, high and low context, power distances, and masculine and feminine cultures.

SELF-TEST

What Are Your Cultural Beliefs and Values?

Here the extremes of 10 cultural differences are identified. For each characteristic indicate your own values:

a. If you feel your values are very similar to the extremes then select 1 or 7,

b. If you feel your values are quite similar to the extremes then select 2 or 6,

c. If you feel your values are fairly similar to the extremes then select 3 or 5, and

d. If you feel you're in the middle, then select 4.

Men and women are equal and are entitled to equality in all areas.	**Gender Equality** 1 2 3 4 5 6 7	Men and women are very different and should stick to the specific roles assigned to them by their culture.
"Success" is measured by your contribution to the group.	**Group and Individual Orientation** 1 2 3 4 5 6 7	"Success" is measured by how far you out-perform others.
You should enjoy yourself as much as possible.	**Hedonism** 1 2 3 4 5 6 7	You should work as much as possible.
Religion is the final arbiter of what is right and wrong; your first obligation is to abide by the rules and customs of your religion.	**Religion** 1 2 3 4 5 6 7	Religion is like any other social institution; it's not inherently moral or right just because it's a religion.
Your first obligation is to your family; each person is responsible for the welfare of his or her family.	**Family** 1 2 3 4 5 6 7	Your first obligation is to yourself; each person is responsible for himself or herself.
Work hard now for a better future.	**Time Orientation** 1 2 3 4 5 6 7	Live in the present; the future may never come.
Romantic relationships, once made, are forever.	**Relationship Permanency** 1 2 3 4 5 6 7	Romantic relationships should be maintained as long as they're more rewarding than punishing and dissolved when they're more punishing than rewarding.
People should express their emotions openly and freely.	**Emotional Expression** 1 2 3 4 5 6 7	People should not reveal their emotions, especially those that may reflect negatively on them or others or make others feel uncomfortable.
Money is extremely important and should be a major consideration in just about any decision you make.	**Money** 1 2 3 4 5 6 7	Money is relatively unimportant and should not enter into life's really important decisions such as what relationship to enter or what career to pursue.
The world is a just place; bad things happen to bad people and good things happen to good people; what goes around comes around.	**Belief in a Just World** 1 2 3 4 5 6 7	The world is random; bad and good things happen to people without any reference to whether they're good or bad people.

This test was designed to help you explore the possible influence of your cultural beliefs and values on communication. If you visualize communication as involving choices, as already noted in Unit 1, then these beliefs will influence the choices you make and thus how you communicate and how you listen and respond to the communications of others. For example, your beliefs and values about gender equality will influence the way in which you communicate with and about the opposite sex. Your group and individual orientation will influence how you perform in work teams and how you deal with your peers at school and at work. Your degree of hedonism will influence the kinds of communications you engage in, the books you read, the television programs you watch. Your religious beliefs will influence the ethical system you follow in communicating. Review the entire list of 10 characteristics and try to identify one *specific* way in which each characteristic influences your communication.

Individual and Collective Orientation

Cultures differ in the extent to which they promote individual values (for example, power, achievement, hedonism, and stimulation) versus collectivist values (for example, benevolence, tradition, and conformity). Americans generally have a preference for the individual values (Kapoor, Wolfe, & Blue 1995).

One of the major differences between these two orientations is the extent to which an individual's goals or the group's goals are given precedence. Individual and collective tendencies are, of course, not mutually exclusive; this is not an all-or-none orientation but rather one of emphasis. You probably have both tendencies. Thus, you may, for example, compete with other members of your basketball team for the most baskets or most valuable player award (and thus emphasize individual goals). At the same time, however, you will—in a game—act in a way that will benefit the entire team (and thus emphasize group goals). In actual practice both individual and collective tendencies will help you and your team each achieve your goals. Yet, most people and most cultures have a dominant orientation; they're more individually oriented or more collectively oriented in most situations, most of the time.

In some instances, however, these tendencies may come into conflict. For example, do you shoot for the basket and try to raise your own individual score or do you pass the ball to another player who is better positioned to score and thus benefit your team? You make this distinction in popular talk when you call someone a team player (**collectivist orientation**) or an individual player (**individualistic orientation**).

In an individualistic-oriented culture members are responsible for themselves and perhaps their immediate family. In a collectivist culture members are responsible for the entire group.

Success, in an individualistic culture, is measured by the extent to which you surpass other members of your group; you would take pride in standing out from the crowd. And your heroes—in the media, for example—are likely to be those who are unique and who stand apart. In a collectivist culture success is measured by your contribution to the achievements of the group as a whole; you would take pride in your similarity to other members of your group. Your heroes, in contrast, are

Going Online

Worldbiz.com Website

Visit this Web site and select a country that you're interested in, but with which you have no cultural connection. Can you identify three things that you did not know about this culture that you learned from this visit?

UNDERSTANDING
Theory and Research

DOES LANGUAGE INFLUENCE THOUGHT?

The *linguistic relativity hypothesis* claims that because the language you speak influences the thoughts you have, people speaking widely differing languages will see the world differently and will think differently.

Theory and research, however, has not been able to find support for this claim. A more modified hypothesis seems currently supported: The language you speak helps you to talk about what you see and perhaps to highlight what you see. For example, if you speak a language that is rich in color terms (English is a good example) you would find it easier to talk about nuances of color than would someone from a culture which has fewer color terms (some cultures, for example, distinguish only two or three or four parts of the color spectrum). But, this doesn't mean that people see the world differently; only that their language helps (or doesn't help) them to talk about certain variations in the world and may make it easier (or more difficult) for them to focus their thinking on such variations. Nor does it mean that people speaking widely differing languages are doomed to misunderstand each other. Translation enables us to understand a great deal of the meaning in a foreign language message. And, of course, we have our communication skills; we can ask for clarification, for additional examples, for restatement. We can listen actively, give feedforward and feedback, use perception checking.

Language differences don't make for very important differences in perception or thought. Difficulties in intercultural understanding are more often due to ineffective communication than to differences in languages.

more likely to be team players who don't stand out from the rest of the group's members.

In an individualistic culture you're responsible to your own conscience, and responsibility is largely an individual matter; in a collectivist culture you're responsible to the rules of the social group, and responsibility for an accomplishment or a failure is shared by all members. Competition is fostered in individualistic cultures while cooperation is promoted in collectivist cultures.

In an individualistic culture you might compete for leadership in a small group setting; there would likely be a very clear distinction between leaders and members. In a collectivist culture leadership would be shared and rotated; there would likely be little distinction between leader and members. These orientations also influence the kinds of communication members consider appropriate in an organizational context. For example, individualistic members favor clarity and directness while collectivists favor "face-saving" and the avoidance of hurting others or arousing negative evaluations (Kim & Sharkey 1995).

Distinctions between in-group members and out-group members are extremely important in collectivist cultures. In individualistic cultures, where the person's individuality is prized, the distinction is likely to be less important.

High- and Low-Context Cultures

Cultures also differ in the extent to which information is made explicit, on the one hand, or is assumed to be in the context or in the persons communicating, on the other. A **high-context culture** is one in which much of the information in communication is in the context or in the person—for example, information that was shared through previous communications, through assumptions about each other, and through shared experiences. The information is thus known by all participants but it is not explicitly stated in the verbal message.

A **low-context culture** is one in which most of the information is explicitly stated in the verbal message. In formal transactions it would be stated in written (or contract) form.

To appreciate the distinction between high and low context, consider giving directions ("Where's the voter registration center?") to someone who knows the neighborhood and to a newcomer to your city. To someone who knows the neighborhood (a high-context situation) you can assume that she or he knows the local landmarks. So, you can give directions such as "next to the laundromat on Main Street" or "the corner of Albany and Elm." To the newcomer (a low-context situation), you could not assume that she or he shares any information with you. So, you would have to use only those directions that even a stranger would understand, for example, "make a left at the next stop sign" or "go two blocks and then turn right."

High-context cultures are also collectivist cultures (Gudykunst, Ting-Toomey, & Chua 1988; Gudykunst & Kim 1992). These cultures (Japanese, Arabic, Latin American, Thai, Korean, Apache, and Mexican are examples) place great emphasis on personal relationships and oral agreements (Victor 1992). Low-context cultures are also individualistic cultures. These cultures (German, Swedish, Norwegian, and American are examples) place less emphasis on personal relationships and more emphasis on the verbalized, explicit explanation and, for example, on the written contracts in business transactions.

It's interesting to note that as relationships become more intimate, they come to resemble high-context interactions. The more you and your partner know each other, the less you have to make verbally explicit. Truman Capote once defined love as "never having to finish your sentences," which is an apt description of high-context relationships. Because you know the other person so well, you can make some pretty good guesses as to what the person will say.

Members of high-context cultures spend lots of time getting to know each other interpersonally and socially before any important transactions take place. Because of this prior personal knowledge a great deal

of information is shared by the members and therefore does not have to be explicitly stated. Members of low-context cultures spend a great deal less time getting to know each other and hence don't have that shared knowledge. As a result everything has to be stated explicitly.

This difference is partly responsible for the differences observed in Japanese and American business groups (alluded to in Unit 1). The Japanese spend lots of time getting to know each other before conducting actual business, whereas Americans get down to business very quickly. The Japanese (and other high-context cultures) want to get to know each other because important information is not made explicit. They have to know you so they can read your nonverbals, for example (Sanders, Wiseman, & Matz 1991). Americans can get right down to business because all important information will be stated explicitly.

To high-context cultural members, what is omitted or assumed is a vital part of the communication transaction. Silence, for example, is highly valued (Basso 1972). To low-context cultural members, what is omitted creates ambiguity. And to these people, this ambiguity is simply something that will be eliminated by explicit and direct communication. To high-context cultural members, ambiguity is something to be avoided; it's a sign that the interpersonal and social interactions have not proved sufficient to establish a shared base of information (Gudykunst 1983).

When this simple difference is not understood, intercultural misunderstandings can easily result. For example, the directness characteristic of the low-context culture may prove insulting, insensitive, or unnecessary to the high-context cultural member. Conversely, to the low-context member, the high-context cultural member may appear vague, underhanded, or dishonest in his or her reluctance to be explicit or engage in communication that a low-context member would consider open and direct.

Another frequent source of intercultural misunderstanding that can be traced to the distinction between high- and low-context cultures can be seen in face-saving (Hall & Hall 1987). High-context cultures place a great deal more emphasis on face-saving. For example, they're more likely to avoid argument for fear of causing others to lose face whereas low-context members (with their individualistic orientation) will use argument to win a point. Similarly, in high-context cultures criticism should only take place in private. Low-context cultures may not make this public–private distinction. Low-context managers who criticize high-context workers in public will find that their criticism causes interpersonal problems and does little to resolve the original difficulty that led to the criticism in the first place (Victor 1992).

Members of high-context cultures are reluctant to say no for fear of offending and causing the person to lose face. And so, for example, it's necessary to be able to read in the Japanese executive's yes when it means yes and when it means no. The difference is not in the words used but in the way in which they're used. It's easy to see how the low-context individual may interpret this reluctance to be direct—to say no when you mean no—as a weakness or as an unwillingness to confront reality.

Power Distances

In some cultures power is concentrated in the hands of a few, and there's a great difference in the power held by these people and by the ordinary citizen. These are called **high power distance cultures**; examples are Mexico, Brazil, India, and the Philippines (Hofstede 1982). In **low power distance cultures**, power is more evenly distributed throughout the citizenry; examples include Denmark,

UNDERSTANDING Theory and Research

HOW CAN YOU REDUCE UNCERTAINTY?

Another way in which cultures differ, as discussed in Unit 3, is in their attitudes toward uncertainty and the importance they place on reducing it. Most important for our purposes here is to note that all communication involves uncertainty and ambiguity. Not surprisingly, this uncertainty and ambiguity are greater when there are large cultural differences (Berger & Bradac 1982, Gudykunst 1989). Drawing from the research and theory on uncertainty reduction, here are some suggestions for reducing uncertainty in communication situations.

Perception checking skills (Unit 3) and active listening skills (Unit 4), for example, help you to check on the accuracy of your perceptions and allow you the opportunity to revise and amend any incorrect perceptions. Being specific reduces ambiguity and the chances of misunderstandings. Misunderstanding is a lot more likely when talking about "neglect" (a highly abstract concept) than when talking about "forgetting your last birthday" (a specific event).

Seeking feedback helps you to correct any possible misconceptions almost immediately. Seek feedback on whether you're making yourself clear ("Does that make sense?" "Do you understand where to put the widget?") as well as on your understanding of what the other person is saying ("Do you mean that you'll never speak with them again? Do you mean that literally?").

Try to resist your natural tendency to judge others quickly and permanently. Prejudices and biases complicate communication further and when combined with high uncertainty are sure to produce judgments you'll have to revise. A judgment made early is likely to be based on too little information. Because of this, flexibility and a willingness to revise opinions are essential skills for reducing uncertainty.

New Zealand, Sweden, and to a lesser extent the United States. These differences impact on communication in a number of ways. For example, in high power distance cultures there's a great power distance between students and teachers; students are expected to be modest, polite, and totally respectful. In low power distance cultures (and you can see this clearly in United States college classrooms) students are expected to demonstrate their knowledge and command of the subject matter, participate in discussions with the teacher, and even challenge the teacher, something many high power distance culture members wouldn't even think of doing.

Friendship and dating relationships will also be influenced by the power distance between groups (Andersen 1991). In India, for example, such relationships are expected to take place within your cultural class; in Sweden, a person is expected to select friends and romantic partners on the basis—not of class or culture—but of individual factors such as personality, appearance, and the like.

In low power distance cultures you're expected to confront a friend, partner, or supervisor assertively; there is in these cultures a general feeling of equality which is consistent with acting assertively (Borden 1991). In high power distance cultures, direct confrontation and assertiveness may be viewed negatively, especially if directed at a superior.

Masculine and Feminine Cultures

Especially important for self-concept is the culture's attitude about gender roles, about how a man or woman should act. In fact, a popular classification of cultures is in terms of their masculinity and femininity (Hofstede 1997). In a highly "**masculine**" **culture** men are viewed as assertive, oriented to material success, and strong; women are viewed as modest, focused on the quality of life, and tender.

BUILDING Communication Skills

TALKING LIKE A MAN? TALKING LIKE A WOMAN?

How do you think a typical man and a typical woman would respond to each of these situations?

1. A supervisor criticizes your poorly written report and says that it must be redone.
2. An associate at work tells you she may be HIV+ and is awaiting results of her blood tests.
3. You see two preteenage neighborhood children fighting in the street; no other adults are around and you worry that they may hurt themselves.
4. An elderly member of your family tells you that he has to go into an old-age home.
5. A colleague confides that she was sexually harassed and doesn't know what to do.
6. You're fed up with neighbors who act decidedly unneighborly—playing the television at extremely high volume, asking you to watch their two young children while they go shopping, and borrowing things they rarely remember returning.

In general, how would you characterize the speech of men? The speech of women? On what evidence do you base your generalizations? For example, were your impressions formed on the basis of actual experience? From the presentations of men and women in the media? From research studies? How does your perception of the way men and women talk influence the way you communicate with them? The next two units discuss some of the differences between men and women in their verbal and nonverbal communications.

In a highly "**feminine**" **culture**, both men and women are encouraged to be modest, oriented to maintaining the quality of life, and tender. On the basis of Hofstede's research, the 10 countries with the highest masculinity score (beginning with the highest) are Japan, Austria, Venezuela, Italy, Switzerland, Mexico, Ireland, Jamaica, Great Britain, and Germany. The 10 countries with the highest femininity score (beginning with the highest) are: Sweden, Norway, Netherlands, Denmark, Costa Rica, Yugoslavia, Finland, Chile, Portugal, and Thailand. Out of the 53 countries ranked, the United States ranks 15th most masculine.

Masculine cultures emphasize success and so socialize their members to be assertive, ambitious, and competitive. For example, members of masculine cultures are more likely to confront conflicts directly and to competitively fight out any differences; they're more likely to emphasize win–lose conflict strategies. Feminine cultures emphasize the quality of life and so socialize their members to be modest and to emphasize close interpersonal relationships. Feminine cultures, for example, are more likely to emphasize compromise and negotiation in resolving conflicts; they're more likely to emphasize win-win solutions.

Similarly, organizations can be viewed as masculine or feminine. Masculine organizations emphasize competitiveness and aggressiveness. They emphasize the bottom line and reward their workers on the basis of their contribution to the organization. Feminine organizations are less competitive and less aggressive. They emphasize worker satisfaction and reward their workers on the basis of need; those who have large families, for example, may get better raises than single people, even if they haven't contributed as much to the organization.

INTERCULTURAL COMMUNICATION

Understanding the role of culture in communication is an essential foundation for understanding intercultural communication as it occurs interpersonally, in small groups, in public speaking, or in the media and for appreciating the principles for effective intercultural communication.

The Nature of Intercultural Communication

Intercultural communication refers to communication between persons who have different cultural

Is your place of employment basically masculine or feminine? What beliefs, attitudes, and values does it teach? What kinds of rewards or punishments does your boss administer for following or not following these teachings?

beliefs, values, or ways of behaving. The model in Figure 6.1 illustrates this concept. The larger circles represent the culture of the individual communicator. The inner circles identify the communicators (the sources/receivers). In this model each communicator is a member of a different culture. In some instances the cultural differences are relatively slight—say, between persons from Toronto and New York. In other instances the cultural differences are great—say, between persons from Borneo and Germany, or between persons from rural Nigeria and industrialized England.

All messages originate from a specific and unique cultural context, and that context influences their content and form. You communicate as you do largely as a result of your culture. Culture (along with the processes of enculturation and acculturation) influences every aspect of your communication experience.

You receive messages through the filters imposed by your cultural context. That context influences what you receive and how you receive it. For example, some cultures rely heavily on television or newspapers and trust them implicitly. Others rely on face-to-face interpersonal interactions, distrusting many of the mass communication systems.

Improving Intercultural Communication

Here is a variety of principles for increasing intercultural communication effectiveness—in conversation, on the job, and in friendly and romantic relationships. These guidelines are based on the intercultural research of a wide variety of researchers

(Barna 1985; Ruben 1985; Gudykunst & Kim 1992; Hofstede 1997).

Recognize and Reduce Your Ethnocentrism

Ethnocentrism, one of the biggest obstacles to intercultural communication, is the tendency to see others and their behaviors through your own cultural filters, often as distortions of your own behaviors. It is the tendency to evaluate the values, beliefs, and behaviors of your own culture as more positive, superior, logical, and natural than those of other cultures. To achieve effective interpersonal communication, you need to see both yourself and others as different but with neither being inferior nor superior—not an easily accomplished task.

Ethnocentrism exists on a continuum. People are not either ethnocentric or not ethnocentric; rather, most are somewhere between these polar opposites (see Table 6.2). Note also that your degree of ethnocentrism depends on the group on which you're focusing. For example, if you're a Greek American, you may have a low degree of ethnocentrism when dealing with Italian Americans but a high degree when dealing with Turkish Americans or Japanese Americans. Most important for our purposes is that your degree of ethnocentrism (and we are all ethnocentric to at least some degree) will influence your interpersonal (intercultural) communications.

Be Mindful

Being mindful rather than mindless (a distinction considered in Unit 9), is generally helpful in intercultural communication situations. When you're in a mindless state, you behave with assumptions that

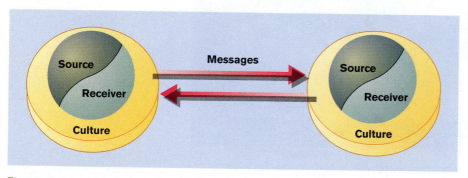

Figure 6.1 **A model of intercultural communication.** This basic model of intercultural communication is designed to illustrate that culture is a part of every communication transaction.

TABLE 6.1   The Ethnocentrism continuum

Drawing from several researchers (Lukens 1978; Gudykunst & Kim 1984; and Gudykunst 1991), this table summarizes some interconnections between ethnocentrism and communication. In this table five degrees of ethnocentrism are identified; in reality, of course, there are as many degrees as there are people. The "communication distances" are simply general terms that highlight the major communication attitude that dominates that level of ethnocentrism. Under "communications" are some ways people might interact given their particular degree of ethnocentrism. How would you have rated yourself on this scale five years ago? How would you rate yourself today?

Degrees of Ethnocentrism	Communication Distance	Communications
Low	Equality	Treats others as equals; evaluates other ways of doing things as equal to one's own
	Sensitivity	Wants to decrease distance between self and others
	Indifference	Lacks concern for others but is not hostile
	Avoidance	Avoids and limits interpersonal interactions with others; prefers to be with one's own kind
High	Disparagement	Engages in hostile behavior; belittles others; views one's own culture as superior to other cultures

would not normally pass intellectual scrutiny. For example, you know that cancer is not contagious and yet you may still avoid touching cancer patients. You know that people who are blind generally don't have hearing problems and yet you may use a louder voice when talking to persons without sight. Approximately one-third of the college students participating in a study said that they would not go swimming in a pool used by mental patients and that they would wash their hands after touching a mental patient (Wheeler, Farina, & Stern 1984). When the discrepancies between available evidence and behaviors are pointed out and your mindful state is awakened, you quickly realize that these behaviors are not logical or realistic.

When you deal with people from other cultures you're often in a mindless state and therefore function "nonrationally" in many ways. When your mindful state is awakened, as it is in textbook discussions such as this one, you may then resort to a more critical thinking mode and recognize, for example, that other people and other cultural systems are different but not inferior or superior. Thus, these suggestions for increasing intercultural communication effectiveness may appear logical (even obvious) to your mindful state but are probably frequently ignored in your mindless state.

Face Fears
Another factor that stands in the way of effective intercultural communication is fear (Stephan & Stephan 1985; Gudykunst 1990). You may fear for your self-esteem. You may become anxious about your ability to control the intercultural situation or you may worry about your own level of discomfort.

You may fear that you'll be taken advantage of by the member of this other culture. Depending upon your own stereotypes you may fear being lied to, financially duped, or made fun of. You may fear that members of this other group will react to you negatively. They may not like you or may disapprove of your attitudes or beliefs or they may even reject you as a person. Conversely, you may fear negative reactions from members of your own group. They might, for example, disapprove of your socializing with the interculturally different.

These fears—coupled with the greater effort that intercultural communication takes and the ease with which you communicate with those who are culturally similar—can easily create sufficient anxiety to make some people give up.

Recognize Differences
When you assume that all people are similar and ignore the differences between yourself and the

Do you agree with the assumption that everyone is ethnocentric to some degree? If so, where would you place yourself on the ethnocentric continuum when the "other" is a person of the opposite sex? A person of a different affectional orientation? A person of a different race? A person of a different religion?

culturally different, your intercultural efforts are likely to fail. This is especially true in the area of values, attitudes, and beliefs. It's easy to see and accept different hairstyles, clothing, and foods. But, when it comes to values and beliefs, it's easier to assume (mindlessly) that deep down we're all similar. We aren't. Henry may be a devout Baptist, while Carol may be an atheist, and Jan may be a Muslim. Each, consequently, sees his or her own life as having very different meanings because of the differences in their religious views. When you assume similarities and ignore differences, you may implicitly communicate to others that you feel your ways are the right ways and their ways are the wrong ways. The result is confusion and misunderstanding on both sides.

Recognize Differences Within Culturally Different Groups

Within every cultural group there are wide and important differences. Just as we know that all Americans are not alike (think of the various groups found in your city or just your own school), so neither are all Jamaicans, Koreans, Mexicans, and so on.

Within each culture there are many smaller cultures. These smaller cultures differ from each other and from the majority culture. Further, members of one smaller culture may share a great deal with members of that same smaller culture in another part of the world. For example, farmers in Indiana may have more in common with farmers in Borneo than with bankers in Indianapolis. For example, all will be concerned with and knowledgeable about weather conditions and their effects on crop growth, crop rotation techniques, and soil composition. Of course, these farmers, so similar when it comes to farming, may differ drastically on such issues as government subsidies, trade regulations, and sales techniques.

Avoid Overattribution

You'll recall from Unit 3 that overattribution is the tendency to attribute too much of a person's behavior or attitudes to one of that person's characteristics (She thinks that way because she's a woman; he believes that because he was raised as a Catholic). In intercultural communication situations, overattribution appears in two ways. First, it's the tendency to see too much of what a person believes or does as caused by the person's cultural identification. Second, it's the tendency to see a person as a spokesperson for that particular culture—to assume that because a person is African American he or she is therefore knowledgeable about the entire African American experience or that the person's thoughts are always focused on African American issues. As demonstrated in the discussion of perception in Unit 3, people's ways of thinking and ways of behaving are influenced by a wide variety of factors; culture is just one of them.

Recognize Differences in Meaning in Verbal and Nonverbal Messages

Earlier, we noted that meaning does not exist in the words we use (Unit 5). Rather, it exists in the person using the words. This principle is especially important in intercultural communication. Consider the

MEDIA WATCH

CULTURAL IMPERIALISM

Political imperialism is a policy of expanding the dominion of one country over that of another. Cultural imperialism refers to a similar process, expanding the dominion of one culture over that of another. This theory of cultural imperialism affords an interesting perspective on the influence of media, especially as they exert influence and dominate other cultures (Becker & Roberts 1992). The theory argues that the media from developed countries such as the United States and western Europe dominate the cultures of countries importing such media.

This cultural dominance is also seen in computer communication where the United States and the English language dominate (also see the Media Watch box in Unit 19). "And some countries," notes one journalist, "already unhappy with the encroachment of American culture—from jeans and Mickey Mouse to movies and TV programs—are worried that their cultures will be further eroded by an American dominance of cyberspace" (Pollack 1995, p. D1). [Although the term "cultural imperialism" is a negative one, the actual process of media influence may be viewed as negative or positive, depending on your cultural perspective.]

Media products from the United States are likely to emphasize its dominant attitudes and values, for example, the preference for competition, the importance of individuality, the advantages of capitalism and democracy, safe sex and health consciousness, and the importance of money. In an extreme form of this theory, it would be argued that the attitudes and values of the dominant media culture will become the attitudes and values of the rest of the world.

Television programs, films, and music from the United States and western Europe are so popular and so in demand in developing countries that they may actually inhibit the growth of the native culture's own talent. So, for example, instead of creating their own vision in an original television drama or film, native writers in developing countries may find it easier and more secure to work as translators for products from more developed countries. And native promoters may find it easier and more lucrative to sell, say, United States rock groups' tapes and CDs than to cultivate and promote native talent. The fact that it is cheaper to import and translate than it is to create original works gives the developed country's products an added advantage and the native culture's productions a decided disadvantage.

The popularity of United States and western Europe's media may also lead artists in developing countries to imitate. For example, media artists and producers may imitate films and television programs from the United States rather than develop their own styles, styles more consistent with their native culture.

From another perspective, however, some people might argue that the media products from the United States are generally superior to those produced elsewhere and hence serve as a kind of benchmark and standard for quality work throughout the world.

Also, it might be argued that such products introduce new trends and perspectives and hence enrich the native culture. Much as people in the United States profit as new cultures exert their influence, the developing cultures profit as United States media introduce new perspectives on government and politics, foods, educational technologies, and health, for example.

What do you think of the influence the media from the United States and western Europe is having on native cultures throughout the world? How do you evaluate it? Do you see advantages? Disadvantages?

The next Media Watch appears on page 120.

---

differences in meaning that might exist for the word *woman* to an American and an Iranian. What about *religion* to a Christian Fundamentalist and to an atheist, and *lunch* to a Chinese rice farmer and a Wall Street executive?

Even when we use the same words, the meanings of many terms may be drastically different. Consider meanings of the words *security, future,* and *family* when used by a New England prep school student and a homeless teenager in Los Angeles.

When it comes to nonverbal messages, the potential differences are even greater. Thus, the over-the-head clasped hands that signify victory to an American may signify friendship to a Russian. To an American, holding up two fingers to make a V signifies victory. To certain South Americans, however, it's an obscene gesture that corresponds to our extended middle finger. Tapping the side of your nose will signify that you and the other person are in on a secret—if in England or Scotland—but that the other person is nosy—if in Wales. A friendly wave of the hand will prove insulting in Greece where the wave of friendship must show the back rather than the front of the hand.

Avoid Violating Cultural Rules and Customs

Each culture has its own rules and customs for communicating. These rules identify what is appropriate and what is inappropriate. Thus, for example, if you lived in a middle-class community in Connecticut, you would follow the rules of the culture and call the person you wish to date three or four days in advance. If you lived in a different culture, you might be expected to call the parents of your future date weeks or even months in advance. In this same Connecticut community, you might say, as a friendly gesture to people you don't ever want to see again, "come on over and pay us a visit." To members of other cultures, this comment is sufficient for them to visit at their convenience.

In some cultures, members show respect by avoiding direct eye contact with the person to whom they're speaking. In other cultures this same eye avoidance would signal lack of interest. In some Mediterranean cultures men walk arm-in-arm. Other cultures consider this inappropriate.

A good example of a series of rules for an extremely large and important culture that many people don't know appears in Table 6.2, "Ten Commandments for Communicating with People with Disabilities." In looking over the list of suggestions, consider if you've seen any violations. Were you explicitly taught any of these principles?

TABLE 6.2   Ten commandments for communicating with people with disabilities

1. Speak directly rather than through a companion or sign language interpreter who may be present.
2. Offer to shake hands when introduced. People with limited hand use or an artificial limb can usually shake hands and offering the left hand is an acceptable greeting.
3. Always identify yourself and others who may be with you when meeting someone with a visual impairment. When conversing in a group, remember to identify the person to whom you're speaking.
4. If you offer assistance, wait until the offer is accepted. Then listen or ask for instructions.
5. Treat adults as adults. Address people who have disabilities by their first names only when extending that same familiarity to all others. Never patronize people in wheelchairs by patting them on the head or shoulder.
6. Don't lean against or hang on someone's wheelchair. Bear in mind that disabled people treat their chairs as extensions of their bodies.
7. Listen attentively when talking with people who have difficulty speaking and wait for them to finish. If necessary, ask short questions that require short answers, a nod, or shake of the head. Never pretend to understand if you're having difficulty doing so. Instead repeat what you've understood and allow the person to respond.
8. Place yourself at eye level when speaking with someone in a wheelchair or on crutches.
9. Tap a hearing impaired person on the shoulder or wave your hand to get his or her attention. Look directly at the person and speak clearly, slowly, and expressively to establish if the person can read your lips. If so, try to face the light source and keep hands, cigarettes, and food away from your mouth when speaking.
10. Relax. Don't be embarrassed if you happen to use common expressions such as "See you later," or "Did you hear about this?" that seem to relate to a person's disability.

BUILDING
Communication Skills

HOW DO YOU CONFRONT INTERCULTURAL DIFFICULTIES?

How might you deal with each of the following obstacles to intercultural understanding and communication? If you have the opportunity, share responses with others. You'll gain a wealth of practical insights.

1. Your friend makes fun of Radha, who comes to class in her native African dress. You feel you want to object to this.
2. Craig and Louise are an interracial couple. Craig's family treats him fairly but virtually ignores Louise. They never invite Craig and Louise as a couple to dinner or to partake in any of the family affairs. The couple decides that they should confront Craig's family.
3. Malcolm is a close friend and is really an open-minded person. But, he has the habit of referring to members of other racial and ethnic groups with the most derogatory language. You decide to tell him that you object to this way of talking.
4. Tom, a good friend of yours, wants to ask Pat out for a date. Both you and Tom know that Pat is a lesbian and will refuse the date, and yet Tom says he's going to have some fun and ask her anyway—just to give her a hard time. You think this is wrong and want to tell Tom you think so.
5. Your parents persist in holding stereotypes about other religious, racial, and ethnic groups. These stereotypes come up in all sorts of conversations. You're really embarrassed by these attitudes and feel you must tell your parents how incorrect you think these stereotypes are.
6. Lenny, a colleague at work, recently underwent a religious conversion. He now persists in trying to get everyone else—yourself included—to undergo this same religious conversion. Every day he tells you why you should convert, gives you literature to read, and otherwise persists in trying to convert you. You decide to tell him that you find this behavior offensive.

Avoid Evaluating Differences Negatively

Be careful not to evaluate negatively the cultural differences you perceive. Be careful that you don't fall into the trap of ethnocentric thinking, evaluating your culture positively and other cultures negatively. For example, many Americans of Northern European descent evaluate negatively the tendency of many Hispanics and Southern Europeans to use the street for a gathering place, for playing Dominos, and for just sitting on a cool evening. Whether you like or dislike using the street in this way, recognize that neither attitude is logically correct or incorrect. This street behavior is simply adequate or inadequate for *members of the culture.*

Remember that you learned your behaviors from your culture. The behaviors are not natural or innate. Therefore, try viewing these variations nonevaluatively. See them as different but equal.

Recognize the Normalcy of Culture Shock

Culture shock refers to the psychological reaction you experience at being in a culture very different from your own (Furnham & Bochner 1986). Culture shock is normal; most people experience it when entering a new and different culture. Nevertheless, it can be unpleasant and frustrating and can sometimes lead to a permanently negative attitude toward this new culture. Understanding the normalcy of culture shock will help lessen any potential negative implications.

Part of culture shock results from your feelings of alienation, conspicuousness, and difference from everyone else. When you lack knowledge of the rules and customs of the new society, you can't communicate effectively. You're apt to blunder frequently and seriously. The person experiencing culture shock may not know some very basic things:

- how to ask someone for a favor or pay someone a compliment
- how to extend or accept an invitation for dinner
- how early or how late to arrive for an appointment or how long to stay
- how to distinguish seriousness from playfulness and politeness from indifference
- how to dress for an informal, formal, or business function
- how to order a meal in a restaurant or how to summon a server

Anthropologist Kalervo Oberg (1960), who first used the term *culture shock*, notes that it occurs in stages. These stages are useful for examining many encounters with the new and the different. Going away to college, getting married, or joining the military, for example, can all result in culture shock.

At the first stage, the **honeymoon**, there's fascination, even enchantment, with the new culture and its people. You finally have your own apartment. You're your own boss. Finally, on your own! When in groups of people who are culturally different, this stage is characterized by cordiality and friendship among these early and superficial relationships. Many tourists remain at this stage because their stay in foreign countries is so brief.

At stage two, the **crisis stage**, the differences between your own culture and the new one create problems. In the new apartment example, no longer do you find dinner ready for you unless you do it yourself. Your clothes are not washed or ironed unless you do them yourself. Feelings of frustration and inadequacy come to the fore. This is the stage at which you experience the actual shock of the new culture. In one study of foreign students coming from over 100 different countries and studying in 11 different countries, it was found that 25 percent of the students experienced depression (Klineberg & Hull 1979).

During the third period, the **recovery**, you gain the skills necessary to function effectively. You learn how to shop, cook, and plan a meal You find a local laundry and figure you'll learn how to iron later. You learn the language and ways of the new culture. Your feelings of inadequacy subside.

At the final stage, the **adjustment**, you adjust to and come to enjoy the new culture and the new experiences. You may still experience periodic difficulties and strains, but on the whole, the experience is pleasant. Actually, you're now a pretty decent cook. You're even coming to enjoy it. You're making a good salary, so why learn to iron?

Simply spending time in a foreign country is not sufficient for the development of positive attitudes; in fact, limited contact with nationals often leads to the development of negative attitudes. Rather, friendships with nationals is what is crucial for satisfaction with the new culture. Contacts only with other expatriates or sojourners is not sufficient (Torbiorn 1982).

People may also experience culture shock when they return to their original culture after living in a foreign culture, a kind of reverse culture shock (Jandt 1999). Consider, for example, the Peace Corps volunteers who work in a rural and economically deprived area. Upon returning to Las Vegas or Beverly Hills they too may experience culture shock. Sailors who served long periods aboard ship and then return to an isolated farming community might also experience culture shock. In these cases, however, the recovery period is shorter and the sense of inadequacy and frustration is less.

SUMMARY

In this unit we introduced the study of culture and its relationship to communication and considered how cultures differ and some of the theories developed to explain how culture and communication impact on one another. In addition, we introduced the study of intercultural communication and its nature and principles.

1. Culture refers to the relatively specialized lifestyle of a group of people, consisting of their values, beliefs, artifacts, ways of behaving and ways of communicating, that is passed on from one generation to the next through communication rather than through genes.

2. Enculturation refers to the process by which culture is transmitted from one generation to the next.

3. Acculturation refers to the processes by which one culture is modified through contact with or exposure to another culture.

4. Cultures differ in terms of individualistic or collectivist orientations, high-context (where the information is

largely in the context or in the person's nonverbals) and low-context (where most of the information is explicitly stated in the message), and in terms of high and low power distance (the degree to which power is concentrated in few or in many of its members).

5. Some theoretical approaches to intercultural communication include (1) language relativity (language helps to structure what you see and how you see it but does not impose any serious barriers to meaningful communication); (2) uncertainty reduction theory (the greater the intercultural differences, the greater the uncertainty and ambiguity, and the greater the communication difficulty); (3) maximizing outcomes (intercultural communication will be guided by the goal of maximizing the outcomes of such interactions, and it often requires

more effort and more time to achieve the desired outcomes); and (4) culture shock (a psychological reaction to being placed in a culture different from one's own, accompanied by a feeling of alienation and conspicuousness over being different).

6. Intercultural communication refers to communication among people who have different cultural beliefs, values, or ways of behaving.

7. Among the principles for more effective intercultural communication are: prepare yourself, recognize and face fears, recognize differences between yourself and the culturally different, recognize differences among the culturally different (avoiding stereotyping), recognize differences in meaning in verbal and nonverbal messages, and follow cultural rules and customs.

KEY TERMS

culture (p. 90)

enculturation (p. 90)

acculturation (p. 90)

collectivist and individualist cultures (p. 92)

high-context culture (p. 93)

low- context culture (p. 94)

high and low power distance cultures (p. 95)

masculine culture (p. 96)

feminine culture (p. 97)

ethnocentrism (p. 98)

culture shock (p. 103)

 ## THINKING CRITICALLY ABOUT
Culture and Communication

1. Social Darwinism or cultural evolution holds that much as the human species evolved from lower life forms to homo sapiens, cultures also evolve. Consequently, some cultures may be considered advanced and others primitive. Most contemporary scholars reject this view because the judgments that distinguish one culture from another have no basis in science and are instead based on individual values and preferences as to what constitutes "civilized" and what constitutes "primitive." Cultural relativism, on the other hand, holds that all cultures are different but that no culture is either superior or inferior to any other (Berry, Poortinga, Segall, & Dasen 1992). Today, this view is generally accepted and guides the infusion of cultural materials into contemporary textbooks on all academic levels. What do you think of these positions?

2. Consider how cultural differences underlie some of the most hotly debated topics in the news today. The following, for example, is a brief list of some of these topics, here identified with specific questions. How would you answer these? How do your cultural attitudes, beliefs, and values influence your responses?

   • Should Christian Science parents be prosecuted for preventing their children from receiving life-saving treat-

   ment such as blood transfusions? Some states, such as Connecticut and Arizona grant Christian Scientists special rights in this regard. Should this special treatment be adopted by all states? Should it be eliminated?

   • Should cock fighting be permitted or declared illegal in all states as "cruelty to animals"? (Some Latin Americans have argued that this is a part of their culture and should be permitted even though it's illegal in most of the United States. In five states and Puerto Rico, cock fighting is legal.)

   • Should same sex marriages be legalized? Test cases of same sex marriage and the Defense of Marriage Act (designed to prohibit such unions) are regularly in the news.

   • Should safe sex practices be taught in the schools? (Recall that President Clinton fired Joslyn Elders from her position as United States Surgeon General for suggesting that masturbation be discussed in the schools.)

   • Should those who commit hate or bias crimes be given harsher sentences?

   • Should doctor-assisted suicides be legalized?

   • Should the race of the child and that of the adopting parents be a relevant issue in adoption decisions?

3. Recently, the U.S. Department of Education issued guidelines (recommendations that are not legally binding on school boards) covering the types of religious communications and activities public schools may permit (*New York Times*, August 26, 1995, Section A, pp. 1, 8). Among the permitted activities are: student prayer, student-initiated discussions of religion, saying grace, proselytizing that would not be considered harassment, and the wearing of religious symbols and clothing. Among the forbidden activities are: prayer endorsed by teachers or administrators, invitations to prayer that could constitute harassment, teaching of a particular religion (rather than about religion), encouraging (officially or through teaching) either religious or antireligious activity, and denying school facilities to religious groups if these same facilities are provided to nonreligious groups. What do you think of these guidelines? If you were a member of a local school board, would you vote to adopt or reject these guidelines? How do your cultural beliefs influence your view of these guidelines?

4. In this age of multiculturalism, how do you feel about Article II, Section 1, of the United States Constitution? The relevant section reads: "No person except a natural born citizen, or a citizen of the United States, at the time of the adoption of this Constitution, shall be eligible to the office of President"?

5. Recently, the Emma Lazarus poem on the Statue of Liberty was changed. The words "the wretched refuse of your teeming shore" were deleted and the poem now reads:

> Give me your tired, your poor,
> Your huddled masses yearning to breathe free, ...

> Send these, the homeless, tempest-tost to me
> I lift my lamp besides the golden door.

Harvard zoologist Stephen Jay Gould, commenting on this change, notes that with the words omitted, the poem no longer has balance or rhyme and, more important, no longer represents what Lazarus wrote (Gould 1995). "The language police triumph," notes Gould, "and integrity bleeds." On the other hand, it can be argued that calling immigrants "wretched refuse" is insulting and degrading and that if Lazarus were writing today, she would not have used that phrase. How do you feel about this? Would you have supported the deletion of this line?

6. How would you go about finding answers to such questions as these?
   - Are relationships between persons of similar individual-collective orientations more or less likely to experience conflicts?
   - Are people living in high and low power distance cultures different in terms of their perceived level of happiness?
   - Do men and women differ in their preference for explicit communications, despite their high- or low-context orientation?
   - Do men and women have different rules for politeness in, say, conversation? In business?
   - Do couples with similar ratings (on the cultural differences scale) stay together longer than couples with dissimilar ratings? Do couples with similar ratings have fewer and less severe conflicts than couples with dissimilar ratings?
   - Are persons with greater education more likely to enter relationships with dissimilar others than are those with lesser education?

UNIT 7

Verbal Messages

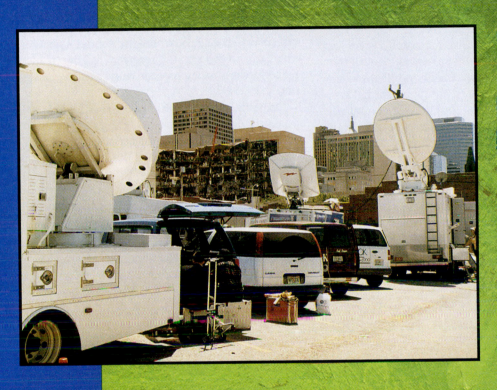

UNIT CONTENTS

The Nature of Language

Disconfirmation and Confirmation

Using Verbal Messages Effectively

UNIT GOALS

After completing this chapter, you should be able to

identify the characteristics of language and their implications for human communication

define *disconfirmation* and *confirmation* and explain the nature of sexist, heterosexist, and racist language as forms of disconfirmation

explain the suggestions for using verbal messages effectively

This unit looks at the nature of language and meaning, the ways in which language can be used to disconfirm or confirm another person, and ways to use verbal messages more effectively.

THE NATURE OF LANGUAGE AND MEANING

In communication you use two major signal systems—the verbal and the nonverbal. This unit focuses on the verbal system: language as a system for communicating meaning and, specifically, how it can be used effectively and how it creates problems when it isn't. The next unit focuses on the nonverbal system. In actual practice, of course, you communicate—in both sending and receiving—with both systems simultaneously.

Language Meanings Are in People

If you wanted to know the definition of the word "love," you'd probably turn to a dictionary. There you'd find, according to Webster's: "the attraction, desire, or affection felt for a person who arouses delight or admiration or elicits tenderness, sympathetic interest, or benevolence." This is the **denotative** meaning.

But where would you turn if you wanted to know what Pedro means when he says "I'm in love?" Of course, you'd turn to Pedro to discover his meaning. It's in this sense that meanings are not in words but in people. This is what is meant by the **connotative** meaning. Consequently, to uncover meaning, you need to look into people and not merely into words.

Also recognize that as you change, you also change the meanings you created out of past messages. Thus, although the message sent may not have changed, the meanings you created from it yesterday and the meanings you create today may be quite different. Yesterday, when a special someone said, "I love you," you created certain meanings. But today, when you learn that the same "I love you" was said to three other people or when you fall in love with someone else, you drastically change the meanings you perceive from those three words.

This principle is especially important in intercultural communication. Consider, for example, the differences in meaning for such words as *woman* to an American and an Iranian, *religion* to a born-again Christian and an atheist, and *lunch* to homeless parents of small children and Wall Street executives. What communication principles might help you more effectively communicate your meaning in these situations?

The Case of Bypassing

A failure to recognize this important principle is at the heart of a common pattern of miscommunication called bypassing. **Bypassing** is a pattern of misevaluation in which people fail to communicate their intended meanings. It's "the miscommunication pattern which occurs when the sender (speaker, writer, and so on) and the receiver (listener, reader, and so forth) miss each other with their meanings" (Haney 1973).

Bypassing can take one of two forms. One type of bypassing occurs when two people use different words but give them the same meaning; on the surface there's disagreement but at the level of meaning there's agreement. That is, two people agree but assume, because they use different words (some of which may actually never be verbalized), that they disagree. Consider the following dialogue:

PAT: I want a permanent relationship. I'm not interested in one-night stands. [Meaning: I want to date you exclusively and I want you to date me exclusively].

CHRIS: I'm not ready for that. [Thinking and meaning: marriage]. Let's keep things the way they are. [Meaning: let's continue dating only each other.]

The second type is more common. This form of bypassing occurs when two people use the same words but give the words different meanings. On the surface it looks like the two people agree (simply because they're using the same words). But if you look more closely you see that the apparent agreement masks real disagreement. Consider this brief dialogue:

PAT: I don't really believe in religion. [Meaning: I don't really believe in God.]

CHRIS: Neither do I. [Meaning: I don't really believe in organized religions.]

Here Pat and Chris assume they agree, but actually they disagree. At some later date the implications of these differences may well become crucial.

Numerous other examples could be cited. Couples who say they're "in love" may mean very different things; one person may mean "a permanent and exclusive commitment" while the other may mean "a sexual involvement." "Come home early" may mean one thing to an anxious parent and quite another to a teenager.

The underlying assumption in bypassing is that words have intrinsic meanings. You incorrectly assume that when two people use the same word they mean the same thing, and when they use different words those words have different meanings. But words don't have meaning; meaning is in the people who use those words.

Meanings Depend on Context

Verbal and nonverbal communications exist in a context, and that context to a large extent determines the meaning of any verbal or nonverbal behavior. The same words or behaviors may have totally different meanings when they occur in different contexts. For example, the greeting, "How are you?" means "Hello" to someone you pass regularly on the street but means "Is your health improving?" when said to a friend in the hospital. A wink to an attractive person on a bus means something completely different from a wink that signifies a put-on or a lie.

Similarly, the meaning of a given signal depends on the other behavior it accompanies or is close to in time. Pounding a fist on the table during a speech in support of a politician means something quite different from that same gesture in response to news of a friend's death. Divorced from the context, it's impossible to tell what meaning was intended from just examining the signals. Of course, even if you know the context in detail, you still might not be able to decipher the meaning of the message.

Especially important is the cultural context, a context emphasized throughout this text. The cultural context will influence not only the meaning assigned to speech and gesture but whether your meaning is friendly, offensive, lacking in respect, condescending, sensitive, and so on.

Messages Are Governed by Rules

Both verbal and nonverbal messages are regulated by a system of rules or norms that state what is and what is not meaningful, appropriate, expected, and permissible in specific social situations. And of course these rules will vary greatly from one culture to another. Rules are cultural (and relative) institutions; they're not universal laws.

You learned the ways to communicate and the rules of meaningfulness and appropriateness from observing the behaviors of the adult community. For example, you learned how to express sympathy along with the rules that your culture has established for expressing it. You learned that touch is permissible under certain circumstances but not under others and you learned which types of touching are permissible and which are not. You learned that women may touch each other in public; for example, they may hold hands, walk arm in arm, engage in prolonged hugging, and even dance together. You also learned that men may not do this, at least not without inviting social criticism.

Another way of looking at the role of cultural rules in regulating verbal and nonverbal messages is to examine its maxims or general communication principles (Grice 1975). For example, in much of the United States you operate with the maxim of quality that holds that communication must be truthful; that is, you expect that what the other person says will be the truth. And you no doubt follow that maxim by telling the truth yourself. Similarly, you operate with the maxim of relevance, that is, what you talk about will be relevant to the conversation. Thus, if you're talking about A, B, and C, and someone brings up D, you would assume that there's a connection between A, B, and C on the one hand and D on the other. These maxims are integrated into just about every communication textbook written in the United States.

Another maxim that we operate with is that of politeness. The maxim of politeness is probably universal across all cultures (Brown & Levinson 1988). Cultures differ, however, in how they define politeness and in how important politeness is compared with, say, openness or honesty. Cultures also differ in the rules for expressing politeness or impoliteness and in the punishments for violating the accepted rules of politeness (Mao 1994; Strecker 1993). Asian cultures, especially Chinese and Japanese, are often singled out because they emphasize politeness more and mete out harsher social punishments for violations than would most people in the United States and Western Europe (Fraser 1990). When this maxim operates, it may actually violate other maxims. For example, the maxim of politeness may require that you not tell the truth, a situation that would violate the maxim of quality.

There are also large gender differences (and some similarities) in the expression of politeness (Holmes 1995). Generally, studies from a number of different cultures show that women use more polite forms than men (Brown 1980; Wetzel 1988; Holmes

1995). For example, in both informal conversation and conflict situations women tend to seek areas of agreement more than do men. Young girls are more apt to try to modify disagreements while young boys are more apt to express "bald disagreements" (Holmes 1995). There are also similarities. For example, men and women in both the United States and New Zealand seem to pay compliments in similar ways (Manes & Wolfson 1981; Holmes 1986, 1995).

Politeness on the Net. The Rules of Netiquette

Not surprisingly, politeness has its own rules in Internet culture. The rules of **netiquette** are the rules for communicating politely over the Internet. Much as the rules of etiquette provide guidance in communicating in social situations, the rules of netiquette provide guidance for communicating over the Net. These rules, as you'll see, are helpful for making Internet communication more pleasant and easier, achieving greater personal efficiency, and putting less strain on the system and on other users. Here are several guidelines suggested by computer researchers (Shea 1994; James & Weingarten 1995; Barron 1995, *Time* (special issue), Spring 1995).

- Read the FAQs. Before asking questions about the system, read the Frequently Asked Questions; your question has probably been asked before and you'll put less strain on the system.
- Don't shout. WRITING IN CAPS IS PERCEIVED AS SHOUTING. It's okay to use caps occasionally to achieve emphasis. If you wish to give emphasis, underline like _this_ or *like this*
- Lurk before speaking. Lurking is reading the posted notices and the conversations without contributing anything; in computer communication, lurking is good, not bad. Lurking will help you learn the rules of the particular group and will help you avoid saying things you'd like to take back.
- Don't contribute to traffic jams. Try connecting during off hours whenever possible. If you're unable to connect, try again later, but not immediately. That only puts added strain on the system and you're likely to be still unable to connect. In securing information, try local information sources before trying more distant sources; it requires fewer connections and less

time. And be economical in using files (for example, photographs) that may tie up lines for long periods of time.
- Be brief. Follow the maxim of quantity by communicating only the information that is needed; follow the maxim of manner by communicating clearly, briefly, and in an organized way.
- Treat newbies kindly; you were once one yourself.

Language is Both Denotative and Connotative

Denotation refers to the meaning you'd find in a dictionary; it's the meaning that members of the culture assign to a word. **Connotation** refers to the emotional meaning that specific speakers-listeners give to a word. Take as an example the word *death*. To a doctor this word might mean (or denote) the time when the heart stops. This is an objective description of a particular event. On the other hand, to the dead person's mother (upon being informed of her son's death), the word means (or connotes) much more. It recalls her son's youth, ambition, family, illness, and so on. To her it's a highly emotional, subjective, and personal word. These emotional, subjective, or personal reactions are the word's connotative meaning.

Semanticist S. I. Hayakawa (Hayakawa & Hayakawa 1990) coined the terms "snarl words" and "purr words" to further clarify the distinction between denotative and connotative meaning. Snarl words are highly negative ("She's an idiot." "He's a pig." "They're a bunch of losers."). Sexist, racist, and heterosexist language and hate speech provide lots of other examples. Purr words are highly positive ("She's a real sweetheart." "He's a dream." "They're the greatest."). Although they may sometimes seem to have denotative meaning and refer to the "real world," snarl and purr words are actually connotative in meaning. They don't describe people or events but, rather, they reveal the speaker's feelings about these people or events.

Language Varies in Directness

Indirect messages are those that communicate your meaning in a roundabout way. You don't really say what you mean, but you imply it. Indirect messages have both advantages and disadvantages.

One of the advantages of indirect messages is that they allow you to express a desire without insulting

BUILDING
Communication Skills

HOW DO YOU USE DIRECTNESS EFFECTIVELY?

Think about how you would respond to someone saying the following sentences.

1A. I'm so bored; I have nothing to do tonight.
2A. I'd like to go to the movies. Would you like to come?
1B. Do you feel like hamburgers tonight?

2B. I'd like hamburgers tonight. How about you?

The statements numbered 1 are relatively indirect; they're attempts to get the listener to say or do something without committing the speaker. The statements numbered 2 are more direct—they state more clearly the speaker's preferences and then ask the listeners if they agree. Can you identify three situations when indirect statements would be more appropriate? Three situations when direct statements would be more appropriate?

---

or offending anyone; they allow you to observe the rules of polite interaction. So instead of saying, "I'm bored with this group," you say, "It's getting late and I have to get up early tomorrow," or you look at your watch and pretend to be surprised by the time. In this way, you're stating a preference but are saying it indirectly so as to avoid offending someone. Sometimes indirect messages allow you to ask for compliments in a socially acceptable manner, such as saying, "I was thinking of getting a nose job." You hope to get the desired compliment: "A nose job? You? Your nose is perfect."

Indirect messages, however, can also create problems. For example, meanings that are expressed too indirectly may be misunderstood; the other person may simply not understand your deeper meaning. When this happens, you may come to resent the other person for not seeing beneath the surface and yourself for not being more up-front. Another disadvantage is that you may be seen as manipulative, that is, trying to get someone to do something without really saying it. For example, you might tell a friend, "I really could use a loan until payday but I really don't want to ask anyone."

The popular stereotype in much of the United States holds that women are indirect in making requests and in giving orders. (cf. Kramarae 1974a, b; 1977; 1981) This indirectness is thought to commu-

nicate their powerlessness and discomfort with their own authority. Men, the stereotype continues, are direct, sometimes to the point of being blunt or rude. This directness communicates power and comfort with one's own authority.

Deborah Tannen (1994) provides an interesting perspective on these stereotypes. Women are more indirect in giving orders and are more likely to say, for example, "It would be great if these letters could go out today" rather than "Have these letters out by three." But, Tannen (1994, p. 84) argues that "issuing orders indirectly can be the prerogative of those in power" and does in no way show powerlessness. Power, to Tannen, is the ability to chose your own style of communication.

Men, however, are also indirect but in different situations (Rundquist 1992). According to Tannen, men are more likely to use indirectness when they express weakness, reveal a problem, or admit an error. Men are more likely to speak indirectly in expressing emotions other than anger. Men are also more indirect when they refuse expressions of increased romantic intimacy. Men are thus indirect, the theory goes, when they're saying something that goes against the masculine stereotype.

Many Asian and Latin American cultures stress the values of indirectness largely because it enables a person to avoid appearing criticized or contradicted and thereby losing face. A somewhat different kind of indirectness is seen in the greater use of intermediaries to resolve conflict among the Chinese than among North Americans, for example (Ma 1992). In most of the United States, however, you're taught that directness is the preferred style. "Be up-front" and "tell it like it is" are commonly heard communication guidelines.

DISCONFIRMATION AND CONFIRMATION

Before reading about confirmation and disconfirmation, take the following self-test to examine your own behavior.

SELF-TEST

How Confirming Are You?

Instructions: In your typical communications, how likely are you to display the following behaviors? Use this scale in responding to each statement: 5 = always; 4 = often; 3 = sometimes; 2 = rarely; and 1 = never.

_____ 1. I acknowledge the presence of another person both verbally and nonverbally.

_____ 2. I acknowledge the contributions of the other person by, for example, supporting or taking issue with what the person says.

_____ 3. During the conversation, I make nonverbal contact by maintaining direct eye contact, touching, hugging, kissing, and otherwise demonstrating acknowledgment of the other person.

_____ 4. I communicate as both speaker and listener, with involvement, and with a concern and respect for the other person.

_____ 5. I signal my understanding of the other person both verbally and nonverbally.

Many people who communicate directly see those who communicate indirectly as being manipulative. According to Tannen (1994, p. 92), however, "'manipulative' is often just a way of blaming others for our discomfort with their styles." Do you agree with Tannen? Or, do you think that indirectness is very often intended to be manipulative?

_____ 6. I reflect back the other person's feelings as a way of showing that I understand these feelings.

_____ 7. I ask questions as appropriate concerning the other person's thoughts and feelings.

_____ 8. I respond to the other person's requests, by, for example, returning phone calls and answering letters within a reasonable time.

_____ 9. I encourage the other person to express his or her thoughts and feelings.

_____ 10. I respond directly and exclusively to what the other person says.

All 10 statements are phrased so that they express confirming behaviors. Therefore, high scores (say, above 35) reflect a strong tendency to engage in confirmation. Low scores (say, below 25) reflect a strong tendency to engage in disconfirmation. Don't assume, however, that all situations call for confirmation and that only insensitive people are disconfirming. You may wish to consider the situations in which disconfirmation would be—if not an effective response— at least a legitimate one. ✔

Disconfirmation is a communication pattern in which you ignore someone's presence as well as that person's communications. You say, in effect, that this person and what this person has to say are not worth serious attention or effort, that this person and this person's contributions are so unimportant or insignificant that there's no reason to concern ourselves with them.

Note that disconfirmation is not the same as *rejection*. In rejection you disagree with the person; you indicate your unwillingness to accept something the other person says or does. In disconfirming someone, however, you deny that person's significance; you claim that what this person says or does simply does not count.

Confirmation is the opposite communication pattern. In confirmation you not only acknowledge the presence of the other person, but you also indicate your acceptance of this person, of this person's definition of self, and of your relationship as defined or viewed by this other person.

A useful way to test your understanding of confirmation and disconfirmation is to consider how you'd talk to someone experiencing grief. Grief is something everyone experiences at some time. It

may be experienced because of illness or death, the loss of a highly valued relationship (for example, a romantic breakup), the loss of certain physical or mental abilities, or the loss of material possessions (your house burning down). Talking with the grief-stricken can be extremely difficult. Consider the following brief monologue, which admittedly exaggerates the wrong way to talk with the grief-stricken:

I just heard that Harry died—I mean—passed away. I'm so sorry. I know exactly how you feel. But, you know, it's for the best. I mean the man was suffering. I remember seeing him last month; he could hardly stand up, he was so weak. And he looked so sad. He must have been in constant pain. It's better this way. He's at peace. You'll get over it. You'll see. Time heals all wounds. It was the same way with me and you know how close we were. I mean we were devoted to each other. Everyone said we were the closest pair they ever saw. And I got over it. So, how about we'll go to dinner tonight? We'll talk about old times. Come on. Come on. Don't be a spoilsport. I really need to get out. I've been in the house all week. Come on, do it for me. After all, you have to forget; you have to get on with your own life. I won't take "no" for an answer. I'll pick you up at seven.

One useful way to talk with the grief-stricken is to confirm the person's feelings. "You must miss him a great deal" confirms the person's feelings, for example. Disconfirming expressions—"You can't cry now; you have to set an example"—are generally less helpful to the person experiencing grief.

Persons grieving often want permission to grieve and to express themselves. They want to know that it's okay with you if he or she grieves in the ways that feel most comfortable—for example, crying or talking about old times. This permission can be communicated in several ways. For example, you can say, quite directly, "just say what you feel." Or, you can use active listening responses (Unit 4) to encourage the other person to continue talking. Another way to communicate this permission is with nonverbal expressions of approval and attention to the grieving person's reactions. Although many people who experience grief welcome the opportunity to talk about it, not all do. Trying to force people to talk about experiences or feelings they may not be ready to share is generally as inappropriate as trying to get them to focus away from their grief.

Many people try to force the grief-stricken to focus on the bright side. Although well-intentioned, this assumes that the grief-stricken person is ready for this change in focus, which is usually not the case. Expressions such as "You're so lucky you still have some vision left" or "It was better this way; Pat was suffering so much" are often resented because of their obvious lack of empathy.

Empathizing with the grief-stricken person and communicating this empathic understanding is often helpful. Letting the grief-stricken person know that you can understand what he or she is going through, but without assuming that your feelings (however empathic) are the same in depth or in kind, is likely to be appreciated.

Part of the art of conversation generally, and especially talking with the grief-stricken, is to develop a sensitivity to leave-taking cues. Trying to force your presence on the grief-stricken or pressing the person to stay with you or a group of people is likely to be resented.

Although these suggestions are likely to be received positively by most people, they're not likely to be received positively in all situations or by all people. Fortunately, there's a useful way to find out, and that is simply to ask. An excellent example of this occurs in the television announcement in communicating with people with AIDS. It goes something like this: "I don't know what to say. But, I want you to know that I care and that I want to help and that I love you. I want you to tell me what I can do."

You can gain insight into a wide variety of offensive language practices by viewing them as types of disconfirmation, as language that alienates and separates. The three obvious practices are sexism, heterosexism, and racism.

Sexism

The National Council of Teachers of English (NCTE) has proposed guidelines for nonsexist (gender-free, gender-neutral, or sex-fair) language. These concern the use of generic "man," the use of generic "he" and "his," and sex-role stereotyping (Penfield, 1987).

Generic Man. The word *man* refers most clearly to an adult male. To use the term to refer to both men and women emphasizes maleness at the expense of femaleness. Similarly, the terms *mankind* or *the common man* or even *cavemen* imply a primary focus on adult males. Gender-neutral terms can easily be substituted. Instead of *mankind*, you can say *humanity*, *people,* or *human beings*. Instead of *the common man*, you can say *the average person* or *ordinary people*. Instead of *cavemen*, you can say *prehistoric people* or *cave dwellers*.

Similarly, terms such as *policeman* or *fireman*, and other terms that presume maleness as the norm and femaleness as a deviation from this norm, are clear and common examples of sexist language. Consider using nonsexist alternatives for these and similar terms; make these alternatives (for example, *police officer* and *firefighter*) a part of your active vocabulary. What alternatives can you offer for each of these words: man, countryman, manmade, manpower, repairman, doorman, fireman, stewardess, waitress, salesman, mailman, and actress?

Generic He and His. The use of the masculine pronoun to refer to any individual regardless of sex is certainly declining. But, it was only as far back as 1975 that all college textbooks, for example, used the masculine pronoun as generic. There seems to be no legitimate reason why the feminine pronoun could not alternate with the masculine pronoun in referring to hypothetical individuals, or why such terms as *he and she* or *her and him* could not be used instead of just *he* or *him*. Alternatively, you can restructure your sentences to eliminate any reference to gender. For example, the NCTE guidelines (Penfield, 1987) suggest that instead of saying, "The average student is worried about his grades," say, "The average student is worried about grades." Instead of saying, "Ask the student to hand in his work as soon as he is finished," say, "Ask students to hand in their work as soon as they're finished."

Sex-Role Stereotyping. The words you use often reflect a sex-role bias, the assumption that certain roles or professions belong to men and others belong to women. In eliminating sex-role stereotyping, avoid, for example, making the hypothetical elementary school teacher female and the college professor male. Avoid referring to doctors as male and nurses as female. Avoid noting the sex of a professional with terms such as "female doctor" or "male nurse." When you're referring to a specific doctor or nurse, the person's sex will become clear when you use the appropriate pronoun: "Dr. Smith wrote the prescription for her new patient" or "The nurse recorded the patient's temperature himself."

BUILDING
Communication Skills

HOW DO YOU CONFIRM, REJECT, AND DISCONFIRM?

To test your mastery of these concepts and the distinctions among them, classify the following responses as confirmation (C), rejection (R), or disconfirmation (D):

Enrique receives this semester's grades in the mail; they're a lot better than previous semesters' grades but are still not great. After opening the letter, Enrique says: "I really tried hard to get my grades up this semester." Enrique's parents respond:

_____ Going out every night hardly seems like trying very hard.

_____ What should we have for dinner?

_____ Keep up the good work.

_____ I can't believe you've really tried your best; how can anyone study with the stereo blasting in his ears?

_____ I'm sure you've tried real hard.

_____ That's great.

_____ What a rotten day I had at the office.

_____ I can remember when I was in school; got all B's without ever opening a book.

Try rewriting each of the sentences you labeled confirming into disconfirming responses, each of the sentences you labeled disconfirming into confirming responses, and each of the sentences you labeled rejecting into either confirming or disconfirming responses.

Heterosexism

A close relative of sexism is heterosexism. The term is a relatively new addition to the list of linguistic prejudices. As the term implies, heterosexism refers to language used to disparage gay men and lesbians. As with racist language, you see heterosexism in the derogatory terms used for lesbians and gay men as well as in more subtle forms of language usage. For example, when you qualify a profession—as in "gay athlete" or "lesbian doctor"—you're in effect stating that athletes and doctors are not normally gay or lesbian. Further, you're highlighting the affectional orientation of the athlete and the doctor in a context where it may have no relevance. This practice, of course, is the same as qualifying by race or gender.

Still another instance of heterosexism—and perhaps the most difficult to deal with—is the presumption of heterosexuality. Usually, people assume the person they're talking to or about is heterosexual. Usually, they're correct since the majority of the population is heterosexual. At the same time, however, note that it denies the lesbian and gay identity a certain legitimacy. The practice is very similar to the presumption of whiteness and maleness that we have made significant inroads in eliminating. Here are a few additional suggestions for avoiding heterosexist, or what some call "homophobic," language.

- Avoid "complimenting" gay men and lesbians because "they don't look it." To gay men and lesbians, it's not a compliment. Similarly, expressing disappointment that a person is gay—often thought to be a compliment when said in such comments as "What a waste!"—is not really a compliment.

- Avoid the assumption that every gay man or lesbian knows what every other gay man or lesbian is thinking. It's very similar to asking a Japanese why Sony is investing heavily in the United States or, as one comic put it, asking an African American "What do you think Jesse Jackson meant by that last speech?"

- Avoid denying individual differences. Saying things like *lesbians are so loyal* or *gay men are so open with their feelings*, which ignore the reality of wide differences within any group, are potentially insulting to all groups.
- Avoid overattribution, the tendency to attribute just about everything a person does, says, and believes to being gay or lesbian. This tendency helps to recall and perpetuate stereotypes (see Unit 3).
- Remember that relationship milestones are important to all people. Ignoring anniversaries or birthdays of, say, a relative's partner is resented by everyone.

Racism

According to Andrea Rich (1974), "any language that, through a conscious or unconscious attempt by the user, places a particular racial or ethnic group in an inferior position is racist." Racist language expresses racist attitudes. It also contributes to the development of racist attitudes in those who use or hear the language.

Racist terms are used by members of one culture to disparage members of other cultures—their customs or their accomplishments. Racist language emphasizes differences rather than similarities and separates rather than unites members of different cultures. Generally, racist language is used by the dominant group to establish and maintain power over other groups. The social consequences of racist language in terms of employment, education, housing opportunities, and general community acceptance are well known.

Many people feel that it's permissible for members of a culture to refer to themselves with racist terms. That is, Asians may use the negative terms referring to Asians, Italians may use the negative terms referring to Italians, and so on. This issue is seen clearly in rap music where performers use such racial terms (*New York Times*, January 24, 1993, Sec. 1, p. 31). The reasoning seems to be that groups should be able to laugh at themselves.

It's interesting to note that the terms denoting some of the major movements in art—for example, "impressionism" and "cubism"—were originally applied negatively. The terms were adopted by the artists themselves and eventually became positive. A parallel can be seen in the use of the word "queer" by some lesbian and gay organizations. Their purpose in using the term is to cause it to lose its negative connotation.

One possible problem, though, is that such terms may not lose their negative connotations and may simply reinforce the negative stereotypes that society has already assigned to certain groups. By using these terms, members may come to accept the labels with their negative connotations and thus contribute to their own stereotyping.

It has often been pointed out (Davis 1973; Bosmajian 1969) that there are aspects of language that may be inherently racist. For example, in one examination of English there were found 134 synonyms for *white*. Of these, 44 have positive connotations (for example, *clean*, *chaste*, and *unblemished*) and only 10 have negative connotations (for example, *whitewash* and *pale*). The remaining are relatively neutral. Of the 120 synonyms for *black*, 60 have unfavorable connotations (*unclean*, *foreboding*, and *deadly*) and none have positive connotations.

Racist, Sexist, and Heterosexist Listening

Just as racist, sexist, and heterosexist attitudes will influence your language, they also influence your listening. In this type of listening you only hear what the speaker is saying through your stereotypes. You assume that what the speaker is saying is unfairly influenced by the speaker's sex, race, or affectional orientation.

Sexist, racist, and heterosexist listening occur in a wide variety of situations. For example, when you dismiss a valid argument or accept an invalid argument, when you refuse to give someone a fair hearing, or when you give less credibility (or more credibility) to a speaker because the speaker is of a particular sex, race, or affectional orientation, you're practicing sexist, racist, or heterosexist listening. Put differently, sexist, racist, or heterosexist listening occurs when you listen differently to a person because of his or her sex, race, or affectional orientation when these characteristics are irrelevant to the communication.

But, there are many instances where these characteristics are relevant and pertinent to your evaluation of the message. For example, the sex of the speaker talking on pregnancy, fathering a child, birth control, or surrogate fatherhood is, most would agree, probably relevant to the message. And so in these examples, it would not be sexist to listen to the topic through the sex of the speaker. It is sexist listening to assume that only one sex has anything to say that's worth hearing or that what one sex says can be discounted without a fair hearing. The same is true when listening through a person's race or affectional orientation.

Do you find this position a reasonable one to take? If not, how would you define sexist, racist, and heterosexist listening? Do you find this a useful concept in understanding effective communication? Do you find these types of listening operating in your classes? In your family? In your community? If you wanted to reduce this type of listening, how would you do it?

Cultural Identifiers

Perhaps the best way to avoid sexism, heterosexism, and racism is to examine the preferred cultural identifiers to use (and not to use) in talking about members of different cultures. As always, when in doubt, find out. The preferences and many of the specific examples identified here are drawn largely from the findings of the Task Force on Bias-Free Language of the Association of American University Presses (Schwartz 1995). Do realize that not everyone would agree with these recommendations; they're presented here—in the words of the Task Force—"to encourage sensitivity to usages that may be imprecise, misleading, and needlessly offensive" (Schwartz 1995, p. ix).

Generally: The term *girl* should only be used to refer to very young females and is equivalent to *boy*. Neither term should be used for people older than, say, 13 or 14. *Girl* is never used to refer to a grown woman, nor is *boy* used to refer to persons in blue-collar positions, as they once were. *Lady* is negatively evaluated by many because it connotes the stereotype of the prim and proper woman. *Woman* or *young woman* is preferred. *Older person* is preferred to *elder, elderly, senior,* or *senior citizen* (which technically refers to someone older than 65).

Generally: *Gay* is the preferred term to refer to a man who has an affectional preference for men and *lesbian* is the preferred term for a woman who has an affectional preference for women. (*Lesbian* means "homosexual woman," so the phrase *lesbian woman* is redundant.) This preference for the term *lesbian* is

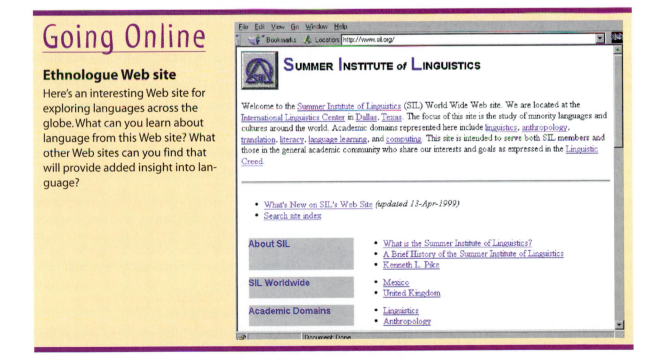

Going Online

Ethnologue Web site

Here's an interesting Web site for exploring languages across the globe. What can you learn about language from this Web site? What other Web sites can you find that will provide added insight into language?

File Edit View Go Window Help

Bookmarks Location: http://www.sil.org/

SUMMER INSTITUTE of LINGUISTICS

Welcome to the Summer Institute of Linguistics (SIL) World Wide Web site. We are located at the International Linguistics Center in Dallas, Texas. The focus of this site is the study of minority languages and cultures around the world. Academic domains represented here include linguistics, anthropology, translation, literacy, language learning, and computing. This site is intended to serve both SIL members and those in the general academic community who share our interests and goals as expressed in the Linguistic Creed.

- What's New on SIL's Web Site *(updated 13-Apr-1999)*
- Search site index

About SIL	• What is the Summer Institute of Linguistics?
	• A Brief History of the Summer Institute of Linguistics
	• Kenneth L. Pike
SIL Worldwide	• Mexico
	• United Kingdom
Academic Domains	• Linguistics
	• Anthropology

Document: Done

not universal among homosexual women; in one survey, for example, 58 percent preferred *lesbian*; 34 percent preferred *gay* (Lever 1995). *Homosexual* refers to both gay men and lesbians, but more often to a sexual orientation to members of one's own sex. *Gay* and *lesbian* refer to a lifestyle and not just to sexual orientation. *Gay* as a noun, although widely used, may prove offensive in some contexts, for example, "We have two gays on the team." Although used within the gay community in an effort to remove the negative stigma through frequent usage, the term *queer*—as in "queer power"—is often resented when used by outsiders. Because most scientific thinking holds that one's sexuality is genetically determined rather than being a matter of choice, the term *sexual orientation* rather than *sexual preference* or *sexual status* (which is also vague) is preferred.

Generally: Most African Americans prefer *African American* to *black* (Hecht, Ribeau, & Collier 1993) though *black* is often used with *white* and is used in a variety of other contexts (for example, Department of Black and Puerto Rican Studies, the *Journal of Black History,* and Black History Month). The American Psychological Association recommends that both terms be capitalized but the *Chicago Manual of Style* (the manual used by most newspapers and publishing houses) recommends using lowercase. The terms *negro* and *colored,* although used in the names of some organizations (for example, the United Negro College Fund and the National Association for the Advancement of Colored People) are not used outside of these contexts. *White* is generally used to refer to those whose roots are in European cultures and usually does not include Hispanics. Analogous to *African American* is the phrase *European American.* Few *European Americans,* however, would want to be called that; most would prefer their national origins emphasized, for example, *German American* or *Greek American.* This preference may well change as Europe moves into a more cohesive and united entity. *People of color*—a more literary sounding term appropriate perhaps to public speaking but sounding awkward in most conversations—is preferred to *nonwhite,* which implies that whiteness is the norm and nonwhiteness is a deviation from that norm. The same is true of the term *non-Christian.*

Generally: *Hispanic* is used to refer to anyone who identifies himself or herself as belonging to a Span-

ish-speaking culture. *Latina* (female) and *Latino* (male) refer to those whose roots are in one of the Latin American countries, for example, Dominican Republic, Nicaragua, or Guatemala. *Hispanic American* refers to those U.S. residents whose ancestry is a Spanish culture and includes Mexican, Caribbean, and Central and South Americans. In emphasizing a Spanish heritage, the term is really inadequate in referring to those large numbers in the Caribbean and in South America whose origins are French or Portuguese. *Chicana* (female) and *Chicano* (male) refer to those with roots in Mexico, though they often connote a nationalist attitude (Jandt 1995) and are considered offensive by many Mexican Americans. *Mexican American* is preferred.

Inuk (plural, *Inuit*) was officially adopted at the Inuit Circumpolar Conference to refer to the group of indigenous people of Alaska, Northern Canada, Greenland, and Eastern Siberia. This term is preferred to *Eskimo* (a term the U.S. Census Bureau uses), which was applied to the indigenous peoples of Alaska by Europeans and derives from a term that means "raw meat eaters" (Maggio 1997).

Indian refers only to someone from India and is incorrectly used when applied to members of other Asian countries or to the indigenous peoples of North America. *American Indian* or *Native American* are preferred, even though many Native Americans refer to themselves as *Indians* and *Indian people.* The term *native American* (with a lowercase *n*) is most often used to refer to persons born in the United States. Although the term technically could refer to anyone born in North or South America, people outside the United States generally prefer more specific designations such as *Argentinean, Cuban,* or *Canadian.* The term *native* means an indigenous inhabitant; it's not used to mean "someone having a less developed culture."

Muslim is the preferred form (rather than the older *Moslem*) to refer to a person who adheres to the religious teachings of Islam. *Quran* (rather than *Koran*) is the preferred term for the scriptures of Islam. The terms *Mohammedan* or *Mohammedanism* are not considered appropriate since they imply worship of Muhammad, the prophet, "considered by Muslims to be a blasphemy against the absolute oneness of God" (Maggio 1997, p. 277).

Although there's no universal agreement, generally *Jewish people* is preferred to *Jews*; and *Jewess* (a

Jewish female) is considered derogatory. *Jew* should only be used as a noun and is never correctly used as a verb or an adjective (Maggio 1997).

When history was being written from a European perspective, it was taken as the focal point and the rest of the world was defined in terms of its location relative to Europe. Thus, Asia became the east or the orient, and Asians became *Orientals*—a term that is today considered inappropriate or "Eurocentric." Thus, people from Asia are *Asians*, just as people from Africa are *Africans* and people from Europe are *Europeans*.

USING VERBAL MESSAGES EFFECTIVELY

A chief concern in using verbal messages is to recognize what critical thinking theorists call "conceptual distortions," that is, mental mistakes, misinterpretations, or reasoning fallacies. Avoiding these distortions and substituting a more critical, more realistic analysis is probably the best way to improve your own use of verbal messages (DeVito 1974).

Language Symbolizes Reality (Partially)

Language symbolizes reality; it's not the reality itself. Of course, this is obvious. But consider: Have you ever reacted to the way something was labeled or described rather than to the actual item? Have you ever bought something because of its name rather than because of the actual object? If so, you were probably responding as if language was the reality, a distortion called intensional orientation.

Intensional Orientation
Intensional orientation (the s in *intensional* is intentional) refers to the tendency to view people, objects, and events in the way they're talked about—the way they're labeled. For example, if Sally is labeled "uninteresting," you would, responding intensionally, evaluate her as uninteresting even before listening to what she had to say. You'd see Sally through a filter imposed by the label "uninteresting." **Extensional orientation**, on the other hand, is the tendency to look first at the actual people, objects, and events and only afterwards at their labels. In this case, it would mean looking at Sally without any

preconceived labels, guided by what she says and does, not by the words used to label her.

To avoid intensional orientation, extensionalize. Labels should never be given greater attention than the actual thing. Give your main attention to the people, things, and events in the world as you see them and not as they're presented in words. For example, when you meet Jack and Jill, observe and interact with them. Then form your impressions. Don't respond to them as "greedy, money-grubbing landlords" because Harry labeled them this way. Don't respond to George as "lazy" just because Elaine told you he was.

Allness
A related distortion is to forget that language only symbolizes a portion of reality, never the whole. When you assume that you can know all or say all about anything you're into a pattern of behavior called **allness**. In reality, you can never see all of anything. You can never experience anything fully. You see a part, then conclude what the whole is like. You have to draw conclusions on the basis of insufficient evidence (you always have insufficient evidence). A useful device to help combat the tendency to think that all can or has been said about anything is to end mentally each statement with "etc."—a reminder that there's more to learn, more to know, and more to say and that every statement is inevitably incomplete. Some people overuse the "etc." They use it not as a mental reminder, but as a substitute for being specific. This obviously is to be avoided and merely adds to the conversational confusion.

To avoid allness, recognize that language symbolizes only a part of reality, never the whole. Whatever someone says—regardless of what it is or how extensive it is—represents only part of the story.

Language Expresses Both Facts and Inferences

Language enables you to form statements of both facts and inferences without making any linguistic distinction between the two. Similarly, when you speak or listen to such statements you often don't make a clear distinction between statements of facts and statements of inference. Yet, there are great differences between the two. Barriers to clear thinking can be created when inferences are treated as facts, a tendency called **fact-inference confusion.**

MEDIA WATCH

HUMAN COMMUNICATION IN CYBERSPACE

To paraphrase a popular advertising slogan, we have all come a long way. From the Summerians' writing system developed around 3500 B.C., to Johannes Gutenberg's invention of the printing press in Germany in 1440, to Alexander Graham Bell's invention of the telephone in the United States in 1846, to the birth of personal computers in the early 1970s, to the Internet in the 1980s and now involving millions of users, the process of sending a message has certainly changed (Dworetsky 1994). And yet, much has remained the same.

Electronic communication—no matter how sophisticated—is still very similar to ordinary face-to-face interactions. For example, electronic communication allows for the same types of communication as does face-to-face interaction, whether interpersonal, small group, or public speaking. Whether you're using the Internet made available by your college or one of the commercially available services such as Compuserve, America OnLine, and Prodigy, for example, you can encode your thoughts through your keyboard and send them via modem in much the same way that you encode your thoughts into words and send these through the air.

E-mail is a good example of interpersonal communication, as is traditional letter writing. Similarly, private chat rooms are available on electronic bulletin boards where you and another party can exchange messages without anyone else participating or even seeing your messages. People engage in written conversation online for all the purposes already noted for communication generally: to discover, to relate, to influence, to play, and to help.

As in face-to-face communication, you can also expand your two-person group to a small group. The number of people you can have in a public chat room will vary somewhat but perhaps a limit of 40 or so participants seems common right now. On any system, there may be hundreds of chat rooms that you may join, just as there are hundreds of groups that you can join on campus, in your community, and so on. And, of course, you can always open your own chat room and invite those who are interested in, say, old movies, carpentry, new software, or communication to join your group.

The public speaking equivalent in cyberspace is the open forum, where you can post a message for anyone to read and then you can read their reactions to your message and so on. Bulletin boards are subject specific and you would obviously post your message on the appropriate bulletin board. If it were about politics then you would post it on a political discussion board; if it were about gardening, then you would post it on a gardening board, and so on.

When you communicate with someone face-to-face, you generally know a great deal about each other—your names, sex, approximate age, general appearance, height, weight, race, and perhaps other things as well. When you communicate electronically, however, this information is only revealed if and when you want to. If you wish, you can remain totally anonymous. Your "handle" or code name is all you need and others will simply know you by this name and no other. Should you wish to reveal who you are—your real name, sex, age, race, religion, occupation, or any other information, you can certainly do so.

(continued on next page)

Notice, for example, that you can say, "She's wearing a blue jacket," as well as "He's harboring an illogical hatred." Although the sentences have similar structures, they're different. You can observe the jacket and the blue color, but how do you observe "illogical hatred"? Obviously, this is not a descriptive but an inferential statement. It's one you make on the basis not only of what you observe, but on

Media Watch *(continued)*

Like all forms of communication, electronic communication has its own cultural norms—it's own system of rules stating what is and what is not appropriate. These rules of "netiquette" include, for example:

- Before you ask a question consult the FAQs (frequently asked questions) so that you don't clog up the system with questions that have already been asked and answered.
- Generally, avoid *flaming* or participating in *flame wars*—personal attacks on other users; it results in too many messages that most people don't want to read and that use up the systems resources.

- Don't reveal the real names of participants who may wish to be known only by their handles.

Electronic communication will obviously increase tremendously in the coming years. How will electronic communication figure into your professional life? Will you be using electronic communication for social purposes, for example, to meet and eventually date someone you get to know online? How are you preparing for this greater role that electronic communication will play in your life?

The next Media Watch appears on page 139.

---

what you infer. For a statement to be considered factual, it must be made by the observer after observation and must be limited to what is observed (Weinberg 1958).

There's nothing wrong with making inferential statements. You must make them to talk about much that is meaningful to you. The problem arises when you act as if those inferential statements are factual. You may test your ability to distinguish facts from inferences by taking the accompanying fact-inference self-test (based on the tests constructed in Haney 1973).

SELF-TEST

Can You Distinguish Facts from Inferences?

Carefully read the following report and the observations based on it. Indicate whether you think the observations are true, false, or doubtful on the basis of the information presented in the report. Write T if the observation is definitely true, F if the observation is definitely false, and ? if the observation may be either true or false. Judge each observation in order. Don't reread the observations after you've indicated your judgment, and don't change any of your answers.

A well-liked college teacher had just completed making up the final examinations and had turned off the lights in the office. Just then a tall, broad figure with dark glasses appeared and demanded the examination. The professor opened the drawer. Everything in the drawer was picked up and the individual ran down the corridor. The dean was notified immediately.

_____ 1. The thief was tall, broad, and wore dark glasses.

_____ 2. The professor turned off the lights.

_____ 3. A tall figure demanded the examination.

_____ 4. The examination was picked up by someone.

_____ 5. The examination was picked up by the professor.

_____ 6. A tall, broad figure appeared after the professor turned off the lights in the office

_____ 7. The man who opened the drawer was the professor.

_____ 8. The professor ran down the corridor.

_____ 9. The drawer was never actually opened.

_____ 10. Three persons are referred to in this report.

After you answer all 10 questions, form small groups of five or six and discuss the answers. Look at each statement from each member's point of view. For each statement, ask yourself "How can you be absolutely certain that the statement is true or false?" You should find that only one statement can be clearly identified as True and only one as False; eight should be marked "?"

UNDERSTANDING
Theory and Research

CAN YOU TALK WITHOUT THE VERB "TO BE"?

The theory of E′ argues that if you wrote and spoke without the verb *to be* (*E-prime*, or *E′*, is simply normal English without the verb *to be*), you'd describe events more accurately (Bourland, 1965–1966; Wilson 1989; Klein 1992). For example, when you say, "Johnny is a failure," the verb "to be" implies that "failure" is *in* Johnny rather than in your observation or evaluation of Johnny. The verb "to be" also implies a fair degree of permanence; the implication is that because failure is in Johnny, it will always be there; Johnny will always be a failure. A more accurate and descriptive statement might be "Johnny failed his last two math exams."

Consider this theory as applied to your thinking about yourself. When you say, for example, "I'm not good at mathematics" or "I'm unpopular" or "I'm lazy," you imply that these qualities are *in* you. But these are simply evaluations that may be incorrect or, if at least partly accurate, may change (Joyner 1993). How would you rewrite the following sentences without using the verb "to be" (*is, are, am, was,* etc)? In what ways are the rewritten versions different from the original versions? How do the rewritten statements differ from those presented here?

1. I'm a poor student.
2. They're inconsiderate.
3. Is this valuable?
4. This Web site is meaningless.
5. Was the movie any good?
6. This class is great.

To avoid fact-inference confusion, label inferential statements as tentative. Inferential statements should leave open the possibility of alternatives. If, for example, you treat the statement "Our biology teacher was fired for poor teaching" as factual, you eliminate any alternatives. But, if you preface your statement with, say, "Pat told me . . ." or "I'm wondering if . . ." the inferential nature of your statement will be clear. Be especially sensitive to this distinction when you're listening. Most talk is inferential. Beware of the speaker who presents everything as fact. Analyze the messages more closely and you'll uncover a world of inferences.

Language Is Relatively Static

Language changes only very slowly, especially when compared to the rapid change in people and things. **Static evaluation** is the tendency to retain evaluations without change while the reality to which they refer is changing. Often a verbal statement you make about an event or person remains static

("That's the way he is; he's always been that way"), while the event or person may have changed enormously. Alfred Korzybski (1933) used an interesting illustration. In a tank there are a large fish and many small fish, the natural food for the large fish. Given freedom in the tank, the large fish will eat the small fish. If you partition the tank, separating the large fish from the small fish by a clear piece of glass, the large fish will continue to attempt to eat the small fish but will fail, knocking instead into the glass partition.

Eventually, the large fish will "learn" the futility of attempting to eat the small fish. If you now remove the partition, the small fish will swim all around the big fish, but the big fish will not eat them. In fact, the large fish will die of starvation while its natural food swims all around. The large fish has learned a pattern of behavior, and even though the actual territory has changed, the map remains static.

The "date" is a device that helps to keep language (and thinking) up-to-date and helps guard against static evaluation. The procedure is simple: date your statements and especially your evaluations. Remember that Pat Smith$_{1984}$ is not Pat Smith $_{2000}$; academic abilities $_{1992}$ are not academic abilities $_{2000}$. T. S. Eliot, in *The Cocktail Party*, said, "What we know of other people is only our memory of the moments during which we knew them. And they have changed since then . . . at every meeting we are meeting a stranger." In listening, look carefully at messages that claim that what was true still is. It may or may not be. Look for change.

Language Can Obscure Distinctions

Language can obscure distinctions among people or events that are covered by the same label but are really quite different (indiscrimination) and make it easy to focus on extremes rather than on the vast middle ground between opposites (polarization).

Indiscrimination

Indiscrimination refers to the failure to distinguish between similar but different people, objects, or events. It occurs when you focus on classes of people and fail to see that each person is unique and needs to be looked at individually. Everything is unique. Everything is unlike everything else.

Our language, however, provides you with common nouns, such as teacher, student, friend, enemy, war, politician, and liberal. These lead you to focus on similarities—to group together all teachers, all students, and all politicians. At the same time, the terms divert attention away from the uniqueness of each person, each object, and each event.

This misevaluation is at the heart of stereotyping on the basis of nationality, race, religion, sex, and affectional orientation. A stereotype, you'll remember from Unit 3, is a fixed mental picture of a group that is applied to each individual in the group without regard to his or her unique qualities. Whether the stereotypes are positive or negative, they create the same problem. They provide you with shortcuts that are often inappropriate.

A useful antidote to indiscrimination (and stereotyping) is the index. This mental subscript identifies each individual as an individual even though both may be covered by the same label. Thus, politician$_1$ is not politician$_2$, teacher$_1$ is not teacher$_2$. The

BUILDING
Communication Skills

HOW DO YOU TALK ABOUT THE MIDDLE?

Think about your own tendency to polarize. Try filling in the word that would logically go where the question mark appears, a word that is the opposite of the term on the left.

hot _____?
high _____?
good _____?
popular _____?
sad _____?

Filling in these opposites was probably easy for you. Also, the words you supplied were probably short. Further, if a number of people supplied opposites, you would find a high degree of agreement among them.

Now try to fill in the middle positions with words meaning, for example, "midway between hot and cold," "midway between high and low." You probably had greater difficulty here. And you probably took more time to think of these middle terms. You also probably used multiword phrases. Further, you would probably find less agreement among different people completing this same task. Although most things and people fall in between these extremes, the common tendency is to concentrate on the extremes and ignore the middle. What implications can you draw about polarization from this brief experience?

index helps you to discriminate among without discriminating against. Although the label ("politician," for example) covers all politicians, the index makes sure that each is thought about as an individual.

Polarization

Another way in which language can obscure differences is in its preponderance of extreme terms and its relative lack of middle terms, a system that often leads to polarization. **Polarization** is the tendency to look at the world in terms of opposites and to describe it in extremes—good or bad, positive or negative, healthy or sick, intelligent or stupid. It's often referred to as the fallacy of "either-or" or "black or white." Most people exist somewhere between the extremes. Yet there's a strong tendency to view only the extremes and to categorize people, objects, and events in terms of these polar opposites.

Problems are created when opposites are used in inappropriate situations. For example, "The politician is either for us or against us." These options don't include all possibilities. The politician may be for us in some things and against us in other things, or may be neutral.

In correcting this tendency to polarize, beware of implying (and believing) that two extreme classes include all possible classes—that an individual must be one or the other, with no alternatives ("Are you prochoice or prolife?"). Most people, most events, most qualities exist between polar extremes. When others imply that there are only two sides or alternatives, look for the middle ground.

Language Can Be Used Unethically as well as Ethically

As mentioned in Unit 1, the messages you formulate and send to others have ethical implications. They may often be judged as moral or immoral, just or unjust, fair or unfair. Two obvious types of messages suggest attention: lying and gossip.

Lying

According to deception researcher Paul Ekman (1985, p. 28) lying occurs when "one person intends to mislead another, doing so deliberately, without prior notification of this purpose, and without having been explicitly asked to do so by the target [the

Using this photo as a basis, can you develop hypothetical scenarios to illustrate some of the major barriers to effective verbal interaction such as intensional orientation, allness, fact inference confusion, static evaluation, indiscrimination, or polarization?

UNDERSTANDING
Theory and Research

HOW DO YOU LIE?

Here are some communication behaviors that are frequently used to detect lying (Knapp & Hall 1992; Miller & Burgoon 1990; O'Hair, Cody, Goss, & Krayer; Leathers 1997). As you review these behaviors, try to imagine a situation in which these behaviors would signal not lying but some other intention. Generally, research finds that liars smile less; respond with shorter answers, often simple "yes" or "no" responses; use fewer specifics and more generalities, for example, "we hung out"; shift their posture more; use more self-touching movements; blink more; use more and longer pauses; avoid direct eye contact with listener; appear less friendly and attentive; and make more speech errors. Which of these behaviors do you use in making assumptions about whether or not people are telling the truth? How reliable do you think these cues are?

person the liar intends to mislead]." As this definition makes clear, lying may be committed by omission as well as commission. When you omit something relevant, and this omission leads others to be misled, you've lied just as surely as if you had made a false statement (Bok 1978, Scott 1994).

Similarly, although most lies are verbal, some are nonverbal and most seem to involve at least some nonverbal elements. The innocent facial expression, despite the commission of some unethical act, and the knowing nod instead of the honest expression of ignorance are common examples of nonverbal lying (Burgoon, Buller, Ebesu, & Rockwell 1994).

Most lies are told to benefit the liar, generally (1) to gain some reward (for example, to increase desirable relationships, to protect one's self-esteem, or to obtain money) or (2) to avoid some punishment. In an analysis of 322 lies, researchers found that 75.8 percent benefited the liar, 21.7 percent benefited the person who was told the lie, and 2.5 percent benefited some third party (Camden, Motley, & Wilson 1984).

You may wish to examine your own beliefs about the ethics of lying by taking the following self-test.

 ## SELF-TEST

[When] Is Lying Unethical?

Each of the situations below presents an occasion for a lie. For the purposes of this exercise let's define a lie as *a deliberate misstatement intended to mislead another person.* Rate each in terms of its ethicality, using this scale: 1 = definitely ethical; 2 = probably ethical; 3 = not sure, need to think more about this one; 4 = probably unethical; 5 = definitely unethical. Note that many of the situations will lead you to look for more specific information before making your decision. For example, you may want to know how old the child in No. 8 is before making your decision or you may want to know kind of lie will be used to get the person in No. 6 to do something good. Because of this you might want to give more than one response for each statement depending upon the specifics of the situation.

_____ 1. to lie to a child to protect a fantasy belief, for example, to protect the child's belief in Santa Claus or the Tooth Fairy

_____ 2. to lie to achieve some greater good, for example, to lie to someone to prevent her or him from committing suicide or from getting depressed, or to lie to prevent a burglary or theft

_____ 3. to lie in an employment interview in answer to a question that is overly personal (and irrelevant) or illegal

_____ 4. to lie to protect the reputation of your family, some specific family member, or some third party

_____ 5. to lie to make another person feel good, for example, to tell someone that he or she looks great or has a great sense of humor

_____ 6. to lie to enable the other person to save face, for example, to voice agreement with an idea you find foolish, to say you enjoyed meeting the person when you didn't, or to compliment the other person when it's totally undeserved

_____ 7. to lie to get what you deserve but can't get any other way, for example, a well-earned promotion or raise or another chance with your relationship partner

_____ 8. to lie to get out of jury duty or to the internal revenue service so as to pay less taxes in April

_____ 9. to lie to keep hidden information about yourself that you simply don't want to reveal to anyone, for example, your religious beliefs, affectional orientation, or financial situation

_____ 10. to lie to your relationship partner to avoid a fight

_____ 11. to lie to get elected to some office; after all, you reason, everyone else does it and if I don't I'll never get elected

_____ 12. to lie to get yourself out of an unpleasant situation, for example, to get out of a date, an extra office chore, or a boring conversation

Each of these situations will be responded to differently by different people, depending on the culture in which they were raised, their beliefs about lying, and their own ethical codes. What cultural beliefs influence the ways in which lying and ethics are looked at? Can you identify situations in which a lie is always unethical? Are there situations in which truth-telling would be unethical and lying would be ethical?

Gossip

There can be no doubt that everyone spends a great deal of time gossiping. In fact, gossip seems universal among all cultures (Laing 1993) and among some it's a commonly accepted ritual (Hall 1993). Gossip refers to third-party talk about another person; the word "now embraces both the talker and the talk, the tattler and the tattle, the newsmonger and the newsmongering" (Bremner 1980, p. 178). Gossip is an inevitable part of daily interactions; to advise anyone not to gossip would be absurd. Not gossiping would eliminate one of the most frequent and enjoyable forms of communication.

In some instances, however, gossip is unethical (Bok 1983). First, it's unethical to reveal information that you've promised to keep secret. Although this principle may seem too obvious to even mention, it seems violated in many cases. For example, in a study of 133 school executives, board presidents, and superintendents, the majority received communications that violated an employee's right to confidentiality (Wilson & Bishard 1994). When it's impossible to keep something secret (Bok offers the example of the teenager who confides a suicide plan), the information should be revealed only to those who must know it, not to the world at large. Second, gossip is unethical when it invades the privacy that everyone has a right to, for example, when it concerns matters that are properly considered private and when the gossip can hurt the individuals involved. And, third, gossip is unethical when it's known to be false and is nevertheless passed on to others.

SUMMARY

In this unit we considered verbal messages. We discussed the nature of language and the ways in which language works, the concept of disconfirmation and how it relates to sexism, heterosexism, and racist language, and the ways in which language can be used more effectively.

1. Language meanings are in people, not in things.
2. Meanings are context-based; the same message in a different context will likely mean something different.
3. Language is both denotative (objective and generally easily agreed upon) and connotative (subjective and generally highly individual in meaning).
4. Language varies in directness; language can state exactly what you mean or it can hedge and state your meaning very indirectly.
5. Language is a cultural institution; each culture has its own rules identifying the ways in which language should be used.

6. Language varies in abstraction; language can vary from extremely general to extremely specific.

7. Disconfirmation refers to the process of ignoring the presence and the communications of others. Confirmation refers to accepting, supporting, and acknowledging the importance of the other person.

8. Sexist, heterosexist, and racist language puts down and negatively evaluates various cultural groups.

9. Using language effectively involves eliminating conceptual distortions and substituting more accurate assumptions about language, the most important of which are:

- Language symbolizes reality; it's not the reality itself.
- Language can express both facts and inferences and distinctions need to be made between them.
- Language is relatively static; because reality changes so rapidly, you need to constantly revise the way you talk about people and things.
- Language can obscure distinctions in its use of general terms and in its emphasis on extreme rather than middle terms.
- Language usage has an ethical dimension.

KEY TERMS

bypassing (p. 108)

language (p. 108)

connotation (p. 110)

denotation (p. 110)

netiquette (p. 110)

confirmation (p. 113)

disconfirmation (p. 113)

sexist language (p. 114)

heterosexist language (p. 115)

racist language (p. 116)

allness (p. 119)

extensional orientation (p. 119)

fact-inference confusion (p. 119)

intensional orientation (p. 119)

static evaluation (p. 122)

indiscrimination (p. 123)

lying (p. 124)

polarization (p. 124)

gossip (p. 126)

THINKING CRITICALLY ABOUT
Verbal Messages

1. When asked what they would like to change about the communication of the opposite sex, men said they wanted women to be more direct and women said they wanted men to stop interrupting and offering advice (Noble 1994). What one change would you like to see in the communication style of the opposite sex? Of your own sex?

2. Visit http://www.ccil.org/jargon/ or any electronic dictionary and browse through the terms and definitions. How is an online dictionary different from a print dictionary? What would a connotative dictionary look like?

3. One theory of politeness claims that you are most polite with friends and considerably less polite with both strangers and intimates (Wolfson 1988, Holmes 1995). Do you find this theory a generally accurate representation of your own level of politeness in different types of relationships?

4. What cultural identifiers to describe yourself do you prefer? Have these preferences changed over time? How can you let other people know the designations that you prefer and those that you don't prefer? An interesting exercise—especially in a large and multicultural class—is for each student to write anonymously his or her preferred cultural identification on an index card and have them all read aloud.

5. Throughout this text, gender differences are discussed in a wide variety of contexts. Holmes (1995) distinguishes three perspectives on gender differences in communication: (1) Gender differences are due to innate biological differences; (2) gender differences are due to different patterns of socialization, which lead to different forms of communication; and (3) gender differences are due to the inequalities in social power; for example, because of women's lesser social power, they're more apt to communicate with greater deference and politeness than are men. What do you think of these three positions? Can you find arguments to support or contradict any of these positions?

6. A widely held assumption in anthropology, linguistics, and communication is that the importance of a concept to a culture can be measured by the number of words the language has for talking about the concept. So, for example, in English there are lots of words for "money" or for transportation or communication. With this principle in mind, consider the findings of Julia Stanley, for example, who researched terms indicating sexual promiscuity. Stanley found 220 terms referring to a sexually promiscuous woman by only 22 terms for a sexually promiscuous man (Thorne, Kramarae, & Henley, 1983). What does this suggest about the culture's attitudes and beliefs about promiscuity in men and women?

7. Consider this situation: an instructor at your school persists in calling the female students girls, refers to gay men and lesbians as queers, and refers to various racial groups with terms that most people would consider inappropriate. To the objection that these terms are offensive, the instructor claims the right to free speech and argues that to prevent instructors from using such terms would be a restriction on free speech, which would be a far greater wrong than being culturally or politically incorrect. How would you comment on this argument?

8. How would you go about finding answers to questions such as these?
   • Does the use of derogatory language about your own groups influence your self-concept?
   • What are the effects of using racist, sexist, and heterosexist language on your campus? At home? With your close friends?
   • Do the definitions of what constitutes confirmation, rejection, and disconfirmation vary from one culture to another?

UNIT 8

Nonverbal Messages

UNIT CONTENTS

Nonverbal Communication

The Channels of Nonverbal Communication

Culture and Nonverbal Communication

UNIT GOALS

After completing this unit, you should be able to

define *nonverbal communication* and identify its major functions

define the nonverbal channels and provide examples of the messages that can be communicated through each

explain how nonverbal messages are influenced by culture

This unit presents the nonverbal aspect of messages and explains the nature of nonverbal communication, the ways people communicate without words, and how culture influences the meanings of nonverbal messages.

NONVERBAL COMMUNICATION

Nonverbal communication is communication without words. You communicate nonverbally when you gesture, smile or frown, widen your eyes, move your chair closer to someone, wear jewelry, touch someone, raise your vocal volume, or even when you say nothing. In this unit we look at these nonverbal messages—how they interact with verbal messages, the types of nonverbal messages, and the cultural variations in nonverbal communication.

In face-to-face communication you blend verbal and nonverbal messages to best convey your meanings (Knapp & Hall 1992). You use nonverbal communication to **accent** or emphasize some part of the verbal message. You might, for example, raise your voice to underscore a particular word or phrase, bang your fist on the desk to stress your commitment, or look longingly into someone's eyes when saying "I love you."

You use nonverbal communication to **complement**, to add nuances of meaning not communicated by your verbal message. Thus, you might smile when telling a story (to suggest that you find it humorous) or frown and shake your head when recounting someone's deceit (to suggest your disapproval).

You may deliberately **contradict** your verbal messages with nonverbal movements—for example, by crossing your fingers or winking to indicate that you're lying.

Movements may be used to **regulate** or control the flow of verbal messages, as when you purse your lips, lean forward, or make hand gestures to indicate that you want to speak. You might also put up your hand or vocalize your pauses (for example, with "um" or "ah") to indicate that you've not finished and aren't ready to relinquish the floor to the next speaker.

You can **repeat** or restate the verbal message nonverbally. You can, for example, follow your verbal "Is that all right?" with raised eyebrows and a questioning look, or motion with your head or hand to repeat your verbal "Let's go."

You may also use nonverbal communication to **substitute** or take the place of verbal messages. For instance, you can signal "okay" with a hand gesture. You can nod your head to indicate yes or shake your head to indicate no.

THE CHANNELS OF NONVERBAL COMMUNICATION

Nonverbal communication is probably most easily explained by identifying the various channels through which messages pass. Here we cover ten channels: body, face, eye, space, artifactual, touch, paralanguage, silence, time, and smell.

The Body

Two areas of the body are especially important in communicating messages. First, the movements you make with your body communicate, and, second, the general appearance of your body communicates.

Body Movements

Nonverbal researchers identify five major types of body movements: emblems, illustrators, affect displays, regulators, and adaptors (Ekman & Friesen 1969, Knapp & Hall 1996).

Emblems are body gestures that directly translate into words or phrases, for example, the okay sign, the thumbs-up for "good job," and the "V" for victory. You use these consciously and purposely to communicate the same meaning as the words. Emblems are culture-specific, so be careful when using your culture's emblems in other cultures. For example, when President Nixon visited Latin America and gestured with the O.K. sign he thought communicated something positive, he was quickly informed that this gesture was not universal. In Latin America the gesture has a far more negative meaning. Here are a few differences in meaning across cultures of the emblems you may commonly use (Axtell 1991):

- In the United States, to say "hello" you wave with your whole hand moving from side to side, but in a large part of Europe that same signal means "no." In Greece it would be considered insulting to the person to whom you're waving.
- The "V" for victory is common throughout much of the world, but if used in England with the

palm facing your face, it's an insult much like the raised middle finger is in the United States.

- In Texas the raised fist with little finger and index finger raised is a positive expression of support because it represents the Texas longhorn steer. But, in Italy it's an insult that means that "your spouse is having an affair with someone else." In parts of South America it's a gesture to ward off evil, and in parts of Africa it's a curse meaning, "may you experience bad times."
- In the United States and in much of Asia hugging is rarely exchanged among acquaintances, but among Latins and Southern Europeans hugging is a common greeting gesture which, if withheld, may communicate unfriendliness.

Illustrators enhance (literally "illustrate") the verbal messages they accompany. For example, when referring to something to the left, you might gesture toward the left. Most often you illustrate with your hands, but you can also illustrate with head and general body movements. You might, for example, turn your head or your entire body toward the left. You might also use illustrators to communicate the shape or size of objects you're talking about.

Affect displays are movements of the face (smiling or frowning, for example) but also of the hands and general body (body tenseness or relaxing posture, for example) that communicate emotional meaning. Affect displays are often unconscious; you smile or frown, for example, without awareness. At other times, however, you may smile with awareness, consciously trying to convey your pleasure or satisfaction.

Regulators are behaviors that monitor, control, coordinate, or maintain the speaking of another individual. When you nod your head, for example, you tell the speaker to keep on speaking; when you lean forward and open your mouth, you tell the speaker that you would like to say something.

Adaptors are gestures that satisfy some personal need, for example, scratching to relieve an itch or moving your hair out of your eyes. *Self-adaptors* are self-touching movements (for example, rubbing your nose). *Alter-adaptors* are movements directed at the person with whom you're speaking, for example, removing lint from someone's jacket or straightening a person's tie or folding your arms in front of you to keep others a comfortable distance from you. *Object-adaptors* are those gestures focused on objects, for

example, doodling on or shredding a styrofoam coffee cup.

Body Appearance

Your general body appearance also communicates. Height, for example, has been shown to be significant in a wide variety of situations. Tall presidential candidates have a much better record of winning the election than do their shorter opponents. Tall people seem to be paid more and are favored by interviewers over shorter applicants (Keyes 1980; Guerrero, DeVito, & Hecht 1999; Knapp & Hall 1992; Jackson & Ervin 1992).

Your body also reveals your race through skin color and tone and may also give clues as to your more specific nationality. Your weight in proportion to your height will also communicate messages to others as will the length, color, and style of your hair.

Your general attractiveness is also a part of body communication. Attractive people have the advantage in just about every activity you can name. They get better grades in school, are more valued as friends and lovers, and are preferred as coworkers (Burgoon, Buller, & Woodall 1995). Although we normally think that attractiveness is culturally determined—and to some degree it is—recent research seems to be showing that definitions of attractiveness are becoming universal (Brody 1994). A person rated as attractive in one culture is likely to be rated as attractive in other cultures—even cultures that are widely different in appearance.

Facial Communication

Throughout your interactions, your face communicates various messages, especially your emotions. Facial movements alone seem to communicate the degree of pleasantness, agreement, and sympathy felt; the rest of the body doesn't provide any additional information. But, for other aspects, for example, the intensity with which an emotion is felt, both facial and bodily cues are used (Graham, Bitti, & Argyle 1975; Graham & Argyle 1975).

Some nonverbal researchers claim that facial movements may express at least the following eight emotions: happiness, surprise, fear, anger, sadness, disgust, contempt, and interest (Ekman, Friesen, & Ellsworth 1972). The emotions are generally called **primary affect displays**. They're relatively pure, single emotions. Other emotional states and other facial displays are combinations of these various primary emotions and are called **affect blends**. You communicate these affects with different parts of your face. Thus, for example, you may experience both fear and disgust at the same time. Your eyes and eyelids may signal fear, and movements of your nose, cheek, and mouth area may signal disgust.

Facial Management Techniques

As you learned the nonverbal system of communication, you also learned certain facial management techniques; for example, to hide certain emotions and to emphasize others. Here are four facial management techniques that you will quickly recognize (Malandro, Barker, & Barker 1989):

- **intensifying** helps you exaggerate a feeling, for example, exaggerating surprise when friends throw you a party to make your friends feel better
- **deintensifying** helps you underplay a feeling, for example, to cover up your own joy in the presence of a friend who didn't receive such good news
- **neutralizing** helps you hide feelings, for example, to cover up your sadness so as not to depress others
- **masking** helps you to replace or substitute the expression of one emotion for the emotion you're really feeling, for example, to express happiness in order to cover up your disappointment in not receiving the gift you had expected

These facial management techniques are learned along with display rules which tell you what emotions to express when; they're the rules of appropriateness. For example, when someone gets bad news in which you may secretly take pleasure, the display rule dictates that you frown and otherwise nonverbally signal your displeasure. If you violate these display rules, you'll be judged insensitive.

Encoding-Decoding Accuracy

Considerable research has addressed the issue of how accurately you can encode and decode facial emotions. One problem in answering this question is that it's difficult to separate the ability of the encoder from the ability of the decoder. Thus, a person may be quite adept at communicating emotions, but the receiver may prove insensitive. On the other hand, the receiver may be good at deciphering emotions, but the sender may be inept. For example, extroverts seem more accurate at decoding nonverbal cues than introverts (Akert & Panter 1986).

Women are better at encoding and decoding nonverbal cues than are men. In 11 different countries, the same results were found (Rosenthal & DePaulo 1979). It may be argued that because men and women play different social roles in society, they've learned different adaptive techniques and skills to help them perform these roles. Thus, in most societies women are expected to be more friendly, nurturing, and supportive and so learn these skills (Eagly 1987).

Accuracy also varies with the emotions themselves. Some emotions are easier to encode and decode than others. In one study, for example, people judged happiness with an accuracy ranging from 55 to 100 percent, surprise from 38 to 86 percent, and sadness from 19 to 88 percent (Ekman, Friesen, & Ellsworth 1972).

Eye Communication

The messages communicated by the eyes (a study known technically as **oculesis**) vary depending on the duration, direction, and quality of the eye behavior. For example, in every culture there are strict, though unstated, rules for the proper duration for eye contact. In our culture, the average length of gaze is 2.95 seconds. The average length of mutual gaze (two persons gazing at each other) is 1.18 seconds (Argyle & Ingham 1972; Argyle 1988). When eye contact falls short of this amount, you may think the person is uninterested, shy, or preoccupied. When the appropriate amount of time is exceeded, you might perceive the person as showing unusually high interest.

The direction of the eye also communicates. In much of the United States, you're expected to glance alternatively at the other person's face, then away, then again at the face, and so on. The rule for the public speaker is to scan the entire audience, not focusing for too long or ignoring any one area of the audience. When you break these directional rules, you communicate different meanings—abnormally high or low interest, self-consciousness, nervousness over the interaction, and so on. The quality—how wide or how narrow your eyes get during interaction—also communicates meaning, especially interest level and such emotions as surprise, fear, and disgust.

UNDERSTANDING
Theory and Research

DO EXPRESSIONS CHANGE ATTITUDES?

The **facial feedback hypothesis** holds that your facial expressions influence physiological arousal (Lanzetta, Cartwright-Smith, & Kleck 1976; Zuckerman, Klorman, Larrance, & Spiegel 1981). In one study, for example, participants held a pen in their teeth to simulate a sad expression and then rated a series of photographs. Results showed that mimicking sad expressions actually increased the degree of sadness the subjects reported feeling when viewing the photographs (Larsen, Kasimatis, & Frey 1992). Further support for this hypothesis comes from a study that compared participants who (1) felt emotions such as happiness and anger with those who (2) both felt and expressed these emotions. In support of the facial feedback hypothesis, subjects who felt and expressed the emotions became emotionally aroused faster than did those who only felt the emotion (Hess, Kappas, McHugo, & Lanzetta 1992).

Generally, research finds that facial expressions can produce or heighten feelings of sadness, fear, disgust, and anger. But, this effect does not occur with all emotions; smiling, for example, doesn't seem to make us feel happier (Burgoon, Buller, & Woodall 1996). Further, it has not been demonstrated that facial expressions can eliminate one feeling and replace it with another. So, if you're feeling sad, smiling will not eliminate the sadness and replace it with gladness. A reasonable conclusion seems to be that your facial expressions can influence some feelings but not all (Burgoon, Buller, & Woodall 1996, Cappella 1993).

Test out this theory yourself or with a few friends. Do your findings support the theory?

The Functions of Eye Contact and Eye Avoidance

Eye contact can serve a variety of functions. One such function is to seek feedback. In talking with someone, we look at her or him intently, as if to say, "Well, what do you think?" As you might predict, listeners gaze at speakers more than speakers gaze at listeners. In public speaking, you might scan hundreds of people to secure this feedback.

A second function is to inform the other person that the channel of communication is open and that he or she should now speak. You see this regularly in conversation when one person asks a question or finishes a thought and then looks to you for a response. Eye contact was also the most frequently noted nonverbal behavior that told library users that the librarian was approachable (Radford 1998).

Eye movements may also signal the nature of a relationship, whether positive (an attentive glance) or negative (eye avoidance). You can also signal your power through "visual dominance behavior" (Exline, Ellyson, & Long 1975). The average speaker, for example, maintains a high level of eye contact while listening and a lower level while speaking. When people want to signal dominance, they may reverse this pattern—maintaining a high level of eye contact while talking but a much lower level while listening.

By making eye contact you psychologically lessen the physical distance between yourself and another person. When you catch someone's eye at a party, for example, you become psychologically close though physically far apart.

Eye avoidance can also serve several different functions. When you avoid eye contact or avert your glance, you may help others to maintain their privacy. You might do this when you see a couple arguing in public. You turn your eyes away (though your eyes may be wide open) as if to say, "I don't mean to intrude; I respect your privacy." Goffman refers to this behavior as **civil inattention**.

Eye avoidance can also signal lack of interest—in a person, a conversation, or some visual stimulus. At times, you might hide your eyes to block off unpleasant stimuli (a particularly gory or violent scene in a movie, for example) or close your eyes to block out visual stimuli and thus heighten other senses. For example, you might listen to music with your eyes closed. Lovers often close their eyes while kissing, and many prefer to make love in a dark or dimly lit room.

Pupil Dilation

In the fifteenth and sixteenth centuries, Italian women put drops of belladonna (which literally means "beautiful woman") into their eyes to enlarge the pupils so that they would look more attractive. Contemporary research supports the intuitive logic of these women; dilated pupils are judged more attractive than constricted ones (Hess 1975; Marshall 1983). In one study, photographs of women were retouched; in half the pupils were enlarged and in the other half they were made smaller (Hess 1975). Men were then asked to judge the women's personalities from the photographs. The photos of women with small pupils drew responses such as cold, hard, and selfish; those with dilated pupils drew responses such as feminine and soft. Interestingly, the male observers could not verbalize the reasons for their different perceptions. Pupil dilation and reactions to changes in the pupil size of others may function below the level of conscious awareness.

Pupil size also reveals your interest and level of emotional arousal. Your pupils enlarge when you're interested in something or when your are emotionally aroused. When homosexuals and heterosexuals were shown pictures of nude bodies, the homosexuals' pupils dilated more when viewing same-sex bodies, while the heterosexuals' pupils dilated more when viewing opposite-sex bodies (Hess, Seltzer, & Schlien 1965). These pupillary responses are also observed in persons with profound mental retardation (Chaney, Givens, Aoki, & Gombiner 1989). Perhaps we judge dilated pupils more attractive because we judge them as indicative of a person's interest in us. And that may be the reason why both models and Beanie Babies® have exceptionally large pupils.

Space Communication

Your use of space to communicate (an area of study known technically as **proxemics**) speaks as surely and loudly as words and sentences. Speakers who stand close to their listener, with their hands on the listener's shoulders and their eyes focused directly on those of the listener, communicate something very different from speakers who stand in a corner with arms folded and eyes downcast. Similarly, for example, the territory you occupy or own and the way you protect this territory also sends a message (an area of study known as **territoriality**). The executive office suite on the top floor with huge windows, private bar, and plush carpeting communicates something totally different than the six-by-six-foot cubicle occupied by the rest of the workers.

Spatial Distances

Edward Hall (1959, 1966) distinguishes four distances that define the type of relationship between people and the type of communication in which they're likely to engage (see Table 8.1). In **intimate distance**, ranging from actual touching to 18 inches, the presence of the other individual is unmistakable. Each person experiences the sound, smell, and feel of the other's breath. You use intimate distance for lovemaking, comforting, and protecting. This distance is so short that most people don't consider it proper in public.

Personal distance refers to the protective "bubble" that defines your personal distance, ranging from 18 inches to 4 feet. This imaginary bubble keeps you protected and untouched by others. You can still hold or grasp another person at this distance but only by extending your arms; allowing you to take certain individuals such as loved ones into your protective bubble. At the outer limit of personal distance, you can touch another person only if both of you extend your arms. At this distance you conduct much of your interpersonal interactions, for example, talking with friends and family.

Social distance ranges from 4 to 12 feet; at this distance you lose the visual detail you have at personal distance. You conduct impersonal business and interact at a social gathering at this social distance. The more distance you maintain in your interactions, the more formal they appear. In offices of high officials, the desks are positioned so the official is assured of at least this distance from clients.

Public distance, from 12 to more than 25 feet, protects you. At this distance you could take defensive action if threatened. On a public bus or train, for example, you might keep at least this distance

TABLE 8.1   Relationships and proxemic distances

Note that these four distances can be further divided into close and far phases and that the far phase of one level (say, personal) blends into the close phase of the next level (social). Do your relationships also blend into one another or are, say, your personal relationships totally separate from your social relationships?

Relationship	Distance
Intimate relationship	**Intimate distance** 0 —————— 18 inches close phase far phase
Personal relationship	**Personal distance** 1½ —————— 4 feet close phase far phase
Social relationship	**Social distance** 4 —————— 12 feet close phase far phase
Public relationship	**Public distance** 12 —————— 25+ feet close phase far phase

from a drunkard. Although at this distance you lose fine details of the face and eyes, you're still close enough to see what is happening.

Influences on Space Communication

Several factors influence the way you relate to and use space in communicating. Here are a few examples of how status, culture, subject matter, gender, and age influence space communication (Burgoon, Buller, & Woodall 1995).

People of equal **status** maintain shorter distances between themselves than do people of unequal status. When status is unequal, the higher-status person may approach the lower-status person more closely than the lower-status person would approach the higher-status person.

Members of different **cultures** treat space differently. For example, those from northern European cultures and many Americans stand fairly far apart when conversing, compared with those from southern European and Middle Eastern cultures who stand much closer. It's easy to see how those who normally stand far apart may interpret the close distances of others as pushy and overly intimate. It's equally easy to appreciate how those who normally stand close may interpret the far distances of others as cold and unfriendly.

When discussing personal **subjects** you maintain shorter distances than with impersonal subjects. Also, you stand closer to someone praising you, than to someone criticizing you.

Your **gender** also influences your spatial relationships. Women generally stand closer to each other than men do. Similarly, when someone approaches another person, he or she will come closer to a woman than to a man. As people **age** there's a tendency for the spaces to become larger. Children stand much closer to each other than do adults. These research findings provide some evidence that maintaining distance is a learned behavior.

The **evaluation** you make of the person (whether positive or negative) will also influence your space.

BUILDING Communication Skills

WHERE DO YOU SIT?

With your recently acquired sensitivity to nonverbal cues, where would you sit in each of the following four situations? What would be your first choice? Your second choice?

A. You want to polish the apple and ingratiate yourself with your boss.

B. You aren't prepared and want to be ignored.

C. You want to challenge your boss on a certain policy that will come up for a vote.

D. You want to be accepted as a new (but important) member of the company.

Why did you make the choices you made? Do you normally make choices based on such

factors as these? What interpersonal factors—for example, the desire to talk to or get a closer look at someone—influence your day-to-day seating behavior?

For example, you stand farther from enemies, authority figures, and higher-status individuals than from friends and peers. You maintain a greater distance from people you see as different from yourself, for example, in race or in physical condition. Typically, you maintain more distance between yourself and people you may unconsciously evaluate negatively.

Territoriality

One of the most interesting concepts in ethology (the study of animals in their natural surroundings) is territoriality, a possessive or ownership reaction to an area of space or to particular objects. Two interesting dimensions of territoriality are territorial types and territorial markers.

Territory Types

Three types of territory are often distinguished: primary, secondary, and public (Altman 1975). **Primary territories** are your exclusive preserve; your desk, room, house, or backyard, for example. In these areas you're in control. It's similar to the home field

advantage that a sports team has when playing in its own ballpark. When you're in these primary areas, you generally have greater influence over others than you would in someone else's territory. For example, when in their own home or office people take on a kind of leadership role; they initiate conversations, fill in silences, assume relaxed and comfortable postures, and maintain their positions with greater conviction. Because the territorial owner is dominant, you stand a better chance of getting your raise, your point accepted, and the contract resolved in your favor if you're in your own primary territory (home, office) rather than in someone else's (Marsh 1988).

Secondary territories, although they don't belong to you, are associated with you perhaps because you've occupied them for a long time or they were assigned to you. For example, your desk in a classroom may be a secondary territory if it was assigned to you or if you regularly occupied it and others treat it as yours. Your neighborhood turf, a cafeteria table that you regularly occupy, or a favorite corner of a local coffee shop may be secondary territories. You feel a certain "ownership-like" attachment to the place although it's really not yours in any legal sense.

Frasier's table at the local coffee shop is a perfect example of a secondary territory. What are your secondary territories?

Public territories are those areas that are open to all people; a park, movie house, restaurant, or beach are examples. The European cafe, the food court in a suburban mall, and the open areas in large city office buildings are public spaces that bring people together and stimulate communication.

The electronic revolution, however, may well change the role of public space in stimulating communication (Drucker & Gumpert 1991; Gumpert & Drucker 1995). For example, home shopping clubs make it less necessary for people to go shopping "downtown" or to the mall, and they consequently have less opportunity to run into other people and to talk and to exchange news. Similarly, electronic mail permits communication without talking and without even going out of one's home to mail a letter. Perhaps the greatest change is telecommuting (Giordano 1989), where workers can go to work without even leaving their homes. The face-to-face communication that normally takes place in an office is replaced by communication via computer.

Territoriality is closely linked to status. Generally, the size and location of your territories signal your status within your social group. For example, male animals will stake out a particular territory and consider it their own. They will allow prospective mates to enter but will defend it against entrance by others, especially other males of the same species. The larger the animal's territory, the higher the animal is in status within the herd. The size and location of human territories also say something about status (Mehrabian 1976; Sommer 1969). An apartment or office in midtown Manhattan or downtown Tokyo, for example, is extremely high-status territory. The cost of the territory restricts it to those who have lots of money.

Territorial Markers

Much as animals mark their territory, humans mark theirs with three types of markers: central, boundary, and earmarkers (Hickson & Stacks 1993). **Central markers** are items you place in a territory to reserve it. For example, you place a drink at the bar, books on your desk, and a sweater over the chair to let others know that this territory belongs to you.

Boundary markers set boundaries that divide your territory from "theirs." In the supermarket checkout line, the bar placed between your groceries and those of the person behind you is a boundary marker. Similarly, the armrests separating your seat from those of the people on either side at a movie theater and the molded plastic seats on a bus or train are boundary markers.

Earmarkers—a term taken from the practice of branding animals on their ears-are those identifying marks that indicate your possession of a territory or object. Trademarks, nameplates, and initials on a shirt or attaché case are all examples of earmarkers.

Artifactual Communication

Artifactual messages are those made by human hands. Thus, color, clothing, jewelry, and the decoration of space would be considered artifactual. Let's look at each of these briefly.

Color Communication

There's some evidence that colors affect us physiologically. For example, respiratory movements increase with red light and decrease with blue light. Similarly, eye blinks increase in frequency when eyes are

UNDERSTANDING
Theory and Research

WHAT HAPPENS WHEN YOU VIOLATE SPACE EXPECTATIONS?

Expectancy violations theory explains what happens when you increase or decrease the distance between yourself and another person in an interpersonal interaction (Burgoon 1978; Burgoon, Buller, & Woodall 1995). Each culture has certain expectancies for the distance that people are expected to maintain in their conversations. And, of course, each person has certain idiosyncrasies. Together these determine "expected distance." If you violate the expected distance to a great extent—small violations most often go unnoticed—then the relationship itself comes into focus. Then the other person begins to turn attention away from the topic of conversation to you and to your relationship with him or her.

If this other person perceives you positively—for example, you're a high-status person or you're particularly attractive—then you'll be perceived even more positively if you violate the expected distance. If, on the other hand, you're perceived negatively and you violate the norm, you'll be perceived even more negatively.

exposed to red light and decrease when exposed to blue. This seems consistent with our intuitive feelings about blue being more soothing and red more arousing. After changing a school's walls from orange and white to blue, the blood pressure of the students decreased while their academic performance increased.

Color also influences perceptions and behaviors (Kanner 1989). People's acceptance of a product, for example, is largely determined by its packaging, especially its color. The very same coffee taken from a yellow can was described as weak, from a dark brown can too strong, from a red can rich, and from a blue can mild. Even your acceptance of a person may depend on the colors worn. Consider, for example, the comments of one color expert (Kanner 1989): "If you have to pick the wardrobe for your defense lawyer heading into court and choose anything but blue, you deserve to lose the case. . . ." Black is so powerful it could work against the lawyer with the jury. Brown lacks sufficient authority. Green would probably elicit a negative response.

Clothing and Body Adornment

People make inferences about who you are—in part—by the way you dress. Whether these infer-ences are accurate or not, they will influence what people think of you and how they react to you. Your socioeconomic class, your seriousness, your attitudes (for example, whether you're conservative or liberal), your concern for convention, your sense of style and perhaps even your creativity will all be judged—in part at least—by the way you dress (Molloy 1977; Burgoon, Buller, & Woodall 1996; Knapp & Hall 1992). Similarly, college students will perceive an instructor dressed informally as friendly, fair, enthusiastic, and flexible, and the same instructor dressed formally as prepared, knowledgeable, and organized (Malandro, Barker, & Barker 1989).

The way you wear your hair says something about who you are—from caring about being up-to-date to a desire to shock to perhaps a lack of concern for appearances. Men with long hair will generally be judged as less conservative than those with shorter hair. Your jewelry also communicates messages about you. Wedding and engagement rings are obvious examples that communicate specific messages. College rings and political buttons likewise communicate specific messages. If you wear a Rolex watch or large precious stones, for example, others are likely to infer that you're rich. Men who wear

MEDIA WATCH

LEGIBLE CLOTHING

Legible clothing is anything that you wear that contains some verbal message; your clothing can literally be read. In some instances it says status; it tells others that you are, for example, rich or stylish or youthful. The Gucci or Louis Vuitton logos on your luggage communicate your status and financial position. In a similar way your sweatshirt saying Bulls or Pirates communicates your interest in sports and perhaps your favorite team.

John Molloy (1981), in *Molloy's Live for Success*, advises you to avoid legible clothing except the kind that says rich. Legible clothing, argues Molloy, communicates lower status and lack of power. And humorist Fran Lebowitz says that legible clothes "are an unpleasant indication of the general state of things. I mean, be realistic. If people don't want to listen to you, what makes you think they want to hear from your sweater?"

But, legible clothing is being bought and worn in record numbers. Many designers and manufacturers have their names integrated into the design of the clothing: DKNY, Calvin Klein underwear, L.L.Bean, and Levi's are just a few examples. At the same time that you're paying extra to buy the brand name, you also provide free advertising for the designer and manufacturer.

To paraphrase Vidal Sassoon, "As long as you look good, so does the advertiser. And, when you look bad, the advertiser looks bad." Imitators—the cheap knockoffs you see on the street—are resisted by the original manufacturers not only because these impact on their own sales. In fact, the impact is probably minimal since the person who would pay $6000 for a Rolex would not buy a $10 imitation on the street. Rather, such knockoffs seem resisted because they're worn by the wrong people—people who would destroy the image the manufacturer wishes to communicate.

T-shirts and sweatshirts are especially popular as message senders. In one study, the types of t-shirt messages were classified into four main categories (Sayre 1992). The order in which these are presented reflects the shirts the subjects (600 male and female college students were surveyed) considered their favorites. Thirty-three percent, for example, considered affiliation message shirts their favorites while 17 percent considered those with personal messages their favorites. The order, starting with most favorite, was

- Affiliation messages, for example, a club or school name. It communicates that you're a part of a larger group.
- Trophy, for example, a shirt from a high-status event such as a concert or perhaps a ski lodge. This is a way of saying that the wearer was in the right place.
- Metaphorical expressions, for example, pictures of rock groups or famous athletes.
- Personal messages, for example, "beliefs, philosophies and causes as well as satirizing current events" (Sayre 1992, p. 77).

Another important dimension of clothing, currently being debated in educational and legal circles, is the use of gang clothing (Burke 1993). Some argue that gang clothing and gang colors contribute to violence in the schools and should therefore be prohibited. Others argue that gang clothing—or any clothing—is covered by the first amendment to the Constitution which guarantees freedom of speech. Consider a specific case. In Harvard, Illinois, you can be arrested for wearing a Star of David in public—not because it's a religious symbol, but because certain gangs are using it as a gang symbol, much as some have with the Dallas Cowboys jacket and the Georgetown baseball cap (*New York Times*, February 7, 1995, p. A 12). In 1993 Harvard passed a law that makes it illegal "for any person within the city to knowingly use, display or wear colors, emblems, or insignia" that would communicate his or her membership in (or sympathy for) gangs.

(continued on next page)

Media Watch *(continued)*

Consider your own use of legible clothing. Do you wear legible clothing? What messages do you wish to communicate? How successful are you in communicating these messages? Do the labels others wear influence your perceptions of them? How do you feel about the law in Harvard, Illinois? Would you support such a law in your own community?

The next Media Watch appears on page 168.

earrings will be judged differently from men who don't. What judgments are made will depend on who the receiver is, the communication context, and all the factors identified throughout this text.

Space Decoration

The way you decorate your private spaces also communicates about you. The office with a mahogany desk and bookcases and oriental rugs communicates your importance and status within the organization just as a metal desk and bare floors indicate a worker much further down in the hierarchy.

Similarly, people will make inferences about you based on the way you decorate your home. The expensiveness of the furnishings may communicate your status and wealth; their coordination may convey your sense of style. The magazines may reflect your interests while the arrangement of chairs around a television set may reveal how important watching television is to you. And bookcases lining the walls reveal the importance of reading. In fact, there's probably little in your home that would not send messages that others would use in making inferences about you. Computers, wide-screen televisions, well-equipped kitchens, and oil paintings of great grandparents, for example, all say something about the people who live in the home.

Similarly, the lack of certain items will communicate something about you. Consider what messages you'd get from a home where there's no television, phone, or books.

Touch Communication

Touch communication, also referred to as **haptics**, is perhaps the most primitive form of communication (Montagu 1971). Developmentally, touch is probably the first sense to be used. Even in the womb the child is stimulated by touch. Soon after birth the child is fondled, caressed, patted, and stroked. In turn, the child explores its world through touch. In short time, the child learns to communicate a wide variety of meanings through touch.

The Meanings of Touch

Touch communicates a wide variety of messages (Jones & Yarbrough 1985). Here are five major ones that will illustrate this great variety.

- Touch communicates **positive feelings** such as support, appreciation, inclusion, sexual interest or intent, composure, immediacy, affection, trust, similarity and quality, and informality (Jones &Yarbrough 1985; Burgoon 1991). Touch also stimulates self-disclosure (Rabinowitz 1991).
- Touch often communicates your intention to **play**, either affectionately or aggressively.
- Touch may **control** the behaviors, attitudes, or feelings of the other person. In compliance, for example, you touch the other person to communicate "move over," "hurry," "stay here," and "do it." You might also touch a person to gain his or her attention, as if to say "look at me" or "look over here."
- **Ritualistic** touching centers on greetings and departures, for example, shaking hands to say "hello" or "good-bye," hugging, kissing, or putting your arm around another's shoulder when greeting or saying farewell.
- **Task-related** touching is associated with the performance of some function, for example, removing a speck of dust from another person's face, helping someone out of a car, or checking someone's forehead for fever.

Touch Avoidance

Much as you have a need and desire to touch and be touched, you also have a tendency to avoid touch from certain people or in certain circumstances (Andersen & Leibowitz 1978). You may

Consider, as Nancy Henley suggests in her *Body Politics* (1977), who would touch whom—say, by putting an arm on the other person's shoulder or by putting a hand on the other person's back—in the following dyads: teacher and student, doctor and patient, manager and worker, minister and parishioner, business executive and secretary. Do your answers reveal that the higher-status person initiates touch with the lower-status person? Henley further argues that in addition to indicating relative status, touching demonstrates the assertion of male power, dominance, and superior status over women. When women touch men, Henley says, the interpretation that it designates a female-dominant relationship is not acceptable (to men) and so the touching is interpreted as a sexual invitation. What do you think of this position?

wish to examine your own tendency by taking the self-test, "Do You Avoid Touch?"

 ## SELF-TEST

Do You Avoid Touch?

This test is composed of 18 statements concerning how you feel about touching other people and being touched. Please indicate the degree to which each statement applies to you by indicating whether you: 1 = strongly agree; 2 = agree; 3 = are undecided; 4 = disagree; and 5 = strongly disagree.

_____ 1. A hug from a same-sex friend is a true sign of friendship.

_____ 2. Opposite-sex friends enjoy it when I touch them.

_____ 3. I often put my arm around friends of the same sex.

_____ 4. When I see two friends of the same sex hugging, it revolts me.

_____ 5. I like it when members of the opposite sex touch me.

_____ 6. People shouldn't be so uptight about touching persons of the same sex.

_____ 7. I think it is vulgar when members of the opposite sex touch me.

_____ 8. When a member of the opposite sex touches me, I find it unpleasant.

_____ 9. I wish I were free to show emotions by touching members of same sex.

_____ 10. I'd enjoy giving a massage to an opposite-sex friend.

_____ 11. I enjoy kissing a person of the same sex.

_____ 12. I like to touch friends that are the same sex as I am.

_____ 13. Touching a friend of the same sex does not make me uncomfortable.

_____ 14. I find it enjoyable when my date and I embrace.

_____ 15. I enjoy getting a back rub from a member of the opposite sex.

_____ 16. I dislike kissing relatives of the same sex.

_____ 17. Intimate touching with members of the opposite sex is pleasurable.

_____ 18. I find it difficult to be touched by a member of my own sex.

To score your Touch Avoidance Questionnaire: Reverse your scores for items 4, 7, 8, 16, and 18. Use these reversed scores in all future calculations.

1. To obtain your same-sex touch avoidance score (the extent to which you avoid touching members of your sex), total the scores for items 1, 3, 4, 6, 9, 11, 12, 13, 16, and 18.
2. To obtain your opposite-sex touch avoidance score (the extent to which you avoid touching members of the opposite sex), total the scores for items 2, 5, 7, 8, 10, 14, 15, and 17.
3. To obtain your total touch avoidance score, add the subtotals from steps 2 and 3.

The higher the score, the higher the touch avoidance–that is, the greater your tendency to avoid touch. In studies by Andersen and Leibowitz (1978), who constructed this test, average opposite-sex touch avoidance scores for males was 12.9 and for females 14.85. Average same-sex touch avoidance scores were 26.43 for males and 21.70 for females. How do your scores compare with those college students in Andersen and Leibowitz's study? Is your touch avoidance likely to be higher when interacting with persons who are culturally different from you? Can you identify types of people and types of situations in which your touch avoidance would be especially high? Especially low?

From Andersen and Leibowitz, "Do You Avoid Touch?" from "Development and Nature of the Construct Touch Avoidence" in *Environmental Psychology and Nonverbal Behavior*, Vol. 3, 1978. Copyright © 1978 Plenum Publishing Corporation. Reprinted by Permission. ✔

Based on the self-test presented here, a number of interesting connections between touch avoidance and other factors were found (Andersen & Liebowitz 1978). For example, touch avoidance is positively related to communication apprehension. If you have a strong fear of oral communication, then you probably also have strong touch avoidance tendencies. Touch avoidance is also high with those who self-disclose less.

Both touch and self-disclosure are intimate forms of communication. People who are reluctant to get close to another person by self-disclosing also seem reluctant to get close by touching.

Older people avoid touch with opposite-sex persons more than do younger people. As people get older they're touched less by members of the opposite sex; this decreased frequency of touching may lead them to avoid touching.

Paralanguage: the Vocal Channel

Paralanguage refers to the vocal (but nonverbal) dimension of speech. It refers to how you say something, not what you say. A traditional exercise to increase a student's ability to express different emotions, feelings, and attitudes is to repeat a sentence while accenting or stressing different words. One popular sentence was, "Is this the face that launched a thousand ships?" Significant differences in meaning are easily communicated depending on where the stress is placed. Consider the following variations:

1. *Is* this the face that launched a thousand ships?
2. Is *this* the face that launched a thousand ships?
3. Is this *the face* that launched a thousand ships?
4. Is this the face *that launched* a thousand ships?
5. Is this the face that launched *a thousand ships*?

Each sentence communicates something different; in fact, each asks a different question even though the words are exactly the same. All that distinguishes the sentences is stress, one aspect of paralanguage. In addition to stress or pitch, paralanguage includes such vocal characteristics as rate, volume, and rhythm as well as the vocalizations you make in crying, whispering, moaning, belching, yawning, and yelling (Trager 1958, 1961; Argyle 1988). A variation in any of these features communicates. When you speak quickly, for example, you communicate something different than when you speak slowly. Even though the words might be the same, if the speed (or volume, rhythm, or pitch) differs, the meanings people receive will also differ.

Judgments About People

Paralanguage cues are often used as a basis for making judgments about people, for example, their emotional state or even their personality. Listeners can accurately judge the emotional states of speakers from vocal expression alone if both speaker and listener speak the same language. Paralanguage cues are not so accurate when used to communicate emotions to those who speak a different language (Albas, McCluskey, & Albas 1976). Some emotions are easier to identify than others; it's easy to distinguish between hate and sympathy but more difficult to distinguish between fear and anxiety. And, of course, listeners vary in their ability to decode, and speakers in their ability to encode emotions (Scherer 1986).

Judgments About Communication Effectiveness

In one-way communication (when one person is doing all or most of the speaking and the other person is doing all or most of the listening), those who talk fast (about 50 percent faster than normal) are more persuasive (MacLachlan 1979). People agree more with a fast speaker than with a slow speaker and find the fast speaker more intelligent and objective.

When we look at comprehension, rapid speech shows an interesting effect. When the speaking rate is increased by 50 percent, the comprehension level drops only by 5 percent. When the rate is doubled, the comprehension level drops only 10 percent. These 5 and 10 percent losses are more than offset by the increased speed; thus the faster rates are much more efficient in communicating information.

If the speeds are more than twice normal speech, however, comprehension begins to fall dramatically.

Do exercise caution in applying this research to all forms of communication (MacLachlan 1979). For example, if you increase your rate to increase efficiency, you may create so unnatural an impression that others will focus on your speed instead of your meaning.

Silence

Like words and gestures, silence too communicates important meanings and serves important functions (Johannesen 1974; Jaworski 1993). Silence allows the speaker *time to think,* time to formulate and organize his or her verbal communications. Before messages of intense conflict, as well as those confessing undying love, there's often silence. Again, silence seems to prepare the receiver for the importance of these future messages.

Some people use silence as a weapon *to hurt* others. We often speak of giving someone "the silent treatment." After a conflict, for example, one or both individuals might remain silent as a kind of punishment. Silence used to hurt others may also take the form of refusing to acknowledge the presence of another person, as in disconfirmation (see Unit 7); here silence is a dramatic demonstration of the total indifference one person feels toward the other.

Sometimes silence is used as a *response to personal anxiety,* shyness, or threats. You may feel anxious or

BUILDING
Communication Skills

WHAT DOES YOUR VOCAL EXPRESSION SAY?

Think about your own ability to communicate different meanings with the use of only paralinguistic cues. Read each of the following statements first to communicate praise and then to communicate criticism. Can others identify which meaning you're communicating? Can you

identify the meanings others are communicating when they try this?

1. You lost weight.
2. You look younger than that.
3. That was some meal.
4. You're so sensitive. I'm amazed.
5. Your parents are really something.
6. Are you ready? Already?

What paralinguistic cues did you use to communicate praise? To communicate criticism?

shy among new people and prefer to remain silent. By remaining silent you preclude the chance of rejection. Only when the silence is broken and an attempt to communicate with another person is made do you risk rejection.

Silence may be used *to prevent communication* of certain messages. In conflict situations silence is sometimes used to prevent certain topics from surfacing and to prevent one or both parties from saying things they may later regret. In such situations silence often allows us time to cool off before expressing hatred, severe criticism, or personal attacks, which, we know, are irreversible.

Like the eyes, face, and hands, silence can also be used *to communicate emotional responses* (Ehrenhaus 1988). Sometimes silence communicates a determination to be uncooperative or defiant; by refusing to engage in verbal communication, you defy the authority or the legitimacy of the other person's position. Silence is often used to communicate annoyance, usually accompanied by a pouting expression, arms crossed in front of the chest, and nostrils flared. Silence may express affection or love, especially when coupled with long and longing stares into each other's eyes.

Of course, you may also use silence when you simply have *nothing to say,* when nothing occurs to you, or when you don't want to say anything. James Russell Lowell expressed this best: "Blessed are they who have nothing to say, and who cannot be persuaded to say it." Silence may also be used to say nothing and thus avoid responsibility for any wrongdoing (Beach 1990, 1991).

Time Communication

Temporal communication (known technically as **chronemics**) concerns the use of time—how you organize it, how you react to it, and the messages it communicates (Bruneau 1985, 1990). Consider, for example, the emphasis you place on the past, present, and future. In a past orientation, you have special reverence for the past. You relive old times and regard the old methods as the best. You see events as circular and recurring, so the wisdom of yesterday is applicable also to today and tomorrow. In a present orientation, however, you live in the present, for now, not tomorrow. In a future orientation, you look toward and live for the future. You save today, work hard in college, and deny yourself luxuries because you're preparing for the future. Before reading more about time, take the accompanying time self-test.

SELF-TEST

What Time Do You Have?

For each statement, indicate whether the statement is true (T) or false (F) of your general attitude and behavior. (A few statements are purposely repeated to facilitate scoring and analyzing your responses.)

_____ 1. Meeting tomorrow's deadlines and doing other necessary work comes before tonight's partying.

_____ 2. I meet my obligations to friends and authorities on time.

_____ 3. I complete projects on time by making steady progress.

_____ 4. I am able to resist temptations when I know there is work to be done.

_____ 5. I keep working at a difficult, uninteresting task if it will help me get ahead.

_____ 6. If things don't get done on time, I don't worry about it.

_____ 7. I think that it's useless to plan too far ahead because things hardly ever come out the way you planned anyway.

_____ 8. I try to live one day at a time.

_____ 9. I live to make better what *is* rather than to be concerned about what will be.

_____ 10. It seems to me that it doesn't make sense to worry about the future, since fate determines that whatever will be, will be.

_____ 11. I believe that getting together with friends to party is one of life's important pleasures.

_____ 12. I do things impulsively, making decisions on the spur of the moment.

_____ 13. I take risks to put excitement in my life.

_____ 14. I get drunk at parties.

_____ 15. It's fun to gamble.

_____ 16. Thinking about the future is pleasant to me.

_____ 17. When I want to achieve something, I set subgoals and consider specific means for reaching those goals.

UNDERSTANDING
Theory and Research

ARE YOU KEEPING PACE WITH YOUR PEERS?

Your culture or, more specifically, your society maintains a schedule for the right time to do a variety of important things, for example, the right time to start dating, to finish college, to buy your own home, to have a child. It provides you with a **social clock**, a clock that will tell you if you're keeping pace with your peers, are ahead of them, or are falling behind (Neugarten 1979). And you no doubt learned about this clock as you were growing up. On the basis of this social clock, you then evaluate your own social and professional development. If you're in pace with the rest of your peers—for example, you all started dating at around the same age or you're all finishing college at around the same age—then you'll feel well adjusted, competent, and a part of the group. If you're late, you'll probably experience feelings of dissatisfaction.

Recent research, however, shows that this social clock is becoming more flexible; people are becoming more willing to tolerate deviations from the established, socially acceptable timetable for accomplishing many of life's transitional events (Peterson 1996). Are you in pace?

_____ 18. It seems to me that my career path is pretty well laid out.

_____ 19. It upsets me to be late for appointments.

_____ 20. I meet my obligations to friends and authorities on time.

_____ 21. I get irritated at people who keep me waiting when we've agreed to meet at a given time.

_____ 22. It makes sense to invest a substantial part of my income in insurance premiums.

_____ 23. I believe that "A stitch in time saves nine."

_____ 24. I believe that "A bird in the hand is worth two in the bush."

_____ 25. I believe it is important to save for a rainy day.

_____ 26. I believe a person's day should be planned each morning.

_____ 27. I make lists of things I must do.

_____ 28. When I want to achieve something, I set subgoals and consider specific means for reaching those goals.

_____ 29. I believe that "A stitch in time saves nine."

This time test measures seven different factors. If you selected true (T) for all or most of the questions within any given factor, you're probably high on that factor. If you selected false (F) for all or most of the questions within any given factor, you're probably low on that factor. As you read down the list of factors, consider how you score on each factor and especially about how your time attitude impacts on your life—as a student, as a friend, as a family member.

The first factor, measured by questions 1–5, is a future, work-motivated, perseverance orientation. People with this orientation have a strong work ethic and are committed to completing a task despite difficulties and temptations.

The second factor (questions 6–10) is a present, fatalistic, worry-free orientation. High scorers on this factor live one day at a time, not necessarily to enjoy the day but to avoid planning for the next day or to avoid anxiety about the future.

The third factor (questions 11–15) is a present, pleasure-seeking, partying orientation. These people enjoy the present, take risks, and engage in a variety of impulsive actions.

The fourth factor (questions 16–18) is a future, goal-seeking, planning orientation. These people derive special pleasure from planning and achieving a variety of goals.

The fifth factor (questions 19–21) is a time-sensitivity orientation. People who score high are especially sensitive to time and its role in social obligations.

The sixth factor (questions 22–25) is a future, practical-action orientation. These people do what they have to do—take practical actions—to achieve the future they want.

The seventh factor (questions 26–29) is a future, somewhat obsessive daily-planning orientation. High scorers on this factor make daily "to do" lists and devote great attention to specific details.

Reprinted with permission from *Psychology Today* magazine, Copyright © 1985 Sussex Publishers, Inc. ✓

The time orientation you develop depends on your socioeconomic class and your personal experiences. Gonzalez and Zimbardo (1985), who developed this scale and upon whose research these findings are based, observe: "A child with parents in unskilled and semiskilled occupations is usually socialized in a way that promotes a present-oriented fatalism and hedonism. A child of parents who are managers, teachers, or other professionals learns future-oriented values and strategies designed to promote achievement." Not surprisingly, in the United States future income is positively related to future orientation; the more future-oriented you are, the greater your income is likely to be.

Different time perspectives also account for much intercultural misunderstanding since different cultures often teach their members drastically different time orientations. For example, members from some Latin cultures would rather be late for an appointment than end a conversation abruptly or before it has come to a natural end. So, the Latin sees this behavior as politeness. But, others may see this as impolite to the person with whom he or she had the appointment (Hall & Hall 1987).

Smell Communication

Smell communication, or **olfactics**, is extremely important in a wide variety of situations and is now "big business" (Kleinfeld 1992). There's some evidence (though clearly not very conclusive evidence), for example, that the smell of lemon contributes to a perception of heath, the smell of lavender and eucalyptus increase alertness, and the smell of rose oil reduces blood pressure. Findings such as these have contributed to the growth of aromatherapy and to a new profession of aromatherapists (Furlow 1996). Because humans possess "denser skin concentrations of scent glands than almost any other mammal" it's been argued that it only remains for us to discover how we use scent to communicate a wide variety of messages (Furlow 1996, p. 41). Here are some of the most important messages scent seems to communicate.

- **Attraction messages**. Humans use perfumes, colognes, after-shave lotions, powders, and the like to enhance their attractiveness to others and to themselves. After all, you also smell yourself. When the smells are pleasant, you feel better about yourself.
- **Taste messages**. Without smell, taste would be severely impaired. For example, it would be extremely difficult to taste the difference between a raw potato and an apple without smell. Street vendors selling hot dogs, sausages, and similar foods are aided greatly by the smells that stimulate the appetites of passersby.
- **Memory messages**. Smell is a powerful memory aid; you can often recall situations from months and even years ago when you happen upon a similar smell.
- **Identification messages**. Smell is often used to create an image or an identity for a product. Advertisers and manufacturers spend millions of dollars each year creating scents for cleaning products and toothpastes, for example, which have nothing to do with their cleaning power. There's also evidence that we can identify specific significant others by smell. For example, young children were able to identify the t-shirts of their brothers and sisters solely on the basis of smell (Porter & Moore 1981).

CULTURE AND NONVERBAL COMMUNICATION

Not surprisingly, nonverbal communication is heavily influenced by culture. Consider a variety of differences. At the sight of unpleasant pictures, members of some cultures (American and European, for example) will facially express disgust. Members of other

Going Online

Biorhythmic compatibility test Web site

The idea behind biorhythms—often discussed in connection with time communication and supported by lots of anecdotal but no hard evidence—is that your physical, intellectual, and emotional lives follow cycles lasting from 23 to 33 days. At certain points in the cycle, you are at your best; at other points, you are at your worst. This Web site enables you to compute your biorhythm analysis. Can you find evidence in your own experiences to support the existence of biorhythms?

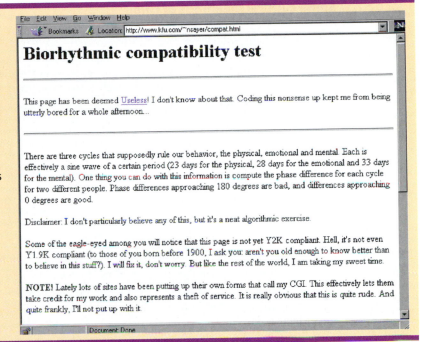

File Edit View Go Window Help

Bookmarks   Location: http://www.kfu.com/~nsayer/compat.html

Biorhythmic compatibility test

This page has been deemed Useless! I don't know about that. Coding this nonsense up kept me from being utterly bored for a whole afternoon...

There are three cycles that supposedly rule our behavior, the physical, emotional and mental. Each is effectively a sine wave of a certain period (23 days for the physical, 28 days for the emotional and 33 days for the mental). One thing you can do with this information is compute the phase difference for each cycle for two different people. Phase differences approaching 180 degrees are bad, and differences approaching 0 degrees are good.

Disclaimer: I don't particularly believe any of this, but it's a neat algorithmic exercise.

Some of the eagle-eyed among you will notice that this page is not yet Y2K compliant. Hell, it's not even Y1.9K compliant (to those of you born before 1900, I ask you: aren't you old enough to know better than to believe in this stuff?). I will fix it, don't worry. But like the rest of the world, I am taking my sweet time.

NOTE! Lately lots of sites have been putting up their own forms that call my CGI. This effectively lets them take credit for my work and also represents a theft of service. It is really obvious that this is quite rude. And quite frankly, I'll not put up with it.

Document Done

---

cultures (Japanese, for example) will avoid facially expressing disgust (Ekman 1985;Matsumoto 1991).

Although Americans consider direct eye contact an expression of honesty and forthrightness, the Japanese often view this as a lack of respect. The Japanese will glance at the other person's face rarely and then only for very short periods (Axtell 1990a). Among some Latin Americans and Native Americans, direct eye contact between, say, a teacher and a student is considered inappropriate, perhaps aggressive; appropriate student behavior is to avoid eye contact with the teacher. Folding your arms over your chest is considered disrespectful in Fiji, pointing with the index finger is considered impolite in many Middle-Eastern countries, and waving your hand can be considered insulting in Greece and Nigeria (Axtell 1993).

In the United States living next door to someone means that you're expected to be friendly and to interact with that person. It seems so natural that Americans and members of many other cultures probably don't even consider that this cultural expectation is not shared by all cultures. In Japan, the fact that your house is next to another's does not imply that you should become close or visit each other. Consider, therefore, the situation in which a Japanese buys a house next to an American. The Japanese may see the American as overly familiar and as taking friendship for granted. The American may see the Japanese as distant, unfriendly, and unneighborly. Yet, each person is merely fulfilling the expectations of his or her own culture (Hall & Hall 1987).

Different cultures also assign different meanings to colors. Some of these cultural differences are illustrated in Table 8.2, but before looking at the table think about the meanings your own culture(s) gives to such colors as red, green, black, white, blue, yellow, and purple.

Touching varies greatly from one culture to another. For example, African Americans touch each other more than do whites. Similarly, touching declines from kindergarten to the sixth grade for white but not for African American children (Burgoon, Buller, & Woodall 1996). Similarly, Japanese touch each other much less than do Anglo-Saxons who in turn touch each other much less than do southern Europeans (Morris 1977; Burgoon, Buller, & Woodall 1996).

Students from the United States reported being touched twice as much as did students from Japan (Barnlund 1975). In Japan there's a strong taboo against touching between strangers. The Japanese are therefore especially careful to maintain sufficient distance.

Another obvious cross-cultural contrast is presented by the Middle East, where same-sex touching in public is extremely common. Middle Easterners, Latin Americans, and southern Europeans touch each

TABLE 8.2   Some cultural meanings of color

This table, constructed from the research reported by Henry Dreyfuss (1971), Nancy Hoft (1995), and Norine Dresser (1996), illustrates only some of the different meanings that colors may communicate and especially how they're viewed in different cultures. Before looking at this accompanying table, jot down on a separate piece of paper the meanings your own culture(s) gives to colors such as red, green, black, white, blue, yellow, and purple.

Color	Cultural Meanings and Comments
Red	In China, red signifies prosperity and rebirth, and is used for festive and joyous occasions; in France and the United Kingdom, masculinity; in many African countries blasphemy, or death; and in Japan, it signifies anger and danger. Red ink, especially among Korean Buddhists, is used only to write a person's name at the time of death or on the anniversary of the person's death, and creates lots of problems when American teachers use red ink to mark homework.
Green	In the United States, green signifies capitalism, go ahead, and envy; in Ireland, patriotism; among some Native Americans, femininity; to the Egyptians, fertility and strength; and to the Japanese, youth and energy.
Black	In Thailand, black signifies old age; in parts of Malaysia, courage; and in much of Europe, death.
White	In Thailand, white signifies purity; in many Muslim and Hindu cultures, purity and peace; and in Japan and other Asian countries, death and mourning.
Blue	In Iran, blue signifies something negative; in Egypt, virtue and truth; in Ghana, joy; and among the Cherokee, defeat.
Yellow	In China, yellow signifies wealth and authority; in the United States, caution and cowardice; in Egypt, happiness and prosperity; and in many countries throughout the world, femininity.
Purple	In Latin America, purple signifies death; in Europe, royalty; in Egypt, virtue and faith; in Japan, grace and nobility; and in China, barbarism.

other while talking a great deal more than do people from "noncontact cultures," Asia and northern Europe, for example. Even such seemingly minor nonverbal differences as these can create difficulties when members of different cultures interact. Southern Europeans may perceive northern Europeans and Japanese as cold, distant, and uninvolved. Southern Europeans in turn may be perceived as pushy, aggressive, and inappropriately intimate.

In the study of touch avoidance discussed earlier, women said that they avoid touching opposite sex members more than do men. This male–female difference, however, is contrary to that found by Jones (1985) who reports that women initiate more opposite-sex touching than do men (especially more opposite-sex touching designed to control). Women also report feeling less positive about opposite-sex touching than do men (Guerrero & Andersen 1994).

Opposite-sex friends touch more than do same-sex friends. Both male and female college students report that they touch and are touched more by their opposite-sex friends than by their same-sex friends. The strong societal bias against same-sex touching

may have influenced these self-reports; people may have reported as they did in order to conform to what is culturally accepted and expected.

Not surprisingly, the role of silence is seen differently in different cultures (Basso 1972). Among the Apache, for example, mutual friends don't feel the need to introduce strangers who may be working in the same area or on the same project. The strangers may remain silent for several days. During this time they're looking each other over, trying to determine if the other person is all right. Only after this period do the individuals talk. When courting, especially during the initial stages, the Apache remain silent for hours; if they do talk, they generally talk very little. Only after a couple have been dating for several months will they have lengthy conversations. These periods of silence are generally attributed to shyness or self-consciousness.

The use of silence is explicitly taught to Apache women, who are especially discouraged from engaging in long discussions with their dates. Silence during courtship is a sign of modesty to many Apache.

In Iranian culture there's an expression, *qahr*, which means to not be on speaking terms with

Here are a few findings from research on nonverbal sex differences (Burgoon, Buller, & Woodall 1995; Eakins & Eakins 1978; Pearson, West, & Turner 1995; Arliss 1991; Shannon 1987): (1) Women smile more than men. (2) Women stand closer to each other than do men and are generally approached more closely than men. (3) Both men and women, when speaking, look at men more than at women. (4) Women both touch and are touched more than men. (5) Men extend their bodies, taking up greater areas of space, than women. What problems might these differences create when men and women try to communicate with each other?

someone, to give someone the "silent treatment." For example, when children disobey their parents, are disrespectful, or fail to do their chores as they should, they're given this silent treatment. With adults *qahr* may be instituted when one person insults or injures another. After a cooling-off period, *ashti* (making up after *qahr*) may be initiated. *Qahr* lasts for a relatively short time between parents and children, but longer when between adults. *Qahr* is more frequently initiated between two women than between two men, but when men experience *qahr* it lasts much longer and often requires the intercession of a mediator to establish *ashti* (Behzadi 1994).

An interesting cultural difference in time orientation is that between **monochronic** and **polychronic time** (Hall 1959, 1976, 1987). Monochronic people or cultures (the United States, Germany, Scandinavia, and Switzerland are good examples) schedule one thing at a time. Time is compartmentalized; there's a time for everything, and everything has its own time. Polychronic people or cultures (Latin Americans, Mediterranean people, and Arabs are good examples), on the other hand, schedule a number of things at the same time. Eating, conducting business with several different people, and taking care of family matters may all be conducted at the same time. No culture is entirely monochronic or polychronic; rather these are general tendencies that are found across a large part of the culture. Some cultures combine both time orientations; Japanese and parts of American culture are examples where both orientations are found.

SUMMARY

In this unit we explored nonverbal communication—communication without words—and considered such areas as body movements, facial and eye movements, spatial and territorial communication, artifactual communication, touch communication, paralanguage, silence, and time communication.

1. The five body movements are emblems (nonverbal behaviors that directly translate words or phrases), illustrators (nonverbal behaviors that accompany and literally "illustrate" the verbal messages), affect displays (nonverbal movements that communicate emotional meaning), regulators (nonverbal movements that coordinate, monitor, maintain, or control the speaking of another individual), and adaptors (nonverbal behaviors emitted without conscious awareness and that usually serve some kind of need, as in scratching an itch).

2. Facial movements may communicate a variety of emotions. The most frequently studied are happiness, surprise, fear, anger, sadness, disgust, and contempt. Facial management techniques enable you to control revealing the emotions you feel.

3. The facial feedback hypothesis claims that facial display of an emotion can lead to physiological and psychological changes.

4. Eye contact may seek feedback, inform others to speak, signal the nature of a relationship, and compensate for increased physical distance. Eye avoidance may help you avoid prying or signal a lack of interest.

5. Pupil size shows one's interest and level of emotional arousal. Pupils enlarge when one is interested in something or is emotionally aroused in a positive way.

6. Proxemics refers to the communicative function of space and spatial relationships. Four major proxemic distances are: (1) intimate distance ranging from actual touching to 18 inches; (2) personal distance, ranging from 18 inches to 4 feet; (3) social distance, ranging from 4 to 12 feet; and (4) public distance, ranging from 12 to more than 25 feet.

7. Your treatment of space is influenced by such factors as status, culture, context, subject matter, sex, age, and positive or negative evaluation of the other person.

8. Territoriality refers to your possessive reaction to an area of space or to particular objects.

9. Artifactual communication refers to messages that are human-made, for example, the use of color, clothing and body adornment, and space decoration.

10. Touch communication (or haptics) may communicate a variety of meanings, the most important being positive affect, playfulness, control, ritual, and task-relatedness.

Touch avoidance refers to our desire to avoid touching and being touched by others.

11. Paralanguage refers to the vocal but nonverbal dimension of speech. It includes rate, pitch, volume, resonance, and vocal quality as well as pauses and hesitations. Based on paralanguage, we make judgments about people, conversational turns, and believability.

12. Silence communicates a variety of meanings, from hurting another with the "silent treatment" to communicating deep emotional responses.

13. Time communication (chronemics) refers to the messages communicated by our treatment of time.

14. Smell can communicate messages of attraction, taste, memory, and identification.

15. Cultural variations in nonverbal communication are great. Different cultures, for example, assign different meanings to facial expressions and to colors, have different spatial rules, and treat time very differently.

KEY TERMS

emblems (p. 130)

illustrators (p. 131)

affect displays (p. 131)

regulators (p. 131)

adaptors (p. 131)

facial management techniques (p. 132)

civil inattention (p. 133)

pupil dilation (p. 134)

proxemics (p. 134)

territoriality (p. 136)

artifactual communication (p. 137)

haptics (p. 140)

paralanguage (p. 142)

chronemics (p. 144)

social clock (p. 145)

THINKING CRITICALLY ABOUT
Nonverbal Messages

1. Status is also signaled by the unwritten law granting the right of invasion. Higher-status individuals have more of a right to invade the territory of others than vice versa. The boss of a large company, for example, can invade the territory of a junior executive by barging into her or his office, but the reverse would be unthinkable. Do you observe this "right" of territorial invasion?

2. A popular defense tactic in sex crimes against women, gay men, and lesbians is to blame the victim by referring to the way the victim was dressed and to imply that the victim, by virtue of the clothing worn, provoked the attack. Currently, New York and Florida are the only states that prohibit defense attorneys from referring to the way a sex-crime victim was dressed at the time of the attack (*New York Times*, July 30, 1994, p. 22). What do you think of this? If you don't live in New York or Florida, have there been proposals in your state to similarly limit this popular defense tactic?

3. Visit one of the Web sites of a large multinational corporation. Most corporations have Web addresses like this: www.CompanyName.com. What can you learn about nonverbal communication from such elements as the general design, colors, movement, fonts, or spacing used? Can you point out any way that the Web site can be visually improved?

4. Test your ability to identify these emotions on the basis of verbal descriptions. Try to "hear" the following voices and to identify the emotions being communicated. Do you hear affection, anger, boredom, or joy (Davitz, 1964)?
   • This voice is soft, with a low pitch, a resonant quality, a slow rate, and a steady and slightly upward inflection. The rhythm is regular, and the enunciation is slurred.
   • This voice is loud, with a high pitch, a moderately blaring quality, a fast rate, an upward inflection, and a regular rhythm.

- This voice is loud, with a high pitch, a blaring quality, a fast rate, and an irregular up-and-down inflection. The rhythm is irregular, and the enunciation is clipped.
- This voice is moderate to low in volume, with a moderate-to-low pitch, a moderately resonant quality, a moderately slow rate, and a monotonous or gradually falling inflection. The enunciation is somewhat slurred.

5. What nonverbal cues should you look for in judging whether someone likes you? List them in the order of their importance, using 1 for the cue that is of most value in making your judgment, 2 for the cue that is next most valuable, and so on down to perhaps 10 or 12. Do you really need two lists? One for judging a woman's liking and one for a man's?

6. How would you go about seeking answers to questions such as these:
   - Do higher-status people touch each other with the same frequency as do lower-status people?
   - Do children who were born blind express emotions with the same facial expressions that sighted children use?
   - Do men and women differ in the way they view time?
   - What is the ideal outfit for a college instructor to wear on the first day of class?
   - Do family photos on an executive's desk contribute to the executive's credibility? Is the relationship between photos and credibility the same for men and women?

UNIT 9

Interpersonal Communication: Conversation

UNIT GOALS

Upon completion of this unit, you should be able to

explain the five-step model of conversation

explain the processes and skills involved in managing conversations

explain the nature and functions of the disclaimer and the excuse

This unit and the next two introduce the first area of communication to be considered in this text—interpersonal communication and relationships. This unit looks at conversation; Unit 10, at interpersonal relationships; and Unit 11, at interpersonal conflict. This unit examines the conversational process—what it is, how you manage a conversation, and how you can be more effective in your own conversations.

CONVERSATION

In this first section we look at the nature of conversation, define what it is, and explain the stages you go through in talking with another person. Second, we look at the nature of conversational turns, the ways the speaker's role is passed from one person to another. Third, we reflect on the model of conversation and suggest some ways to use it to better understand conversation (cf. Hecht 1978a, b).

The Conversation Process in Five Stages

Figure 9.1 provides a model of the process of conversation and divides the process into five main stages: opening, feedforward, business, feedback, and closing. Examining each stage in turn will give us a convenient overview of what goes on when two people talk.

The Opening

The first step is to open the conversation, usually with some kind of greeting: "Hi," "How are you?" "Hello, this is Joe." Greetings can be verbal or nonverbal and are usually both (Krivonos & Knapp 1975; Knapp and Vangelisti 1992). Verbal greetings include, for example, verbal salutes ("Hi," "Hello"), initiation of the topic ("The reason I called . . . "), making reference to the other ("Hey, Joe, what's up?"), and personal inquiries ("What's new?" "How are you doing?"). Nonverbal greetings include waving, smiling, shaking hands, and winking. Usually, you greet another person both verbally and nonverbally: You smile when you say "Hello."

In normal conversation, your greeting is reciprocated with a greeting from the other person that is similar in degree of formality or informality and in intensity. When it isn't—when the other person turns away or responds coldly to your friendly "good morning"—you know that something is wrong. Openings are also generally consistent in tone with the main part of the conversation; a cheery "How ya doing today, big guy?" is not normally followed by news of a family death.

In opening a conversation, consider two general principles. First, be positive. Lead off with something positive rather than something negative. Say, for example, "I really enjoy coming here" instead of "Don't you just hate this place?" Second, don't be too revealing; don't self-disclose too early in an interaction. If you do, you risk making the other person feel uncomfortable. An interesting perspective on opening lines is provided in the Understanding Theory and Research box "What's Your Line?" (p. 156).

Feedforward

At the second step, there's usually some kind of feedforward. Here you give the other person a general idea of what the conversation will focus on: "I've got

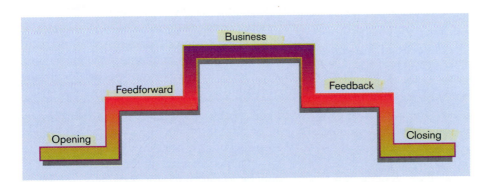

Figure 9.1   **The Process of Conversation.**   As with the model of interpersonal relationships, this model of the stages of conversation is best seen as a way of talking about conversation and not as the unvarying stages all conversations follow. How accurately do you think this model reflects the normal progression of a conversation?

Greetings serve different functions (Knapp & Vangelisti 1992; Krivonos & Knapp 1975). For example, greetings may signal a stage of access, opening up the channels of communication for more meaningful interaction. Greetings may also reveal important information about the relationship; for example, a big smile and a warm "Hi, it's been a long time" signals that the relationship is still a friendly one. Greetings may also help maintain the relationship. When workers in an office greet each other as they pass through the office, it assures them that even though they don't stop and talk for an extended period, they still have access to each other. What functions did your last three greetings serve?

to tell you about Jack," "Did you hear what happened in class yesterday?" or "We need to talk about our vacation plans." Feedforward may also identify the tone of the conversation ("I'm really depressed and need to talk with you") or the time required ("This will just take a minute") (Frentz 1976; Reardon 1987) or it may preface the conversation to ensure that your message will be understood and will not reflect negatively on you (see Unit 1).

Business

The third step is the "business," the substance or focus of the conversation. "Business" is a good term to use for this stage because it emphasizes that most conversations are goal-directed. You converse to fulfill one or several of the general purposes of interpersonal communication: to learn, relate, influence, play, or help (Unit 1). The term is also sufficiently general to incorporate all kinds of interactions.

The business is conducted through an exchange of speaker and listener roles. Usually, brief (rather than long) speaking turns characterize most satisfying conversations. Here you talk about Jack, what happened in class, or your vacation plans. This is obviously the longest part of the conversation and the reason for both the opening and the feedforward.

Feedback

The fourth step is the reverse of the second. Here you reflect back on the conversation to signal that as far as you're concerned, the business is completed: "So, you may want to send Jack a get well card," "Wasn't that the craziest class you ever heard of?" or "I'll call for reservations while you shop for what we need" (see Unit 1).

Of course, the other person may not agree that the business is completed and may therefore counter with, for example, "But what hospital is he in?" When this happens, you normally go back a step and continue the business.

Closing

The fifth and last step, the opposite of the first step, is the closing, the good-bye (Knapp, Hart, Friedrich, & Shulman 1973; Knapp & Vangelisti 1992). Like the opening, the closing may be verbal or nonverbal but is usually a combination of both verbal and nonverbal. Most obviously, the closing signals the end of accessibility. Just as the opening signaled access, the closing signals the end of access. The closing usually also signals some degree of supportiveness, for example, you express your pleasure in interacting: "Well, it was good talking with you." The closing may also summarize the interaction.

Closing a conversation is almost as difficult as opening a conversation. It's frequently an awkward and uncomfortable part of interpersonal interaction. Here are a few ways you might consider for closing a conversation.

- Reflect back on the conversation and briefly summarize it so as to bring it to a close. For example, "I'm glad I ran into you and found out what happened at that union meeting. I'll probably be seeing you at the meetings."
- State the desire to end the conversation directly and to get on with other things. For example, "I'd like to continue talking but I really have to run. I'll see you around."

UNDERSTANDING
Theory and Research

HOW DOES INTERPERSONAL COMMUNICATION DEVELOP?

In the developmental approach, interpersonal communication is seen as the end of a progression from impersonal communication at one extreme to highly personal or intimate communication at the other end. This progression signals or defines the development of interpersonal communication. According to communicologist Gerald Miller's (1978) analysis, interpersonal communication is characterized by and distinguished from impersonal communication on the basis of at least three factors: psychologically based predictions, explanatory knowledge, and personally established rules.

In impersonal encounters you respond to another person on the basis of sociological data—the classes or groups to which the person belongs. For example, you respond to a particular college professor the way you respond to college professors in general. Similarly, the college professor responds to a particular student in the way professors respond to students generally. As the relationship becomes more personal, however, both the professor and the student begin to respond to each other not as members of their groups but as individuals. You respond to another person on the basis of **psychological data**, on the ways this person differs from the members of his or her group.

In interpersonal interactions you base your communications on **explanatory knowledge** of each other. When you know a particular person, you can predict how that person will act in a variety of situations. As you get to know that person better, however, you can predict not only how a person will act but also why the person behaves as he or she does. The college professor may, in an impersonal relationship, know that Pat will be five minutes late to class each Friday. That is, the professor is able to predict Pat's behavior. In an interpersonal situation, however, the professor can also offer explanations for the behavior (giving reasons for Pat's lateness).

Society sets up rules for interaction in impersonal situations. As noted in the previous example of the student and professor, the social rules of interaction set up by the culture lose importance as the relationship becomes more personal. In the place of these social rules, the individuals set up **personal rules**. When individuals establish their own rules for interacting with each other rather than using the rules set down by the society, the situation is interpersonal.

These three factors vary in degree. You respond to another on the basis of psychological data to some degree. You can explain another's behavior to some degree. And you interact on the basis of mutually established rules rather than on socially established norms to some degree. A developmental approach to communication implies a continuum ranging from highly impersonal to highly intimate. "Interpersonal communication" occupies a part of this continuum, though each person might draw its boundaries a bit differently.

- Refer to future interaction. For example, "Why don't we get together next week sometime and continue this discussion?"
- Ask for closure. For example, "Have I explained what you wanted to know?"
- State that you enjoyed the interaction. For example, "I really enjoyed talking with you."

With any of these closings, it should be clear to the other person that you're attempting to end the conversation. Obviously, you'll have to use more direct methods with those who don't take these subtle hints—those who don't realize that both persons are responsible for bringing the conversation to a satisfying close.

UNDERSTANDING
Theory and Research

WHAT'S YOUR LINE?

How do you strike up a conversation? How have people tried to open a conversation with you? In research on this question, Chris Kleinke (1986) found three basic types of opening lines.

Cute-flippant openers are humorous, indirect, and ambiguous as to whether or not the one opening the conversation really wants an extended encounter. Examples include: "Is that really your hair?" "Bet I can outdrink you." "I bet the cherries jubilee isn't as sweet as you are."

Innocuous openers are highly ambiguous as to whether these are simple comments that might be made to just anyone or whether they're in fact openers designed to initiate an extended encounter. Examples include: "What do you think of the band?" "I haven't been here before. What's good on the menu?" "Could you show me how to work this machine?"

Direct openers clearly demonstrate the speaker's interest in meeting the other person. Examples include: "I feel a little embarrassed about this, but I'd like to meet you." "Would you like to have a drink after dinner?" "Since we're both eating alone, would you like to join me?"

According to Kleinke (1986), the most preferred opening lines by both men and women are generally those that are direct or innocuous. The least preferred lines by both men and women are those that are cute-flippant; women, however, dislike these openers more than men. Men generally underestimate how much women dislike the cute-flippant openers and probably continue to use them because they're indirect enough to cushion any rejection. Men also underestimate how much women actually like innocuous openers.

Women prefer men to use openers that are relatively modest and to avoid coming on too strong. Women generally underestimate how much men like direct openers. Most men prefer openers that are very clear in meaning, which may be because men are not used to having a women initiate a meeting. Women also overestimate how much men like innocuous lines.

Do you find support for these conclusions from your own experience?

Maintaining Conversations

The defining feature of conversation is that the roles of speaker and listener are exchanged throughout the interaction. You accomplish this by using a wide variety of verbal and nonverbal cues to signal **conversational turns**—the changing (or maintaining) of the speaker or listener role during the conversation. Combining the insights of a variety of communication researchers (Burgoon, Buller, & Woodall 1995; Duncan 1972; Pearson & Spitzberg 1990), we can look at conversational turns in terms of speaker cues and listener cues.

Speakers regulate the conversation through two major types of cues: turn-maintaining cues and turn-yielding cues. Their effective use not only insures communication efficiency but also increases likability (Place & Becker 1991, Heap 1992). The ways of

using the conversational turns identified here have been derived largely from studies conducted in the United States. Each culture appears to define the types and appropriateness of turns differently (for example, Iizuka 1993). Polychronic people, for example, will often disregard the turn-taking principles used by monochronic people. The effect is that to monochronic people—who carefully follow these rules—polychronic people will often appear rude, as they interrupt and overlap conversations, for example (Lee 1984, Grossin 1987).

Turn-maintaining Cues

These are designed to enable the speaker to maintain the role of speaker and may be communicated in a variety of ways (Burgoon, Buller, & Woodall 1995; Duncan 1972):

- audibly inhaling breath to show that the speaker has more to say
- continuing a gesture or series of gestures to show that the thought is not yet complete
- avoiding eye contact with the listener so there's no indication that the speaker is passing the speaking turn on to the listener
- sustaining the intonation pattern to indicate that more will be said
- vocalizing pauses (*er, umm*) to prevent the listener from speaking and to show that the speaker is still talking

In most cases you expect the speaker to maintain relatively brief speaking turns and to willingly turn over the speaking role to the listener (when so signaled by the listener). Those who don't are likely to be evaluated negatively.

Turn-yielding Cues

These cues tell the listener that the speaker is finished and wishes to exchange the role of speaker for the role of listener. They tell the listener (and sometimes they're addressed to a specific listener rather than to just any listener) to take over the role of speaker. For example, you may at the end of a statement add some paralinguistic cue such as "oh?" which asks one of the listeners to assume the role of speaker. You can also indicate that you've finished speaking by dropping your intonation, by a prolonged silence, by making direct eye contact with a listener, by asking some general question, or by nodding in the direction of a particular listener.

In much the same way that you expect a speaker to yield the role of speaker, you also expect the listener to willingly assume the speaking role. Those who don't may be regarded as reticent or unwilling to involve themselves and take equal responsibility for the conversation. For example, in an analysis of turn-taking violations in the conversations of married couples, the most common violation found was that of no response (DeFrancisco 1991). Forty-five percent of the 540 violations identified involved a lack of response to an invitation to take on the role of speaker. Of these "no response" violations, 68 percent were committed by men and 32 percent by women. Other turn-taking violations include interruptions, delayed responses, and inappropriately brief responses. DeFrancisco argues that with these violations, all of which are committed more frequently by men, men silence women in marital interactions.

As a listener you can regulate the conversation by using three types of cues: turn-requesting cues, turn-denying cues, and backchanneling cues.

Turn-requesting Cues

These cues let the speaker know that you would like to say something, that you would like to take a turn as speaker. Sometimes you can do this by simply saying, "I'd like to say something," but often it's done more subtly through some vocalized *er* or *um* that tells the speaker that you would now like to speak. This request to speak is also often made with facial and mouth gestures. Frequently a listener will indicate a desire to speak by opening his or her eyes and mouth wide as if to say something, by beginning to gesture with a hand, or by leaning forward.

Turn-denying Cues

You would use turn-denying cues to indicate your reluctance to assume the role of speaker, for example, intoning a slurred "I don't know" or by giving some brief grunt that signals you have nothing to say. Often turn denying is accomplished by avoiding eye contact with the speaker who wishes you to now take on the role of speaker, or by engaging in some behavior that is incompatible with speaking—for example, coughing or blowing your nose.

Backchanneling Cues

These are used to communicate various types of information back to the speaker without assuming the role of the speaker. You can send a variety of messages with backchanneling cues (Burgoon, Buller, & Woodall 1995; Pearson & Spitzberg 1990). You can indicate your agreement or disagreement with the speaker through smiles or frowns, gestures of approval or disapproval, brief comments such as "right" or "never," or a vocalization such as *uh-huh*.

You can also indicate your degree of involvement or boredom with the speaker. Attentive posture, forward leaning, and focused eye contact will tell the speaker that you're involved in the conversation just as an inattentive posture, backward leaning, and avoidance of eye contact will communicate your lack of involvement.

Giving the speaker pacing cues helps regulate the speed of speech. You can, for example, ask the speaker to slow down by raising your hand near your ear and leaning forward and to speed up by continuously nodding your head. You can also do this verbally by simply asking the speaker to slow down ("Slow down,

BUILDING
Communication Skills

HOW DO YOU OPEN A CONVERSATION?

Think about how you might open a conversation with the persons described in each of these situations. What general approaches would meet with a favorable response? What general approaches seem frowned on?

1. On the first day of class, you and another student are the first to come into the classroom and are seated in the room alone.
2. You're a guest at a friend's party. You're one of the first guests to arrive and are now there with several other people to whom you've only just been introduced. Your friend, the host, is busy with other matters.
3. You've just started a new job in a large office where you're one of several computer operators. It seems as if most of the other people know each other.
4. You're in the college cafeteria eating alone. You see another student who is also eating alone and who you've seen in your English Literature class. You're not sure if this person has noticed you in class.

I want to make sure I'm getting all this"). Similarly, you can tell the speaker to speed up by saying something like "and . . . " or "go on, go on . . ."

A request for clarification is still another function of backchanneling cues. A puzzled facial expression, perhaps coupled with a forward lean, will probably tell most speakers that you want some clarification. Similarly, you can ask for clarification by interjecting some interrogative: Who? When? Where?

Some of these backchanneling cues are actually interruptions. These interruptions, however, are generally confirming rather than disconfirming. They tell the speaker that you are listening and are involved (Kennedy & Camden 1988).

Figure 9.2 provides an illustration of the various turn-taking cues and how they correspond to the conversational wants of speaker and listener.

Reflections on the Model

Not all conversations will be easily divided into these five steps. Often the opening and the feedforward are combined, as when you see someone on campus and say "Hey, listen to this" or when in a work situation, someone says, "Well, folks, let's get the meeting going." In a similar way, the feedback and the closing might be combined: "Look, I've got to think more about this commitment, okay?"

As already noted, the business is the longest part of the conversation. The opening and the closing are usually about the same length and the feedforward and feedback are usually about equal in length. When these relative lengths are severely distorted, you may feel that something is wrong. For example, when someone uses a long feedforward or a too-short opening, you might suspect that what is to follow is extremely serious.

It's also important to note that effectiveness or competence in conversation and following the appropriate conversational rules will contribute to your own interpersonal attractiveness. For example, in a study of 10-year-old girls, four conversational skills were studied: making an appropriate request, turn taking, responding without excessive delay when spoken to, and following the logic of the conversation. The girls who demonstrated these skills were liked more and were described in more positive terms than those who lacked these conversational skills (Place & Becker 1991).

Of course, each culture will alter these basic steps in different ways. In some cultures, the openings are

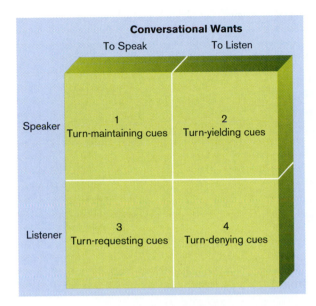

Conversational Wants

	To Speak	To Listen
Speaker	1 Turn-maintaining cues	2 Turn-yielding cues
Listener	3 Turn-requesting cues	4 Turn-denying cues

Figure 9.2   **Turn-taking and conversational wants.**   Quadrant 1 represents the speaker who wants to speak (continue to speak) and uses turn-maintaining cues; Quadrant 2, the speaker who wants to listen and uses turn-yielding cues; Quadrant 3, the listener who wants to speak and uses turn-requesting cues; and Quadrant 4, the listener who wants to listen (continue listening) and uses turn-denying cues. Backchanneling cues would appear in Quadrant 4, since they're cues that listeners use while they continue to listen.

especially short, whereas in others the openings are elaborate, lengthy, and, in some cases, highly ritualized. It's easy in intercultural communication situations to violate another culture's conversational rules. Being overly friendly, too formal, or too forward may easily hinder the remainder of the conversation (Murata 1994).

The reasons such violations may have significant consequences is that you may not be aware of these rules and hence may not see violations as cultural differences but rather as aggressiveness, stuffiness, or pushiness—and almost immediately dislike the person and put a negative cast on the future conversation. Table 9.1 identifies some of the more common conversational problems.

MANAGING CONVERSATION

In developing conversational competence or effectiveness we need to look at interpersonal skills on two levels. On one level there are the skills of effectiveness such as openness and supportiveness.

On another level, however, are skills that guide us in regulating our openness and our supportiveness. They're skills about skills, or **metaskills**. These qualities will provide a good foundation for communicating interpersonally, in small groups, in public speaking, and especially in intercultural communication.

Metaskills

Because each conversation is unique, the qualities of interpersonal competence can't be applied indiscriminately. You need to know how the skills themselves should be applied. You should be mindful, flexible, and culturally sensitive.

Mindfulness

After you've learned a skill or a rule you often apply it without thinking; you apply it "mindlessly," without considering the novel aspects of this unique situation. Instead, conversational skills need to be applied mindfully, a concept that was introduced briefly in Unit 6 (Langer 1989). For example, after learning the skills of active listening, many will respond to all situations with active listening responses. Some of these responses will be appropriate but others will prove inappropriate and ineffective. Before responding, think about the unique communication situation you face and consider your alternatives. Be alert and responsive to small changes in the situation that may cue which behaviors will be effective and which ineffective. Be especially mindful of the cultural differences among people, as outlined in the section "Cultural Sensitivity."

Langer (1989) offers several suggestions for increasing mindfulness that will prove useful in most conversations and, in fact, in most communications generally. As you read through these suggestions, try to provide a specific example or application for each of these suggestions.

- Create and recreate categories. See an object, event, or person as belonging to a wide variety of categories. Avoid storing in memory an image of a person, for example, with only one specific label; it will be difficult to recategorize it later.
- Be open to new information even if it contradicts your most firmly held stereotypes.
- Be open to different points of view. This will help you avoid the tendency to blame outside forces for your negative behaviors ("that test

TABLE 9.1 Conversational rule violations

What other rule violations can you identify?

- Using openings that are insensitive, for example, "Wow, you've gained a few pounds!"
- Using overly long feedforwards that make you wonder if the other person will ever get to the business
- Omitting feedforward before a truly shocking message (for example, the death or illness of a friend or relative), which leads one to see the other person as insensitive or uncaring
- Doing business without the normally expected greeting, as when you go to a doctor who begins the conversation by saying, "Well, what's wrong?"
- Omitting feedback, which leads you to wonder if the other person heard what you said or cared about it
- Omitting an appropriate closing, which makes one wonder if the other person is disturbed or angry

was unfair") and internal forces for the negative behaviors of others ("Pat didn't study," "Pat isn't very bright"). Be willing to see your own and others' behaviors from a variety of perspectives.

- Beware of relying too heavily on first impressions, what psychologists call "premature cognitive commitment" (Chanowitz & Langer 1981; Langer 1989). Treat your first impressions as tentative, as hypotheses.

Flexibility

Flexibility can be best explained by examining specific communication situations and thinking about the way you would act in each. The following self-test, "How Flexible Are You in Communication?" will help you with this introspection.

✔ SELF-TEST

How Flexible Are You in Communication?

Here are some situations that illustrate how people sometimes act when communicating with others. The first part of each situation asks you to imagine that you are in the situation. Then, a course of action is identified and you are asked to determine how much your own behavior would be like the action described in the scenario. If it is *exactly* like you, mark a 5; if it is *a lot* like you, mark a 4; if it is *somewhat* like you, mark a 3; if it is *not much* like you, mark a 2; and if it is *not at all* like you, mark a 1.

Imagine

_____ 1. Last week, as you were discussing your strained finances with your family, family members came up with several possible solutions. Even though you already decided on one solution, you decided to spend more time considering all the possibilities before making a final decision.

_____ 2. You were invited to a Halloween party, and assuming it was a costume party, you dressed as a pumpkin. When you arrived at the party and found everyone else dressed in formal attire, you laughed and joked about the misunderstanding, and decided to stay and enjoy the party.

_____ 3. You have always enjoyed being with your friend Chris, but do not enjoy Chris's habit of always interrupting you. The last time you met, every time Chris interrupted you, you then interrupted Chris to teach Chris a lesson.

_____ 4. Your daily schedule is very structured and your calendar is full of appointments and commitments. When asked to make a change in your schedule, you replied that changes are impossible before even considering the change.

_____ 5. You went to a party where over 50 people attended. You had a good

BUILDING
Communication Skills

HOW DO YOU CLOSE A CONVERSATION?

How might you bring each of the following conversations to an end? What types of closings seem most effective? Which seem least effective?

- You and a friend have been talking on the phone for the last hour but not much new is being said. You have a great deal of work to get to and would like to close the conversation. Your friend just doesn't seem to hear your subtle cues.
- You're at a party and are anxious to meet a person with whom you've exchanged eye contact for the last 10 minutes. The problem is that a friendly and talkative former teacher of yours is demanding all your attention. You don't want to insult the instructor but at the same time you want to make contact with this other person.
- You've had a conference with a teacher and have learned what you needed to know. This teacher, however, doesn't seem to know how to end the conversation, seems very ill at ease, and just continues to go over what has already been said. You have to get to your next class and must close the conversation.
- You're at a party and notice a person you would like to get to know. You initiate the conversation but after a few minutes realize that this person is not the kind of person with whom you would care to spend any more time. You want to close this conversation as soon as possible.

time, but spent most of the evening talking to one close friend rather than meeting new people.

_____ 6. When discussing a personal problem with a group of friends, you noticed that many different solutions were offered. Although several of the solutions seemed feasible, you already had your opinion and did not listen to any of the alternative solutions.

_____ 7. You and a friend planned a fun evening and you were dressed and ready ahead of time. You found that you are unable to do anything else until your friend arrived.

_____ 8. When you found your seat at the ball game, you realized you did not know anyone sitting nearby. However, you introduced yourself to the people sitting next to you and attempted to strike up a conversation.

_____ 9. You had lunch with your friend Chris, and Chris told you about a too-personal family problem. You quickly finished your lunch and stated that you had to leave because you had a lot to do that afternoon.

_____ 10. You were involved in a discussion about international politics with a group of acquaintances and you assumed that the members of the group were as knowledgeable as you on the topic; but, as the discussion progressed, you learned that most of the group knew little about the subject. Instead of explaining your point of view, you decided to withdraw from the discussion.

_____ 11. You and a group of friends got into a discussion about gun control and, after a while, it became obvious that your opinions differed greatly from the rest of the group. You explained your position once again, but you agreed to respect the group's opinion also.

_____ 12. You were asked to speak to a group you belong to, so you worked hard preparing a 30-minute presentation; but at the meeting, the organizer asked you to lead a question-and-answer session instead of giving your presentation. You agreed, and answered the group's questions as candidly and fully as possible.

_____ 13. You were offered a managerial position where every day you would face new tasks and challenges and a changing day-to-day routine. You decided to accept this position instead of one that has a stable daily routine.

_____ 14. You were asked to give a speech at a Chamber of Commerce breakfast. Because you did not know anyone at the breakfast and would feel uncomfortable not knowing anyone in the audience, you declined the invitation.

To compute your score:

1. Reverse the scoring for items 4, 5, 6, 7, 9, 10, and 14. That is, for each of these questions, substitute as follows:

   a. If you answered 5, reverse it to 1
   b. If you answered 4, reverse it to 2
   c. If you answered 3, keep it as 3
   d. If you answered 2, reverse it to 4
   e. If you answered 1, reverse it to 5

2. Add the scores for all 14 items. Be sure that you use the reversed scores for items 4, 5, 6, 7, 9, 10, and 14 instead of your original responses. Use your original scores for items 1, 2, 3, 8, 11, 12, and 13.

In general, you can interpret your score as follows:

- 65–70 = much more flexible than average
- 57–64 = more flexible than average
- 44–56 = about average
- 37–43 = less flexible than average
- 14–36 = much less flexible than average

Do you agree with the assumption made that flexibility is an essential ingredient in communication competence? Are you satisfied with your level of flexibility? What might you do to cultivate flexibility in general and communication flexibility in particular?

From "Development of a Communication Flexibility Measure" by Matthew M. Martin and Rebecca B. Rubin, *The Southern Communication Journal* 59 (Winter 1994) pp. 171–178.

From "How Flexible Are You in Communication?" from "Communication Flexibility Scale" by Matthew Martin and Rebecca Rubin in *The Southern Communication Journal*, 59, Winter 1994 pp. 171–178. Reprinted by permission of the Southern States Communication Association.

Keep in mind this concept of flexibility as you examine the general principles for conversational effectiveness presented next. For example, you may need to be frank and spontaneous when talking with a close friend about your feelings, but you may not want to be so open when talking with your grandmother about the dinner she prepared that you disliked.

Cultural Sensitivity

In applying the skills for interpersonal effectiveness, be sensitive to the cultural differences among people (Unit 6, Guo-Ming & Starosta 1995). What may prove effective for upper-income people working in the IBM subculture of Boston or New York may prove ineffective for lower-income people working as fruit pickers in Florida or California. What works in Germany may not work in Mexico. The direct eye contact that signals immediacy in most of the United States may be considered rude or too intrusive in other cultures. The specific skills discussed in the next section are considered to be generally effective in the United States and among most people living in the United States; but do be aware that these skills and the ways you communicate them may not apply to other cultures (Kim 1991).

Effectiveness in intercultural settings, according to Kim, requires that you be

- open to new ideas and to differences among people
- flexible in ways of communicating and in adapting to the communications of the culturally different
- tolerant of other attitudes, values, and ways of doing things
- creative in seeking varied ways to communicate

From another perspective, the successful sojourner—one who enters another culture for a rela-

Going Online

The Exchange Web site

The Exchange is a Web site set up by the Longman publishing company to complement this textbook's coverage of interpersonal communication. Review the interpersonal scenarios. What insights into interpersonal communication do these scenarios provide?

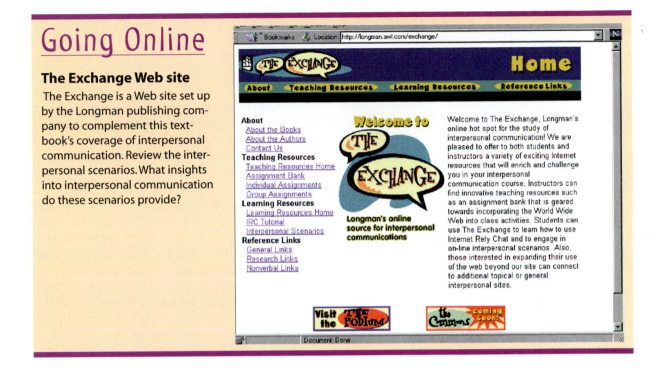

tively short period of time, such as a traveler or one who spends a year or so working in this other culture—is one who is self-confident, interested in others, open, flexible, and competent professionally (Kealy & Ruben 1983; Berry, Poortinga, Segall, & Dasen 1992).

In another study, persons were more likely to be competent in intercultural communication when they had a high positive self-concept and when they were appropriate self-disclosers, high self-monitors, behaviorally flexible, highly involving (attentive and responsive, for example), adaptable, and culturally aware (Chen 1990).

These qualities—along with some knowledge of the other culture and the general skills of effectiveness—"should enable a person to approach each intercultural encounter with the psychological posture of an interested learner . . . and to strive for the communication outcomes that are as effective as possible under a given set of relational and situational constraints" (Kim 1991).

Skills in Conversational Competence

The skills of conversational competence discussed here are (1) openness, (2) empathy, (3) positiveness, (4) immediacy, (5) interaction management, (6) expressiveness, and (7) other-orientation (Bochner &

Kelly 1974; Bochner & Yerby 1977; Spitzberg & Hecht 1984; Spitzberg & Cupach 1984). As you read the discussions of these concepts, keep in mind that the most effective communicator is one who is flexible and who adapts to the individual situation. To be always open or empathic, for example, will probably prove ineffective. Although these qualities are generally appropriate to most interpersonal interactions, do remember that the ability to control these qualities—rather than exhibiting them reflexively—should be your aim.

These qualities would not be effective in all cultures, nor would the specific verbal and nonverbal behaviors carry the same meanings in all cultures. For example, assertiveness is evaluated differently by African Americans and Hispanics (Rodriguez 1988). Similarly, whites, African Americans, and Hispanics define what is satisfying communication in different ways. What follows then are general suggestions that should prove useful most of the time. Always go to the specific culture for specific recommendations.

Openness

Openness refers to three aspects of interpersonal communication. First, you should be willing to self-disclose—to reveal information about yourself. Of course, these disclosures need to be appropriate to the entire communication act (see Unit 3). There must also be an openness in regard to listening to the other person; you should be open to the thoughts and feelings of the person with whom you're communicating.

A second aspect of openness refers to your willingness to listen and react honestly to the messages and situations that confront you. You demonstrate openness by responding spontaneously and honestly to the communications and the feedback of others.

Third, openness calls for the "owning" of feelings and thoughts. To be open in this sense is to acknowledge that the feelings and thoughts you express are yours and that you bear the responsibility for them; you don't try to shift the responsibility for your feelings to others. For example, consider these comments:

1. Your behavior was grossly inconsiderate.
2. Everyone thought your behavior was grossly inconsiderate.
3. I was really disturbed when you told my father he was an old man.

Comments 1 and 2 don't evidence ownership of feelings. In 1, the speaker accuses the listener of being inconsiderate without assuming any of the responsibility for the judgment. In 2, the speaker assigns responsibility to the convenient but elusive "everyone" and again assumes none of the responsibility. In comment 3, however, a drastic difference appears. Note that here the speaker is taking responsibility for his or her own feelings ("I was really disturbed").

When you own your own messages you use I-messages instead of you-messages. Instead of saying, "You make me feel so stupid when you ask what everyone else thinks but don't ask my opinion," the person who owns his or her feelings says "I feel stupid when you ask everyone else what they think but don't ask me." When you own your feelings and thoughts, when you use I-messages, you say in effect, "This is how I feel," "This is how I see the situation," "This is what I think," with the "I" always paramount. Instead of saying, "This discussion is useless," one would say, "I'm bored by this discussion," or "I want to talk more about myself," or any other such statement that includes a reference to the fact that "I" am making an evaluation and not describing objective reality. By doing so, you make it explicit that your feelings are the result of the interaction between what is going on in the world out-

side your skin (what others say, for example) and what is going on inside your skin (your preconceptions, attitudes, and prejudices, for example).

Empathy

When you empathize with someone, you're able to experience what the other is experiencing from that person's point of view. Empathy does not mean that you agree with what the other person says or does. You never lose your own identity or your own attitudes and beliefs. To sympathize, on the other hand, is to feel for the individual—to feel sorry for the person. To empathize is to feel the same feelings in the same way as the other person does. **Empathy**, then, enables you to understand, emotionally and intellectually, what another person is experiencing.

Most people find it easier to communicate empathy in response to a person's positive statements (Heiskell & Rychiak 1986). Similarly, empathy will be more difficult to achieve with persons who are culturally different from you than for persons who are culturally similar. So perhaps you'll have to exert special effort to communicate empathy for negative statements and in intercultural situations.

Of course, empathy will mean little if you're not able to communicate this empathic understanding back to the other person. Here are a few suggestions for communicating empathy both verbally and nonverbally:

- Confront mixed messages. Confront messages that seem to be communicating conflicting feelings to show you're trying to understand the other person's feelings. For example, "You say that it doesn't bother you but I seem to hear a lot of anger coming through."
- Avoid judgmental and evaluative (nonempathic) responses. Avoid should- and ought-statements that try to tell the other person how he or she should feel. For example, avoid expressions such as "Don't feel so bad," "Cheer up," "In time you'll forget all about this," and "You should start looking for another job; by next month you won't even remember this place."
- Use reinforcing comments. Let the speaker know that you understand what the speaker is saying and encourage the speaker to continue talking about this issue. For example, use comments such as "I see," "I get it," "I understand," "Yes," and "Right."

- Demonstrate interest by maintaining eye contact (avoid scanning the room or focusing on objects or persons other than the person with whom you're interacting), maintaining physical closeness, leaning toward (not away from) the other person, and showing your interest and agreement with your facial expressions, nods, and eye movements.

Although empathy is almost universally considered positive, there's some evidence to show that even it has a negative side. For example, people are most empathic with those who are similar—racially and ethnically as well as in appearance and social status. The more empathy one feels towards one's own group, the less empathy—possibly even hostility—one feels toward other groups. The same empathy that increases your understanding of your own group decreases your understanding of other groups. So, while empathy may encourage group cohesiveness and identification, it can also create dividing lines between one's own group and "them" (Angier 1995).

Positiveness

You can communicate **positiveness** in interpersonal communication in at least two ways. First, you can state positive attitudes. Second, you can "stroke" the person with whom you interact.

People who feel negative about themselves invariably communicate these feelings to others, who in turn probably develop similar negative feelings. On the other hand, people who feel positive about themselves convey this feeling to others, who then return the positive regard.

Positiveness in attitudes also refers to a positive feeling for the general communication situation. A negative response to a communication makes you feel almost as if you're intruding, and communication is sure to break down.

Positiveness is most clearly evident in the way you phrase statements. Consider these two sentences:

1. You look horrible in stripes.
2. You look your best, I think, in solid colors.

The first sentence is critical and will almost surely encourage an argument. The second sentence, on the other hand, expresses the speaker's thought clearly and positively and should encourage responses that are cooperative.

You also communicate positiveness through "stroking." Stroking behavior acknowledges the importance of the other person. It's the opposite of indifference. When you stroke someone, whether positively or negatively, you acknowledge him or her as a person, as a significant human being.

Stroking may be verbal, as in "I like you," "I enjoy being with you," or "You're a pig." Stroking may also be nonverbal. A smile, a hug, or a slap in the face are also examples of stroking. Positive stroking generally takes the form of compliments or rewards. Positive strokes bolster your self-image and make you feel a little bit better than you did before you received them. Negative strokes, on the other hand, are punishing. Sometimes, like cruel remarks, they hurt you emotionally. Sometimes, like a punch in the mouth, they hurt you physically.

Immediacy

Immediacy refers to the joining of the speaker and listener, the creation of a sense of togetherness. The communicator who demonstrates immediacy conveys a sense of interest and attention, a liking for and an attraction to the other person. Here are a few ways immediacy may be communicated nonverbally and verbally:

- Maintain appropriate eye contact and limit looking around at others
- Maintain a physical closeness which suggests a psychological closeness
- Use a direct and open body posture, for example, by arranging your body to keep others out
- Smile and otherwise express your interest and concern for the other person.
- Use the other person's name; for example, say "Joe, what do you think?" instead of "What do you think?" Say, "I like that, Mary" instead of "I like that."
- Focus on the other person's remarks. Make the speaker know that you heard and understood what was said and will base your feedback on it. For example, use questions that ask for clarification or elaboration, such as "Do you think the same thing is true of baseball?" or "How would your argument apply to the Midwest?" Also, refer to the speaker's previous remarks, as in "I never thought of that being true of all religions" or "Colorado does sound like a great vacation spot."

- Reinforce, reward, or compliment the other person. Make use of such expressions as "I like your new outfit" or "Your comments were really to the point."
- Incorporate self-references into evaluative statements rather than depersonalizing them. Say, for example, "I think your report is great" rather than "Your report is great" or "Everyone likes your report."

Do realize that these immediacy behaviors will be evaluated differently in different cultures. For example, in the United States these immediacy behaviors are generally seen as friendly and appropriate. In other cultures, however, the same immediacy behaviors may be viewed as overly familiar, as presuming that a close relationship exists when it's only one of acquaintanceship. In the United States, to take one specific example, we move rather quickly from Mr. LastName and Ms. LastName to Fred and Ginger. In more formal countries (Japan and Germany are two examples) a much longer period of acquaintanceship would be necessary before first names would be considered appropriate (Axtell 1993).

Interaction Management

The effective communicator controls the interaction to the satisfaction of both parties. In effective **interaction management**, neither person feels ignored or on stage. Each contributes to the total communication interchange. Maintaining your role as speaker or listener and passing back and forth the opportunity to speak are interaction management skills. If one person speaks all the time and the other listens all the time, effective conversation becomes difficult if not impossible. Depending on the situation, one person may speak more than the other person. This imbalance, however, should be a function of the situation and not that one person is a "talker" and another a "listener."

Generally, effective interaction managers also avoid interrupting the other person. Interruptions often signal that what you have to say is more important than what the other person is saying and puts the other person in an inferior position. The result is dissatisfaction with the conversation. In the United States some interruptions may be seen as signs of involvement and interest in the conversa-

tion. In other cultures, however, these same interruptions may be seen as rude and insulting. Similarly, keeping the conversation flowing and fluent without long and awkward pauses that make everyone uncomfortable are signs of effective interaction management.

One of the best ways to look at interaction management is to take the following self-test. This test will help you to identify the qualities that make for the effective management of interpersonal communication situations.

SELF-TEST

Are You a High Self-Monitor?

These statements concern personal reactions to a number of different situations. No two statements are exactly alike, so consider each statement carefully before answering. If a statement is true, or mostly true, as applied to you, mark it T. If a statement is false or not usually true as applied to you, mark it F.

_____ 1. I find it hard to imitate the behavior of other people.

_____ 2. At parties and social gatherings, I do not attempt to do or say things that others will like.

_____ 3. I can only argue for ideas that I already believe.

_____ 4. I can make impromptu speeches on topics about which I have almost no information.

_____ 5. I guess I put on a show to impress or entertain people.

_____ 6. I would probably make a good actor.

_____ 7. In a group of people I am rarely the center of attention.

_____ 8. In different situations and with different people, I often act like very different persons.

_____ 9. I am not particularly good at making other people like me.

_____ 10. I'm not always the person I appear to be.

_____ 11. I would not change my opinions (or the way I do things) in order to please someone or win a person's favor.

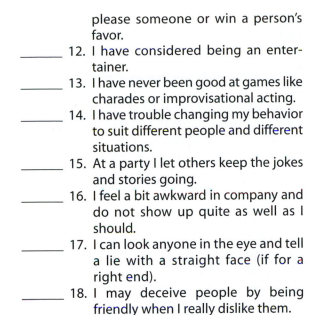

_____ 12. I have considered being an entertainer.

_____ 13. I have never been good at games like charades or improvisational acting.

_____ 14. I have trouble changing my behavior to suit different people and different situations.

_____ 15. At a party I let others keep the jokes and stories going.

_____ 16. I feel a bit awkward in company and do not show up quite as well as I should.

_____ 17. I can look anyone in the eye and tell a lie with a straight face (if for a right end).

_____ 18. I may deceive people by being friendly when I really dislike them.

Give yourself one point for each true response you gave to questions 4, 5, 6, 8, 10, 12, 17, and 18, and give yourself one point for each false response you gave to questions 1, 2, 3, 7, 9, 11, 13, 14, 15, and 16. According to Snyder (1987), scores may be interpreted roughly as follows: 13 or higher = very high self-monitoring; 11–12 = high self-monitoring; 8–10 = low self-monitoring; 0–7 = very low self-monitoring.

Although there seem to be two clear-cut types of persons—high and low self-monitors—we all engage more or less in selective monitoring, depending on the situation. If you go to a job interview, you're likely to monitor your behaviors very carefully. On the other hand, you're less likely to monitor your performance with a group of friends. In what situations and with what people are you most likely to self-monitor? Least likely to self-monitor? How do these situations and people differ?

From *Public Appearances/Private Realities* by Snyder. ©1987 by W. H. Freeman and Company. Used with permission ✔

Self-monitoring, the manipulation of the image that you present to others in your interpersonal interactions, is integrally related to interpersonal interaction management. High self-monitors carefully adjust their behaviors on the basis of feedback from others so that they produce the most desirable effect. Low self-monitors are not concerned with the image they present to others. Rather, they communicate their thoughts and feelings with no attempt to manipulate the impressions they create. Most of us lie somewhere between the two extremes.

When you compare high and low self-monitors, you find several interesting differences. For example, high self-monitors are more apt to take charge of a situation, are more sensitive to the deceptive techniques of others, and are better able to detect self-monitoring or impression management techniques when used by others. High self-monitors prefer to interact with low self-monitors, over whom they're able to assume positions of influence and power.

Expressiveness

The expressive speaker communicates genuine involvement in the interpersonal interaction. He or she plays the game instead of just watching it as a spectator. **Expressiveness** is similar to openness in its emphasis on involvement (Cegala, Savage, Brunner, & Conrad 1982). It includes taking responsibility for your thoughts and feelings, encouraging expressiveness or openness in others, and providing appropriate feedback. Do recognize that here too there are wide cultural differences. For example, in the United States women are expected to participate fully in business discussions, to smile, laugh, and initiate interactions. These behaviors are so expected and seemingly so natural that it seems strange even mentioning them. In many other countries (Arab countries and many Asian countries), however, this expressiveness would be considered inappropriate (Lustig & Koester 1993; Axtell 1993; Hall & Hall 1987).

Expressiveness also includes taking responsibility for both talking and listening and in this way is similar to equality. In conflict situations, expressiveness involves fighting actively and stating disagreement directly. Expressiveness means using I-messages in which you accept responsibility for your thoughts and feelings, for example, "I'm bored when I don't get to talk" or "I want to talk more," rather than you-messages ("you ignore me," "you don't ask my opinion"). It's the opposite of fighting passively, withdrawing from the encounter, or attributing responsibility to others.

More specifically, expressiveness may be communicated in a wide variety of ways. Here are a few guidelines:

MEDIA WATCH

THE SPIRAL OF SILENCE

Consider your own tendency to discuss your attitudes and beliefs with others. Are you equally likely to voice opinions that agree with others as those that disagree? The spiral of silence theory would argue that you're more likely to voice agreement positions than disagreement ones (Noelle-Neumann 1973, 1980, 1991; Becker & Roberts 1992; Windahl, Signitzer, & Olson 1992).

The spiral of silence theory claims that when a controversial issue arises, you estimate the opinions of others; you try to estimate public opinion on the issue. You estimate which views are popular and which are not and you estimate *how* popular these positions are. At the same time, you also judge the likelihood of being punished for expressing minority opinions and the severity of that punishment. And you do this largely by attending to the media. Once these assumptions about the popularity of an issue are formed, you use these to regulate your expression of your own opinions on that issue.

According to the theory, when you feel your opinions are in agreement with the majority, you're more likely to voice them than if you feel they're in disagreement. Of course there are many reasons you might be reluctant to voice minority opinions. After all, you don't want to be isolated from the majority. Another reason is that disagreement often means confrontation with the possibility of being proven wrong, both unpleasant results. And, you may assume that the majority, because they're a majority, must be right; and you want to be right, not wrong.

Not all people seem affected by this spiral equally (Noelle-Neumann 1991). For example, younger people and men are more likely to express minority opinions than are older people and women. Educated people are more likely to express minority opinions than are those who are less educated. This is not surprising since the expression of a minority opinion often requires some defense, which the educated feel competent to present but the uneducated don't.

As these people remain silent, the media position gets stronger (because those who agree with it are the only ones who are speaking). As the media's position grows stronger, the silence of the opposition also grows. The silence becomes an ever-widening spiral.

One of the problems this situation creates is that the media are likely to express the same general opinions, values, and beliefs and thus present a false picture of the extent to which people are in agreement. Those who take their cues from the media are therefore likely to misestimate the real degree of agreement and disagreement.

Consider your own part in the spiral of silence. How much, if any, do you contribute to this spiral of silence? How much do your peers contribute? To what degree does your college provide for the presentation of minority values, opinions, and beliefs? How does this theory relate to interpersonal communication in general? Can you apply this theory to the way in which small groups within organizations operate? To contemporary political speaking?

The next Media Watch appears on page 191.

- Practice active listening by paraphrasing, expressing understanding of the thoughts and feelings of the other person, and asking relevant questions (as explained in Unit 5).
- Avoid clichés and trite expressions that signal a lack of personal involvement and originality.

- Address mixed messages—messages (verbal or nonverbal) that are communicated simultaneously but that contradict each other.
- Address messages that somehow seem unrealistic to you (for example, statements claiming that the breakup of a long-term relationship is

completely forgotten or that failing a course doesn't mean anything).

- Use I-messages to signal personal involvement and a willingness to share your feelings. Instead of saying "You never give me a chance to make any decisions," say "I'd like to contribute to the decisions that affect both of us."
- Communicate expressiveness nonverbally by using appropriate variations in vocal rate, pitch, volume, and rhythm to convey involvement and interest, and by allowing your facial muscles to reflect and echo this inner involvement.
- Similarly, use gestures appropriately to communicate involvement. Too few gestures signal disinterest, while too many may communicate discomfort, uneasiness, and awkwardness.

Other Orientation

Some people are primarily self-oriented and talk mainly about themselves, their experiences, their interests, and their desires. They do most of the talking, and pay little attention to verbal and nonverbal feedback from the other person. Other-orientation is the opposite of self-orientation. It involves the ability to communicate attentiveness and interest in the other person and in what is being said. Without other-orientation each person pursues his or her own goal instead of cooperating and working together to achieve a common goal.

Other-orientation is especially important (and especially difficult) when you're interacting with people who are very different from you as in, for example, talking with people from other cultures. Here are some methods to improve your other-orientation:

- Use focused eye contact, smiles, and head nods.
- Lean toward the other person.
- Display feelings and emotions through appropriate facial expression.
- Avoid focusing on yourself (as in preening, for example) or on anyone other than the person to whom you're speaking (through frequent or prolonged eye contact or body orientation).
- Ask the other person for suggestions, opinions, and clarification as appropriate. Statements such as "How do you feel about it?" or "What

do you think?" will go a long way toward focusing the communication on the other person.

- Express agreement when appropriate. Comments such as "You're right" or "That's interesting" help to focus the interaction on the other person, which encourages greater openness.
- Use minimal responses to encourage the other person to express himself or herself. Minimal responses are those brief expressions that encourage another to continue talking without intruding on their thoughts and feelings or directing them to go in any particular direction. For example, "yes," "I see," or even "aha" or "hmm" are minimal responses that tell the other person that you're interested in his or her continued comments.
- Use positive affect statements to refer to the other person and to his or her contributions to the interaction; for example, "I really enjoy your presentation at the department meeting today" or "That was a clever way of looking at things" are positive affect statements that are often felt but rarely expressed.

Other-orientation demonstrates consideration and respect—for example, asking if it's all right to dump your troubles on someone before doing so or asking if your phone call comes at an inopportune time before launching into your conversation. Other-orientation involves acknowledging others' feelings as legitimate: "I can understand why you're so angry; I would be, too."

CONVERSATION PROBLEMS: PREVENTION AND REPAIR

In conversation, you may anticipate a problem and seek to prevent it. Or you may discover that you said or did something that will lead to disapproval, and you may seek to excuse yourself. Here we give just one example of a device to prevent potential conversational problems (the disclaimer) and one example of a device to repair conversational problems (the excuse). The purpose is simply to illustrate the complexity of these processes and not to present you with an exhaustive listing of the ways in which conversational problems may be prevented or repaired.

Preventing Conversational Problems: The Disclaimer

Let us say, for example, that you fear your listeners will think your comment is inappropriate in the present context, or that they may rush to judge you without hearing your full account, or that you're not in full possession of your faculties. In these cases, you may use some form of disclaimer. A **disclaimer** is a statement that aims to ensure that your message will be understood and will not reflect negatively on you.

Think about your own use of disclaimers as you read about these five types (Hewitt and Stokes 1975; McLaughlin 1984). **Hedging** helps you to separate yourself from the message so that if your listeners reject your message, they need not reject you (for example, "I may be wrong here, but . . ."). Hedges decrease the attractiveness of both women and men (Wright and Hosman 1983) if they're seen as indicating a lack of certainty or conviction because of some inadequacy. On the other hand, if the hedges are seen as indicating a belief in "nonallness" (that no one can know all about any subject) and a belief that tentative statements are all one can reasonably make (Hosman 1989; Pearson, West, & Turner 1995), they will be more positively received.

Credentialing helps you to establish your special qualifications for saying what you're about to say (for example, "Don't get me wrong, I'm not homophobic . . ."). **Sin licenses** ask listeners for permission to deviate in some way from some normally accepted convention (for example, "I know this may not be the place to discuss business, but . . ."). **Cognitive disclaimers** help you to make the case that you're in full possession of your faculties (for example, "I know you'll think I'm crazy, but let me explain the logic of the case"). **Appeals for the suspension of judgment** ask listeners to hear you out before making a judgment (for example, "Don't hang up on me until you hear my side of the story").

Generally, disclaimers are effective when, for example, you think you might offend listeners by telling a joke (for example, "I don't usually like these types of jokes, but . . ."). In one study, for example, 11-year-old children were read a story about someone whose actions created negative effects. Some children heard the story with a disclaimer and others here the same story without the disclaimer. When the children were asked to indicate how the person should be punished, those who heard the story with the disclaimer recommended significantly lower punishments (Bennett 1990).

But, disclaimers can also get you into trouble. For example, to inappropriately preface remarks with "I'm no liar" may well lead listeners to think that perhaps the speaker is a liar. Also, if you use too many disclaimers you may be perceived as someone who doesn't have any strong convictions or as one who wants to avoid responsibility for just about everything. This seems especially true of hedges.

In responding to statements containing disclaimers, it's often necessary to respond to both the disclaimer and to the statement. By doing so, you let the speaker know that you heard the disclaimer and that you aren't going to view this communication negatively. Appropriate responses might be: "I know you're no sexist but I don't agree that . . ." or "Well, perhaps we should discuss the money now even if it doesn't seem right."

Repairing Conversational Problems: The Excuse

Earlier we examined the concept of irreversibility, the idea that once something is said, it cannot be *un*communicated (Unit 2). In part because of this fact, we need at times to defend or justify messages that may be perceived negatively. Perhaps the most common method for doing so is "the excuse." Excuses pervade all forms of communication and behavior. Although we emphasize their role in conversation, recognize that the excuse is applicable to all human behaviors, not just conversational ones.

You learn early in life that when you do something that will be perceived negatively, an excuse is in order to justify your poor performance. The excuse, as C. R. Snyder (1984) notes, "plays a central role in how we get along in life, both with yourself and with other people."

The excuse usually follows from three conditions:

1. You say something.
2. Your statement is viewed negatively; you desire to disassociate yourself from it.
3. Someone hears the message or the results of the message. (The "witness" may be an outsider, for example, a boss, a friend, a colleague, but also could be yourself—you're a witness to your own messages.)

More formally, Snyder (1984; Snyder, Higgins, & Stucky 1983) defines **excuses** as "explanations or actions that lessen the negative implications of an actor's performance, thereby maintaining a positive image for oneself and others."

Excuses seem especially in order when we say or are accused of saying something that runs counter to what is expected, sanctioned, or considered "right" by the people involved or by society in general. The excuse, ideally, lessens the negative impact of the message.

Three kinds of excuses can be identified (Snyder 1984; Snyder, Higgins, & Stucky 1983). In the *I didn't do it* type, you claim not to have done the behavior of which you're accused: "I didn't say that." "I wasn't even near the place when it happened." In the *It wasn't so bad* type, you claim that the behavior was not really so bad, certainly not as bad as others may at first think: "I only copied one answer." In the *Yes, but* type, you claim that extenuating circumstances accounted for the behavior: "It was the liquor talking." "I really tried to help him; I didn't mean to hurt his feelings."

Some Motives for Excuse-Making

The major motive for excuse-making seems to be to maintain our self-esteem, to project a positive image to ourselves and to others. Excuses are also offered to reduce the stress that may be created by a bad performance. We feel that if we can offer an excuse—especially a good one that is accepted by those around us—it will lessen the negative reaction and the subsequent stress that accompanies a poor performance.

Excuses enable you to take risks and engage in behavior that may be unsuccessful; you may offer an anticipatory excuse: "My throat's a bit sore but I'll give the speech a try." The excuse is designed to lessen the criticism should we fail to deliver an acceptable speech.

Excuses also enable us to maintain effective interpersonal relationships even after some negative behavior. For example, after criticizing a friend's behavior and observing the negative reaction to our criticism, we might offer an excuse such as, "Please forgive me; I'm really exhausted. I'm just not thinking straight." Excuses enable us to place our messages—even our possible failures—in a more favorable light.

Good and Bad Excuses

The most important question to most people is what makes a good excuse and what makes a bad excuse (Snyder 1984; Slade 1995). How can you make good excuses and thus get out of problems, and how can you avoid bad excuses and thus only make matters worse? Good excuse-makers use excuses in moderation; bad excuse-makers rely on excuses too often. Good excuse-makers avoid using excuses in the presence of those who know what really happened; bad excuse-makers make excuses

For 6,000 yen a month (about $70) a Japanese cable radio network provides listeners with several "excuse" stations. These stations broadcast background noise, for example, the sound of a train station, coffee shop, or telephone booth. Thus, when you want to have someone believe you're at a train station you can play the radio while you're on the phone to say that you can't be home on time (*New York Times Magazine*, July 16, 1995, p. 8). What do you think of this service? Would you subscribe to it? Would you invest money in it? Would it be more popular with one sex than another? Would it be more popular in some cultures than in others?

even in these inappropriate situations. Good ex-cuse-makers avoid blaming others, especially those they work with; bad excuse-makers blame even their work colleagues. In a similar way, good ex-cuse-makers don't attribute their failure to others or to the company; bad excuse-makers do. Good excuse-makers acknowledge their own responsi-bility for the failure by noting that they did some-thing wrong (not that they lack competence); bad excuse-makers refuse to accept any responsibility for their failure.

The best excuses are apologies because they contain three essential elements for a good excuse (Slade 1995):

- acknowledge some of the responsibility
- ask forgiveness
- suggest that things will be done better in the future

The worst excuses are the *I didn't do it* type be-cause they fail to acknowledge responsibility, and also because they offer no assurance that this failure will not happen again.

SUMMARY

In this unit we covered the conversation process, from open-ing to closing; the principles of conversational effectiveness; and conversational problems, their prevention and repair.

1. Conversation consists of five general stages: opening, feedforward, business, feedback, and closing.
2. Initiating conversations can be accomplished in various ways, for example, with self, other, relational, and con-text references.
3. The business of conversation is maintained by the pass-ing of speaking and listening turns; turn-maintaining and turn-yielding cues are used by the speaker, and turn-requesting, turn-denying, and backchanneling cues are used by the listener.
4. Closing a conversation may be achieved through a va-riety of methods; for example: reflect back on the conversation as in summarizing, directly state your

desire to end the conversation, refer to future inter-action, ask for closure, and state your pleasure with interaction.
5. The metaskills of conversational effectiveness need to be applied with mindfulness, flexibility, and cultural sensi-tivity (as appropriate).
6. Among the skills of conversational effectiveness are openness, empathy, positiveness, immediacy, interaction management, expressiveness, and other-orientation.
7. One way potential conversational problems may be averted is through the disclaimer, a statement that helps to ensure that your message will be understood and will not reflect negatively on the speaker.
8. One way to repair a conversational problem is with the excuse, a statement designed to lessen the negative im-pact of a speaker's messages.

KEY TERMS

conversation (p. 153)

conversational turns (p. 156)

turn-maintaining cues (p. 156)

turn-yielding cues (p. 157)

turn-requesting cues (p. 157)

turn-denying cues (p. 157)

backchanneling cues (p. 157)

metaskills (p. 159)

mindfulness (p. 159)

flexibility (p. 160)

openness (p. 163)

empathy (p. 164)

positiveness (p. 165)

immediacy (p. 165)

interaction management (p. 166)

self-monitoring (p. 166)

expressiveness (p. 167)

other-orientation (p. 169)

disclaimer (p. 170)

excuse (p. 170)

THINKING CRITICALLY ABOUT
Conversation

1. After reviewing the research on the empathic and lis-tening abilities of men and women, Pearson, West, and Turner (1994) conclude: "Men and women do not dif-fer as much as conventional wisdom would have us be-lieve. In many instances, she thinks like a man, and he

thinks like a woman because they both think alike." Does your experience support or contradict this obser-vation?
2. Animal researchers have argued that some animals show empathy. For example, consider the male gorilla

who watched a female try in vain to get water that collected in an automobile tire and who then secured the tire and brought it to the female. This gorilla, it has been argued, demonstrated empathy; he felt the other gorilla's thirst (Angier 1995). Similarly, the animal who cringes when another of its species gets hurt seems also to be showing empathy. What evidence would you demand before believing that animals possess empathic abilities? What evidence would you want before believing that a relationship partner or a friend feels empathy for you?

3. Try collecting examples of disclaimers from your interpersonal interactions as well as from the media. Consider, for example, what type of disclaimer is being used? Why is it being used? Is the disclaimer appropriate? What other kinds of disclaimers could have been used more effectively?

4. How would you go about answering such questions as these?
   - Are high self-monitors generally more successful in interpersonal relationships than low self-monitors? In business relationships?
   - Do happy and unhappy couples use disclaimers in the same way? Do effective and ineffective managers use disclaimers in the same way?
   - Are people who demonstrate the qualities of effective conversational management better liked than those who don't?
   - Which quality of effectiveness is the most important in communication between health-care provider and patient?
   - What role does other-orientation play in first dates?
   - Do men and women use the same kind of excuses?

5. Visit one of the IRCs and lurk for 5 to 10 minutes. What characterizes the conversation on the channel you observed? What is the topic of conversation? What is the most obvious purpose of the group? If possible try comparing your reactions with others who visited other channels.

6. Access ERIC, Medline, Psychlit, or Sociofile (databases of citations and abstracts of thousands of articles on communication and education, medicine, psychology, and sociology) and locate an article dealing with some aspect of conversation. What can you learn about conversation and interpersonal communication from this article?

UNIT 10
Interpersonal Relationships

UNIT CONTENTS

Relationship Processes

Relationship Types

Relationship Theories

UNIT GOALS

After completing this unit, you should be able to

explain the factors and processes involved in interpersonal relationship development, deterioration, maintenance, and repair

explain the types of friendships, loves, and primary relationships that have been identified

explain the basic assumptions of attraction, relationship rules, reinforcement, social exchange, and equity theories

This unit examines interpersonal relationships. After a brief overview of the nature of interpersonal relationships and its general stages, we discuss relationship processes—including relationship development, deterioration, maintenance, and repair. Second, we look into relationship types and the wide differences among friendship, love, and family relationships. Third, we cover some of the theories that try to explain how relationships work.

Interpersonal relationships are established in stages. You don't become intimate friends with someone immediately upon meeting. Rather, you grow into an intimate relationship gradually, through a series of steps from the initial contact, through intimacy, and perhaps on to dissolution. And the same is probably true with most other relationships as well. In all, six major stages are identifiable (see Figure 10.1): contact, involvement, intimacy, deterioration, repair, and dissolution. Each stage can be divided into an early and a late phase, as noted in the diagram. For each specific relationship, you might wish to modify and revise the basic model in various ways. As a general description of relationship development, however, the stages seem fairly standard.

These stages are not static; rather, within each there are dynamic tensions between various opposites (Rawlins 1989, 1992). Within each relationship and within each relationship stage, there are dynamic tensions between several opposites. For example, research has found three such opposites (Baxter 1988, 1990; Baxter & Simon 1993). The tension between **autonomy and connection** expresses your desire to remain an individual but also to be intimately connected to another person and to a relationship. This theme is also seen in women's magazines and seems to teach readers to want both autonomy and connection (Prusank, Duran, & DeLillo 1993). The tension between **novelty and predictability** focuses on the dual desires for newness and adventure on the one hand and sameness and comfortableness on the other. The tension between **closedness and openness** relates to the desires to be in an exclusive relationship and one that is open to different people. So, view each of the stages as dynamic transactions rather than as static events.

RELATIONSHIP PROCESSES

In this section, we look at relationship processes. These include the processes of relationship development (the contact, involvement, and intimacy stages

noted in the six-stage model presented in Figure 10.1), deterioration and dissolution, maintenance (where we maintain a certain level of involvement—neither moving more toward intimacy nor more toward deterioration), and repair (both of the relationship and of yourself).

Relationship Development

There's probably nothing as important to most people than contact with others. So important is this contact that when it's absent for prolonged periods, depression sets in, self-doubt surfaces, and people find it difficult to conduct even the basics of daily living.

Reasons for Relationship Development
Of course, each person pursues a relationship for unique reasons. Yet there are also some general reasons for developing relationships: to lessen loneliness, to secure stimulation, to acquire self-knowledge, and to maximize pleasures and minimize pain.

Think about the development of your own relationships as you read through these reasons. Are these reasons adequate to explain why you've developed the relationships you did? Are there other reasons that motivated your relationships that are not noted here?

One reason we enter relationships is because contact with another human being helps **lessen loneliness**. It doesn't always, of course. At times, for example, you may experience loneliness even though you're with other people. And at other times you don't feel lonely even when physically alone (Perlman & Peplau 1981). Yet, generally, contact with other people helps lessen the uncomfortable feelings of loneliness (Peplau & Perlman 1982; Rubenstein & Shaver 1982).

Human beings need **stimulation,** and interpersonal relationships provide one of the best ways to get this stimulation. Because you are, in part, an intellectual creature and need intellectual stimulation, you talk about ideas, attend classes, and argue about different interpretations of a film or novel. Because you're also a physical creature who needs physical stimulation, you touch and are touched, hold and are held. Because you're an emotional creature who needs emotional stimulation, you laugh and cry, feel hope and surprise, and experience warmth and affection. Such stimulation comes most easily within an interpersonal

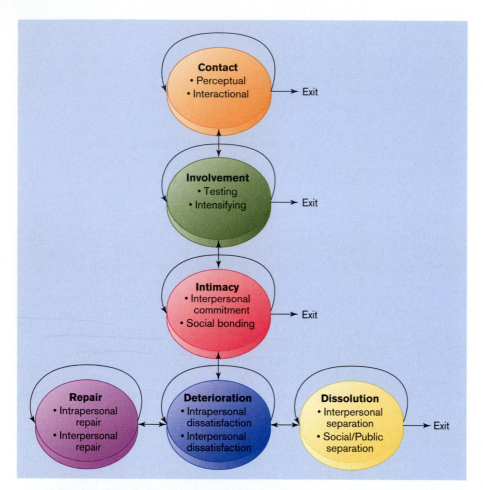

Figure 10.1 **A six-stage relationship model.** This model of relationships is best viewed as a tool for talking about relationships rather than as a specific map that indicates how you move from one relationship position to another.

relationship—a friendship, love, or family relationship.

It's largely through contact with other human beings that you gain **self-knowledge**. As noted in the discussion of self-awareness (Unit 5) you see yourself in part through the eyes of others. And those with the best eyesight are usually your friends, lovers, or family members.

The most general reason to establish relationships, and one that could include all the others, is that you seek human contact to **maximize your pleasures and minimize your pains**. Most people want to share with others both their good fortune and their emotional or physical pain. The first impulse upon

having something extreme happen (positive or negative) is often to tell it to a relationship partner.

Initiating Relationships: The First Encounter

Perhaps the most difficult and yet the most important aspect of relationship development is the beginning. Meeting the person, presenting yourself, and somehow moving to another stage is a difficult process. Three major phases can be identified in the first encounter: examining the qualifiers, determining clearance, and communicating your desire for contact. Before reading about this first encounter you may wish to take the following apprehension self-test.

SELF-TEST

How Apprehensive Are You in Conversations?

Although we often think of apprehension or fear of speaking in connection with public speaking, each of us has a certain degree of apprehension in all forms of communication. The following brief test is designed to measure your apprehension in interpersonal conversations and is especially appropriate for exploring your own apprehension in initiating relationships.

This questionnaire consists of six statements concerning your feelings about interpersonal conversations. Indicate in the space provided the degree to which each statement applies to you by marking whether you (1) Strongly Agree, (2) Agree, (3) Are Undecided, (4) Disagree, or (5) Strongly Disagree with each statement. There are no right or wrong answers. Some of the statements are similar to other statements. Do not be concerned about this. Work quickly; just record your first impression.

_____ 1. While participating in a conversation with a new acquaintance, I feel very nervous.

_____ 2. I have no fear of speaking up in conversations.

_____ 3. Ordinarily I am very tense and nervous in conversations.

_____ 4. Ordinarily I am very calm and relaxed in conversations.

_____ 5. While conversing with a new acquaintance, I feel very relaxed.

_____ 6. I'm afraid to speak up in conversations.

To obtain your apprehension score, use the following formula: Add 18 to your score for items 2, 4, and 5; then subtract your scores for items 1, 3, and 6. A score above 18 shows some degree of apprehension.

This self-test is the first of several that deal with communication apprehension, one of the most important obstacles to effective communication interaction. Apprehension, as explained throughout this text, is especially strong in intercultural situations where there's greater uncertainty and

ambiguity. As you take these tests, think about the reasons for your apprehension and the ways in which you might be able to more effectively manage apprehension.

From James C. McCroskey, *An Introduction to Rhetorical Communication,* 6th edition, 1993, Prentice-Hall, Upper Saddle River, NJ. Reprinted by permission.

Your first step is to **examine the qualifiers**, those qualities that make the individual you wish to meet an appropriate choice (Davis, 1973). Some qualifiers are obvious, such as beauty, style of clothes, jewelry, and the like. Others are hidden, such as personality, health, wealth, talent, and intelligence. These qualifiers tell you something about who the person is and help you to decide if you wish to pursue this initial encounter.

Your second step is to **determine clearance**, to see if the person is available for the type of meeting you're interested in (Davis 1973). If you're interested in a date, then you might look to see if the person is wearing a wedding ring. Does the person seem to be waiting for someone else?

The next stage is to **make contact**. You need to open the encounter nonverbally and verbally. Nonverbally you might signal this desire for contact in a variety of ways. Here are just a few things you might do.

- Establish eye contact. The eyes communicate awareness of and interest in the other person.
- While maintaining eye contact, smile and further signal your interest in and positive response to this other person.
- Concentrate your focus. Nonverbally shut off from your awareness the rest of the room. Be careful, however, that you don't focus so directly that you make the person uncomfortable.
- Establish physical closeness or at least lessen the physical distance between the two of you. Approach the other person, but not to the point of discomfort, so your interest in making contact is obvious.
- Maintain an open posture. Throughout the encounter, maintain a posture that communicates a willingness to enter into interaction with the other person. Hands crossed over the chest or clutched around your stomach communicate a closedness, an unwillingness to let others enter your space.

- Reinforce the positive behaviors of the other person to signal continued interest and a further willingness to make contact. Again, nod, smile, or somehow communicate your favorable reaction.

Although nonverbal contact is signaled first, much of the subsequent nonverbal contact takes place at the same time that you're communicating verbally. Here are some methods for making verbal contact:

- Introduce yourself. Try to avoid trite opening lines, such as "Haven't I seen you here before?" It's best simply to say, "Hi, my name is Pat."
- Focus the conversation on the other person. Get the other person talking about himself or herself. No one enjoys talking about any topic more than this one. Also, you'll gain an opportunity to learn something about the person you want to get to know. For example, the hidden qualifiers or disqualifiers such as intelligence or the lack of it will begin to emerge here.
- Exchange favors and rewards. Compliment the other person. If you can't find anything to compliment, then you might want to reassess your interest in this person.
- Stress the positives. Positiveness contributes to a good first impression simply because people are more attracted to positive than to negative people.
- Avoid negative or too intimate self-disclosures. Enter a relationship gradually and gracefully. Disclosures should come slowly and should be reciprocal (see Unit 5). Anything too intimate or too negative, when revealed too early in the relationship, will create a negative image. If you can't resist self-disclosing, try to stick to the positives and to issues that are not overly intimate.
- Establish commonalities. Seek to discover in your interaction those things you have in common with the other person—attitudes, interests, personal qualities, third parties, places—anything that will stress a connection.

Relationship Deterioration

The opposite end of relationship development is deterioration and possible dissolution. **Relational deterioration**, the weakening of the bonds that hold people together, may be gradual or sudden, slight or extreme. Murray Davis (1973), in his *Intimate Relations*, uses the terms "passing away" to designate gradual deterioration and "sudden death" to designate immediate or sudden deterioration. An example of passing away occurs when one of the parties develops close ties with a new intimate and this new relationship gradually pushes out the old. An example of sudden death occurs when one or both of the parties break a rule that was essential to the relationship (for example, the rule of fidelity). As a result, both realize that the relationship must be terminated.

Although you may be accustomed to thinking of relationship breakup as negative, this is not necessarily so. At times a relationship may be unproductive for one or both parties, and a breakup is often the best thing that could happen. Ending a relationship may provide a period for the individuals to regain their independence and self-reliance. Some relationships are so absorbing that there's little time available for reflection about oneself, others, and the relationship itself. In these cases, distance often helps. For the most part, it's up to you to draw out of any decaying relationship some positive characteristics and some learning that can be used later on.

Causes of Relationship Deterioration

The causes of relationship deterioration are as numerous as the individuals involved. All these causes may also be seen as effects of relational deterioration. For example, when things start to go sour, the individuals may remove themselves physically from one another in response to the deterioration. This physical separation may in turn cause further deterioration by driving the individuals farther apart emotionally and psychologically. Or it may encourage them to seek other partners.

When the **reasons you developed the relationship change drastically**, your relationship may deteriorate. For example, when loneliness is no longer lessened, the relationship may be on the road to decay. When the stimulation is weak, one or both may begin to look elsewhere. If self-knowledge and self-growth prove insufficient, you may become dissatisfied with yourself, your partner, and your relationship. When the pains (costs) begin to exceed the pleasures (rewards), you begin to look for ways to exit the relationship or in some cases ways to improve or repair it.

BUILDING
Communication Skills

HOW DO YOU GET SOMEONE TO LIKE YOU?

One way to make yourself more attractive to the other person is to use a broad class of behaviors known as affinity-seeking strategies (Bell & Daly 1984; Frymier & Thompson 1992). For example, it's been found that when teachers use these affinity-seeking strategies, students evaluate the teachers as being more competent than those who don't use the strategies (Prisbell 1994). Students also come to like the instructors who use affinity-seeking strategies (offering evidence that they work) and feel they're learning more (Roach 1991). As you read down the list of these strategies, try to develop one way in which you could use each of the strategies.

- Altruism. Be of help to Other.
- Control. Appear "in control," as a leader, as one who takes charge.
- Equality. Present yourself as socially equal to Other.
- Comfortable self. Present yourself as comfortable and relaxed when with Other.
- Dynamism. Appear active, enthusiastic, and dynamic.
- Disclosures. Stimulate and encourage Other to talk about himself or herself; reinforce disclosures and contributions of Other.
- Inclusion of Other. Include Other in your social activities and groupings.
- Listening. Listen to Other attentively and actively.
- Openness. Engage in self-disclosure with Other.
- Optimism. Appear optimistic and positive rather than pessimistic and negative.
- Self-concept confirmation. Show respect for Other and help Other to feel positively about himself or herself.
- Self-inclusion. Arrange circumstances so that you and Other come into frequent contact.
- Sensitivity. Communicate warmth and empathy to Other.
- Similarity. Demonstrate that you share significant attitudes and values with Other.
- Trustworthiness. Appear to Other as honest and reliable.

Relational changes in one or both parties may encourage relational deterioration. Psychological changes such as the development of different intellectual interests or incompatible attitudes may create relational problems. Behavioral changes such as preoccupation with business or schooling may strain the relationship and create problems. Status changes may also create difficulties for a couple.

Sometimes one or both parties maintain **unrealistic expectations**. This often occurs early in a relationship when, for example, the individuals think that they will want to spend all their time together. When they discover that neither one does, each resents this "lessening" of feeling in the other. The resolution of such conflicts lies not so much in meeting these unrealistic expectations as in discovering why they were unrealistic and substituting more attainable expectations.

Few sexual relationships are free of **sexual difficulties**. In fact, sexual problems rank among the top three problems in almost all studies of newlyweds (Blumstein & Schwartz 1983). Although sexual frequency is not related to relational breakdown, sexual satisfaction is. It's the quality and not the quantity of a sexual relationship that is crucial. When the quality is poor, the partners may seek sexual satisfaction outside the primary relationship. Extrarelational affairs contribute significantly to breakups for all couples, whether married or cohabiting, whether heterosexual or homosexual. Even "open relationships"—ones that are based on sexual freedom outside the primary relationship—experience these problems and are more likely to break up than the traditional "closed" relationship.

Unhappiness with work often leads to difficulties in relationships. Most people can't separate problems with work from their relationships (Blumstein & Schwartz 1983). This is true for all types of couples. With heterosexual couples (both married and cohabiting), if the man is disturbed over the woman's job—for example, if she earns a great deal more than he does or devotes a great deal of time to the job—the relationship is in for considerable trouble. And this is true whether the relationship is in its early stages or is a well-established one. One research study, for example, found that husbands whose wives worked were less satisfied with their own jobs and lives than were men whose wives did not work (Staines, Pottick, & Fudge 1986). Often the man expects the woman to work but does not reduce his expectations concerning her household responsibilities. The man may become resentful if the woman does not fulfill these expectations, and the woman may become resentful if she takes on both outside work and full household duties.

In surveys of problems among couples, **financial difficulties** loom large. Money is seldom discussed by couples beginning a relationship. Yet it proves to be one of the major problems faced by all couples as they settle into their relationship. Dissatisfaction with money usually leads to dissatisfaction with the relationship. This is true for married and cohabiting heterosexual couples and gay male couples. It's not true for lesbian couples, who seem to care a great deal less about financial matters. This difference has led some researchers to speculate that concern over money and its equation with power and relational satisfaction are largely male attitudes (Blumstein & Schwartz 1983).

Money also creates problems in heterosexual relationships because men and women view it differently. To men, money is power. To women, it is security and independence. Conflicts over how the couple's money is to be spent or invested can easily result from such different perceptions (Blumstein & Schwartz, 1983).

Communication in Relationship Deterioration

Like relational development, relational deterioration involves unique and specialized communication. These communication patterns are in part a response to the deterioration itself. However, these patterns are also causative. The way you communicate influences the course of a relationship.

Nonverbally, **withdrawal** is seen in the greater space each person seems to require and the ease with which tempers are aroused when that space is encroached on. When people are close emotionally, they can comfortably occupy close physical quarters, but when they're growing apart, they need wider spaces. Withdrawal of another kind may be seen in the decrease in similarities in clothing and in the display of "intimate trophies" such as bracelets, photographs, and rings (Knapp & Vangelisti 1992). Other nonverbal signs include the failure to engage in eye contact, to look at each other generally, and to touch each other (Miller & Parks 1982).

Verbally, withdrawal is seen in a number of ways. Where once there was a great desire to talk and listen, there's now less desire—perhaps none. At times small talk is engaged in as an end in itself. Whereas small talk is usually a preliminary to serious conversation (as in phatic communion) here it's used as an alternative to or a means of forestalling serious talk. Thus people in the throes of dissolution may talk a great deal about insignificant events—the weather, a movie on television, a neighbor down the hall. By focusing on these topics, they avoid confronting serious issues.

Self-disclosure declines significantly when a relationship deteriorates. Self-disclosure may not be thought worth the effort if the relationship is dying. Or, you may also limit self-disclosures because you feel that the other person may not be supportive or may use the disclosures against you. Probably the most general reason is that you no longer have a desire to share intimate thoughts and feelings with someone for whom your positive feelings are decreasing.

Deception generally increases as relationships break down. Lies may be seen as a way to avoid arguments over staying out all night, not calling, or being seen in the wrong place with the wrong person. At other times lies are used because of some feeling of shame. Perhaps you want to save the relationship and don't want to add another obstacle or you may not want to appear to be the cause of any further problems and so you lie. Sometimes deception takes the form of avoidance—the lie of omission. You talk about everything except the crux of the difficulty. Whether by omission or commission, deception has a way of escalating and creating a climate of distrust and disbelief.

Relational deterioration often brings an increase in negative **evaluations** and a decrease in positive evaluations. Where once you praised the other's behaviors, talents, or ideas, you now criticize them. Often the behaviors have not changed significantly. What has changed is your way of looking at them. Negative evaluation frequently leads to outright fighting and conflict. And although conflict is not necessarily bad (Unit 16), in relationships that are deteriorating, the conflict (often coupled with withdrawal) is often not resolved.

During relational deterioration there's little **favor exchange**. Compliments, once given frequently and sincerely, are now rare. Positive stroking is minimal. Nonverbally, eye contact, smiling, touching, caressing, and holding each other occur less frequently.

Relationship Maintenance

Relationship maintenance concerns that part of the relationship process in which you act to continue (maintain, retain) the relationship. Of course, maintenance behaviors can serve a variety of functions, for example:

- to keep the relationship intact, to retain the semblance of a relationship, to prevent completely dissolving the relationship
- to keep the relationship at its present stage, to prevent it from moving too far either toward less or toward greater intimacy
- to keep the relationship satisfying, to maintain a favorable balance between rewards and penalties

Some people, after entering a relationship, assume that the relationship will continue unless something catastrophic happens. And so, while they may seek to prevent any major mishaps, they're unlikely to engage in much maintenance behavior. Others will be ever on the lookout for something wrong and will seek to patch it up as quickly and as effectively as possible. In between lie most people, who will engage in maintenance behaviors when things are going wrong and when there's the possibility that the relationship can be improved. Behaviors directed at improving badly damaged or even broken relationships are considered under the topic of "repair," later in this unit.

Think about the relationships you're in now. What maintains these relationships? Put differently, why have they survived rather than deteriorated or dissolved? What keeps your relationships together? Can you identify reasons other than those given here that might account for relationship maintenance? Here are some of the more popular and frequently cited reasons.

The most obvious reason for maintaining a relationship is that the individuals have an **emotional attachment**, they like or love each other and want to preserve their relationship. They don't find alternative couplings as inviting or as potentially enjoyable—the individuals' needs are being satisfied and so the relationship is maintained. In some cases, these needs are predominantly for love and mutual caring, but in other cases, the needs being met may not be quite so positive. For example, one individual may maintain a relationship because it provides a means of exercising control over another. Another might continue the relationship because it provides ego gratification, each according to his or her specific need.

Often the relationship involves neither great love nor great need satisfaction but is maintained for reasons of **convenience**. Perhaps both partners may jointly own a business or have mutual friends who are important to them. In these cases it may be more convenient to stay together than to break up and go through the difficulties involved in finding another person to live with or another business partner or another social escort.

Relationships are often maintained because there are **children** involved. Children are sometimes brought into the world to save a relationship. In some cases they do. The parents stay together because they feel, rightly or wrongly, that it's in the best interests of the children. In other cases, the children provide a socially acceptable excuse to mask the real reason—convenience, financial advantage, a fear of being alone, and so on. In childless relationships, both parties can be more independent and can make life choices based more on individual needs and wants. These individuals, therefore, are less likely to remain in relationships they find unpleasant or uncomfortable.

Fear motivates many couples to stay together. The individuals may fear the outside world; they may fear being alone and of facing others as "singles." They may remember the horrors of the singles bars, the one-night stands, and the lonely weekends. As a result they may elect to preserve their current relationship as the better alternative. Sometimes the fear may be of social criticism: "What will our friends say? They'll think I'm a failure because I can't hold on to another person." Sometimes the fear concerns the consequences of violating some religious or parental tenet that tells you to stay together, no matter what happens.

Financial advantages motivate many couples to stick it out. Divorces and separations are both emotionally and financially expensive. Some people fear a breakup that may cost them half their wealth or even more. And, depending on where the individuals live and their preferred lifestyle, being single can be expensive. The cost of living in Boston, Tokyo, Paris, and many other cities is almost prohibitive for single people. Many couples stay together to avoid facing additional economic problems.

A major reason for the preservation of many relationships is **inertia**, the tendency for a body at rest to remain at rest and a body in motion to remain in motion. Many people just go along with the program, and it hardly occurs to them to consider changing their status; change seems too much trouble. Inertia is greatly aided by the media. It's easier for many individuals to remain in their present relationship and to seek vicarious satisfactions from situation comedies, dramas, and especially soap operas wherein the actors do all the things the viewer would do if he or she were not so resistant to change.

An important factor influencing the course of relationship deterioration (as well as relationship maintenance) is the degree of **commitment** the individuals have toward each other and toward the relationship. It will depend, for example, on your answers to such questions as these: Do I *want to* stay in this relationship? Do I *have a moral obligation* to stay in this relationship? Do I *have to* stay in this relationship: are there no acceptable alternatives? (Johnson, 1973, 1982, 1991; Knapp & Taylor, 1995; Kurdek, 1995). All relationships are held together, in part, by one or some combination of *want*, *obligation*, and *necessity*. And the strength of the relationship, including its resistance to possible deterioration, is also related to this degree of commitment. When a relationship shows signs of deterioration and yet there's a strong commitment to preserving it, the individuals may well surmount the obstacles and reverse the process. When commitment is weak and the individuals doubt that there are good reasons for staying together, the relationship deteriorates faster and more intensely.

Obviously, the patterns of **communication** used by the individuals also contribute to the mainte-

nance of the relationship. In one research study, four communication patterns were identified (Gao 1991).

Openness. The willingness to maintain open and honest communication.

Involvement. A strong sense of being a pair, a couple; lots of time put into the relationship.

Shared meanings. Mutual understanding of each other's nonverbal communication messages.

Relationship assessment. Both individuals see the relationship and its future in similar and mutually compatible ways.

More generally we might say that the communication patterns that help maintain a relationship are those singled out for effective conversation such as openness, empathy, positiveness, immediacy, interaction management, expressiveness, and other-orientation—performed mindfully, flexibly, and with cultural sensitivity. Add to these appropriate self-disclosure, active listening, and confirmation—and in fact all the skills considered throughout this text—and you have a pretty comprehensive list of potentially useful communication tools for maintaining a relationship.

Few couples stay together for a single reason. Rather, there are usually a multiplicity of reasons that vary in intensity and from one relationship to another. Obviously, the more urgent the reason, the more likely it is that the relationship will be preserved. But because so many of the reasons for relational preservation are unconscious, it's difficult to discover why a particular couple stays together or breaks up, or to predict which relationships will last and which will not.

Maintenance Behaviors

Another reason relationships last is that people try to make them work. A number of researchers have focused on the maintenance strategies that people use in their various relationships (Ayres 1983; Canary & Stafford 1994a, 1994b; Dindia & Baxter 1987; Canary, Stafford, Hause & Wallace 1993); Dainton & Stafford 1993; Guerrero, Eloy, & Wabnik 1993.

- **Prosocial behaviors** include being polite, cheerful, and friendly; avoiding criticism; and compromising even when it involves self-sacrifice. Prosocial behaviors also include talking about a shared future; for example, talking about a future vacation or buying a house together.

- **Ceremonial behaviors** include celebrating birthdays and anniversaries, discussing past pleasurable times, and eating at a favorite restaurant.
- **Communication behaviors** include calling just to say, "How are you?", talking about the honesty and openness in the relationship, and talking about shared feelings. Responding constructively in a conflict (even when your partner may act in ways harmful to the relationship) is another type of communicative maintenance strategy (Rusbult and Buunk 1993).
- **Togetherness behaviors** include spending time together visiting mutual friends, doing specific things as a couple, and sometimes just being together with no concern for what is done. Controlling extrarelational activities would be another type of togetherness behavior (Rusbult and Buunk 1993).
- **Openness behaviors** include engaging in direct discussion and listening to the other, for example, self-disclosing, talking about what the person wants from the relationship, giving advice, expressing empathy (rather than judgment)
- **Assurance behaviors** include assuring the other of the significance of the relationship, for example, comforting each other, putting the partner first, expressing love for the person
- **Sharing joint activities** involves spending time with the other, for example, playing ball together, going to events together, or simply talking
- **Positivity behaviors** include trying to make interactions pleasant and upbeat, for example, holding hands, giving in to make the other person happy, doing favors for the other person
- **Sending cards and letters and making calls.**
- **Avoidance behaviors** include staying away from the other or from certain issues, for example, doing some things with third parties or not talking about potentially sensitive issues
- **Sharing tasks** with the other, for example, cleaning the house together
- **Using social networks,** relying on friends and relatives for support and to help with various problems

Also found were such strategies as *humor* (making jokes or teasing the other); *talk* (engaging in small talk and establishing specific times for talking);

affection, including sexual intimacy, (acts affectionately and romantically); and *focus on self* (making oneself look good)[Canary, Stafford, Hause, & Wallace 1993; Dainton & Stafford 1993].

Relationship Repair

When a relationship begins to deteriorate, you may wish to try to save it by repairing the problems and differences. Sometimes, you'll suffer emotional damage from relationships and you may need to repair yourself. Each of these types of repair are considered here.

Interpersonal Repair

If you wish to salvage a relationship, you may try to do so by changing your communication patterns and, in effect, putting into practice the insights and skills learned in this course. You can look at the strategies for repairing a relationship in terms of the following six suggestions, which conveniently spell out the word REPAIR (Figure 10.2), a useful reminder that repair is not a one-step but a multistep process:

Recognize the problem

Engage in productive conflict resolution

Propose possible solutions

Affirm each other

Integrate solutions into normal behavior

Risk

Your first step is to **recognize the problem** and to recognize it both intellectually and emotionally. Specify what is wrong with your present relationship (in concrete, specific terms) and what changes would be needed to make it better (again, in specific terms). Without this first step there's little hope for improving any interpersonal relationship. It sometimes helps to create a picture of your relationship as you would want it to be and compare that picture to the way the relationship looks now. You can then specify the changes that would have to take place to have the present picture become the idealized picture.

Try to see the problem from your partner's point of view and to have your partner see the problem from yours. Exchange these perspectives, empathically and with open minds. Try to be descriptive when discussing grievances, being especially careful

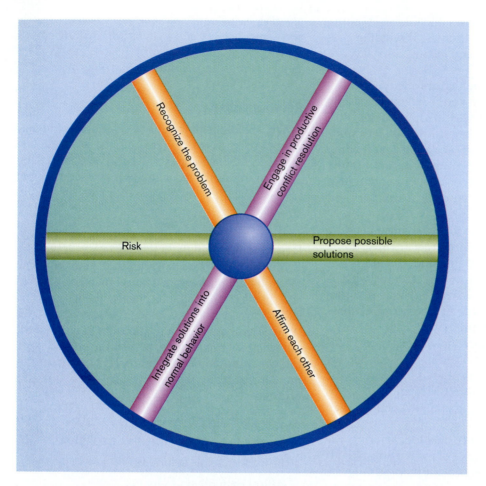

Figure 10.2   **The Relationship Repair Wheel.**   This metaphorical wheel is designed to suggest that (1) relationship repair consists of several processes, and that (2) these processes must work together so that (3) the relationship can move from one place to another, and (4) the process works best when another wheel (propelled by the other person) is moving in the same direction. You may find it interesting to create your own metaphor for relationship repair and for how the process of repair works.

to avoid such troublesome terms as *always* and *never*. Also, own your own feelings and thoughts; use I-messages and take responsibility for your feelings instead of blaming your partner.

Engage in productive conflict resolution. Interpersonal conflict is an inevitable part of relationship life. It's not so much the conflict that causes relationship difficulties but rather the way in which the conflict is pursued. If it's confronted with productive strategies, the conflict may be resolved and the relationship may actually emerge stronger and healthier. If, on the other hand, unproductive and destructive strategies are used, the relationship may well deteri-

orate further. Because this topic is so crucial, Unit 16 is devoted exclusively to the process of conflict and especially to the ways to engage in productive interpersonal conflict.

After the problem is identified, you need to **propose possible solutions**, to identify ways to lessen or eliminate the difficulty. Look for solutions that will enable both of you to win. Try to avoid "solutions" where one person wins and the other person loses, in which case resentment and hostility are likely to fester. The suggestions offered in our discussion of the problem-solving group (Unit 13) are especially applicable to this phase of relationship repair.

UNDERSTANDING
Theory and Research

IS RELATIONSHIP RESEARCH CULTURALLY BIASED?

The models and explanations of interpersonal relationships presented in this unit come mainly from research conducted in the United States and reflect the way most relationships are viewed in the United States. So, it's important to pause and examine some of the ways in which this reporting is culturally biased. For example, we assume—in the model and in the discussion of relationship development—that we voluntarily choose our relationship partners. In some cultures, however, your romantic partner is chosen for you by your parents, perhaps to solidify two families or to bring some financial advantage to your family or village.

In the United States, researchers study and textbook authors write about dissolving relationships and how to manage after a relationship breaks up. We assume that the individual has the right to exit an undesirable relationship. But, that's not always true. In some cultures, you simply can't dissolve a relationship once it's formed or once there are children. In other cultures only the man may dissolve a relationship.

In most of the United States, interpersonal friendships are drawn from a relatively large pool. Out of all the people you come into regular contact with, you choose relatively few of these as friends. And now with computer chat groups, the number of friends people can have has increased enormously as has the range from which these friends can be chosen. In rural areas and in small villages throughout much of the world, however, you would have very few choices. The two or three other children your age become your friends; there's no real choice because these are the only possible friends you could make.

A cultural bias is also seen in the research on maintenance; it's assumed that relationships should be permanent or at least long lasting. It's also assumed that people want to keep relationships together. There's little research that studies how people move from one intimate relationship to another or that advises you how to do this effectively and efficiently.

In what ways has your own thinking about relationships been influenced by your cultural training? Can you identify how you came to have any of your current relationship beliefs?

It should come as no surprise to find that happily married couples **affirm** each other; that is, they engage in greater positive behavior exchange. They communicate more agreement, approval, and positive affect than do unhappily married couples (Dindia & Fitzpatrick 1985). Clearly, these behaviors result from the positive feelings these spouses have for each other. But it can also be argued that these expressions help to increase the positive regard that each person has for his or her partner. Other affirming messages are also needed, such as the exchange of favors, compliments, positive stroking, and all the nonverbals that say "I care."

Often solutions that are reached after an argument are followed for only a very short time; then the couple goes back to its previous unproductive behavior patterns. Instead, **integrate solutions into your normal behavior**, so that the solutions become integral to your everyday relationship interactions. Exchanging favors, compliments, and cherishing behaviors needs to become a part of everyday communication.

Take **risks** in trying to improve your relationship. Risk giving favors without any certainty of reciprocity. Risk rejection; make the first move to make up or say you're sorry. Be willing to change, to adapt,

BUILDING
Communication Skills

HOW DO YOU TALK CHERISHING?

Cherishing behaviors are an especially insightful way to affirm another person and to increase favor exchange, a concept that comes from the work of William Lederer (1984). Cherishing behaviors are those small gestures you enjoy receiving from your partner (a smile, a wink, a squeeze, a kiss). If you think this idea has merit, consider exchanging cherishing behaviors with a partner—a lover, best friend, or sibling, for example. You would each make a list of, say, 10 behaviors that you'd like to receive from your partner—on occasion and

as is appropriate. Identify cherishing behaviors that are (1) specific and positive—nothing overly general or negative, (2) focused on the present and future rather than related to issues about which the partners have argued in the past, (3) capable of being performed daily, and (4) easily executed—nothing for which you really have to go out of your way to accomplish. Once you have each prepared your lists, you would exchange them and, ideally, perform the cherishing behaviors your partner would like. At first, these behaviors may seem self-conscious and awkward. In time, however, they'll become a normal part of your interaction, which is exactly what you hope to achieve.

and to take on new tasks and responsibilities. And, of course, be willing to try new and different communication strategies.

Self-Repair

Of course, some relationships end. Sometimes there's simply not enough to hold the couple together or there are problems that can't be resolved. Sometimes the costs are too high and the rewards too few, or the relationship is recognized as destructive and escape seems the only alternative. Given the inevitability that some relationships will break up, here are some suggestions to ease the difficulty that is sure to follow. These suggestions can apply to the termination of any type of relationship, between friends or lovers, through death, separation, or breakup. The language of romantic breakups is used because these are the ones we deal with most frequently.

Break the loneliness-depression cycle. Loneliness and depression, the two most experienced feelings following the ending of a relationship, are serious. Depression, for example, may lead to physical illness. Ulcers, high blood pressure, insomnia, stomach pains, and sexual difficulties frequently accompany or are seriously aggravated by depression. In most cases lone-

liness and depression are temporary. Your task then is to eliminate or lessen these uncomfortable and potentially dangerous feelings by changing the situation. When depression does last or proves particularly upsetting, it's time to seek professional help.

Take time out. Take time out for yourself. Renew your relationship with yourself. If you were in a long-term relationship, you probably saw yourself as part of a team, as part of a couple. Now get to know yourself as a unique individual, standing alone now but fully capable of entering a meaningful relationship in the near future.

Bolster your self-esteem. When relationships fail, self-esteem often falls. You may feel guilty for having been the cause of the breakup or inadequate for not holding on to a permanent relationship. You may feel unwanted and unloved. All of these feelings contribute to lowering self-esteem. Your task here is to regain the positive self-image that is needed to function effectively as an individual and as a member of another relationship. Take positive action to raise your self-esteem. Oddly enough, helping others is one of the best ways to do this (Rubenstein & Shaver 1982). When you do things for others, either informally for people you know or by volunteer work in some community agency, you get the positive stroking from others, which helps you feel better about yourself. Positive and successful experiences are extremely helpful in building self-esteem, so engage in activities that you enjoy, that you do well, and that are likely to result in success.

Seek support. Although many people feel they should bear their burdens alone (men, in particular, have been taught that this is the only "manly" way to handle things), seeking the support of others is one of the best antidotes to the unhappiness caused when a relationship ends. Avail yourself of your friends and family for support. Tell your friends of your situation—in only general terms, if you prefer—and make it clear that you need support now. Seek out people who are positive and nurturing. Make the distinction between seeking support and seeking advice. If you feel you need advice, seek out a professional. For support, friends are best.

Avoid repeating negative patterns. Many people enter second and third relationships with the same blinders, faulty preconceptions, and unrealistic expectations with which they entered earlier relationships. It's possible, however, to learn from failed relationships and not repeat the same patterns. Ask yourself at the start of a new relationship if you're entering a relationship modeled on the previous one. If the answer is yes, be especially careful not to fall into old behavior patterns. At the same time, don't become a prophet of doom. Don't see in every new relationship vestiges of the old. Treat the new relationship as the unique relationship it is and don't evaluate it through past experiences. Past relationships and experiences should be guides, not filters.

RELATIONSHIP TYPES

Relationships, whether friendship, love, or primary relationships, are each unique. Yet, there are general types that research has identified and that give unusual insight into interpersonal relationships.

Types of Friendships

One theory of friendship identifies three major types: reciprocity, receptivity, and association (Reisman 1979, 1981). The friendship of **reciprocity** is the ideal type, characterized by loyalty, self-sacrifice, mutual affection, and generosity. A friendship of reciprocity is based on

equality: each individual shares equally in giving and receiving the benefits and rewards of the relationship.

In the friendship of **receptivity**, in contrast, there is an imbalance in giving and receiving; one person is the primary giver and one the primary receiver. This imbalance, however, is a positive one because each person gains something from the relationship. The different needs of both the person who receives and the person who gives affection are satisfied. This is the friendship that may develop between a teacher and a student or between a doctor and a patient. In fact, a difference in status is essential for the friendship of receptivity to develop.

The friendship of **association** is a transitory one. It might be described as a friendly relationship rather than a true friendship. Associative friendships are the kind we often have with classmates, neighbors, or coworkers. There is no great loyalty, no great trust, no great giving or receiving. The association is cordial but not intense.

Types of Lovers

Like friends, lovers come in different styles as well. Before reading about these styles, take the following self-test to identify your own love style.

SELF-TEST

What Kind of Lover Are You?

Respond to each of the following statements with T (if you believe the statement to be a generally accurate representation of your attitudes about love) or F (if you believe the statement does not adequately represent your attitudes about love).

_____ 1. My lover and I have the right physical "chemistry" between us.

_____ 2. I feel that my lover and I were meant for each other.

_____ 3. My lover and I really understand each other.

_____ 4. I believe that what my lover doesn't know about me won't hurt him/her.

_____ 5. My lover would get upset if he/she knew of some of the things I've done with other people.

_____ 6. When my lover gets too dependent on me, I want to back off a little.

_____ 7. I expect to always be friends with my lover.

_____ 8. Our love is really a deep friendship, not a mysterious, mystical emotion.

_____ 9. Our love relationship is the most satisfying because it developed from a good friendship.

_____ 10. In choosing my lover, I believed it was best to love someone with a similar background.

_____ 11. An important factor in choosing a partner is whether or not he/she would be a good parent.

_____ 12. One consideration in choosing my lover was how he/she would reflect on my career.

_____ 13. Sometimes I get so excited about being in love with my lover that I can't sleep.

_____ 14. When my lover doesn't pay attention to me, I feel sick all over.

_____ 15. I cannot relax if I suspect that my lover is with someone else.

_____ 16. I would rather suffer myself than let my lover suffer.

_____ 17. When my lover gets angry with me, I still love him/her fully and unconditionally.

_____ 18. I would endure all things for the sake of my lover.

This scale is designed to enable you to identify those styles that best reflect your own beliefs about love. "True" answers represent your agreement and "false" answers represent your disagreement with the type of love to which the statements refer.

Statements 1–3 are characteristic of the **eros lover**. If you answered "true" to these statements, you have a strong eros component to your love style. If you answered "false," you have a weak eros component. The eros lover seeks beauty and sensuality and focuses on physical attractiveness, sometimes to the exclusion of qualities we might consider more important and more lasting. The erotic lover has an idealized image of beauty that is unattainable in reality. Consequently, the erotic lover often feels unfulfilled.

Statements 4–6 refer to **ludus love**, a love that seeks entertainment and excitement and sees love as fun, a game. To the ludic lover, love is not to be taken too seriously; emotions are to be held in check lest they get out of hand and make trouble. The ludic lover retains a partner only so long as the partner is interesting and amusing. When the partner is no longer interesting enough, it's time to change.

Statements 7–9 refer to **storge love**, a love that is peaceful and tranquil. Like ludus, storge lacks passion and intensity. Storgic lovers do not set out to find lovers but to establish a companion-like relationship with someone they know and can share interests and activities. Storgic love is a gradual process of unfolding thoughts and feelings and is sometimes difficult to separate from friendship.

Statements 10–12 refer to **pragma love**, a love that seeks the practical and traditional and wants compatibility and a relationship in which important needs and desires will be satisfied. The pragma lover is concerned with the social qualifications of a potential mate even more than personal qualities; family and background are extremely important to the pragma lover, who relies not so much on feelings as on logic.

Statements 13–15 refer to **manic love**, an obsessive love that needs to give and to receive constant attention and affection. When this is not given or when an expression of increased commitment is not returned, such reactions as depression, jealousy, and self-doubt are often experienced and can lead to the extreme lows characteristic of the manic lover.

Statements 16–18 refer to **agapic love**, a compassionate and selfless love. The agapic lover loves the stranger on the road and the annoying neighbor. Jesus, Buddha, and Gandhi practiced and preached this unqualified, spiritual love, a love that is offered without concern for personal reward or gain, and without any expectation that the love will be returned or reciprocated.

Do your scores seem accurate reflections of what you think about love?

From "What Kind of Lover are You?" from "A Relationship: Specific Version of the Love Attitudes Scale" by C. Hendrick and S. Hendrick in *Journal of Social Behavior and Personality*, 5, 1990, pp.239-245. Reprinted by permission of Select Press.

Types of Primary Relationships

A most interesting typology of primary relationships (based on responses from more than 1,000 couples to questions concerning their degree of sharing, their space needs, their conflicts, and the time they spend together—all identified in the headings of the accompanying self-test) identifies three basic types: traditionals, independents, and separates (Fitzpatrick

1983, 1988, 1991; Noller & Fitzpatrick 1993). At this point, you may wish to examine your own relational attitudes and style by taking the "What Type of Relationship Do You Prefer?" self-test. If you have a relational partner, you might wish to have him or her also complete the test and then compare your results.

SELF-TEST

What type of relationship do you prefer?

Respond to each of the following 16 statements by indicating the degree to which you agree with each. Circle *high* if you agree strongly, *med* if you agree moderately (medium), and *low* if you feel little agreement. For now, do not be concerned with the fact that these terms appear in different positions in the columns. Note that in some cases there are only two alternatives. When you agree with an alternative that appears twice, circle it both times.

Ideology of Traditionalism

1. A woman should take her husband's last name when she marries.

   High   Low   Med

2. Our wedding ceremony was (will be) very important to us.

   High   Low   Med

Ideology of Uncertainty and Change

3. In marriage/close relationships, there should be no constraints or restrictions on individual freedom.

   Low   High   Med

4. The ideal relationship is one marked by novelty, humor, and spontaneity.

   Low   High   Med

Sharing

5. We tell each other how much we love or care about each other.

   High   Low   Med

6. My spouse/mate reassures and comforts me when I am feeling low.

   High   Low   Med

Autonomy

7. I have my own private work space (study, workshop, utility room, etc.).

   Low   High   High

8. My spouse has his/her own private work space (workshop, utility, etc.).

   Low   High   High

Undifferentiated Space

9. I feel free to interrupt my spouse/mate when he/she is concentrating on something if he/she is in my presence.

   High   High   Low

10. I open my spouse/mate's personal mail without asking permission.

    High   Med   Low

Temporal Regularity

11. We eat our meals (i.e., the ones at home) at the same time every day.

    High   Low   High

12. In our house, we keep a fairly regular daily time schedule.

    High   Low   High

Conflict Avoidance

13. If I can avoid arguing about some problems, they will disappear.

    Med   Low   High

14. It is better to hide one's true feelings in order to avoid hurting your spouse/mate.

    Med   Low   High

Assertiveness

15. We are likely to argue in front of friends or in public places.

    Low   Med   Med

16. My spouse/mate tries to persuade me to do something I do not want to do.

    Low   Med   Med

The responses noted in column 1 are characteristic of traditionals. The number of circled items in this column, then, indicates your agreement with and similarity to those considered "traditionals."

Responses noted in column 2 are characteristic of independents; those noted in column 3 are characteristic of separates.

Traditional couples share a basic belief system and philosophy of life. They see themselves as a blending of two persons into a single couple rather than as two separate individuals. They're interdependent and believe that an individual's independence must be sacrificed for the good of the relationship. Traditionals believe in mutual sharing and do little separately. This couple holds to the traditional sex roles, and there are seldom any role conflicts. There are few power struggles and few conflicts because each person knows and adheres to a specified role within the relationship. In their communications, traditionals are highly responsive to each other. Traditionals lean toward each other, smile, talk a lot, interrupt each other, and finish each other's sentences.

Independents stress their individuality. The relationship is important but never more important than each person's individual identity. Although independents spend a great deal of time together, they do not ritualize it, for example, with schedules. Each individual spends time with outside friends. Independents see themselves as relatively androgynous, as individuals who combine the traditionally feminine and the traditionally masculine roles and qualities. The communication between independents is responsive. They engage in conflict openly and without fear. Their disclosures are quite extensive and include high-risk and negative disclosures that are typically absent among traditionals.

Separates live together but view their relationship more as a matter of convenience than a result of their mutual love or closeness. They seem to have little desire to be together and, in fact, usually are together only at ritual functions, such as mealtime or holiday get-togethers. It's important to these separates that each has his or her own physical as well as psychological space. Separates share little; each seems to prefer to go his or her own way. Separates hold relatively traditional values and beliefs about sex roles, and each person tries to follow the behaviors normally assigned to each role. What best characterizes this type, however, is that each person sees himself or herself as a separate individual and not as a part of a "we."

In addition to these three pure types, there are also combinations. For example, in the separate-traditional couple one individual is a separate and one a traditional. Another common pattern is the traditional-independent, in which one individual believes in the traditional view of relationships and one in autonomy and independence.

From Mary Anne Fitzpatrick, *Relational Dimensions Instrument*. Reprinted by permission of Mary Anne Fitzpatrick.

RELATIONSHIP THEORIES

Several theories offer insight into why and how we develop and dissolve our relationships. Here we single out five such theories: attraction, relationship rules, social penetration, social exchange, and equity.

Attraction Theory

You're no doubt attracted to some people and not attracted to others. In a similar way, some people are attracted to you and some people are not. If you're like most people, then you're attracted to others on the basis of four major factors: attractiveness (physical appearance and personality), similarity, proximity, and reinforcement.

Attractiveness: Physical and Personality

When you say, "I find that person attractive," you probably mean either that (1) you find that person physically attractive or (2) you find that person's personality or behavior attractive. For the most part you probably like physically attractive people rather than physically unattractive people, and you like people who have a pleasant rather than an unpleasant personality. Of course, we each would define "attractive" somewhat differently. However, recent research seems to be finding universals of attraction. For example, in one study both Japanese and Britons ranked faces as attractive when they had large eyes, looked youthful, had high cheekbones, and had a narrow jaw (*New York Times* March 21, 1994, p. A14).

Generally, people attribute positive characteristics to people they find attractive and negative characteristics to people they find unattractive. Those who are perceived as attractive are also perceived as more competent in general. Interestingly enough, those who are perceived as more competent in communication are

MEDIA WATCH

PARASOCIAL RELATIONSHIPS

A parasocial relationship is one that a viewer perceives himself or herself to have with a media personality (Rubin & McHugh 1987). At times viewers develop these relationships with real media personalities—Rosie O'Donnell, Kathy Lee Gifford, or Geraldo Rivera, for example. As a result they may watch these personalities faithfully and communicate with the individual in their own imaginations. At other times, the relationship is with the fictional character—a doctor on "ER," Jesse, or Walker. In fact, those who play doctors frequently get mail asking their medical advice. And soap opera stars who are about to be "killed" frequently get warning letters from their parasocial relationship partners. Most people obviously don't go quite this far. Yet, many viewers consider the role real enough to make that actor in that role a bankable spokesperson for a product. For example, actor Susan Sullivan, who played a nurse on television some 10 years ago, is still a spokesperson for a particular medication.

CD ROM and Internet videos of our television heroes that we can play over and over provide a natural source for parasocial relationships. The chat sessions that many of these stars hold on the Internet (usually on one of the commercial carriers) where you can talk with them help create the illusion of a real interpersonal relationship. The screen savers of television stars (those from Friends, Seinfeld, Home Improvement, and Frasier are currently popular) make it difficult not to think of them in relationship terms when they face you every time you leave your computer idle for a few minutes.

Parasocial relationships develop from an initial attraction with the character's social and task roles, to a perceived relationship, and finally to a sense that this relationship is an important one (Rubin & McHugh 1987). A viewer's ability to predict the behavior of a character seems to contribute to the development of parasocial relationships (Perse & Rubin 1989). As can be expected, these parasocial relationships are most important to those who spend a great deal of time with the media and who have few interpersonal relationships (Rubin, Perse, & Powell 1985).

Even the relationship between talk show host and guest is a parasocial one, media researcher Janice Peck (1995) argues. The reason is that such relationships are basically one-sided and the roles are not interchangeable. The interaction is not one of dialogue but rather one in which the host controls the interaction and the guests essentially answer the questions the host asks.

In many instances, relationships are not that easy to classify into real or parasocial classes. For example, most of us can probably recall at least one real relationship we have had where the talk was basically one-sided, where the roles were not interchangeable, and where the interaction was largely controlled by one person.

Further, in the talk shows where viewers can often write in to meet the guests from the show, the relationships may begin as parasocial but quickly move to real. For example, a "Sally Jesse Raphael" show in early 1995 was devoted to viewers who had crushes on former guests and whom the show got together for another show. Viewers can now see the characters on television—and in some ways talk show panelists are very much like dramatic characters in a play—as potential relationship partners. Even though such occurrences are infrequent, they seem to happen often enough for people to write in with the possibility of meeting a guest. On home-shopping programs, you may develop a parasocial relationship with the host (Grant, Guthrie, & Ball-Rokeach 1991). On some shows you can often talk

(continued on next page)

Media Watch *(continued)*

with the host or with a product's spokesperson. You can, for example, call the number on the screen and talk to some minor or even major celebrity. As the ability to interact with the television programs increases, the distinction between real and parasocial relationships will become increasingly blurred (Auter & Moore 1993).

Do you see both advantages and disadvantages to parasocial relationships? What are the major advantages? The major disadvantages? Do you maintain parasocial relationships with media personalities? If so, what functions do these relationships serve for you?

The next Media Watch appears on page 222.

---

also perceived as more attractive, both socially and physically (Duran & Kelly, 1988).

Similarity

If you could construct your mate, it's likely that your mate would look, act, and think very much like you (Burleson, Samter, & Luccetti 1992; Burleson, Kunkel, & Birch 1994). By being attracted to people like us, we validate ourselves; we tell ourselves that we are worthy of being liked, that we are attractive. Although there are exceptions, we generally like people who are similar to ourselves in nationality, race, ability, physical characteristics, intelligence, attitudes, and so on.

Sometimes people are attracted to their opposites, for example, a dominant person might be attracted to someone who is more submissive. Generally, however, people much prefer relationships with people who are similar. And, not surprisingly, relationships between persons who are similar last longer than relationships between dissimilar people (Blumstein & Schwartz 1983).

Proximity

If you look around at people you find attractive, you would probably find that they are the people who live or work close to you. People who become friends are the people who have the greatest opportunity to interact with each other. Physical closeness is most important in the early stages of interaction, for example, during the first days of school (in class or in dormitories). It decreases (but always remains significant) as the opportunity to interact with more distant others increases.

Reinforcement

Not surprisingly, we are attracted to people who give us rewards or reinforcements. These may be social,

It has been argued that you don't actually develop an attraction for those who are similar to you but rather develop a repulsion for those who are dissimilar (Rosenbaum 1986). For example, you may be repulsed by those who disagree with you and therefore exclude them from those with whom you might develop a relationship. You're therefore left with a pool of possible partners who are similar to you. What do you think of this repulsion hypothesis? How would you go about testing it?

as in the case of compliments or praise, or material, as in the case of the suitor whose gifts eventually win the hand of the beloved. When overdone, of course, reward can lose its effectiveness and may even lead to negative responses. The people who reward you constantly soon become too sweet to take, and in a short period you probably learn to discount whatever they say. Also, if the reward is to work, it must be perceived as genuine and not motivated by selfish concerns.

You're also attracted to people *you* reward (Jecker & Landy, 1969; Aronson, 1980). You come to like people for whom you do favors. For example, you have probably increased your liking for persons after buying them an expensive present or going out of your way to do them a special favor. In these situations, you justify your behavior by believing that the person was worth your efforts; otherwise, you would have to admit to spending your money and effort on people who do not deserve it.

Relationship Rules Approach

You can gain an interesting perspective on interpersonal relationships by looking at them in terms of the rules that govern them (Shimanoff 1980). The general assumption of this view is that relationships—friendship and love in particular—are held together by adherence to certain rules. When those rules are broken, the relationship may deteriorate and even dissolve.

Discovering relationship rules serves several functions. Ideally, these rules help identify successful versus destructive relationship behavior. In addition,

these rules help pinpoint more specifically why relationships break up and how they may be repaired. Further, if we know what the rules are we will be better able to teach the social skills involved in relationship development and maintenance. Since these rules vary from one culture to another, it will be necessary to identify those unique to each culture so that intercultural relationships may be more effectively developed and maintained.

Friendship Rules

Column 1 in Table 10.1 presents some important rules of friendship (Argyle & Henderson 1984, Argyle 1986). When these rules are followed, the friendship is strong and mutually satisfying. When these rules are broken, the friendship suffers and may die. Column 2 presents the abuses that are most significant in breaking up a friendship (Argyle & Henderson 1984). Note that some rules for maintaining a friendship directly correspond to the abuses that break up friendships. For example, it's important to "demonstrate emotional support" to maintain a friendship, but when emotional support is not shown, the friendship will prove less satisfying and may well break up. The strategy for maintaining a friendship would then depend on your knowing the rules and having the ability to apply the appropriate interpersonal skills (Trower 1981; Blieszner & Adams 1992).

Romantic Rules

Other research has identified the rules that romantic relationships establish and follow. Leslie Baxter (1986), for example, has identified eight major rules.

TABLE 10.1   **Keeping and breaking up a friendship**

Do these rules adequately describe the ways in which your friendships have been maintained or broken up? Can you think of additional rules that are important in friendships?

To Keep a Friendship	*To Break Up a Friendship*
Stand up for Friend in his or her absence.	Be intolerant of Friend's friends.
Share information and feelings about successes.	Discuss confidences between yourself and Friend with others.
Demonstrate emotional support	Don't display any positive regard for Friend.
Trust each other; confide in each other.	Don't demonstrate any positive support for Friend.
Offer to help Friend when in need.	Nag Friend.
Try to make Friend happy when you're together.	Don't trust or confide in Friend.

Baxter argues that these rules both keep the relationship together and, when broken, lead to deterioration and eventually dissolution. The general form for each rule, as Baxter phrases it, is "If parties are in a close relationship, they should . . ."

1. acknowledge one another's individual identities and lives beyond the relationship
2. express similar attitudes, beliefs, values, and interests
3. enhance one another's self-worth and self-esteem
4. be open, genuine and authentic with one another
5. remain loyal and faithful to one another
6. have substantial shared time together
7. reap rewards commensurate with their investments relative to the other party
8. experience a mysterious and inexplicable 'magic' in one another's presence

Social Penetration Theory

Social penetration theory is a theory not of why relationships develop but of what happens when they do develop; it describes relationships in terms of the number of topics that people talk about and their degree of "personalness" (Altman & Taylor 1973). The *breadth* of a relationship refers to the number of topics you and your partner talk about. The *depth* of a relationship refers to the degree to which you penetrate the inner personality—the core of the individual.

We can represent an individual as a circle and divide that circle into various parts. These parts represent the topics or areas of interpersonal communication, or breadth. Further, visualize the circle and its parts as consisting of concentric inner circles, rather like an onion. These represent the different levels of communication, or the depth (see Figure 10.3). The circles contain eight topic areas (A through H) and five levels of intimacy (represented by the concentric circles).

Depenetration

When a relationship begins to deteriorate, the breadth and depth will, in many ways, reverse themselves, a process called *depenetration*. For example, while ending a relationship, you might cut out certain topics from your interpersonal communications. At the same time you might discuss the remaining topics in less depth. In some instances of relational deterioration, however, both the breadth and the depth of interaction increase. For example, when a couple breaks up

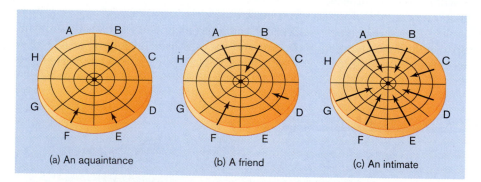

(a) An acquaintance   **(b) A friend**   **(c) An intimate**

Figure 10.3 **Social Penetration with (a) an acquaintance, (b) a friend, and (c) an intimate.**   Note that in circle (a) you discuss only three topic areas. You penetrate two only to the first level and one to the second level. In this type of interaction, you discuss the three topic areas at fairly superficial levels. This is the type of relationship you might have with an acquaintance. Circle (b) represents a more intense relationship. It's both broader and deeper. This is the type of relationship you might have with a friend. Circle (c) is a still more intense relationship, one with considerable breadth and depth. This is the type of relationship you might have with a lover, a parent, or a sibling. Does this theory adequately describe the types of communication you have with acquaintances, friends, and intimates? Does it adequately describe both face-to-face and online relationships?

Going Online

Cyrano Server Web site

Visit Cyrano and ask him to write you a love letter or a relationship-ending letter. What would the relationship theories discussed in this section say about Cyrano's letters? Can you use the theories to explain the logic of Cyrano's letters?

and each is finally free from an oppressive relationship, they may—after some time—begin to discuss problems and feelings they would never have discussed when they were together. In fact, they may become extremely close friends and come to like each other more than when they were together. In these cases the breadth and depth of their relationship may increase rather than decrease (Baxter 1983).

Social Exchange Theory

Social exchange theory claims that you develop relationships that will enable you to maximize your profits (Chadwick-Jones 1976; Gergen, Greenberg, & Willis 1980; Thibaut & Kelley 1986), a theory based on an economic model of profits and losses. The theory begins with the following equation: Profits = Rewards − Costs. Rewards are anything that you would incur costs to obtain. Research has identified six types of rewards in a love relationship: money, status, love, information, goods, and services (Baron & Byrne 1984). For example, to get the reward of money, you might have to work rather than play. To earn the status of an "A" in interpersonal communication, you might have to write a term paper or study more than you want to.

Costs are those things that you normally try to avoid. These are the things you consider unpleasant or difficult. Working overtime; washing dishes and ironing clothes; watching your partner's favorite television show, which you find boring; and doing favors for those you dislike might all be considered costs.

Using this basic economic model, social exchange theory claims that you seek to develop friendship and romantic relationships that will give you the greatest profits; that is, relationships in which the rewards are greater than the costs. The most preferred relationships, according to this theory, are those that give you the greatest rewards with the least costs.

You enter a relationship with a **comparison level**—a general idea of the kinds of rewards and profits that you feel you ought to get out of such a relationship. This comparison level comprises your realistic expectations concerning what you feel you deserve from this relationship. For example, in a study of married couples it was found that most people expect high levels of trust, mutual respect, love, and commitment. Their expectations are significantly lower for time spent together, privacy, sexual activity, and communication (Sabatelli & Pearce, 1986). When the rewards that you get equal or surpass this comparison level, you feel satisfied with your relationship.

However, you also have a **comparison level for alternatives**. That is, you compare the profits that you get from your current relationship with the profits you think you can get from alternative relationships. Thus, if you see that the profits from your present relationship are below the profits that you could get from an alternative relationship, you might decide to leave your current relationship and enter a new, more profitable relationship.

Equity Theory

Equity theory uses the ideas of social exchange but goes a step further and claims that you develop and maintain relationships in which the *ratio* of your rewards compared to costs is approximately equal to your partner's (Walster, Walster, & Berscheid 1978; Messick & Cook 1983). For example, if you and a friend start a business and you put up two-thirds of the money and your friend puts up one-third, equity would demand that you get two-thirds of the profits and your friend get one-third. An equitable relationship, then, is simply one in which each party derives rewards that are proportional to their costs. If you contribute more toward the relationship than your partner, then equity requires that you should get greater rewards. If you each work equally hard then equity demands that you should each get approximately equal rewards. Conversely, inequity would exist in a relationship if you pay more of the costs (for example, you do more of the unpleasant tasks) but your partner enjoys more of the rewards. Inequity would also exist if you and your partner work equally hard, but one of you gets more of the rewards.

Much research supports this idea that people want equity in their interpersonal relationships

UNDERSTANDING
Theory and Research

WHAT DO THE THEORIES SAY?

Read each of the following letters and *describe* each of the problems in terms of (1) attraction, (2) relationship rules, (3) social penetration, (4) social exchange, or (5) equity theories.

Love and Age Difference

I'm in love with an older woman. She's 43 and I'm 19 but very mature; in fact, I'm a lot more mature than she is. I want to get married but she doesn't; she says she doesn't love me but I know she does. She wants to break up our romance and "become friends." How can I win her over?

/Signed/ 22 and Determined

Love and Sports

My relationship of the last 20 years has been great—except for one thing: I can't watch sports on television. If I turn on the game Pat moans and groans until I turn it off. Pat wants to talk; I want to watch the game. I work hard during the week and on the weekend I want to watch sports, drink beer, and fall asleep on the couch. This problem has gotten so bad that I'm seriously considering separating. What should I do?

/Signed/ Sports Lover

Love and the Dilemma

I'm 29 and have been dating fairly steadily two really great people. Each knows about my relationship with the other and for a while they went along with it and tolerated what they felt was an unpleasant situation. They now threaten to break up if I don't make a decision. To be perfectly honest, I like both of them a great deal and simply need more time before I can make the decision and ask one to be my life mate. How can I get them to stay with the status quo for maybe another year or two or three?

/Signed/ Simply Undecided

Do the theories make any predictions about how these situations are likely to be resolved? Do they offer any suggestions as to what the individuals should do? Which theory offers the greatest insights into problems such as these?

(Ueleke et al. 1983). The general idea behind this is that if you are underbenefited (you get less than you put in), you'll be angry and dissatisfied. If, on the other hand, you are overbenefited (you get more than you put in), you'll feel guilty. Some research, however, has questioned this rather neat but intuitively unsatisfying assumption and finds that the overbenefited person is often quite happy and contented; guilt from getting more than you deserve seems easily forgotten (Noller & Fitzpatrick 1993).

Equity theory puts into clear focus the sources of relational dissatisfaction seen every day. For example, in a relationship both partners may have full-time jobs but one may also be expected to do the major share of the household chores. Thus, although both may be deriving equal rewards—they have equally good cars, they live in the same three-bedroom house, and so on—one partner is paying more of the costs. According to equity theory, this partner will be dissatisfied because of this lack of equity.

Equity theory claims that you will develop and maintain relationships and will be satisfied with relationships that are equitable. You will not develop, will terminate, and will be dissatisfied with relationships that are inequitable. The greater the inequity, the greater the dissatisfaction, and the greater likelihood that the relationship will end.

A summary of these basic theories is presented in Table 10.2.

TABLE 10.2 Relationship theories and relationship movement

This table summarizes the theories just considered and their basic assumptions on relationship development, maintenance, and deterioration. Can you think of specific examples in which the theories effectively explained what happened in a relationship? Can you think of examples where the relationship contradicted the theory's predictions?

Relationship Theories / Relationship Movement	Attraction	Relationship Rules	Social Penetration	Social Exchange	Equity
Development; increases toward intimacy	When attraction is great	When the relationship partners follow the rules	Depth and breadth increase	When the rewards are greater than the costs, and especially when these rewards are more than you could get elsewhere	When the rewards and costs are distributed between the partners equitably
Maintenance, keeping the relationship much as it is	When attraction is satisfactory	When the relationship rules are maintained or are broken with acceptable frequency	Depth and breadth remain at acceptable levels	When the rewards are greater and the costs are less than you expected or that you could get elsewhere	When the rewards and costs are distributed equitably or within acceptable limits of inequity
Deterioration; movements away from intimacy	When attraction is less than desired	When relationship rules are broken	Depth and breadth decrease	When the costs exceed the rewards or when you could get greater profit in another relationship	When the rewards and costs are distributed to an unacceptable inequitable degree

How equitable are your friendships? How equitable are your romantic relationships? If any are not equitable, are you the overbenefitted or the underbenefitted partner? How do you feel about this?

SUMMARY

In this unit we looked at interpersonal relationships, their nature, stages, and types and at the theories that try to explain what happens in an interpersonal relationship.

1. Relationships develop for a variety of reasons; some of the most important are to lessen loneliness, secure stimulation, gain self-knowledge, and maximize pleasures and minimize pain.

2. We establish relationships in stages. Recognize at least these: contact, involvement, intimacy, deterioration, repair, and dissolution.

3. Three main phases in initiating relationships may be noted: examining the qualifiers, determining clearance, and communicating your desire for contact.

4. The following nonverbal behaviors are useful in initiating relationships: establish eye contact, signal positive response, concentrate your focus, establish proximity, maintain an open posture, respond visibly, use positive behaviors, and avoid overexposure. The following verbal behaviors are helpful in initiating relationships: introduce yourself, focus the conversation on the other person, exchange favors and rewards, be energetic, stress the positives, avoid negative or too intimate self-disclosures, and establish commonalities.

5. Relationship deterioration—the weakening of the bonds holding people together—may be gradual or sudden and may have positive as well as negative effects.

6. Among the causes for relationship deterioration are diminution of the reasons for establishing the relationship, relational changes, undefined expectations, sex conflicts, work problems, financial difficulties, and the inequitable distribution of rewards and costs.

7. Among the communication changes that take place during relationship deterioration are general withdrawal, a decrease in self-disclosure, an increase in deception, a decrease in positive and an increase in negative evaluative responses, and a decrease in the exchange of favors.

8. Relationship maintenance focuses on behaviors designed to continue the relationship, to keep it intact, to keep the relationship confined to one stage, or to keep it from deteriorating.

9. Relationships may stay together because of emotional attachments, convenience, children, fear, financial considerations, inertia, commitment, and effective communication patterns.

10. A useful approach to relationship repair is first to recognize the problem, engage in productive conflict resolution, pose possible solutions, affirm each other, integrate solutions into relationship behaviors, and take risks.

11. If the relationship does end, engage in self-repair. Break the loneliness–depression cycle, take time out, bolster self-esteem, seek emotional support, and avoid repeating negative patterns.

12. Friendships may be classified as those of reciprocity, receptivity, and association.

13. Six primary love styles have been identified: eros, ludus, storge, mania, pragma, and agape.

14. Primary relationships may be classified into traditionals, independents, and separates.

15. Attraction, relationship rules, social penetration, social exchange, and equity theories are five explanations of what happens when we develop, maintain, and dissolve interpersonal relationships.

16. Attraction depends on four factors: attractiveness (physical and personality), similarity (especially attitudinal), proximity (physical closeness), and reinforcement.

17. The relationship rules approach views relationships as held together by agreement and adherence to an agreed upon set of rules.

18. Social penetration describes relationships in terms of breadth and depth. Breadth refers to the number of topics we talk about. Depth refers to the degree of personalness with which we pursue topics.

19. Social exchange theory holds that we develop relationships that yield the greatest profits. We seek relationships in which the rewards exceed the costs and are more likely to dissolve relationships when the costs exceed the rewards.

20. Equity theory claims that we develop and maintain relationships in which rewards are distributed in proportion to costs. When our share of the rewards is less than would be demanded by equity, we are likely to experience dissatisfaction and exit the relationship.

KEY TERMS

interpersonal relationship (p. 175)

relationship development (p. 175)

relationship deterioration (p. 178)

relationship maintenance (p. 181)

commitment (p. 182)

interpersonal repair (p. 183)

self-repair (p. 186)

friendships of reciprocity, receptivity, and association (p. 187)

eros, ludus, storge, pragma, mania, and agape love styles (p. 188)

traditional, independent, and separate styles in primary relationships (p. 190)

attraction theory (p. 190)

similarity (p. 192)

proximity (p. 192)

reinforcement (p. 192)

relationship rules theory (p. 193)

social penetration theory (p. 194)

depenetration (p. 194)

breadth (p. 194)

depth (p. 194)

social exchange theory (p. 195)

comparison level (p. 195)

comparison level for alternatives (p. 196)

equity theory (p. 196)

THINKING CRITICALLY ABOUT
Interpersonal Relationships

1. It was only as recently as 1967—after nine years of trials and appeals—that the United States Supreme Court forbade any state laws against interracial marriage (Crohn 1995). How would you describe the state of interracial romantic relationships today? What obstacles do such relationships face? What advantages do they offer?

2. How would you go about finding answers to such questions as these?
   • Are the reasons for developing relationships similar for female–male, female–female, or male–male relationships?
   • Do the reasons for developing relationships change with age? How do the reasons differ between, say, 20-year-olds, on the one hand, and 50–60-year-olds, on the other?
   • Do men and women use the same maintenance strategies?
   • How do the maintenance strategies differ for friends and for romantic relationships?

3. One way to improve communication during difficult times is to ask your partner for positive behaviors rather than to stop negative behaviors. How might you use this suggestion to replace such statements as: (1) I hate it when you ignore me at business functions. (2) I can't stand going to these cheap restaurants; when are you going to start spending a few bucks? (3) Stop being so negative; you criticize everything and everyone.

4. The "matching hypothesis" claims that people date and mate people who are very similar to themselves in physical attractiveness (Walster & Walster 1978). When this does not happen—when a very attractive person dates someone of average attractiveness—the person may begin to look for "compensating factors," factors that the less attractive person possesses that compensate or make up for being less physically attractive. What evidence can you find to support or contract this theory? How would you go about testing this theory?

5. Test out the predictions of the five theories on your own relationships. For example, are you attracted to people who are physically attractive, have a pleasing personality, who are near to you, who are similar to you, and reinforce you? Do you maintain relationships when rules are followed and break up when rules are broken? Do you talk about more topics and in greater depth in close relationships than in mere acquaintanceships? Do you pursue and maintain relationships that give you profits (where rewards are greater than costs)? Were the relationships that you did not pursue or that you ended unprofitable, that is, those in which costs were greater than rewards? Are you more satisfied with equitable relationships than with inequitable ones?

UNIT 11
Interpersonal Conflict

UNIT GOALS

After completing this unit, you should be able to

define *interpersonal conflict* and distinguish between content and relationship conflict

explain the strategies of conflict management

describe the suggestions for preparing for and following up an interpersonal conflict

This unit focuses on interpersonal conflict, what it is, how it can go wrong, and, most important, what you can do to resolve effectively the inevitable conflicts that are a part of all interpersonal relationships.

INTERPERSONAL CONFLICT

Pat wants to go to the movies with Chris; Chris wants to stay home. Pat's insisting on going to the movies interferes with Chris's staying home and Chris's determination to stay home interferes with Pat's going to the movies.

Jim and Bernard own a small business. Jim wants to expand the business and open a branch in California. Bernard wants to sell the business and retire. Each has opposing goals and each interferes with each other's attaining these goals.

As experience shows, relational conflicts can be of various types:

- goals to be pursued ("We want you to go to college and become a teacher or a doctor, not a disco dancer")
- allocation of resources such as money or time ("I want to spend the tax refund on a car, not on new furniture")
- decisions to be made ("I refuse to have the Jeffersons over for dinner")
- behaviors that are considered appropriate or desirable by one person and inappropriate or undesirable by the other ("I hate it when you get drunk/pinch me/ridicule me in front of others/flirt with others/dress provocatively")

Myths About Conflict

One of the problems in studying and in dealing with interpersonal conflict is that you may be operating with false assumptions about what conflict is and what it means. Think about your own assumptions about conflict, which were probably derived from the communications you witnessed in your family and in your social interactions. For example, do you think the following are true or false?

- If two people are in a relationship fight, it means their relationship is a bad one.
- Fighting damages an interpersonal relationship.
- Fighting is bad because it reveals our negative selves—our pettiness, our need to be in control, our unreasonable expectations.

Simple answers are usually wrong. The three assumptions above may all be true or may all be false. It depends. In and of itself, conflict is neither good nor bad. Conflict is a part of every interpersonal relationship, between parents and children, brothers and sisters, friends, lovers, coworkers. If it isn't, then the relationship is probably dull, irrelevant, or insignificant. Conflict is inevitable in any meaningful relationship.

It's not so much the conflict that creates the problem as the way in which you approach and deal with the conflict. Some ways of approaching conflict can resolve difficulties and actually improve the relationship. Other ways can hurt the relationship; they can destroy self-esteem, create bitterness, and foster suspicion. Your task, therefore, is not to try to create relationships that will be free of conflict but rather to learn appropriate and productive ways of managing conflict.

Similarly, it's not the conflict that will reveal your negative side but the fight strategies you use. Thus if you personally attack the other person, use force, or use personal rejection or manipulation you'll reveal your negative side. But in fighting you can also reveal your positive self—your willingness to listen to opposing points of view, your readiness to change unpleasant behaviors, and your willingness to accept imperfection in others.

Content and Relationship Aspects of Conflict

Using concepts developed earlier (Unit 2), we may distinguish between content conflict and relationship conflict. Content conflict centers on objects, events, and persons in the world that are usually, but not always, external to the parties involved in the conflict. These include the millions of issues that you argue and fight about every day—the value of a particular movie, what to watch on television, the fairness of the last examination or job promotion, and the way to spend your savings.

Relationship conflicts are equally numerous and include such conflict situations as a younger brother who does not obey his older brother, two partners who each want an equal say in making vacation plans, and the mother and daughter who each want to have the final word concerning the daughter's lifestyle. Here the conflicts are concerned not so much with some external object as with the relationships between the individuals, with such issues as who is in charge, the equality of a primary relationship, and who has the right to set down rules of behavior.

Content conflicts are usually manifest; they're clearly observable and identifiable. Relationship conflicts are often latent; they're often hidden and much more difficult to identify. Thus, a conflict over where you should vacation may on the surface, or manifest, level center on the advantages and disadvantages of Mexico versus Hawaii. On a relationship and often latent level, however, it may center on who has the greater right to select the place to vacation, who should win the argument, who is the decision maker in the relationship, and so on. Here are two studies identifying the issues that most frequently create conflict. In the first study gay, lesbian, and heterosexual couples were surveyed on the issues they argued about most; the findings are presented in Table 11.1 (Kurdek 1994).

In another study four conditions led up to a couple's "first big fight" (Siegert & Stamp 1994):

- uncertainty over commitment
- jealousy
- violation of expectations
- personality differences

Rarely are conflicts all content- or all relationship-oriented. In fact, the vast majority of conflicts contain elements of both content and relationship. Try identifying the possible relationship aspects and the possible content aspects in each of the causes of conflict just listed as well as the causes of your own conflicts. Distinguishing the content from the relationship dimensions of any given conflict is one of the first steps toward conflict resolution.

The Context of Conflict

Conflict, like any form of communication, takes place in a context that is physical, sociopsychological, temporal, and cultural.

The **physical context**, whether you engage in conflict privately or publicly, alone or in front of children or relatives, for example, will influence the way the conflict is conducted as well as the effects that this conflict will have.

The **sociopsychological context** will also influence the conflict. If the atmosphere is one of equality, for example, the conflict is likely to progress very differently than if in an atmosphere of inequality. A

TABLE 11.1   Relationship conflict issues

This table presents the rank order of the six most frequently argued-about issues (1 = the most argud-about). Note that these issues involve both content and relationship dimensions. Note also the striking similarity among all couples. It seems that affectional orientation has little to do with the topics people argue about.

Issue	Gay (N = 75)	Lesbian (N = 51)	Heterosexual (N = 108)
Intimacy issues such as affection and sex	1	1	1
Power issues such as excessive demands or possessiveness, lack of equality in the relationship, friends, and leisure time	2	2	2
Personal flaws issues such as drinking or smoking, personal grooming, and driving style	3	3	4
Personal distance issues such as frequently being absent and school or job commitments	4	4	5
Social issues such as politics and social issues, parents, and personal values	5	5	3
Distrust issues such as previous lovers and lying	6	6	6

friendly or a hostile context will exert different influences on the conflict.

The **temporal context** will likewise prove important to understand. A conflict after a series of similar conflicts will be seen differently than a conflict after a series of enjoyable experiences and an absence of conflict. A conflict immediately after a hard day of work will engender feelings different from a conflict after an enjoyable dinner.

The **cultural context** is influential in conflict as it is with all other types of human communication. Culture will influence the issues that people fight about as well as what is considered appropriate and inappropriate ways of dealing with conflict. For example, cohabitating 18-year-olds are more likely to have conflict with the parents on their living style if they lived in the United States than if they lived in Sweden, where cohabitation is much more accepted. Similarly, male infidelity is more likely to cause conflict among American couples than among Southern European couples. Students from the United States are more likely to pursue a conflict with another United States student than with someone from another culture. Chinese students, on the other hand, are more likely to pursue a conflict with another Chinese student than with a non-Chinese (Leung 1988).

The types of conflicts that arise will depend on the cultural orientation of the individuals. For example, it's likely that in high-context cultures conflicts are more likely to center on violating collective or group norms and values. Conversely, it's likely that in low-context cultures conflicts are more likely to come up when individual norms are violated (Ting-Toomey 1985).

In Japan it's especially important that you not embarrass the person with whom you're in conflict, especially if that conflict occurs in public. This face-saving principle prohibits the use of such strategies as personal rejection or verbal aggressiveness. In the United States men and women, ideally at least, are both expected to express their desires and complaints openly and directly. Many Middle Eastern and Pacific Rim cultures would discourage women from such expressions. Rather, a more agreeable and permissive posture would be expected. African Americans and European Americans engage in conflict in very different ways (Kochman 1981). The issues that cause conflict and that aggravate conflict, the conflict strategies that are expected and accepted, and the entire attitude toward conflict vary from one group to the other.

Different cultures also view conflict management techniques differently. For example, in one study (Collier 1991) it was found that African American men preferred clear arguments and a focus on problem-solving. African American women, however, preferred assertiveness and respect. In another study African American females were found to use more direct controlling strategies (for example, assuming control over the conflict and arguing persistently for their point of view) than did white females. White females, on the other hand, used more problem-solution-oriented conflict styles than did African American females. African American and white men were very similar in their conflict strategies; both tended to avoid or withdraw from relationship conflict. They preferred to keep quiet about their differences or make them seem insignificant (Ting-Toomey 1986).

Mexican American men emphasized mutual understanding achieved through discussing the reasons for the conflict while women focused on support for the relationship. Anglo-American men preferred direct and rational argument while women preferred flexibility. These, of course, are merely examples, but the underlying principle is that techniques for dealing with interpersonal conflict are viewed differently by different cultures.

The following brief dialogue (from an idea by Crohn 1995) is designed to illustrate the issue of cultural differences in conflict and some of the problems these may create. As you read it, try to explain what is possibly going on interculturally.

PAT: Why did you tell her I was home? I told you an hour ago that I didn't want to speak with her. You just don't listen.

CHRIS: I'm sorry. I completely forgot. But, you seemed to have had a nice talk. So, no harm done—right?

PAT: Wrong. You just don't understand. I didn't want to talk with her.

CHRIS: Okay. Sorry.

Chris withdraws to next room and remains silent. To Pat's repeated comments and criticisms, he says nothing. After about two hours:

PAT: I can't stand your silent treatment; you're making me the villain. You're the one who screwed up.

CHRIS: I'm sorry. [Walks away]

Communication continued in this way for the rest of the evening—with Pat ranting and raving every several minutes and with Chris saying hardly anything and always trying to walk away. Pat comes from a culture where anger is regularly and expectedly expressed. Yelling and screaming are customary ways of dealing with conflict. Chris comes from a culture where anger is expressed by silence. The extent to which you remain silent is a clear measure of your anger.

From Chris's silence it's easy for Pat to conclude that Chris doesn't care about what happened and is indifferent to Pat's anger. From Pat's outburst Chris may easily conclude that Pat is unhappy in their relationship.

If Pat and Chris came from the same culture—with the same rules for expressing anger—or had sufficient intercultural awareness, their argument would have been no less real. Don't let us fool ourselves into thinking that cultural awareness will resolve all conflicts or that culture is the only factor that can cause such differences; it won't and it isn't. But, it would have prevented a large part of the conflict—for example, the anger over the way the other person expressed anger—and would have prevented each from making inaccurate assumptions about the other. The problem is made even more difficult to resolve because these cultural rules are so deeply ingrained that we assume everyone has the same rules. And we never get to explore the problem from the point of view of intercultural communication differences because we assume this underlying similarity.

The Negatives and Positives of Conflict

The kind of conflict focused on here is conflict among or between "connected" individuals. Interpersonal conflict occurs frequently between lovers, best friends, siblings, and parent and child. Interpersonal conflict is made all the more difficult because, unlike many other conflict situations, you often care for, like, even love the individual with whom you're in disagreement. There are both negative and positive aspects or dimensions to interpersonal conflict, and each of these should be noted.

Some Negatives

Conflict often leads to increased negative regard for the opponent, and when this opponent is someone you love or care for very deeply, it can create serious problems for the relationship. One problem is that many conflicts involve unfair fighting methods that aim largely to hurt the other person. When one person hurts the other, increased negative feelings are inevitable; even the strongest relationship has limits.

Conflict frequently leads to a depletion of energy better spent on other areas. This is especially true when unproductive conflict strategies are used, as we'll examine later in this unit.

At times conflict leads you to close yourself off from the other individual. Though it would not be to your advantage to reveal your weaknesses to your "enemy," when you hide your true self from an intimate, you may prevent meaningful communication from taking place. One possible consequence is that one or both parties may seek intimacy elsewhere. This often leads to further conflict, mutual hurt, and resentment—qualities that add heavily to the costs carried by the relationship. As these costs increase, exchanging rewards may become difficult—perhaps impossible. The result is a situation in which the costs increase and the rewards decrease—a situation that often results in relationship deterioration and eventual dissolution.

Some Positives

The major value of interpersonal conflict is that it forces you to examine a problem and work toward a potential solution. If productive conflict strategies are used, the relationship may well emerge from the encounter stronger, healthier, and more satisfying than before.

Conflict enables you to state what you each want and—if the conflict is resolved effectively—perhaps to get it. In fact, a better understanding of each other's feelings has been found to be one of the main results of the "first big fight" (Siegert & Stamp 1994). For example, let's say that you want to spend your money on a new car (your old one is unreliable) and your partner wants to spend it on a vacation (your partner feels the need for a change of pace). Through your conflict and its resolution, you hopefully learn what each really wants—in this case, a reliable car and a break from routine. You may then be able to figure out a way for each to get what he or she wants. You might

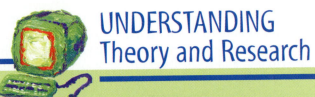

UNDERSTANDING
Theory and Research

DO WOMEN AND MEN FIGHT IN THE SAME WAY?

Do men and women engage in conflict differently? Research shows that men are more apt to withdraw from a conflict situation than are women. It's been argued that this may be due to the fact that men become more psychologically and physiologically aroused during conflict (and retain this heightened level of arousal much longer than do women) and so may try to distance themselves and withdraw from the conflict to prevent further arousal (Gottman & Carrere 1994; Canary, Cupach, & Messman 1995; Goleman 1995). Women, on the other hand, want to get closer to the conflict; they want to talk about it and resolve it. Even adolescents reveal these differences; in a study of boys and girls 11–17, boys withdrew more than girls but were more aggressive when they didn't withdraw (Lindeman, Harakka, & Keltikangas-Jarvinen 1997; Heasley, Babbitt, & Burbach 1995).

Other research has found that women are more emotional and men are more logical when they argue (Schaap, Buunk, & Kerkstra 1988; Canary, Cupach, & Messman 1995). Women have been defined as conflict "feelers" and men as conflict "thinkers" (Sorenson, Hawkins, & Sorenson 1995). Another difference found is that women are more apt to reveal their negative feelings than are men (Schaap, Buunk, & Kerkstra 1988; Canary, Cupach, & Messman 1995).

Do you observe gender differences in conflict? What do you mean by "fighting like a woman"? What do you mean by "fighting like a man"?

accept a good used car or a less expensive new car and your partner might accept a shorter or less expensive vacation. Or you might buy a used car and take an inexpensive motor trip. Each of these solutions would satisfy both of you—they're win-win solutions.

Conflict also prevents hostilities and resentments from festering. Suppose you're annoyed at your partner talking with colleagues from work for two hours on the phone instead of giving that time to you. If you say nothing, your annoyance and resentment are likely to grow. Further, by saying nothing you implicitly approve of such behavior and so it's likely that such phone calls will be repeated.

Through your conflict and its resolution you stop resentment from increasing. In the process you also let your own needs be known—that you need lots of attention when you come home from work and that your partner needs to review and get closure on his or her day's work. If you both can appreciate the legitimacy of these needs, then solutions may be easily identified. Perhaps the phone call can be made after your attention needs are met or perhaps you can delay your need for attention until your partner gets closure about work. Or perhaps you can learn to provide for your partner's closure needs and in doing so may also get the attention you need.

Consider too that when you try to resolve conflict within an interpersonal relationship, you're saying in effect that the relationship is worth the effort; otherwise you would walk away from such a conflict. Although there may be exceptions—as when you confront conflict to save face or to gratify some ego need—usually confronting a conflict indicates concern, commitment, and a desire to preserve the relationship.

Online Conflicts

Just as you experience conflict in face-to-face communication, you can experience the same conflicts online. A few conflict situations that are unique to online communication may be noted here.

Sending commercial messages to those who didn't request them often creates conflict. Junk mail is junk mail; but on the Internet, the receiver has to pay for the time it takes to read and delete these unwanted messages.

Spamming often causes conflict. **Spamming** is sending someone unsolicited mail, repeatedly sending the same mail, or posting the same message on lots of bulletin boards, even when the message is irrelevant to the focus of the group. One of the very practical reasons spamming is frowned upon is that it generally costs people money. And even if the e-mail is free, it takes up valuable time and energy to read something you didn't want in the first place. Another reason, of course, is that it clogs the system, slowing it down for everyone.

Flaming, especially common in newsgroups, refers to sending messages that personally attack another user. Frequently, flaming leads to flame wars where everyone in the group gets into the act and attacks each other. Generally, flaming and flame wars prevent us from achieving our goals, and so are counterproductive.

CONFLICT MANAGEMENT

The conflict management strategies that you choose will be influenced by a variety of considerations. Understanding these factors may help you select more appropriate and more effective strategies.

For example, the goals (short-term and long-term) you wish to achieve will influence what strategies seem appropriate to you. If you just want to save today's date, you might want to simply "give in" and basically ignore the difficulty. On the other hand, if you want to build a long-term relationship, you might want to fully analyze the cause of the problem and look for strategies that will enable both parties to win.

Your emotional state will influence your strategies. You're unlikely to select the same strategies when you're sad as when you're angry. Different strategies will be used if you're seeking to apologize or looking for revenge.

Your cognitive assessment of the situation will exert powerful influence. For example, your attitudes and beliefs about what is fair and equitable will influence your readiness to acknowledge the fairness in the other person's position. Your own assessment of who (if anyone) is the cause of the problem will also influence your conflict style. You might also assess the likely effects of your various strategies. For example, what do you risk if you fight with your boss by using blame or personal rejection? Do you risk alienating your teenager when you use force?

Your personality and level of communication competence will influence the way you engage in conflict. For example, if you're shy and unassertive, you may be more likely to want to avoid a conflict rather than fight actively. If you're extroverted and have a strong desire to state your position, then you may be more likely to fight actively and to argue forcefully.

In what other ways is face-to-face conflict different from online conflict?

Your cultural background will influence your strategies. As noted earlier, many Asian cultures emphasize the importance of saving face, that is, not embarrassing another person, especially in public. Consequently, Asians are probably less likely to use conflict strategies such as blame and personal rejection since these are likely to result in a loss of face. Of course many Asians are more likely to use other strategies to preserve and enhance one's public image. Those from cultures that look more favorably upon the open discussion of conflict might be more apt to use argumentativeness and to fight actively. Students from collective cultures preferred mediation and bargaining as conflict resolution strategies whereas students from individual cultures preferred a conflict style that was more adversarial and confrontational (Leung 1987; Berry, Poortinga, Segall, & Dasen 1992).

And of course many cultures have different rules for men and women engaging in conflict. Asian cultures are more strongly prohibitive of women's conflict strategies. Asian women are expected to be exceptionally polite; this is even more important when women are in conflict with men and when the conflict is public (Tannen 1994b). In the United States, there's a verbalized equality; men and women have equal rights when it comes to permissible conflict strategies. In reality, there are many who expect women to be more polite, to pursue conflict is a nonargumentative way. And men are expected to argue forcefully and logically.

You might wish to pause at this point and ask yourself what your own culture teaches about conflict and its management. What strategies does it prohibit? Are some strategies prohibited when in conflict with certain people (say, your parents) but not with others (say, your friends)? Does your culture prescribe certain ways of dealing with conflict? Does it have different expectations for men and for women? To what degree have you internalized these teachings? What effect do these teachings have on your actual conflict behaviors?

Win–Lose and Win–Win Strategies

In any interpersonal conflict, you have a choice. You can look for solutions in which one person wins, usually you, and the other person loses, usually the other person (win–lose solutions). Or you can look for solutions in which you and the other person both win (win–win solutions). Obviously, win–win solu-

tions are the more desirable, at least when the conflict is interpersonal. Too often, however, we fail to even consider the possibility of win–win solutions and what they might be.

For example, let's say that I want to spend our money on a new car (my old one is unreliable) and you want to spend it on a vacation (you're exhausted and feel the need for a rest). Through our conflict and its resolution, we hopefully learn what each really wants. We may then be able to figure out a way for each of us to get what we want. I might accept a good used car and you might accept a less expensive vacation. Or we might buy a used car and take an inexpensive road trip. Each of these win–win solutions will satisfy both of us; each of us wins, each of us gets what we wanted. Additional examples of win–win strategies as they might be used in an actual problem situations, are provided in "Building Communication Skills. How Do You Find Win–Win Solutions?" (p 208).

Avoidance and Active Fighting

Avoidance may involve actual physical flight. You may leave the scene of the conflict (walk out of the apartment or go to another part of the office), fall asleep, or blast the stereo to drown out all conversation. It may also take the form of emotional or intellectual avoidance. Here you may leave the conflict psychologically by not dealing with any of the arguments or problems raised. In the United States men are more likely to use avoidance than women (Markman, Silvern, Clements, & Kraft-Hanak 1993; Oggins, Veroff, & Leber 1993), often coupled with denials that anything is wrong (Haferkamp 1991–92).

Nonnegotiation is a special type of avoidance. Here you refuse to discuss the conflict or to listen to the other person's argument. At times nonnegotiation takes the form of hammering away at one's own point of view until the other person gives in, a method referred to as **steamrolling**.

Instead of avoiding the issues, take an active role in your interpersonal conflicts. Don't close your ears (or mind), blast the stereo, or walk out of the house during an argument. This is not to say that a cooling-off period is not at times desirable. But if you wish to resolve conflicts, you need to confront them actively.

Involve yourself on both sides of the communication exchange. Participate actively as a speaker–listener; voice your own feelings and listen carefully to

BUILDING Communication Skills

HOW DO YOU FIND WIN–WIN SOLUTIONS?

In any interpersonal conflict, you have a choice. You can look for solutions in which one person wins, usually you, and one person loses, usually the other person (win–lose solutions). Or you can look for solutions in which you and the other person both win (win–win solutions). Obviously, win–win solutions are the more desirable, at least when the conflict is interpersonal. Often, however, people fail to even consider if there are possible win–win solutions and what they might be. To get into the habit of looking for win–win solutions, consider the following conflict situations, either alone or in groups of five or six. For each of the situations, try generating as many possible win–win solutions that you feel the individuals involved in the conflict could reasonably accept. Give yourself two minutes for each case. Write down all win–win solutions that you (or the group) think of; don't censor yourself or any members of the group.

1. Pat and Chris plan to take a two-week vacation in August. Pat wants to go to the shore and relax by the water. Chris wants to go the mountains, hiking and camping.

2. Pat recently got a $3,000 totally unexpected bonus. Pat wants to buy a new computer and printer to augment the office; Chris wants to take a much-needed vacation.

3. Pat hangs around the house in underwear. Chris really hates this and they argue about it almost daily.

4. Philip has recently come out as gay to his parents. He wants them to accept him and his lifestyle (which includes a committed relationship with another man). His parents refuse to accept him and want him to seek religious counseling to change.

5. Workers at the local bottling plant want a 20 percent raise to bring them into line with the salaries of similar workers at other plants. Management has repeatedly turned down their requests.

If possible, share your win–win solutions with other individuals or groups. From this experience it should be clear that win–win solutions exist for most conflict situations but not necessarily all. And, of course, some situations will allow for the easy generation of a lot more win–win solutions than others. Not all conflicts are equal. How might you incorporate win–win strategies into your own conflict management behavior?

---

the voicing of your opponent's feelings. Although periodic moratoriums are sometimes helpful, be willing to communicate as both sender and receiver—to say what is on your mind and to listen to what the other person is saying,

Another part of active fighting involves taking responsibility for your thoughts and feelings. For example, when you disagree with your partner or find fault with her or his behavior, take responsibility for these feelings. Say, for example, "I disagree with . . ." or "I don't like it when you . . . "Avoid statements that deny your responsibility, as in, "Everybody thinks you're wrong about . . ." or "Even Chris thinks you shouldn't . . ."

Force and Talk

When confronted with conflict, many people prefer not to deal with the issues but rather to physically **force** their position on the other person. The force may be emotional or physical. In either case, the issues are avoided and the person who "wins" is the one who exerts the most force. This is the technique of warring nations, children, and even some normally

One of the most puzzling findings on violence is that many victims interpret it as a sign of love. For some reason, they see being beaten or verbally abused as a sign that their partner is fully in love with them. Also, many victims blame themselves for the violence instead of blaming their partners (Gelles & Cornell 1985). Why do you think this is so? What part does force or violence play in your own interpersonal relationship conflicts?

sensible and mature adults. This is surely one of the most serious problems confronting relationships today, but many approach it as if it were of only minor importance or even something humorous.

Over 50 percent of both single and married couples reported that they had experienced physical violence in their relationship. If we add symbolic violence (for example, threatening to hit the other person or throwing something), the percentages are above 60 percent for singles and above 70 percent for marrieds (Marshall & Rose 1987). In a study of divorced couples, 70 percent reported at least one episode of violence in their premarital, marital, or postmarital relationship. Violence during marriage was higher than for pre- or postmarital relationships (Olday & Wesley 1990). In another study, 47 percent of a sample of 410 college students reported some experience with violence in a dating relationship (Deal & Wampler 1986). In most cases the violence was reciprocal—each person in the relationship used violence. In cases where only one person was violent, the research results are conflicting. For example, Deal and Wampler (1986) found that in cases were one partner was violent, the aggressor was significantly more often the female partner. Earlier research found similar sex differences (for example, Care et al. 1982). Other research, however, has found that the popular conception of men being more likely to use force than women is indeed true (DeTurck 1987): Men are more apt than women to use violent methods to achieve compliance.

Findings such as these point to problems well beyond the prevalence of unproductive conflict strategies that you want to identify and avoid. They demonstrate the existence of underlying pathologies that we are discovering are a lot more common than were thought previously, when issues like these were never mentioned in college textbooks or lectures. Awareness, of course, is only a first step in understanding and eventually combating such problems.

The only real alternative to force is **talk**. Instead of using force, you need to talk and listen. The qualities of empathy, openness, and positiveness (see Unit 9), for example, are suitable starting points.

Blame and Empathy

Conflict is rarely caused by a single, clearly identifiable problem or by only one of the parties. Usually, conflict is caused by a wide variety of factors, in which both individuals play a role. Any attempt to single out one person for blame is sure to fail. Yet, a frequently used fight strategy is to **blame** the other person. Consider, for example, the couple who fight over their child's getting into trouble with the police. The parents may—instead of dealing with the conflict itself— blame each other for the child's troubles. Such blaming, of course, does nothing to resolve the problem or to help the child.

Often when you blame someone you attribute motives to the person, a process often referred to as mind reading. Thus, if the person forgot your birthday and

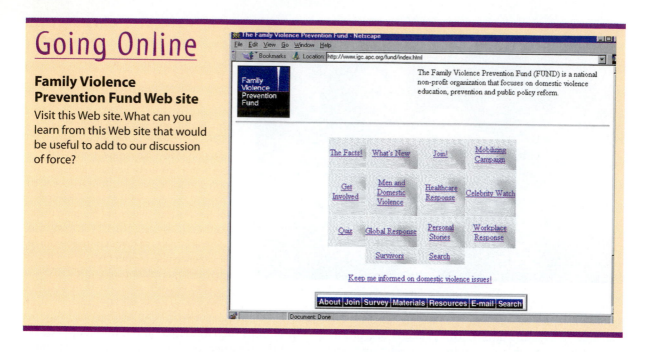

Going Online

Family Violence Prevention Fund Web site

Visit this Web site. What can you learn from this Web site that would be useful to add to our discussion of force?

---

this disturbs you, fight about the forgetting of the birthday (the actual behavior). Try not to presuppose motives: "Well, it's obvious you just don't care about me. If you really cared, you could never have forgotten my birthday!"

Empathy is an excellent alternative to blame. Try to feel what the other person is feeling and to see the situation as the other person does. Try to see the situation as punctuated by the other person and think about how this differs from your own punctuation.

Demonstrate empathic understanding (Unit 9). Once you've empathically understood your opponent's feelings, validate those feelings where appropriate. If your partner is hurt or angry, and you feel that such feelings are legitimate and justified (from the other person's point of view), say so; say, "You have a right to be angry; I shouldn't have called your mother a slob. I'm sorry. But I still don't want to go on vacation with her." In expressing validation you're not necessarily expressing agreement on the issue in conflict; you're merely stating that your partner has feelings that are legitimate and that you recognize them as such.

Silencers and Facilitating Open Expression

Silencers cover a wide variety of fighting techniques that literally silence the other individual. One frequently used silencer is crying. When a person is unable to deal with a conflict or when winning seems

unlikely, he or she may begin to cry and thus silence the other person.

Another silencer is to feign extreme emotionalism—to yell and scream and pretend to be losing control of yourself. Still another is to develop some "physical" reaction—headaches and shortness of breath are probably the most popular. One of the major problems with silencers is that you can never be certain whether they are strategies to win the argument or real physical reactions that you should pay attention to. Regardless of what you do, the conflict remains unexamined and unresolved.

To facilitate open expression, grant the other person permission to express himself or herself freely and openly, to be himself or herself. Avoid power tactics that suppress or inhibit freedom of expression. Such tactics are designed to put the other person down and to subvert real interpersonal equality.

Gunnysacking and Present Focus

A gunnysack is a large bag usually made of burlap. As a conflict strategy, **gunnysacking** refers to the practice of storing up grievances so you may unload them at another time (Back & Wyden 1968). The immediate occasion may be relatively simple (or so it might seem at first), such as someone's coming home late without calling. Instead of arguing about this, the gunnysacker unloads all past grievances. The birthday you forgot, the time you arrived late for dinner, the hotel reservations you forgot to make are all noted. As you probably know from experience, gunnysacking begets gunnysacking. When one person gunnysacks, the other person gunnysacks. The result is two people dumping their stored-up grievances on one another. Frequently the original problem never gets addressed. Instead, resentment and hostility escalate.

Focus your conflict on the here and now rather than on issues that occurred two months ago. Similarly, focus your conflict on the person with whom you're fighting, and not on the person's mother, child, or friends.

Manipulation and Spontaneity

Manipulation involves an avoidance of open conflict. The individual attempts to divert the conflict by being especially charming (disarming, actually). The manipulator gets the other individual into a receptive and noncombative frame of mind. Then the manipulator presents his or her demands to a weakened opponent. The manipulator relies on your tendency to give in to people who are especially nice to you.

Instead of manipulating, try expressing your feelings with spontaneity and honesty. Remember that in interpersonal conflict situations there's no need to plan a strategy to win a war. The objective is not to win but to increase mutual understanding and to reach a decision that both parties can accept.

Personal Rejection and Acceptance

A person practicing personal **rejection** withholds love and affection from his or her opponent in conflict. He or she seeks to win the argument by getting the other person to break down in the face of this withdrawal. The individual acts cold and uncaring in an effort to demoralize the other person. In withdrawing affection, the individual hopes to make the other person question his or her own self-worth. Once the other is demoralized and feels less than worthy, it's relatively easy for the "rejector" to get his or her way. The renewal of love and affection is held out as a reward for resolving the conflict in the manipulator's favor.

Instead of rejection, express positive feelings for the other person and for the relationship between the two of you. Throughout any conflict, many harsh words will probably be exchanged, later to be regretted. The words cannot be unsaid or uncommunicated, but they can be partially offset by the expression of positive statements. If you're engaged in combat with someone you love, remember that you're fighting with a loved one and express that feeling. "I love you very much, but I still don't want your mother on vacation with us. I want to be alone with you."

Fighting Below and Above the Belt

Much like boxers in a ring, each of us has a "beltline." When you hit someone below it, a tactic called **beltlining**, you can inflict serious injury. When you hit above the belt, however, the person is able to absorb the blow. With most interpersonal relationships, especially those of long standing, we know where the beltline is. You know, for example, that to hit Pat with the inability to have children is to hit below the belt. You know that to hit Chris with the failure to get a permanent job is to hit below the belt. Hitting below the beltline causes everyone involved added problems. Keep blows to areas your opponent can absorb and handle.

Remember that the aim of a relationship conflict is not to win and have your opponent lose. Rather, it's to resolve a problem and strengthen the relationship. Keep this ultimate goal always in clear focus, especially when you're angry or hurt.

Face-Detracting and Face-Enhancing Strategies

Another dimension of conflict strategies is that of face orientation. **Face-detracting** or **face-attacking** orientation involves treating the other person as incompetent or untrustworthy, as unable or bad (Donahue & Kolt 1992). Such attacks can vary from mildly embarrassing the other person to severely damaging his or her ego or reputation (Imahori & Cupach 1994). When such attacks become extreme they may be similar to verbal aggressiveness—a tactic explained in the next section.

Face-enhancing techniques involve helping the other person to maintain a positive image, an image as competent and trustworthy, able and good. There's some evidence to show that even when you get what you want, say, at bargaining, it is wise to help the other person retain positive face. This makes it less likely that future conflicts will arise (Donahue & Kolt 1992). Not surprisingly, people are more likely to make a greater effort to support the listener's "face" if they like the listener than if they don't (Meyer 1994).

Confirming the other person's definition of self (Unit 7), avoiding attack and blame, and using excuses and apologies as appropriate are some generally useful face positive strategies.

Aggressiveness and Argumentativeness

An especially interesting perspective on conflict is emerging from the work on verbal aggressiveness and argumentativeness (Infante 1988; Rancer 1998; Wigley 1998). Understanding these two concepts will help in understanding some of the reasons why things go wrong and some of the ways in which you can use conflict to actually improve your relationships.

Verbal Aggressiveness

Verbal aggressiveness is a method of winning an argument by inflicting psychological pain, by attacking the other person's self-concept. The technique relies on many of the unproductive conflict strategies just considered. It's a type of disconfirmation in that it seeks to discredit the individual's view of self (see Unit 7). To explore this tendency further, take the following self-test of verbal aggressiveness.

 **SELF-TEST**

How Verbally Aggressive Are You?

This scale is designed to measure how people try to obtain compliance from others. For each statement, indicate the extent to which you feel it's true for you in your attempts to influence others. Use the following scale: 1 = almost never true; 2 = rarely true; 3 = occasionally true; 4 = often true; and 5 = almost always true.

_____ 1. I am extremely careful to avoid attacking individuals' intelligence when I attack their ideas.

_____ 2. When individuals are very stubborn, I use insults to soften the stubbornness.

_____ 3. I try very hard to avoid having other people feel bad about themselves when I try to influence them.

_____ 4. When people refuse to do a task I know is important, without good reason, I tell them they are unreasonable.

_____ 5. When others do things I regard as stupid, I try to be extremely gentle with them.

_____ 6. If individuals I am trying to influence really deserve it, I attack their character.

_____ 7. When people behave in ways that are really in very poor taste, I insult them in order to shock them into proper behavior.

_____ 8. I try to make people feel good about themselves even when their ideas are stupid.

_____ 9. When people simply will not budge on a matter of importance, I lose my temper and say rather strong things to them.

_____ 10. When people criticize my shortcomings, I take it in good humor and do not try to get back at them.

_____ 11. When individuals insult me, I get a lot of pleasure out of really telling them off.

_____ 12. When I dislike individuals greatly, I try not to show it in what I say or how I say it.

_____ 13. I like poking fun at people who do things which are very stupid in order to stimulate their intelligence.

_____ 14. When I attack a person's ideas, I try not to damage their self-concepts.

_____ 15. When I try to influence people, I make a great effort not to offend them.

_____ 16. When people do things which are mean or cruel, I attack their character in order to help correct their behavior.

_____ 17. I refuse to participate in arguments when they involve personal attacks.

_____ 18. When nothing seems to work in trying to influence others, I yell and scream in order to get some movement from them.

_____ 19. When I am not able to refute others' positions, I try to make them feel defensive in order to weaken their positions.

_____ 20. When an argument shifts to personal attacks, I try very hard to change the subject.

To compute your verbal aggressiveness score, follow these steps:

1. Add your scores on items 2, 4, 6, 7, 9, 11, 13, 16, 18, 19.
2. Add your scores on items 1, 3, 5, 8, 10, 12, 14, 15, 17, 20.
3. Subtract the sum obtained in step 2 from 60.
4. To compute your verbal aggressiveness score, add the total obtained in step 1 to the result obtained in step 3.

If you scored between 59 and 100, you're high in verbal aggressiveness; if you scored between 39 and 58, you're moderate in verbal aggressiveness; and if you scored between 20 and 38, you're low in verbal aggressiveness. Can you identify relationships in which verbal aggressiveness is the customary way of dealing with conflict? What do you see as the primary disadvantage of verbal aggressiveness as a conflict strategy? Can you identify any advantages of verbal aggressiveness?

Think about your own tendency toward aggressiveness. In reviewing your score, for example, make special note of the characteristics identified in the 20 statements that refer to the tendency to act aggressively. Note those inappropriate behaviors that you're especially prone to commit. Review your previous encounters when you acted aggressively. What effect did such actions have on your subsequent interaction? What effect did they have on your relationship with the other person? What alternative ways of getting your point across might you have used? Might these have proved more effective?

Argumentativeness

Contrary to popular belief, **argumentativeness** is a quality to be cultivated rather than avoided. Argumentativeness refers to your willingness to argue for a point of view, your tendency to speak your mind on significant issues. It's the mode of dealing with disagreements that is the preferred alternative to verbal aggressiveness. Before reading about ways to increase your argumentativeness, take the following heavily researched self-test (Infante & Rancer 1995).

SELF-TEST

How Argumentative Are You?

This questionnaire contains statements about controversial issues. Indicate how often each statement is true for you personally according to the following scale: 1 = almost never true; 2 = rarely true; 3 = occasionally true; 4 = often true; and 5 = almost never true.

_____ 1. While in an argument, I worry that the person I am arguing with will form a negative impression of me.

_____ 2. Arguing over controversial issues improves my intelligence.

_____ 3. I enjoy avoiding arguments.

_____ 4. I am energetic and enthusiastic when I argue.

_____ 5. Once I finish an argument, I promise myself that I will not get into another.

_____ 6. Arguing with a person creates more problems for me than it solves.

_____ 7. I have a pleasant, good feeling when I win a point in an argument,

_____ 8. When I finish arguing with anyone, I feel nervous and upset.

_____ 9. I enjoy a good argument over a controversial issue.

_____ 10. I get an unpleasant feeling when I realize I am about to get into an argument.

_____ 11. I enjoy defending my point of view on an issue.

_____ 12. I am happy when I keep an argument from happening.

_____ 13. I do not like to miss the opportunity to argue a controversial issue.

_____ 14. I prefer being with people who rarely disagree with me.

_____ 15. I consider an argument an exciting intellectual challenge.

_____ 16. I find myself unable to think of effective points during an argument.

_____ 17. I feel refreshed and satisfied after an argument on a controversial issue.
_____ 18. I have the ability to do well in an argument.
_____ 19. I try to avoid getting into arguments.
_____ 20. I feel excitement when I expect that a conversation I am in is leading to an argument.

To compute your argumentativeness score, follow these steps:

1. Add your scores on items 2, 4, 7, 9, 11, 13, 15, 17, 18, and 20.
2. Add 60 to the sum obtained in step 1.
3. Add your scores on items 1, 3, 5, 6, 8, 10, 12, 14, 16, 19.
4. To compute your argumentativeness score, subtract the total obtained in step 3 from the total obtained in step 2.

Interpreting Your Score

Scores between 73 and 100 indicate high argumentativeness.

Scores between 56 and 72 indicate moderate argumentativeness.

Scores between 20 and 55 indicate low argumentativeness.

Can you identify relationships in which argumentativeness is the customary way of dealing with conflicts? What is the primary advantage of argumentativeness? Can you identify any disadvantages?

Generally, those who score high in argumentativeness have a strong tendency to state their position on controversial issues and argue against the positions of others. A high scorer sees arguing as exciting, intellectually challenging, and as an opportunity to win a kind of contest.

The moderately argumentative person possesses some of the qualities of the high argumentative and some of the qualities of the low argumentative. The person who scores low in argumentativeness tries to prevent arguments. This person experiences satisfaction not from arguing, but from avoiding arguments.

The low argumentative sees arguing as unpleasant and unsatisfying. Not surprisingly, this person has little confidence in his or her ability to argue effectively.

Men generally score higher in argumentativeness (and in verbal aggressiveness) than women. Men are also more apt to be perceived (by both men and women) as more argumentative and verbally aggressive than women (Nicotera & Rancer 1994). High and low argumentatives also differ in the way in which they view argument (Rancer, Kosberg, & Baukus 1992). High argumentatives see arguing as enjoyable and its outcomes as pragmatic. They see arguing as having a positive impact on their self-concept, to have functional outcomes, and to be highly ego-involving. Low argumentatives, on the other hand, believe that arguing has a negative impact on their self-concept, that it has dysfunctional outcomes, and that it's not very ego-involving. They see arguing as having little enjoyment or pragmatic outcomes.

The researchers who developed this test note that both high and low argumentatives may experience communication difficulties. The high argumentative, for example, may argue needlessly, too often, and too forcefully. The low argumentative, on the other hand, may avoid taking a stand even when it seems necessary.

Persons scoring somewhere in the middle are probably the most interpersonally skilled and adaptable, arguing when it's necessary but avoiding the many arguments that are needless and repetitive.

Here are some suggestions for cultivating argumentativeness and for preventing it from degenerating into aggressiveness (Infante 1988).

- Treat disagreements as objectively as possible; avoid assuming that because someone takes issue with your position or your interpretation that they're attacking you as a person.
- Avoid attacking the other person (rather than the person's arguments) even if this would give you a tactical advantage—it will probably backfire at some later time and make your relationship more difficult. Center your arguments on issues rather than personalities.
- Reaffirm the other person's sense of competence; compliment the other person as appropriate.
- Avoid interrupting; allow the other person to state her or his position fully before you respond.
- Stress equality and stress the similarities that you have with the other person; stress your areas of agreement before attacking the disagreements.

- Express interest in the other person's position, attitude, and point of view.
- Avoid presenting your arguments too emotionally; using an overly loud voice or interjecting vulgar expressions will prove offensive and eventually ineffective.
- Allow the other person to save face; never humiliate the other person.

BEFORE AND AFTER THE CONFLICT

If you are to make conflict truly productive you will need to consider a few suggestions for preparing for the conflict and for using the conflict as a method for relational growth.

Before the Conflict

Try to fight in private. When you air your conflicts in front of others you create a wide variety of other problems. You may not be willing to be totally honest when third parties are present; you may feel you have to save face and therefore must win the fight at all costs. This may lead you to use strategies to win the argument rather than strategies to resolve the conflict. Also, of course, you run the risk of embarrassing your partner in front of others, which will incur resentment and hostility.

Be sure you're both ready to fight. Although conflicts arise at the most inopportune times, you can choose the time when you will try to resolve them. Confronting your partner when she or he comes home after a hard day of work may not be the right time for resolving a conflict. Make sure you're both relatively free of other problems and ready to deal with the conflict at hand.

Know what you're fighting about. Sometimes people in a relationship become so hurt and angry that they lash out at the other person just to vent their own frustration. The "content" of the conflict is merely an excuse to express anger. Any attempt at resolving this "problem" will of course be doomed to failure since the problem addressed is not what gave rise to the conflict. Instead, it may be the underlying hostility, anger, and frustration that needs to be dealt with.

At other times, people argue about general and abstract issues that are poorly specified, for example, the person's lack of consideration or failure to accept responsibility. Only when you define your differences in specific terms can you begin to understand them and hence resolve them.

BUILDING
Communication Skills

HOW DO YOU AVOID CONFLICT?

Think about the major productive and unproductive conflict strategies just discussed as they might apply to the specific situations described next. Assume that the statements below are made by someone close to you. Try developing an unproductive and an alternative productive strategy for each situation.

1. You're late again. You're always late. Your lateness is so inconsiderate of my time and my interests. What is wrong with you?

2. I just can't bear another weekend of sitting home watching television. You never want to do anything. I'm just not going to do that again and that's final.

3. Guess who forgot to phone for reservations again? Don't you remember anything?

4. You can't possibly go out with Pat. We're your parents and we simply won't allow it. And we don't want to hear any more about it. It's over.

5. Why don't you stay out of the neighbors' business? You're always butting in and telling people what to do. Why don't you mind your own business and take care of your own family instead of trying to run everybody else's?

Fight about problems that can be solved. Fighting about past behaviors or about family members or situations over which you have no control solves nothing; instead, it creates additional difficulties. Any attempt at resolution is naturally doomed to failure since the problems can't be solved. Often such conflicts are concealed attempts at expressing one's frustration or dissatisfaction.

Consider what beliefs you hold that may need to be reexamined. Unrealistic beliefs are often at the heart of interpersonal conflict. The following self-test, "What Do You Believe about Relationships?" will help you examine your relationship beliefs to see if some may be unrealistic and causing conflict.

✔ SELF-TEST

What Do You Believe about Relationships?

For each of the following statements, use the following scale to show how much you agree or disagree: agree completely = 7; agree a good deal = 6; agree somewhat = 5; neither agree nor disagree = 4; disagree somewhat = 3; disagree a good deal = 2; and disagree completely = 1.

_____ 1. If a person has any questions about the relationship, then it means there is something wrong with it.

_____ 2. If my partner truly loved me, we would not have any quarrels.

_____ 3. If my partner really cared, he or she would always feel affection for me.

_____ 4. If my partner gets angry at me or is critical in public, this indicates he or she doesn't really love me.

_____ 5. My partner should know what is important to me without my having to tell him or her.

_____ 6. If I have to ask for something that I really want, it spoils it.

_____ 7. If my partner really cared, he or she would do what I ask.

_____ 8. A good relationship should not have any problems.

_____ 9. If people really love each other, they should not have to work on their relationship.

_____ 10. If my partner does something that upsets me, I think it is because he or she deliberately wants to hurt me.

_____ 11. When my partner disagrees with me in public, I think it is a sign that he or she doesn't care for me very much.

_____ 12. If my partner contradicts me, I think that he or she doesn't have much respect for me.

_____ 13. If my partner hurts my feelings, I think that it is because he or she is mean.

_____ 14. My partner always tries to get his or her own way.

_____ 15. My partner doesn't listen to what I have to say.

Aaron Beck, one of the leading theorists in cognitive therapy and the author of the popular *Love Is Never Enough*, claims that all of these beliefs are unrealistic and may well create problems in your interpersonal relationships. The test was developed to help people identify potential sources of difficulty for relationship development and maintenance. The more statements that you indicated you believe in, the more unrealistic your expectations are.

Do you agree with Beck that these beliefs are unrealistic and that they will cause problems? Which belief is the most dangerous to the development and maintenance of an interpersonal relationship?

"Self-Text. What Do You Believe about Relationships." from *Love is Never Enough* by Aaron T. Beck Copyright © by Aaron T. Beck, M.D. Reprinted by permission of HarperCollins*Publishers*, Inc.   ✔

After the Conflict

After the conflict is resolved, there's still work to be done. Often after one conflict is supposedly settled, another conflict will emerge because, for example, one person feels harmed and feels the need to retaliate and take revenge in order to restore self-worth (Kim & Smith 1993). So it's especially important that the conflict be resolved and not allowed to generate other, perhaps more significant, conflicts.

Learn from the conflict and from the process you went through in trying to resolve the conflict. For example, can you identify the fight strategies that aggravated the situation? Does the other person need a cooling-off period? Do you need extra space when upset? Can you identify when minor issues are going to escalate into major arguments? Does avoidance make matters worse? What issues are particularly disturbing and likely to cause difficulties? Can these be avoided?

Keep the conflict in perspective. Be careful not to blow it out of proportion, defining your relationship in terms of conflict. Avoid the tendency to see disagreement as inevitably leading to major blowups. Conflicts in most relationships actually occupy a very small percentage of real time, and yet in recollection they often loom extremely large. Also, don't allow the conflict to undermine your own or your partner's self-esteem. Don't view yourself, your part-

ner, or your relationships as failures just because you had an argument or even lots of arguments.

Negative feelings frequently arise after an interpersonal conflict, most often because unfair fight strategies were used to undermine the other person—for example, personal rejection, manipulation, or force.

Resolve surely to avoid such unfair tactics in the future, but at the same time let go of guilt and blame for yourself and your partner. If you think it would help, discuss these feelings with your partner or even a therapist.

Increase the exchange of rewards and cherishing behaviors to demonstrate your positive feelings and that you're over the conflict. It's a good way of saying you want the relationship to survive and to flourish.

SUMMARY

In this unit we explored interpersonal conflict, the types of conflicts that occur, the don'ts and do's of conflict management, and what to do before and after the conflict.

1. Relationship conflict refers to a situation in which two persons have opposing goals and interfere with each other's attaining these goals. Conflicts may occur face-to-face or on the Internet, through e-mail or newsgroups, for example.
2. Content conflict centers on objects, events, and persons in the world that are usually, but not always, external to the parties involved in the conflict.
3. Relationship conflicts are concerned not so much with some external object as with the relationships between the individuals, with such issues as who is in charge, the equality of a primary relationship, and who has the right to set down rules of behavior.
4. Unproductive and productive conflict strategies include: win–lose and win–win solutions, avoidance and fighting actively, force and talk, blame and empathy, si-

lencers and facilitating open expression, gunnysacking and present focus, manipulation and spontaneity, personal rejection and acceptance, fighting below and above the belt, and fighting aggressively and argumentatively.

5. To cultivate argumentativeness, treat disagreements objectively and avoid attacking the other person; reaffirm the other's sense of competence; avoid interrupting; stress equality and similarities; express interest in the other's position; avoid presenting your arguments too emotionally; and allow the other to save face.
6. Prepare for the conflict and try to fight in private and when you're both ready to fight. Have a clear idea of what you want to fight about and be specific; fight about things that can be solved.
7. After the conflict, assess what you've learned, keep the conflict in perspective, let go of negative feelings, and increase the positiveness in the relationship.

KEY TERMS

interpersonal conflict (p. 201)
content conflict (p. 201
relationship conflict (p. 201)
avoidance (p. 207)
nonnegotiation (p. 207)

win-lose strategies (p. 207)
win-win strategies (p. 207)
blame (p. 209)
empathy (p. 209)
silencers (p. 210)

gunnysacking (p. 210)
beltlining (p. 211)
manipulation (p. 211)
verbal aggressiveness (p. 212)
argumentativeness (p. 213)

THINKING CRITICALLY ABOUT
Interpersonal Conflict

1. Why are men more likely to withdraw from a conflict than are women? What arguments can you present for or against any of these reasons (Noller 1993): Because men have difficulty dealing with conflict? Because the culture has taught men to avoid it? Because withdrawal is an expression of power?

2. How would you go about finding answers to such questions as these:

   • Are more-educated people less likely to use verbal aggressiveness and more likely to use argumentativeness than less-educated people?

   • Do men and women differ in the satisfaction or dissatisfaction they derive from a conflict experience?

   • What types of strategies are more likely to be used by happy couples than by unhappy couples?

   • How do man–man, woman–woman, and woman–man interpersonal conflicts differ from each other?

3. Access ERIC, Medline, Psychlit, or Sociofile and locate an article dealing with interpersonal conflict. What can you learn about conflict and interpersonal communication from this article?

4. Visit some game Web sites (for example, http://www.games-domain.co.uk or http://www.gamepen.com/yellowpages/) and examine the rules of the games. What kinds of conflict strategies do these game rules embody? Do you think these influence people's interpersonal conflict strategies?

5. Assume that you're a manager of a small office and two employees have complained that they received smaller bonuses than workers who had been with the company for a shorter amount of time and who were not as productive. These two employees are extremely angry and have just voiced their complaint to you. Can you develop responses—or even a dialogue—that would incorporate these four suggestions for dealing with complaints? (1) What do you say to let the person know that *you're open to complaints and that you do view them as essential sources of information*? (2) What do you say to show that *you're following the suggestions for effective listening already discussed, for example, listening supportively and with empathy*? (3) What do you say to make sure that *you understand both the thoughts and the feelings that go with the complaint*? (4) What do you say to show the other person that *you want to know what he or she would like you to do about the complaint*?

UNIT 12
Interviewing

UNIT GOALS

After completing this unit, you should be able to

define *interviewing* and its major types

describe the sequence of steps for information interviews

explain the principles of employment interviewing

distinguish between lawful and unlawful questions

You'll no doubt find yourself in a wide variety of interviewing situations throughout your social and professional life. And, as you'll see throughout this chapter, your effectiveness—whether as interviewer or interviewee—in this form of communication will prove crucial in helping you achieve many of your goals. Interviewing includes a wide range of communication situations. Here are just a few examples:

- A salesperson tries to sell a client a new car.
- A teacher talks with a student about the reasons the student failed the course.
- A counselor talks with a family about their communication problems.
- A recent graduate applies to IBM for a job in the product development division.
- A building owner talks with a potential apartment renter.
- A minister talks with a church member about relationship problems.
- A lawyer examines a witness during a trial.
- A theatrical agent talks with a potential client.
- A client discusses with a dating service employee some of the qualities desired in a potential mate.
- An employer talks with an employee about the reasons for terminating his or her employment.

THE INTERVIEW PROCESS

Interviewing is a particular form of communication in which you interact largely through a question-and-answer format to achieve specific goals. These goals guide and structure the interview in both content and format. In an employment interview, for example, the goal for the interviewer is to find an applicant who can fulfill the tasks of the position. The interviewee's goal is to get the job, if it seems desirable. These goals guide the behaviors of both parties, are relatively specific, and are usually clear to both parties.

The interview is distinctly different from other forms of communication because it proceeds through questions and answers. Both parties in the interview ask and answer questions, but most often the interviewer asks the questions and the interviewee answers them.

Usually, we think of interviewing as a face-to-face experience and often it is. But, interviewing is increasingly being conducted through e-mail, chat groups, video conferences, and, of course, telephone. Especially when a company, say, interviews candidates in a series of three or four interviews, the first one or two interviews might well be held through chat groups or by telephone and the later ones in a face-to-face setting.

Two-Person and Team Interviews

Most interviews follow a two-person structure but team interviews are becoming more popular. In the media, on "Nightline," for example, several journalists might interview a political candidate or one journalist might interview several candidates. On the ubiquitous television talk show (see Media Watch box in this unit, p. 222), a moderator interviews several people at the same time.

In employment situations team interviews are extremely important, especially as you go up the organizational hierarchy. It's not uncommon, for example, for an entire academic department to interview a candidate for a teaching position, often followed by a similar team interview with the administration. In business organizations, three or four vice presidents might interview a candidate for a middle management position.

The main advantage of the team interview is that it gives the audience or the organization different viewpoints and perspectives on the person being interviewed. It also helps ensure that the interview does not lag but follows a relatively rapid pace.

Team interviews, however, are expensive (in an organization, time *is* money), may degenerate into what may appear to be an interrogation (which may be desirable on television but inappropriate in an employment setting), and may result in focusing too much time on those conducting the interview and not enough on the person being interviewed (see Kanter 1995).

General Interview Structures

Interviews vary from relatively informal talks that resemble everyday conversations to those that ask rigidly prescribed questions in a set order (Hambrick 1991). Depending on your specific purpose, you can select the interview structure, or combine various types to create a unique interview structure, that best fits your needs.

In the **informal interview** two friends might discuss what happened on their respective dates or employment interviews. This type of interview resembles

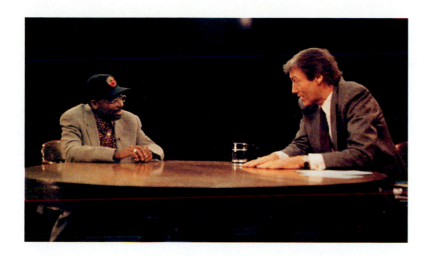

How would you characterize the interviewing style of Charlie Rose, pictured here with film director Spike Lee, or of, say, Jay Leno or Oprah Winfrey?

conversation; a general theme for the interview is chosen in advance but the specific questions are formed during the interaction. You use this type of interview to obtain information informally.

In the **guided interview** a guest on "The Tonight Show" might be interviewed about a new television series or CD. Here the topics are chosen in advance but specific questions and wordings are guided by the ongoing interaction. The guided interview is useful because it assures maximum flexibility and responsiveness to the dynamics of the situation.

The **standard open interview** might be used for interviewing several candidates for a job. Open-ended questions and their order are selected in advance. This type of interview would be useful when standardization is needed, when you want to be sure to ask each person the same question in exactly the same way.

In the **quantitative interview** a researcher might survey students' political opinions. In this form, questions and their order are selected in advance as are the possible response categories, for example, A, B, C, D; agree-disagree; check from 1 to 10. The quantitative interview is useful when statistical analyses are to be performed and when large amounts of information are to be collected.

Interview Questions and Answers

Understanding the different types of questions may help you respond to questions more effectively—as in an employment interview—and ask questions more effectively—as in an information-gathering interview. Questions may be analyzed in terms of at

least the following dimensions: open–closed, neutral–biased, primary–follow-up, and direct–indirect.

Open–Closed

Openness refers to the degree of freedom you have to respond, both in content and format. At times there's almost unlimited latitude in what may constitute an answer, for example, "What are your goals?" "Why do you want to work at Peabody and Peabody?" At the opposite extreme are *closed* questions that require only a "yes" or "no," for example, "Are you willing to relocate to San Francisco?" "Can you use Lotus 1–2–3?" Between these extremes are short-answer questions; those that are relatively closed and to which you have only limited freedom in responding, for example, "What would you do as manager here?" "What computer skills do you have?" Part of the art of successful interviewing is to respond with answers that are appropriate to the question's level of openness. Thus, if you're asked a question like "Why do you want to work at Peabody and Peabody?" you're expected to speak at some length. If you're asked, "Are you willing to relocate to San Francisco?" then a simple yes or no (with or without a qualification) will suffice, for example, "Absolutely, though it would take me a few months to close my affairs here in Boston."

Neutral–Biased

Neutrality and its opposite, *bias*, refer to the extent to which the question provides the answer the interviewer wants from the interviewee. Some questions are neutral and don't specify any answer as more appropriate than any other. At the other extreme are

MEDIA WATCH

THOSE TELEVISION TALK SHOWS

Interviewing is a form of communication used widely in the media—in newspapers and magazines as well as on talk radio and on television. But it's the television talk show that has most captured the attention of the television viewer and a media phenomenon that needs to be examined (Jacobs 1995). In an article entitled "Talk Shows Are Good for You," frequent talk show psychologist Gilda Carle (1995) identifies some of the benefits of talks shows: they show us new communication techniques, teach us about new topics, break down myths, show us celebrities as real people, and make us laugh.

Mass communication researcher Janice Peck (1995) notes, from an analysis of "Oprah Winfrey" and "Sally Jessy Raphael," that the talk shows have made public issues that were once hidden and have given a public platform to groups who have generally not had media exposure (for example, women).

But, consider some of the disadvantages. For example, talk shows dispense advice on a variety of issues—especially in the monologue that closes many of the shows—from someone with little to no professional training in the topic. Do you really want to take relationship advice from Ricki Lake or Montel Williams or Richard Bey? They regularly give communication advice with no basis in scientific research and generally foster myths about communication. Perhaps the most prevalent myth about communication is that communication will solve all problems and that the more communication a couple has the better the relationship will be. Talk shows are entertaining but they often present themselves as educational, as therapy for the masses, and as arbiters of how you and your parents and your friends should live your lives.

Talk shows also create an impression that the world is divided into two extremes. Polarizing guests—the gay activist and the fundamentalist preacher, the pro- and anti-abortionist, the liberal and the conservative—makes for interesting debate and generally holds viewer attention. But, the extremes don't represent the world. They're extreme precisely because they don't represent the vast majority of the world.

Many talk shows seek to resolve the conflict or the problem during the one hour show. They often give the impression that therapy takes one hour—the problem is introduced, the therapy is given, the catharsis takes place, and the cure emerges. Janice Peck (1995, p. 76) argues: "The programs discourage critical engagement with and reflection on those problems in favor of immediate identification and catharsis, and undermine the ability to take these problems seriously in the service of making them entertaining."

Do you watch talk shows? If so, what do you get out of them? What is to you the main advantage of television talk shows? The main disadvantage? What can you learn about interviewing techniques from television talk show hosts?

The next Media Watch appears on page 245.

---

questions that are biased, or loaded. These indicate quite clearly the particular answer the interviewer expects or wants. Compare the following questions:

- How did you feel about managing your own Web design firm?
- You must really enjoy managing your own Web design company, don't you?

The first question is neutral and allows you to respond in any way; it asks for no particular answer.

The second question is biased; it specifies that the interviewer expects a "yes." Between the neutrality of "How did you feel about your previous job?" and the bias of "You must have loved your previous job, didn't you?" there are questions that specify with varying degrees of strength the answer the interviewer expects or prefers. For example:

- Did you like your previous job?
- Did you dislike your previous job very much?
- It seems like it would be an interesting job, no?

An interviewer who asks too many biased questions will not learn about the interviewee's talents or experiences, but only about the interviewee's ability to give the desired answer. As an interviewee, pay special attention to any biases in the question. Don't give the responses your interviewer expects if they're not what you believe to be correct or know to be true. This would be unethical. However, when your responses are not what the interviewer expects, consider explaining why you're responding as you are. For example, to the biased question, "It seems like it would be an interesting job, no?" you might respond: "It was interesting most of the time, but it didn't allow for enough creativity."

Primary–Follow-Up

Primary questions introduce a topic and follow-up questions ask for elaboration on what was just said. Too many primary questions and not enough follow-up questions will often communicate a lack of interest and perhaps a failure to listen as effectively as possible. When we introduce a topic we expect people to ask follow-up questions. When they don't, we feel that they're not interested in what we're saying or aren't really listening.

The stereotypical psychiatric interviewer would ask a lot of follow-up questions, probing each and every thought the patient expresses. The stereotypical unresponsive partner would ask no follow-up questions. A balance between primary and follow-up questions, determined in large part by the situation and by your own communication goals, is the desired goal.

One way to judge whether you're balancing these appropriately is to mentally pause and ask yourself how you and your listener are enjoying the conversation or interview. If your listener seems not to be enjoying the interaction, try increasing your follow-up responses. Use the active listening responses discussed in Unit 4. If you're not finding it satisfactory, then probably your listener is not asking enough follow-up questions, not giving your statements enough attention. One helpful guide is to talk in specifics about yourself. Instead of "life is difficult," say "I'm going through a bad time." Also, clue your listener in a more obvious way to your desire to pursue this topic. So, instead of just saying "I'm going through a bad time," continue with "and I'm not sure what I should do" and, even more directly, "and I need advice."

Direct–Indirect

This aspect of questions will vary greatly from one culture to another. In the United States, be prepared for rather direct questions, whether you're being interviewed for information or for a job. In Japan, on the other hand, the interviewee is expected to reveal himself or herself despite the indirectness of the questions.

Similarly, cultures vary in what they consider appropriate directness in speaking of one's accomplishments, say, in a job interview. In many Asian cultures, the interviewee is expected to appear modest and unassuming and should allow his or her competencies to emerge indirectly during the interview. In the United States, on the other hand, you're expected to state your competencies without any significant modesty. In fact, many interviewers expect a certain amount of hyperbole and exaggeration.

Types of Interviews

We can distinguish the different types of interviews on the basis of the goals of interviewer and interviewee. Here we identify briefly the persuasive, appraisal, exit, and counseling interviews (Stewart & Cash 1988; Zima 1983). The information and employment interviews are probably the most important for most college students, and so these are covered at length later in the unit.

The Persuasive Interview

In the **persuasive interview** the goal is to change an individual's attitudes, beliefs, or behaviors. The interviewer may either ask questions that will lead the interviewee to the desired conclusion or answer questions in a persuasive way. For example, if you go into a showroom to buy a new car, you interview the salesperson. The salesperson's goal is to get you to buy a particular car. He or she attempts to accomplish this by answering your questions persuasively. You ask about mileage, safety features, and finance terms. The salesperson discourses eloquently on the superiority of this car above all others.

All interviews contain elements of both information and persuasion. When, for example, a guest appears on "The Tonight Show" and talks about a new movie, information is communicated. But the performer is also trying to persuade the audience to see the movie. Informing and persuading usually go together in actual practice.

The Appraisal Interview

In the **appraisal** or evaluation **interview**, the interviewee's performance is assessed by management or more experienced colleagues. The general aim is to discover what the interviewee is doing well (and to praise this), and not doing well and why (and to correct this). These interviews are important because they help new members of an organization see how their performance matches up with the expectations of those making promotion and firing decisions.

The Exit Interview

The **exit interview** is used widely by organizations in the United States and throughout the world. All organizations compete in one way or another for superior workers. When an employee leaves a company voluntarily, it's important to know why, to prevent other valuable workers from leaving as well. Another function of this interview is to provide a way of making the exit as pleasant and as efficient as possible for both employee and employer.

The Counseling interview

Counseling interviews are conducted to provide guidance. The goal here is to help the person deal more effectively with problems; to work more effectively; to get along better with friends or lovers; or to cope more effectively with day-to-day living. For the interview to be of any value, the interviewer must learn a considerable amount about the person—habits, problems, self-perceptions, goals, and so on. With this information, the counselor then tries to persuade the person to alter certain aspects of his or her thinking or behaving. The counselor may try to persuade you, for example, to listen more attentively when your spouse argues or to devote more time to your classwork.

THE INFORMATION INTERVIEW

In the **information interview**, the interviewer tries to learn something about the interviewee. In the informative interview—unlike the employment interview—the person interviewed is usually a person of some reputation and accomplishment. The interviewer accomplishes this goal by asking a series of questions designed to elicit the interviewee's views, beliefs, insights, perspectives, predictions, life history, and so on. Examples of the information interview include those published in popular magazines;

the TV interviews conducted by David Letterman, Katie Couric, and Barbara Walters; and those conducted by a lawyer during a trial. All aim to elicit specific information from someone who supposedly knows something others don't know. In this discussion, we concentrate on your role as the interviewer, since that is the role you're likely to find yourself serving now and in the near future.

Let's say that your interview is designed to get information about a particular field, for example, Web design. You want to know about the available job opportunities and the preparation you would need to get into this field. Here are a few guidelines for conducting such information-gathering interviews.

Select the Person You Wish to Interview

There are several ways to find a likely person to interview. Let's say that you wish to learn something about Web publishing. You might, for example, look through your college catalog; there you find that a course on this general topic is offered by Professor Bernard Brommel. You think it might be worthwhile to interview him. Or, you visit a variety of newsgroups and discover that one particular person has posted extremely well-reasoned articles and you'd like to interview her to get her opinion on Web design and advice on how you might break into this field. If you want to contact a book author, you can always write to the author in care of the publisher or editor (listed on the copyright page), though many authors are now including their e-mail address. You can often find the address and phone number of most professional people by calling the appropriate professional association for a directory listing (the *Encyclopedia of Associations* lists just about every professional association in the country). Or, you can write to the person via the association's Web site. Newsgroup and listserv writers are of course the easiest to contact since their e-mail addresses are included with their posts. Last, you can often find experts through *The Yearbook of Experts, Authorities, and Spokespersons* and a variety of Web sites, for example, http://www.experts.com and http://www.usc.edu/dept/news_service/experts_directory.html.

After you've selected one of the people you hope to interview but before you pursue the interview, try to learn something about this person. Consult an online library or bookstore to see if this person has written a book, or go through a CD ROM database to see if this person has written any research articles.

Search through the databases covering computers, the Internet, and the World Wide Web. Search the Web and Usenet groups to see if the person has a Web page or posts to newsgroups. You may find that the person encourages people to correspond via e-mail.

Secure an Appointment

Phone the person or send a letter or e-mail requesting an interview. In your call or letter, identify the purpose of your request and that you would like a brief interview. For example, you might say: "I'm preparing for a career in Web design and I would appreciate it if I could interview you to learn more about the subject. The interview would take about 15 minutes." (It's helpful to let the person know it will not take too long; he or she is more likely to agree to being interviewed.) Generally, it's best to be available at the interviewee's convenience. So indicate flexibility on your part, for example, "I can interview you any afternoon this week."

You may find it necessary to conduct the interview by phone. In this case, call to set up a time for a future interview call. For example, you might say, "I'm interested in a career in Web design and I would like to interview you on the job opportunities in this field. If you agree, I can call you back at a time that's convenient for you." In this way, you don't run the risk of asking the person to hold still for an interview while eating lunch, talking with colleagues, or running to class.

Prepare Your Questions

Preparing questions ahead of time will ensure that you use the time available to your best advantage. Of course, as the interview progresses other questions will come to mind and should be asked. But having a prepared list of questions will help you obtain the information you need most easily.

Establish Rapport with the Interviewee

Open the interview with an expression of thanks for making the time available to you. Many people receive lots of requests and it helps if you also remind the person of your specific purpose. You might say something like this: "I really appreciate your making time for this interview. As I mentioned, I'm interesting in learning about the job opportunities in Web design and your expertise and experience in this area will help a great deal."

Ask Permission to Tape the Interview

Generally, it's a good idea to tape the interview. It will enable you to secure a more complete record of the interview, which you'll be able to review as you need to. It will also free you to concentrate on the interview rather than on trying to write down the person's responses. But ask permission first. Some people prefer not to have informal interviews taped. Even if the interview is being conducted by phone, ask permission if you intend to tape the conversation.

Ask Open-ended Questions

Use questions that provide the interviewee with room to discuss the issues you want to raise. Thus, instead of asking "Do you have formal training in Web publishing?" (a question that requires a simple "yes" or "no" and will not be very informative), you might ask, "Can you tell me something about your background in this field?" (a question that is open-ended and allows the person greater freedom). You can then ask follow-up questions to pursue more specifically the topics considered in the answers to your open-ended questions.

Close the Interview with an Expression of Appreciation

Thank the person for making the time available for the interview, for being informative, cooperative, helpful, or whatever. Showing your appreciation will make it a great deal easier if you want to return for a second interview.

Follow Up the Interview

Follow up the interview with a brief note of thanks in which you might express your appreciation for the time given you, your enjoyment in speaking with the person, and your accomplishing your goal of getting the information you needed.

These general principles will also prove useful in the other types of interviews, especially in the employment interview, which we consider next.

THE EMPLOYMENT INTERVIEW

Perhaps of most concern to college students is the **employment** or **selection interview**. In this type of interview, a great deal of information and persuasion will be exchanged. The interviewer will learn about

UNDERSTANDING Theory and Research

ARE YOU A TALKAHOLIC?

A concept especially important in interviewing is talkaholism—the tendency to talk too much, to be a compulsive talker (McCroskey & Richmond 1995). Not surprisingly, talkaholics were found to be especially assertive, more willing to communicate, and more positive about their own communication skills than those who were not talkaholics. Talkaholics were also more likely to be planning for careers that have high communication demands (for example, public relations and advertising). A high number of talkaholics were majoring in journalism or communication. Persons who were low talkaholics were likely to be more shy, introverted, and apprehensive than high talkaholics. In interviews with some of the high talkaholics, researchers found that talkaholics know they're compulsive talkers, but none of the 21 students studied in depth felt that their talkaholism was a problem.

On the basis of this study, what additional questions about this concept of compulsive communication might be worth researching? How might the concept of talkaholism and the conclusions reached in this study help you to understand better your own interviewing communication tendencies or those of others?

you, your interests, your talents—and, if clever enough, some of your weaknesses and liabilities. In turn, you'll be informed about the nature of the company, its benefits, its advantages—and, if you're clever enough, some of its disadvantages and problems. For the purpose of this discussion, assume you're the interviewee.

As with the other forms of communication considered throughout this text, each culture has its own rules for employment interviewing. In the United States you would be advised to express confidence in your ability and to "blow your own horn." In Japan and China, on the other hand, you would be expected to demonstrate modesty and a willingness to learn from those who know more. This would be doubly true if you were a woman.

In some cultures, a job is seen as a lifetime deal. Once you're hired, you're expected to stay with that firm throughout your entire professional life. Consequently, your prospective employer will want to know a great deal about you and your family. In other cultures, jobs are seen as more temporary and you're expected to move from one job to another several times during your professional career.

In China, Japan, Korea, and other Asian cultures, your family is looked at just as carefully as you are. In other cultures (the United States, for example), it would be illegal to ask a job candidate if she or he is married.

Prepare Yourself

Before going into a job interview, do your homework. One interviewing counselor suggests that this homework should consist of researching four areas: the field, the position, the company, and current events (Taub 1997).

First, research the career field you're entering and its current trends. With this information you'll be able to demonstrate that you're up-to-date and committed to your field of expertise.

Second, research the specific position you're applying for so you'll be able to show how your skills and talents mesh with the position. A good way to do this is to visit the company's Web site. Most large corporations and, increasingly, many small firms, maintain Web sites and frequently include detailed job descriptions. Be prepared to demonstrate your ability to perform each of the tasks noted in the job description. The Monster Board Web site shown here will give you a good starting place to search the Web to learn about jobs and specific companies and even improve your résumé.

Going Online

The Monster Board Web site

This screen presents the Monster Board homepage. This Web site lists some 50,000 jobs you can access by keyword, location, or industry; it's just one of the many Web sites that are useful for finding jobs. Take a look at a few others, for example: http://www.adamsonline.com—discussion groups about jobs and career opportunities, http://www.careermosaic.com—listings of thousands of jobs, and http://www.espan.com—over 10,000 job listings and profiles of employers (Heenehan 1997). What can you learn about the job opportunities in your field from these Web sites?

Third, research the company or organization—its history, mission, and current directions. If it's a publishing company, familiarize yourself with its books and software products. If it's an advertising agency, familiarize yourself with its major clients and major advertising campaigns. A good way to do this is to call and ask the company to send you company brochures, newsletters, or perhaps a quarterly or annual report. And be sure to visit the company's Web site; not only will you learn lots of useful information about this company, but you will also show the interviewer that you make use of the latest technology. With extensive knowledge of the company, you'll be able to show your interest and focus on this specific company.

Fourth, research what is going on in the world in general and in the business world in particular. This will increase your breadth of knowledge and allow you to demonstrate that you're a knowledgeable individual who continues to learn. Reading a good daily newspaper or weekly news magazine will help you master current events.

With the employment interview, both you and the company are trying to fill a need. You want a job that will help build your career and the company wants an effective employee who will be an asset to the company. View the interview as an opportunity to engage in a joint effort to each gain something beneficial. If you approach the interview in this cooperative frame of mind, you're less likely to become defensive, which, in turn, will make you a more appealing potential colleague.

The most important element you can prepare is your résumé. The résumé is a summary of essential information about your experience, education, and abilities. Often, a job applicant submits a résumé in response to a job listing, and if the employer thinks the applicant's résumé is promising, the candidate is invited for an interview. Because of the importance of the résumé and its close association with the interview, a sample one-page résumé and some guidelines to assist you in preparing your own are provided next. A variety of computer programs is available to help you in preparing your résumé; most offer an extensive array of templates that you fill in (or customize if you wish) with your specific data. The one presented here was customized from a Corel Office Suite template.

You can also post your résumé on the Net by e-mailing your résumé to **occ-resumes@msen.com**. It will remain there for 90 days for virtually anyone to see.

Also, recognize that employment interviews are anxiety provoking and that you're likely to experience some communication apprehension. You may wish to take the following self-test to assess your job interviewing apprehension before reading about this interview type.

② For some people, employment objectives may be more general than indicated here, for example,"to secure a management trainee position with an international investment bank." If you do have more specific objectives, put them down. Don't imply that you'll take just anything but also don't appear too specific or demanding.

③ List work experience in chronological order, beginning with your latest position and working back. Depending on your work experience, you may have to pare down what you write. Or, you may have little or nothing to write, so you will have to search through your employment history for some relevent experience. Often the dates of the various positions are included. If you have little or no paid work experience or large gaps in employment history due, say, to time off raising a family, include volunteer work or other unpaid work that requires skills important to the job, for example, coordinator of a little league team or treasurer of the PTA.

④ Provide more information than simply your educational degree. For example, include your major and your minor and perhaps sequences of courses in communication or management or some other field which will further establish your suitability for the job. List honors or awards if they're relevant to your education or job experience. If the awards are primarily educational (for example, Dean's List), list them under the Education heading; if job-related, list them under the Work Experience heading.

⑤ Identify those activities that are relevant to the job skills you want to demonstrate (for example, debating) and also those that attest to the personal qualities you want to stress (for example, reliability and trustworthiness as shown in being treasurer).

⑥ Highlight your special skills. Do you have some foreign language ability? Do you have experience with business or statistical software? If you do, put it down. Such competencies are relevant to many jobs.

① Your name, address, phone and fax number, and e-mail are generally centered at the top of the résumé.

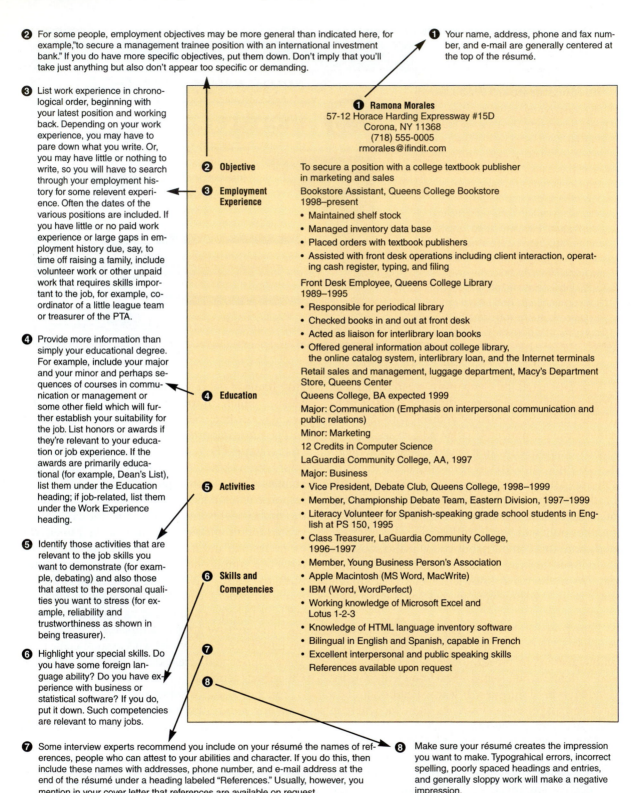

① Ramona Morales
57-12 Horace Harding Expressway #15D
Corona, NY 11368
(718) 555-0005
rmorales@ifindit.com

② Objective
To secure a position with a college textbook publisher in marketing and sales

③ Employment Experience
Bookstore Assistant, Queens College Bookstore
1998–present
- Maintained shelf stock
- Managed inventory data base
- Placed orders with textbook publishers
- Assisted with front desk operations including client interaction, operating cash register, typing, and filing

Front Desk Employee, Queens College Library
1989–1995
- Responsible for periodical library
- Checked books in and out at front desk
- Acted as liaison for interlibrary loan books
- Offered general information about college library, the online catalog system, interlibrary loan, and the Internet terminals

Retail sales and management, luggage department, Macy's Department Store, Queens Center

④ Education
Queens College, BA expected 1999
Major: Communication (Emphasis on interpersonal communication and public relations)
Minor: Marketing
12 Credits in Computer Science
LaGuardia Community College, AA, 1997
Major: Business

⑤ Activities
- Vice President, Debate Club, Queens College, 1998–1999
- Member, Championship Debate Team, Eastern Division, 1997–1999
- Literacy Volunteer for Spanish-speaking grade school students in English at PS 150, 1995
- Class Treasurer, LaGuardia Community College, 1996–1997
- Member, Young Business Person's Association

⑥ Skills and Competencies
- Apple Macintosh (MS Word, MacWrite)
- IBM (Word, WordPerfect)
- Working knowledge of Microsoft Excel and Lotus 1-2-3
- Knowledge of HTML language inventory software
- Bilingual in English and Spanish, capable in French
- Excellent interpersonal and public speaking skills
  References available upon request

⑦

⑧

⑦ Some interview experts recommend you include on your résumé the names of references, people who can attest to your abilities and character. If you do this, then include these names with addresses, phone number, and e-mail address at the end of the résumé under a heading labeled "References." Usually, however, you mention in your cover letter that references are available on request.

⑧ Make sure your résumé creates the impression you want to make. Typographical errors, incorrect spelling, poorly spaced headings and entries, and generally sloppy work will make a negative impression.

SELF-TEST

How Apprehensive Are You in Employment Interviews?

This questionnaire is composed of five questions concerning your feelings about communicating in the job interview setting. Indicate in the spaces provided the degree to which each statement adequately describes your feelings about the employment interview. Use the following scale: (1) strongly agree, (2) agree, (3) undecided, (4) disagree, or (5) strongly disagree.

_____ 1. While participating in a job interview with a potential employer, I am not nervous.

_____ 2. Ordinarily, I am very tense and nervous in job interviews.

_____ 3. I have no fear of speaking up in job interviews.

_____ 4. I'm afraid to speak up in job interviews.

_____ 5. Ordinarily, I am very calm and relaxed in job interviews.

To compute your score, follow these steps:

1. Reverse your scores for items 2 and 4 as follows:

if you said	reverse it to
1	5
2	4
3	3
4	2
5	1

2. Add the scores from all five items; be sure to use the reverse scores for items 2 and 4 and the original scores for 1, 3, and 5.

The higher your score, the greater your apprehension. Since this test is still under development, specific meanings for specific scores are not possible. A score of 25 (the highest possible score) would indicate an extremely apprehensive individual while a score of 5 (the lowest possible score) would indicate an extremely unapprehensive individual. How does your score compare with those of your peers? What score do you think would ensure optimum performance at the job interview?

Your apprehension will probably differ somewhat depending on the type of job interview, your responsibilities, the need and desire you have for the job, and so on. What factors would make you especially apprehensive? Do these answers give you clues as to how to lessen your apprehension?

It seems clear that a person demonstrating apprehension during a job interview will be perceived less positively than will someone demonstrating confidence and composure. How might you learn to better display confidence?

"How Apprehensive Are You in Employment Interviews?" from "A Progress Report on the Development of an Instrument to Measure Communication Apprehension in Employment Interviews" by Joe Ayres, et al., in *Communication Research Reports,* 10, 1993 pp. 87–94. Reprinted by permission of Eastern Communication Association, West Haven, Ct.

Establish Goals

All interviews have specific objectives. As part of your preparation, fix these goals firmly in your mind. Use them as guides to the remainder of your preparation and also to your behavior during and even after the interview. After establishing your objectives clearly in your own mind, relate your preparation to these goals. For example, in considering how to dress, what to learn about the specific company, and what questions to ask during the interview, ask yourself how your goals might help you answer these questions.

Prepare Answers and Questions

If the interview is at all important to you, you'll probably think about it for some time. Use this time productively by rehearsing the predicted course of the interview.

Think about the questions that are likely to be asked and how you'll answer them. Table 12.1 presents a list of questions commonly asked in employment interviews organized around the major topics on the resume, drawn from a variety of interviewing experts (Seidman 1991; Sincoff & Goyer 1984; Skopec 1986; Stewart & Cash 1988; Zima 1983). As you read down this list, visualize yourself at a job interview and try responding to the questions in the middle column. After you've formulated a specific response, look at the suggestions opposite each set of questions. Did you follow the suggestions? Can you rephrase your responses for greater effectiveness? You may also find it helpful to rehearse with this list before going into the interview. Although not all of these questions would be asked in any one interview, be prepared to answer all of them.

Even though the interviewer will ask most of the questions, you too will want to ask questions. In addition to rehearsing some answers to predicted questions, fix firmly in mind the questions you want to ask the interviewer.

After the preparations, you're ready for the interview proper. Several suggestions may guide you through this sometimes difficult procedure.

Make an Effective Presentation of Self

This is probably the most important part of the entire procedure. If you fail here and make a bad initial impression, it will be difficult to salvage the rest of the interview. So devote special care to the way in which you present yourself.

A great number of jobs are won or lost on the basis of physical appearance alone, so also give attention to your physical presentation. Dress in a manner that shows that you care enough about the interview to make a good impression. At the same time, dress comfortably. To avoid extremes is perhaps the most specific advice to give you. When in doubt, it's probably best to err on the side of formality: wear the tie, high heels, or dress.

Bring with you the appropriate materials, whatever they may be. At the very least bring a pen and paper, an extra copy or two of your résumé and, if appropriate, a business card. If you're applying for a job in an area where you've worked before, you might bring samples of your previous work.

Arrive on Time

In interview situations this means 5 to 10 minutes early. This will allow you time to relax, to get accustomed to the general surroundings, and perhaps to fill out any forms that may be required. And it gives you a cushion should something delay you on the way.

Be sure you know the name of the company, the job title, and the interviewer's name. Although you'll have much on your mind when you go into the interview, the interviewer's name is not one of the things you can afford to forget (or mispronounce).

In presenting yourself, don't err on the side of too much casualness or too much formality. When there's doubt, act on the side of increased formality.

Slouching back in the chair, smoking, and chewing gum or candy are obvious behaviors to avoid when you're trying to impress an interviewer.

Demonstrate Effective Interpersonal Communication

Throughout the interview, be certain that you demonstrate the skills of interpersonal communication that are spelled out in this book. The interview is the ideal place to put into practice all the skills you've learned. Here, for example, are the seven characteristics of conversational effectiveness considered in Unit 9 with special reference to the interview situation.

- **Openness.** Answer questions fully. Avoid one-word answers that may signal a lack of interest or knowledge.
- **Empathy.** See the questions from the asker's point of view. Focus your eye contact and orient your body toward the interviewer. Lean forward as appropriate.
- **Positiveness.** Emphasize your positive qualities. Express positive interest in the position. Avoid statements critical of yourself and others.
- **Immediacy.** Connect yourself with the interviewer throughout the interview, for example, by using the interviewer's name, focusing clearly on the interviewer's remarks, and expressing responsibility for your thoughts and feelings.
- **Interaction Management.** Ensure the interviewer's satisfaction by being positive, complimentary, and generally cooperative.
- **Expressiveness.** Let your nonverbal behaviors (especially facial expression and vocal variety) reflect your verbal messages and your general enthusiasm. Avoid fidgeting and excessive moving about.
- **Other-orientation.** Focus on the interviewer and on the company. Express agreement and ask for clarification as appropriate.

In addition to demonstrating these qualities of effectiveness, avoid behaviors that create negative impressions during employment interviews. Here are a few of the most frequent mistakes:

- Being unprepared; they forgot to bring their résumé, don't show that they know anything about the company

TABLE 12.1   **Common interview questions**

Question Areas	Examples	Suggestions
Objectives and Career Goals:	What made you apply to Datacomm? Do you know much about Datacomm? What did you like most about Datacomm? If you took a job with us, where would you like to be in five years? What benefits do you want to get out of this job?	Be positive (and as specific as you can be) about the company. Demonstrate your knowledge of the company. Take a long range view; no firm wants to hire someone who will be looking for another job in six months.
Education:	What do you think of the education you got at Queens College? Why did you major in communication? What was majoring in communication at Queens like? What kinds of courses did you take? Did you do an internship? What were your responsibilities?	Be positive about your educational experience. Try to relate your educational experience to the specific job. Demonstrate competence but at the same time the willingness to continue your education (either formally or informally).
Previous Work Experience:	Tell me about your previous work experience. What did you do exactly? Did you enjoy working at Happy Publications? Why did you leave? How does this previous experience relate to the work you'd be doing here at Datacomm? What kinds of problems did you encounter at your last position?	Again, be positive; never knock a previous job. If you do, the interviewer will think you may be criticizing them in the near future. Especially avoid criticizing specific people with whom you worked.
Special Competencies:	I see here you have a speaking and writing knowledge of Spanish. Could you talk with someone on the phone in Spanish or write letters in Spanish to our customers? Do you know any other languages? How much do you know about computers? Accessing databases?	Before going into the interview, review your competencies. Explain your skills in as much detail as needed to establish their relevance to the job and your own specific competencies.
Personal:	Tell me. Who is Chris Williams? What do you like? What do you dislike? Are you willing to relocate? Are there places you would not consider relocating to? Do you think you'd have any trouble giving orders to others? Do you have difficulty working under deadlines?	Place yourself in the position of the interviewer and ask yourself what kind of person you would hire. Stress your ability to work independently but also as a member of a team. Stress your flexibility in adapting to new work situations.
References:	Do the people you listed here know you personally or academically? Which of these people know you the best? Who would give you the best reference? Who else might know about your abilities that we might contact?	Be sure the people you list know you well and especially that they have special knowledge about you that is relevant to the job at hand.

- Demonstrating poor communication skills; they avoid looking at the interviewer, slouch, slur their words, speak in an overly low or rapid voice, give one word answers, fidget, dress inappropriately
- Appearing to have an unpleasant personality; they appear defensive, cocky, lacking in assertiveness, extremely introverted, overly aggressive
- Showing little initiative; they fail to pick up on ramifications of interviewer's questions, give one word answers, don't ask questions as would be appropriate
- Listening ineffectively; they're easily distracted, need to have questions repeated, fail to maintain appropriate eye contact0

Demonstrate Confidence

A special type of communication skill is that of communicating confidence. Make the interviewer see you as someone who can get the job done, who is confident. Here are some suggestions for communicating confidence that are not limited in their application to interviewing but have relevance of all forms of communication.

- Control your emotions. Once your emotions get the best of you, you will have lost your power and influence and will appear to lack the confidence necessary to deal with the relevant issues.
- Admit mistakes. Attempting to cover up obvious mistakes communicates a lack of confidence. Only a confident person can openly admit her or his mistakes and not worry about what others will think.
- Take an active role in the interview. Initiate topics or questions when appropriate. Avoid appearing as a passive participant, waiting for some stimulus.
- Don't ask for agreement from the interviewer by using tag questions, for example, "That was appropriate, don't you think?" or by saying normally declarative sentences with a rising intonation and thereby turning them into questions, for example, "I'll arrive at nine?" By asking for agreement you communicate a lack of confidence in making decisions and in expressing opinions.

- Avoid excessive movements, especially self-touching movements. Tapping a pencil on a desk, crossing and uncrossing your legs in rapid succession, or touching your face or hair all communicate an uneasiness, a lack of social confidence.
- Maintain eye contact with the interviewer. People who avoid eye contact are often judged to be ill at ease, as if they're afraid to engage in meaningful interaction.
- Avoid vocalized pauses—the "ers" and "ahs", the "you knows" and "like I mean"—that frequently punctuate conversations and that communicate that you lack certainty and are hesitating, not quite sure what to say.

Acknowledge Cultural Rules and Customs

Each culture—and each organization is much like a culture—has its own rules for communicating (Barna 1991; Ruben 1985; Spitzberg 1991). These rules—whether in the interview situation or in friendly conversation—prescribe appropriate and inappropriate behavior, rewards and punishments, and what will help you get the job and what won't. For example, earlier general advice was given here to emphasize your positive qualities, to highlight your abilities and positive qualities, and to minimize any negative characteristics or failings. But in some cultures—especially collectivist cultures such as China, Korea, and Japan, interviewees are expected to show modesty (Copeland & Griggs 1985). Should you stress your own competencies too much, you may be seen as arrogant, brash, and unfit to work in an organization where teamwork and cooperation are emphasized.

In collectivist cultures, great deference is to be shown to the interviewer who represents the company. If you don't treat the interviewer with great respect, you may appear to be disrespectful of the entire company. On the other hand, in individualist cultures, such as the United States, too much deference may make you appear unassertive, unsure of yourself, and unable to assume a position of authority.

And recall (as mentioned earlier) that cultures also vary greatly in attitudes toward directness. Too direct an approach may offend people of one culture while too indirect an approach might offend people of another.

Mentally Review the Interview

By reviewing the interview, you'll fix it firmly in your mind. What questions were asked? How did you answer them? Review and write down any important information the interviewer gave. Ask yourself what you could have done more effectively. Consider what you did effectively that you could repeat in other interviews. Ask yourself how you might correct your weaknesses and capitalize on your strengths.

Follow Up

In most cases, follow up an interview with a thank-you note to the interviewer. In this brief, professional letter, thank the interviewer for his or her time and consideration. Reiterate your interest in the company and perhaps add that you hope to hear from him or her soon. Even if you did not get the job, you might in a follow-up letter ask to be kept in mind for future openings.

This letter provides you with an opportunity to resell yourself—to mention again those qualities you possess and wish to emphasize, but may have been too modest to discuss at the time. It will help to make you stand out in the mind of the interviewer, since not many interviewees write thank-you letters. It will help to remind the interviewer of your interview. It will also tell the interviewer that you're still interested in the position. It's a kind of pat on the back to the interviewer that says, in effect, that the interview was an effective one.

THE LAWFULNESS OF QUESTIONS

Through the Equal Employment Opportunity Commission, the federal government has classified some interview questions as unlawful. These are federal guidelines and therefore apply in all 50 states; individual states, however, may have added further restrictions. You may find it interesting to take the following self-test (constructed with the good help of Stewart & Cash 1988 and Zincoff & Goyer 1984) to see if you can identify which questions are lawful and which are unlawful (see Pullum 1991).

SELF-TEST

Can You Identify Unlawful Questions?

For each question write L (Lawful) if you think the question is legal for an interviewer to ask in an employment interview and U (Unlawful) if you think the question is illegal. For each question you consider unlawful, indicate why you think it's so classified.

_____ 1. Are you married, Tom?
_____ 2. When did you graduate from high school, Mary?
_____ 3. Do you have a picture so I can attach it to your resume?
_____ 4. Will you need to be near a mosque (church, synagogue)?
_____ 5. I see you taught courses in "gay and lesbian studies." Are you gay?
_____ 6. Is Chinese your native language?
_____ 7. Will you have difficulty getting a baby-sitter?
_____ 8. I notice that you walk with a limp. Is this a permanent injury?
_____ 9. Where were you born?
_____ 10. Have you ever been arrested for a crime?

All 10 questions are unlawful. The remaining discussion illustrates why each of these and similar questions are unlawful. But, before reading the text discussion try to develop general principles of what is and what is not legal from the questions given here. Put differently, can you predict the generalizations about illegal questions that will be presented on the basis of knowing that these 10 questions are illegal?

Unlawful Information Requests

Some of the more important areas in which unlawful questions are frequently asked concern age, marital status, race, religion, nationality, citizenship, physical condition, and arrest and criminal records. For example, it's legal to ask applicants whether they meet the legal age requirements for the job and could provide proof of that. But it's unlawful to ask their exact age, even in indirect ways as illustrated in

BUILDING
Communication Skills

HOW CAN YOU PRACTICE INTERVIEWING SKILLS?

Form three-person groups, preferably among persons who don't know each other well or who have had relatively little interaction. One person should be designated the interviewer, another the interviewee, and the third the interview analyst. The interview analyst should choose one of the following situations:

1. An interview for the position of camp counselor for children with disabilities.
2. An interview for a part in a new Broadway musical.
3. An appraisal interview to focus on communication problems in relating to superiors.
4. A teacher–student interview in which the teacher is trying to discover why the course taught last semester was such a dismal failure.

5. An interview between the Chair of the Communication Department and a candidate for the position of instructor of Human Communication.

After the situation is chosen, the interviewer should interview the interviewee for approximately 10 minutes. The analyst should observe but not interfere in any way. After the interview is over, the analyst should offer a detailed analysis, considering each of the following:

1. What happened during the interview (essentially a description of the interaction)?
2. What was well handled?
3. What went wrong? What aspects of the interview were not handled as effectively as they might have been?
4. What could have been done to make the interview more effective?

The analysts for each interview may then report their major findings to the class as a whole. A list of "common faults" or "suggestions for improving interviews" may then be developed by the group leader.

---

question 2 in the self-test. It's unlawful to ask about a person's marital status (question 1) or about family matters that are unrelated to the job (question 7). An interviewer may ask you, however, to identify a close relative or guardian if you're a minor, or any relative who currently works for the company.

Questions concerning your race (questions 3 and 6), religion (question 4), national origin (question 9), affectional orientation (question 5), age (question 2), handicaps unrelated to job performance (question 8), or even arrest record (question 10) are unlawful, as are questions that get at this same information in oblique ways. (Note, for example, that requiring a picture may be a way of discriminating against an applicant on the basis of sex, race, and age.)

Thus, for example, the interviewer may ask you what languages you're fluent in but may not ask what

your native language is (question 6), what language you speak at home, or what language your parents speak. The interviewer may ask you if you if are in this country legally but may not ask if you were born in this country or naturalized (question 9).

The interviewer may inquire into your physical condition only insofar as the job is concerned. For example, the interviewer may ask, "Do you have any physical problems that might prevent you from fulfilling your responsibilities at this job?" But the interviewer may not ask about any physical disabilities (question 8). The interviewer may ask you if you've been convicted of a felony but not if you've been arrested (question 10).

These are merely examples of some of the lawful and unlawful questions that may be asked during an interview. Note that even the questions used as examples here might be lawful in specific situations. The test to apply is simple: Is the information related to your ability to perform the job? Such questions are referred to as BFOQ—Bona Fide Occupational Qualification—questions.

Once you've discovered what questions are unlawful, consider how to deal with them if they come up during an interview.

Strategies for Dealing with Unlawful Questions

Your first strategy should be to deal with such questions by answering the part you don't object to and omitting any information you don't want to give. For example, if you're asked the unlawful question concerning what language is spoken at home, you may respond with a statement such as "I have some language facility in German and Italian," without specifying a direct answer to the question. If you're asked to list all the organizations of which you're a member (an unlawful question in many states, since it's often a way of getting at political affiliation, religion, nationality, and various other areas), you might respond by saying something like: "The only organizations I belong to that are relevant to this job are the International Communication Association and the National Communication Association."

This type of response is preferable to the one that immediately tells the interviewer he or she is asking an unlawful question. In many cases, the interviewer may not even be aware of the legality of various questions and may have no intention of trying to get at information you're not obliged to give. For example, the interviewer may recognize the nationality of your last name and simply want to mention that he or she is also of that nationality. If you immediately take issue with the question, you may be creating problems where none really exist.

On the other hand, do recognize that in many employment interviews, the unwritten intention is to keep certain people out, whether it's people who are older or those of a particular marital status, affectional orientation, nationality, religion, and so on. If you're confronted by questions that are unlawful and that you don't want to answer, and if the gentle method described above does not work and your interviewer persists—saying, for example, "Is German the language spoken at home?" or "What other organizations have you belonged to?"—you might counter by saying that such information is irrelevant to the interview and to the position you're seeking. Again, be courteous but firm. Say something like "This position does not call for any particular language skill and so it does not matter what language is spoken in my home." Or you might say, "The organizations I mentioned are the only relevant ones; whatever other organizations I belong to will certainly not interfere with my ability to perform in this company at this job."

If the interviewer still persists—and it's doubtful that many would after these rather clear and direct responses—you might note that these questions are unlawful and that you're not going to answer them.

Can you identify possible legitimate reasons for asking each of the questions given in the self-test on the lawfulness of questions? Do you agree that certain questions should be considered illegal in a job interview? What types of questions do you think should be considered illegal?

BUILDING
Communication Skills

HOW CAN YOU RESPOND TO UNLAWFUL QUESTIONS?

This exercise is designed to raise some of the unlawful questions that you don't have to answer, and provide you with some practice in developing responses that protect your privacy while maintaining a positive relationship with the interviewer. In the self-test, "Can you identify unlawful questions?" 10 questions were presented.

Assume that you did not want to answer the questions; how would you respond to each of them? One useful procedure is to write your responses and then compare them with those of other students, either in groups or with the class as a whole. Or form two-person groups and role-play the interviewer–interviewee situation. To make this realistic, the person playing the interviewer should press for an answer, while the interviewee should continue to avoid answering, yet respond positively and cordially. You'll discover this is not always easy; tempers often flare in this type of interaction.

SUMMARY

In this unit we introduced the process of interviewing, explored the nature of questions and answers, and identified the major forms of interviewing (focusing on the information gathering and the employment interviews).

1. Interviewing is a form of interpersonal communication in which two persons interact largely through a question-and-answer format to achieve specific goals.
2. Six types of interviewing are the persuasive interview, the appraisal interview, the exit interview, the counseling interview, the information interview, and the employment interview.
3. Questions may be viewed as varying in their degree of openness, neutrality, primacy (or follow-up), and directness.

4. In the informative interview the following guidelines should prove useful: select the person you wish to interview, secure an appointment, prepare your questions, establish rapport with the interviewer, ask permission to tape the interview, ask open-ended questions, and follow up the interview.
5. In the employment interviews the following guidelines should prove useful: prepare yourself intellectually and physically for the interview, establish your objectives, prepare answers to predicted questions, make an effective presentation of yourself, mentally review the interview, and follow up the interview with a brief letter.
6. Interviewees should familiarize themselves with possible unlawful questions and develop strategies for dealing with these questions.

KEY TERMS

interviewing (p. 220)

informal interview (p. 220)

guided interview (p. 221)

standard open interview (p. 221)

quantitative interview (p. 221)

persuasion interview (p. 223)

exit interview (p. 224)

counseling interview (p. 224)

information interview (p. 224)

appraisal interview (p. 224)

employment interview (p. 225)

unlawful questions (p. 233)

BFOQ questions (p. 235)

THINKING CRITICALLY ABOUT
   Interviewing

1. How is a blind date like an interview? How is the first day of class like an interview?

2. How would you prepare a short interview guide to study one of the following questions: (1) Why do students select the elective courses they do? (2) Why do people become teachers (or law enforcement officers or health care workers)? (3) Why do people watch the television shows they watch?

3. Visit one of the Web sites noted in this chapter and locate a job that you think might be appropriate for yourself or for someone in the class. What do you see as the advantages and disadvantages of job searching on the Web?

4. Some positions ask for a reference list, people the employer could contact who could comment on your suit-ability for the position. Who would you include on your reference list? Why would they be appropriate for such a list? What (ideally) would each person say about you?

5. How would you go about finding answers to such questions as these?

   • Are men and women equally effective in interviewing for information? Are men and women equally effective in job interview situations?

   • What questions do people ask about perspective blind dates? Do these questions change as people get older?

   • Who are the most credible television interviewers?

   • What characteristics do television talk show hosts have in common? How do they differ?

UNIT 13
Small Group Communication

UNIT CONTENTS

UNIT GOALS

After completing this unit, you should be able to

describe the nature of a small group, its stages, formats, and channels

explain the four principles of brainstorming

describe the types and nature of personal growth groups

explain the function of the learning group and the focus group

identify the steps that should be followed in problem-solving discussions

Everyone is a member of a wide variety of small groups. The family is the most obvious example, but you also function as members of a team, a class, a collection of friends, and so on. Some of your most important and most personally satisfying communications take place within small groups.

In this unit we look into the nature of the small group and identify its characteristics. With this as a foundation, we examine four major types of small groups (brainstorming, personal growth, information-sharing, and problem-solving,) and the procedures you may follow in participating in these groups. Last, we examine four popular small group formats.

SMALL GROUPS

A small group is a relatively small collection of individuals who are related to each other by some common purpose and have some degree of organization among them. Each of these characteristics needs to be explained a bit further.

A small group is, first, a collection of individuals, few enough in number so all members may communicate with relative ease as both senders and receivers. Generally, a small group consists of approximately 5 to 12 people. The important point to keep in mind is that each member should be able to function as both source and receiver with relative ease. If the group gets much larger than 12 this becomes difficult.

Second, the members of a group must be connected to one another in some way. People on a bus would not constitute a group, since they're not working at some common purpose. Should the bus get stuck in a ditch, the riders may quickly become a group and work together to get the bus back on the road. In a small group the behavior of one member is significant for all other members. This does not mean that all members must have exactly the same purpose in being members of the group. But generally there must be some similarity in the individuals' reasons for interacting.

Third, the members must be connected by some organizing rules or structure. At times the structure is rigid—as in groups operating under parliamentary procedure, where each comment must follow prescribed rules. At other times, as in a social gathering, the structure is very loose. Yet in both groups there's

some organization and some structure: Two people don't speak at the same time, comments or questions by one member are responded to by others rather than ignored, and so on.

Small Group Apprehension

Just as you have some apprehension in interpersonal conversations (Unit 9), you probably experience apprehension to some degree in group discussions. Because small groups vary so widely, you're likely to experience different degrees of apprehension depending on the nature of the specific group. Work groups, for example, may cause greater apprehension than groups of friends. And interacting with superiors is likely to generate greater apprehension than meeting with peers or subordinates. Similarly, the degree of familiarity you have with the group members and the extent to which you see yourself as a part of the group (as opposed to outsider) will also influence your apprehension. You may wish at this point to take the following apprehension self-test to measure your own apprehension in group discussions and meetings.

 **SELF-TEST**

How Apprehensive Are You in Group Discussions and Meetings?

Just as you have apprehension in conversations (Unit 9), and in interviewing (Unit 12), you probably have some degree of apprehension in group discussions and in meetings. This brief test is designed to measure your apprehension in these small group situations.

This questionnaire consists of 12 statements concerning your feelings about communication in group discussions and meetings. Please indicate in the space provided the degree to which each statement applies to you by marking whether you (1) strongly agree, (2) agree, (3) are undecided, (4) disagree, or (5) strongly disagree. There are no right or wrong answers. Some of the statements are similar to other statements. Don't be concerned about this. Work quickly; just record your first impression.

_____ 1. I dislike participating in group discussions.

_____ 2. Generally, I am comfortable while participating in group discussions.

_____ 3. I am tense and nervous while parti-cipating in group discussions.

_____ 4. I like to get involved in group discussions.

_____ 5. Engaging in a group discussion with new people makes me tense and nervous.

_____ 6. I am calm and relaxed while partici-pating in group discussions.

_____ 7. Generally, I am nervous when I have to participate in a meeting.

_____ 8. Usually, I am calm and relaxed while participating in meetings.

_____ 9. I am very calm and relaxed when I am called upon to express an opin-ion at a meeting.

_____ 10. I am afraid to express myself at meetings.

_____ 11. Communicating at meetings usually makes me uncomfortable.

_____ 12. I am very relaxed when answering questions at a meeting.

This test will enable you to obtain two subscores, one for group discussions and one for meetings. To obtain your scores use the following formulas:

For group discussions compute your score as follows:

1. Begin with the number 18; this is just used as a base so that you won't wind up with nega-tive numbers
2. To 18, add your scores for items 2, 4, and 6
3. Subtract your scores for items 1, 3, and 5 from your step 2 total.

For meetings compute your score as follows:

1. Begin with the number 18; this is just used as a base so that you won't wind up with nega-tive numbers
2. To 18, add your scores for items 8, 9, and 12
3. Subtract your scores for items 7, 10, and 11 from your step 2 total.

Scores above 18 show some degree of appre-hension. Can you identify the specific aspects of small groups that influence your apprehension? For example, what group factors help reduce ap-prehension? What group factors help increase apprehension? What might you do to reduce the factors that increase apprehension and increase the factors that reduce it?

From James C. McCroskey, _An Introduction to Rhetorical Communication_, 7th edition, Prentice-Hall, Upper saddle River, NJ. Reprinted by permissions.

Small Group Culture

Many groups—especially those of long standing like work groups—develop into a kind of small culture with its own **norms**. These are the rules or standards of behavior identifying which behaviors are consid-ered appropriate (for example, willingness to take on added tasks or directing conflict toward issues rather than toward people) and which are considered in-appropriate (for example, coming late or not con-tributing actively). Sometimes these rules for appropriate behavior are explicitly stated in a com-pany contract or policy: all members must attend de-partment meetings. Sometimes the rules are implicit: members should be well-groomed. Regardless of whether norms are spelled out or not, they're pow-erful regulators of members' behaviors.

Norms may apply to individual members as well as to the group as a whole and, of course, will differ from one group to another (Axtell 1990a, 1993). For example, in the United States men and women in business are expected to interact when making busi-ness decisions as well as when socializing. In Mus-lim and Buddhist societies, however, there are religious restrictions that prevent mixing the sexes. In the United States, Bangladesh, Australia, Ger-many, Finland, and Hong Kong, for example, punc-tuality for business meetings is very important. But, in countries like Morocco, Italy, Brazil, Zambia, Ire-land, and Panama, for example, time is less highly regarded and being late is no great insult and is even expected. In the United States, and in much of Asia and Europe, meetings are held between two groups. In many Persian Gulf states, however, the business executive is likely to conduct meetings with several different people—sometimes dealing with totally dif-ferent issues—at the same time. In this situation, you have to expect to share what in the United States would be "your time" with these other parties. In the United States very little interpersonal touching goes on during business meetings; in Arab countries, however, touching (for example, hand holding) is common and is a gesture of friendship.

Norms that regulate a particular member's behav-ior, called role expectations, identify what each per-son in an organization is expected to do, for example,

Pat has a great computer setup and so should play the role of secretary.

Think about the situations in which you would be most likely to accept the norms of your group. When are you more likely to violate these norms? According to research on group norms, you're more likely to accept the norms of your group's culture when you answer "yes" to the following questions (Napier & Gershenfeld 1989). "Yes" responses indicate your willingness to accept your group's norms.

- Do you want to continue your membership in the group?
- Do you feel that your group membership is important?
- Is your group cohesive? Are you and the other members closely connected? Are you attracted to each other? Do you depend on each other to meet individual needs?
- Would you be punished by negative reactions or exclusion from the group for violating the group norms?

Small Group Phases

The small group develops in much the same way that a conversation develops. As in conversation, there are five stages: opening, feedforward, business, feedback, closing. The **opening** period is usually a getting-acquainted time where members introduce themselves and engage in phatic communion. After this preliminary get-together, there's usually some **feedforward**, some attempt to identify what needs to be done, who will do it, and so on. In a formal group, the agenda (which is a perfect example of feedforward) might be reviewed and the tasks of the group identified. In more informal social groups, the feedforward might consist simply of introducing a topic of conversation or talking about what the group's members should do. The **business** portion is the actual discussion of the tasks—the problem solving, the sharing of information, or whatever else the group needs to do. At the **feedback** stage, the group might reflect on what it has done and perhaps what remains to be done. Some groups may even evaluate their performance at this stage. At the **closing** stage, the group members again return to their focus on individuals and will perhaps exchange closing comments—good seeing you again, etc. A typical pattern would look like Figure 13.1.

These stages are rarely separate from one another. Rather, like the colors of the rainbow, they seem to blend into one another. For example, the opening stage is not completely finished before the feedforward begins. Rather, as the opening comments are completed, the group begins to introduce feedforward and as the feedforward begins to end, the business starts.

Electronic Channels

Small groups use a wide variety of channels. Often, of course, they take place face-to-face. This is the type of group that probably comes to mind when you think of group interaction. But, especially today,

Each culture has its own group norms. Can you identify the norms that your culture taught you about what's proper and what's improper in a business group?

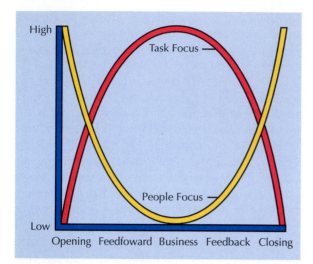

Figure 13.1 **Small group stages and the focus on task and people.** Of course, different types of groups will evidence different patterns. For example, a problem-solving group is likely to spend a great deal more time focused on the task whereas an informal social group, say two or three couples who get together for dinner, will spend more time focused on people concerns. Similarly, the amount of time spent on the opening or business or closing, for example, will vary with the type of group and with the purposes that the group wishes to accomplish.

much small group interaction takes place online. Online groups are proliferating and are becoming a part of people's experience throughout the world. They're important personally and socially as well as professionally. Two major online groups may be noted here: the mailing list group and the Internet Relay Chat (IRC) group. In conjunction with the following discussions, take a look at the Credo for Free and Responsible Use of Electronic Communication Networks (p. 243). It's one attempt by a national communication association to articulate some of the ethical issues in electronic communication.

The Mailing List Group

The mailing list group or listserv consists of a group of people interested in a particular topic who communicate with each other through e-mail. Generally, you subscribe to a list and communicate with all other members by addressing your mail to the group e-mail address. Any message you send to this address

will be sent to each member who subscribes to the list. Your message is sent to all members at the same time; there are no asides to the person sitting next to you (as in face-to-face groups).

The mailing list Web site shown on page 224 will provide you with a list of 1500 mailing lists categorized by topic. A list of frequently asked questions (FAQs) and mailing list addresses can be found at http://www.cis.ohio-state.edu/hypertext/faq/usenet/mail/mailing-lists/top.html. Of course you could also go to one of the search engines and search for mailing lists. To locate a mailing list you might be interested in, you might e-mail your request to listserv@listserv.net. Send the message: **list topic-of-interest**, for example, **list politics** or **list politics international**.

Communication through mailing lists does not take place in real time. It's like regular e-mail; you may send your message today but it may not be read until next week and you may not get an answer for another week. Much of the spontaneity created by real time communication is lost here. You may, for example, be very enthusiastic about a topic when you send your e-mail but practically forget it by the time someone responds.

Internet Relay Chat

IRC groups have proliferated across the Internet. These groups enable members to communicate with each other in real time in discussion groups called channels. At any one time, there may be perhaps 4000 channels and 20,000 users, so your chances of finding a topic you're interested in are fairly high.

Unlike mailing lists, IRC communication takes place in real time; you see a member's message as it's being sent, there's virtually no delay. Like mailing lists and face-to-face conversation, the purposes of IRCs vary from communication that simply maintains connection with others—what many would call "idle chatter," or phatic communion—to extremely significant—for example, IRCs were used to gather information on military activities during the Persian Gulf war and to provide an information database during the California earthquake in 1994 (Estabrook 1997).

Communication on an IRC resembles the conversation you'd observe at a large party. The guests divide up into small groups of two or more people, and each small group discusses its own topic or version of a general topic. For example, in an

CREDO FOR FREE AND RESPONSIBLE USE OF ELECTRONIC COMMUNICATION NETWORKS

The principles of free and responsible communication have long been a hallmark of communication study. Since 1963, the National Communication Association has included among its core documents a Credo for Free and Responsible Communication in a Democratic Society. Recognizing the advent of electronic means of global communication that are accessible to the general public, we members of the National Communication Association endorse the following statement of principles relating to electronic communication:

We take the concept of "free speech" literally: there is limited freedom of expression if access to the means of expression is limited by financial ability. We, therefore, urge the development of free and low-cost means of accessing the means for processing and distributing information in electronic forms.

We realize that access is limited if specialized expertise is required to take advantage of the necessary technology. We, therefore, urge the development of hardware and software that requires minimal training but that still allows wide use of worldwide electronic resources.

We support freedom of expression and condemn attempts to constrain information processing or electronic communication, especially expressions that are offensive to some or even most of the populace. Likewise, we support a right to privacy, both in the ability to maintain the integrity of individual message exchanges and in the ability to shield oneself from unwanted messages.

While supporting free expression, we nevertheless consider the maintenance of intellectual property rights to be crucial to the encouragement of creativity and originality. We, therefore, urge the designers and regulators of electronic forms of communication to use special vigilance to insure that the works of individuals or groups are protected from unfair use by others.

We encourage communication researchers to produce findings that will guide policy decisions concerning the social impact of electronic communication and to make those findings available widely.

Likewise, we encourage the designers and regulators of electronic forms of communication to take credible findings about the social impact of their work into account as they implement new products and services.

We accept the need to teach students not only how to use electronic forms of communication but how to use them both wisely and well.

Finally, we call upon users of information processing and distribution networks to do so responsibly, with respect for language, culture, gender, sexuality, ethnicity, and generational and economic differences they may encounter in others.

Adopted 1994.

From *The National Communication Association*, "Credo for Free and Responsible Use of Electronic Communication Networks," 1994. Reprinted by Permission.

IRC about food, six people may be discussing food calories, four people may be discussing restaurant food preparation, and two people may be discussing the basic food groups—all on this one channel dealing with food. So, although you may be communicating in one primary group (say, dealing with restaurant food), you also have your eye trained to pick up something particularly interesting in another group (much as you do at a party). IRCs also notify you when someone new comes into the group and when someone leaves. IRCs, like mailing lists, have the great advantage that they enable you to communicate with people you would never meet and interact with otherwise. Because IRCs are international, they provide excellent exposure to other cultures, other ideas, and other ways of communicating.

IRCs, unlike e-mail, also allow you to "whisper," to communicate with just one other person without giving access to your message to other participants. In this situation, IRCs resemble interpersonal rather than small group communication.

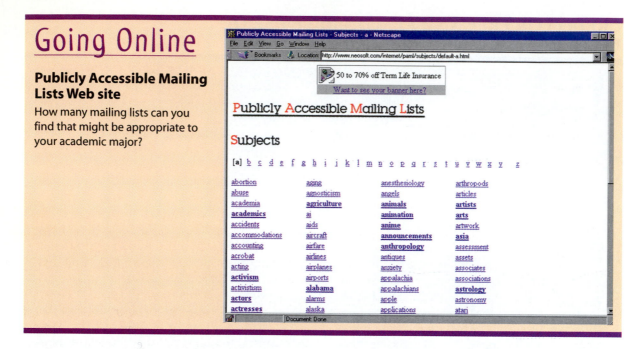

Going Online

Publicly Accessible Mailing Lists Web site

How many mailing lists can you find that might be appropriate to your academic major?

In face-to-face group communication, you're expected to contribute to the ongoing discussion. In IRCs you can simply observe; in fact, you're encouraged to lurk—to observe the group's interaction before you say anything yourself. In this way, you'll be able to learn the customs of the group and not violate any of its rules or norms.

Power in the Small Group

Power permeates all small groups and in fact all relationships. It influences what you do, when, and with whom. It influences the employment you seek and the employment you get. It influences the friends you choose and don't choose and those who choose you and those who don't. It influences your romantic and family relationships—their success, failure, and level of satisfaction or dissatisfaction.

Power is what enables one person (the one with power) to control the behaviors of the others. Thus, if A has power over B and C, then A, by virtue of this power and through the exercise of this power (or the threat of its being exercised), can control the behaviors of B and C. Differences in the amount and type of power influence who makes important decisions, who will prevail in an argument, and who will control the finances.

Although all relationships are the same in that they all involve power, they differ in the types of

power that the people use and to which they respond. The following self-test will help you identify the six major types of power.

SELF-TEST

How Powerful Are You?

For each statement, indicate which of the following descriptions is most appropriate: 1 = true of 20 percent or less of the people I know; 2 = true of about 21 to 40 percent of the people I know; 3 = true of about 41 to 60 percent of the people I know; 4 = true of about 61 to 80 percent of the people I know; and 5 = true of 81 percent or more of the people I know.

_____ 1. My position is such that I often have to tell others what to do. For example, a mother's position demands that she tell her children what to do, a manager's position demands that he or she tells employees what to do, and so on.

_____ 2. People wish to be like me or identified with me. For example, high school football players may admire the former professional football

MEDIA WATCH

WHO ARE THE GATEKEEPERS?

As you were growing up, your parents gave you certain information and withheld other information. For example, depending on the culture in which you were raised, you may have been told about Santa Claus and the tooth fairy but not about cancer or mutual funds. That is, your parents served as gatekeepers—they regulated what information you were exposed to. When you went to school, your teachers served a similar function. They taught you about certain historical events, for example, but not others. Gatekeepers are all around us; the most important of these are the media.

In the passage of a message from the source of mass media to the viewer, a gatekeeper intervenes. The term *gatekeeping* was originally used by Kurt Lewin in his *Human Relations* (1947). It refers to (1) the process by which a message passes through various gates, as well as to (2) the people or groups that allow the message to pass (gatekeepers).

A gatekeeper's main function is to filter the messages an individual receives. Teachers are perfect examples of gatekeepers. Teachers read the various books in an area of study. They read journal articles and listen to convention papers. They share information among themselves and conduct their own research in the field. From all this information, they pass some of it on to their students. Textbook authors are also gatekeepers. For example, in a thorough review of the research used in history textbooks, one researcher concluded that the content included was designed "to preserve political and economic power" rather than truth (Robinson 1993). Editors of newspapers, magazines, publishing houses are also gatekeepers as are those who regulate and monitor Internet messages (Lewis 1995). They allow only certain information to get through.

The media, usually on the basis of their own codes and sometimes because of legal regulations, censors what gets through to viewers. For example, MTV serves as a gatekeeper and rejects a variety of video clips because they violate some standard. Thus, for example, Madonna's "Justify My Love" was rejected because of its depiction of group sex, and David Bowie's "China Girl" was rejected because of a nude beach scene. Neil Young's "This Note's for You" and Seaweed's "Kid Candy" were rejected because they showed brand name products (Banks 1995). Newspapers and magazines regularly reject stories they consider too sexual and photos they consider too graphic.

The gatekeeper, then, limits the messages we receive. The teacher, for example, limits the information the students receive. However, the teacher enables the students to learn a great deal more by distilling, organizing, and analyzing information for them. That is, without gatekeepers we would not get half the information we now receive.

You may find it interesting to ask yourself how the following people function as gatekeepers:

- The editor of your local or college newspaper
- Jerry Springer and Oprah Winfrey
- Your romantic partner (past or present)
- The president of the United States
- Network news shows
- General Motors' advertising department

The next Media Watch appears on page 273.

player who is now their coach and want to be like him.

_____ 3. People see me as having the ability to give them what they want. For example, employers have the ability to give their employees increased pay,

longer vacations, and improved working conditions.

_____ 4. People see me as having the ability to administer punishment or to withhold things they want. For example, employers have the ability to reduce

_____ voluntary overtime, shorten vacation time, and fail to improve working conditions.

_____ 5. Other people realize that I have expertise in certain areas of knowledge. For example, a doctor has expertise in medicine and so others turn to the doctor to tell them what to do. Someone knowledgeable about computers similarly possesses expertise.

_____ 6. Other people realize that I possess the communication ability to present an argument logically and persuasively.

These statements refer to the six major types of power. Low scores (1s and 2s) indicate your belief that you possess little of this particular type of power and high scores (4s and 5s) indicate your belief that you possess a great deal of this particular type of power. How satisfied are you with your level of power? If you're not satisfied, what might you do about it? ✔

The six types of power covered in the self-test are legitimate, referent, reward, coercive, expert, and information or persuasion power (from French & Raven 1968, Raven, Centers, & Rodrigues 1975). You have **legitimate power** (self-test statement 1) over another when this person believes you have a right—by virtue of your position (for example, you're the appointed group leader)—to influence or control his or her behavior. This type of power stems from the belief that certain people, because of their position in society or in a group, have a right to influence others. Legitimate power usually comes from the roles people occupy. Teachers are often seen to have legitimate power and this is doubly true for religious teachers. Parents are seen as having legitimate power over their children. Employers, judges, managers, doctors, and police officers are others who may hold legitimate power. What these people share is that they occupy positions of leadership.

You have **referent power** (statement 2) over another person when that person wishes to be like you or identified with you. For example, an older brother may have referent power over a younger brother because the younger wants to be like his older brother. The assumption made by the younger brother is that he will be more like his older brother if he behaves and believes as his brother does. Your referent power increases when you're well liked and well respected, when you're seen as attractive and prestigious, when you're of the same sex, and when you have similar attitudes and experiences as this other person. And this is why role models are so important; role models, by definition, possess referent power and exert great influence on those looking up to them.

You have **reward power** (statement 3) over a person if you have the ability to give that person rewards—either material (money, promotions, jewelry) or social (love, friendship, respect). Conversely, you have **coercive power** (statement 4) if you have the ability to remove rewards from that person or to administer punishments. Usually, the two go hand in hand, and if you have one type of power, you also have the other. A good example of this is parents who may grant as well as deny privileges to their children.

Reward power increases attractiveness; we like those who have the power to reward us and who do in fact give us rewards. Coercive power, on the other hand, decreases attractiveness; we dislike those who have the power to punish us and who threaten us with punishment, whether they actually follow through or not. Thus, as a parent, manager, teacher, or group leader, you'll be better liked and more persuasive if you reward people for their desirable behaviors instead of punishing them for undesirable behaviors.

You possess **expert power** (statement 5) if group members regard you as having expertise or knowledge (whether or not you truly possess such expertise). Often your position will communicate your expertise and so generally, for example, the lawyer is viewed as an expert in legal matters and the doctor in medical matters. Expert power increases when you are seen as unbiased, with nothing to gain personally from influencing others. It decreases if you are seen as biased and as having something to gain from securing the compliance of others.

You have **information** or **persuasion power** (statement 6) if you are seen as someone who can communicate logically and persuasively. If people see you as having the ability to communicate effectively, they will be more likely to believe and follow you. Generally, persuasion power is attributed to people who are perceived as possessing significant information and the ability to use that information in presenting a well-reasoned argument. Information or persuasive power is also enhanced by the use of powerful speech (discussed in Unit 7). So, an effective department report or a persuasive argument presented at a company meeting will contribute significantly to your information or persuasion power.

Here are a few ways you can communicate your power in a small group or in any communication setting (Lewis 1989; Burgoon, Buller, & Woodall 1995).

1. Respond visibly but in moderation; an occasional nod of agreement or a facial expression that says "that's interesting" are usually sufficient. Responding with too little or too much reaction is likely to be perceived as powerless. Too little response says you aren't listening and too much response says you aren't listening critically. Use backchanneling cues— head nods and brief oral responses that say you're listening.

2. Avoid adaptors—playing with your hair or a pencil or drawing pictures on a styrofoam cup; they signal that you're uncomfortable and hence that you lack power. The lack of adaptors, on the other hand, makes you appear in control and comfortable.

3. When you break eye contact, direct your gaze downward; otherwise you'll communicate a lack of interest to the other person.

4. To communicate dominance with your handshake, exert more pressure than usual and hold the grip a bit longer than normal.

5. Walk slowly and deliberately. To appear hurried is to appear as without power, as if you were rushing to meet the expectations of someone with power over you.

6. Maintain an open posture. When around a table or in an audience, resist covering your face, chest, or stomach with your hands. This type of posture is often interpreted as indicating defensiveness and may lead others to see you as vulnerable and powerless.

Small Group Formats

Small groups serve their functions in a variety of formats. Among the most popular formats for relatively formal groups are the roundtable, the panel, the symposium, and the symposium-forum (Figure 13.2).

The Round Table

In the round table format, group members arrange themselves in a circular or semicircular pattern. They share the information or solve the problem without any set pattern of who speaks when. Group interaction is informal and members contribute as they see fit. A leader or moderator may be present who may, for example, try to keep the discussion on the topic or encourage more reticent members to speak up.

The Panel

In the panel, group members are "experts" and participate informally and without any set pattern of who speaks when. The difference is that there's an audience whose members may interject comments or ask questions. Many talk shows, such as *Jerry Springer* and *The Oprah Winfrey Show*, use this format.

A variation is the two-panel format, with an expert panel and a lay panel. The lay panel discusses the topic but when in need of technical information, additional data, or direction, they may turn to the expert panel members to provide the needed information.

The Symposium

In the symposium, each member delivers a prepared presentation, much like a public speech. All speeches are addressed to different aspects of a single topic. In the symposium, the leader introduces the speakers, provides transitions from one speaker to another, and may provide periodic summaries.

The Symposium-Forum

The symposium-forum consists of two parts: a symposium, with prepared speeches, and a forum, with questions from the audience and responses by the speakers. The leader introduces the speakers and moderates the question-and-answer session.

IDEA-GENERATION GROUPS

Many small groups exist solely to generate ideas and often follow a formula called **brainstorming** (Beebe & Masterson 1997; DeVito 1996; Osborn 1957). Brainstorming is a technique for bombarding a problem and generating as many ideas as possible. In this system the process occurs in two phases. The first is the brainstorming period proper; the second is the evaluation period.

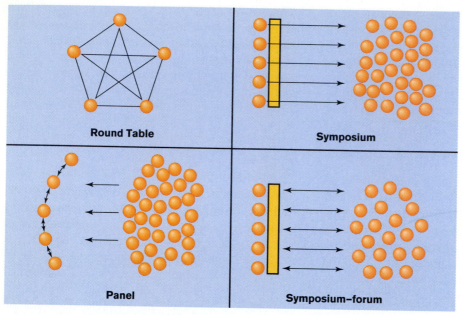

Figure 13.2   **Small Group Formats.**   These four formats are general patterns that may describe a wide variety of groups. Within each type, there will naturally be considerable variation. For example, in the symposium-forum there's no set pattern for how much time will be spent on the symposium part and how much time will be spent on the forum part. Similarly, combinations may be used. Thus, for example, group members may each present a position paper (basically a symposium) and then participate in a roundtable discussion.

The procedures are simple. A problem is selected that is amenable to many possible solutions or ideas. Group members are informed of the problem to be brainstormed before the actual session, so they can think about the topic. When the group meets, each person contributes as many ideas as he or she can think of. All ideas are recorded either in writing or on tape. During this idea-generating session, four general rules are followed.

Brainstorm Rule 1: Don't Criticize

All ideas are recorded. They're not evaluated, nor are they even discussed. Any negative criticism—whether verbal or nonverbal—is itself criticized by the leader or the members. This is a good general rule to follow in all creative thinking. Allow your idea time to develop before you look for problems with it. At the same time, don't praise the ideas either. All evaluations should be suspended during the brainstorming session.

Brainstorm Rule 2: Strive for Quantity

Linus Pauling, Nobel Prize winner for chemistry (1954) and peace (1962), once said, "The best way to have a good idea is to have lots of ideas." This second rule of brainstorming uses this concept. If you need an idea, you're more likely to find it in a group of many than in a group of few. Thus, in brainstorming, the more ideas the better.

Brainstorm Rule 3: Combine and Extend Ideas

While you may not criticize a particular idea, you may extend it or combine it in some way. The value of a particular idea may be the way it stimulates someone to combine or extend it. Even if your modification seems minor or obvious, say it. Don't censor yourself.

Brainstorm Rule 4: Develop the Wildest Ideas Possible

The wilder the idea, the better. It's easier to tone an idea down than to build it up. A wild idea can easily

UNDERSTANDING
Theory and Research

HOW DOES YOUR GROUP DISTRIBUTE POWER?

Earlier (Unit 6) the theory of high and low power distance cultures was noted. There it was pointed out that high power distance cultures are those in which power is concentrated in the hands of a few and there's a great difference in the power held by these people and by the ordinary citizen (Hofstede 1997). In low power distance cultures, power is relatively evenly distributed throughout the citizenry. Groups may also be viewed in terms of high and low power distance. In high power distance groups, the leader is far more powerful than the members. In low power distance groups, the leaders and members differ much less in their power.

Consider the implications of this theory for your own small group behavior. Of the groups in which you'll participate—as a member or a leader—some will be high power distance groups and others will be low. The skill is to recognize which is which, to follow the rules generally, and to break them only after you've thought through the consequences. For example, in low power distance cultures and groups you're expected to confront a group leader (or friend or supervisor) assertively; acting assertively denotes the general feeling of equality (Borden 1991). In high power distance groups and cultures, direct confrontation and assertiveness toward the leader (or any person in authority such as a teacher or doctor) may be viewed negatively (Westwood, Tang, & Kirkbride 1992; also see Bochner & Hesketh 1994).

---

be tempered, but it's not so easy to elaborate on a simple or conservative idea.

At times, the brainstorming session may break down, with members failing to contribute new ideas. At this point, the moderator may prod the members with statements such as the following:

- Let's try to get a few more ideas before we close this session.
- Can we piggyback any other ideas or add extensions on the suggestion to. . . .
- Here's what we have so far. As I read the list of contributed suggestions, additional ideas may come to mind.
- Here's an aspect we haven't focused on. . . . Does this stimulate any ideas?

After all the ideas are generated—a period lasting no longer than 15 or 20 minutes—the entire list of ideas is evaluated, using the critical thinking skills covered throughout this textbook. The ones that are

unworkable are thrown out; the ones that show promise are retained and evaluated. During this phase negative criticism is allowed.

Although brainstorming was designed as a group experience, there's some evidence to show that individual brainstorming can work even more effectively than group brainstorming (Peters 1987). As with group brainstorming, individuals brainstorming alone need to follow the same rules as the group. Be especially careful that you don't censor yourself and that you record (on paper or tape) every idea that comes to you. Remember that these are ideas not necessarily solutions; don't be afraid to record even the seemingly most absurd ideas.

PERSONAL GROWTH GROUPS

Some **personal growth groups**, sometimes referred to as support groups, aim to help members cope with particular difficulties, such as drug addiction, having an alcoholic parent, being an exconvict, or

Generating new ideas through brainstorming or some other process needs to be complemented by giving these new ideas a fair hearing, by listening openly and honestly to the idea and only then to what others are saying about it. What other suggestions would you offer that would be helpful in listening to new ideas? (Also see Building Communications Skills box on page 257.)

having an overactive child or a promiscuous spouse. Other groups are more clearly therapeutic and are designed to change significant aspects of one's personality or behavior.

Some Popular Personal Growth Groups

There are many varieties of support or personal growth groups. The *encounter group*, for example, tries to facilitate personal growth and the ability to deal effectively with other people (Rogers 1970). One of its assumptions is that the members will be more effective psychologically and socially if they get to know and like themselves better. Consequently, the atmosphere of the encounter group is one of acceptance and support. Freedom to express one's inner thoughts, fears, and doubts is stressed.

The *assertiveness-training group* aims to increase the willingness of its members to stand up for their rights and to act more assertively in a wide variety of situations (Adler 1977).

The *consciousness-raising group* aims to help people cope with the problems society confronts them with. The members of a consciousness-raising group all have one characteristic in common (for example, they're all women, all unwed mothers, all gay fathers, or all recently unemployed executives). It's this commonality that leads the members to join together and assist one another. In the consciousness-raising group the assumption is that similar people are best equipped to assist each other's personal growth. Structurally, the consciousness-raising group is leaderless. All members (usually ranging from 6 to 12) are equal in their control of the group and in their presumed knowledge.

Although all personal growth groups will function somewhat differently, we can illustrate at least one possible pattern by looking at the steps and procedures that a sample consciousness-raising group might follow. These procedures are generally much more flexible than those followed in a problem-solving group, for example.

Some Rules and Procedures

To illustrate how such groups might work, let's look at a fairly typical consciousness-raising group. Here the group might start with selecting a topic, usually by majority vote of the group. This topic may be drawn from a prepared list or suggested by one of the group members. But regardless of what topic is selected, it's always discussed from the point of view of the larger topic that brings these particular people together—let's say, sexual harassment. Whether the topic is men, employment, or family, it's pursued in light of the issues and problems of sexual harassment.

After a topic is selected, a starting point is established through some random procedure. That member speaks for about 10 minutes on his or her feelings, experiences, and thoughts. The focus is always on oneself. No interruptions are allowed. After the member has finished, the other group members may ask questions of clarification. The feedback from other members is to be totally supportive.

After questions of clarification have been answered, the next member speaks. The same procedure is followed until all members have spoken. After the last member has spoken, a general discussion follows. During this time members may relate different aspects of their experience to what the others have

BUILDING Communication Skills

HOW DO YOU COMBAT IDEA KILLERS?

Think about how you can be on guard against negative criticism and how you can respond to such "idea killers" or "killer messages" as those listed below. These phrases are directed at stopping an idea from being developed, to kill it in its tracks, before it can even get off the ground. As you read down the list of these commonly heard killer messages, formulate at least one response you might use if someone used one of these on you. Also consider responses you might make on occasions when you use these terms to censor your own creative thinking.

- We tried it before and it didn't work.
- It'll never work.
- No one would vote for it.
- It's too complex.
- It's too simple.
- It would take too long.
- It's too expensive.
- It's not logical.
- We don't have the facilities.
- It's a waste of time and money.
- What we have is good enough.
- It won't fly.
- It just doesn't fit us.
- It's impossible.

said. Or they may tell the group how they feel about some of the issues raised by others.

With this procedure your consciousness is raised by formulating and verbalizing your thoughts on a particular topic, hearing how others feel and think about the same topic, and formulating and answering questions of clarification.

INFORMATION-SHARING GROUPS

The purpose of information-sharing groups is to acquire new information or skill through a sharing of knowledge. In most information-sharing groups, all members have something to teach and something to learn. In others, the interaction takes place because some have information and some don't.

Educational or Learning Groups

In learning groups, the members pool their knowledge to the benefit of all. Members may follow a variety of discussion patterns. For example, a historical topic might be developed chronologically, with the discussion progressing from the past into the present and perhaps predicting the future. Issues in developmental psychology such as language development in the child or physical maturity might also be discussed chronologically. Some topics lend themselves to spatial development. For example, the development of the United States might take a spatial pattern going from east to west or a chronological pattern going from 1776 to the present. Other suitable patterns, depending on the nature of the topic and the needs of the discussants, might be developed in terms of causes and effects, problems and solutions, or structures and functions.

Perhaps the most popular is the topical pattern. A group might discuss the problems in raising a hyperactive child by itemizing and discussing each of the major problems. The structure of a corporation might also be considered in terms of its major divisions. As can be appreciated, each of these topics may be further systematized, for instance, by ordering the problems of hyperactivity in terms of their importance or complexity and ordering the major structures of the corporation in terms of decision-making power.

Focus Groups

A different type of learning group is the focus group, a kind of in-depth interview of a small group. The aim here is to discover what people think about an issue or product; for example, what do men between 18 and 25 think of the new aftershave lotion and its packaging? What do young executives earning over $70,000 think of buying a foreign luxury car?

In the focus group the leader tries to discover the beliefs, attitudes, thoughts, and feelings that members have so as to better guide decisions on changing the scent or redesigning the packaging or constructing advertisements for luxury cars. It is the leader's task to prod members to analyze their thoughts and feelings on a deeper level and to use the thoughts of one member to stimulate the thoughts of others.

For example, in one study the researcher tried "to collect supplementary data on the perceptions graduates have of the Department of Communication at ABC University" (Lederman 1990). Two major research questions, taken directly from Lederman's study, motivated this focus group: (1) What do graduates of the program perceive the educational effectiveness of their major to be at ABC? and (2) What would they want implemented in the program as it exists today? Group participants then discussed their perceptions, organized around such questions as these (Lederman 1990):

- The first issue to discuss is what the program was like when you were a major in the department. Let's begin by going around the table and making introductions. Will you tell me your name, when you graduated from ABC, what you're doing now, and what the program was like when you were here, as you remember it?
- Based on what you remember of the program and what you have used from your major since graduating, what kinds of changes, if any, would you suggest?

PROBLEM-SOLVING GROUPS

A problem-solving group is a collection of individuals who meet to solve a problem or to reach a decision. In one sense this is the most exacting kind of group to participate in. It requires not only a knowledge of small group communication techniques, but a thorough knowledge of the particular problem. And it usually demands faithful adherence to a somewhat rigid set of rules. We look at this group

first in terms of the classic and still popular problem-solving approach, whereby we identify the steps to go through in solving a problem. Next we look at several types of groups that are popular in organizations today: the nominal group, the Delphi method, quality circles, improvement groups, and task groups. Lastly, we consider the major decision-making methods.

The Problem-Solving Sequence

The approach developed by philosopher John Dewey, the **problem-solving sequence,** is probably the one used most often. Six steps are identified (see Figure 13.3) and are designed to make problem solving more efficient and effective.

Define and Analyze the Problem

In many instances the nature of the problem is clearly specified. For example, a group of designers might discuss how to package the new soap project. In other instances, however, the problem may be vague, and it remains for the group to define it in concrete terms. Thus, for example, the general problem may be poor campus communications. But such a vague and general topic is difficult to tackle in a problem-solving discussion, so it's helpful to specify the problem clearly.

Limit the problem so that it identifies a manageable area for discussion. A question such as, "How can we improve the university?" is too broad and general. Rather, it would be more effective to limit the problem and to identify one subdivision of the university on which the group might focus. You might, for example, choose from among such subdivisions as the college Web site, student newspaper, student–faculty relationships, registration, examination scheduling, or student advisory services.

Generally, it's best to define the problem as an open-ended question ("How can we improve the college Web site?") rather than as a statement ("The college Web site needs to be improved") or a yes/no question ("Does the Web site need improvement?"). The open-ended question allows for greater freedom of exploration. It doesn't restrict the ways in which the group may approach the problem.

In defining the problem, the group seeks to identify its dimensions. Appropriate questions (for most problems) revolve around the following issues: (1) Duration—How long has the problem ex-

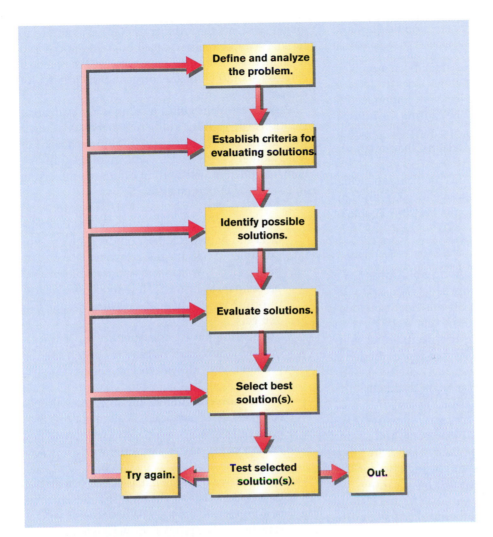

Figure 13.3 **Steps in problem-solving discussion.** While most small group theorists would advise you to follow the problem-solving pattern as presented here, others would alter it somewhat. For example, the pattern here advises you to first define the problem and then establish criteria for identifying possible solutions. You would then keep these criteria in mind as you generate possible solutions (step 3). Another school of thought, however, would advise you to generate solutions first and only consider how they will be evaluated after these solutions are proposed (Brilhart & Galanes 1986). The advantage of this second approach is that you're likely to generate more creative solutions since you won't be restricted by standards of evaluation. The disadvantage is that you might spend a great deal of time generating very impractical solutions that would never meet the standards you'll eventually propose.

isted? Is it likely to continue in the future? What is the predicted course of the problem? For example, will it grow or lessen in influence? (2) Causes— What are the major causes of the problem? How certain can we be that these are the actual causes?

(3) Effects—What are the effects of the problem? How significant are they? Who is affected by this problem? How significantly are they affected? Is this problem causing other problems? How important are these other problems? Applied to our

student newspaper example, the specific questions might look something like this:

- Duration: How long has there been a problem with securing advertising? Does it look as though it will grow or lessen in importance?
- Causes: What seems to be causing the newspaper problem? Are there specific policies (editorial, advertising, or design) that might be causing the problem?
- Effects: What effects is this problem producing? How significant are these effects? Who is affected? Students? Alumni? Faculty? People in the community?

Establish Criteria for Evaluating Solutions

Before any solutions are proposed, you need to decide how to evaluate them. At this stage you identify the standards or criteria that you'll use in evaluating the solutions or in selecting one solution over another. Generally, two types of criteria need to be considered. First, there are the practical criteria. For example, you might decide that the solutions must not increase the budget, must lead to a higher number of advertisers, must increase the readership by at least 10 percent, and so on. Second, there are the value criteria. These are more difficult to identify. These might include, for example, that the newspaper must be a learning experience for all those who work on it, that it must reflect the attitudes of the board of trustees, the faculty, or the students.

Identify Possible Solutions

At this stage identify as many solutions as possible. Focus on quantity rather than quality. Brainstorming may be particularly useful at this point (see discussion of idea-generation groups). Solutions to the student newspaper problem might include incorporating reviews of faculty publications; student evaluations of specific courses; reviews of restaurants in the campus area; outlines for new courses; and employment information.

Evaluate Solutions

After all the solutions have been proposed, you would go back and evaluate each according to the criteria established for evaluating solutions. For example, to what extent does incorporating reviews of

area restaurants meet the criteria for evaluating solutions? Would it increase the budget? Would it lead to an increase in advertising revenue? Each potential solution should be matched against the criteria for evaluating solutions.

An especially insightful technique for evaluating solutions (or gaining a different perspective on a problem) is offered by critical thinking pioneer Edward deBono (1987). The skill involves thinking with six different hats and, in doing so, subjecting an issue to a six-part analysis.

- The **fact hat** focuses attention on the data, the facts and figures that bear on the problem. For example, What are the relevant data on the newspaper? How can you get more information on the paper's history? How much does it cost to print? How much advertising revenue can you get?
- The **feeling hat** focuses attention on our feelings, emotions, and intuitions concerning the problem. How do you feel about the newspaper and about making major changes?
- The **negative argument hat** asks that you become the devil's advocate. Why might this proposal fail? What are the problems with publishing reviews of courses? What is the worst-case scenario?
- The **positive benefits hat** asks that you look at the upside. What are the opportunities that this new format will open up? What benefits will reviewing courses provide for the students? What would be the best thing that could happen?
- The **creative new idea hat** focuses attention on new ways of looking at the problem and can be easily combined with the techniques of brainstorming discussed earlier in this chapter. What other ways can you use to look at this problem? What other functions can a student newspaper serve that have not been thought of? Can the student paper provide a service to the nonacademic community as well?
- The **control of thinking hat** helps you analyze what you have done and are doing. It asks that you reflect on your own thinking processes and synthesize the results of your thinking. Have you adequately defined the problem? Are you focusing too much on insignificant issues? Have you given enough attention to the possible negative effects?

UNDERSTANDING
Theory and Research

HOW DO YOU EVALUATE RESEARCH?

Just as you need to evaluate the proposed solutions to a problem, you also need to evaluate research—its methods and its conclusions. After all, not all research is good research. Evaluate research by asking, for example, the following questions:

Are the results reliable? Reliability is a measure of the extent to which research findings are consistent and is always important to consider in evaluating research findings. In investigating reliability, you would ask if another researcher, using the same essential tools, would find the same results. Would the same people respond in the same way at other times? If the answer to such questions is yes, then the results are reliable. If the answer is no, then the results may be unreliable.

Are the results valid? Validity is a measure of the extent to which a measuring instrument measures what it claims to measure. Do the instruments measure what they claim to measure? For example, does your score on an intelligence test really measure what we think of as intelligence? Does your score on a test of communication apprehension measure what most people think of as constituting apprehension?

Do the results justify the conclusion? Results and conclusions are two different things. Results are objective findings such as "men scored higher than women on this test of romanticism." Conclusions are the researcher's (or reader's) interpretation of the results and might include, for example, "Men are more romantic than women."

The topic of evaluating research is returned to in Unit 15, where we discuss how to evaluate information generally and especially material from the Internet.

Select the Best Solution(s)

At this stage the best solution or solutions are selected and put into operation. Thus, for example, if "reviews of faculty publications" and "outlines for new courses" best met the criteria for evaluating solutions, the group might then incorporate these two new items in the next issue of the newspaper.

Test Selected Solution(s)

After the solution(s) are put into operation, test their effectiveness. The group might, for example, poll students about the new newspaper or examine the number of copies purchased. Or you might analyze the advertising revenue or see if readership did increase 10 percent.

If these solutions prove ineffective, you would go back to one of the previous stages and repeat part of the process. Often this takes the form of selecting other solutions to test. But, it may also involve going further back to, for example, a reanalysis of the problem, an identification of other solutions, or a restatement of criteria.

Problem Solving at Work

The problem-solving sequence discussed here is used widely in business in a variety of different types of groups. Here are three groups popular in business that rely largely on the problem-solving techniques just discussed: the nominal group technique, the Delphi method, and quality circles.

The Nominal Group Technique

The **nominal group technique** is a method of problem solving that uses limited discussion and confidential voting to obtain a group decision. It's especially helpful when some members may be reluctant to voice their opinions in a regular problem-solving group or when the issue is controversial or sensitive. With this technique, each member contributes equally and each contribution is treated equally. Another advantage of this technique is that it can be accomplished in a relatively short period of time. The nominal group technique can be divided into seven steps (Kelly 1994):

1. The problem is defined and clarified for all members.
2. Each member writes down (without discussion or consultation with others) his or her ideas on or possible solutions to the problem.
3. Each member—in sequence—states one idea from his or her list, which is recorded on a board or flip chart so everyone can see it. This process is repeated until all suggestions are stated and recorded. Duplicates are then eliminated. Group agreement is secured before ideas are combined.
4. Each suggestion is clarified (without debate). Ideally, each suggestion would be given equal time.
5. Each member rank orders the suggestions.
6. The rankings of the members are combined to get a group ranking, which is then written on the board.
7. Clarification, discussion, and possible reordering may follow.

The highest-ranking solution might then be selected to be tested, or perhaps several high ranking solutions may be put into operation.

The Delphi Method

In the **Delphi method**, a group of experts is established but there's no interaction among them; instead they communicate by repeatedly responding to questionnaires (Tersine & Riggs 1980; Kelly 1994). The method is especially useful when you want to involve people who are geographically distant from each other, when you want all members to act a part of the solution and to uphold it, or when you want to minimize the effects of dominant members or even of peer pressure. The method is best explained as a series of steps (Kelly 1994).

1. The problem is defined (for example, "We need to improve intradepartmental communication"). What each member is expected to do is specified (for example, each member should contribute five ideas on this specific question).

2. Each member then anonymously contributes five ideas in writing. This stage used to be completed through questionnaires sent through traditional mail but is now more frequently done through e-mail, which greatly increases the speed with which this entire process can be accomplished.
3. The ideas of all members are combined, written up, and distributed to all members who may be asked to, say, select the three or four best ideas from this composite list.
4. Members then select the three or four best ideas and submit these.
5. From these responses another list is produced and distributed to all members, who may be asked to select the one or two best ideas.
6. Members then select the one or two best ideas and submit these.
7. From these responses another list is produced and distributed to all members. The process may be repeated any number of times, but usually three rounds are sufficient for achieving a fair degree of agreement.
8. The "final" solutions are identified and are communicated to all members.

Quality Circles

Quality circles are groups of workers (usually from about 6 to 12) whose task it is to investigate and make recommendations for improving the quality of some organizational function. The members are drawn from the workers whose area is being studied. Thus, for example, if the problem were to improve advertising on the Internet, then the quality circle membership would be drawn from the advertising and computer departments. Generally, the motivation for establishing quality circles is economic; the company's aim is to improve quality and profitability. Another related goal is to improve worker morale; because quality circles involve workers in decision making, workers may feel empowered and more essential to the organization (Gorden & Nevins 1993).

The basic idea is that people who work on similar tasks will be better able to improve their departments or jobs by pooling their insights and working through problems they share. The quality circle style of problem solving is often considered one of the major reasons for the success of Japanese businesses, where it is widely used. In the United States, hundreds of organizations use quality circles but generally with less success than those in Japan (Gorden & Nevins 1993).

Quality circle members investigate problems using any method they feel might be helpful, for example, face-to-face problem-solving groups, nominal groups, or delphi methods. The group then reports its findings and its suggestions to those who can do something about it. In some cases the quality circle members may implement their solutions without approval from upper management levels.

A somewhat similar type of group is the **improvement group** or what is often called "kaizen," a Japanese word that means "continual improvement" (Beebe & Masterson 1994). These groups are based on the assumption that every process or product in any organization can be improved. Such groups may be set up for a certain amount of time or may be permanent.

Decision-Making Methods

Groups may use different decision-making methods in deciding, for example, which criterion to use or which solution to accept. Generally, groups use one of three methods.

Authority

In decision making by authority, members voice their feelings and opinions but the leader, boss, or CEO makes the final decision. This is surely an efficient method; it gets things done quickly and the amount of discussion can be limited as desired. Another advantage is that experienced and informed members (for example, those who have been with the company longest) will probably exert a greater influence on the decision maker.

The great disadvantage is that members may not feel the need to contribute their insights and may

BUILDING
Communication Skills

HOW DO YOU LISTEN TO NEW IDEAS?

A useful skill for listening to new ideas is PIP'N, a technique that derives from the insights of Carl Rogers (1970), specifically his emphasis on paraphrase as a means for ensuring understanding, and Edward deBono's (1976) PMI (plus, minus, interesting) technique. PIP'N involves four steps:

P = **Paraphrase**. State in your own words what you think the other person is saying. This will ensure that you and the person proposing the idea are talking about the same thing. Your paraphrase will also provide the other person with the opportunity to elaborate or clarify his or her ideas.

I = **Interesting**. State something interesting that you find in the idea. Say why you think this idea might be interesting to you, to others, to the organization.

P = **Positive**. Say something positive about the idea. What is good about it? How might it solve a problem or make a situation better?

N = **Negative**. State any negatives that you think the idea might entail. Might it prove expensive? Difficult to implement? Is it directed at insignificant issues?

You may want to try using PIP'N the next time you hear about a new idea, say, in conversation or in a small group. For practice, you may want to try PIP'N on the PIP'N technique itself: (1) paraphrase the PIP'N technique, (2) say why the technique is interesting, (3) say something positive about it, and (4) say something negative about it.

become distanced from the power within the group or organization. Another disadvantage is that it may lead members to give the decision maker what they feel she or he wants to receive, a condition that can easily lead to groupthink (Unit 14).

Majority Rule

With this method the group agrees to abide by the majority decision and may vote on various issues as the group progresses to solve its problem. Majority rule is efficient since there's usually an option to call for a vote when the majority are in agreement. This is a useful method for issues that are relatively unimportant (What company should service the water cooler?) and where member satisfaction and commitment is not needed.

One disadvantage is that it can lead to factioning, where various minorities align against the majority.

The method may also lead to limiting discussion once a majority has agreed and a vote is called.

Consensus

The group operating under consensus reaches a decision only when all group members agree, as in the criminal jury system. This method is especially important when the group wants the satisfaction and commitment of each member to the decision and to the decision-making process as a whole (DeStephen & Hirokawa 1988; Rothwell 1992).

Consensus obviously takes longest and can lead to a great deal of wasted time if members wish to prolong the discussion process needlessly or selfishly. This method may also put great pressure on the person who honestly disagrees but who doesn't want to prevent the group from making a decision.

SUMMARY

In this unit we introduced the nature of the small group and discussed four major types of groups and their functions.

1. A small group is a collection of individuals that is small enough for all members to communicate with relative ease as both senders and receivers. The members are related to each other by some common purpose and have some degree of organization or structure among them.
2. Most small groups develop norms or rules, which operate much like a culture's norms, identifying what is considered appropriate behavior for its members.
3. Power operates in all groups. Six types of power may be identified: referent, legitimate, reward, coercive, expert, and information or persuasion.
4. Small groups make use of four major formats: the roundtable, the panel, the symposium, and the symposium-forum.
5. The idea-generation or brainstorming group attempts to generate as many ideas as possible.
6. The personal growth group helps members to deal with personal problems and to function more effectively. Popular personal growth groups are the encounter group, the assertiveness-training group, and the consciousness-raising group.

7. The educational or learning group attempts to acquire new information or skill through a mutual sharing of knowledge or insight.
8. The focus group aims to discover what people think about an issue or product through a kind of in-depth group interview.
9. The problem-solving group attempts to solve a particular problem or at least to reach a decision that may be a preface to the problem solving itself
10. The six steps in the problem-solving approach are: define and analyze the problem; establish criteria for evaluating solutions; identify possible solutions; evaluate solutions; select best solution(s); and test solution(s).
11. The six hats technique is especially useful in analyzing problems and consists of focusing on different aspects of the problem: facts, feelings, negative arguments, positive benefits, creative or new ways of viewing problems, and your thinking processes.
12. Decision-making methods include authority, majority rule, and consensus.
13. Small groups that are widely used in business today include the nominal group, the Delphi method, and quality circles.

KEY TERMS

small group (p. 239)

small group norm (p. 240)

small group phases (p. 241)

IRC channel (p. 242)

mailing list group (p. 242)

referent power (p. 246)

legitimate power (p. 246)

reward power (p. 246)

coercive power (p. 246)

expert power (p. 246)

information power (p. 246)

brainstorming (p. 247)

small group formats (p. 247)

round table (p. 247)

panel (p. 247)

symposium (p. 247)

symposium-forum (p. 247)

idea-generation group (p. 247)

personal growth group (p. 249)

educational or learning group (p. 251)

focus group (p. 251)

problem-solving sequence (p. 252)

problem-solving group (p. 252)

nominal group technique (p. 255)

Delphi method (p. 256)

quality circles (p. 257)

THINKING CRITICALLY ABOUT
Small Group Communication

1. Studies find that persons high in communication apprehension are generally less effective in idea-generation groups than are those low in apprehension (Jablin 1981; Comadena 1984; Cragan & Wright 1990). Why do you think this is so?

2. What norms govern your class in human communication? What norms govern your family? Your place of work? Do you have any difficulty with these norms?

3. Is this problem-solving sequence also appropriate for resolving interpersonal conflicts? Can you trace an example through this sequence?

4. What type of criteria would an advertising agency use in evaluating a campaign to sell soap? A university in evaluating a new multicultural curriculum? Parents in evaluating a preschool for their children?

5. How might you go about finding answers to such questions as these:
   - Are group memberships more important to men or to women?
   - How effective is peer group instruction compared to instruction by lecture?
   - What personality or cultural factors are correlated with one's tendency to abide by the rules or norms of the group?
   - Is communication apprehension related to one's effectiveness in personal growth groups? In information-sharing groups? In problem-solving groups?

UNIT 14
Members and Leaders

UNIT CONTENTS

Members in Small Group Communication

Leaders in Small Group Communication

Membership, Leadership, and Culture

UNIT GOALS

After completing this unit, you should be able to

identify the three major types of member roles and give examples of each type

explain the theories of leadership, the three leadership styles, and the functions leaders serve in small group communication

explain the influence of culture on group membership and leadership

This unit looks at the roles or functions of small group members and leaders. By understanding the roles of both members and leaders, you'll be in a better position to analyze your own small group behavior (as member and leader) and to modify it as you wish.

MEMBERS IN SMALL GROUP COMMUNICATION

Membership in small group communication situations can be viewed from a variety of perspectives—the roles that members serve, the types of contributions they make, and the principles for more effective participation.

Member Roles

Member roles fall into three general classes: group task roles, group building and maintenance roles, and individual roles, a classification introduced in early research (Benne & Sheats 1948) and still widely used today (Lumsden & Lumsden 1996; Beebe & Masterson 1997). These roles are, of course, frequently served by leaders as well.

Think about your own behavior, your own membership style, as you read down these lists. Which of these do you regularly serve? Are there productive roles that you never or rarely serve? Are there destructive roles that you often serve?

Group Task Roles

Group task roles are those that help the group focus more specifically on achieving its goals. In serving any of these roles, you don't act as an isolated individual, but rather as a part of the larger whole. The needs and goals of the group dictate the roles you serve. As an effective group member you would serve several of these functions.

Some people, however, lock into a few specific roles. For example, one person may almost always seek the opinions of others, another may concentrate on elaborating details, still another on evaluating suggestions. Usually, this single focus is counterproductive. It's usually better for the roles to be spread more evenly among the members so that each may serve many group task roles. The 12 specific group task roles are these:

- The **initiator-contributor** presents new ideas or new perspectives on old ideas; suggests new goals, or new procedures or organizational strategies.

- The **information seeker** asks for facts and opinions; seeks clarification of the issues being discussed.
- The **opinion seeker** tries to discover the values underlying the group's task.
- The **information giver** presents facts and opinions to the group members.
- The **opinion giver** presents values and opinions and tries to spell out what the values of the group should be.
- The **elaborator** gives examples and tries to work out possible solutions, trying to build on what others have said.
- The **coordinator** spells out relationships among ideas and suggested solutions; coordinates the activities of the different members.
- The **orienter** summarizes what has been said and addresses the direction the group is taking.
- The **evaluator-critic** evaluates the group's decisions; questions the logic or practicality of the suggestions and thus provides the group with both positive and negative feedback.
- The **energizer** stimulates the group to greater activity.
- The **procedural technician** takes care of the various mechanical duties such as distributing group materials and arranging the seating.
- The **recorder** writes down the group's activities, suggestions, and decisions; serves as the memory of the group.

Group Building and Maintenance Roles

Most groups focus not only on the task to be performed but on interpersonal relationships among members. If the group is to function effectively, and if members are to be both satisfied and productive, these relationships must be nourished. When these needs are not met, group members may become irritable when the group process gets bogged down, engage in frequent conflicts, or find the small group process unsatisfying. The group and its members need the same kind of support that individuals need. The group building and maintenance roles serve this general function. Group building and maintenance are broken down into seven specific roles:

- The **encourager** supplies members with positive reinforcement in the form of social approval or praise for their ideas.

- The **harmonizer** mediates the various differences among group members.
- The **compromiser** tries to resolve conflict between his or her ideas and those of others; offers compromises.
- The **gatekeeper-expediter** keeps the channels of communication open by reinforcing the efforts of others.
- The **standard setter** proposes standards for the functioning of the group or for its solutions.
- The **group observer** and commentator keeps a record of the proceedings and uses this in the group's evaluation of itself.
- The **follower** goes along with the members of the group; passively accepts the ideas of others and functions more as an audience than as an active member.

Individual Roles

The group task and the group building and maintenance roles are productive roles; they aid the group in achieving its goals. The roles are group-oriented. Individual roles, on the other hand, are counterproductive. These roles, often termed dysfunctional, hinder the group's productivity and member satisfaction largely because they focus on serving individual rather than group needs. Eight specific types are identified:

- The **aggressor** expresses negative evaluation of the actions or feelings of the group members; attacks the group or the problem being considered.
- The **blocker** provides negative feedback, is disagreeable, and opposes other members or suggestions regardless of their merit.
- The **recognition seeker** tries to focus attention on himself or herself rather an the task at hand, boasts about own accomplishments.
- The **self-confessor** expresses his or her own feelings and personal perspectives rather than focusing on the group.
- The **playboy/playgirl** jokes around without any regard for the group process.
- The **dominator** tries to run the group or the group members by pulling rank, flattering members of the group, or acting the role of the boss.
- The **help seeker** expresses insecurity or confusion or deprecates himself or herself and thus tries to gain sympathy from the other members.

- The **special-interest pleader** disregards the goals of the group and pleads the case of some special group.

Interaction Process Analysis

Another way of looking at the contributions group members make is through **interaction process analysis** (IPA), developed by Robert Bales (1950). In this system you analyze the contributions of members in four general categories: (1) social-emotional positive contributions, (2) social-emotional negative contributions, (3) attempted answers, and (4) questions. Each of these four areas contains three subdivisions, yielding a total of 12 categories into which you can classify group members' contributions (Table 14.1). Note that the categories under social-emotional positive are the natural opposites of those under social-emotional negative, and those under attempted answers are the natural opposites of those under questions.

Try out Bales' system by listening to a small group discussion and recording the interactions using Table 14.1. In the spaces at the top write in the participants' names. In the column under each participant's name, place a slash mark for each contribution in one of the 12 categories. You can also try this out when watching a video tape of a film or a television sitcom such as "Seinfeld," "Frasier," or "Friends" and classify the contributions of the characters. After completing such an analysis—even for, say, 10 or 20 minutes of a discussion—you should find that IPA enables you to identify the different types of contributions individual members make during a discussion, and it also enables you to identify problems with the participant's contributions. You should also be in a better position to offer improvement suggestions for individual members based on this interaction process analysis.

Both the three-part member role classification and the categories of interaction process analysis are useful in viewing the contributions that members make in small group situations. When you look at member contributions through these systems, you can see, for example, if one member is locked into a particular role or if the group process breaks down because too many people are serving individual rather than group goals or because social-emotional negative comments dominate the discussion. These systems are designed to help you see more clearly what is going on in a group and what specific contributions may mean to the entire group process.

TABLE 14.1   Interaction process analysis form

Social-Emotional Positive	Shows solidarity								
	Shows tension release								
	Shows agreement								
Social-Emotional Negative	Shows disagreement								
	Shows tension								
	Shows antagonism								
Attempted Answers	Gives suggestions								
	Gives opinions								
	Gives information								
Questions	Asks for suggestions								
	Asks for opinions								
	Asks for information								

Member Participation

Another perspective on group membership may be gained from looking at the recommendations for effective participation in small group communication. Look at these suggestions as an elaboration and extension of the characteristics of effective conversation (Unit 9).

Be Group- or Team-Oriented

In the small group you're a member of a team, a larger whole. Your participation is of value to the extent that it advances the goals of the group and promotes member satisfaction. Your task is to pool your talents, knowledge, and insight so that the group may arrive at a better solution than any one person could have developed. Solo performances hinder the group.

This call for group orientation is not to be taken as a suggestion that members abandon their individuality or give up their personal values or beliefs for the sake of the group. Individuality with a group orientation is what is advocated here.

Center Conflict on Issues

Conflict in small group situations is inevitable and its management should follow the general rules for dealing with conflict already covered in Unit 11. As in interpersonal communication, conflict is a natural part of the small group process.

It's particularly important in the small group to center conflict on issues rather than on personalities. When you disagree, make it clear that your disagreement is with the solution suggested or the ideas expressed, and not with the person who expressed them. Similarly, when someone disagrees with what you say, don't take this as a personal attack. Rather, view this as an opportunity to discuss issues from an alternative point of view.

Be Critically Open-Minded

One common but unproductive development occurs when members come to the group with their minds already made up. When this happens, the small group process degenerates into a series of individual debates in which each person argues for his or her own position. Instead, members should come to the group equipped with relevant information that will be useful to the discussion. They should not have decided on the solution or conclusion they will accept. Any solutions or conclusions should be advanced tentatively rather than with certainty. Members should be willing to alter their suggestions and revise them in light of the discussion.

Listen openly but critically to the comments of all other members. Don't accept or reject any member's suggestions without critically evaluating them. Be judiciously open-minded. Be judiciously critical of your own contributions as well as of the contributions of others.

Ensure Understanding

Make sure that your ideas and information are understood by all participants. If something is worth saying, it's worth saying clearly. When in doubt, ask: "Is that clear?" "Did I explain that clearly?"

Make sure, too, that you understand fully the contributions of the other members, especially before you take issue with them. In fact, it's often wise to preface any extended disagreement with some kind of paraphrase. For example, you might say "As I understand it, you want to exclude freshmen from playing on the football team. Is that correct? I disagree with that idea and I'd like to explain why I think that would be a mistake." Then you would go on to state your objections. In this way you give the other person the opportunity to clarify, deny, or otherwise alter what was said.

Beware of Groupthink

Groupthink is a way of thinking that people use when agreement among members becomes extremely important in a cohesive ingroup. So important is agreement among members that it tends to shut out realistic and logical analysis of a problem or of possible alternatives (Janis 1983). The term itself is meant to signal a "deterioration in mental efficiency, reality testing, and moral judgments as a result of group pressures" (Janis 1983). Both members and leaders need to be able to listen to the symptoms of groupthink and combat its negative effects.

Many specific behaviors of group members can lead to groupthink. One of the most significant occurs when the group limits its discussion to only a small number of alternative solutions, overlooking other possibilities. Another occurs when the group does not reexamine its decisions even when there are indications of possible dangers. Another is when the group spends little time discussing why certain initial alternatives were rejected. For example, if the group rejected a certain alternative because it was too costly, members will devote little time, if any, to the ways in which the cost may be reduced.

In groupthink, the group members are extremely selective in the information they consider seriously. Facts and opinions contrary to the position of the group are generally ignored. Facts and opinions that support the position of the group, however, are easily and uncritically accepted.

The following list of symptoms should help you listen critically for the possible existence of groupthink in the groups you observe or participate in (Janis 1983):

- Group members think the group and its members are invulnerable to dangers.
- Members create rationalizations to avoid dealing directly with warnings or threats.
- Group members believe their group is moral.
- Those opposed to the group are perceived in simplistic, stereotyped ways.
- Group pressure is put on any member who expresses doubts or who questions the group's arguments or proposals.
- Group members censor their own doubts.
- Group members believe all members are in unanimous agreement, whether such agreement is stated or not.
- Group members emerge whose function it is to guard the information that gets to other members of the group, especially when such information may create diversity of opinion.

Have you ever been in a group when groupthink was operating? If so, what were its symptoms? What effect did groupthink have on the process and conclusions of the group?

LEADERS IN SMALL GROUP COMMUNICATION

A leader is one who influences the thoughts and behaviors of others; a leader is one who establishes the direction that others follow. In many small groups,

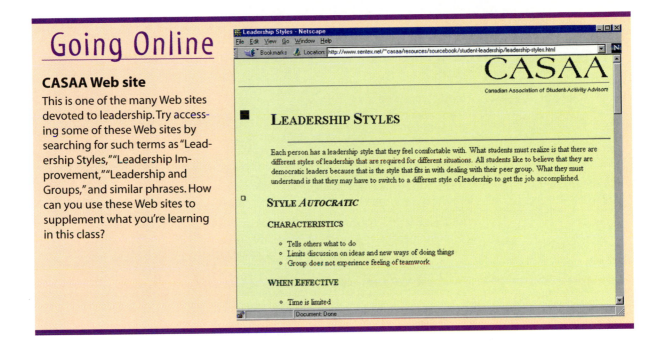

Going Online

CASAA Web site

This is one of the many Web sites devoted to leadership. Try accessing some of these Web sites by searching for such terms as "Leadership Styles," "Leadership Improvement," "Leadership and Groups," and similar phrases. How can you use these Web sites to supplement what you're learning in this class?

one person serves as leader. In others, leadership may be shared by several persons. In some groups, a person may be appointed the leader or may serve as leader because of her or his position within the company or hierarchy.

In still other groups, the leader may emerge as the group proceeds in fulfilling its functions or may be voted as leader by the group members. The single most important factor in determining who emerges as the group leader is the extent of active participation; the one who talks the most emerges leader (Muller, Salas, & Driskell 1989; Shaw & Gouran 1990). The "emergent leader" performs the duties of leadership, though not asked or expected to and gradually becomes recognized by the members as the group's leader. Since this person has now proven herself or himself an effective leader, it's not surprising that this emergent leader often becomes the designated leader for future groups. Generally, the emergent leader serves as leader as long as the group members are satisfied. When they're not, they may encourage another member to emerge as leader. But, as long as the emergent leader serves effectively, the group will probably not look to others.

In any case the role of the leader or leaders is vital to the well-being and effectiveness of the group. Even in leaderless groups, where all members are equal, leadership functions must still be served.

Approaches to Leadership

Not surprisingly, leadership has been the focus of considerable attention from theorists and researchers who have used a number of approaches to understand this particular communication behavior. Four of these are summarized in Table 14.2. Although contemporary theorists favor the situational approach, the traits, functional, and transformational approaches continue to have considerable merit.

The Traits Approach

The **traits approach** merits consideration because it emphasizes that leaders must possess certain qualities if they're to function effectively. Some of the traits found to be associated with leadership are intelligence, dominance, honesty, foresight, altruism, popularity, sociability, cooperativeness, knowledge, and dependability (Hackman & Johnson 1991). The problem with the traits approach is that these qualities will vary with the situation, with the members, and with the culture in which the leader functions. Thus, for example, the leader's knowledge and personality are generally significant factors. But, for some groups a knowledge of financial issues and a serious personality might be effective, whereas for other groups a knowledge of design and a more humorous personality might be effective.

TABLE 14.2   What is a leader?

Which of the four approaches identified here do you think best clarifies what you mean by "leader"?

Approach	Definition	Actions Identified
Traits approach	A leader is one who possesses those characteristics (or traits) that contribute to leadership	Is a high achiever, popular; has higher status, intelligence
Functional approach	A leader is one who behaves (or functions) as a leader	Serves task roles, ensures member satisfaction, energizes group members
Transformational approach	A leader is one who enables and empowers group members	Demonstrates charisma, competence, and morality, serves as role model
Situational approach	A leader is one who balances task accomplishment and member satisfaction on the basis of the unique situation	Delegates, participates, sells, and tells depending on the members and the situation

The Functional Approach

The **functional approach** is significant because it helps identify what the leader should do in a given situation. Some of these functions have already been examined in the discussion of group membership in which group roles were identified. Other functions found to be associated with leadership are setting group goals, giving the group members direction, and summarizing the group's progress (Schultz 1986). Additional functions are identified in the section entitled, "Functions of Leadership," later in this unit.

The Transformational Approach

In the **transformational approach** the leader elevates the group's members, enabling them not only to accomplish the group task but to also emerge as more empowered individuals. At the center of the transformational approach is the concept of *charisma*, that quality of an individual that makes us believe or want to follow him or her. Gandhi, Martin Luther King, and John F. Kennedy may be cited as examples of transformational leaders. These leaders were role models of what they asked of their members, were seen as extremely competent and able leaders, and articulated moral goals (Northouse 1997). We return to this concept of charisma and to these qualities in our discussion of credibility in Unit 19.

The Situational Approach

The **situational approach** deserves attention because it focuses on the two major tasks of the leader—accomplishing the task at hand and ensuring the satisfaction of the members—and because it recognizes that the leader's style must vary on the basis of the specific situation. Just as you adjust your interpersonal style in conversation or your motivational appeals in public speaking on the basis of the uniqueness of the situation, so you must adjust your leadership style.

Leaders must be concerned with getting the task accomplished (the task dimension) and with ensuring that members are satisfied (the people dimension). Leadership effectiveness, then, depends on combining the concerns for task and people according to the specifics of the situation—hence, the "situational theory of leadership." Some situations, for example, will call for high concentration on task issues but will need little in the way of people encouragement. For example, a group of scientists working on AIDS research would probably need a leader who provides them with the needed information to accomplish their task. They would be self-motivating and would probably need little in the way of social and emotional encouragement. On the other hand, a group of recovering alcoholics might require leadership that stresses the social and emotional needs of the members.

The situational theory of leadership visualizes these two dimensions as in the figure in the leadership self-test (Hersey & Blanchard 1988), which you may wish to take at this point. It will help you visualize more specifically the task and people dimensions included in this theory.

 **SELF-TEST**

What Kind of Leader Are You?

The following items describe aspects of group member behavior. Respond to each item according to the way you would be most likely to act if you were in a problem-solving group. Circle whether you would be likely to behave in the described way: always (A), frequently (F), occasionally (O), seldom (S), or never (N).

IF I WERE A MEMBER OF A PROBLEM-SOLVING GROUP:

A F O S N   1.   I would be very likely to act as the spokesperson of the group.
A F O S N   2.   I would encourage overtime work.
A F O S N   3.   I would allow members complete freedom in their work.
A F O S N   4.   I would encourage the use of uniform procedures.
A F O S N   5.   I would permit the others to use their own judgment in solving problems.
A F O S N   6.   I would stress being ahead of competitive groups.
A F O S N   7.   I would speak as a representative of the group.
A F O S N   8.   I would encourage members toward greater effort.
A F O S N   9.   I would try out my ideas in the group.
A F O S N   10.   I would let the others do their work the way they think best.
A F O S N   11.   I would be working hard for personal recognition.
A F O S N   12.   I would be able to tolerate postponement and uncertainty.
A F O S N   13.   I would speak for the group when visitors were present.
A F O S N   14.   I would keep the work moving at a rapid pace.
A F O S N   15.   I would help to identify a task and let the others do it.
A F O S N   16.   I would settle conflicts when they occur in the group.
A F O S N   17.   I would be likely to get swamped by details.
A F O S N   18.   I would represent the group at outside meetings.
A F O S N   19.   I would be reluctant to allow the others freedom of action.
A F O S N   20.   I would decide what should be done and how it should be done.
A F O S N   21.   I would push for better results.
A F O S N   22.   I would let other members have some authority.
A F O S N   23.   Things would usually turn out as I predicted.
A F O S N   24.   I would allow the others a high degree of initiative.
A F O S N   25.   I would try to assign group members to particular tasks.
A F O S N   26.   I would be willing to make changes.
A F O S N   27.   I would ask the others to work harder.
A F O S N   28.   I would trust the group members to exercise good judgment.
A F O S N   29.   I would try to schedule work to be done.
A F O S N   30.   I would refuse to explain my actions when questioned.
A F O S N   31.   I would persuade others that my ideas are to their advantage.
A F O S N   32.   I would permit the group to set its own pace.
A F O S N   33.   I would urge the group to beat its previous record.
A F O S N   34.   I would act without consulting the group.
A F O S N   35.   I would ask that group members follow standard rules and regulations.

To compute your score, follow these detailed but simple directions.

1. Circle the item letter for 1, 4, 7, 13, 16, 17, 18, 19, 20, 23, 29, 30, 31, 34, and 35.
2. Put an X in front of only those circled item numbers for items to which you responded S (seldom) or N (never).
3. Put an X in front of those items whose numbers were not circled only when you responded to such items with A (always) or F (frequently).
4. Circle any X that you have put in front of any of the following item numbers: 3, 5, 8, 10, 12, 15, 17, 19, 22, 24, 26, 28, 30, 32, and 34.
5. Count the circled Xs. This is your Person Orientation (P) Score.
6. Count the uncircled Xs. This is your Task Orientation (T) Score.

Your T and P scores are then plotted on the grid and are interpreted in terms of the descriptive elements given in the appropriate cell. To locate yourself on the grid below, find your score on the Person dimension (P) on the horizontal axis of the graph. Next, start up the column above your P score to the cell that corresponds to your Task score (T). Place an X in the cell that represents your two scores.

The horizontal axis is the people dimension. The farther you go to the right on this axis, the greater your concern for the members' social and emotional satisfaction (high P). The vertical axis is the task dimension. The more you move toward the top, the greater your concern for accomplishing the task (high T).

Leaders in the upper left area of the chart have little concern for people but great concern for accomplishing the task (high T, low P). Those in the lower left have little concern for either people or task (low T, low P). Those in the upper right have great concern for both task and people (high T, high P). Those in the lower right have little concern for task but high concern for people (low T, high P). Those in the middle have average concern for both task and people.

Does your score coincide with your image of your leadership focus? Can you identify specific people who would fit into each of the five major cells of this grid?

From "What Kind of Leader Are You?" from *Decision-Making: Group Interaction* by B. R. Patton, K. Giffin, & E. N. Patton, 3rd ed. 1989, pp. 179–181; adapted from J. W. Pfeiffer and J. E. Jones, *Structured Experiences for Human Relations Training*, 1969, pp. 9–10. Reprinted by permission.

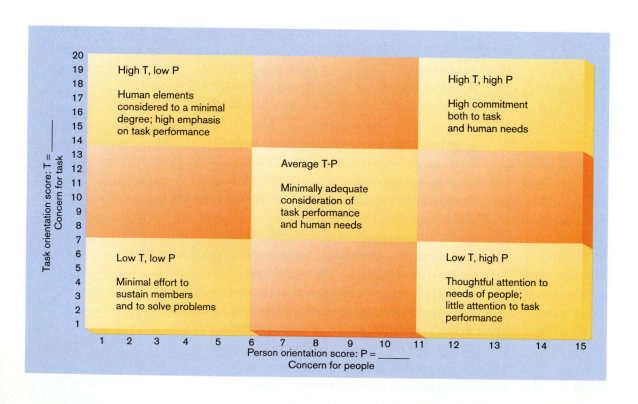

Styles of Leadership

In addition to looking at the concerns of leadership for both task and function, as we did with the situational theory of leadership, we can also look at leadership in terms of its three major styles: laissez-faire, democratic, and authoritarian (Bennis & Nanus 1985; Hackman & Johnson 1991).

Think about your own leadership style and the leadership styles of those you've worked with as you read these descriptions. Which of these styles are you likely to feel most comfortable using? Most comfortable working with as a group member?

Laissez-Faire Leader

As a **laissez-faire leader** you would take no initiative in directing or suggesting alternative courses of action. Rather, you would allow the group to develop and progress on its own, even allowing it to make its own mistakes. You would in effect give up or deny any real authority. As a laissez-faire leader you would answer questions or provide relevant information, but only when specifically asked. You would give little if any reinforcement to the group members. At the same time you would not punish members either. As a result you would be seen as nonthreatening. Generally this type of leadership results in a satisfied but inefficient group.

Democratic Leader

As a **democratic leader** you would provide direction but allow the group to develop and progress the way its members wish. You would encourage group members to determine their own goals and procedures. You would stimulate self-direction and self-actualization of the group members. Unlike the laissez-faire leader, a democratic leader would give members reinforcement and contribute suggestions for direction and alternative courses of action. Always, however, you would allow the group to make its own decisions. Generally, this form of leadership results in both satisfaction and efficiency.

Authoritarian Leader

As an **authoritarian leader** you would be the opposite of the laissez-faire leader. You would determine the group policies or make decisions without consulting or securing agreement from the members. You would be impersonal and would encourage communication that goes to you and from you but not from member to member; you would seek to minimize intragroup communication. In this way, you would enhance your own importance and control.

As an authoritarian leader you assume the greatest responsibility for the progress of the group and would not want interference from members. You would be concerned with getting the group to accept your decisions rather than making its own decisions. You might satisfy the group's psychological needs. You would reward and punish the group much as a parent does. If the authoritarian leader is a competent one, the group members may be highly efficient but are likely to be less personally satisfied.

The moderator of an Internet group, say a mailing list or an IRC channel, is a kind of group leader. For example, a person usually sets up a mailing list, serves as leader for a time, and then lets it operate as an automated system. IRC groups also have "channel operators" who are like leaders; these too are usually the ones who established the group. The moderator (who may be a person or a computer program) may also serve as a filter or gatekeeper who allows certain messages to go through and others to not go through. Much like a supervisor in an organization, the Internet group moderator may on occasion decide to exclude a particular member from further group participation, usually for violating the rules of the particular Internet group. Most Internet group moderators are laissez-faire leaders; they usually don't intrude in the group's ongoing interaction.

Each of these leadership styles has its place; one style should not be considered superior to the others. Each is appropriate for a different purpose and for a different situation. In a social group at a friend's house, any leadership other than laissez-faire would be difficult to tolerate. But, when speed and efficiency are paramount, authoritarian leadership may be more appropriate. Authoritarian leadership may also be more appropriate when group members continue to show lack of motivation toward the task despite democratic efforts to move them. When all members are about equal in their knowledge of the topic or when the members are very concerned with their individual rights, the democratic leadership style seems more appropriate.

With which leadership style are you most comfortable—as a leader? As a member?

Functions of Leadership

With the situational view of leadership and the three general styles of leadership in mind, we can look at some of the major functions leaders serve. In relatively formal small group situations, as when politicians plan a strategy, advertisers discuss a campaign, or teachers consider educational methods, the leader has several specific functions. Keep in mind that these functions are not the exclusive property of the leader. Nevertheless, when there's a specific leader, he or she is expected to perform them.

Prediscussion Functions

It often falls to the leader to provide members with necessary materials prior to the meeting. It may involve, for example, arranging a convenient meeting time and place, informing members of the purposes and goals of the meeting, providing them with materials they should read or view, and recommending that they come to the meeting with, for example, general ideas or specific proposals.

Similarly, groups form gradually and need to be eased into meaningful discussion. Diverse members should not be expected to sit down and discuss a problem without becoming familiar with each other. Put more generally, the leader is responsible for any preparations and preliminaries necessary to insure an orderly and productive group experience.

Activate the Group Agenda

Most groups have an agenda. An agenda is simply a list of the tasks the group wishes to complete. It's an itemized listing of what the group should devote its attention to. At times, the agenda is prepared by the supervisor or consultant or CEO and is simply presented to the group. The group is then expected to follow the agenda item by item. At other times, the group will develop its own agenda, usually as its first or second order of business.

Generally, the more formal the group, the more important this agenda becomes. In informal groups, the agenda may simply be general ideas in the minds of the members (for example, we'll review the class assignment and then make plans for the weekend). In formal business groups the agenda will be much more detailed and explicit. Some agendas specify not only the items that must be covered, but the order in which they should be covered, and even the amount of time that should be devoted to each item.

The agenda must be agreed upon by the group members. At times, the leader might initiate a brief discussion on the agenda and secure a commitment from all members to follow it.

Activate Group Interaction

Many groups need some prodding and stimulation to interact. Perhaps the group is newly formed and the members feel a bit uneasy with one another. As the group leader you would stimulate the members to interact. You would also serve this function when members act as individuals rather than as a group. In this case you would want to focus the members on their group task.

UNDERSTANDING
Theory and Research

WHAT CAN YOU LEARN FROM ATTILA THE HUN?

From a totally different perspective, consider these leadership qualities, paraphrased from Wes Roberts's *The Leadership Secrets of Attila the Hun* (1987).

- **Empathy.** Leaders must develop an appreciation for and an understanding of other cultures and the values of their members.
- **Courage.** Leaders should be fearless and have the courage to complete their assignments; they must not complain about obstacles nor be discouraged by adversity.
- **Accountability.** Leaders must hold themselves responsible for their own actions and for those of their members.
- **Dependability.** Leaders must be dependable in carrying out their responsibilities; leaders must

also depend upon their members to accomplish matters they themselves can't oversee.
- **Credibility.** Leaders must be believable to both friends and enemies; they must possess the integrity and intelligence needed to secure and communicate accurate information.
- **Stewardship.** Leaders must be caretakers of their members' interests and well-being; they must guide and reward subordinates.

In addition to these six, Attila also identified loyalty, desire, emotional stamina, physical stamina, decisiveness, anticipation, timing, competitiveness, self-confidence, responsibility, and tenacity. You might find it profitable to review these 11 additional qualities and explain how you think they can contribute to effective group leadership. How would you go about finding evidence bearing on this approach to leadership?

Maintain Effective Interaction

Even after the group is stimulated to group interaction, you would strive to see that members maintain effective interaction. When the discussion begins to drag, you would prod the group to effective interaction: "Do we have any additional comments on the proposal to eliminate required courses?" "What do those of you who are members of the college curriculum committee think about the English Department's proposal to restructure required courses?" "Does anyone want to make any additional comments on eliminating the minor area of concentration?" As the leader you would want to ensure that all members have an opportunity to express themselves.

Empower Group Members

An important function to at least some leadership style (though not limited to leadership) is to empower others, to help other group members (but also, your relational partner, coworkers, employees, other students, or siblings) to gain increased power

over themselves and their environment. Some ways you might use to empower others are to:

- Raise the person's self-esteem. Compliment, reinforce. Resist fault-finding; it doesn't benefit anyone and in fact disempowers.
- Share skills and decision-making power and authority.
- Be constructively critical. Be willing to offer your perspective, to lend an ear to a first try singing effort, or to listen to a new poem. Be willing to react honestly to suggestions from all group members and not just those in high positions.
- Encourage growth in all forms, academic, relational, and professional. The growth and empowerment of the other person enhances your own growth and power.

Manage Conflict

As in interpersonal relationships, conflict is a part of small group interaction. And it's a function of

UNDERSTANDING
Theory and Research

HOW DO YOU SIGNAL LEADERSHIP?

Think about the types of cues you use to get members to do certain things. Do you think you would get greater power from emphasizing your ability to do a task (task cues) or from threats (dominance cues)? Consider the results from one interesting study (Driskell, Olmstead, & Salas 1993). In this study, task cues included, for example, maintaining eye contact, sitting at the head of the table, using a relatively rapid speech rate, speaking fluently, and gesturing appropri-

ately. Dominance cues, on the other hand, included speaking in a loud and angry voice, pointing fingers, maintaining rigid posture, using forceful gestures, and lowering the eyebrows. Which leader would you be more apt to follow? Results showed that most people will be more influenced by speakers using task cues. They will also see such speakers as more competent and more likable. Persons using dominance cues, on the other hand, are perceived as less competent, less influential, less likable, and more self-oriented. The implication, from at least this one study, is that if you wish to gain influence in a group (and be liked), use task cues and avoid dominance cues.

---

leadership to deal effectively with it. Small group communication researchers distinguish between procedural and people conflicts and offer a wide variety of conflict management strategies (Patton, Giffin, & Patton 1989; Folger, Poole, & Stutman 1997; Kindler 1996).

Procedural and People Conflicts. *Procedural conflicts* involve disagreements over who is in charge (who is the leader or who should be the leader), what the agenda or task of the group should be, and how the group should conduct its business. The best way to deal with procedural problems is to prevent them from occurring in the first place by establishing early in the group's interaction who is to serve as leader and what the agenda should be. If procedural problems arise after these agreements are reached, members or the leader can refer the conflicting participants to the group's earlier decisions. When members disagree or become dissatisfied with these early decisions, they may become negative or antagonistic and cease to participate in the discussion. When this happens (or if members want to change procedures), a brief discussion on the procedures

can be held. The important point to realize is that the procedural conflicts should be dealt with as procedural conflicts and should not be allowed to escalate into something else.

People conflicts can occur when one member dominates the group, when several members battle for control, or when some members refuse to participate. The leaders should try to secure the commitment of all members and to convince them that the progress of the group depends on everyone's contributions. At times, it may be necessary to redirect the focus of the group to concentrate on people needs, on satisfying members' needs for group approval, for periodic rewards, or for encouragement.

People conflicts are also created when people rather than ideas are attacked. The leader needs to ensure that attacks and disagreements are clearly focused on ideas, not people. And if a personal attack does get started, the leaders should step in to refocus the difference in opinion to the idea and away from the person.

Conflict Management Strategies for Small Groups. The conflict management strategies presented in Unit 11

MEDIA WATCH

AGENDA-SETTING THEORY

In much the same way that a small group has an agenda, so do the media. In fact, the media establish the agenda for viewers by focusing attention on certain people and events (McCombs & Shaw 1972, 1993). The media tell you—by virtue of what they cover—who is important and what events are significant. They tell you, in effect, that these are the people and the events to which you should give your attention.

Agenda-setting theory, as Agee, Ault, and Emery (1997) put it, refers to the "ability of the media to select and call to the public's attention both ideas and events." The media tell us what is and what is not important. The media "do not tell people 'what to think' but 'what to think about'" (Edelstein 1993). The things you think are important and the things you discuss are very probably the very things on which the media concentrate. In fact, it may be argued that nothing important can happen without media coverage. If the media don't cover it, then it isn't important.

Although there's clearly no one-to-one relationship between media attention and popular perception of importance (interpersonal factors are also operating), the media do probably set your agendas to some significant degree by leading you to focus attention on certain subjects and away from others.

Recognize too that most media are controlled by persons of enormous wealth and power (network owners and executives, advertisers, or directors of multimillion-dollar corporations). These people want to retain and increase such wealth and power. What gets attention from the media and influences what the media present is dictated largely by this small but extremely influential group. The media exist to make profit for this group. Of course, there are public service media that don't focus on financial gain. But they too have agendas. All communicators have agendas, and the messages from any person or organization establish agendas for the receiver.

To what extent does the media establish your agenda?

The next Media Watch appears on page 355.

---

are also applicable to the small group situation. In addition, here are four principles that have special relevance to the small group situation (Kindler 1996):

- Preserve the dignity and respect of all members. Assume, for example, that each person's disagreement is legitimate and stems from a genuine concern for the good of the group. Therefore, treat disagreements kindly; even if someone attacks you personally, it's generally wise not to respond in kind but to redirect the criticism to the issues at hand.
- Listen empathically. See the perspectives of the other members, try to feel what they're feeling without making any critical judgments. Try to ask yourself why these other people see the situation differently from the way you see it.

- Seek out and emphasize common ground. Even in the midst of disagreement, there are areas of common interest, common beliefs, and common aims. Find these and build on them.
- Value diversity and differences. Creative solutions often emerge from conflicting perspectives. So, don't gloss over differences; instead, explore them for the valuable information they can give you.

Keep Members on Track

Many individuals are egocentric and will pursue only their own interests and concerns. As the leader it's your task to keep all members reasonably on track. You might accomplish this by asking questions, by interjecting internal summaries, or by providing transitions so that the relationship of an issue just discussed to one about to be considered is clear. If there's a formal agenda, it may assist you in serving this function.

Ensure Member Satisfaction

Members have different psychological needs and wants, and many people enter groups to satisfy these personal concerns. Even though a group may, for example, deal with political issues, the members may have come together for reasons that are more psychological than political. If a group is to be effective, it must meet not only the surface purposes of the group, but also the underlying or interpersonal purposes that motivated many of the members to come together in the first place.

Depending on the specific members, special adjustments may have to be made to accommodate those with handicaps. One such group that is often ignored in discussions of leadership functions is those with hearing problems. Table 14.3 offers some suggestions.

Encourage Ongoing Evaluation and Improvement

Most groups encounter obstacles as they try to solve a problem, reach a decision, or generate ideas. Therefore, most could use some improvement. If the group is to improve, it must focus on itself. Along with trying to solve some external problem, it must try to solve its own internal problems as well, for example, personal conflicts, failure of members to meet on time, or members who come unprepared. As the leader, try to identify any such difficulties and encourage and help the group to analyze and resolve them.

Postdiscussion Functions

Just as the leader is responsible for prediscussion functions, so is the leader also responsible for postdiscussion functions. Such functions might include summarizing the group's discussion, organizing future meetings, or presenting the group's decisions to some other group. Again, the leader is responsible

TABLE 14.3   Facilitating small group communications with deaf people

- Set the deaf person to his or her best advantage. This usually means a seat near the speaker, so that the deaf person can see the speaker's lips.
- Provide new vocabulary in advance. If new vocabulary cannot be presented in advance, write the terms on paper, a chalkboard, or an overhead projector, if possible.
- Avoid unnecessary pace and speaking when writing on a chalkboard. It is difficult to speechread a person in motion, and impossible to speechread one whose back is turned.
- Use visual aids if possible.
- Make sure the deaf person doesn't miss vital information. Write out any changes in meeting times, special assignments, additional instructions, etc.
- Slow down the pace of communication slightly to facilitate understanding.
- Repeat questions and statements made from the back of the room and point to the person who's speaking.
- Allow full participation by the deaf person in the discussion. It is difficult for deaf persons to participate in group discussions because they are not sure when speakers have finished. The group leader or teacher should recognize the deaf person from time to time to allow full participation by that person.
- Use hands-on experience whenever possible in training situations.
- Use an interpreter in a large group setting.
- Use a notetaker when possible to record information. It is difficult for many deaf persons to pay attention to a speaker and take notes simultaneously.

*From *Tips for Communicating with Deaf People.* Reprinted by permission of the Rochester Institute of Technology, National Technical Institute for the Deaf, 52 Lomb Memorial Drive, Rochester, NY 14623-0887.

BUILDING
Communication Skills

HOW DO YOU DEAL WITH SMALL GROUP COMPLAINTS?

Assume that you're the leader of a work team consisting of members from each of the major departments in your company. For each of the following complaints explain: (1) what you would say and (2) what objective your response would be designed to achieve.

1. Reducing costs is an impossible task; we're wasting our time here. Costs have gone up; there's no way we can reduce costs. Period. The end.

2. Look, we've been at this for two hours and I still haven't heard anything about accounting, which is my department. I really don't know why I'm here. How can the accounting department help reduce costs?

3. You're calling these meetings much too often and much too early to suit us. We'd like fewer meetings scheduled for later in the day.

4. That's not fair. Why do I always have to take the minutes of these meetings? Can't we have real secretary here?

5. There's a good reason why I don't contribute to the discussion. I don't contribute because no one listens to what I say.

for whatever needs to be done to insure that the group's experience proves to be a productive one.

Qualities of Leadership

In addition to the leader's functions, a mixture of task and people functions, an effective leader needs two major qualities: knowledge and communication competence.

Knowledge

The leader needs knowledge in both the substance of the discussion and in the ways of effectively leading a group. The leader needs to understand the problem facing the group and be able to identify alternatives for viewing and solving the problem and to assess both the positive and the negative consequences of each alternative (Hirokawa 1985, 1988).

Communication Competence

The effective leader needs also to be an effective communicator as both listener and speaker. The qualities noted in the discussion of effective conversation (Unit 9) are obvious qualities that an effective leader needs: mindfulness, flexibility, and cultural sensitivity plus the more specific skills of openness, empathy, positiveness, immediacy, interaction management, expressiveness, and other-orientation.

Some researchers have proposed that small groups have a natural tendency to take detours and divert their attention from the task at hand. As a result, they view the effective leader as one whose communications prevent the group from these natural but unproductive diversions (Gouran & Hirokawa 1986).

MEMBERSHIP, LEADERSHIP, AND CULTURE

Most of the research and theory of small group communication, membership, and leadership has been conducted in universities in the United States and reflects American culture. For example, in the United States—and in individualistic cultures generally—the individual group member is extremely important. In collectivist cultures, the individual is less important; it's the group that is the significant entity. In Japan, for example, group researchers find that "individual fulfillment of self is attained through finding and maintaining one's place within the group" (Cathcart & Cathcart 1985, p. 191). In the United States, individual fulfillment of self is attained by the individual and through his or her own efforts, not by the group.

It's often thought that because group membership and group identity are so important in collectivist cultures that it's the group that makes important decisions. Actually this does not seem to be the case. In fact, in a study of 48 Japanese organizations (highly collectivist) participating in decision-making groups did not give the members decision-making power. Members are encouraged to contribute ideas but the decision-making power is reserved for the CEO and for managers higher up the organizational ladder (Brennan 1991).

In the discussion of member roles earlier in this unit, an entire category was devoted to individual roles, roles that individuals played to satisfy individual rather than group goals. In other cultures (no-

tably collectivist cultures), these roles would probably not even be mentioned simply because they wouldn't be acted out often enough to deserve such extended discussion. In many collectivist cultures, the group orientation is too pervasive for individuals to violate it by acting as the blocker, the recognition seeker, or dominator, for example.

One obvious consequence of this difference can be seen when a group member commits a serious error; for example, a team member submits the wrong advertising copy to the media. In a group governed by individualistic norms, that member is likely to be singled out, reprimanded, and perhaps fired. Further, the leader or supervisor, say, is likely to distance himself or herself from this member for fear that this error will rub off. In a more collectivist culture, this error is more likely to be seen as a group mistake. The individual is unlikely to be singled out—especially not in public—and the leader is likely to bear part of the blame. The same is true when one member comes up with a great idea. In individualistic cultures, that person is likely to be rewarded and only indirectly does this person's work group benefit. In a collectivist culture, it is the group that gets recognized and rewarded for the idea.

In a similar way, each culture maintains its own belief system that influences group members' behavior. For example, members of many Asian cultures, influenced by Confucian principles, believe that "the protruding nail gets pounded down" and are therefore not likely to voice disagreement with the majority of the group. Americans, on the other hand, influenced by the belief that "the squeaky wheel gets the grease," are more likely to voice disagreement or to act in ways different from other group members in order to get what they want.

Also, each culture has its own rules of preferred and expected leadership style. In the United States the general and expected style for a group leader is democratic. Our political leaders are elected by a democratic process; similarly, CEOs are elected by the shareholders of a corporation. In other situations, of course, leaders are chosen by those in authority. The president of the company will normally decide who will supervise and who will be supervised. Even in this situation, however, we expect the supervisor to behave democratically—to listen to the ideas of the members, to take their views into consideration when decisions are to be made, to keep them informed of corporate developments, and to generally

How does the cultural background of members influence the small group communication that takes place in your class? On the job?

respect their interests. Also, we expect that leaders will be changed fairly regularly. We elect a president every four years and company elections are normally held each year.

In other cultures, leaders are chosen by right of birth. They're not elected, nor are they expected to behave democratically. Similarly, their tenure as leaders is usually extremely long, and may in fact last their entire lives and then be passed on to their children. In other cases, leaders in a wide variety of situations may be chosen by the military dictator.

The important point to realize is that your membership and your leadership style are influenced by the culture in which you were raised. Consequently, when in a group with members of different cultures, consider the differences in both membership and leadership style that individuals bring with them. For example, a member who plays individual roles may be tolerated in many groups in the United States and in some may even be thought amusing and different. That same member playing the same roles in a group with a more collectivist orientation is likely to be much more negatively evaluated. Multicultural groups may find it helpful to discuss the views they have of group membership and leadership and what constitutes comfortable interaction for them.

SUMMARY

In this unit we examined the role of members and leaders and the principles that govern effective group interaction.

1. A popular classification of small group member roles divides them into group task roles, group building and maintenance roles, and individual roles.
2. Twelve group task roles are: initiator-contributor, information seeker, opinion seeker, information giver, opinion giver, elaborator, coordinator, orienter, evaluator-critic, energizer, procedural technician, and recorder.
3. Seven group building and maintenance roles are: encourager, harmonizer, compromiser, gatekeeper-expediter, standard setter or ego ideal, group observer and commentator, and follower.
4. Eight individual roles are: aggressor, blocker, recognition seeker, self-confessor, playboy or playgirl, dominator, help seeker, and special-interest pleader.
5. Interaction process analysis categorizes contributions into four areas: social-emotional positive, social-emotional negative, attempted answers, and questions.
6. Member participation should be group-oriented, should center conflict on issues, should be critically open-minded, and should ensure understanding.
7. Groupthink is defined as the mode of thinking that persons engage in when concurrence seeking becomes so dominant in a cohesive ingroup that it tends to override realistic appraisal of alternative course of action.
8. The traits approach to leadership focuses on the characteristics that contribute to leadership, the functional approach centers on what the leader does (the functions the leader serves), and the transformational approach focuses on the leader's empowerment of the group members.
9. In the situational theory of leadership, leadership is seen as concerned with accomplishing the task and serving the interpersonal needs of the members. The degree to which either concern is emphasized should depend on the specific group and the unique situation.
10. Three major leadership styles are: laissez-faire, democratic, and authoritarian.
11. Among the leader's functions are: to activate the group interaction, maintain effective interaction, keep members on track, ensure member satisfaction, encourage ongoing evaluation and improvement, and prepare members for the discussion.
12. The effective leader values people, listens actively, is tactful, gives credit, is consistent, admits mistakes, has a sense of humor, and sets a good example.
13. The culture in which one is raised will greatly influence the ways in which members and leaders interact in small groups.

KEY TERMS

group task roles (p. 261)

group building and maintenance roles (p. 261)

individual roles (p. 262)

interaction process analysis (p. 262)

groupthink (p. 264)

leadership (p. 264)

traits approach to leadership (p. 265)

functional approach to leadership (p. 266)

transformational approach to leadership (p. 266)

situational approach to leadership (p. 266)

laissez-faire leader (p. 269)

democratic leader (p. 269)

authoritarian leader (p. 269)

agenda-setting (p. 273)

➡ THINKING CRITICALLY ABOUT
Members and Leaders in Group Communication

1. Can you identify roles that you habitually serve in certain groups? Do you serve these roles in your friendship, love, and family relationships as well?

2. How would you characterize the leadership style of one of your local politicians, religious leaders, college instructors, or talk show hosts? How would you characterize your own leadership style? For example, are you usually more concerned with people or with tasks? Are you more likely to be a laissez-faire, democratic, or authoritarian leader?

3. How would you go about finding answers to such questions as these?
   - Does serving individual functions in a group make a member unpopular with other group members?
   - Can leadership styles be used to describe approaches to teaching? To parenting? To managing?
   - Do women and men respond similarly to the different leadership styles? Do women and men exercise the different leadership styles with equal facility?

4. It's been found that the person with the highest rate of participation in a group is the one most likely to be chosen leader (Muller, Salas, & Driskell 1989). Do you find this to be true of the groups in which you have participated? Why do you suppose this relationship exists?

5. In a social group at a friend's house, any leadership other than laissez-faire would be difficult to tolerate. When all members are about equal in their knowledge of the topic or when the members are very concerned with their individual rights, the democratic leader seems the most appropriate. When time and efficiency are critical or when group members continue to lack motivation despite repeated democratic efforts, authoritarian leadership may be the most effective. In what other situations would laissez-faire, democratic, or authoritarian leadership style be appropriate?

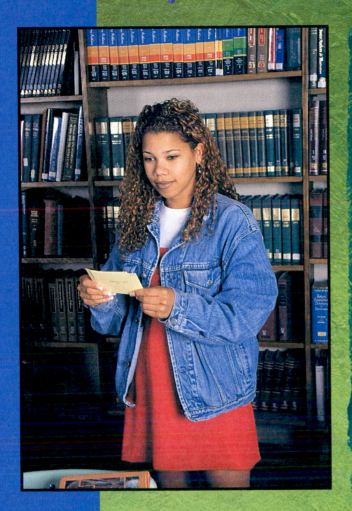

UNIT 15

Public Speaking Topics, Audiences, and Research

UNIT CONTENT

Introducing Public Speaking

Step 1. Select Your Topic and Purpose

Step 2. Analyze Your Audience

Step 3. Research Your Speech Topic

UNIT GOALS

After reading this unit, you should be able to

define *public speaking* and explain the methods for managing communication apprehension

explain the nature of suitable public speaking topics and purposes and how to select and narrow them

explain the factors that need to be considered in audience analysis

explain the strategies and sources for researching speech topics

This unit introduces public speaking and explains what public speaking is, gives you a glimpse at its history and breadth, and looks into apprehension in public speaking and especially how you can manage it. With this as a foundation, the public speaking preparation process is discussed as a 10-step process, and its first three steps are explained. The next two units cover the remaining seven steps.

INTRODUCING PUBLIC SPEAKING

Fair questions to ask of a large section of a book or course are "What will I get out of this?" "How will the effort and time I put into public speaking benefit me?" Here are just a few of the benefits you'll derive from this introduction to public speaking.

- Enhanced personal and social abilities. Public speaking provides training in a variety of personal and social competencies. For example, in the pages that follow you'll read about such skills as self-awareness, self-confidence, and dealing with the fear of communicating. These certainly are skills that you'll apply in public speaking, but they will also prove valuable in all of your social interactions.
- Improved academic and career skills. As you learn public speaking, you'll also learn a wide variety of academic and career skills. Among these are the ability to conduct research; explain complex concepts; support an argument with logical, emotional, and ethical appeals; organize a variety of messages; and evaluate the validity of persuasive appeals.
- Refined communication abilities. Speakers aren't born; they're made. Through instruction, exposure to different speeches, feedback, and individual learning experiences, you can become an effective speaker. Regardless of your present level of competence, you can improve through proper training. As you acquire the skills of public speaking, you'll also develop and refine your general communication abilities, such as developing a more effective communication style, giving and responding appropriately to criticism, improving listening skills, and refining your delivery skills.

In public speaking *a speaker presents a relatively continuous message to a relatively large audience in a unique context* (see Figure 15.1). Like all forms of communication, public speaking is a transactional process (Watzlawick, Beavin, & Jackson 1967; Watzlawick 1978). The elements next are interdependent, never independent. Each element in the public speaking process depends on and interacts with all other elements. For example, the way in which you organize a speech will depend on such factors as the speech topic, the specific audience, the purpose you hope to achieve, and a host of other variables—all of which are explained in the remainder of this unit and in the units to follow.

Especially important to appreciate is the mutual interaction and influence between speaker and listener. True, when you give a public speech you do most of the speaking and the listeners do most of the listening. The listeners, however, also send messages in the form of feedback, for example, applause, bored looks, nods of agreement or disagreement, and attentive glances. The audience also influences how you'll prepare and present your speech. It influences your arguments, language, method of organization, and, in fact, every choice you make. You would not, for example, present the same speech on saving money to high school students as you would to senior citizens.

Historical Roots of Public Speaking

Public speaking is both a very old and very new art. It's likely that public speaking principles were developed soon after our species began to talk. Much of contemporary public speaking, however, is based on the works of the ancient Greeks and Romans who articulated an especially insightful system of rhetoric or public speaking. This tradition has been enriched by experiments, surveys, field studies, and historical studies that have been done since then.

Aristotle's *Rhetoric*, written some 2300 years ago, was one of the earliest systematic studies of public speaking. It was in this work that the three kinds of proof—*logos* (or logical proof), *pathos* (emotional appeals), and *ethos* (appeals based on the character of the speaker)—were introduced. This three-part division is still followed today.

Roman rhetoricians added to the work of the Greeks. Quintilian, who taught in Rome during the first century, built an entire educational system—from childhood through adulthood—based on the development of the effective and responsible orator. Throughout these 2300 years, the study of public speaking has grown and developed.

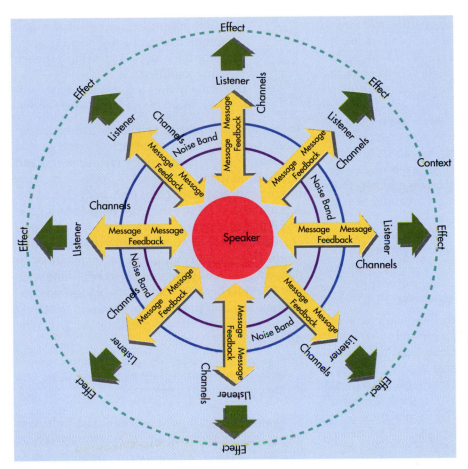

Figure 15.1 The public speaking transaction. How would you diagram the process of public speaking?

Contemporary public speaking builds on this classical heritage and also incorporates insights from the humanities, the social and behavioral sciences, and, now, computer science and technology. Likewise, perspectives from different cultures are being integrated into our present study of public speaking.

Ethics in Public Speaking

As a public speaker, you design and deliver your speeches to influence listeners: politicians give campaign speeches to secure your vote; advertisers give sales pitches to get you to buy their products; teachers give lectures to influence your thinking about history, psychology, or communication. Because your speeches will have effects, you have an obligation to consider the moral implications of your messages throughout the public speaking process. When

you develop your topic, present your research, create your persuasive appeals, and do any of the other tasks related to public speaking, there are ethical issues to be considered (Jaksa & Pritchard 1994; Bok 1978; Johannesen 1994). And the listener and the critic also have ethical obligations; for example, listeners have an obligation to give a speaker a fair hearing and critics have an obligation to render a fair and unbiased evaluation.

Ethics—the morality of an act—is an integral part of all public speaking for speaker, listener, and critic. Here are just a few ethical issues that the public speaker is likely to confront at some point in preparing and presenting a speech to an audience. As you read down the list consider what you *would* do if confronted with this issue. What do you feel you *should* do (if this is different from what you *would* do)? What general principle of ethics are you using in making these *would* and *should* judgments?

- Would it be ethical to use questionable means to achieve a worthwhile end? For example, would it be wrong for a speaker to exaggerate if by doing so he or she might achieve some respectable goal, for example, getting teens to stop smoking?
- Would it be ethical to persuade an audience by scaring or threatening them if your goal was to get them to do something that would be beneficial to them, for example, exercise? To get them to follow a particular religious belief? To get them to do something that would benefit, say, the poor and homeless?
- Would it be ethical to assume leadership of a group to get the group to do as you wish?

Apprehension in Public Speaking

Before beginning the actual speech preparation process, let's look first at what is probably your number one concern, stage fright, or what is now called **communication apprehension.** People experience apprehension in all forms of communication (as illustrated throughout this text), but it's in the public speaking situation that apprehension is most common and most severe (Richmond & McCroskey 1998; Daly, McCroskey, Ayres, Hopf, & Ayres 1997). Take the following apprehension test to measure your own fear of speaking in public.

SELF-TEST

How Apprehensive Are You in Public Speaking?

This questionnaire consists of six statements concerning your feelings about public speaking. Indicate the degree to which each statement applies to you by marking whether you (1) strongly agree, (2) agree, (3) are undecided, (4) disagree, or (5) strongly disagree with each statement. There are no right or wrong answers. Don't be concerned that some of the statements are similar to others. Work quickly; just record your first impression.

_____ 1. I have no fear of giving a speech.
_____ 2. Certain parts of my body feel very tense and rigid while giving a speech.
_____ 3. I feel relaxed while giving a speech.
_____ 4. My thoughts become confused and jumbled when I am giving a speech.
_____ 5. I face the prospect of giving a speech with confidence.
_____ 6. While giving a speech, I get so nervous that I forget facts I really know.

To obtain your public speaking apprehension score, begin with the number 18 (selected so that you won't wind up with negative numbers) and add to it the scores for items 1, 3, and 5. Then, from this total, subtract the scores from items 2, 4, and 6. A score above 18 shows some degree of apprehension. Most people score above 18, so if you scored relatively high, you're among the vast majority of people. You may find it interesting to compare your several apprehension scores (Units 9, 12, and 13). Most people would score highest on public speaking and the job interview and relatively low on conversations and group discussions. Why do you think this is true?

From James C. McCroskey, *An Introduction to Rhetorical Communication*, 6th edition, 1993, Prentice-Hall, Upper Saddle River, NJ. Reprinted by permission.

There are several ways you can deal with your own public speaking anxiety: (1) reverse the factors that cause anxiety, (2) practice performance visualization, (3) systematically desensitize yourself, and (4) use some basic skills.

Reduce Apprehension by Reversing the Factors that Cause Apprehension

There are five factors that contribute to speaker apprehension; if you can reverse these factors or lessen their impact, you'll be able to reduce your anxiety. These five factors are: the new and the different, subordinate status, conspicuousness, lack of similarity, and prior history (Beatty 1988).

New and different situations will make you anxious. Since public speaking is likely to be relatively new and different to many of you, it's a situation that is likely to generate anxiety. So, gaining as much experience in public speaking as you can (making it less new and different) will lessen your anxiety. Try to familiarize yourself with the public speaking context. Try, for example, to rehearse in the room in which you will give your speech. Or, stand in the front of the room before the actual presentation, as if you were giving your speech.

When you see yourself as having **subordinate status**, when, for example, you feel that others are better speakers or that they know more than you do, your anxiety increases. Thinking positively about yourself and being thorough in your preparation reduces this particular cause of anxiety.

When you're the center of attention, as you normally are in public speaking, you feel **conspicuous** and your anxiety increases. Therefore, try thinking of public speaking as another type of conversation (some theorists call it "enlarged conversation"). Or, if you're comfortable talking in small groups, visualizing your audience as an enlarged small group will likely dispel some of the anxiety you feel.

When you feel you **lack similarity** with your audience, that you have little in common with your listeners, you may feel that your audience doesn't empathize with you and so you may become anxious. Try emphasizing the commonalities you share with your listeners as you plan your speeches as well as during the actual presentation. This will help you see yourself as a part of the audience and is also likely to suggest areas of similarity that you may integrate into your speech.

If you have a **prior history of apprehension**, that is, you've experienced public speaking anxiety before, you're more likely to dwell on such past experiences and become even more anxious. Your positive public speaking experiences in this class will help reduce this cause of anxiety.

Reduce Apprehension with Performance Visualization

Performance visualization is designed specifically to reduce the outward manifestations of speaker apprehension and also to reduce the negative thinking that often creates anxiety (Ayres & Hopf 1992, 1993; Ayres, Hopf, & Ayres 1994).

The first part of performance visualization is to develop a positive attitude and a positive self-perception. This involves visualizing yourself in the role of being an effective public speaker. Visualize yourself walking to the front of the room—fully and totally confident. You scan the audience and slowly begin your speech. Throughout the speech you're fully in control of the situation. The audience is at rapt attention and, as you finish, bursts into wild applause. Throughout this visualization, avoid all negative thoughts. As you visualize yourself as an effective public speaker, take note of how you walk, look at your listeners, handle your notes, and respond to questions; and, especially, think about how you feel about the whole experience.

The second part of performance visualization is designed to help you model your performance on that of an especially effective speaker. Here you would view a particularly competent public speaker on video and make a mental movie of it. As you review the actual and mental movie, you begin to shift yourself into the role of speaker. You, in effect, become this effective speaker.

Reduce Apprehension by Systematically Desensitizing Yourself

Systematic desensitization is a technique for dealing with a variety of fears including those involved in public speaking (Wolpe 1957; Goss, Thompson, & Olds 1978; Richmond & McCroskey 1998). The general idea is to create a hierarchy of behaviors leading up to the desired but feared behavior (say, speaking before an audience). One specific hierarchy might look like this:

5. Giving a speech in class
4. Introducing another speaker to the class
3. Speaking in a group in front of the class
2. Answering a question in class
1. Asking a question in class

You would begin at the bottom of this hierarchy and rehearse this behavior mentally over a period of days until you can clearly visualize asking a question in class without any uncomfortable anxiety. Once you can accomplish this, you can move to the second level. Here you would visualize the somewhat more threatening behavior, answering a question. Once you can do this, you can move to the third level, and so on until you get to the desired behavior.

In creating your hierarchy, try to use small steps. This will enable you to get from one step to the next more easily. Each success will make the next step easier. You might then go on to engage in the actual behaviors after you have comfortably visualized them: ask a question, answer a question, and so on.

Reduce Apprehension by Using Some Basic Skills

The last general approach to dealing with speaker apprehension is to use some of the specific skills and techniques for achieving greater control over apprehension (Richmond & McCroskey 1998; Watson & Dodd 1984 Caducci & Zimbardo 1995).

Prepare and Practice Thoroughly. Much of the fear you experience is a fear of failure. Adequate and even extra preparation will lessen the possibility of failure and the accompanying apprehension. Jack Valenti (1982), president of the Motion Picture Association of America and speechwriter for Lyndon Johnson, put it this way: "The most effective antidote to stage fright and other calamities of speechmaking is total, slavish, monkish preparation." Because apprehension is greatest during the beginning of the speech, try memorizing the first few sentences of your speech to eliminate any possibility of not saying them correctly or forgetting them. If there are complicated facts or figures, be sure to write these out and plan to read them. Again, this procedure will help lessen your fear of making a mistake.

Gain Experience. Learning to speak in public is similar to learning to drive a car or ski down a mountain. With experience, the initial fears and anxieties give way to feelings of control, comfort, and pleasure. Experience will prove to you that a public speech can be effective despite your fears and anxieties. It will show you that the feelings of accomplishment in public speaking are rewarding and will outweigh any initial anxiety.

Move About and Breathe Deeply. Physical activity—gross bodily movements as well as the small movements of the hands, face, and head—eases or lessens apprehension. Using a visual aid, for example, will temporarily divert attention from you and will allow you to get rid of your excess energy. Deep breathing relaxes the body. By breathing deeply a few times before getting up to speak, you will sense your body relax. This will help you overcome your initial fear of getting out of your seat and walking to the front of the room. If you find yourself getting a bit more nervous than you had hoped during your speech, just breathe deeply during a pause.

Avoid Chemicals as Tension Relievers. Unless prescribed by a physician, avoid any chemical means for reducing apprehension. Tranquilizers, marijuana, alcohol, or artificial stimulants, for example, are more likely to create problems rather than reduce them.

They will probably impair other functions. For example, chemicals may interfere with your ability to remember the parts of your speech, to accurately read audience feedback, and to regulate the timing of your speech.

Put Your Apprehension in Perspective. Fear increases when you feel that the audience's expectations are very high (Ayres 1986). So, maintain realistic expectations. Compete with yourself. Your second speech does not have to be better than that of the previous speaker, but it should be better than your own first one. Your audience does not expect perfection, either.

You're going to give a speech and you're anxious and unsure of what to say. What do you do? What do you speak about? How do you decide what to include in the speech? How should you organize a speech? At this point you probably have a lot more questions than answers but that's the way it should be. We will now begin to answer these questions by providing a brief overview of the public speaking process. In this way you'll be able to begin public speaking almost immediately. By following the 10 steps outlined in this unit and the next two, you'll be able to prepare and present effective speeches.

Figure 15.2 presents these 10 steps in a linear fashion. The process of constructing a public speech, however, doesn't always follow a logical and linear sequence. That is, you'll probably not progress simply from step 1 to 2 to 3 and so on. Instead, your progression might go more like this: step 1, step 2, back again to step 1, step 3, back again to step 2, and so on throughout the preparation of your speech. For example, after selecting your subject and purpose (step 1), you may progress to step 2 and analyze your audience. On the basis of this analysis, however, you may wish to go back and modify your subject, your purpose, or both. Similarly, after you research the topic (step 3), you may want more information on your audience. You may, therefore, return to step 2.

Going from one step to another and then back again should not throw you off track. This is the way most people prepare speeches. So, although the steps are presented in the order a speaker normally follows, remember that you're in charge of the

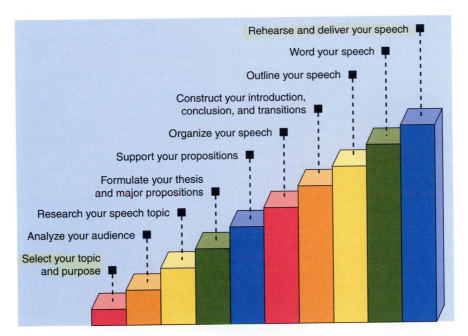

Figure 15.2   **The steps in preparing and delivering a public speech.**

process. Use the order of these steps as guidelines but break the sequence as you need to. As long as you cover all 10 steps thoroughly, you'll accomplish your goal.

STEP 1. SELECT YOUR TOPIC AND PURPOSE

Your first step is to select your topic and purpose.

Your Topic

A suitable speech topic should be (1) worthwhile and deal with matters of substance, (2) appropriate to you and your audience, and (3) sensitive and appropriate to the culture in which the speech takes place.

The topics should be **worthwhile**. Such topics should address issues that have significant implications for the audience. Topics that are worthwhile have consequences (social, educational, political, and so on) that are significant for your listeners. The topic must be important enough to merit the time and attention of a group of intelligent and educated persons.

A suitable topic is **appropriate** to you as the speaker, to the audience you'll address, and to the occasion. When you select a topic you're interested

in you'll enjoy thinking and reading about it and this will come through in your speech. Look also at your topic in terms of its appropriateness to the audience. What are they interested in? What would they like to learn more about? On what topics would they find the time listening to your speech well spent? It's a lot easier to please an audience when the topic interests them.

The topic should also be appropriate for the occasion. While the classroom offers few problems created by the "occasion," it imposes a number of serious restrictions outside the classroom. Some occasions call for humorous subjects that would be out of place in other contexts. Others call for speeches of personal experience that may be inappropriate in another context. Similarly, time limitations will force you to exclude certain topics because they're too complex to cover in the time you have available.

Topics need to be **culture-sensitive**. In many Arab, Asian, and African cultures, discussing sex in an audience of both men and women would be considered obscene and offensive. In other cultures (Scandinavia is a good example), sex is expected to be discussed openly and without embarrassment or discomfort. Each culture has its own taboo topics, subjects that should be avoided, especially by visitors from other cultures. For example, Roger Axtell in *Do's and Taboos Around the World* (1993) recommends that visitors from the United States avoid discussing politics, language differences between French and Flemish, and religion in Belgium; family, religion, jobs, and negative comments on bullfighting in Spain; religion and Middle East politics in Iraq; World War II in Japan; politics, religion, corruption, and foreign aid in the Philippines; and race, local politics, and religion in the Caribbean.

Your college or communication classroom very likely has its own cultural norms as to what would be considered an appropriate topic. Consider, for example, if the following speeches would be considered "appropriate" by members of your public speaking class or by the general college community.

- A speech that seeks to convert listeners to a specific religious cult
- A speech supporting neo-Nazi values
- A speech supporting racial segregation
- A speech that teaches listeners how to cheat on their income tax

Finding Topics

Perhaps the first question you have is "What will I talk about?" "I'm not knowledgeable about international affairs, the Middle East, or environmental issues." "I'm not up on issues such as mass transit, national health insurance, or gay rights." This situation is not uncommon; many, if not most, college students feel the same way. This need not lead to despair; all is not lost. Since the objective of your classroom speeches is to learn the skills of public speaking, there are literally thousands of subjects to talk about. Searching for speech topics is a relatively easy process. Here are four ways to find topics: topic lists, surveys, news items, and brainstorming.

Topic Lists. Most public speaking textbooks contain suggestions for topics suitable for public speeches (DeVito 2000; Osborn & Osborn 2000; Verderber 2000) as do books for writers (for example, Lamm 1991). A useful list of over 250 debate topics that can be modified for both informative and persuasive speeches can be found at the International Islamic University Malaysia's Web site at http://www.iiu.edu.my/stadd/spice/topics.html. *The Speech Writer's Guide* (1995) contains a computerized list of hundreds of topics. Another resource for topics

is the list of the best-selling nonfiction books in most newspapers or the well-stocked bookstore. The popularity of these books tell you that people are interested in these topics.

Surveys. Survey data are now easier than ever to get since many of the larger poll results are available on the Internet. For example, the Gallup organization maintains a Web site at http://www.gallup.com/, which includes national and international surveys on political, social, consumer, and other issues speakers often talk about. Another way is to go to a search directory and examine the major topics and any subdivisions of those you'd care to pursue—a process that's explained later in this unit. These topics are exactly the topics that people are talking about and that therefore often make excellent speech topics. For example, in one survey 10,000 executives and meeting planners identified the 10 topics that they consider the most important and that will continue to be important for the next few years: dealing with change, customer service, global marketplace opportunities, future strategies, total quality, new technologies, productivity and performance in business, diversity, legal issues, and health and fitness (Weinstein 1995).

News Items. Another useful starting point is a good newspaper or magazine. Here you'll find the important international and domestic issues, the financial issues, and the social issues all conveniently packaged in one place. The editorial page and the letters to the editor are also useful in learning what people are concerned about. News magazines like *Time* and *Newsweek* and financial magazines such as *Forbes*, *Money*, and *Fortune* will provide a wealth of suggestions. Similarly, news shows like "20/20," "60 Minutes," "Meet the Press," and even the ubiquitous talk shows often identify the very issues that people are concerned with and on which there are conflicting points of view. The fasting growing news sources are the news Web sites, for example, http://www.cnn.com/, http://www.sfgate.com/, or http://www.usatoday.com/). These will provide excellent suggestions for speech topics.

Brainstorming. Another useful method is to brainstorm, a technique discussed in more detail in Unit 13. Using brainstorming to help you generate topics is simple. You begin with your "problem," which in this case is "What will I talk about?" You then record any idea that occurs to you. Allow your mind to free associate. Don't censor yourself; instead, allow your ideas to flow as freely as possible. Record all your thoughts—regardless of how silly or inappropriate they may seem. Write them down or record them on tape. Try to generate as many ideas as possible. The more ideas you think of, the more chance there is of a suitable topic being in the pile. After you've generated a sizable list—it should take no longer than five minutes—read over the list or replay the tape. Do any of the topics on your list suggest other topics? If so, write these down as well. Can you combine or extend your ideas? Which ideas seem workable?

Limiting Topics

To be suitable for a public speech—or any type of communication—a topic must be limited in scope; it must be narrowed down to fit the time constraints. Probably the major problem for beginning speakers is that they attempt to cover a huge topic in too short a time. The inevitable result is that nothing specific is covered—everything is touched on, but only superficially. Because you can't go into any depth with a broad topic, you often succeed only in telling the audience what it already knows.

Narrowing your topic will also help you focus your collection of research materials. If your topic is too broad, you'll be forced to review a lot more re-search material than you're going to need. Here are three methods for narrowing and limiting your topic.

Topoi, *The System of Topics.* This technique comes to us from the classical rhetorics of ancient Greece and Rome. Using this method of *topoi*, you would ask yourself a series of questions about your general subject. The process will enable you to see divisions or aspects of your general topic on which you might want to focus. For example, asking the typical reporter's questions (Who? What? Why? When? Where? How? and So?) and a series of subquestions, you'll see the different aspects of a topic. Let's say you want to give a speech on homelessness. Applying the system of *topoi*, you would ask such questions as:

- Who are the homeless?
- What does homelessness do to the people themselves and to society in general?
- Why are there so many homeless people?
- Where is homelessness most prevalent?
- How does someone become homeless?
- How can we help the homeless and prevent others from becoming homeless?
- Why must we be concerned with homelessness?

Tree Diagrams. The construction of tree diagrams (actually, they resemble upside-down trees) might also help you narrow your topic. Let's say, for example, that you want to do a speech on mass communication.

BUILDING
Communication Skills

HOW DO YOU LIMIT A TOPIC?

Here are a few overly general topics. Using one of the methods discussed in this unit (or any other method you're familiar with), limit each of these topics to ones that would be reasonable for a 5- to 10-minute speech.

1. Dangerous sports
2. Race relationships
3. Parole
4. Censorship on the Internet
5. Ecological problems
6. Problems faced by college students
7. Morality
8. Health and fitness
9. Ethical issues in politics
10. Urban violence

You might develop a tree diagram with branches for the division that interests you most, as shown in Figure 15.3. Thus you can divide mass communication into film, television, radio, newspapers, and magazines. If television interests you most, then develop branches from television. Comedy, news, soaps, sports, and quiz shows would be appropriate. Now, let's say that it's the soaps that most interest you. In this case you'd create branches from soaps, perhaps primetime and daytime. Keep dividing the topic until you get something that is significant, appropriate to you and your audience, and that you can cover in some depth in the allotted time.

Search Directories. A more technologically sophisticated way of both selecting and limiting your topic is to let a search directory do some of the work for you. A search directory is simply a nested list of topics. You go from the general to the specific by selecting a topic, and then a subdivision of that topic,

and then a subdivision of that topic. The process is illustrated in Table 15.1.

Your Purpose

The purpose of your speech is your goal; it's what you hope to achieve during your speech. It identifies the effect that your want your speech to have on your audience. In constructing your speech, first identify your general purpose and second, your specific purpose.

General Purposes

The two major purposes of public speeches are to **inform** and to **persuade**. In the informative speech you seek to create understanding: to clarify, enlighten, correct misunderstandings, demonstrate how to do something, describe how something works, or define a concept. In this type of speech you rely most heavily on materials that support—examples, illustra-

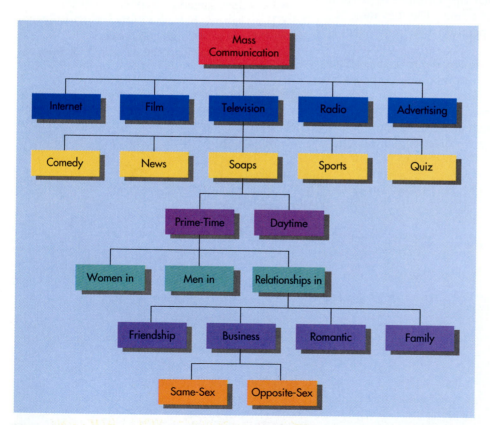

Figure 15.3 **A tree diagram for limiting speech topics.**   How would you draw a tree diagram for limiting topics beginning with such general subjects as *immigration, education, sports, transportation,* or *politics*?

TABLE 15.1   Using search directories to find and limit your speech topics

This table is based on material found on Hotbot (July 15, 1998). Your search-and-limit mission begins with selecting a topic from the first level, say, "society & politics." This would give you the list of second level topics in column 2. Selecting "crime & justice" produced the third level list in column 3. Selecting any one of the topics on the third level will result in a list of Websites and links to other sites.

First Level Topics	Second Level Topics	Third Level Topics
automotive	community & culture	crime by type
business & finance	**crime & justice**	crime prevention
computers & Internet	environment	criminal law
entertainment & media	gender & sexuality	criminology
hobbies & interests	government	District Attorneys
home & family	international affairs	famous crimes
people & chat	issues & policy	law enforcement
reference & education	law	missing persons
shopping & services	news & magazines	news & research
society & politics	politics	prisons & sentencing
sports & recreation	religion & belief	services
travel & vacations	world cultures	victims & complainant

tions, definitions, testimony, audiovisual aids, and the like. In the persuasive speech you try to influence attitudes or behaviors; you seek to strengthen or change existing attitudes or get the audience to take some action. In this type of speech you rely heavily on materials that offer proof—on evidence, argument, and psychological appeals, for example.

Any persuasive speech is in part an informative speech and as such contains materials that amplify, illustrate, define, and so on. In its focus on strengthening or changing attitudes and behaviors, however, the persuasive speech must go beyond simply providing information. Logical, motivational, and credibility appeals (discussed in the next unit) are essential.

Specific Purposes

After you have established your general purpose, identify your specific purpose, which states more precisely what you aim to accomplish. For example, in an informative speech, your specific speech purpose would identify that information you want to convey to your audience, for example, "to inform my audience of the recent progress in AIDS research" or "to inform my audience of the currently used tests for HIV infection."

In a persuasive speech, your specific purpose identifies what you want your audience to believe, to think, or perhaps to do, for example, "to persuade my audience that they should be tested for HIV infection" or "to persuade my audience to become better informed about how AIDS can be transmitted."

In formulating your specific purpose, be sure to limit it to what you can reasonably develop in the allotted time. Instead of the too-broad purpose "to inform my audience about clothing design," a more limited and appropriate one would be "to inform my audience of the importance of color in clothing design."

Use an infinitive phrase. Begin the statement of your specific purpose with the word "to," for example: *to persuade my audience to contribute a book to the library fundraiser.*

STEP 2. ANALYZE YOUR AUDIENCE

The characteristic that seems best to define an audience is common purpose; a public speaking audience is a group of individuals gathered together to hear a speech. If you're to be a successful speaker, then you must know your audience. This knowledge will help you in selecting your topic; phrasing your purpose; establishing a relationship between yourself and your audience; and choosing examples, illustrations, and logical and emotional appeals.

Your first step in audience analysis is to construct an audience profile in which you analyze their sociological or demographic characteristics. These characteristics help you estimate the attitudes, beliefs, and values of your audience. If you want to effect changes in these attitudes, beliefs, and values, you have to know what they are.

Attitudes, Beliefs, and Values

Attitude refers to your tendency to act for or against a person, object, or position. If you have a positive attitude toward the death penalty, you're likely to argue or act in favor of instituting the death penalty (for example, vote for a candidate who supports the death penalty). If you have a negative attitude toward the death penalty, then you're likely to argue or act against it. Attitudes influence how favorably or unfavorably listeners will respond to speakers who support or denounce the death penalty.

Belief refers to the confidence or conviction you have in the existence or truth of some proposition. For example, you may believe that there is an afterlife, that education is the best way to rise from poverty, that democracy is the best form of government, or that all people are born equal. If your listeners believe that the death penalty is a deterrent to crime, for example, then they will be more likely to favor arguments for (and speakers who support) the death penalty than will listeners who don't believe in the connection between the death penalty and deterrence.

Value refers to your perception of the worth or goodness (or worthlessness or badness) of some concept or idea. For example, you probably have positive values for financial success, education, and contributing to the common welfare. At the same time, you probably have negative values for chemical weapons, corrupt politicians, and selling drugs to children. Because the values an audience holds will influence how it responds to ideas that are related to those values, it's essential that you learn the values of your specific audience. For example, if your audience places a high positive value on child

welfare, then it is likely to vote for legislation that protects children or allocates money for breakfasts and lunches in school, and they might consider signing a petition, volunteering their time, or donating their money to advance the welfare of children. If you find that your audience places a negative value on big business, you might want to reconsider using the testimony of corporate leaders or the statistics compiled by corporations.

Analyzing the Sociology of the Audience

In analyzing an audience be careful not to assume that people covered by the same label are necessarily all alike. As soon as you begin to use a sociological characteristic with the expressed or implied "all," consider the possibility that you may be stereotyping. Don't assume that all women or all older people or all highly educated people think or believe the same things. They don't. Nevertheless, there are characteristics that seem to be more common among one group than another, and it is these characteristics that you want to explore in analyzing your audience. Let's look at four major sociological or demographic variables: (1) cultural factors, (2) age, (3) gender, and (4) religion and religiousness.

Cultural Factors

Cultural factors such as nationality, race, and cultural identity are crucial in audience analysis. Largely because of different training and experiences, the interests, values, and goals of various cultural groups will also differ. Further, cultural factors will also influence each of the remaining factors; for example, attitudes toward age and gender will differ greatly from one culture to another. Perhaps the primary question to ask is, "Are the cultural beliefs and values of the audience relevant to your topic and purpose?" Might the cultural membership of your audience members influence the way they see the topic? If so, find out what these beliefs and values are and take these into consideration as you build your speech.

Consider too that the cultural beliefs that you might wish to use in your speeches as basic assumptions vary from one group to another. For example, how favorably or unfavorably (on, say, a 10-point scale) would members of this class respond to the following cultural beliefs?

- God is good and just.
- The welfare of the family must come first, even before your own.
- Sex outside of marriage is wrong and sinful.
- Winning is all important; it's not how you play the game, it's whether or not you win that matters.
- Intercultural relationships are okay in business, but should be discouraged when it comes to intimate or romantic relationships; generally, the races should be kept "pure."
- Doing good for others is the goal of life; personal happiness is secondary.
- Money is good; the quest for financial success is a perfectly respectable one.
- United States immigration should be curtailed, at least until the current immigrants are assimilated.
- In a heterosexual relationship, "a wife is to submit graciously to the servant leadership of her husband" (a directive of the Southern Baptist Convention) (Woodward 1998).
- Keeping the United States militarily superior is the best way to preserve world peace.

Age

Different age groups have different attitudes and beliefs largely because they have had different experiences in different contexts. Take these differences into consideration in preparing your speeches. For example, let's say that you're an investment counselor and you want to persuade your listeners to invest their money to increase their earnings. Your speech would have to be very different if you were addressing an audience of retired people (say in their 60s) and an audience of young executives (say in their 30s). In considering the age of your audience, ask yourself if the age groups differ in the goals, interests, and day-to-day concerns that may be related to your topic and purpose. Graduating from college, achieving corporate success, raising a family, and saving for retirement are concerns that differ greatly from one age group to another. Ask too if the groups differ in their ability to absorb and process information. Will they differ in their responses to visual cues? With a young audience, it may be best to keep up a steady, even swift pace. With older persons, you may wish to maintain a more moderate pace.

Gender

Gender is one of the most difficult audience variables to analyze. The rapid social changes taking place today make it difficult to pin down the effects of gender. As you analyze your audience in terms of gender, ask yourself if men and women differ in the values they consider important and that are related to your topic and purpose. Traditionally, men have been found to place greater importance on theoretical, economic, and political values. Traditionally, women have been found to place greater importance on aesthetic, social, and religious values. In framing appeals and in selecting examples, use the values your audience members consider most important.

Ask too if your topic will be seen as more interesting by one sex? Will men and women have different attitudes toward the topic? Men and women do not, for example, respond in the same way to such topics as abortion, rape, and equal pay for equal work. Select your topics and supporting materials in light of the sex of your audience members. When your audience is mixed, make a special effort to relate "women's" topics to men and "men's" topics to women.

Religion and Religiousness

The religion and religiousness of your audience will often influence their responses to your speech. Religion permeates all topics and all issues. On a

Generally, do you think you're at an advantage speaking to a same-sex or an opposite-sex audience? As a listener, are you more responsive to a same-sex speaker or an opposite-sex speaker? Does your answer depend on the speech topic?

most obvious level, we know that such issues as birth control, abortion, and divorce are closely connected to religion. Similarly, premarital sex, marriage, child-rearing, money, cohabitation, responsibilities toward parents, and thousands of other issues are clearly influenced by religion. Religion is also important, however, in areas where its connection is not so obvious. For example, religion influences one's ideas concerning such topics as obedience to authority, responsibility to government, and the usefulness of such qualities as honesty, guilt, and happiness.

Ask yourself if your topic or purpose might be seen as an attack on the religious beliefs of any segment of your audience? If so, then you might want to make adjustments, not necessarily to abandon your purpose but to rephrase your arguments or incorporate different evidence. When dealing with any religious beliefs (and particularly when disagreeing with them), recognize that you're going to meet stiff opposition. Proceed slowly and inductively. Present your evidence and argument before expressing your disagreement.

Analyzing The Psychology of the Audience

In addition to looking at an audience's sociological characteristics, it's often useful to consider their psychological characteristics, particularly, their willing-ness to listen to you, their favorableness to your purpose, and their knowledge.

How Willing Is Your Audience?

Your immediate concern, of course, is with the willingness of your fellow students to listen to your speeches. Do they come to class because they have to or do they come because they're interested in what you'll say? If they're a willing group, then you have few problems. If they're an unwilling group, all is not lost; you just have to work a little harder in adapting your speech. The unwilling audience demands special and delicate handling. Here are a few suggestions to help change your listeners from unwilling to willing.

- Secure their interest and attention as early in your speech as possible and reinforce this throughout the speech by using little-known facts, quotations, startling statistics, examples, narratives, audiovisual aids, and the like.
- Reward the audience for their attendance and attention. Let the audience know you're aware they're making a sacrifice in coming to hear you speak. Tell them you appreciate it.
- Relate your topic and supporting materials directly to your audience's needs and wants. Show the audience how they can save time, make more money, solve their problems, or

UNDERSTANDING
Theory and Research

ARE YOU FROM A SACRED OR A SECULAR CULTURE?

Some cultures may be viewed as secular cultures in which religion does not dominate the attitudes and views of the people or greatly influence political or educational decisions (Dodd 1995). Liberal Protestant cultures such as the Scandinavian countries would be clearly secular. Other cultures are sacred; in these cultures reli-gion and religious beliefs and values dominate everything a person does and influence politics, education, and just about every topic or issue imaginable. Islamic cultures would be traditional examples of sacred cultures. Technically, the United States would be a secular culture (the Constitution, for example, expressly separates church and state) but in some areas of the country, religion exerts powerful influence on schools (from prayers to condom distribution to sex education) and politics (from the selection of political leaders to concern for social welfare to gay rights legislation).

become more popular. If you fail to do this, then your audience has good reason for not listening.

How Favorable Is Your Audience?

Audiences vary in the degree to which they're favorable or unfavorable toward you, your topic, or point of view. If you conclude that your audience is unfavorable, the following suggestions should help.

- Clear up any possible misapprehensions that may be causing the disagreement. So, for example, if the audience is hostile to your team approach because they wrongly think it will result in a reduction in their autonomy, then tell them very directly that it won't and perhaps explain why it won't.
- Build on commonalities; stress what you and the audience share as people, as interested citizens, as fellow students. When an audience sees similarity or "common ground" between itself and you, it becomes more favorable to both you and your speech.
- Organize your speech inductively. Try to build your speech from areas of agreement, through areas of slight disagreement, up to the major differences between the audience's attitudes and your position. Once areas of agreement are established, it's easier to bring up differences.
- Strive for small gains. Don't try to convince a pro-life group to contribute money for the new abortion clinic or a pro-choice group to vote against liberalizing abortion laws in a five-minute speech. Be content to get them to see some validity in your position and to listen fairly.
- Acknowledge the differences explicitly. If it's clear to the audience that they and you are at opposite ends of the issue, it may be helpful to acknowledge this directly. Show the audience that you understand their position and that you respect it, but that you'd like them to consider a different way of looking at things.

How Knowledgeable Is Your Audience?

Listeners differ greatly in the knowledge they have. Some listeners will be quite knowledgeable about the topic, others will be almost totally ignorant. Mixed audiences are the most difficult ones. Treat audiences that lack knowledge of the topic very carefully. Never confuse a lack of knowledge with a lack of ability to understand.

- Don't talk down to your audience. No one wants to listen to a speaker putting them down.
- Don't confuse a lack of knowledge with a lack of intelligence. An audience may have no knowledge of your topic but be quite capable of following a clearly presented, logically developed argument. Try especially hard to use concrete examples, audiovisual aids, and simple language. Fill in background details as required. Avoid jargon and specialized terms that may not be clear to someone new to the subject. Never overestimate your audience's knowledge but never underestimate their intelligence. Audiences with much knowledge also require special handling because their response may well be, "Why should I listen to this? I already know about this topic."
- Let the audience know that you're aware of their knowledge and expertise. Try to do this as early in the speech as possible. Emphasize that what you have to say will not be redundant. Tell them that you'll be presenting recent developments or new approaches. In short, let them know that they will not be wasting their time listening to your speech.
- Emphasize your credibility, especially your competence in this general subject area.

Analysis and Adaptation During the Speech

In your classroom speeches, you'll face a known audience, an audience you've already analyzed and for which you've made appropriate adaptations. At other times, however, you may face an audience that you haven't been able to analyze beforehand or one that differs greatly from the audience you thought you would address. In these cases you'll have to analyze and adapt to them as you speak. Here are a few suggestions:

As you prepare your speech, keep your audience clearly in mind. For example, let's say you've been told that you're to explain the opportunities available to the nontraditional student at your college. You've been told that your audience will consist mainly of working women in their 30s and 40s who are just beginning college. As you prepare your speech with this audience in mind, ask yourself, for example: What if the audience has a large number of men? What if the audience consisted of women much older than 40? What if the audience members also came with their spouses or their children? Keeping such questions in mind will force you to consider alternatives as you prepare your speech. And you'll find them readily available as you face this new or different audience.

Focus on listeners as message senders. As you're speaking, look at your listeners. Remember that just as you're sending messages to your audience, they're also sending messages to you. Just as they're responding to what you're communicating, you need to respond to what they're communicating. Pay attention to these messages and on the basis of what these tell you, make the necessary adjustments. If your audience shows signs of boredom, you might increase your volume, move closer to them, or tell them that what you're going to say will be of value to them. If your audience shows signs of disagreement or hostility, you might stress some similarity you have with them. If your audience looks puzzled or confused, you might pause a moment and rephrase your ideas, provide necessary definitions, or insert an internal summary. If your audience seems impatient, you might say, for example, "my last argument . . ." instead of your originally planned "my third argument . . . ."

Another way of dealing with audience responses is to confront them directly and say to those who seem puzzled, "I know this plan may seem confusing, but bear with me; it will become clear in a moment." Or, to those who seem impatient, you might respond: "I know this has been a long day but give me just a few more minutes and you'll be able to save hours recording your accounts." By responding to your listeners' reactions and feedback, you acknowledge your audience's needs. You let them know that you hear them, that you're with them, and that you're responding to their needs.

Audience Analysis and Ethics

When advertisers conduct audience research, they're interested in learning about their audience so they can develop more effective persuasive strategies to help them make a greater profit by enabling them to sell more products or services. And while the profit motive isn't unethical, it does raise ethical issues when it takes precedence over audience welfare, for example, when advertising is directed at selling products that are dangerous or unhealthy for the audience or simply overpriced. Cigarettes and cigars, cereals and snacks loaded with sugar and high-cholesterol fats, and certain brand name sneakers come to mind most quickly. This is quite different from the purpose of audience research as explained here. The objective of the public speaker is surely to be more persuasive, but the audience's best interests and welfare must come first.

This isn't to say that you shouldn't speak out of personal interest. It is to argue, however, that speakers should never exploit their audiences or speak out of a self-interest that may be harmful to the listeners. If a speaker asks an audience to listen to a speech and to do certain things, it should be for their ultimate benefit. It would be unethical, for example, to persuade an audience to take up arms in a self-destructive war, to buy homes in a flood zone, or to donate money to an embezzling organization.

STEP 3. RESEARCH YOUR SPEECH TOPIC

Suppose that you're to speak on immigration policies. Where do you go for information? How can you learn about the different immigration policies? How do you find the evidence and arguments bearing on current policies and proposed changes? What are the legal issues involved? What were the prominent legal battles? What are the moral implications of the varied immigration policies and proposals? How does granting asylum to political dissidents impact on immigration policy? Research will enable you to answer these and hundreds of other questions.

Traditional printed books, journals, magazines, newspapers, and pamphlets are now used alongside computerized sources such as e-mail, newsgroups, the World Wide Web, and a vast array of computerized databases. Because the information available on just about any topic is so vast, it's understandably daunting for many people. At the same time, however, the same technology that has produced this tremendous expansion of available information has also made searching through it relatively easy and efficient.

General Principles of Research

After you've selected your topic, you'll need to find information on it—statistics, arguments for or against a proposition, examples, biographical data,

UNDERSTANDING
Theory and Research

WHAT ARE YOUR RESEARCH COMPETENCIES?

Indicate the research competencies you possess by responding to each of the following items with the following scale: A = finding this would be simple; B = finding this would be possible, but would take some effort; and C = finding this would be impossible without asking someone for help.

_____ An article on India that appeared in the *New York Times* sometime in 1998

_____ Ten newsgroups dealing with the topic of computers

_____ 10 listservs dealing with topics relating to your professional goal

_____ The most recent stock quotation for IBM

_____ Ten abstracts of articles dealing with hepatitis

_____ The communication courses (or pick another department) offered at Kansas State University (or pick another school)

_____ The population of Toronto and Tokyo

_____ The speeches given during the last session of Congress

_____ The biography of a state political figure

_____ Recent law cases dealing with sexual harassment

One way to review this test and this topic generally is to share your responses and your own research strengths and weaknesses in a small group of five or six others. As you discuss the various responses also consider: Which avenues of research are the most efficient? Which are the most reliable? Which will prove the most credible with your peers?

---

or research findings, for example. Here are some general principles to help you do your research more efficiently and effectively.

- Examine what you know. Do you know about books or Web sites on the topic or persons who might know something about the topic? Do you have personal experiences and observations that can be used?

- Work from the general to the specific. An encyclopedia article will serve this purpose well as will a visit to the Web and querying a few search engines for a general overview. Many of these articles contain references or links that will direct you to more specific and detailed information.

- Take accurate notes. Accuracy in the beginning will save you from wasting time going back to sources to check something or to sources you've already consulted. If you want to collect your material on paper, a looseleaf notebook works well to keep everything relating to a

speech or article in the same place. If you want to file your material electronically, create a folder and title it something like *PublicSpeaking/Speech1:Immigration*. This will work especially well if you have a scanner and can scan into your folder material you find in print.

- Learn the available sources of information. Learn where the most useful materials are located or how they can be accessed. Learn the computer search facilities available at your college for accessing newspapers, research articles, corporate reports, magazines, or any type of media you may wish to use. Find out what databases are available. And, perhaps the most useful suggestion of all: talk with your librarian. Librarians are experts in the very issues that may be giving you trouble and will be able to help you in accessing biographical material, indexes of current articles, materials in specialized collections at other libraries, and a wide variety of computerized databases.

General Internet Resources

Although you will no doubt use a variety of research sources—both print and electronic—it's important to realize at the start that it's a lot easier to do your research by computer. Perhaps the greatest advantage is that in computer research you browse through a larger number of sources in less time and with greater accuracy and thoroughness than you could do manually. And, in many cases, you can do this research at your own convenience, since electronic sources are available 24 hours a day, and from your own home. A further convenience is that you can download the information to your computer or print it out instead of copying it longhand as had to be done just a few years ago. There are three major Internet avenues you'll want to consider in researching your speeches: e-mail, newsgroups, and the World Wide Web.

E-mail

Through **e-mail** you can write to specific people or a group or a listserv, which is an e-mail list of several to perhaps hundreds of people who exchange messages on a relatively specific topic at a rate of perhaps several to hundreds a week. Some messages will be from other members and some will be postings from, for example, the press, which some member copies and distributes.

E-mail may prove useful in public speaking in several ways. For example, you can write to specific people who may be experts in the topic you're researching. Internet services are now making it quite easy to locate a person's e-mail address. Try, for example, the Netscape people page, which you can access from Netscape's home page or by going to http://guide.netscape.com/guide/people.html, or Yahoo's directory (http://www.yahoo.com/search/people/) and its links to numerous other directories such as Yahoo's white pages (http://www.yahoo.com/Reference/White-Pages/). Another useful people search tool is http://www.procd.com/hl/direct.htm. Also, try the sites that specialize in e-mail addresses such as Four11 (http://www.four11.com), Who Where? (http://www.whowhere.com), and Switchboard (www.switchboard.com). Four11 also provides a directory of regular telephone numbers as well as special directories for government personnel and celebrities.

You can use e-mail to join a mailing list or listserv that focuses on the topic you're researching and learn from the collective insights of all members. You can explore potentially useful listservs by using Liszt (www.liszt.com), a directory of information about a wide variety of listservs and whether new members are welcomed (see Going Online, on page 297). When joining a listserv, remember to lurk before contributing; get a feel for the group and for the types of messages its members send. Read the FAQs to avoid asking questions that have already been answered. The types of questions listserv members seem to favor are those that ask for ideas and insights rather than those that ask for information readily available elsewhere.

If your class were set up as a listserv, you would be able to communicate with everyone else through e-mail. You would be able, for example, to distribute an audience analysis questionnaire to see what your audience knows about your topic or what their attitudes are about a variety of issues. You'd also be able to set up a critique group with a few accepting and supportive others in your class to get feedback on your speech or outline. Such a group would also be helpful for people who want to ask questions or try out an idea before presenting it in the actual speech.

Newsgroups

Newsgroups are discussion forums for the exchange of ideas on a wide variety of topics. There are thousands of newsgroups on the Internet (the overall system of newsgroups is referred to as Usenet) where you can post your messages (also called "articles" or "posts"), read the messages of others, and respond to the messages you read. Messages, replies to them, replies to the replies, and so on constitute a thread, a collection of messages unified by a focus on a specific topic. Newsgroups are much like listservs in that they bring together a group of people interested in communicating about a common topic. Some newsgroups also include messages from news services such as the Associated Press or Reuters.

Newsgroups are useful sources of information; they contain news items, letters, and papers on just about any topic you can think of. Because there are so many newsgroups, you should have no problem finding several that deal with topics on which you'll be speaking. You can also save the news items you're particularly interested in to your own file.

Going Online

Liszt Web site

This is currently the most widely used search engine for information on listservs. But, notice that it also searches for newsgroups and IRC groups. Try accessing this. Can you find any listservs that focus on topics relevant to your next speech?

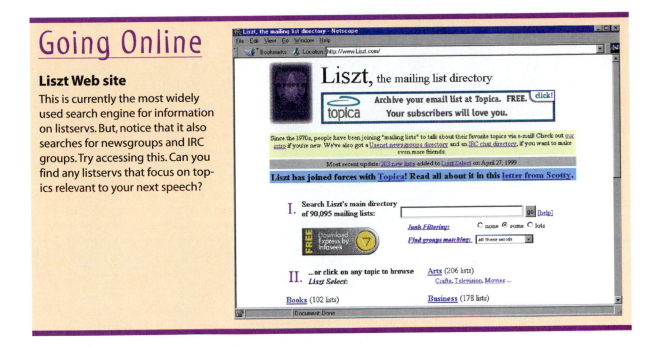

Search engines such as Deja News, or any of a variety of others will search the available newsgroups for the topics you request. You simply submit keywords that best describe your research topic and the program will search its database of newsgroups and return a list of article titles and authors along with the date on which they were written and a relevance score for each article. You can then click on any of the titles that seem most closely related to what you're looking for.

Those newsgroups that get news feeds are especially useful because the information is current and very likely in greater detail than you'd find in newspapers, which have to cut copy to fit space limitations. You're also more likely to find a greater diversity of viewpoints than you'd find in, say, the standard news magazines like *Time* or *Newsweek*. Another advantage is that through newsgroups you can ask questions and get the opinions of others for your next speech. Newsgroups also provide an easily available and generally receptive audience to whom you can communicate your thoughts and feelings. Reading through the FAQ file (frequently asked questions)—http://sunsite.unc.edu/usenet-i/info-center-faq.html—will help you get the maximum benefit from Usenet connections.

The World Wide Web

The **World Wide Web** is the most interesting and most valuable part of the Internet for research; it's a collection of documents—some containing graphic, audio, and video components. Some documents appear in abstract and increasingly in full-text form. Newspapers, newsmagazines, and numerous books are available in full text through a publisher or library. Some Web sites are available to the general public and others are available only by subscription.

In some instances you may know the Web address of the source you want to consult. In this case you would access the Web site by simply entering the address in your Web browser. Fortunately, Web addresses are becoming more standardized, making it easier for you to predict many relevant addresses. For example, the Web address of most corporations follow the same general format: www.NameOfCorporation.com, for example, www.Microsoft.com. You can access these Web sites for copies of speeches, annual reports, or other information you might need for your speech. Generally, this information will be sent to your e-mail address so you'd be able to print out whatever they send.

In most cases, however, searching the Web efficiently for speech topics requires the use of a search engine and some knowledge of how they operate. A **search engine** is a program that enables you to

One cyberlibrarian draws a distinction between "technophiles" who think everything on the Web is accurate and trustworthy and "technophobes" who think just the reverse and try to discredit information on the Internet (James-Catalano 1996). How do you feel about information on the Internet? Do these attitudes influence the way you use and evaluate Internet information?

search a database or index of Internet sites for the specific words you submit. These search engines are easily accessed through your Internet browser. And, in fact, the popular browsers—Netscape and Internet Explorer, for example—have search functions as a part of their own home pages; they also provide convenient links to the most popular search engines and directories.

Most search engines operate similarly; you type in a word or phrase and the program searches its databases and returns a list of sites (sometimes with an indication of how relevant the source will be to you and sometimes with a brief description of the site you can click on to visit).

A **directory** serves a similar function, but does it in a different way. A directory is a list of subjects or categories of Web links. You begin the process by selecting the category you're most interested in, and then a subcategory of that, and then a subcategory of that until you reach the specific topic you're interested in. Many search engines also provide directories. Yahoo, Excite, and Infoseek (among others), for example, are both search engines and directories. Other popular directories include Magellan (http://www.mckinley.com/) and Point (http://www.pointcom.com/).

Because the databases these engines search are so vast and because they search for all occurrences of the words you submit, they invariably pull up lots of noise—documents that are totally unrelated to what you're looking for. Because of this it's important to learn to narrow your search and ask the search engine to look for specific rather than general topics. Further, most of the search engines and directories—despite their frequent updates—will include a variety of expired links. Expect this; it's one of the inevitable problems created by a system that's so vast in size and changing so rapidly.

Because each search engine or directory uses a somewhat different database and a different method for searching, no two search engines will yield the exact same results even when the exact same request is submitted to each. So, when conducting research, be sure to use several of these search engines and directories. A good practice is to bookmark or list among your "favorites" each of the major search engines and directories, for example, Yahoo at http://www.yahoo.com, Excite at http://www.excite.com, HotBot at http://www.hotbot.com, Alta Vista at http://altavista.digital.com, Infoseek at http://www.infoseek.com, and Lycos at http://www.lycos.com.

Databases

A **database** is organized information contained in one place. A dictionary, an encyclopedia, and an index to magazines are all examples of databases. A database may be in print, for example, *Psychological Abstracts*, or computerized, for example, *Psychlit*.

Here we look at databases under four headings: general reference sources, news, research and general interest articles and posts, and books.

General Reference Sources

General reference sources are often your first stop in conducting research. These resources provide you with some basic information that can help you think more clearly about your topic and provide you with leads to more specialized sources. Here, we discuss just a few general sources: encyclopedias, biographical dictionaries, almanacs, and a somewhat dissimilar source, museum collections and exhibits.

Encyclopedias. One of the best places to start researching your topic is a standard **encyclopedia**. It will give you a general overview of the subject and suggestions for additional reading. Many encyclopedias are available on personal CD ROMS and online (for example, *Encyclopedia Britannica*, *Encarta*, *Collier's*, *Comptoms*, and *Grolier's*). Many of these also have Web sites that provide frequent updates and other additional material. There are also many specialized encyclopedias. Those devoted to religion include the *New Catholic Encyclopedia* (15 volumes), *Encyclopedia Judaica* (16 volumes plus yearbooks), *Encyclopedia of Islam*, and *Encyclopedia of Buddhism*. Supplement these with appropriate Web sites devoted to specific religions, for example, http://www.utm.edu/martinarea/fbc/bfm.html (Southern Baptist), http://www.catholic.org/index.html (Catholic), http://www.geocities.com/RodeaDrive/1415/indexd.html (Hinduism), http://www.utexas.edu/students/amso (Islam), and http://jewishnet.net (Jewish-related sites).

Biographical Material. When you want information about a person, take a look at the *Biography and Genealogy Master Index*; it indexes over 350 biographical indexes. This index will lead you to the best index for the information you want. There are numerous specialized works to which this index will send you. Here are just a few to give you an idea of the breadth and depth of biographical research: *Dictionary of American Biography* (for deceased Americans), *Current Biography*, and *Who's Who in America* (both covering living Americans).

Not surprisingly, there are lots of Internet sources for biographical information. For example, http://mgm.mit.edu:8080/pevzner/Nobel.html, provides links to biographical information on all Nobel Prize winners. If you want information on members of the House of Representatives try http://www.house.gov. And http://www.biography.com/ will provide you with brief biographies of some 15,000 famous people, living and dead. Still another way to search for information on a person is to simply type the name of the person into one or more search engines or directories.

Almanacs. Should you want information on the world's languages, household income, presidential elections, the countries of the world, national defense, sports, noted personalities, economics and employment, the environment, awards and prizes, science and technology, health and medicine, maps, world travel information, or postal rates, an almanac will prove extremely useful. Numerous inexpensive versions published annually are among the most up-to-date sources of information on many topics. The most popular are *The World Almanac and Book of Facts* (also available on CD-ROM), the *Information Please Almanac*, *The Universal Almanac*, and *The Canadian Almanac and Directory*.

The annual *Statistical Abstract of the United States* contains the most complete statistical data on population, vital statistics, health, education, law, geography and environment, elections, finances and employment, defense, insurance, labor, income, prices, banking, and a wide variety of other topics. Useful Web sites include http://cedr.1b1.gov/cdrom/doc/lookup_doc.html for U. S. census data and http://www.cs.cmu.edu/Web/references.html, which provides links to a wide variety of relevant reference materials.

News Sources

Often you'll want to read reports on accidents, political speeches, congressional actions, obituaries, financial news, international developments, United Nations actions, or any of a host of other topics. Or you may wish to locate the time of a particular event and learn something about what else was going on in the world at that particular time. For this type of information you may want to consult a reliable newspaper. Many speeches rely to some extent on news, whether local, national, or international. Especially relevant are newspaper indexes, newspaper databases, newspaper and magazine Web sites, news wire services, and news networks on line.

One way to start a newspaper search is to consult one of the newspaper indexes your college has, for example, the *National Newspaper Index*, which covers

27 newspapers, including the *Christian Science Monitor*, *The New York Times*, *The Wall Street Journal*, *The Los Angeles Times*, and *The Washington Post*. Each of these newspapers also has its own index.

Many newspapers can be accessed online or through CD ROM databases to which your college library probably subscribes. The *New York Times* database, for example, contains the full editorial content of the paper, one of the world's most comprehensive newspapers. All aspects of news, sports, editorials, columns, obituaries, New York and regional news, and the *New York Times Book Review* and *Magazine* are included. You can search this database by subject terms, personal names, or company names. Many features also contain brief 25 word abstracts.

Most newspapers maintain their own Web sites from which you can access current and past issues. Here are a few to get you started: Http://www.latimes.com/ (Los Angeles Times), http://www.usatoday.com/ (USA Today), http://journal.link.wsj.com/ (Wall Street Journal), http://www.washingtonpost.com/ (Washington Post). A particularly useful Web site is http://www.newslink.org/menu.html, which provides access to a variety of online newspapers and magazines. Http://nt.excite.com/?uid= offers a variety of news items and allows you to search the news index.

Two wire services should prove helpful. The Associated Press can be accessed at http://www1.trib.com/ NEWS/Apwire.html and Reuters at http://www.reuters.com/. The advantage of getting your information from a news wire service is that it's more complete than you would find in a newspaper, which has to cut copy to fit space requirements and, in some cases, may put a politically or socially motivated spin on the news.

All of the television news stations maintain extremely useful Web sites. Here are some of the most useful: Access CNN at http://www.cnn.com/, ESPN at http://espn.sportszone.com/, ABC News at http://www.abcnews.com/newsflash, CBS News at http://www.cbs.com/news/, and MSNBC News at http://www.msnbc.com/news.

Research and General Interest Articles and Posts

Very often you'll want to read academic research articles in professional research journals or general interest articles in magazines or in postings online. **Academic research** forms the core of what we know about people and the world. These are reports of studies conducted by researchers from a wide variety of fields. For the most part, this research is conducted by unbiased researchers using the best research methods available. Further, this research is subjected to careful critical review by experts in the specific research field and is the most valid and the most reliable information you're likely to find. On occasion, however, poorly researched articles as well as small and large mistakes may get published in these journals, so don't assume one hundred percent accuracy and reliability.

Each college library subscribes to a somewhat different package of CD ROM and online databases to access these academic journals. Unlike the personal CD ROM encyclopedias and almanacs, these CD ROMs are vastly larger and are available by subscription. Some of those your college library is likely to have include: *America: History and Life* (contains citations and abstracts of the major scholarly literature in history and surveys over 2,100 journals); Psychlit and Sociofile contain citations from approximately 1,300 journals in psychology and from about 1,600 journals in sociology, respectively; *Medline* (the definitive source in the United States for biomedical literature, contains citations from over 3700 journals "selected for inclusion because of their importance to health professions"); ERIC (covers over 750 journals and provides complete citations and abstracts of 200 to 300 words).

General interest articles in magazines differ greatly from the research articles in professional journals. For example, they're most often written by professional writers rather than researchers. Magazine articles may be summaries of the research by others or they may be largely in the nature of opinion. Often, they're simplified accounts of rather complex issues written for the general public rather than an audience of professional researchers. Further, they seldom undergo the rigorous review process that accompanies publication in a professional academic journal. As a result, articles appearing in popular magazines are much less reliable than those appearing in such professional research journals as, say, *Communication Monographs*, *Journal of Experimental Psychology*, or *The New England Journal of Medicine*. Nevertheless, magazine articles and general posts are often very helpful for speakers. Here are a few suggestions for finding the information you want.

Indexes. The *Readers' Guide to Periodical Literature* (in print or electronic form) covers magazine articles for the period from 1900 to the present. This guide indexes by subject and by author (in one convenient alphabetical index) articles published in about 180 different magazines. *Readers' Guide* is valuable for its broad coverage, but it's limited in that it covers mostly general publications and only a few of the more specialized ones. The *Alternative Press Index* indexes almost 200 magazines, newspapers, and journals that might be labeled "radical." This index is valuable for speakers dealing with such issues as the Third World, minority rights, socialism, and the like. *Access* also indexes publications not covered in *Reader's Guide*. The online LEXIS/NEXIS System allows you to retrieve the complete text of articles from hundreds of newspapers, magazines, journals, and even newsletters in addition to a wide variety of legal and statutory records.

Listservs, Usenet groups, and the World Wide Web.

These resources, as explained earlier in this unit, contain a wide variety of articles, many more than you could possibly use in one or even many speeches. Explore relevant listservs through Liszt (www.liszt.com), newsgroups through DejaNews (www.DejaNews.com), and the vast array of World Wide Web documents with the help of the numerous search engines.

Book Sources

There are two major ways to find books—through a library and through a bookstore. Generally, you would access your material by looking up your major subject heading(s). A good way to do this is to make a list of the five or six major concepts that appear in your speech and look each of these up in the library catalog. Create a complete bibliography of available sources and examine each one. Sometimes, you may want to locate the works by or about a particular person. In this case, you would simply look up the author's name much as you would a concept or, even better, consult one of the available biographical sources (explained previously).

Both general and specialized online libraries are available. The Library of Congress (http://www.loc.gov/) provides an online catalog of all its holdings as well as links to Internet search engines and a variety of useful indexes for researching a wide variety of topics. Useful directories to libraries, most in North America and Europe, can be found at http://www.llv.com/~msauers/libs/libs/html. And an

especially rich source of links to reference cites can be found at http://www.state.wi.us/agencies/dpi/www/lib_res.html.

If you're talking about something that people are interested in today, there's likely to be a book dealing with it. Visit your local bookstore as well as some of the online bookstores, for example, Amazon.com, BarnesandNobel.com, or Borders.com. Visit the Library of Congress (http://lcweb.loc.gov) to discover any book at all—the Library of Congress maintains records on all books published in the United States. In addition, other useful sites include: http://aaup.pupress.princeton.edu/ (Association of American University Presses), http://www.cs.cmu.edu/Web/People/spok/banned-books.html (contains links to texts of books that have been banned in the United States and elsewhere), and http://www.booksite.com/ (contains search tools for locating over two million books).

Critically Evaluating Research

Collecting research materials—whether from traditional print sources, listservs and the Web, or interviews with experts—is only part of the process; the other part is critically evaluating them. Here are some questions to ask in critically evaluating research.

Is the Information Current?

Generally, the more recent the material, the more useful it will be. With some topics, for example, unemployment statistics, developments in AIDS research, and tuition costs, the recency of the information is crucial to its usefulness. Check important figures in a recent *Almanac*, newspaper, or frequently updated Internet source.

The date of a newspaper, the copyright date of a book, or the date of a cited article or e-mail will help you identify the recency of the information. Unfortunately, not all Internet documents are dated and so at times you won't be able to tell when the document was written. You may, however, be able to write to the author and ask since many Internet writers include their e-mail address.

Is the Information Fair and Unbiased?

Bias is not easy to determine, but do try to examine any sources of potential bias. Obvious examples come quickly to mind: cigarette manufacturers' statements on the health risks from smoking; newspaper

BUILDING
Communication Skills

HOW DO YOU CONDUCT ELECTRONIC RESEARCH?

This exercise is designed to illustrate the wide variety of information you can easily secure from computer searches and to focus attention on the process of conducting research rather than simply on finding the answer. As you attempt to find the answer to one or more of these items, try to focus on the processes you're following—take note, for example, of wrong turns and how you might develop more efficient strategies for locating such information.

- An article on public speaking that appears in the ERIC database in the last five years
- An article on a psychological study on fear from the Psychlit database

- An article on persuasion from the Sociofile database
- An article appearing in *The Quarterly Journal of Speech*, *Communication Monographs*, or *Communication Education* that is of some interest to you
- An article from a business journal dealing with communication skills
- An article from any online newspaper dealing with college education
- An article on diabetes from *Medline* and one from the Web
- A list of listservs or Usenet groups concerned with ecological issues
- An article on divorce from any database, using any of the major search engines
- An article on immigration patterns during the last 20 years from *America: History and Life*
- A review of Frank McCourt's *Angela's Ashes*

and network editorials on the fairness of news reporting; and the National Rifle Association's arguments against gun control. Try checking the credibility of your sources in a biographical dictionary or in relevant newspaper articles. Reviewing the research in the area will enable you to see how other experts view the author of a particular article. It will also enable you to see if the author's view of the situation takes into consideration all sides of the issue and if these sides are represented fairly and accurately. In some cases, the author presents her or his credentials, and these can easily be checked should you wish to.

Distinguish between primary and secondary source material. Primary sources include, for example, the original research study as reported in an academic journal or a corporation's annual report. Secondary sources include, for example, summaries of the research appearing in popular

magazines and television news reports on a corporation's earnings. When using secondary sources, examine the information for any particular spin the writer may be giving the material. If possible, you may wish to check with the primary source to see what might have been left out or if the conclusions are really warranted on the basis of the primary evidence.

Recognize that anyone can "publish" on the Internet. An article on the Internet can be written by world-renowned scientists or by elementary school students, by fair and objective reporters or by those who would spin the issues to serve political or religious or social purposes. And it's not always easy to tell which is which. Find out what the author's qualifications are. Look carefully at any statistics or figures. Are these cited from reliable and recent sources? One useful technique used by many Web writers is to include Internet links in

Going Online

Teaching Undergrads Web Evaluation

This Web page, although addressed to librarians, provides 5 criteria for evaluating Internet materials. Try applying these criteria to Web site material. How effectively does this system help you evaluate Internet material? Other Web sites addressed to this issue include: Alastair Smith's http://www.vuw.ac.nz, Elizabeth Kirk's http://milton.mse.jhu.edu:8001/ research/education/net.html (both suggested by Harnack & Kleppinger, 1997), and Janice Walker's http:longman.awl.com/podium/citation_walker_eval.htm.

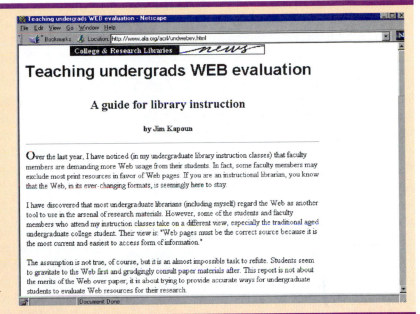

Teaching undergrads WEB evaluation - Netscape

College & Research Libraries *news*

Teaching undergrads WEB evaluation

A guide for library instruction

by Jim Kapoun

Over the last year, I have noticed (in my undergraduate library instruction classes) that faculty members are demanding more Web usage from their students. In fact, some faculty members may exclude most print resources in favor of Web pages. If you are an instructional librarian, you know that the Web, in its ever-changing formats, is seemingly here to stay.

I have discovered that most undergraduate librarians (including myself) regard the Web as another tool to use in the arsenal of research materials. However, some of the students and faculty members who attend my instruction classes take on a different view, especially the traditional aged undergraduate college student. Their view is: "Web pages must be the correct source because it is the most current and easiest to access form of information."

The assumption is not true, of course, but it is an almost impossible task to refute. Students seem to gravitate to the Web first and grudgingly consult paper materials after. This report is not about the merits of the Web over paper; it is about trying to provide accurate ways for undergraduate students to evaluate Web resources for their research.

---

their document to the sources from which they derived, say, their statistics or predictions or arguments. If you find these links, it's often worth checking them to see if the author did in fact fairly and accurately present the information.

Recognize also, however, that much information on the Internet is identical to the information you regularly read in print. Encyclopedias, newspapers and newsmagazines, and professional journals that appear on the Internet are often identical to the print copies, so there's no need to draw distinctions between print and Internet information when dealing with sites such as these.

Is the Evidence Reliable and the Reasoning Logical?

The most important question in evaluating research must focus on the evidence and reasoning used in arriving at a conclusion. Ask yourself if the conclusions have been arrived at logically rather than, say, emotionally. Does the author offer clear evidence and sound arguments to support conclusions rather than, say, anecdotes or testimonials from like-minded people?

Another way to estimate reliability is look at the publisher. Note especially if the publisher is a special interest group with a specific corporate, reli-

gious, political, or social agenda. If so, try to balance this perspective with information that represents the other sides of the issue.

On the other hand, if an article appears in a journal sponsored by the American Psychological Association or the National Communication Association, for example, you can be pretty sure that the article has been carefully reviewed by experts before publication. If an article appears in *The New York Times*, *The Washington Post*, *The Wall Street Journal* or any of the major newsmagazines or news networks, again, you can be pretty sure that the information is reliable. Both textbook and trade book publishers go to enormous effort to insure the accuracy of what appears in print. A textbook, for example, is normally reviewed by perhaps 10 to 20 professionals in the specific field before it ever sees the light of day.

This claim of accuracy is, of course, a generalization that has on occasion been proven false. Recently, for example, a writer from *The Boston Globe* was found to have fabricated stories in her columns. *The Cincinnati Enquirer* paid the Chiquita corporation over $10 million for stories the newspaper later said were "untrue." And, in perhaps the most widely publicized example, both CNN and *Time* magazine apologized for claiming that the United States military had used lethal gas in Laos that was intended to kill American defectors (*The New York Times*, Section 4, July 5, 1998, p. 2). So, inaccuracies do creep into even the most respected sources.

Some Internet sources contain "about" files that will help you learn more about the author and perhaps the author's sources. Sometimes you'll be able to contact the author via e-mail. An interesting exercise for evaluating sources may be found on http://long-man.awl.com/podium/citation_walker_eval.htm.

Integrating Research into the Speech

By integrating and acknowledging your sources of information in the speech, you'll give fair credit to those whose ideas and statements you're using and at the same time you'll help establish your own reputation as a responsible researcher. Here are a few suggestions for integrating your research into your speech.

Mention the sources in your speech by citing at least the author and, if helpful, the publication and the date.

Provide smooth transitions between your words and the words of the author you're citing. Notice how, in this excerpt, Nancy Dickenson-Hazard (1998, p. 495) mentions the source and smoothly quotes from the book:

> David McNally, author of *Even Eagles Need a Push*, believes inspired persons know why they do what they do and why they want what they want. Furthermore, he says, "people perform at their best when contributing their talents to something they believe in."

Avoid useless expressions such as "I have a quote here" or "I want to quote an example." Let the audience know that you're quoting by pausing before the quote, taking a step forward, or referring to your notes to read the extended quotation. Marilyn Loden (1986, p. 473) does this effectively:

> Mary Kay Ash believes in feminine leadership. Recently she said: "A woman can no more duplicate the male style of leadership than an American businessman can exactly reproduce the Japanese style."

If you feel it's crucial that the audience know you're quoting and you want to state that this is a quotation, you might do it this way:

> Recently, Mary Kay Ash put this in perspective, and I quote: "A woman can no more duplicate the male style of leadership than an American businessman can exactly reproduce the Japanese style."

Use "signal verbs" in your speech to let the audience know your own evaluation of the material (Harnack & Kleppinger 1997). Let's say, for example, that in an Internet article by Pat Doe you read the statement "Low self-esteem influences speaker apprehension." You can preface that information with a variety of signal verbs such as *has proven that, says, argues that, speculates that, has found that, thinks,* and *wonders if,* for example, and say "Pat Doe *speculates that* low self-esteem influences speaker apprehension," which, of course, is quite different from "Pat Doe *has proven that* low self-esteem influences speaker apprehension" (you might then go on to explain briefly how this was proven). Select the verb that best represents what Pat Doe said and meant and at the same time the support or lack of support that you're attributing to Pat's statement. You may find it helpful to modify your verb in some way, for example, "convincingly argues" or "wildly speculates" to further indicate your support or lack of it.

Avoid Even the Suggestion of Plagiarism. Plagiarism is committed when you use material from another source without properly crediting it. There are a number of forms this can take.

- **Using the exact words of another person.** If you're going to use another person's exact words, then cite them exactly as they were written or spoken and credit the source. For example, in a speech on nonverbal communication in different cultures, you might say something like this:

> According to Roger Axtell, in his *Gestures: The Do's and Taboos of Body Language Around the World*, touching varies from one culture to another. Axtell says, for example, "In the Middle East, two Arab male friends may even be seen walking down the street hand-in-hand and all it signifies is friendship."

In your outline, give the full bibliographic reference just as you would in a history paper. Be sure you use quotation marks for any citation in which you use the person's exact words, just as you would in a written essay. And, make it clear to your listeners that you're using the person's exact words as was done in the example above. You can do this by changing your inflection, stepping forward, or reading the specific words from your notes. In this way, the audience will know that the exact words belong to someone else.

- **Using the ideas of another person.** Even if you're not quoting directly, you still have to acknowledge your source if you're using the ideas, arguments, insights, examples, or even organizational structure taken from another source. If you're using the ideas of another, simply acknowledge this in your speech and in any written materials such as an outline. Much as readers of an essay have the right to know where your arguments or data came from, so do listeners. Therefore, weave into your speech the sources of your materials. Do this with subtlety and without disturbing the natural flow and rhythm of your speech. Here are a few examples.

A recent article in *Time* magazine noted that. . . .

Professor Fox, in her lecture last week on Western Civilization, argued that. . . .

This week Nielsen reported that the number of homes with color televisions. . . .

- **Using the organizational structure of another.** Even if you're "only" following the organizational structure of another source, you need to acknowledge your indebtedness. In these cases, you can say something like this:

I'm here following the arguments given by Professor Marishu in her lecture on culture and racism.

This pattern for explaining how a car is designed comes from the work of Edward Frid in his new book, *Designing a Car*.

SUMMARY

This unit introduced the nature of public speaking and covered selecting and limiting the topic and purpose, analyzing and adapting to your audience, and researching your speech.

1. The preparation of a public speech involves ten steps: (1) select the topic and purpose, (2) analyze the audience, (3) research the topic, (4) formulate the thesis and identify the major problems, (5) support the major propositions, (6) organize the speech materials, (7) construct the conclusion, introduction, and transitions, (8) outline the speech, (9) word the speech, and (10) rehearse and deliver the speech. The first four of these were discussed in this unit; the remaining six are discussed in the next two units.

2. Speech topics should deal with significant issues that interest the audience. Subjects and purposes should be limited in scope.

3. In analyzing the audience, consider age; sex; cultural factors; occupation, income, and status; religion and religiousness; the occasion; and the specific context.

4. Formulate the thesis of the speech. Develop your major propositions by asking relevant questions about this thesis.

5. Research the topic, beginning with general sources and gradually exploring more specific and specialized sources.

KEY TERMS

public speaking (p. 281)

public speaking apprehension (p. 282)

systematic desensitization (p. 283)

performance visualization (p. 283)

topic (p. 285)

taboos (p. 285)

brainstorming (p. 286)

topoi (p. 287)

tree diagrams (p. 287)

search directories (p. 288)

general purpose (p. 288)

specific purpose (p. 289)

audience (p. 289)

audience analysis (p. 289)

attitude (p. 290)

belief (p. 290)

value (p. 290)

sociological analysis (p. 290)

audience willingness (p. 292)

audience favor (p. 293)

audience knowledge (p. 293)

e-mail (p. 296)

newsgroups (p. 296)

World Wide Web (p. 297)

search engine (p. 297)

directory (p. 298)

database (p. 298)

primary and secondary source material (p. 302)

THINKING CRITICALLY ABOUT
Public Speaking Topics, Audiences, and Research

1. Access the Psychlit, Sociofile, or ERIC database and search for the key terms and concepts discussed in this unit: for example, attitude, value, belief, and audience psychology. On the basis of this search what might you add to this unit's discussion?

2. Using Liszt (www.liszt.com) explore the listservs that deal with topics related to your next speech. How many can you find? Using DejaNews (www.dejanews.com) investigate the available newsgroups dealing with topics related to your next speech. Try to find at least three.

3. One of the common beliefs about religious people is that they're more honest, more charitable, and more likely to reach out to those in need than would the nonreligious. A review of research, however, finds even this seemingly logical connection not true (Kohn 1989). For example, in a study of cheating among college students, religious beliefs bore little relationship to honesty; in fact, atheists were less likely to cheat than those who identified themselves as religious. Other studies have found that religious people were not any more likely to help those in need, for example, to give time to work with retarded children or to comfort someone lying in the street. What assumptions about people's behavior can you make from knowing only that they are very religious?

4. Jack is scheduled to give a speech on careers in computer technology to a group of high school students who have been forced to attend career day on a Saturday and attend at least three of the speeches. The audience is definitely an unwilling one. What advice can you give Jack to help him deal with this type of audience?

5. Jill wants to give a speech on television talk shows and wants to include biographical information on some of the talk show hosts. What sources might Jill go to in order to get authoritative and current information on these hosts? What sources might she go to in order to get "fan" type information? What advice would you give Jill for distinguishing the two types of sources and information?

6. Prepare and deliver a two-minute speech in which you
   - evaluate the topics of recent talk shows against the criteria for a worthwhile and appropriate topic
   - explain the cultural factors operating in this class that need to be taken into consideration by the speaker selecting a topic and purpose
   - explain a particularly strong belief that you hold
   - describe members of your class in terms of how willing, favorable, and knowledgeable you see them to be about any specific topic or speaker
   - describe the audience of a popular magazine or television show or movie
   - explain the value of one reference book, Web site, database, listserv, or newsgroup for research in public speaking

UNIT 16

Supporting and Organizing Your Speech

UNIT CONTENTS

Step 4. Formulate Your Thesis and Major Propositions

Step 5. Support Your Propositions

Step 6. Organize Your Speech

Step 7. Construct Your Introduction, Conclusion, and Transitions

UNIT GOALS

After completing this unit, you should be able to:

explain how a thesis may be developed and how major propositions may be derived from it

explain how propositions may be supported with a wide variety of appropriate materials such as examples, testimony, statistics, and presentation aids

explain the major patterns for organizing a public speech

explain the functions and methods for introducing and concluding the speech and for connecting its parts

This unit continues the discussion of the steps in preparing and presenting a public speech and covers four steps: formulating your thesis and major propositions; supporting your propositions; organizing the body of your speech; and constructing your introduction, conclusion, and transitions.

STEP 4. FORMULATE YOUR THESIS AND MAJOR PROPOSITIONS

Your thesis is your main assertion; it's what you want the audience to absorb from your speech. The thesis of the "Rocky" movies was that the underdog can win; the thesis of the Martin Luther King, Jr., "I Have a Dream" speech was that true equality must be granted to African Americans and to all people. Your major propositions are the main ideas that will clarify, prove, or support your thesis.

Your Thesis

Let's say, for example, that you are planning to present a speech against using animals for experimentation. Your thesis statement might be something like this: "Animal experimentation should be banned." This is what you want your audience to believe as a result of your speech. In an informative speech the thesis statement focuses on what you want your audience to learn. For example, a suitable thesis for a speech on jealousy might be: "There are two main theories of jealousy." Be sure to limit the thesis statement to one central idea. Statements such as "Animal experimentation should be banned and companies engaging in it should be prosecuted" contain not one but two basic ideas. Notice that in persuasive speeches, the thesis statement puts forth a point of view, an opinion. The thesis is an arguable, debatable proposition. In informative speeches, the thesis is relatively neutral and objective.

Use the thesis statement to help you generate your main ideas or assertions. Each thesis contains an essential question within it; this question allows you to explore and subdivide the thesis. Your objective is to find this question and pose it of your thesis. For example, let's say your thesis is: "The Hart bill provides needed services for senior citizens." Stated in this form, the obvious question suggested is "What are they?" The answer to this question suggests the main parts of your speech, for example, health, food, shelter, and recreational services. These four areas then become the four main points of your speech.

Use the thesis to help focus the audience's attention on your central idea. The thesis sentence also focuses the audience's attention on your central idea. In some speeches you may wish to state your thesis early in your speech. In cases where your audience might be hostile to your thesis, it may be wise to give your evidence first and gradually move the audience into a more positive frame of mind before stating your thesis. Here are a few guidelines to help you make the right decision about when to introduce your thesis:

- In an informative speech, state your thesis early, clearly, and directly.
- In a persuasive speech where your audience is neutral or positive, state your thesis explicitly and early in your speech.
- In a persuasive speech where your audience is hostile to your position, delay stating your thesis until you have moved them closer to your position.
- Recognize that there are cultural differences in the way a thesis should be stated. In some Asian cultures, for example, making a point too directly or asking directly for audience compliance may be considered rude or insulting.

Word the thesis as a simple declarative sentence: "Animal experimentation must be banned." This will help you focus your thinking, your collection of materials, and your organizational pattern. You may, however, phrase your thesis in other ways when you present it to your audience, for example, as a question ("Should animal experimentation be banned?" or "Why must we ban animal experimentation?").

Major Propositions

The major propositions are your principal assertions, your main points. If your speech were a play, the propositions would be its acts. Let's look at how you can select and word your propositions and how you can logically arrange them.

In discussing the thesis, you saw how you can develop your main points or propositions by asking strategic questions. To see how this works in detail, imagine that you are giving a speech to a group of high school students on the values of a college education. Your thesis is: "A college education is valuable." You then ask, "Why is it valuable?" From this question you generate your major propositions. Your

BUILDING
Communication Skills

HOW DO YOU GENERATE MAJOR PROPOSITIONS?

One of the skills in organizing a speech is to ask a question of your thesis and from the answer generate your major propositions. Next we present 10 thesis statements suitable for a variety of informative or persuasive speeches. For each thesis statement, ask a question and generate two, three, or four major propositions that would be suitable for an informative or persuasive speech. Here is an example to get you started:

Thesis Statement: Mandatory retirement should (should not) be abolished.

Question: Why should mandatory retirement be abolished?

I.   Mandatory retirement leads us to lose many of the most productive workers.
II. Mandatory retirement contributes to psychological problems of those forced to retire.
III. Mandatory retirement costs corporations economic hardship because they have to train new people.

1. Tax (don't tax) property assets owned by religious organizations.
2. Require (don't require) adoption agencies to reveal the names of birth-parents to all children when they reach 18 years of age.
3. Permit (don't permit) condom advertisements in all media.
4. Make (don't make) the death penalty mandatory for those convicted of selling drugs to minors.
5. Elected political officials should (not) be allowed to serve as lobbyists at any time after their term of office has expired.
6. Courses on women's issues should (not) be required for all students at this college.
7. Legalize (don't legalize) soft drugs.
8. Build (don't build) houses for the homeless.
9. Support (don't support) mandatory instruction in AIDS prevention in all elementary and high schools.
10. Grant (don't grant) full equality to gay men and lesbians in the military.

---

first step might be to brainstorm this question and generate as many answers as possible without evaluating them. You may come up with answers such as the following:

1. It helps you get a good job.
2. It increases your earning potential.
3. It gives you greater job mobility.
4. It helps you secure more creative work.
5. It helps you to appreciate the arts more fully.
6. It helps you to understand an extremely complex world.
7. It helps you understand different cultures.
8. It allows you to avoid taking a regular job for a few years.
9. It helps you meet lots of people and make new friends.
10. It helps you increase your personal effectiveness.

There are, of course, other possibilities, but for purposes of illustration, these 10 possible main points will suffice. But not all 10 are equally valuable or relevant to your audience, so you should look over the list to see how to make it shorter and more meaningful. Try these suggestions:

1. Eliminate those points that seem least important to your thesis. On this basis you might want to eliminate No. 8 since this seems least consistent with your intended emphasis on the positive values of college.

TABLE 16.1   Additional forms of support

As you read this table, consider how you might use each of these forms in your next speech.

Form of Support	Uses	Cautions
Quotations, the exact words of another person	Useful for adding spice and wit as well as authority to your speeches	Make sure they're relatively short, easily understood, and directly related to your point.
Definitions, the meaning of a term	Helpful when complex terms are introduced or when you wish to provide a unique perspective on a subject	Don't overdo definitions; if too many definitions are needed then your subject may be too complex for a short speech.
Comparisons and contrasts, the similarities and differences between words or concepts	Useful for highlighting similarities and differences between, say, two health care plans or between cultures	A few major points of comparison and contrast may work better than an exhaustive list of similarities and differences which listeners won't be able to remember.
Facts or a series of facts, verifiable truths	Useful to help you support a main idea	Don't allow the individual facts to cloud your major propositions; make sure the facts are clearly linked to the proposition they support.
Repetition (repeating your idea in the same words at strategic places throughout your speech) and restatement (repeating your idea in different words).	Helpful for emphasizing a particular point and often especially helpful when addressing listeners who learned your language as a second language and may not easily understand idioms and figures of speech	Repetition and restatement can be overdone and get boring; limit yourself to what is reasonable for increasing audience comprehension.

2. Combine those points that have a common focus. Notice, for example, that the first four points all center on the values of college in terms of jobs. You might, therefore, consider grouping these four items into one proposition: A college education helps you get a good job.

This point might be one of the major propositions that could be developed by defining what you mean by a "good job." This main point or proposition and its elaboration might look like this:

I. A college education helps you get a good job.
   A. College graduates earn higher salaries.

   B. College graduates enter more creative jobs.

   C. College graduates have greater job mobility.

Note that A, B, and C are all aspects or subdivisions of a "good job."

3. Select points that are most relevant to or that interest your audience. You might decide that high school students would be more interested in increasing personal effectiveness, so you might select No. 10 for inclusion as a second major proposition.

4. Use two, three, or four main points. For your class speeches, which will generally range from 5 to 15 minutes, use two, three, or four main propositions. Too many main points will result in a speech that is confusing, contains too much information and too little amplification, and proves difficult to remember.

5. Word each of your major propositions in the same (parallel) style. Phrase points labeled with Roman numerals in a similar (parallel) style. Likewise, phrase points labeled with capital letters and subordinate to the same Roman numeral (for example, A, B, and C under point I or A, B, and C under point II) in a similar style. Parallel style was used in the example on college education and getting a good job, above in No. 2. This parallel styling helps the audience follow and remember your speech.

6. Develop your main points so they are separate and discrete. Don't allow your main points to overlap each other. Each section labeled with a Roman numeral should be a separate entity.

STEP 5. SUPPORT YOUR PROPOSITIONS

Now that you've identified your major propositions and you know how to search for information, you can devote attention to your next step, supporting your propositions. Among the most useful sources of support are examples, narration, testimony, statistics, and presentation aids, which we cover in depth. In addition, however, there are a wide variety of other forms of support (see Table 16.1).

Examples

Examples are specific instances that are explained in varying degrees of detail. Examples are useful when you wish to make an abstract concept or idea concrete. It's easier for an audience to understand what you mean by, say, "love" or "friendship" if you provide them with a specific example (as well as your definition).

In using examples, keep in mind that their function is to make your ideas vivid and easily understood. They're useful for explaining a concept; they're not ends in themselves. Make them only as long as necessary to ensure that your purpose is achieved.

Use enough examples to make your point. Make sure that the examples are sufficient to re-create your meaning in the minds of your listeners, but be careful not to use so many that the audience loses the very point you are making.

Make the relationship between your assertion and your example explicit. Show the audience exactly how your example relates to the assertion or concept you are explaining.

Narration

Narratives are stories and are often useful as supporting materials in a speech. Narratives give the audience what it wants: a good story. It helps you maintain attention since listeners automatically perk up when a story is told. The main value of narration is that it allows you to bring an abstract concept down to specifics. Narratives may be of different types and each serves a somewhat different purpose. Following Clella Jaffe (1998) we can distinguish three types of narrative: explanatory, exemplary, and persuasive.

- **Explanatory narratives** explain the way things are. The biblical book of Genesis, for example, explains the development of the world from a particular religious viewpoint. An eye witness report might explain the events leading up to an accident.
- **Exemplary narratives** provide examples of excellence, examples to follow or admire. The stories of the lives of saints and martyrs are exemplary narratives as are the Horatio Alger success stories. Similarly, many motivational speakers such as Susan Powter and Tony Little often include exemplary narratives in their speeches and will tell the story of what they were like when they were out of shape.
- **Persuasive narratives** try to strengthen or change beliefs and attitudes. When Sally Struthers tells us of the plight of the starving children, she's using a persuasive narrative. The parables in religious writings are persuasive in urging listeners to lead life in a particular way.

Keep your narratives relatively short and few in number. In most cases, one or possibly two narratives are sufficient in a short five- to seven-minute speech. Make explicit the connection between your story and the point you are making. If the people in the audience don't get this connection, you not only lose the effectiveness of the story but you also lose their attention as they try to figure out why you told that story.

Testimony

Testimony refers to the opinions of experts or to the accounts of witnesses. Testimony helps to amplify your speech by adding a note of authority to your arguments. For example, you might want to use the testimony of a noted economist to support your predictions about inflation or the testimony of someone who spent two years in a maximum-security prison to discourage young people from committing crimes.

UNDERSTANDING
Theory and Research

DO THE ENDS JUSTIFY THE MEANS?

A long-standing debate in ethics focuses on means and ends. Do the ends justify the means? For example, would it be ethical for a public speaker to say things that would normally be considered unethical, say, making up statistics if the end she or he hoped to achieve was a worthy one, for example, keeping children from using drugs? Those taking an objective position would argue that the ends do not justify the means, that the lie, for example, is always wrong regardless of the specific situation. Those taking a subjective position would argue that at times the end would justify the means and at times it wouldn't; it would depend on the specific means and ends in question.

You'll probably make at least some of your public speaking decisions on the basis of a means-ends analysis. Consider you own feelings about means and ends by asking yourself if it would it be ethical to:

1. Pretend to be culturally similar to an audience (without actually saying so, but just allowing them to believe it) to better achieve your purpose, which will benefit the audience members?
2. Exaggerate your skills and experience to make yourself more credible?
3. Misrepresent yourself in an Internet newsgroup to spice things up?
4. Make up statistics to support your point of view in a public speech because you know that what you're advocating will benefit the audience?
5. Work on an advertising team writing an ad using only emotional and credibility appeals (nothing logical about it) to get children to buy expensive sneakers? To get teens to avoid potentially dangerous sexual practices?

When you cite testimony, stress first the competence of the person, whether that person is an expert or a witness. To cite the predictions of a world-famous economist of whom your audience has never heard will mean little unless you first explain the person's competence. You might say, for example: "This prediction comes from the world's leading economist, who has successfully predicted all major financial trends over the past 20 years." Now the audience will be prepared to lend credence to what this person says.

Second, stress the unbiased nature of the testimony. If the audience perceives the testimony to be biased—whether or not it really is—it will have little effect. You want to check out the biases of a witness so that you may present accurate information. But you also want to make the audience see that the testimony is in fact unbiased.

Third, stress the recency of the statement to the audience. Notice that in the first excerpt that follows, we have no way of knowing when the state- ment was made and therefore no way of knowing how true this statement would be today. In the second excerpt, however, the recency of the statement is stressed.

Statistics

Let's say you want to show that significant numbers of people are now getting their news from the Internet, that the cost of film making has skyrocketed over the last 20 years, or that women buy significantly more books and magazines than men. To communicate these types of information, you'd use statistics—summary numbers that help you communicate the important characteristics of an otherwise complex set of numbers. Statistics help the audience see, for example, the percentage of people getting their news from the Internet, the average cost of films in 1998 versus previous years, and the difference between male and female book and magazine purchases.

BUILDING
Communication Skills

HOW DO YOU LIVEN UP SUPPORTING STATEMENTS?

Here are some rather bland, uninteresting statements. Select one of them and amplify it by using at least three different methods of amplification. Identify each method used. Since the purpose of this exercise is to provide greater insight into forms and methods of amplification, you may, for this exercise, manufacture, fabricate, or otherwise invent facts, figures, illustrations, examples, and the like. In fact, it may prove even more beneficial if you go to extremes in constructing these forms of support.

1. Bullfighting is morally wrong.
2. The Sears Tower in Chicago is tall.
3. Williams was my favorite instructor.
4. My grandparents left me a fortune in their will.
5. The college I just visited seems ideal.
6. The writer of this article is a real authority.
7. I knew I was marrying into money as soon as I walked into the house.
8. Considering what they did, punishment to the fullest extent of the law would be mild.
9. The psychic gave us good news.
10. The athlete lived an interesting life.

- *Make the statistics clear to your audience.* Remember, they'll hear the figures only once. Round off figures so they are easy to understand and retain.
- *Make the statistics meaningful.* When using statistics, it's often helpful to remind the audience of what the statistic itself means. So, for example, if you say that "the median co-op apartment in San Francisco is $243,000" remind the audience that this means the middle price—that half of the homes are above $243,000 and half are below. Also, present numbers so that the audience can appreciate the meaning you want to convey. To say, for example, that the Sears Tower in Chicago is 1559 feet tall doesn't visualize its height. So, consider saying something like: "The Sears Tower is 1559 feet tall. Just how tall is 1559 feet? Well, it's as tall as the length of more than four football fields. That's how tall. It's as tall as 260 six-foot people standing on each other's heads."
- *Connect the statistics with the proposition.* Make explicit the connection between the statistics and what they show. To say, for example, that college professors make an average

of $52,000 per year needs to be related specifically to the proposition that teachers' salaries should be raised or lowered, depending on your point of view.
- *Visually (and verbally) reinforce the statistics.* Because numbers are difficult to grasp and remember when they are presented without some kind of visual reinforcement, it's often helpful to complement your oral presentation of statistics with some type of presentation aid—perhaps a graph or a chart.
- *Use statistics in moderation.* In most cases statistics should be used sparingly. Most listeners' capacity for numerical data presented in a speech is limited, so use statistics in moderation.

Presentation Aids

When you're planning to give a speech, consider using some kind of presentation aid—a visual or auditory means for clarifying ideas. Ask yourself how you can visualize in your aid what you want your audience to remember. How can you reinforce your ideas with additional media? If you want your audience to see the increases in sales tax, consider showing them a chart

Going Online

Federal Statistics Web site

This Web site contains a vast array of statistical information. Can you locate statistics that would help you support one of the propositions for your next speech? (If you're unclear about any statistics concept or simply want to learn more about statistics, you can download an electronic statistics textbook from http://www.stat-soft.com/textbook/stathome.html.)

of rising sales tax over the last 10 years. If you want them to see that Brand A is superior to Brand X, consider showing them a comparison chart identifying the superiority of Brand A.

Types of Presentation Aids

Among the presentation aids you have available are the actual object, models of the object, graphs, word charts, maps, people, photographs and illustrations, and tapes and CDs.

As a general rule (to which there are many exceptions), the best presentation aid is **the object** itself; bring it to your speech if you can. Notice that infomercials sell their product not only by talking about it but by showing it to potential buyers. You see what George Forman's Lean Mean Grilling Machine looks like and how it works. You see the jewelry, the clothing, and the new mop from a wide variety of angles and in varied settings. If you want to explain some tangible thing and you can show it to your audience, do so.

Models—replicas of the actual object—are useful for a variety of purposes. For example, if you wanted to explain complex structures such as the hearing or vocal mechanism, the brain, or the structure of DNA, you would almost have to use a model. You may remember from science classes that these models (and the pictures of them in the textbooks)

make a lot more sense than just the verbal explanations. These models help to clarify relative size and position and how each part interacts with each other part. These are good examples of how large models can be used to help listeners visualize objects that are too small (and unavailable) to appreciate otherwise. In other cases, small models of large objects—objects that are too large to bring to your speech—are helpful. For example, in a speech on stretching exercises, one student used a 14-inch wooden artist's model.

Graphs are useful for showing differences over time, for showing how a whole is divided into parts, and for showing different amounts or sizes. Figure 16.1 contains a variety of graphs that can be drawn freehand or generated with the graphics capabilities of any word-processing or presentation software.

Word charts (which can also contain numbers and even graphics) are useful for lots of different types of information. For example, you might use a word chart to identify the key points that you cover in one of your propositions or in your entire speech—in the order in which you cover them, of course. Slide No. 5 in Figure 16.2 is a good example of a simple word chart that identifies the major topics discussed in the speech. Or, you could use word charts to identify the steps in a process, for example, the steps in programming a VCR, in dealing with

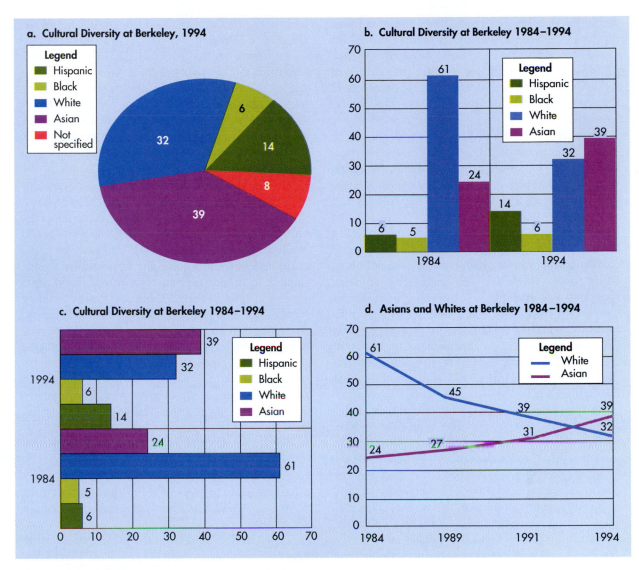

Figure 16.1 **Assorted Graphs.**   Notice that each of the graphs serves a somewhat different purpose. The pie chart (a) is especially useful if you want to show how some whole is divided into its parts and the relative sizes of the parts. From the pie chart you can easily see the relative percentage of students of different cultural groups at a particular time. Only use a pie chart to show a division that's numerically significant; that is, the sizes of the pie's slices should bear some relationship to numerical values. Pie charts are especially helpful when you have three to five values to illustrate; any more than five creates a pie that is difficult to read at a glance. The two bar graphs (b and c) both illustrate the same data but in different ways. Both graphs enable you to see at a glance the changing cultural composition of the Berkeley student body. (b) This graph makes it easier to see the differences over time. (c) This graph makes it easier to see the differences within each cultural group for the two years studied. As with the pie chart, try not to create bar graphs that will require more than five color distinctions. (d) The line graph shows how comparisons can be illustrated with this very simple graph. Notice that the graph is especially clear because it focuses on only two groups. Had it focused on 8 or 10 groups, it would have been difficult for an audience to understand.

Data for these four graphs come from the University of California at Berkeley as reported in *The New York Times,* June 4, 1995, p. 22).

sexual harassment, or in installing a new computer program. Another use of charts is for information you want your audience to write down. Emergency phone numbers, addresses to write to, or titles of recommended books and Web sites are examples of the type of information that listeners will welcome in written form.

Maps are useful for illustrating a wide variety of issues. If you want to illustrate the location of cities, lakes, rivers, or mountain ranges, for example, maps will obviously prove useful as presentation aids. One speaker, for example, used a map to show the size and location of the rain forests. Maps are also helpful for illustrating, for example, population densities, immigration patterns, varied economic conditions, the spread of diseases, and hundreds of other issues you may wish to develop in your speeches. For example, in a speech on natural resources, one speaker used a variety of maps to illustrate the location of large reserves of oil, gas, and precious metals. Another speaker used maps to illustrate the concentration of wealth while another used maps to show differences in the mortality rate throughout the world.

You can also use maps to illustrate numerical differences. For example, you may want to use a map to show the wide variation in literacy rates throughout the world. So, for example, you might color the countries that have 90–100 percent literacy red, the countries having 80–89 percent literacy green, and so on. When you use maps in this way, it's often useful to complement them with charts or graphs that, for example, give the specific literacy rates for the specific countries on which you want to concentrate. Although theses maps may seem overly complex to construct, computer programs now make the creation of such maps relatively simple. Further, a wide variety of maps may be downloaded from the Internet, which you can then show as slides or transparencies. Chances are you'll find a map on the Internet for exactly the purpose you need.

Oddly enough, **people** can function effectively as "presentation aids." For example, if you wanted to demonstrate the muscles of the body, you might use a bodybuilder. If you wanted to demonstrate different voice patterns, skin complexions, or hairstyles, you might use people as your aids. Aside from the obvious assistance they provide in demonstrating their muscles or voice qualities, people

help to secure and maintain the attention and interest of the audience.

And don't overlook yourself as a (kind of) presentation aid. For example, if you are giving a speech on boxing strategies, exercise techniques, or sitting and standing postures that can lead to backaches, you might demonstrate them yourself. As an added plus, going through these demonstrations is likely to reduce your apprehension and make you more relaxed.

Photographs and illustrations are useful aids for a variety of purposes. Speeches on types of trees, styles of art or architecture, or types of exercise machines would profit greatly from a few well chosen photographs or illustrations. If you want to show these and you don't have the opportunity to put them onto slides, you may try to simply hold them up as you refer to them. There are, however, many hazards involved in using this type of aid, so they're recommended only with reservations. If the picture is large enough for all members of the audience to see clearly (say, poster size), if it clearly illustrates what you want to illustrate, and if it's mounted on cardboard, then use it; otherwise, don't. Fortunately, it's relatively easy to have photos enlarged or put onto slides.

Don't pass pictures around the room. This only draws attention away from what you are saying. Listeners will look for the pictures before the pictures circulate to them, will wonder what the pictures contain, and will miss a great deal of your speech in the interim.

Tapes and CDs can be useful for many other types of speeches as well. A speech on advertising would be greatly helped, for example, by having actual samples of advertisements as played on radio or television; it would go a long way in helping the audience to see exactly what you are talking about. It would also provide variety by breaking up the oral presentation.

The Media of Presentation Aids

Once you've decided on the type of presentation aid you'll use, you need to decide on the medium you'll use to present it. Some of these media are low tech, for example, the chalkboard, transparencies, and flip charts. These media are generally more effective in smaller, informal situations, especially those that arise without prior notice, which you simply don't have the time to prepare high-tech resources for. Low-tech devices are also useful for highly interactive sessions—for example, the flip chart is still one of the best ways to record group members' contributions. Other media, for example, slides and slide shows, are high tech. High-tech materials are generally more effective with larger, more formal groups, in which you do most of the talking and the audience does most of the listening. High-tech materials may also be your only choice if the material you have to communicate is extremely complex or if the norms of your organization simply require that you use high-tech presentation formats.

The best advice anyone could offer is to encourage you to learn how to use both low- and high-tech resources. The decisions you make concerning which types of media to use should be based on the message you want to communicate and on the audience to whom you'll be speaking.

The **chalkboard** is the easiest to use, but not necessarily the most effective. All classrooms have such boards, and you have seen them used by teachers with greater or lesser effect; in some way, you've had "experience" with them. The chalkboard may be used effectively to present key terms or important definitions or even to outline the general structure of your speech. Don't use it when you can present the same information with a preplanned chart or model. It takes too long to write out anything substantial. Be careful if you do write on the board not to turn your back to the audience. In this brief time, you can easily lose their attention.

Chartboards are useful when you have just one or two relatively simple charts that you want to display during your speech. If you want to display them for several minutes, be sure you have a way of holding them up. For example, bring masking tape if you intend to secure them to the chalkboard or enlist the aid of an audience member to hold them up. Use a light colored board; white generally works best. Write in black; it provides the best contrast and is the easiest for people to read.

Flip charts, large pads of paper (usually about 24 by 24 inches) mounted on a stand, can be used to record a variety of types of information that you reveal by flipping the pages as you deliver your speech. For example, if you were to discuss the various departments in an organization, you might have the key points relating to each department on a separate page of your flip chart. As you discuss the advertising department, you would show the chart relevant to the advertising department. When you move on to discuss the personnel department, you would flip to the chart dealing with personnel. You may find this device useful if you have a large number of word charts that you want to have easy control over. Make sure that the chart is positioned so that everyone in the audience can see it clearly and that the folding legs are positioned securely so it doesn't collapse when you flip the first page. Make sure you write large enough so that the people in the back can read it without straining their eyes.

Flip charts are especially useful to record ideas at small group meetings (see Unit 13). Unlike the chalkboard, the flip chart enables you to retain a written record of the meeting; should you need to, you can easily review the group's contributions.

Slides and transparency projections are helpful in showing a series of visuals that may be of very different types, for example, photographs, illustrations, charts, or tables. The slides can easily be created with many of the popular computer programs (see the section called Computer Assisted Presentations). To produce actual 35mm slides, you'll need considerable lead time; so be sure to build this into your preparation time.

If you don't have access to slide projectors or if you don't have the lead time needed to construct slides, consider somewhat less sophisticated transparencies. You can create your visual in any of the word-processing or spreadsheet programs you normally use and probably find a printer that will enable you to print transparencies. Another alternative is to use a copier that will produce transparencies.

When using any presentation aid, but especially with slides and transparencies, make sure that you have the proper equipment, for example, projector, table, a working outlet nearby, control over the lighting in the room, and whatever else you'll need to have the audience see your projections clearly.

An advantage of transparencies is that you can write on the transparencies (and on slides in computer presentations as we discuss later) while you're speaking. You can circle important items, underline key terms, and draw lines connecting different terms.

Videotapes may serve a variety of purposes in public speaking. Basically, you have two options with videotapes. First, you can tape a scene from a film or television show with your VCR and show it at the appropriate time in your speech. Thus, for example, you might videotape examples of sexism in television sitcoms, violence on television talk shows, or types of transitions used in feature films and show these excerpts during your speech. As you can see, however, this type of video takes a great deal of time and preplanning, so if you are going to use this you must plan well in advance. As a teacher, I use a variety of films and film excerpts to illustrate some of the breakdowns in interpersonal communication, the studies in teaching animals to communicate, the nature of nonverbal communication, and various other topics.

Second, you can create your own video with a simple camcorder. One student created a video of ethnic store signs to illustrate the "interculturalization" of the city. With the help (and agreement to be videotaped) of a few friends, another student created a three-minute video of religious holidays as celebrated by members of different religions and carefully coordinated each excerpt with her discussion of each holiday.

In using videotapes do make sure that they don't occupy too much of your speaking time; after all, your main objective is to learn the principles of public speaking.

Handouts are printed materials that you distribute to members of the audience and are especially helpful in explaining complex material and also in providing listeners with a permanent record of some aspect of your speech. Handouts are also useful for presenting complex information that you want your audience to refer to throughout the speech. Handouts encourage listeners to take notes—especially if you leave enough white space or even provide a specific place for notes—which keeps them actively involved in your presentation. Handouts reward the audience by giving them something for their attendance and attention. A variety of handouts can be easily prepared with many of the computer presentation packages that we consider in the last section of this unit.

You can distribute them at the beginning of, during, or after your speech, but realize that whichever system you use has potential difficulties. If you distribute them before or during your speech, you run the risk of your listeners' reading the handout and not concentrating on your speech. On the other hand, if they are getting the information you want to communicate—even if primarily from the handout—that isn't too bad. And, in a way, handouts allow listeners to process the information at their own pace.

You can encourage listeners to listen to you when you want them to and to look at the handout when you want them to by simply telling them: "Look at the graph on the top of page two of the handout; it summarizes recent census figures on immigration" or "We'll get back to the handout in a minute; now, however, I want to direct your attention to this next slide [or the second argument]."

If you distribute your handouts at the end of the speech, they will obviously not interfere with your presentation but they may not be read at all. After all, listeners might reason, they heard the speech, why bother going through the handout? To counteract this very natural tendency, you might include additional material on the handout and mention this to your audience. When you distribute your handout you might say something like: "This handout contains all the slides shown here and three additional slides that provide economic data for Thailand, Cambodia, and Vietnam, which I didn't have time to cover. When you look at the data, you'll see that it mirrors exactly the data provided in my talk of the other countries." When you provide additional information on your handout, it's more likely that it will get looked at and thus provide the reinforcement you want.

Preparing Presentation Aids

Once you have the idea of an aid you want to present and you know the medium you want to use, direct your attention to preparing your aid so it can best serve your purposes. Make sure that it adds clarity to your speech, that it's appealing to the listeners, and that it's culturally sensitive.

Clarity is the most important test of all. Make sure that the aid is clearly relevant to your speech purpose—in the minds of your listeners. It may be attractive, well-designed, and easy to read, but if the listeners don't understand how it relates to your speech, leave it at home. Make sure your aid is large enough to be seen by everyone from all parts of the room. Use typefaces that are easy to see and easy to read. Use colors that will make your message instantly clear; light colors on dark backgrounds or dark colors on light backgrounds provide the best contrast and seem to work best for most purposes. Be careful of using yellow, which is often difficult to see, especially if there's glare from the sun.

- Use direct phrases (not complete sentences); use bullets to highlight your points or your support (see Figure 16.2). Just as you phrase your propositions in parallel style, phrase your bullets in parallel style; in many cases this is done by using the same part of speech (for example, all nouns or all infinitive phrases). And make sure that any connection between a graphic and its meaning is immediately clear. If it isn't, explain it.
- Use the aid to highlight a few essential points; don't clutter it with too much information. Four bullets on a slide or chart, for example, is about as much information as you should include. Make sure the aid is simple rather than complicated; like your verbal message, the aid should be instantly intelligible.

Presentation aids work best when they're **appealing**. Sloppy, poorly designed, and worn-out aids will detract from the purpose they are intended to serve. Presentation aids should be attractive enough to engage the attention of the audience, but not so attractive that they're distracting. The almost nude body draped across a car may be effective in selling underwear, but would probably detract if your object is to explain the profit-and-loss statement of Intel Corporation.

Make sure your presentation aids are **culturally sensitive** and are easily interpreted by people from other cultures. For example, the symbols you use that you may assume are universal may not be known by persons new to a culture. And, of course, when speaking to international audiences, use universal symbols or explain those that are not universal. Be careful that your icons don't reveal an ethnocentric bias. For example, using the American dollar sign to symbolize "wealth" may be quite logical in your public speaking class but might be interpreted as ethnocentric if used with an audience of international visitors. Also, the meanings that different colors communicate vary greatly from one culture to another, as already illustrated in Unit 8. Revisit that unit and particularly the section on color to make sure that the colors you use don't send messages that you don't want to send.

Using Presentation Aids

Keep the following guidelines clearly in mind when using presentation aids.

- Know your aids intimately. Be sure you know in what order they are to be presented and how you plan to introduce them. Know exactly what goes where and when.
- Test the aids before using them. Test the presentation aids prior to your speech. Be certain that they can be easily seen from all parts of the room.
- Rehearse your speech with the presentation aids incorporated into the presentation. Practice your actual movements with the aids you'll use. If you're going to use a chart, how will you use it? Will it stand by itself? Can you tape it somewhere? Do you have tape with you?
- Integrate your aids into your speech seamlessly. Just as a verbal example should flow naturally into the text and seem an integral part of the speech, so should the presentation aid. It should not appear as an afterthought but as an essential part of the speech.
- Don't talk to your aid. Both you and the aid should be focused on the audience. Know your aids so well that you can point to what you want without breaking eye contact with your audience. Or, at the least, break audience eye contact for only very short periods of time.
- Use the aid when it's relevant. Show it when you want the audience to concentrate on it and then remove it. If you don't remove it, the audience's attention may remain focused on the visual when you want them to focus on what you'll be saying next.

Computer Assisted Presentations

There are a variety of presentation software packages available: PowerPoint™, Corel Presentations™, and Lotus Freelance™ are among the most popular and are very similar in what they do and how they do it. Figure 16.2 illustrates what a set of slides might look like; the slides are built around the speech outline discussed in unit 17 (pp.337–339) and were constructed in PowerPoint™ (though a similar slide show could be produced with most presentation software programs). As you review this figure, try to visualize how you

Slide 1

Speech title

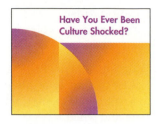

This first slide introduces the topic with the title of the speech. Follow the general rules for titling your speech: Keep it short, provocative, and focused on your audience. If you put a graphic on this page, make sure that it doesn't detract from your title. What graphics might work well here?

Slide 2

The thesis of the speech

You may or may not want to identify your thesis right at the beginning of your speech. Consider the arguments for and against identifying your thesis—both cultural and strategic and the suggestions for when and how to state the thesis on page 308. As a listener, do you prefer it when speakers state their thesis right at the beginning or do you prefer it when the thesis is only implied and left for you to figure out?

Slide 3

Attention-getting device; corresponds to the Introduction's "I A-B"

This slide gains attention by relating the topic directly to the audience; it answers the listener's obvious question, "Why should I listen to this speech?"

Slide 4

S-A-T connection; corresponds to the Introduction's "II A-B"

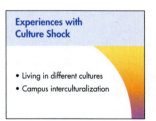

This slide connects the speaker, the audience, and the topic. Because you talk about yourself in this part of your speech, some speakers may prefer to eliminate a verbal slide and use a graphic or a photo. Another alternative is to include your S-A-T connection with the previous attention-getting slide.

Slide 5

Orientation; corresponds to the Introduction's "III A-D"

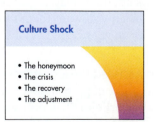

In this slide, you give your orientation by identifying your major propostions. These four bullets will become your four major propositions.

Slide 6

First major proposition; corresponds to the Body's "I A-B"

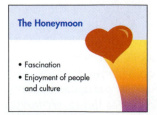

This is your first major proposition, and you would introduce it, perhaps, by saying, "The honeymoon occurs first." If you want your audience to keep track of the stage number, you could use numbers in your slide, e.g., "1. The Honeymoon" or "Stage 1, the Honeymoon." The graphic of the heart is meant to associate culture shock with good times and a romantic-like experience. As a listener, would you prefer that the speaker explain this graphic or say nothing about it?

Figure 16.2   **A Slide Show**

Slide 7

Second major proposition; corresponds to the Body's "II A-B"

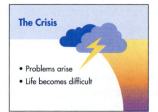

This is your second proposition and follows in the format of the previous slide. Again, a graphic is used. Can you think of a better graphic?

Slide 8

Third major proposition; corresponds to the Body's "III A-B"

This is your third major proposition and again follows the format of the previous two slides.

Slide 9

Fourth major proposition; corresponds to the Body's "IV A-B"

This is your fourth major proposition, and, as noted in the text, the sound of applause is programmed to come on with this slide, reinforcing the idea that we do adjust to this shock. Examine the sound effects you have available; what other sound effects would you use in this speech?

Slide 10

Summary; corresponds to the Conclusion's "I A-D"

This is your summary of your four major propositions; notice that it's the same as your orientation (Slide 5). This slide violates the general rule to use graphics in moderation. What do you think of the repetition of graphics? Do you think they add reinforcement? Do they detract from the verbal message?

Slide 11

Motivation; corresponds to the Conclusion's "II A-B"

This part of the summary ideally motivates your listeners to pursue the topic in more detail.

Slide 12

Closure; corresponds to the Conclusion's "III"

This slide is intended to wrap up the speech—it contains the title and two graphics, which will support the speaker's concluding statement: "By knowing about culture shock you'll be in a better position to deal with it at school and on the job." Notice that the conclusion is tied to the introduction by a similarity in font and text color; it helps signal that this is the last slide and the end of the speech.

would use a slide show to present your next speech. Also, realize that you could easily import photographs and have slides of these inserted into your slide show or add video clips.

Ways of Using Presentation Package Software. Computer presentation software enables you to produce a variety of aids; the software will produce what you want. For example, you can construct slides on your computer, save them on a disk, and then have 35 mm slides developed from the disk. To do this, you would have to have a slide printer or send them out (you can do this via modem) to a lab specializing in converting electronic files into 35mm slides. You may have access to a slide printer at your school, so check there first. Similarly, your local office supply store or photocopy shop, such as Staples, Office Max, or Kinko, may have exactly the services you need.

Or, you can create your slides and then show them on your computer screen. If you are speaking to a very small group, it may be possible to have your listeners gather around your computer as you speak. With larger audiences, however, you'll need a computer projector or an LCD projection panel. Assuming that you have a properly equipped computer in the classroom, you can copy your entire presentation to a floppy disk and bring it with you on the day of the speech.

Computer presentation software also enables you to print out a variety of handouts:

- The slides shown during your speech as well as additional slides that you might not have time to include in the speech, but which you nevertheless want your listeners to look at when they read your handout
- The slides plus speaker's notes, the key points that you made as you showed each of the slides (the function that was used to produce Figure 16.2)
- The slides plus places for listeners to write notes next to each of them
- An outline of your talk
- Any combination of the above

Overhead transparencies can also be created from your computer slides. They can be made on many printers and most copiers by just substituting transparency paper for computer paper. If you create your slides with a computer presentation package, you'll be able to produce professional-looking transparencies.

Suggestions for Using Presentation Software. The templates and the suggestions of the program "Wizards" will follow the suggestions offered here. Nevertheless, it's important to understand the qualities of effective slides should you want to make changes in the suggested formats or if you want to start from scratch.

In developing your slides, strive for clarity and consistency. For example, choose typeface styles, sizes, and colors to help you clearly distinguish the major propositions from the supporting materials. At the same time, use a consistent combination of fonts, colors, backgrounds, and graphics throughout your slides to give your presentation unity.

Use color (of type and background) and graphics sparingly—remember that clarity is your goal; you want your audience to remember your ideas and not just that all you slides were red, white, and blue. Likewise, too many graphics will distract your audience's attention from your verbal message. Also, be sure to choose graphics that support your tone. If your speech is on a serious topic, then the graphics (and photographs or illustrations) should contribute to this tone. Also, try to use graphics that are consistent with one another; generally it's better to use all shadow figures or all stick figures or all Victorian images than to mix them.

Generally, put one complete thought on a slide; don't try to put too many words on one slide; use few words for the slides and expand on these during your speech. Try not to use more than two levels of thought in a slide—a major statement and two to four subordinate phrases (bulleted)—is about all you can put on one slide. Avoid using subheads of subheads of subheads. Generally, use a sans-serif type (more attention-getting) for headings and a serif type (easier to read) for text (see Table 16.2).

A good guideline to follow in designing your slides is to give each item in your outline that has the same level head (for example, all the Roman numeral heads) the same typeface, size, and color throughout your presentation. Similarly, use the same font for all the A level heads, etc. This will help your listeners follow the organization of your speech. Notice that this principle is followed for the most part in the slides in Figure 16.2. It's broken in one case to connect the introduction with the conclusion by doing these in a color and typeface different from the rest of the slides.

Consider using charts and tables; you have a tremendous variety of chart types (for example, pie, bar, and cumulative charts) and tables to choose from. If you are using presentation software that's part of a suite, then you'll find it especially easy to import files from your word processor or spread sheet.

If there's a question-and-answer period following your speech, consider preparing a few extra slides for your responses to questions you anticipate being asked. Then when someone asks you a predicted question, you can say: "I anticipated that someone might ask that question; it raises an important issue. The data I've been able to find are presented in this chart." You'd then show the slide and explain it more fully. This is surely going the extra mile but it can easily make your speech a real standout.

Use transitions wisely. Just as verbal transitions help you move from one part of your speech to another, presentational transitions help you move from one slide to the next with the desired effect—blinds folding from left or right or top or bottom or a quick fade.

Generally, consistency works best. Don't try to use too many different transitions in the same talk; it will detract attention from what you are saying. Generally, use the same transitions for all the slides in a single presentation. You might vary this a bit by, say, having the last slide introduced by a somewhat different transition, but any more variation is likely to work against the listeners' focusing on your message.

TABLE 16.2   Some typefaces

You have an enormous number of typefaces to choose from. Generally, select typefaces that are easy to read and that are consistent in tone to the message of your speech.	
Typeface	*Comments*
Palatino Century Schoolbook Garamond Times	Serif typefaces retain some of the cursive strokes found in writing by pen. The cursive stroke is illustrated especially in the "m" and "n" which begin with a slight upsweep. Serif styles are easy to read and useful for blocks of text.
Helvetica Bauhaus Ariel Futura	Sans-serif typefaces (a style that is more bold and doesn't include the serif or upsweep) are useful for titles and headings but make reading long text difficult. Helvetica was used in Slides 1 and 12 in Figure 16.2. Futura is the typeface used in the headings for Slides 2 through 11.
Serif Gothic Black **STENCIL** **Gill Sans Ultra Bold**	These extremely bold typefaces are tempting to use, but as you can see, they're not easy to read. They're most appropriate for short titles.
Akzidenz Grotesk **Radiant Condensed** **Franklin Gothic**	These compressed typefaces are useful when you have to fit a lot of text into a small space. They are, however, difficult to read and so should generally be avoided (or, at least, used sparingly) when creating slides. It would be better to use an easier-to-read typeface and spread out the text over additional slides.
CASTELLAR ROSEWOOD **JAZZ** kiek Linotext	Decorative styles like these, although difficult to read for extended text, make great headings or titles. Be careful, however, that the originality of your typefaces doesn't steal attention away from your message.
Mistral Pablo Freestyle Script Pepita	These typefaces are interesting and will give your presentation a personal look, as if you wrote it longhand. But, they'll be difficult to read. If you're going to read the slides word for word along with the audience, then typefaces that are a bit more difficult to read may still be used with considerable effect.

In choosing transitions select one that's consistent with your speech purpose; don't use a frivolous black and yellow checkerboard transition in a speech on "child abuse," for example.

Consider using sound effects with your transitions but again go easy; overdoing it is sure to make your speech seem carelessly put together. In the slides in Figure 16.2, I programmed "applause" (one of the readily available sound effects) to come on as Slide No. 9—the adjustment—comes on. As you read through the slides you might find additional places where sound could be used effectively.

Use build effects to help you focus your listeners' attention. *Build effects* refer to the way in which your bulleted items come to the screen. For example, you can have each bulleted phrase fly from the top of the screen into its position; with the next mouse click, the second bullet flies into position. Or you can have your bullets slide in from right to left or from left to right, and so on.

In listing four or five bulleted items, consider the value of hiding or dimming the previous bullet as you introduce the next one. Making the previous bullet disappear or fade into a lighter color when the next bullet appears further enables you to focus your listeners' attention on exactly the point you're discussing. Do be careful that you allow the audience time to read each bullet, otherwise they'll be disappointed when it disappears.

Use the spell check. You don't want professionally prepared slides with misspellings; it can ruin your credibility and seriously damage the impact of your speech.

STEP 6. ORGANIZE YOUR SPEECH

When you organize your ideas, you derive a variety of benefits. Organization, for example, will help you prepare the speech. For example, as you organize your speech you'll be able to see if you have adequately and fairly supported each of your main points and if you are devoting approximately equal time to each of your main propositions. Organization also makes your speech easy to understand and remember. When you organize perhaps 30 pieces of specific information (for example, statistics, statement of thesis, examples, illustrations, testimonials, transitions) into, say, three or four or five chunks, you're making it much easier for the audience to remember what you want them to remember. An added bonus here is that organization will also help you remember your speech more easily. You'll be less likely to forget a carefully organized speech than you would a disorganized one. Organization will also contribute to your credibility. The audience is more likely to see the well-organized speaker as more competent, more knowledgeable and more in control of the information in the speech.

Once you've identified the major propositions you wish to include in your speech, you need to devote attention to how you'll arrange these propositions in the body of your speech. When you follow a clearly identified organizational pattern, your listeners will be able to see your speech as a whole and will be able to see more clearly the connections and relationships among your various pieces of information. Should they have a momentary lapse in attention—as they surely will at some point in just about every speech—you will be able to refocus their attention.

Consider each pattern in terms of the topics to which it's most applicable and the ways in which you can arrange your main points and supporting materials. The introduction, conclusion, and transitions are considered in depth in Step 7 of this unit. The mechanical aspects of outlining and additional guidance in preparing the outline are presented in Unit 17.

Temporal Pattern

Organization on the basis of some temporal (time) relationship is a pattern listeners will find easy to follow. Generally, when you use this pattern, you organize your speech into two, three, or four major parts, beginning with the past and working up to the present or the future, or beginning with the present or the future and working back to the past.

The temporal (sometimes called "chronological") pattern is especially appropriate for informative speeches in which you wish to describe events or processes that occur over time. It's also useful when you wish to tell a story, demonstrate how something works, or the steps involved in doing something. The events leading up to the Civil War, the steps toward a college education, or the history of writing would all be appropriate for temporal patterning. A speech on the development of language in the child might be organized in a temporal pattern and could be broken down something like this:

I. Babbling occurs around the fifth month.
II. Lallation occurs around the sixth month.

III. Echolalia occurs around the ninth month.
IV. "Communication" occurs around the twelfth month.

Spatial Pattern

You can also organize your main points on the basis of space. This pattern is especially useful when you wish to describe objects or places. Like the temporal pattern, it's an organizational pattern that listeners will find easy to follow as you progress, from top to bottom, left to right, inside to outside, or from east to west, for example. The structure of a place, object, or even animal is easily placed into a spatial pattern. You might describe the layout of a hospital, school, skyscraper, or perhaps even the structure of a dinosaur with a spatial pattern of organization.

Topical Pattern

When your topic conveniently divides itself into subdivisions, each of which is clear and approximately equal in importance, the topical pattern is most useful. A speech on important cities of the world might be organized into a topical pattern, as might be speeches on problems facing the college graduate, great works of literature, the world's major religions, and the like. The topical pattern would be an obvious one for organizing a speech on the powers of the government. The topic itself divides into three parts: legislative, executive, and judicial. A sample outline might look like this:

I. The legislative branch is controlled by Congress.
II. The executive branch is controlled by the president.
III. The judicial branch is controlled by the courts.

Problem–Solution Pattern

The problem–solution pattern is especially useful in persuasive speeches in which you want to convince the audience that a problem exists and that your solution would solve or lessen the problem. Let's say that you believe that jury awards for damages have gotten out of hand. You might want to persuade your audience, then, that jury awards for damages should be limited. A problem–solution pattern might be appropriate here. In this first part of your speech you'd identify the problem(s) created by these large awards and in the second part, the solution. A sample outline for such a speech might look something like this:

I. Jury awards for damages are out of control. [the general problem]
    A. These awards increase insurance rates. [a specific problem]
    B. These awards increase medical costs. [a second specific problem]
    C. These awards place unfair burdens on business. [a third specific problem]
II. Jury awards need to be limited. [the general solution]
    A. Greater evidence should be required before a case can be brought to trial. [a specific solution]

What other suggestions would you offer to a speaker giving a speech with a slide show?

B. Part of the award should be turned over to the state. [a second specific solution]

C. Realistic estimates of financial damage must be used. [a third specific solution]

Cause–Effect/Effect–Cause Pattern

Similar to the problem-solution pattern is the cause–effect or effect–cause pattern. This pattern is useful in persuasive speeches in which you want to convince your audience of the causal connection existing between two events or elements. In the cause–effect pattern you divide the speech into two major sections, causes and effects. For example, a speech on the reasons for highway accidents or birth defects might lend itself to a cause–effect pattern. Here you might first consider, say, the causes of highway accidents or birth defects and then some of the effects, for example, the number of deaths, the number of accidents, and so on.

Let's say you wanted to demonstrate the causes for the increase in AIDS in your state. You might use an effect–cause pattern that might look something like this:

I. AIDS is increasing. [general effect]
   A. AIDS is increasing among teenagers. [a specific effect]
   B. AIDS is increasing among IV drug users. [a second specific effect]
   C. AIDS is increasing among women. [a third specific effect]
II. Three factors contribute to this increase. [general causal statement]
   A. Teenagers are ignorant about how the HIV virus is transmitted. [a specific cause]
   B. IV drug users exchange tainted needles. [a second specific cause]
   C. Women are not practicing safe sex. [a third specific cause]

As you can see from this example, this type of speech is often combined with the problem–solution type. For example, after identifying the causes, the speaker might then treat the causes as problems and offer solutions for each problem/cause (for example: education programs for teens, free needle exchange, and education programs for men and women).

The Motivated Sequence

The motivated sequence is a pattern of arranging your information so as to motivate your audience to respond positively to your purpose (Gronbeck, McKerrow, Ehninger, & Monroe 1997). The previous organizational patterns provided ways of organizing the main ideas in the body of the speech. The motivated sequence is a pattern for organizing the entire speech. Here the speech (introduction, body, and conclusion) is divided into five parts or steps: (1) attention, (2) need, (3) satisfaction, (4) visualization, and (5) action.

1. The **attention step** makes the audience give you their undivided attention. If you execute this step effectively, your audience should be anxious and ready to hear what you have to say. You can gain audience attention through a variety of means, for example, asking a question (rhetorical or actual) or making reference to audience members. These methods are presented in the discussion of the Introduction.

2. In the second part of your speech, you **establish need**; you demonstrate that a need exists for some kind of change. The audience should feel that something has to be learned or something has to be done because of this demonstrated need.

3. You **satisfy** the need by presenting the "answer" or the "solution" to the need you demonstrated in step 2. On the basis of this satisfaction step, the audience should now believe that what you are informing them about or persuading them to do will satisfy the need.

4. Visualization intensifies the audience's feelings or beliefs. In this step you take the people in the audience beyond the present time and place and enable them to imagine the situation as it would be if the need were satisfied as you suggested in step 3. You might, for example, demonstrate the benefits that the audience would receive if your ideas were put into operation or perhaps demonstrate the negative effects that the audience would suffer if your plan were not put into operation.

5. Tell the audience what **action** they should take to ensure that the need (as demonstrated in step 2) is satisfied (as stated in step 3) as visualized (as stated in step 4). Here you want to move the audience in a particular direction, for example, to contribute free time to read to the blind. You can accomplish this step by stating what the audience members should do, using a variety of supporting materials and logical, emotional, and ethical appeals.

Additional Organizational Patterns

The six patterns just considered are the most common and the most useful for organizing most public

UNDERSTANDING
Theory and Research

WHAT DOES CULTURE HAVE TO DO WITH ORGANIZATION?

Members of low-context cultures (see Unit 6) are usually direct in their reactions to others. This directness is generally appreciated by other low-context culture members. But it may prove insulting, insensitive, or unnecessary to the high-context cultural member. Conversely, to the low-context member, the high-context cultural member may appear vague, underhanded, or dishonest in his or her reluctance to be explicit or engage in communication that a low-context member would consider open and direct.

Speakers in Japan, to take one well-researched example, need to be careful lest they make their point too obvious or too direct and insult the audience. Speakers in Japan are expected to lead their listeners to the conclusion through example,

illustration, and various other indirect means (Lustig & Koester 1999).

High-context cultures prefer indirectness. Effective speakers seem to lead the audience in the general direction of the thesis but not explicitly and directly to it, at least, not as directly as would low-context culture members. In the United States, speakers are encouraged to be explicit and direct, to tell the audience, for example, exactly what the speaker wants them to do (see the earlier discussion on focusing audience attention on the thesis in this unit).

In the United States each major proposition of a speech or written composition should be developed by itself. Only when this is fully developed and finalized would the speaker or writer move on to the next point. Hindi culture, however, is less rigid and allows for many ideas being considered in the same paragraph of an essay or in the same part of a speech (Lustig & Koester 1999).

---

speeches. But, there are other patterns that might be appropriate for different topics.

Structure–Function. The structure–function pattern is useful in informative speeches in which you want to discuss how something is constructed (its structural aspects) and what it does (its functional aspects). This pattern might be useful, for example, in a speech to explain what an organization is and what it does, the parts of a university and how they operate, or the sensory systems of the body and their various functions. This pattern might also be useful in discussing the nature of a living organism: its anatomy (that is, its structures) and its physiology (that is, its functions).

Comparison and Contrast. Arranging your material in a comparison-and-contrast pattern is useful in informative speeches in which you want to analyze two different theories, proposals, departments, or products in terms of their similarities and differences. In this type of speech you would not only be concerned with explaining each theory or

proposal, but also with how they're similar and how they're different.

Pro and Con, Advantages and Disadvantages. The pro-and-con pattern, sometimes called the advantages–disadvantages pattern, is useful in informative speeches in which you want to explain objectively the advantages (the pros) and the disadvantages (the cons) of each plan, method, or product.

Claim and Proof. The claim-and-proof pattern is especially useful in a persuasive speech in which you want to prove the truth or usefulness of a particular proposition. It's the pattern that you see frequently in trials where the claim made by the prosecution is that the defendant is guilty and the proof is the varied evidence: the defendant had a motive; the defendant had the opportunity; the defendant had no alibi. In this pattern your speech would consist of two major parts. In the first part you'd explain your claim (tuition must not be raised, library hours must be expanded, courses in Caribbean studies must be instituted). In the second part you'd offer your evidence or proof as to why tuition must not be raised, for example.

Multiple Definition. The multiple definition pattern is often useful for explaining specific concepts (What is a born-again Christian? What is a scholar? What is multiculturalism?). In this pattern each major heading would consist of a different type of definition or way of looking at the concept. A variety of definition types is discussed in Unit 18.

Who? What? Why? Where? When? This 5W pattern is the pattern of the journalist and is useful when you wish to report or explain an event, for example, a robbery, political coup, war, ceremony, or trial. Here you'd have five major parts to the body of your speech, each dealing with the answers to one of these five questions.

STEP 7. CONSTRUCT YOUR INTRODUCTION, CONCLUSION, AND TRANSITIONS

Now that you have the body of your speech organized, devote your attention to the introduction, conclusion, and transitions that will hold the parts of your speech together.

Introduction

Begin collecting suitable material for your introduction as you prepare the entire speech, but wait until all the other parts are completed before you put the pieces together. In this way you'll be better able to determine which elements should be included and which should be eliminated.

Together with your general appearance and your nonverbal messages, the introduction gives your audience its first impression of you and your speech. Your introduction sets the tone for the rest of the speech; it tells your listeners what kind of a speech they'll hear.

Your introduction should serve three functions: gain attention, establish a speaker-audience-topic connection, and orient the audience as to what is to follow. Let's look at each of these functions and at the ways you can serve these functions.

Gain Attention

In your introduction, gain the attention of your audience and focus it on your speech topic. And, of course, maintain that attention throughout your speech. You can secure attention in a number of ways; here are just a few of them.

- *Ask a question*. Questions are effective because they are a change from declarative statements and they call for an active response from listeners.
- *Refer to audience members*. Referring to the audience makes them perk up and pay attention, because you are involving them directly in your talk.
- *Refer to recent happenings*. Citing a previous speech, recent event, or prominent person currently making news helps gain attention because the audience is familiar with this and will pay attention to see how you are going to connect it to your speech topic.
- *Use humor*. A clever (and appropriate) anecdote is often useful in holding attention.
- *Use an illustration or dramatic story*. Much as people are drawn to soap operas, so are we drawn to illustrations and stories about people.
- *Stress importance of topic*. People pay attention to what they feel is important to them and ignore what seems unimportant and irrelevant. If your topic focuses on the interests of the audience, you might begin by referring directly to it.
- *Use a presentation aid*. Presentation aids are valuable because they are new and different. They engage our senses and thus our attention.
- *Tell the audience to pay attention*. A simple, "I want you to listen to this frightening statistic," or "I want you to pay particularly close attention to . . . ," used once or twice in a speech, will help gain audience attention.
- *Use a quotation*. Quotations are useful because the audience is likely to pay attention to the brief and clever remarks of someone they've heard of or read about. Do make sure, however, that the quotation relates directly to your topic.
- *Cite a little known fact or statistic*. Little-known facts or statistics will help perk up an audience's attention. Headlines on unemployment statistics, crime in the schools, and political corruption sell newspapers because they gain attention.

Establish a Speaker-Audience-Topic Relationship

In addition to gaining attention, use your introduction to establish a connection among yourself as the speaker, the audience members, and your topic. Try to answer your listeners' inevitable question: Why should we listen to you speak on this topic? You can establish an effective speaker-audience-topic relationship in a number of ways.

- *Refer to others present.* Not only will this help you to gain attention, it will also help you to establish an effective speaker-audience-topic relationship.
- *Refer to the occasion.* Often your speech will be connected directly with the occasion. By referring to the reason the audience has gathered, you can establish a connection between yourself, the audience, and the topic.
- *Express your pleasure or interest in speaking.*
- *Establish your competence in the subject.* Show the audience that you are really interested in and knowledgeable about the topic.
- *Compliment the audience.* Pay the people in the audience an honest and sincere compliment, and they will not only give you their attention, they will feel a part of your speech. In some cultures—Asian cultures such as Japan and Korea are good examples—the speaker is expected to compliment the audience. It's one of the essential parts of the introduction. Visitors from the United States are often advised when speaking in a foreign country to compliment the country itself, its beauty, its culture.
- *Express similarities with the audience.* By stressing your own similarity with members of the audience, you create a bond with them and become an "insider" instead of an "outsider."

Orient the Audience

The introduction should orient the audience in some way as to what is to follow in the body of the speech. Preview for the audience what you are going to say by giving them a general idea, for example, "Tonight I'm going to discuss atomic waste"; giving a detailed preview, perhaps outlining your major propositions; or identifying your goal, for example, stating your thesis.

Conclusion

Your conclusion is especially important because it's often the part of the speech that the audience remembers most clearly. It's your conclusion that in many cases determines what image of you is left in the minds of the audience. Devote special attention to this brief but crucial part of your speech. Let your conclusion serve three major functions: to summarize, motivate, and provide closure.

Summarize

The summary function is particularly important in an informative speech, less so in persuasive speeches or in speeches to entertain. You may summarize your speech in a variety of ways.

- *Restate your thesis or purpose.* In this type of brief summary, you restate the essential thrust of your speech, repeating your thesis or perhaps the goals you hoped to achieve.
- *Restate the importance of the topic.* Tell the audience again why your topic or thesis is so important.
- *Restate your major propositions.* Restate your thesis and the major propositions you used to support it.

Motivate

A second function of the conclusion—most appropriate in persuasive speeches—is to motivate the people in audience to do what you want them to do. In your conclusion you have the opportunity to give the audience one final push in the direction you wish them to take. Whether it's to buy stock, vote a particular way, or change an attitude, you can use the conclusion for a final motivation, a final appeal. Here are two excellent ways to motivate.

- *Ask for a specific response.* Specify what you want the audience to do after listening to your speech.
- *Provide directions for future action.* Spell out, most often in general terms, the direction you wish the audience to take.

Close

The third function of your conclusion is to provide closure. Often your summary will accomplish this, but in some instances it will prove insufficient. End your speech with a conclusion that is crisp and definite. Make the audience know that you have definitely and clearly ended. Some kind of wrap-up, some sort of final statement, is helpful in providing this feeling of closure. You may achieve closure through a variety of methods.

- *Use a quotation.* A quotation is often an effective means of providing closure.
- *Refer to subsequent events.* You may also achieve closure by referring to future events taking place either that day or soon afterwards.
- *Refer back to the introduction.* It's sometimes useful to connect your conclusion with your introduction.
- *Pose a challenge or question.* You may close your speech by leaving the audience with a provocative question to ponder or a challenge to consider. Or, you can pose a question and answer it by recapping your thesis and perhaps some of your major arguments or propositions.
- *Thank the audience.* Speakers frequently conclude their speeches by thanking the audience for their attention or their invitation to you to address them.

Transitions

Transitions are words, phrases, or sentences that connect the various parts of your speech. They provide the audience with guideposts that help them follow the development of your thoughts and arguments. Use transitions in at least the following places:

- between the introduction and the body of the speech
- between the body and the conclusion
- between the main points in the body of the speech

Here are the major transitional functions and some stylistic devices that you might use to serve these functions.

To announce the start of a major proposition or piece of evidence: First, . . . , A second argument . . . , A closely related problem . . . , If you want further evidence, look at. . . .

To signal that you're drawing a conclusion from previously given evidence and argument: Thus, . . . , Therefore, . . . , So, as you can see . . . , It follows, then, that . . . .

To alert the audience to your introducing a qualification or exception: But, . . . , However, also consider . . . .

To remind listeners of what has just been said and that it's connected with another issue that will now be considered: In contrast to . . . , consider also . . . , Not only . . . , but also . . . , In addition to . . . , we also need to look at . . . .

To signal the part of your speech you're approaching: By way of introduction . . . , In conclusion . . . , Now, let's discuss why we're here today . . . .

To signal your organizational structure: I'll first explain the problems with jury awards and then propose a workable solution.

To summarize some section of your speech and to point to the next section: The three arguments advanced here were (1) . . . , (2) . . . , (3) . . . . Now, what can we do about them? I think we can do two things. First, ..."

You can enhance your transitions by pausing between your transition and the next part of your speech. This will help the audience see that a new part of your speech is coming. You might also take a step forward or to the side after saying your transition. This will also help to reinforce the movement from one part of your speech to another.

SUMMARY

This unit covered ways of supporting and organizing your main thoughts and introducing and concluding your speech.

1. Reinforce your major propositions with a variety of materials that support them.
2. Suitable supporting materials include examples, narration, testimony, statistics, and presentation aids as well as such materials as quotations, definitions, comparisons, statements of facts, and repetition and restatement.
3. Organize the speech materials into a clear, easily identifiable thought pattern.
4. Suitable organizational patterns include: time, space, topical, problem–solution, cause–effect/effect–cause, motivated sequence, structure–function, comparison and contrast, pro and con, claim and proof, multiple definition, and who-what-why-where-when.
5. Conclusions should summarize the main ideas, provide a final motivation, and provide a crisp closing to the speech.
6. Introductions should gain attention, establish a connection between the speaker, audience, and topic, and orient the audience as to what is to follow.
7. Transitions and internal summaries help connect the parts of the speech so that they flow into one another and also help the listeners better remember the speech.

KEY TERMS

presentation aid (p. 313)

temporal pattern (p. 324)

spatial pattern (p. 325)

topical pattern (p. 325)

problem–solution pattern (p. 325)

cause–effect pattern (p. 326)

motivated sequence (p. 326)

structure–function pattern (p. 327)

pro-and-con pattern (p. 327)

claim-and-proof pattern (p. 327)

comparison and contrast pattern (p. 327)

multiple definition (p. 328)

5W pattern (p. 328)

speaker-audience-topic connection (p. 328)

attention (p. 328)

orientation (p. 329)

summary (p. 329)

motivation (p. 329)

closure (p. 329)

transition (p. 330)

 ## THINKING CRITICALLY ABOUT
Supporting and Organizing a Public Speech

1. What strategies of arrangement would you use if you were giving a proabortion speech to an antiabortion audience? What strategies would you use if you were giving a speech in favor of domestic partnership insurance to the leadership of a variety of gay rights organizations?

2. Jamie, a student at a community college in Texas, wants to give a speech on the cruelty of cock fighting. The audience is predominantly Hispanic, most coming from Mexico, where cock fighting is a legal and popular sport. Among the visuals Jamie's considering are extremely vivid photographs of cocks literally torn to shreds by their opponents who have razor blades strapped to their feet. Would you advise Jamie to use these photographs if the audience was, say, moderately in favor of cock fighting? What if they were moderately against cock fighting? What general principle underlies your recommendations?

3. Visit one of the Web sites for quotations, for example: http://www.columbia.edu/acis/bartleby/bartlett (Barlett's Quotations), http://us.imdb.com/ (a database of quotations from films), and http://isleuth.com/quote.html (a combined reference of different collections of quotations). Select a quotation suitable for use with the slide show of the speech on culture shock and explain how you would use this on a new slide or on one of the 12 presented in Figure 16.2.

4. Shana wants to illustrate the rise and fall in the prices of 12 stocks over the last 10 years. She wants to show that the investment club (an audience of 16 members who are active participants in the club's investments) should sell three of the stocks and keep the other nine. This is the first time Shana will be using visual aids and she needs advice on what types of aids might best serve her purpose. What suggestions do you have for Shana?

5. Dave wants to set up a system of folders so he can conveniently store all the information he collects for his next three speeches, all of which will be built around the general topic of suicide. The first speech will deal with cultural views of suicide, the second on the current laws governing doctor-assisted suicides, and third a persuasive speech on doctor-assisted suicides. Dave wants to store all his outlines, research, speech critique forms, and anything else in a series of folders, which he's heard about but doesn't really know how to use. What advice can you give Dave to help him organize his speech folders? (The assumption here is that these are computer folders but physical folders would also work, though not as efficiently.)

6. Prepare and deliver a two-minute speech in which you
   - explain how you'd outline a speech on the geography of the United States, the structure of a table lamp, the need for improved sex education on campus, or why members should contribute to UNICEF
   - tell a personal story to illustrate a specific point, being sure to follow the suggestions offered in this unit
   - explain a print ad that relies on statistics and show how the advertiser uses statistics to make a point
   - select an advertisement and analyze it in terms of the motivated sequence
   - describe the events portrayed in a recently seen television program using a temporal pattern
   - discuss a recent newspaper editorial or op-ed letter in terms of a problem–7solution or cause–effect pattern
   - explain how television commercials get your attention
   - describe the introductions and conclusions used on television talk shows or on news programs
   - explain a print ad that contains a visual and explain how the visual and the text complement each other

UNIT 17

Style and Delivery in Public Speaking

UNIT GOALS

After reading this unit, you should be able to:

explain the values of outlining and the structure and function of the preparation, skeletal, and delivery outlines

explain how to achieve an oral style that is clear, vivid, appropriate, personal, and forceful.

explain the suggestions for efficient and effective rehearsal, the advantages and disadvantages of the different methods of delivery, and the characteristics of effective vocal and bodily delivery

This unit completes the steps for preparing and presenting a speech and focuses on the techniques of outlining, suggestions for wording your speech, and guides for rehearsal and delivery.

STEP 8. OUTLINE YOUR SPEECH

The outline is a blueprint for your speech; it lays out the elements of the speech and their relationship to each other. With this blueprint in front of you, you can see at a glance all the elements of organization—the functions of the introduction and conclusion, the transitions, the major propositions and their relationship to the thesis and purpose, and the adequacy of the supporting materials. And, like a blueprint for a building, the outline enables you to spot weaknesses that might otherwise go undetected.

Begin outlining at the time you begin constructing your speech. In this way you'll take the best advantage of one of the major functions of an outline—to tell you where change is needed. Change and alter the outline as necessary at every stage of the speech construction process.

Outlines may be extremely detailed or extremely general. Since you're now in a learning environment where the objective is to make you a more proficient public speaker, a detailed, full sentence outline will serve best. The more detail you put into the outline, the easier it will be to examine the parts of the speech for all the qualities and characteristics that make a speech effective.

Constructing the Outline

After you've completed your research and have an organizational plan for your speech mapped out, put this plan (this blueprint) on paper. Construct a "preparation outline" of your speech using the following guidelines.

Preface the Outline with Identifying Data. Before you begin the outline proper, identify the general and specific purposes as well as your thesis. This prefatory material should look something like this:

General purpose: to inform

Specific purpose: to inform my audience of four major functions of the mass media

Thesis: the mass media serve four major functions

These identifying notes are not part of your speech proper. They're not, for example, mentioned in your oral presentation. Rather, they're guides to the preparation of the speech and the outline. They're like road signs to keep you going in the right direction and to signal when you've gone off course. One additional bit of identifying data should preface the preface: the title of your speech.

Outline the Introduction, Body, and Conclusion as Separate Units. Each of these three parts of the speech, although intimately connected, should be labeled separately and should be kept distinct in your outline. Like the identifying data above, these labels are not spoken to the audience but are further guides to your preparation.

By keeping the introduction, body, and conclusion separate, you'll be able to see at a glance if they do, in fact, serve the functions you want them to serve. You'll be able to see where further amplification and support are needed. In short, you'll be able to see where there are problems and where repair is necessary.

At the same time, do make sure that you examine and see the speech as a whole—where the introduction leads to the body and the conclusion summarizes your propositions and brings your speech to a close.

Insert Transitions. Insert [using square brackets] transitions between the introduction and the body, the body and the conclusion, the major propositions of the body, and wherever else you think they might be useful.

Append a List of References. Some instructors require that you append a list of references to your speeches. If this is requested, then do so at the end of the outline or on a separate page. Some instructors require that only sources cited in the speech be included in the list of references, whereas others require that the full list of sources consulted be provided (those mentioned in the speech as well as those not mentioned).

Whatever the specific requirements, remember that these sources will prove most effective with your audience if you carefully integrate them into the speech. It will count for little if you consulted the latest works by the greatest authorities but never mention this to your audience. So, when appropriate, weave into your speech the source material you've consulted. In your outline, refer to the source material by author's name, date, and page in parentheses and then provide the complete citation in your list of references.

In your actual speech it might prove more effective to include the source with your statement. It might be phrased something like this:

> According to John Naisbitt, author of the nationwide bestseller, *Megatrends*, the bellwether states are California, Florida, Washington, Colorado, and Connecticut.

Regardless of what specific system is required (find out before you prepare your outline), make certain to include all sources of information, not just written materials. Personal interviews, information derived from course lectures, and data learned from television should all be included in your list of references.

Use a Consistent Set of Symbols. The following is the standard, accepted sequence of symbols for outlining.

    I.
      A.
        1.
          a.
            (1)
              (a)

Begin the introduction, the body, and the conclusion with Roman numeral I. Treat each of the three major parts as a complete unit.

Use Visual Aspects to Reflect the Organizational Pattern. Use proper and clear indentation. The outlining function of word processing programs has many of these suggestions built into them.

Not This:
I. Television caters to the lowest possible intelligence.
II. Talk shows illustrate this.
III. "General Hospital"

This:
I. Television caters to the lowest possible intelligence.
  A. Talk shows illustrate this.
    1. "Geraldo"
    2. "Ricki Lake"
    3. "Jerry Springer "
  B. Soap operas illustrate this.
    1. "As the World Turns"

2. "General Hospital"
3. "Young and the Restless"

Use One Discrete Idea Per Symbol. If your outline is to reflect the organizational pattern among the various items of information, use just one discrete idea per symbol. Compound sentences are sure giveaways that you have not limited each item to a single idea. Also, be sure that each item is discrete, that is, that it does not overlap with any other item. Instead of the overlapping, "Education might be improved if teachers were better trained and if students were better motivated," break it into two propositions: I. Education would be improved if teachers were better trained and II. Education would be improved if students were better motivated.

Use Complete Declarative Sentences. Phrase your ideas in the outline in complete declarative sentences rather than as questions or as phrases. This will further assist you in examining the essential relationships. It's much easier, for example, to see if one item of information supports another if both are phrased in the declarative mode. If one is a question and one is a statement, this will be more difficult.

Three Sample Outlines

Now that the principles of outlining are clear, here are some specific examples to illustrate how those principles are used in specific outlines. Presented here are a full sentence preparation outline with annotations to guide you through the essential steps in outlining a speech, a skeletal outline that will provide a kind of template for a speech outline, and a delivery outline which will illustrate the type of outline you might use in delivering your speech.

The Preparation Outline

Here's a relatively detailed outline similar to the ones you might prepare in constructing your speech. The side notes should clarify both the content and the format of a full sentence outline. This is the outline from which the PowerPoint™ slide show presented in the previous unit was designed.

Have You Ever Been Culture Shocked?

Thesis: Culture shock can be described in four stages.

General Purpose: To Inform

Specific Purpose To inform my audience of the four phases of culture shock.

Generally the title, thesis, general, and specific purpose of the speech are prefaced to the outline. When the outline is an assignment that is to be handed in, additional information may be requested.

Note the general format for the outline; note that the headings are clearly labeled and that the indenting helps you to see clearly the relationship that one item bears to the other. For example, in Introduction II, the outline format helps you to see that A and B are explanations (amplification, support) for II.

Introduction

I. Many of you have or will experience culture shock.
    A. Many people experience culture shock, that reaction to being in a culture very different from what you were used to.
    B. By understanding culture shock, you'll be in a better position to deal with it if and when it comes.
II. I've lived in four different cultures myself.
    A. I've always been interested in the way in which people adapt to different cultures.
    B. With our own campus becoming more culturally diverse every semester, the process of culture shock becomes important for us all.
III. Culture shock occurs in four stages (Oberg 1960).
    A. The Honeymoon occurs first.
    B. The Crisis occurs second.
    C. The Recovery occurs third.
    D. The Adjustment occurs fourth.

Note that the introduction, body, and conclusion are clearly labeled and separated visually.

The speaker assumes that the audience knows the general nature of culture shock and so does not go into detail as to its definition. But, just in case some audience members don't know and to refresh the memory of others, the speaker includes a brief definition.

Here the speaker attempts to connect the speaker, audience, and topic by stressing intercultural experiences and an abiding interest in the topic. Also, the speaker makes the topic important to the audience by referring to their everyday surroundings.

Note that references are integrated throughout the outline just as they would be in a term paper. In the actual speech, the speaker might say: "Anthropologist Kalervo Oberg, who coined the term *culture shock*, said it occurs in four stages."

The introduction serves the three functions noted: it gains attention (by involving the audience and by stressing the importance of the topic to the audience's desire to gain self-understanding), it connects the speaker, audience, and topic in a way that establishes the credibility of the speaker, and it orients the audience as to what is to follow. This particular orientation identifies both the number of stages and their names. If this speech were a much longer and more complex one, the orientation might also have included brief definitions of each stage.

[Let's follow the order in which these four stages occur and begin with the first stage, the honeymoon.]

This transition cues the audience into a four-part presentation. Also, the numbers repeated throughout the outline will further aid the audience in keeping track of where you are in the speech. Most important, it tells the audience that the speech will follow a temporal thought pattern.

Body

I. The Honeymoon occurs first.
   A. The honeymoon is the period of fascination with the new people and culture.
   B. You enjoy the people and the culture.
      1. You love the people.
         a. For example, the people in Zaire spend their time very differently from the way New Yorkers do.
         b. For example, my first 18 years living on a farm was very different from life in a college dorm.
      2. You love the culture.
         a. The great number of different religions in India fascinated me.
         b. Eating was an especially great experience.

[But, like many relationships, life is not all honeymoon; soon there comes a crisis.]

II. The Crisis occurs second.
   A. The crisis is the period when you begin to experience problems.
      1. One-third of American workers abroad fail because of culture shock (Samovar & Porter 1991, p. 232).
      2. The personal difficulties are also great.
   B. Life becomes difficult in the new culture.
      1. Communication is difficult.
      2. It's easy to offend people without realizing it.

[As you gain control over the crises, you begin to recover.]

III. The Recovery occurs third.
   A. The recovery is the period where you learn how to cope.
   B. You begin to learn intercultural competence (Lustig & Koester 1999).
      1. You learn how to communicate.
         a. Being able to go to the market and make my wants known was a great day for me.
         b. I was able to ask for a date.

Notice the parallel structure throughout the outline. For example, note that I, II, III, and IV in the body are all phrased in exactly the same way. Although this may seem unnecessarily redundant, it will help your audience follow your speech more closely and will also help you in logically structuring your thoughts.

Notice that there are lots of examples throughout this speech. These examples are identified only briefly in the outline and would naturally be elaborated on in the speech.

Notice too the internal organization of each major point. Each main assertion in the body contains a definition of the stage (IA, IIA, IIIA, and IVA) and examples (IB, IIB, IIIB, and IVB) to illustrate the stage.

Because this is a specific fact, some style manuals require that the page number should be included.

Note that each statement in the outline is a complete sentence. You can easily convert this outline into a phrase or keyword outline for use in delivery. The full sentences, however, will help you see more clearly relationships among items.

2. You learn the rules of the culture.
   a. The different religious ceremonies each have their own rules.
   b. Eating is a ritual experience in lots of places throughout Africa.

[Your recovery leads naturally into the next and final stage, the adjustment.]

IV. The Adjustment occurs fourth.
   A. The adjustment is the period where you come to enjoy the new culture.
   B. You come to appreciate the people and the culture.

[Let me summarize the stages you go through in experiencing culture shock.]

Conclusion

I. Culture shock can be described in four stages.
   A. The honeymoon is first.
   B. The crisis is second.
   C. The recovery is third.
   D. The adjustment is fourth.

II. Culture shock is a fascinating process; you may want to explore it more fully.
   A. Lots of books on culture shock are on reserve for Communication 325: Culture and Communication.
   B. Sunday's "60 Minutes" is going to have a piece on culture shock.

III. By knowing the four stages, you can better understand the culture shock you may now be experiencing on the job, at school, or in your private life.

REFERENCES

Lustig, Myron W., and Jolene Koester (1999). *Intercultural Competence: Interpersonal Communication across Cultures*, 3rd ed. New York: Longman.

Oberg, Kalervo (1960). Culture Shock: Adjustment to New Cultural Environments. *Practical Anthropology* 7:177–182.

Samovar, Larry A., and Richard E. Porter (1995). *Communication Between Cultures*. Belmont, CA: Wadsworth.

The transitions are inserted between all major parts of the speech. Although they may seem too numerous in this abbreviated outline, they will be appreciated by your audience because the transitions will help them follow your speech.

Notice that these four points correspond to I, II, III, and IV of the body and to III A, B, C, and D of the introduction. Notice how the similar wording adds clarity.

This step in which the speaker motivates the listeners to continue learning about culture shock is optional in informative speeches.

This step provides closure; it makes it clear that the speech is finished. It also serves to encourage reflection on the part of the audience as to their own culture shock.

This reference list includes just those sources that appear in the completed speech.

The Skeletal Outline

Here's a skeletal outline—a kind of template for structuring a speech. This particular outline would be appropriate for a speech using a time, spatial, or topical organization pattern. Note that in this skeletal outline there are three major propositions (I, II, and III in the body). These correspond to the III A, B, and C in the introduction (where you'd orient the audience) and to the I A, B, and C in the conclusion

(where you'd summarize your major propositions). The transitions are signaled by square brackets. As you review this outline—the faintly printed watermarks will remind you of the functions of each outline item—you'll be able to see how it can be adapted for use with other organization patterns, for example, problem–solution, cause–effect, or the motivated sequence.

Thesis: your main assertion; the core of your speech
_____.

General Purpose: your general aim (to inform, to persuade, to entertain)
_____.

Specific Purpose: what you hope to achieve from this speech
_____.

Introduction

I. gain attention _____.

II. establish s-a-t connection _____.

III. orient audience _____.

  A. first major proposition; same as I in body

  B. second major proposition; same as II in body

  C. third major proposition; same as III in body

[Transition: connect the introduction to the body]

Body

I. first major proposition _____.

  A. support for I (the first major proposition)

  B. further support for I

[Transition: connect the first major proposition to the second]

II. second major proposition _____.

  A. support for II (the second major proposition)

  B. further support for II

[Transition: connect the second major proposition to the third]

III. third major proposition _____.

  A. support for III

  B. further support for III

[Transition: connect the third major proposition (or all major propositions) to the conclusion]

Conclusion

I. summary _____.

  A. first major proposition; same as I in body

  B. second major proposition; same as II in body

  C. third major proposition; same as III in body

II. motivation _____.

III. closure _____.

References

1.

2.

3.

The Delivery Outline

Now that you've constructed a preparation outline, you need to construct a delivery outline, an outline that will assist you in delivering the speech. Resist the temptation to use your preparation outline to deliver the speech. If you use your preparation outline, you'll tend to read from the outline, instead of presenting an extemporaneous speech where you attend to and respond to audience feedback. Instead, construct a brief delivery outline, one that will assist rather than hinder your delivery of the speech. Here are some guidelines in preparing this delivery outline.

- *Be brief.* Try to limit yourself to one side of one sheet of paper.
- *Be clear.* Be sure that you can see the outline while you're speaking. Use different colored ink, underlining, and whatever system will help you communicate your ideas.
- *Be delivery-minded.* Include any guides to delivery that will help while you're speaking. Note in the outline when you'll use your presentation aid and when you'll remove it. A simple "show PA" or "remove PA" should suffice. You might also wish to note some speaking cues such as "slow down" when reading a poetry excerpt, or perhaps a place where an extended pause might help.
- *Rehearse with the delivery outline.* In your rehearsals, use the delivery outline only. Remember, the objective is to make rehearsals as close to the real thing as possible.

The following is a sample delivery outline constructed from the preparation outline on culture shock. Note that the outline is brief enough so that you'll be able to use it effectively without losing eye contact with the audience. It uses abbreviations (for example, CS for culture shock) and phrases rather than complete sentences. And yet, it's detailed enough to include all essential parts of your speech, including transitions. It contains delivery notes specifically tailored to your own needs, for example, pause suggestions and guides to using visual aids. Note also that it's clearly divided into introduction, body, and conclusion and uses the same numbering system as the preparation outline.

PAUSE!

LOOK OVER THE AUDIENCE!

I. Many experience CS

   A. CS: the reaction to being in a culture very different from your own

   B. By understanding CS, you'll be better able to deal with it

PAUSE SCAN AUDIENCE
II. I've experienced CS
III. CS occurs in 4 stages (WRITE ON BOARD)

   A. Honeymoon

   B. Crisis

   C. Recovery

   D. Adjustment

[Let's examine these stages of CS]

PAUSE/STEP FORWARD

I. Honeymoon

   A. fascination w/ people and culture

   B. enjoyment of people and culture
      1. Zaire example
      2. farm to college dorm

[But, life is not all honeymoon—the crisis]

II. Crisis

   A. problems arise
      1. 1/3 Am workers fail abroad
      2. personal difficulties

   B. life becomes difficult
      1. communication
      2. offend others

[As you gain control over the crises, you learn how to cope]

PAUSE

(continued on next page)

III. Recovery
   A. period of learning to cope
   B. you learn intercultural competence
      1. communication becomes easier
      2. you learn the culture's rules

[As you recover, you adjust]

IV. Adjustment
   A. learn to enjoy (again) the new culture
   B. appreciate people and culture

[These then are the four stages; let me summarize]

PAUSE BEFORE STARTING CONCLUSION

I. CS occurs in 4 stages: honeymoon, crisis, recovery, & adjustment
II. You can learn more about CS: books, 60 minutes
III. By knowing the 4 stages, you can better understand the culture shock you may now be experiencing on the job, at school, or in your private life.

PAUSE
ANY QUESTIONS?

STEP 9. WORD YOUR SPEECH

You're a successful public speaker when your listeners create in their minds the meanings you want them to create. You're successful when your listeners adopt the attitudes and behaviors you want them to adopt. The language choices you make—the words you select and the sentences you form—will greatly influence the meanings your listeners receive and, thus, how successful you are.

Oral Style

Oral style is a quality of spoken language that differentiates it from written language. You do not speak as you write (Akinnaso 1982). The words and sentences you use differ. The major reason for this difference is that you compose speech instantly. You select your words and construct your sentences as you think your thoughts. There's very little time in between the thought and the utterance. When you write, however, you compose your thoughts after considerable reflection. Even then you probably often rewrite and edit as you go along. Because of this, written language has a more formal tone. Spoken language is more informal, more colloquial.

Generally, spoken language consists of shorter, simpler, and more familiar words than does written language. There's more qualification in speech than in writing. For example, when speaking you probably make greater use of such expressions as *although*, *however*, *perhaps*, and the like. When writing, you probably edit these out.

Spoken language has a greater number of self-reference terms (terms that refer to the speaker herself or himself): *I*, *me*, *our*, *us*, and *you*. Spoken language also has a greater number of "allness" terms such as *all*, *none*, *every*, *always*, and *never*. You're probably more careful when you write to edit out such allness terms when you realize that such terms are probably not very descriptive of reality.

Spoken language has more pseudo-quantifying terms (for example, *many, much, very, lots*) and terms that include the speaker as part of the observation (for example, *it seems to me that . . .* or *as I see it . . .*). Further, speech contains more verbs and adverbs; writing contains more nouns and adjectives.

Spoken and written language not only do differ, they should differ. The main reason why spoken and written language should differ is that the listener hears a speech only once; therefore, speech must be *instantly intelligible*. The reader, on the other hand, can reread an essay or look up an unfamiliar word. The reader can spend as much time as he or she wishes with the written page. The listener, however, must move at the pace set by the speaker. The reader may reread a sentence or paragraph if there's a temporary attention lapse. The listener doesn't have this option.

For the most part, it's wise to use "oral style" in your public speeches. The public speech, however, is composed much like a written essay. There's considerable thought and deliberation and much editing and restyling. Because of this, you'll need to devote special effort to retaining and polishing your oral style. In the following section specific suggestions for achieving this goal are presented.

Choosing Words

Choose carefully the words you use in your public speeches. Choose words to achieve clarity, vividness, appropriateness, a personal style, and forcefulness.

Clarity

Clarity in speaking style should be your primary goal. Here are some guidelines to help you make your speech clear.

Be Economical. Don't waste words. Notice the wasted words in such expressions as "at 9 am *in the morning,*" "we *first* began the discussion," "I *myself personally,*" and "blue *in color.*" By withholding the italicized terms you eliminate unnecessary words and move closer to a more economical and clearer style.

Use Specific Terms and Numbers. As we get more and more specific, we get a clearer and more detailed picture. Be specific. Don't say "dog" when you want your listeners to picture a St. Bernard. Don't say "car" when you want them to picture a limousine. The same is true of numbers. Don't say "earned a good salary" if you mean "earned $90,000 a year." Don't say "taxes will go up" when you mean "taxes will increase .07 percent."

Use Guide Phrases. Use guide phrases to help listeners see that you're moving from one idea to another. Use phrases such as "now that we have seen how . . . , let us consider how . . . ," and "my next argument . . . ." Terms such as *first, second, and also, although,* and *however* will help your audience follow your line of thinking.

Use Short, Familiar Terms. Generally, favor the short word over the long one. Favor the familiar word over the unfamiliar word. Favor the more commonly used term over the rarely used term.

Distinguish Between Commonly Confused Words. Many words, because they sound alike or are used in similar situations, are commonly confused. Try the accompanying self-test, which covers 10 of the most frequently confused words.

SELF-TEST

Can You Distinguish Commonly Confused Words?

Underline the word in parentheses that you would use in each sentence.

1. She (accepted, excepted) the award and thanked everyone (accept, except) the producer.
2. The teacher (affected, effected) his students greatly and will now (affect, effect) an entirely new curriculum.
3. Are you deciding (between, among) red and green or (between, among) red, green, and blue?
4. I (can, may) scale the mountain but I (can, may) not reveal its hidden path.
5. The table was (cheap, inexpensive) but has great style; the chairs cost a fortune but look (cheap, inexpensive).
6. We (discover, invent) uncharted lands but (discover, invent) computer programs.
7. He was (explicit, implicit) in his denial of the crime but was (explicit, implicit) concerning his whereabouts.
8. She (implied, inferred) that she'd seek a divorce; we can only (imply, infer) her reasons.
9. The wedding was (tasteful, tasty) and the food most (tasteful, tasty).
10. The student seemed (disinterested, uninterested) in the lecture. The teacher was (disinterested, uninterested) in who received what grades.

Here are the principles that govern correct usage: (1) Use *accept* to mean to receive and *except* to mean with the exclusion of. (2) Use *to affect* to mean to have an effect or to influence, and *to effect* to mean to produce a result. (3) Use *between* when referring to two items and *among* when referring to more than two items. (4) Use *can* to refer to ability and *may* to refer to permission. (5) Use *cheap* to refer to something that is inferior and *inexpensive* to something that costs little. (6) Use *discover* to refer to the act of finding something out or to learn something previously unknown and use *invent* to refer to the act of originating something new. (7) Use *explicit* to mean specific and *implicit* to mean the act of expressing something without actually stating it. (8) Use *to imply* to mean to state indirectly and *to infer* to mean to draw a conclusion. (9) Use *tasteful* to refer to one's good taste and use *tasty* to refer to something that tastes good. (10) Use *uninterested* to mean a lack of interest and use *disinterested* to mean objective or unbiased. What other commonly confused words can you think of? ✓

Carefully Assess Idioms. Idioms are expressions that are unique to a specific language and whose meaning cannot be deduced from the individual words used. Expressions such as "to kick the bucket," or "doesn't have a leg to stand on" are idioms; you either know the meaning of the expression or you don't; you can't figure it out from only a knowledge of the individual words.

The positive side of idioms is that they give your speech a casual and informal style; they make your speech sound like a speech and not like a written essay. The negative side of idioms is that they create problems for listeners who are not native speakers of your language. Many will simply not understand the meaning of your idioms. This problem is especially important because audiences are becoming increasingly intercultural and because the number of idioms we use is extremely high. If you're not convinced of this, read through any of the speeches in this text, especially in an intercultural group, and underline all idioms. You will no doubt have underlined a great deal more than most people would have suspected.

Vividness

Select words to make your ideas vivid and come alive in the minds of your listeners: use active verbs, strong verbs, figures of speech, and imagery.

Use Active Verbs. Favor verbs that communicate activity rather than passivity. The verb to be, in all its forms—is, are, was, were, will be—is relatively inactive. Try using verbs of action instead. Rather than saying "The teacher was in the middle of the crowd," say "The teacher stood in the middle of the crowd." Instead of saying "The report was on the President's desk for three days," try "The report rested (or slept) on the President's desk for three days." Instead of saying "Management will be here tomorrow," consider "Management will descend on us tomorrow" or "Management jets in tomorrow."

Use Strong Verbs. The verb is the strongest part of your sentence. Choose verbs carefully, and choose them so they accomplish a lot. Instead of saying "He

walked through the forest," consider such terms as wandered, prowled, rambled, or roamed. Consider whether one of these might not better suit your intended meaning. Consult a thesaurus for any verb you suspect might be weak.

Use Figures of Speech. Figures of speech help achieve vividness. Figures of speech are stylistic devices that have been a part of rhetoric since ancient times. Here are a few of the more popular ones:

- *Alliteration*, repeating the same initial sound in two or more words: for example, fifty famous flavors, the cool calculating leader.
- *Antithesis*, presenting contrary ideas in parallel form: for example, my loves are many, my enemies are few; "It was the best of times, it was the worst of times." (Charles Dickens)
- *Metaphor*, comparing two unlike things: for example, she's a lion when she wakes up, all nature is science, he's a real bulldozer. When the words *like* or *as* are used, the comparison is called a simile: for example, he takes charge like a bull, the manager is as gentle as a lamb.
- *Metonymy*, substituting a name for a title with which it's closely associated: for example, "City Hall issued the following news release" where City Hall is used instead of the mayor or the city council.
- *Rhetorical question*, using a question to make a statement or to produce a desired effect rather than secure an answer: for example, do you want to be popular? do you want to get well?

Use Imagery. Appeal to the senses, especially our visual, auditory, and tactile senses. Make your audience see, hear, and feel what you're talking about.

In describing people or objects, **create visual images**, pictures that your listeners can see. When appropriate, describe such visual qualities as height, weight, color, size, shape, length, and contour. Let your audience see the sweat pouring down the faces of the coal miners; let them see the short, overweight executive in a pin-striped suit smoking a cigar.

Use **auditory imagery** to describe sounds; let your listeners hear the car screeching, the wind whistling, the bells chiming, the angry professor roaring.

Use terms referring to temperature, texture, and touch to create **tactile imagery**. Let your listeners

UNDERSTANDING
Theory and Research

CAN IMAGERY BE TOO VIVID?

The suggestions for using imagery were offered as aids to making your speech more vivid than it would normally be in, say, conversation. However, there's some evidence to show that too vivid images may actually make your speech less memorable and less persuasive than it would be without these vivid images (Frey & Eagly 1993). When images are too vivid, they divert the brain from following a logically presented series of thoughts or arguments. The brain focuses on these extremely vivid images and loses the speaker's train of thought. The advice, therefore, is to use vividness when it adds clarity to your ideas. When there's the suspicion that your listeners may concentrate on the imagery rather than the idea, drop the imagery.

feel the cool water running over their bodies and the punch of the fighter; let them feel the smooth skin of the newborn baby.

Appropriateness

Use language that is appropriate to you as the speaker. Also, use language that is appropriate to your audience, the occasion, and the speech topic. Here are some general guidelines to help you achieve this quality.

Speak on the Appropriate Level of Formality. The most effective public speaking style is less formal than the written essay but more formal than conversation. One way to achieve an informal style is to use contractions. Say *don't* instead of *do not*, *I'll* instead of *I shall*, and *wouldn't* instead of *would not*. Contractions give a public speech the sound and rhythm of conversation, a quality that most listeners react to favorably. Use personal pronouns rather than impersonal expressions. Say "I found" instead of "it has been found," or "I will present three arguments" instead of "three arguments will be presented."

Avoid Unfamiliar Terms. Avoid using terms the audience doesn't know. Avoid foreign and technical terms unless you're certain the audience is familiar with them. Similarly, avoid jargon (the technical vocabulary of a specialized field) unless you're sure the meanings are clear to your listeners. Some acronyms (NATO, UN, NOW, and CORE) are probably familiar to most audiences; many, however, are not. When you wish to use any of these types of expression, explain fully their meaning to the audience.

Avoid Slang. Avoid offending your audience with language that embarrasses them or makes them think you have little respect for them. Although your listeners may themselves use such expressions, they often resent their use by public speakers.

Avoid Ethnic Expressions (Generally). Ethnic expressions are words and phrases that are peculiar to a particular ethnic group. At times these expressions are known only by members of the ethnic group and at other times they are known more widely but still recognized as ethnic expressions.

In speaking to a multicultural audience it's generally best to avoid ethnic expressions unless they're integral to your speech and you explain them. Such expressions are often interpreted as exclusionist; they highlight the connection between the speaker and the members of that particular ethnic group and the lack of connection between the speaker and all others who are not members of that ethnic group. And, of course, ethnic expressions should never be used if you're not a member of the ethnic group.

If, on the other hand, you're speaking to an audience from one ethnic group and if you're also a member, then such expressions are fine. In fact, they may well prove effective since they are part of the common language of speaker and audience and will help to stress your own similarities with the audience.

Personal Style

Audiences favor speakers who speak in a personal rather than an impersonal style, who speak with them rather than at them. You can achieve a more personal style by using personal pronouns, asking questions, and creating immediacy.

Use Personal Pronouns. Say *I*, *me*, *he*, *she*, and *you*. Avoid such impersonal expressions as *one* (as in "One is lead to believe . . . ."); or *this speaker*; or *you, the listeners*. These expressions distance the audience and create barriers rather than bridges.

Use Questions. Ask the audience questions to involve them. In a small audience, you might even briefly entertain responses. In larger audiences, you might ask the question, pause to allow the audience time to consider their responses, and then move on. When you direct questions to your listeners, they feel a part of the public speaking transaction.

Create Immediacy. Immediacy is a connectedness, a relatedness with one's listeners. Immediacy is the opposite of disconnected and separated. Here are some suggestions for creating immediacy through language:

- Use personal examples.
- Use terms that include both you and the audience, for example, *we* and *our.*
- Address the audience directly; say *you* rather than *students*; say "you'll enjoy reading" instead of "everyone will enjoy reading"; say "I want you to see" instead of "I want people to see."
- Use specific names of audience members when appropriate.
- Express concern for the audience members.
- Reinforce or compliment the audience.
- Refer directly to commonalities between you and the audience; for example, "we are all children of immigrants" or "we all want to see our team in the playoffs."
- Refer to shared experiences and goals; for example, "we all want, we all need a more responsive PTA."

Would you be offended by slang and vulgar expressions if you overheard strangers in the street use them? If your instructor used them? If students gave speeches using them? Under what circumstances, if any, would it be acceptable to use these expressions?

- Recognize audience feedback and refer to it in your speech. Say, for example, "I can see from your expressions that we're all anxious to get to our immediate problem."

Forcefulness/Power

Forceful or powerful language will help you achieve your purpose, whether it be informative or persuasive. Forceful language enables you to direct the audience's attention, thoughts, and feelings. To make your speech more forceful, eliminate weakeners, vary intensity, and avoid overused expressions.

Eliminate Weakeners. Delete phrases that weaken your sentences. Among the major weakeners are uncertainty expressions and weak modifiers. Uncertainty expressions such as *I'm not sure of this, but*; *perhaps it might*; or *maybe it works this way* communicate a lack of commitment and conviction and will make your audience wonder if you're worth listening to. Weak

UNDERSTANDING Theory and Research

WHEN IS SPEECH UNETHICAL?

Here are just a few examples of speech that many people are beginning to see as unethical. For example, it's considered unethical (and it's illegal as well) to defame another person, to falsely attack his or her reputation, causing damage to it. When this attack is done in print or in pictures it is called *libel*, when done through speech it is called *slander*.

Whereas just decades ago it would have been considered quite respectable to use racial, sexist, or homophobic terms in conversation or tell jokes at the expense of various cultural groups, today it would be considered unethical to demean another person because of that person's sex, age, race, na-

tionality, affectional orientation, or religion. It would also be considered unethical to speak in cultural stereotypes—fixed images of groups that deny differences and that promote generally negative pictures. Public speakers are usually expected to follow a more socially conscious speech than would be expected in, say, a small group of culturally similar persons.

Sexual harassment (against either sex by either sex) would be considered unethical and a form of speech that would not be protected by the First Amendment.

Another form of speech that would be considered unethical is verbal abuse. Verbally abusing people because of their position on a particular issue or because of their cultural identification would be considered unethical.

---

modifiers such as "It works *pretty* well," "It's *kind of like* . . . ," or "It *may be* the one we want" make you seem unsure and indefinite about what you're saying.

Cut out any unnecessary phrases that reduce the impact of your meaning. Instead of saying "There are lots of things we can do to help," say "We can do lots of things to help." Instead of saying "I'm sorry to be so graphic, but Senator Bingsley's proposal . . . ," say "We need to be graphic. Senator Bingsley's proposal . . . ." Instead of saying "It should be observed in this connection that, all things considered, money is not productive of happiness," say "Money does not bring happiness." Consider the suggestions in Table 17.1 for achieving more powerful language. These suggestions are not limited in application to public speaking; they relate as well to interpersonal and small group communication.

Vary Intensity as Appropriate. Just as you can vary your voice in intensity, you can also phrase your ideas with different degrees of stylistic intensity. You can, for example, refer to an action as "failing to support our position" or as "stabbing us in the back"; you can say that

a new proposal will "endanger our goals" or "destroy us completely"; you can refer to a child's behavior as "playful," "creative," or "destructive." Vary your language to express different degrees of intensity—from mild through neutral to extremely intense.

Avoid Bromides and Clichés. Bromides are sentences that are worn out because of constant usage. Here are some examples.

- She's as pretty as a picture.
- Honesty is the best policy.
- If I can't do it well, I won't do it at all.
- I don't understand modern art, but I know what I like.

When we hear them, we recognize them as unoriginal and uninspired.

Clichés are phrases that have lost their novelty and part of their meaning through overuse. Clichés call attention to themselves because of their overuse. Here are some clichés to avoid:

- in this day and age
- tell it like it is

TABLE 17.1   Suggestions for more powerful speech

| What other suggestions can you offer for making speech more powerful? | | |
Avoid	Examples	Reasons
Hesitations	I, er, want to say that, ah, this one is, er, the best, you know.	Hesitations make you sound unprepared and uncertain.
Too many intensifiers	Really, this was the greatest; it was truly phenomenal.	Too many intensifiers make your speeches all sound the same and don't allow for intensifying what should be emphasized.
Tag questions	I'll review the report now, okay? That's a great proposal, don't you think?	Tag questions ask for another's agreement and therefore signal your need for approval and your own uncertainty or lack of conviction.
Self-critical statements	I'm not very good at this. This is my first speech.	Self-critical statements signal a lack of confidence and make public your inadequacies.
Slang and vulgar expressions	"!!#//***," No problem	Slang and vulgarity signal a low social class and hence little power; it may also communicate a lack of respect for your audience.

- free as a bird
- in the pink
- no sooner said than done
- it goes without saying
- few and far between
- over the hill
- no news is good news
- the life of the party
- keep your shirt on

Phrasing Sentences

Give the same careful consideration that you give to words to your sentences as well. Some guidelines follow.

Use Short Sentences

Short sentences are more forceful and economical. They are easier to comprehend and remember. Listeners don't have the time or the inclination to unravel long and complex sentences. Help them to listen more efficiently. Use short rather than long sentences.

Use Direct Sentences

Direct sentences are easier to understand. They are also more forceful. Instead of saying, "I want to tell you of the three main reasons why we should not adopt Program A," say "We should not adopt Program A. There are three main reasons."

Use Active Sentences

Active sentences are easier to understand than passive ones. They also make your speech seem livelier and more vivid. Instead of saying "The lower court's decision was reversed by the Supreme Court," say "The Supreme Court reversed the lower court's decision." Instead of saying "The proposal was favored by management," say "Management favored the proposal."

Use Positive Sentences

Positive sentences are easier to comprehend and remember. Notice how sentences (a) and (c) are easier to understand than sentences (b) and (d).

a. The committee rejected the proposal.
b. The committee did not accept the proposal.
c. This committee works outside the normal company hierarchy.
d. This committee does not work within the normal company hierarchy.

Listen to a good network anchorperson. How forceful or powerful is her or his language? Can you identify specific examples of powerful and powerless language?

Vary the Types of Sentences

The advice to use short, direct, active, and positive sentences is valid most of the time. Yet too many sentences of the same type or length will make your speech sound boring. Use variety while following (generally) the preceding advice.

Making Your Speech Easy to Remember

If your aim is to communicate information and argument to a listener, then surely part of your job is to ensure that your listeners remember what you say. Here are a few techniques you might use in helping your audience remember your speech.

- *Stress interest and relevance.* Listeners will think more about material they find interesting and relevant with the result that this "active rehearsal" significantly aids all kinds of memorization. You would probably have little trouble remembering the address for a job interview that promises $1500 per week to start, nor are you likely to forget the amount of money being offered.
- *Create connections.* Associate your material with what the audience already knows. If a new theory resembles a theory the audience is familiar with, mention this and then point out the differences between the two. If, for example, feedback in communication works like feedback in a thermostat (with which the audience is already familiar), mention that.
- *Pattern your messages.* Things are more easily remembered if they're presented in an organized pattern. The organizational patterns considered in the discussion of organization and outlining

(in the previous section) help you to present the listeners with patterns to aid their memory. Time sequences and spatial sequences, for example, are obvious examples of using known organizational patterns to assist memory.

- *Focus audience attention.* The best way to focus the listeners' attention is to tell them to focus their attention. Simply say, "I want you to focus on three points that I will make in this speech. First, ..." Then repeat at least once again (but preferably two or three times) these very same points. With experience in public speaking, you'll be able to do this with just the right combination of subtlety and directness.

STEP 10. REHEARSE AND DELIVER YOUR SPEECH

Your last step is to rehearse and deliver your speech. Let's look first at rehearsal.

Rehearsal

Use your rehearsal time effectively and efficiently to achieve the following goals:

- To develop a delivery that will help you achieve the purposes of your speech.
- To time your speech; if you time your rehearsals, you'll be able to see if you can add material or if you have to delete something.
- To see how the speech will flow as a whole and to make any changes and improvements you think necessary.

Going Online

The Douglas Web site

Visit the Douglas Web site. What resources does this Web site contain that might be of value to you in learning public speaking?

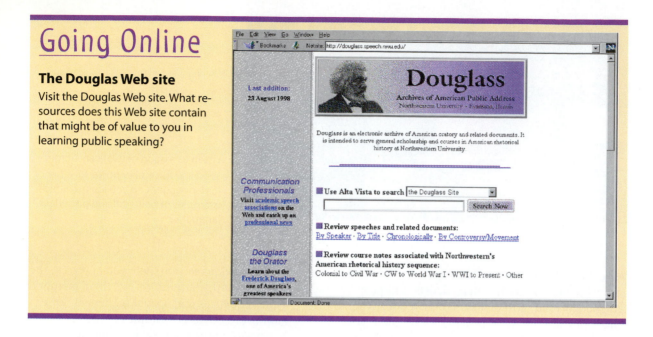

- To test the presentation aids, detect any technological problems, and resolve them.
- To help you learn the speech effectively.
- To reduce apprehension and give you confidence.

The following procedures should assist you in achieving these goals.

Rehearse the Speech as a Whole

Rehearse the speech from beginning to end. Do not rehearse the speech in parts. Rehearse it from getting out of your seat through the introduction, body, and conclusion, to returning to your seat. Be sure to rehearse the speech with all the examples and illustrations (and any audiovisual aids) included. This will enable you to connect the parts of the speech and see how they interact with each other.

Time the Speech

Time the speech during each rehearsal. Make the necessary adjustments on the basis of this timing. If you're using computer presentation software, you'll be able to time your speech very precisely. It will also enable you to time the individual parts of your speech so you can achieve the balance you want—for example, you might want to spend twice as much time on the solutions as on the problems or you might want to balance the introduction and conclu-

sion so that they each constitute about 10 percent of your speech.

Approximate the Actual Speech Situation

Rehearse the speech under conditions as close as possible to those under which you'll deliver it. If possible, rehearse the speech in the same room in which you'll present it. If this is impossible, try to simulate the actual conditions as close as you can—in your living room or even bathroom. If possible, rehearse the speech in front of a few supportive listeners. It's always helpful (but especially for your beginning speeches) that your listeners be supportive rather than too critical. Merely having listeners present during your rehearsal will further simulate the conditions under which you'll eventually speak. Get together with two or three other students in an empty classroom where you can each take turns as speaker and listener.

See Yourself as a Speaker

Rehearse the speech in front of a full-length mirror. This will enable you to see yourself and see how you'll appear to the audience. This may be extremely difficult at first, and you may have to force yourself to watch. After a few attempts, however, you'll begin to see the value of this experience. Practice your eye contact, your movements, and your gestures in front of the mirror.

Incorporate Changes and Make Delivery Notes

Make any changes in the speech that seem appropriate between rehearsals. Do not interrupt your rehearsal to make notes or changes. If you do, you may never experience the entire speech from beginning to end. While making these changes, note too any words whose pronunciation you wish to check. Also, insert pause notations ("slow down" warnings, and other delivery suggestions) into your outline.

If possible, record your speech (ideally, on videotape) so you can hear exactly what your listeners will hear: your volume, rate, pitch, pronunciation, and pauses. You'll thus be in a better position to improve these qualities.

Rehearse Often

Rehearse the speech as often as seems necessary. Two useful guides are: (1) rehearse the speech at least three or four times; less than this is sure to be too little; (2) rehearse the speech as long as your rehearsals result in improvements in the speech or in your delivery. Some suggestions for a long-term delivery improvement program are provided in the next section.

Undertake a Long-Term Delivery Improvement Program

Approach your long-term delivery program with positive thinking. This will help a great deal in setting up an attitude that will help you become a truly effective public speaker. Tell yourself that you can do it and that you will do it.

1. Seek feedback from someone whose opinion and insight you respect. Your public speaking instructor may be a logical choice, but someone majoring in communication or working in a communication field might also be appropriate. Get an honest and thorough appraisal of both your voice and your bodily action.
2. Learn to hear, see, and feel the differences between effective and ineffective patterns. Learn to hear, for example, the patterned nature of your pitch or your too-loud volume. A tape recorder will be very helpful. Learn to feel your rigid posture or your lack of arm and hand gestures. Once you've perceived these differences, concentrate on learning more effective patterns. Practice a few minutes each day. Avoid becoming too conscious of any source of ineffectiveness. Just try to increase your awareness and

work on one problem at a time. Do not try to change all your patterns at once.
3. Seek additional feedback on the changes. Make certain that listeners agree that the new patterns you're practicing are really more effective. Remember that you hear yourself through air transmission as well as through bone conduction. Others hear you only through air transmission. So, what you hear and what others hear will be different.
4. For voice improvement, consult a book on voice and diction for practice exercises and for additional information on the nature of volume, rate, pitch, and quality.
5. If any of these difficulties persist, see a professional. For voice problems, see a speech clinician. Most campuses have a speech clinic. You can easily avail yourself of its services. For bodily action difficulties, talk with your public speaking instructor.
6. Seek professional help if you're psychologically uncomfortable with any aspect of your voice or bodily action. It may be that all you have to do is to hear yourself or see yourself on a videotape—as others see and hear you—to convince yourself that you sound and look just fine. Regardless of what is causing this discomfort, however, if you're uncomfortable, do something about it. In a college community there's more assistance available to you at no cost than you'll ever experience again. Make use of it.

Delivery

If you're like my own students, delivery creates more anxiety for you than any other aspect of public speaking. Few speakers worry about organization or audience analysis or style. Many worry about delivery, so you have lots of company. In this unit the general methods and principles for effectiveness in presentation are examined. You can then adapt them to your own personality. In the next unit, specific suggestions for effectively presenting your speech are offered.

Methods of Delivery

Speakers vary widely in their methods of delivery: some speak "off-the-cuff", with no apparent preparation; others read their speeches from manuscript; some memorize their speeches word for word; others construct a detailed outline and actualize the speech itself at the moment of delivery. Speakers use all four of these general methods of delivery: impromptu, manuscript, memorized, and extemporaneous. Each has advantages and disadvantages.

Speaking Impromptu. When you speak impromptu you speak without any specific preparation. You and the topic meet for the first time and immediately the speech begins. On some occasions you will not be able to avoid speaking impromptu. In a classroom, after someone has spoken, you might comment on the speaker and the speech you just heard—this requires a brief impromptu speech of evaluation. In asking or answering questions in an interview situation you're giving impromptu speeches, albeit extremely short ones. At meetings, you may find yourself explaining a proposal or defending a plan of action. These too are impromptu speeches.

The impromptu experience provides excellent training in the different aspects of public speaking, for example, maintaining eye contact, responding to audience feedback, or gesturing. The impromptu speech experience can also provide practice in basic organization and in development of examples, arguments, and appeals.

The major disadvantage is that it focuses on appearances. The aim is often to *appear* to give an effective and well-thought-out speech. Another disadvantage is that it does not permit attention to the details of public speaking such as audience adaptation, research, and style. Because of this inadequacy, the audience is likely to get bored. This in turn may make the speaker feel uncomfortable.

Speaking from Manuscript. In the manuscript method, you read the entire speech. The speech is constructed in the same way you'd construct any speech. After you've constructed the detailed preparation outline, you'd write out the entire speech, exactly as you want it to be heard by your audience. You'd then read this speech to the audience.

The major advantage of a manuscript speech is that you can control the timing precisely. This is particularly important when delivering a recorded speech (on television, for example). You don't want your conclusion cut off so the fifty-ninth rerun of "Roseanne" can go on as scheduled. Also, there's no danger of forgetting, no danger of being unable to find the right word. Everything is there for you on

paper, so you'll probably be less anxious. Still another advantage is that it allows you to use the exact wording you (or a team of speech writers) want. In the political arena this is often crucial. The manuscript speech also has the advantage that it's already written out so you can distribute copies and are, therefore, less likely to be misquoted.

The most obvious disadvantage is that audiences don't like speakers to read their speeches; they prefer speakers who speak with them. Reading a manuscript makes it difficult (even impossible) to respond to feedback from your listeners. With a manuscript you're committed to the speech word for word and cannot make adjustments on the basis of audience feedback. When the manuscript is on a stationary lectern, as it most often is, it's impossible for you to move around. You have to stay in one place. The speech controls your movement or, rather, your lack of movement. It's also difficult to read a speech and sound natural and nonmechanical. Reading material from the printed page with liveliness and naturalness (or even from a teleprompter) is itself a skill that's difficult to achieve without lots of practice. Still another disadvantage is that it takes lots of time to write out a speech word for word, time that is much better spent working on the substance of your speech.

Speaking from Memory. The memorized method involves writing out the speech word for word (as does the manuscript speech) but instead of reading it, you commit it to memory and recite it or "act it out."

The memorized method has all the advantages of the manuscript method; at the same time, however, it allows you freedom to move about and otherwise concentrate on delivery. The major disadvantage, of course, is that you might forget your speech. In a memorized speech each sentence cues the recall of the following sentence. Thus, when you forget one sentence, you may forget the rest of the speech. This danger, along with the natural nervousness that speakers feel, makes this method a poor choice in most situations. Another disadvantage is that the memorized method is even more time-consuming than the manuscript method since it involves additional time for memorization. Still another disadvantage is that the memorized method doesn't allow easy adjusting to feedback. In fact, there's less opportunity to adjust to listener feedback than even in the manuscript method. And if you're not going to

BUILDING
Communication Skills

HOW DO YOU SPEAK IMPROMPTU?

The following experience may prove useful as an exercise in delivery. Students should be given three index cards each. Each student should write an impromptu speech topic on each of the cards. The topics to be used for impromptu speaking should be familiar but not clichés. They should be worthwhile and substantive, not trivial. They should be neither too simplistic nor too complex. The cards should be collected and placed face down on a table. A speaker is chosen through some random process and selects two cards, reads the topics, selects one of them and takes approximately one or two minutes to prepare a two-to-three minute impromptu speech. A few guidelines may prove helpful.

1. Don't apologize. Everyone will have difficulty with this assignment, so there is no need to emphasize any problems you may have.

2. Don't express verbally or nonverbally any displeasure or any negative responses to the experience, the topic, the audience, or even to yourself. Approach the entire task with a positive attitude and a positive appearance. It will help make the experience more enjoyable for both you and your audience.

3. When you select the topic, jot down two or three subtopics that you will cover and perhaps two or three bits of supporting material that you will use in amplifying these two or three subtopics.

4. Develop your conclusion. It is probably best to use a simple summary conclusion in which you restate your main topic and the subordinate topics that you discussed.

5. Develop an introduction. Here it is probably best simply to identify your topic and orient the audience by telling them the two or three subtopics that you will cover.

---

adjust to feedback, you lose the main advantage of face-to-face contact.

Speaking Extemporaneously. Extemporaneous delivery involves thorough preparation but no commitment to the exact wording to be used during the speech. It often involves memorizing your opening lines (perhaps the first few sentences), your closing lines (perhaps the last few sentences), and your major propositions and the order in which you will present them. Memorizing the opening and closing lines will help you to focus your complete attention on the audience and will also put you more at ease. Once you know exactly what you'll say in opening and closing the speech, you'll feel more in control.

The extemporaneous method is useful in most speaking situations. Good college lecturers use the extemporaneous method. They prepare thoroughly and

know what they want to say and in what order they want to say it, but they have given no commitment to exact wording. This method allows you to respond easily to feedback. Should a point need clarification, you can elaborate on it when it will be most effective. This method makes it easy to be natural because you're being yourself. It's the method that comes closest to conversation or, as some theorists have put it, enlarged conversation. With the extemporaneous method, you can move about and interact with the audience. The major disadvantage is that you may stumble and grope for words. If you've rehearsed the speech a number of times, however, this is not likely to happen. Another disadvantage is that you cannot give the speech the attention to style that you can with other methods. You can get around this disadvantage too by memorizing those phrases you want to say exactly. There is nothing in the extemporaneous method that prevents your committing to memory selected phrases, sentences, or quotations.

Characteristics of Effective Delivery

Strive for a delivery that is natural, reinforces the message, is varied, and conversational.

Effective Delivery Is Natural. Listeners will enjoy and believe you more if you speak naturally, as if you were conversing with a small group of people. Don't allow your delivery to call attention to itself. Your ultimate aim should be to deliver the speech so naturally that the audience won't even notice your delivery. This will take some practice, but you can do it. When voice or bodily action is so prominent that it's distracting, the audience concentrates on the delivery and will fail to attend to your speech.

Effective Delivery Reinforces the Message. Effective delivery should aid instant intelligibility. Your main objective is to make your ideas understandable to an audience. A voice that listeners have to strain to hear, a decrease in volume at the ends of sentences, and slurred diction will obviously hinder comprehension.

When you give a public speech, everything about you communicates. You cannot prevent yourself from sending messages to others. The way in which you dress is no exception. In fact, your attire will figure significantly in the way your audience assesses your credibility and even the extent to which they give you attention. In short, it will influence your effectiveness in all forms of persuasive and informative speaking. Unfortunately, there are no rules that will apply to all situations for all speakers. Thus, only general guidelines are offered here. Modify and tailor these for yourself and for each unique situation.

- Avoid extremes: don't allow your clothes to detract attention from what you're saying.
- Dress comfortably: be both physically and psychologically comfortable with your appearance so that you can concentrate your energies on what you're saying.
- Dress appropriately: your appearance should be consistent with the specific public speaking occasion.

Effective Delivery Is Varied. Listening to a speech is hard work. Flexible and varied delivery relieves this difficulty. Be especially careful to avoid monotonous and predictable patterns.

Speakers who are monotonous keep their voices at the same pitch, volume, and rate throughout the speech. The monotonous speaker maintains one level from the introduction to the conclusion. Like the drone of a motor, it easily puts the audience to sleep. Vary your pitch levels, your volume, and your rate of speaking. In a similar way, avoid monotony in bodily action. Avoid standing in exactly the same position throughout the speech. Use your body to express your ideas, to communicate to the audience what is going on in your head.

A predictable vocal pattern is one in which, for example, the volume levels vary but always in the same pattern. Through repetition, the pattern soon becomes predictable. For example, each sentence may begin at a loud volume and then decline to a barely audible volume. In bodily action, the predictable speaker repeatedly uses the same movements or gestures. For example, a speaker may scan the audience from left to right to left to right throughout the entire speech. If the audience can predict the pattern of your voice or your bodily action, your speech will almost surely be ineffective. A patterned and predictable delivery will draw the audience's attention away from what you're saying.

Effective Delivery Is Conversational. Although more formal than conversation, delivery in public speaking should have some of the most important features of conversation. These qualities are immediacy, eye contact, expressiveness, and responsiveness to feedback.

Just as you can create a sense of **immediacy** through language, you can also create it with delivery. Make your listeners feel that you're talking directly and individually to each of them. You can communicate immediacy through delivery in a number of ways:

- Maintain appropriate eye contact with the audience members.
- Maintain a physical closeness that reinforces a psychological closeness; don't stand behind a desk or lectern.
- Smile.

BUILDING
Communication Skills

HOW DO YOU RESPOND STRATEGICALLY AND ETHICALLY?

Consider the following situations that might arise in a public speaking situation. How would you respond to achieve your purpose and yet not violate any of your own ethical standards?

1. You've just given a speech to a racially diverse high school class on why they should attend your college. One audience member asks how racially diverse your faculty and students are. Your faculty is 94 percent European American, 4 percent Asian American, and 2 percent African American. You do know that the administration has been talking about making a major effort to recruit a more racially diverse faculty, but so far no action has been taken. Your student population is approximately 40 percent European American, 40 percent African American, 10 percent Hispanic, and 10 percent Asian American. What do you say?

2. You've just given a speech advocating banning alcohol on campus and in the speech you claimed that over 70 percent of the students favored banning alcohol. At the end of the speech, you realize that you made a mistake and that only 30 percent favored banning alcohol. Because you were nervous, you mixed up the figures. There's a question and answer period but no one asks about the figures. What do you say?

3. You represent the college newspaper and are asking the Student Government to increase the funding for the paper. The Student Government objects to giving extra money because the paper has taken on lots of causes that are unpopular with the majority of students. You feel that it's essential for the paper to represent the disenfranchised and fully expect to continue to do just exactly as you have in the past. But, if you say this, you won't get the funding that is essential to the life of the paper; the paper won't be able to survive unless the funding is increased. You would get the funding if you say you'll give primary coverage to majority positions. What do you say?

- Move around a bit; avoid the appearance of being too scared to move.
- Stand with a direct and open body posture.
- Talk directly to your audience and not to your notes or to your visual aid.

When you maintain **eye contact**, you make the public speaking interaction more conversational (in addition to communicating immediacy). Look directly into your listeners' eyes. Make a special effort to make eye contact. Lock eyes with different audience members for short periods.

When you're **expressive,** you communicate genuine involvement in the public speaking situation. You can communicate this quality of expressiveness, of involvement, in several ways:

- Express responsibility for your own thoughts and feelings.
- Vary your vocal rate, pitch, volume, and rhythm to communicate involvement and interest in the audience and in the topic.
- Allow your facial muscles and your entire body to reflect and echo this inner involvement.
- Use gestures to communicate involvement— too few gestures may signal disinterest, too many may communicate uneasiness, awkwardness, or anxiety.

Read carefully the **feedback** signals sent by your audience. Then respond to these signals with verbal, vocal, and bodily adjustments. For example, respond to audience feedback signals communicating lack of comprehension or inability to hear with added explanation or increased volume.

Using Notes. For many speeches it may be helpful to use notes. A few simple guidelines may help you avoid some of the common errors made in using notes.

1. *Keep notes to a minimum.* The fewer notes you take with you, the better off you will be. The reason so many speakers bring notes with them is that they want to avoid the face-to-face interaction required. With experience, however, you should find this face-to-face interaction the best part of the public speaking experience.
2. *Resist the normal temptation to bring with you the entire speech outline.* You may rely on it too heavily and lose the direct contact with the audience. Instead, compose a delivery outline, using only key words. Bring this to the lectern with you— one side of an index card or at most an 8-1/2 by 11-inch page should be sufficient. This will relieve anxiety over the possibility of your forgetting your speech but will not be extensive enough to interfere with direct contact with your audience.
3. *Don't make your notes more obvious than necessary.* But, at the same time, don't try to hide them. Don't gesture with your notes and thus make them more obvious than they need be. At the same time, don't turn away from the audience to steal a glance at them either. Use them openly and honestly but gracefully, with "open subtlety." To do this effectively, you'll have to know your notes intimately. Rehearse at least twice with the same notes that you will take with you to the speaker's stand.
4. *When referring to your notes, pause to examine them.* Then regain eye contact with the audience and continue your speech. Don't read from your notes, just take cues from them. The one exception to this is an extensive quotation or complex set of statistics that you have to read; then, almost immediately, resume direct eye contact with the audience.

Voice

Three dimensions of voice are significant to the public speaker: volume, rate, and pitch. Your manipulation of these elements will enable you to control your voice to maximum advantage.

Volume refers to the relative intensity of the voice. Loudness, on the other hand, refers to the perception of that relative intensity. In an adequately controlled voice, volume will vary according to a number of factors. For example, the distance between speaker and listener, the competing noise, and the emphasis the speaker wishes to give an idea will all influence volume.

The problems with volume are easy to identify in others, though difficult to recognize in ourselves. One obvious problem is a voice that is too soft. When speech is so soft that listeners have to strain to hear, they will soon tire of expending so much energy. On the other hand, a voice that is too loud will prove disturbing because it intrudes on our psychological space. However, it's interesting to note that a voice louder than normal communicates assertiveness (Page & Balloun, 1978) and will lead people to pay greater attention to you (Robinson & McArthur, 1982). On the other hand, it can also communicate aggressiveness and give others the impression that you'd be difficult to get along with.

The most common problem is too little volume variation. A related problem is a volume pattern that, although varied, varies in an easily predictable pattern. If the audience can predict the pattern of volume changes, they will focus on it and not on what you're saying.

Fading away at the end of sentences is particularly disturbing. Here the speaker uses a volume that is appropriate, but ends sentences speaking the last few words at an extremely low volume. Be particularly careful when finishing sentences; make sure the audience is able to hear these at an appropriate volume.

If you're using a microphone, test it first. Whether it's a microphone that clips around your neck, one you hold in your hand, or one that is stationed to the podium, try it out first. Some speakers—talk show host Montel Williams is a good example—use the hand microphone as a prop and flip it in the air or from hand to hand as they emphasize a particular point. For your beginning speeches, it's probably best to avoid such techniques and to use the microphone as unobtrusively as you can.

Rate refers to the speed at which you speak. About 150 words per minute seems average for speaking as well as for reading aloud. The problems of rate are speaking too fast or too slow, or with too little variation or too predictable a pattern. If you talk too fast you deprive your listeners of time they need to understand and digest what you're saying.

MEDIA WATCH

REVERSING MEDIA'S INFLUENCE

Although the media are generally analyzed for their effects on the individual, recognize that viewers and readers also exert influence on each other and may ultimately affect the media (radio, television, newspapers and magazines, film, CDs, and the Internet). For example, you may influence your friends or your family. They, in turn, will influence others, who will influence still others. Through these interpersonal channels, the influence of one person can be considerable. The larger and more influential these groups become, the more influence they will exert on the media through their selective attention and their buying habits. You may also influence the media more directly. Kathleen Hall Jamieson and Karlyn Kohrs Campbell, in their perceptive *Interplay of Influence* (1997) suggest that you can effectively influence the media in several important ways (see also Postman & Powers 1992).

Register individual complaints. For example, you can write letters to (or call) a television station or an advertiser expressing your views on the content of a program or topics to which you think more attention should be given. You can also write letters to a public forum, such as letters to the editor of a newspaper, or call a television talk show. And of course you can write letters to the Federal Communication Commission or to other regulatory agencies, which in turn will exert pressure on the media.

These letters and phone calls count a great deal more than most people think. Because most people do not write or call, the media give such messages considerable weight. Letters and phone calls, for example, may also help other audience members crystallize their own thinking and, depending on your persuasiveness, may even convince them to believe and to act as you do.

Exert group pressure. When you join with others who think the same way you do, group pressure can be brought to bear on television networks, newspapers, advertisers, and manufacturers. Threatening a boycott or legal action can quickly gain attention and often some measure of compliance (and potentially, at least, damage the economic base of an organization).

Protest through an established organization. Obviously the larger the organization you use to influence the media, the better. Similarly, the more economically powerful, the more persuasive your appeal will be. The AIDS epidemic has led to the creation of a wide variety of organizations that have exerted pressure for increased research funding and services to people with AIDS. ACT UP (AIDS Coalition to Unleash Power) is perhaps the most visible of such organizations.

Protesting with a social movement. This technique has been used throughout history to gain civil rights for minority groups and for women. Forming such movements or aligning yourself with an established movement can enable you to secure not only a large number of petitioners but also the accompanying media coverage that would enable you to put forth your own position.

Create legislative pressure. You can exert influence on the state or federal level by influencing your local political representatives (through your own voting, calls, and letters), who will in turn influence representatives on higher levels of the political hierarchy. And of course you can help to influence the groups to which you belong to exert influence.

Do recall that communication is inevitable and that silence communicates just as surely as do words and gestures—principles we covered throughout this text and especially in the Media Watch box, the Spiral of Silence (Unit 9). Because of this, when you do not talk back to the media, your silence is interpreted by the media as basically approval. If approval is not what you wish to register, then you have little choice but to talk back.

The next Media Watch appears on page 364.

If the rate is extreme, the listeners will simply not spend the time and energy needed to understand your speech.

If your rate is too slow, it will encourage your listeners to wander to matters unrelated to your speech. Be careful, therefore, not to bore the audience by presenting information at too slow a rate; yet do not give them information at a pace that is too rapid for listeners to absorb. Strike a happy medium. Speak at a pace that engages the listeners and allows them time for reflection but without boring them.

Like volume, rate variations may be underused or totally absent. If you speak at the same rate throughout the entire speech, you're not making use of this important speech asset. Use variations in rate to call attention to certain points and to add variety. If you speak of, for example, the dull routine of an assembly line worker in a rapid and varied pace, or of the wonder of a circus in a pace with absolutely no variation, you're surely misusing this important vocal dimension. Again, if you're interested in and conscious of what you're saying, your rate variations should flow naturally and effectively. Too predictable a rate pattern is sometimes as bad as no variation at all. If the audience can predict—consciously or unconsciously—your rate pattern, you're in a vocal rut. You're not communicating ideas but words you've memorized.

Pitch refers to the relative highness or lowness of your voice as perceived by your listener. More technically, pitch results from the rate at which your vocal folds vibrate. If they vibrate rapidly, listeners will perceive your voice as having a high pitch. If they vibrate slowly, listeners will perceive your voice as having a low pitch.

Pitch changes often signal changes in the meanings of many sentences. The most obvious is the difference between a statement and a question. Thus, the difference between the declarative sentence, "So this is the proposal you want me to support" and the question "So this is the proposal you want me to support?" is inflection or pitch. This, of course, is obvious. But note that, depending on where the inflectional change is placed, the meaning of the sentence changes drastically. Note also that all of the following questions contain exactly the same words, but they each ask a different question when you emphasize different words:

- Is **this** the proposal you want me to support?
- Is this the **proposal** you want me to support?
- Is this the proposal you want **me** to support?
- Is this the proposal you want me to **support**?

The obvious problems of pitch are levels that are too high, too low, and too patterned. Neither of the first two problems is common in speakers with otherwise normal voices, and you can correct a pitch pattern that is too predictable or monotonous with practice. With increased speaking experience, pitch changes will come naturally from the sense of what you're saying. Because each sentence is somewhat different from every other sentence, there should be a normal variation—a variation that results not from some predetermined pattern but rather from the meanings you wish to convey to the audience.

Pauses

Pauses come in two basic types: filled and unfilled. Filled pauses are pauses in the stream of speech that we fill with vocalizations such as *-er, -um, -ah*, and the like. Even expressions such as *well* and *you know*, when used just to fill up silence, are called filled pauses. These pauses are ineffective and weaken the strength of your message. They will make you appear hesitant, unprepared, and unsure of yourself.

Unfilled pauses are silences interjected into the normally fluent stream of speech. Unfilled pauses can be especially effective if used correctly. Here are just a few examples of places where unfilled pauses—silences of a few seconds—should prove effective.

1. Pause at transitional points. This will signal that you're moving from one part of the speech to another or from one idea to another. It will help the listeners separate the main issues you're discussing.
2. Pause at the end of an important assertion. This will allow the audience time to think about the significance of what you're saying.
3. Pause after asking a rhetorical question. This will provide the necessary time so the members of the audience can think of how they would answer the question.
4. Pause before an important idea. This will help signal that what comes next is especially significant.

In addition, pauses are helpful before beginning your speech and after you've concluded your speech. Don't start speaking as soon as you get to the front of the room; rather, pause to scan the audience and gather your thoughts. Also, don't leave the podium as you speak your last word; pause to allow your speech to sink in and avoid giving the audience the impression that you're anxious to leave them.

Bodily Action

Your body is a powerful instrument in your speech. You speak with your body as well as with your mouth. The total effect of the speech depends not only on what you say but also on the way you present it. It depends on your movements, gestures, and facial expressions as well as your words.

Six aspects of bodily action are especially important in public speaking: eye contact, facial expression, posture, gestures, movement, and proxemics.

Eye Contact. The most important single aspect of bodily communication is eye contact. The two major problems with eye contact are not enough eye contact and eye contact that does not cover the audience fairly. Speakers who do not maintain enough eye contact appear distant, unconcerned, and less trustworthy than speakers who look directly at their audience. And, of course, without eye contact, you will not be able to secure that all-important audience feedback.

Maintain eye contact with the entire audience. Involve all listeners in the public speaking transaction. Communicate equally with the members on the left and on the right, in both the back and the front.

Use eye contact to secure audience feedback. Are they interested? Bored? Puzzled? In agreement? In disagreement? Use your eyes to communicate your commitment to and interest in what you're saying. Communicate your confidence and commitment by making direct eye contact; avoid staring blankly through your audience or glancing over their heads, at the floor, or out the window.

Facial Expression. Facial expressions are especially important in communicating emotions—your anger and fear, boredom and excitement, doubt and surprise. If you feel committed to and believe in your thesis, you'll probably display your meanings appropriately and effectively.

Nervousness and anxiety, however, may at times prevent you from relaxing enough so that your emotions come through. Fortunately, time and practice will allow you to relax, and the emotions you feel will reveal themselves appropriately and automatically.

Generally, members of one culture will be able to recognize the emotion displayed facially by members of other cultures. But, there are differences in what each culture considers appropriate to display. Each culture has its own "display rules" (Ekman, Friesen, & Ellsworth 1972). For example, Japanese Americans watching a stress-inducing film spontaneously displayed the same facial emotions as did other Americans when they thought they were unobserved. But, when an observer was present, the Japanese masked (tried to hide) their emotional expressions more than did the Americans (Gudykunst & Kim 1992).

Posture. When delivering your speech, stand straight but not stiff. Try to communicate a command of the situation without communicating the discomfort that is actually quite common for beginning speakers.

Avoid the common mistakes of posture: avoid putting your hands in your pockets and leaning on the desk, the podium, or the chalkboard. With practice you'll come to feel more at ease and will communicate this by the way you stand before the audience.

Gestures. Gestures in public speaking help illustrate your verbal messages. We do this regularly in conversation. For example, when saying "come here," you probably move your head, hands, arms, and perhaps your entire body to motion the listener in your direction. Your body as well as your verbal message say "come here."

Avoid using your hands to preen, for example, fixing your hair or adjusting your clothing. Avoid fidgeting with your watch, ring, or jewelry. Avoid keeping your hands in your pockets or clasped in front or behind your back.

Effective bodily action is spontaneous and natural to you as the speaker, to your audience, and to your speech. If they seem planned or rehearsed, they'll appear phony and insincere. As a general rule, don't do anything with your hands that doesn't feel right for you; the audience will recognize it as unnatural. If you feel relaxed and comfortable with yourself and your audience, you'll generate natural bodily action without conscious and studied attention.

Movement. Movement here refers to your large bodily movements. It helps to move around a bit. It keeps both the audience and you more alert. Even when speaking behind a lectern, you can give the illusion of movement. You can step back or forward or flex your upper body so you appear to be moving more than you are.

Avoid these three problems of movement: too little, too much, and too patterned movement. Speakers who move too little often appear strapped to the podium, afraid of the audience, or too disinterested to involve themselves fully. With too much movement, the audience begins to concentrate on the movement itself, wondering where the speaker will wind up next. With too patterned a movement, the audience may become bored—too steady and predictable a rhythm quickly becomes tiring. The audience will often view the speaker as nonspontaneous and uninvolved.

Use gross movements to emphasize transitions and to emphasize the introduction of a new and important assertion. Thus, when making a transition, you might take a step forward to signal that something new is coming. Similarly, this type of movement may signal the introduction of an important assumption, bit of evidence, or closely reasoned argument.

Proxemics. Proxemics refers to the way you use space in communication. In public speaking the space between you and your listeners and among the listeners themselves is often a crucial factor. If you stand too close to the people in the audience, they might feel uncomfortable, as if their personal space is being violated. If you stand too far away from your audience, you might be perceived as uninvolved, uninterested, and uncomfortable. Watch where your instructor and other speakers stand and adjust your own position accordingly.

If you're using a lectern, you may wish to signal transitions by stepping to the side or in front of it and then behind it again as you move from one point to another. Generally, it's best to avoid the extremes; too much movement around the lectern and no movement are both to be avoided. You may wish to lean over it when, say, posing a question to your listeners or when advancing a particularly important argument. But, never lean on the lectern; never use it as support.

SUMMARY

This unit focused on outlining, style, rehearsal, and delivery and offered suggestions for using preparation, skeletal, and delivery outlines; choosing words and phrasing sentences; and rehearsing and delivering your speech.

1. An outline is blueprint of your speech that helps you organize and evaluate your speech. The preparation outline is extremely detailed and includes your main points, all supporting materials, introduction, conclusion, transition, and references. The skeletal outline is a kind of template that can help you see where certain material can be placed. The delivery outline is a brief version of your preparation outline that you use as a guide when delivering your speech.

2. Compared with written style, oral style contains shorter, simpler, and more familiar words; greater qualification; and more self-referential terms.

3. Effective public speaking style is clear (be economical and specific; use guide phrases; and stick to short, familiar, and commonly-used terms), vivid (use active verbs, strong verbs, figures of speech, and imagery), appropriate to your audience (speak on a suitable level of formality; avoid written style expressions; avoid slang, vulgar, and offensive terms), and personal (use personal pronouns, ask questions, and create immediacy).

4. In constructing sentences for public speeches, favor short, direct, active, and positively phrased sentences. Vary the type and length.

5. There are three basic methods of delivering a public speech. The impromptu method involves speaking without any specific preparation. The manuscript method involves writing out the entire speech and reading it to the audience. The extemporaneous method involves thorough preparation and memorizing the main ideas and their order of appearance, without a commitment to exact wording.

6. Use rehearsal to time your speech; perfect your volume, rate, and pitch; incorporate pauses and other delivery notes; and perfect your bodily action.

7. When you deliver your speech, regulate your voice for greatest effectiveness. Adjust your volume on the basis of the distance between you and your audience and the emphasis you wish to give certain ideas, for example. Adjust your rate on the basis of time constraints, the speech's content, and the listening conditions.

8. Use pauses to signal a transition between the major parts of the speech, to allow the audience time to think, to allow the audience to ponder a rhetorical question, and to signal the approach of a particularly important idea. Avoid filled pauses; they weaken your message.

9. Effective body action involves maintaining eye contact with your entire audience, allowing your facial expressions to convey your feelings, using your posture to communicate command of the public speaking interaction, gesturing naturally, and moving around a bit.

KEY TERMS

outline (p. 333)

preparation outline (p. 334)

skeletal outline (p. 338)

delivery outline (p. 339)

oral style (p. 340)

language clarity (p. 341)

vividness (p. 342)

figures of speech (p. 342)

slang (p. 343)

personal style (p. 344)

language immediacy (p. 344)

weakeners (p. 344)

clichés (p. 345)

impromptu speaking (p. 350)

manuscript speaking (p. 350)

memorized delivery (p. 350)

extemporaneous speaking (p. 351)

monotonous patterns (p. 352)

predictable patterns (p. 352)

vocal volume (p. 354)

vocal rate (p. 354)

vocal pitch (p. 356)

pause (p. 356)

THINKING CRITICALLY ABOUT
Style and Delivery

1. Shandra is being interviewed for a managerial position at Cybox Corporation. As part of the second interview, Shandra is asked to give a speech to a group of analysts she'll supervise (as well as to the management that will make the hiring decision). What advice would you give Shandra concerning her speaking style? For example, should she strive for a personal style or an impersonal one? A powerful style? Should she strive for immediacy or should she signal distance? Would your advice differ if Shandra was significantly older than the group she'll be supervising? Would your advice differ is Shandra was significantly younger than the group?

2. Francisco is scheduled to give two speeches, one to a predominantly female audience of health professionals and one to a predominantly male audience of small business owners. His topic for both groups is the same: neighborhood violence. What advice—if any—would you give Francisco for tailoring his speech to the two different audiences? If you would not offer advice, why not?

3. John has this great joke that is only tangentially related to his speech topic. But the joke is so great that it will immediately get the audience actively involved in his speech and this, he thinks, outweighs the fact that it isn't integrally related to the speech. John asks your advice; what do you suggest?

4. Michael has a very formal-type personality; he's very restrained in everything he does. But he wants to try to project a different image—a much more personable, friendly, informal type of guy—in his speeches. What advice would you give Michael?

5. Whether or not you speak English as a second language, visit a Web site devoted to this (for example, http://www.lang.uiuc.edu/r-li5/esl/). What can you learn from this Web site that could supplement what was covered in this unit?

6. Mary comes from a background very different from the students in this class—Mary's family dressed for dinner, women were encouraged to be accepting rather than assertive, and politeness was emphasized above all else. If Mary communicates this image of herself, she thinks that the class will see her as an outsider, not only as a speaker but also as a person. She wonders if there's anything she can do in her speeches to present herself in a light that others will respond to positively. What advice would you give Mary?

7. Prepare and deliver a two-minute speech in which you
   - describe the language of a noted personality (television, politics, arts, etc.)
   - describe the delivery of a speaker you consider effective and the delivery of one you consider ineffective
   - describe the delivery style of a prominent comedian or compare the delivery styles of any two comedians
   - introduce an excerpt from literature and read the excerpt as you might a manuscript speech
   - analyze an advertisement in terms of one or two of the characteristics of effective style: clarity, vividness, appropriateness, personal style, or forcefulness
   - describe an object in the room using visual, auditory, and tactile imagery

UNIT 18
The Informative Speech

UNIT OUTLINE

Principles of Informative Speaking

The Speech of Description

The Speech of Definition

The Speech of Demonstration

A Sample Informative Speech

UNIT GOALS

After completing this unit, you should be able to:

explain the principles for informative speaking

define and identify the strategies for developing the speech of description

define and identify the strategies for developing the speech of definition

define and identify the strategies for developing the speech of demonstration

analyze a speech according to the principles for informative speaking

In this unit we look at the informative speech. First, a series of general principles useful for all informative speaking is presented and second, the three types of informative speeches (descriptive, definition, and demonstration) are explained. Finally, a sample informative speech is presented as a summary of the principles for speech preparation.

PRINCIPLES OF INFORMATIVE SPEAKING

When you communicate "information" you tell your listeners something they don't know, something new. You may tell them of a new way of looking at old things or an old way of looking at new things. You may discuss a theory not previously heard of or a familiar one not fully understood. You may talk about events that the audience may be unaware of or may have misconceptions about. Regardless of what type of informative speech you intend to give, the following principles should help.

Limit the Amount of Information

There's a limit to the amount of information that a listener can take in at one time. Resist the temptation to overload your listeners with information. Limit the breadth of information you communicate and, instead, expand its depth. It's better to present two new items of information and explain these with examples, illustrations, and descriptions than to present five items without this needed amplification. Here, for example, is the type of thing you should avoid:

> In this speech I want to discuss the differences between women and men. I'm going to focus on the physiological, psychological, social, and linguistic differences.

Clearly you'd be trying to cover too much. You'd be forced to cover these four areas only superficially with the result that you'd communicate little new information. Instead, select one area and develop it in depth:

> In this speech I want to discuss some of the linguistic differences between women and men. I'm going to focus on two linguistic differences: differences in language development and differences in language problems. Let's look first at the way in which girls and boys develop language.

In this speech, you'd now have the opportunity to cover an area in depth. As a result the listeners are more likely to learn something that they didn't know.

Adjust the Level of Complexity

As you know from attending college classes, information can be presented in a very simplified form or in an extremely complex form. The level of complexity that you communicate your information on should depend on a wide variety of factors considered throughout: the level of knowledge your audience has, the time you have available, the purpose you hope to achieve, the topic on which you're speaking, and so on. If you simplify a topic too much, you risk boring or, even worse, insulting your audience. If your talk is too complex, you risk confusing your audience and failing to communicate the desired information.

Generally, however, beginning speakers err on the side of being too complex and do not realize that a five or ten minute speech is not very long to make an audience understand sophisticated concepts or how a complicated process works. At least in your beginning speeches, try to keep it simple rather than complex. For example, make sure the words you use are familiar to your audience or, if not, explain and define them as you use them. Remember too that jargon and technical vocabulary familiar to the computer hacker may not be familiar to the person who still uses a typewriter. Always see your topic from the point of view of the members of the audience; ask yourself how much they know about your topic and its unique language.

Stress Relevance and Usefulness

Listeners will remember your information best when they see it as relevant and useful to their own needs or goals. Notice that as a listener you follow this principle all the time. For example, in class you might attend to and remember the stages in the development of language in children simply because you'll be tested on the information and you want to earn a high grade. Or you might attend to information because it will help you make a better impression in your job interview, make you a better parent, or enable you to deal with relationship problems. Like you, listeners attend to information that will prove useful to them.

If you want the audience to listen to your speech, relate your information to their needs, wants, or

UNDERSTANDING
Theory and Research

WHAT'S INFORMATION?

In the 1940s, the mathematical theory of communication—which became known as *information theory*—was developed by mathematicians and engineers working at Bell Telephone Laboratories (Shannon & Weaver 1949). This theory defined information as that which reduces uncertainty. For example, if I tell you my name and you already know it, then I haven't communicated information because my message (my name) did-

n't reduce uncertainty; you already knew my name and so had no uncertainty in this connection. Although this theory doesn't explain the complexities of human communication very well—for example, it views communication as a linear process (see Unit 1), this view of information is especially helpful in thinking about the purpose of the informative speech—to communicate information, to tell the members of the audience something they didn't already know, or to send messages that reduce the uncertainty of your listeners about your speech topic.

goals. Throughout your speech, but especially in the beginning, make sure your audience knows that the information you're presenting is relevant and useful to them now or in the immediate future. For example, you might say something like:

> We all want financial security. We all want to be able to buy those luxuries we read so much about in magazines and see every evening on television. Wouldn't it be nice to be able to buy a car without worrying about where you're going to get the down payment or how you'll be able to make the monthly payments? Actually, that is not an unrealistic goal as I'll demonstrate in this speech. In fact, I will show you several methods for investing your money that will enable you to increase your income by at least 20 percent.

In recent research on relevance, communication researchers investigated what students felt made their college lectures relevant to their personal and professionals goals (Frymier & Shulman 1995). They found that the greater the relevance of the lecture, the more the students were motivated to study. It seems reasonable to extend these findings and argue that the more relevant a speech, the more listeners will be motivated to listen and even to pursue the topic further. Here are a few of the most frequently noted ways for stressing relevance that the researchers found, stated in the form of suggestions for informative speaking:

- Use examples that make content relevant.
- Use exercises or explanations to show the content's importance to your listeners.
- Explain how the content is related to career goals of your listeners.
- Stimulate your listener's thinking about how the content applies to their goals.
- Use your own or your listeners' own experiences to stress the importance of the content of your talk.
- Relate current events to the content of your talk.

Relate New Information to Old

Listeners will learn information more easily and retain it longer when you relate it to what they already know. So, relate the new to the old, the unfamiliar to the familiar, the unseen to the seen, the untasted to the tasted. Here, for example, Betsy Heffernan, a student from the University of Wisconsin (Reynolds & Schnoor 1991), relates the problem of sewage to a familiar historical event:

> During our nation's struggle for independence, the citizens of Boston were hailed as heroes for dumping tea into Boston Harbor. But not to be outdone, many modern day Bostonians are also dumping things into the harbor. Five thousand gallons of human waste every second. The New England Aquarium of Boston

states that since 1900, Bostonians have dumped enough human sewage into the harbor to cover the entire state of Massachusetts chest deep in sludge. Unfortunately, Boston isn't alone. All over the country, bays, rivers, and lakes are literally becoming cesspools.

Vary the Levels of Abstraction

You can talk about freedom of the press in the abstract by talking about the importance of getting information to the public, by referring to the Bill of Rights, and by relating a free press to the preservation of democracy. That is, you can talk about the topic on a relatively high level of abstraction. But, you can also talk about freedom of the press by citing specific examples: how a local newspaper was prevented from running a story critical of the town council or about how Lucy Rinaldo was fired from the Accord *Sentinel* after she wrote a story critical of the mayor. You can talk about the topic on a relatively low level of abstraction, a level that is specific and concrete.

Combining the high abstraction and the specific seems to work best. Too many high abstractions without the specifics or too many specifics without the high abstractions will generally prove less effective than the combination of abstract and specific.

Here, for example, is an excerpt from a speech on the homeless. Note that in the first paragraph we have a relatively abstract description of homelessness. In the second paragraph, we get into specifics. In the last paragraph the abstract and the concrete are connected.

Homelessness is a serious problem for all metropolitan areas throughout the country. It's currently estimated that there are now over 200,000 homeless in New York City alone. But, what is this really about? Let me tell you what it's about.

It's about a young man. He must be about 25 or 30, although he looks a lot older. He lives in a cardboard box on the side of my apartment house. We call him Tom, although we really don't know his name. All his possessions are stored in this huge box. I think it was a box from a refrigerator. Actually, he doesn't have very much and what he has easily fits in this box. There's a blanket my neighbor threw out, some plastic bottles he puts water in, and some styrofoam containers he picked up from the garbage from Burger King. He uses these to store whatever food he finds.

What is homelessness about? It's about Tom and 200,000 other "Tom's" in New York and thousands of others throughout the rest of the country. And not all of them even have boxes to live in.

THE SPEECH OF DESCRIPTION

When you prepare a speech of description, you're concerned with explaining an object, person, event, or process. Here are a few examples:

Describing an Object or Person
- the structure of the brain
- the contributions of Thomas Edison
- the parts of a telephone
- the layout of the Alamo

Can you identify any additional principles that might be useful in informing an audience?

MEDIA WATCH

THE KNOWLEDGE GAP

The knowledge gap refers to the difference in knowledge between one group and another; it's the division between those who have a great deal of knowledge and those who have significantly less. Much of the research in this area has focused on the influence of the media in widening this knowledge gap (Tichenor, Donohue, & Olien 1970; Severin & Tankard 1988; Viswanath & Finnegan 1995).

Information is, of course, valuable. It brings wealth and gives power. It even gives people the information they need to live healthy lives (Viswanath et al. 1993). More generally, information enables you to do more things more effectively.

But, information is expensive and not everyone has equal access to it. This is especially true as we live more of our lives in cyberspace. The new communication technologies—computers, CD ROMS, the Internet, satellite and cable television, for example—are major ways for gaining information. Technologies, however, are expensive and require skills that uneducated people don't have. (In fact, we're increasingly coming to define "educated" as the ability to use the technologies of communication.) Thus, the better educated have the skills and the money to own and master the new technologies and thus acquire more information. The less educated don't have the skills or the money to own and master the new technologies and thus cannot acquire more information. For example, in 1995, 53 percent of children in families with incomes under $20,000 had access to computers in elementary and high school, but 68 percent of those in families with incomes over $75,000 had this access. This difference of 15 percent is small when we compare it with home computer access. Only 15 percent of the children in families with incomes under $20,000 had a computer in the home. But 74 percent of the children in families with incomes over $75,000 had home computers (*Newsweek*, February 27, 1995, p. 50).

The knowledge gap hypothesis may also be applied to different cultures. Developed countries, for example, have the new technologies in their schools and offices and many people can afford to buy their own computers and satellite systems. Access to the new technologies help these countries develop further. Undeveloped countries, with little or no access to such technologies, cannot experience the same gain in knowledge and information as those with this technological access.

Even the language of a culture may influence the extent of the knowledge gap. For example, English dominates the Internet and so the Internet is therefore more easily accessible to people in the United States and other English-speaking countries (and also to educated people in non-English-speaking countries who learned English as a second language). As one South Korean computer user put it, "It's not only English you have to understand but American culture, even slang. All in all, there are many people who just give up" (Pollack 1995, p. D4). Still another factor is that more than half the world's people do not use the Latin Alphabet; Chinese, Japanese, Korean, and Arab people, for example, use alphabets that make software development and Internet access more difficult—at least at the present time.

Efforts are being made to reduce this knowledge gap, for example, by developing translation software, by equipping computers with fonts used by non-Latin alphabet languages, and even by concerted United Nations action (UNESCO 1993). Right now, however, Japanese companies are having great difficulty developing software that will sell throughout the world whereas India, where most educated people speak English, is enjoying an enormously successful software industry (Pollack 1995).

The next Media Watch appears on page 379.

- the hierarchy of a corporation
- the human body
- the components of a computer system

Describing an Event or Process
- the bombing in Oklahoma City
- the events leading to World War II
- organizing a body-building contest
- the breakdown of Russian communism
- how a newspaper is printed
- the process of buying a house
- purchasing stock
- how a child acquires language
- how to read a textbook

Strategies for Describing

Here are some suggestions for describing objects, people, events, and processes.

Select an Appropriate Organizational Pattern

Consider using a spatial or a topical organization when describing objects and people. Consider using a temporal pattern when describing events and processes. For example, if you were to describe the layout of Philadelphia, you might start from the north and work down to the south (using a spatial pattern). If you were to describe the contributions of Thomas Edison, you might select the three or four major contributions and discuss each of these equally (using a topical pattern).

If you were describing the events leading up to World War II, you might use a temporal pattern and start with the earliest and work up to the latest. A temporal pattern would also be appropriate for describing how a hurricane develops or how a parade is put together.

Use a Variety of Descriptive Categories

Describe the object or event with lots of descriptive categories. Use physical categories and ask yourself questions such as these:

- What color is it?
- How big is it?
- What is it shaped like?
- How high is it?
- How much does it weigh?
- How long or short is it?

- What is its volume?
- How attractive/unattractive is it?

Also, consider its social, psychological, and economic categories. In describing a person, for example, consider such categories as friendly/unfriendly, warm/cold, rich/poor, aggressive/meek, and pleasant/unpleasant.

Consider Using Presentation Aids

Presentation aids such as those described in Unit 16 will help you describe almost anything. Use them if you possibly can. In describing an object or person, show your listeners a picture of, for example, the brain, the inside of a telephone, or the skeleton of the body. In describing an event or process, show them a diagram or flowchart to illustrate the stages or steps, for example, representing the stages in buying stock, in publishing a newspaper, or in putting a parade together.

Consider Who? What? Where? When? and Why?

These categories are especially useful when you want to describe an event or process. For example, if you're going to describe how to purchase a house, you might want to consider the people involved (who?), the steps you have to go through (what?), the places you'll have to go (where?), the time or sequence in which each of the steps have to take place (when?), and the advantages and disadvantages of buying the house (why?).

Developing the Speech of Description

Here are two examples of how you might go about constructing a speech of description. In this first example, the speaker describes four suggestions for increasing assertiveness (following a temporal sequence). Notice that the steps follow the order one would follow in becoming more assertive.

General purpose: to inform

Specific purpose: to describe how we can become more assertive

Thesis: assertiveness can be increased (How can assertiveness be increased?)

I. Analyze assertive behaviors.
II. Record your own assertive behaviors.
III. Rehearse assertive behaviors.
IV. Act assertively.

In this second example, the speaker describes the way in which fear works in intercultural communication.

General purpose: to inform

Specific purpose: to describe the way fear works in intercultural communication

Thesis: fear influences intercultural communication (How does fear influence intercultural communication?)

I. We fear disapproval.
II. We fear embarrassing ourselves.
III. We fear being harmed.

In delivering such a speech a speaker might begin by saying:

There are three major fears that interfere with intercultural communication. First, there's the fear of disapproval—from members of our own group as well as from members of the other person's group. Second, we fear embarrassing ourselves, even making fools of ourselves by saying the wrong thing or appearing insensitive. And third, we may fear being harmed—our stereotypes of the other group may lead us to see their members as dangerous or potentially harmful to us.

Let's look at each of these fears in more detail and we'll be able to see how they influence our own intercultural communication behavior.

Consider, first, the fear of disapproval.

THE SPEECH OF DEFINITION

What is leadership? What is a born-again Christian? What is the difference between sociology and psychology? What is a cultural anthropologist? What is safe sex? These are all topics for informative speeches of definition.

A **definition** is a statement of the meaning or significance of a concept or term. Use definitions when you wish to explain difficult or unfamiliar concepts or when you wish to make a concept more vivid or forceful.

In defining a term or in giving an entire speech of definition, you may focus on defining a term, a system or theory, or the similarities and/or differences among terms or systems. It may be a subject new to the audience or one familiar to them but presented in a new and different way.

Here are some examples:

Defining a Term
- What is multiculturalism?
- What is drug addiction?
- What is machismo?
- What is creativity?
- What is affirmative action?
- What is classism?
- What is political correctness?
- What is inflation?

Defining a System or Theory
- What is the classical theory of public speaking?
- What are the parts of a generative grammar?
- What are the major beliefs of Confucianism?
- What is expressionism?
- What is futurism?
- What is the "play theory" of mass communication?

Defining Similar and Dissimilar Terms or Systems
- Football and soccer: What's the difference?
- Communism and socialism: What are the similarities and differences?
- What do Christians and Muslims have in common?
- Oedipus and Electra: How do they differ?
- How do genetics and heredity relate to each other?
- What do ballet and square dancing have in common?
- What are the differences between critical and creative thinking?
- What do animal and human rights have in common?
- What are keyword and directory searches?
- How do freshwater and saltwater fishing differ?

Strategies for Defining
There are several approaches to defining your topic. Here are some suggestions.

Use a Variety of Definitions
When explaining a concept, it's helpful to define it in a number of different ways. Here are some of the most important ways to define a term.

Going Online

The Podium Web site

Visit the Podium. What can you find here that might be useful as you prepare an informative speech?

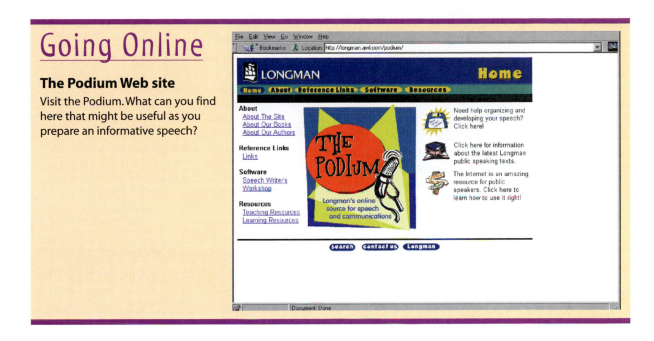

Define by Etymology. If you look up the word *communication*, you might note that it comes from the Latin *communis*, meaning "common"; in communicating you seek to establish a commonness, a sameness, a similarity with another individual. And *woman* comes from the Anglo-Saxon *wifman*, which meant literally a "wife man," where the word man was applied to both sexes. Through phonetic change *wifman* became *woman*. Most larger dictionaries and, of course, etymological dictionaries will help you find useful etymological definitions.

Define by Authority. You might, for example, define *lateral thinking* by authority and say that Edward deBono, who developed lateral thinking in 1966, has stated that "lateral thinking involves moving sideways to look at things in a different way. Instead of fixing on one particular approach and then working forward from that, the lateral thinker tries to find other approaches."

Or you might use the authority of cynic and satirist Ambrose Bierce and define *love* as nothing but "a temporary insanity curable by marriage," and *friendship* as "a ship big enough to carry two in fair weather, but only one in foul."

Define by Negation. You might also define a term by noting what the term is not, that is, defining by negation. "A wife," you might say, "is not a cook, a cleaning person, a baby sitter, a seamstress, a sex partner. A wife is . . . ." or "A teacher is not someone who tells you what you should know but rather one who . . . ." Here Michael Marien (1992) defines futurists first negatively and then positively:

> Futurists do not use crystal balls. Indeed, they're generally loathe to make firm predictions of what will happen. Rather, they make forecasts of what is probable, sketch scenarios of what is possible, and/or point to desirable futures—what is preferable and what strategies we should pursue to get there.

Define by Direct Symbolization. You might also define a term by direct symbolization, by showing the actual thing or a picture or model of it. For example, a sales representative explaining a new computer keyboard would obviously use an actual keyboard in the speech. Similarly, a speech on magazine layout or types of fabrics would include actual layout pages and fabric samples.

Use Definitions to Add Clarity

If the purpose of the definition is to clarify, then it must do just that. This would be too obvious to mention except for the fact that so many speakers, perhaps for want of something to say, define terms that don't need extended definitions. Some speakers use definitions that don't clarify, and that, in fact, complicate an already complex concept. Make sure your definitions define only what needs defining.

Use Credible Sources

When you use an authority to define a term, make sure the person is in fact an authority. Tell the audience who the authority is and the basis for the individual's expertise. In the following excerpt, note how Russell Peterson (1985) uses the expertise of Robert McNamara in his definition:

> When Robert McNamara was president of the World Bank, he coined the term "absolute poverty" to characterize a condition of life so degraded by malnutrition, illiteracy, violence, disease and squalor, to be beneath any reasonable definition of human decency. In 1980, the World Bank estimated that 780 million persons in the developing countries lived in absolute poverty. That's about three times as many people as live in the entire United States.

Proceed from the Known to the Unknown

Start with what your audience knows and work up to what is new or unfamiliar. Let's say you want to explain the concept of phonemics (with which your audience is totally unfamiliar). The specific idea you wish to get across is that each phoneme stands for a unique sound. You might proceed from the known to the unknown and begin your definition with something like this:

> We all know that in the written language each letter of the alphabet stands for a unit of the written language. Each letter is different from every other letter. A *t* is different from a *g* and a *g* is different from a *b* and so on. Each letter is called a *grapheme*. In English we know we have 26 such letters.
>
> We can look at the spoken language in much the same way. Each sound is different from every other sound. A *t* sound is different from a *d* and a *d* is different from a *k* and so on. Each individual sound is called a *phoneme*.
>
> Now, let me explain in a little more detail what I mean by a *phoneme*.

Developing the Speech of Definition

Here are two examples of how you might go about constructing a speech of definition. In this first example, the speaker explains the parts of a resume and follows a spatial order, going from the top to the bottom of the page.

General purpose: to inform

Specific purpose: to define the essential parts of a resume

Thesis: there are four major parts to a résumé. (What are the four major parts of a résumé?)

I. Identify your career goals.
II. Identify your educational background.

Going Online

Gifts of Speech Web site

Visit this Web site devoted to women speakers and read one of the speeches. In what specific ways does the speaker follow or not follow the suggestions for communicating information discussed in this unit?

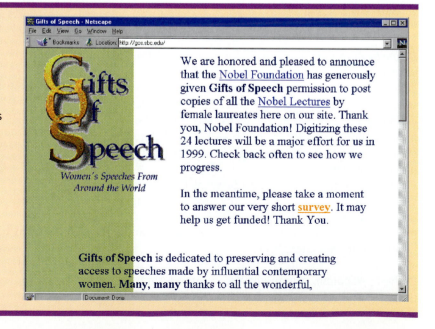

III. Identify your work experience.
IV. Identify your special competencies.

In this second example, the speaker selects three major types of lying for discussion and arranges these in a topical pattern.

General purpose: to inform

Specific purpose: to define lying by explaining the major types of lying misdirection

Thesis: there are three major kinds of lying (What are the three major kinds of lying?)

I. Concealment is the process of hiding the truth.
II. Falsification is the process of presenting false information as if it were true.
III. Misdirection is the process of acknowledging a feeling but misidentifying its cause.

In delivering such a speech, a speaker might begin the speech by saying:

A lie is a lie is a lie. True? Well, not exactly. Actually, there are a number of different ways we can lie. We can lie by concealing the truth. We can lie by falsification, by presenting false information as if it were true. And, we can lie by misdirection, by acknowledging a feeling but misidentifying its cause. Let's look at the first type of lie—the lie of concealment.

Most lies are lies of concealment. Most of the time when we lie we simply conceal the truth. We don't actually make any false statements. Rather, we simply don't reveal the truth. Let me give you some examples I overheard recently.

THE SPEECH OF DEMONSTRATION

In using demonstration (or in a speech devoted entirely to demonstration), you would explain how to do something or how something operates. Here are some examples:

Demonstrating How to Do Something
- how to give mouth-to-mouth resuscitation
- how to balance a checkbook
- how to pilot a plane
- how to drive defensively
- how to mix colors
- how to say "no"
- how to prevent burnout
- how to ask for a raise
- how to burglar-proof your house
- how to develop your body

Demonstrating How Something Operates
- how the body maintains homeostasis
- how a thermostat operates
- how perception works
- how the Internet works
- how divorce laws work
- how e-mail works
- how probate works
- how a hurricane develops
- how a heart bypass operation is performed

What types of definitions might you use in an informative speech on "technological advances in communication"?

BUILDING
Communication Skills

HOW CAN YOU DEFINE A TERM?

Select one of the following terms and define it with at least three different types of definitions (etymology, authority, negative, or direct symbolism): *communication, love, friendship, conflict, leadership, audience.* You'll find it helpful to visit a few online dictionaries or thesauruses: http://c.gp.cs.cmu.edu:5103/prog/webster/; http://www.m-w.com/netdict.htm; http://humanities.uchicago.edu/forms_unrest/ROGET.html. A useful Web site containing links to varied types of dictionaries is http://www.bucknell.edu/~rbeard/diction.html.

Strategies for Demonstrating

In demonstrating how to do something or how something operates, consider the following guidelines.

Use Temporal Organization

In most cases, a temporal pattern will work best in speeches of demonstration. Demonstrate each step in the sequence in which it's to be performed. In this way, you'll avoid one of the major difficulties in demonstrating a process, backtracking. Don't skip steps even if you think they're familiar to the audience. They may not be.

Connect each step to the other with appropriate transitions. For example, in explaining the Heimlich maneuver you might say:

> Now that you have your arms around the choking victim's chest, your next step is to . . . ."

Assist your listeners by labeling the steps clearly, for example, "the first step," "the second step," and so on.

Begin with an Overview

It's often helpful when demonstrating to give a broad general picture and then present each step in turn. For example, let's say you were talking about how to prepare a wall for painting. You might begin with a general overview and say this:

> In preparing the wall for painting, you want to make sure that the wall is smoothly sanded, free of dust, and dry. Sanding a wall is not like sanding a block of wood. So, let's look at the proper way to sand a wall.

In this way, your listeners will have a general idea of how you'll go about demonstrating the process.

Consider the Value of Presentation Aids

Visual aids are especially helpful in showing the steps of a process in sequence. A good example of this is the signs in all restaurants demonstrating the Heimlich maneuver. These signs demonstrate each of the steps with pictures as well as words. The combination of verbal and graphic information makes it easy to understand this important process. In a speech on this topic, however, the best aid would be just the pictures so that the written words would not distract your audience from your oral explanation.

Developing the Speech of Demonstration

Here are two examples of the speech of demonstration. In this first example, the speaker explains the proper way to argue by identifying the ways we should not argue. As you can see, these unproductive fight strategies are all about equal in value and are arranged in a topical order.

General purpose: to inform

Specific purpose: to demonstrate how to fight fairly by identifying and demonstrating four unfair conflict strategies.

Thesis: conflict can be made more productive (How can conflict be made more productive?)

I. Blame the other person.
II. Unload all your previous grievances.

III. Make light of the other person's displeasure.
IV. Hit the other person with issues he or she cannot handle effectively.

In the next example, the speaker identifies and demonstrates how to listen actively.

General purpose: to inform

Specific purpose: to demonstrate three techniques of active listening Thesis: we can learn active listening (How can we learn active listening?)

I. Paraphrase the speaker's meaning.
II. Express understanding of the speaker's feelings.
III. Ask questions.

In delivering the speech, the speaker might begin by saying:

Active listening is a special kind of listening. It's listening with total involvement, with a concern for the speaker. It's probably the most important type of listening you can engage in. Active listening consists of three steps: paraphrasing the speaker's meaning, expressing understanding of the speaker's feelings, and asking questions.

Your first step in active listening is to paraphrase the speaker's meaning. What is a paraphrase? A paraphrase is a restatement in your own words of the speaker's meaning. That is, you express in your own words what you think the speaker meant. For example, let's say that the speaker said . . . .

The three types of informative speeches identified here are just a few examples of informative speaking. Table 18.1 provides additional types of informative speeches offered by other textbook writers.

A SAMPLE INFORMATIVE SPEECH

This speech is presented as a kind of summary of this unit, as well as Units 15, 16, and 17, which covered the 10 steps of preparing a public speech. It will help you see all 10 steps in completed form and also help you identify the major parts of an informative speech and the way they fit together. First, carefully read the speech by Cindy Weisenbeck, "False Memory Syndrome," presented next. For your first reading, ignore the Critical Thinking questions to the side. After you've read the entire speech, reread it, this time reading and responding to the Critical Thinking questions. These questions should help you analyze the speech and see the principles of public speaking in clear application.

TABLE 18.1   Informative speeches: some other types

The table is based on the classifications of Engleberg (1994), Lucas (1998), Rodman & Adler (1997), and Ayres & Miller (1994).

Informative Speech Types	Examples
New information	telling your audience how to do something
Enhance information	detailing the recent research in AIDS
Clarify information	safe ways to lose weight
Speeches about objects, persons, places, or things	the contributions of a noted scientist or philosopher
Speeches about processes or a series of actions	explaining how to do something
Speeches about events or happenings	your first date
Speeches about concepts, beliefs, or ideas	theories of economics
Introductions	of yourself as well as of objects, events, and concepts
Instructions to do something	how to use a scanner
Explanations of why something works	why cocaine has the effects it does
Lecture	the classroom lecture
Report	the classroom oral report

FALSE MEMORY SYNDROME

Connie Chung on the CBS evening news of August 25, 1993, stated, "(But) memories are far from perfect; there are some things that happen that we can't remember, then there are things we remember that never happened." Stephen Cook might finally agree. After his suit accusing Cardinal Bernardin of childhood sexual abuse was highly publicized, the Boston Globe of March 1, 1994, reported that he has since dropped all charges realizing his memories of abuse were purely fictitious. Stephen Cook's story embodies what the psychological community terms False Memory Syndrome. *Time* of November 29, 1993, describes False Memory Syndrome as "a troubling psychological phenomenon that is harming patients, devastating families, influencing legislation, taking up courtroom time and stirring fierce controversy." The magnitude of this problem is highlighted by the fact that both *Time* and *U.S. News & World Report* featured False Memory Syndrome as their cover stories during the week of November 29, 1993. Considering the sheer number of Americans in counseling or therapy today, the reality is that any one of us could either be manipulated into developing our own false memories or be accused of abuse or other crimes based on someone else's false memories. In order to realize how we can protect ourselves from this phenomenon, we first need to investigate how False Memory Syndrome is destroying the lives of both the accused as well as the accuser. Then, we'll come to see how the psychological and legal communities are perpetuating this syndrome. And finally, we'll pursue solutions to ensure that none of us are wrongly accused of childhood sexual abuse based solely on someone's false memories.

There is little question, given the number of cases throughout the country, that False Memory Syndrome both exists and is devastating individuals. The Gannett News Service on March 16, 1994, reported that the False Memory Syndrome Foundation, headquartered in Philadelphia, fielded calls from over 11,000 individuals who were either therapy patients persuaded to believe they were victims of sexual abuse or by individuals accused of abusing someone in the past. Through therapy, memories of abuse are "discovered," and given current legal trends, are then used to potentially convict the accused. States the *Skeptical Inquirer* of Summer 1993, juries

What functions does this introduction serve?
What specifically gains your attention?

What connects the speaker, audience, and topic?

How does the speaker orient the audience?

Does the speaker draw you into the topic and make it interesting to you? How?

Are you convinced that the accusation of Stephen Cook against Cardinal Bernardin was a case of false memory syndrome? If not, what evidence would you want?

What organizational structure is signaled by this orientation? How else might this have been presented?

today are finding patients guilty with no evidence except therapist-induced memories.

The result, as described by Dr. Richard Ofshe in *Society* of March/April 1993, is that "because the memories implicate family and community members of horrible crimes, the trauma of this therapy radiates outward to involve often dozens of innocent people. . . . Thousands of families have already been shattered. The possibilities for fracturing family groups are all being realized: the accused spouse is divorced; siblings are forced to choose sides; grandparents are denied access to their grandchildren; grandchildren lose contact with their grandparents and so on."

Unfortunately, False Memory Syndrome does not only harm the accused, for the therapy patients themselves are also victimized. The November 29, 1993, issue of *Time* magazine relates the story of 39-year-old Melody Gavigan. She had checked herself into a local psychiatric hospital for depression. There, her counselor suggested incest. Through a therapist, she recovered extensive memories of molestation from ages one through five. She became so convinced of the memories that she confronted her father, severed all ties with him and formed an incest survivors group. Once away from therapy, Melody realized that her memories were simply not true. She is currently seeking to repair her familial relationships and is suing the hospital for malpractice. The devastation for Ms. Gavigan, as well as all victims of False Memory Syndrome, was expressed by Psychiatrist John J. Cannell in the *Missoulian* of February 21, 1993. "[But] there is no healing if someone relies on something that is false to explain their problems. The pain is still there. People won't get well unless you search for the real causes of their pain." Clearly, our society's attempts to aid the true victims of childhood sexual abuse have left us with extensive and destructive problems.

With this devastation in mind, let's try to understand how and why false memories are created. Three critical underlying factors are responsible, for false memories are created through hypnosis and sustained because of a profit motive and current laws.

In examining how false memories are created, it is important to keep in mind that repressed memories themselves are not the problem, but rather how those memories are uncovered. The *U.S. News & World Report* of November 29, 1993, reports that

What level of credibility do you ascribe to the *Skeptical Inquirer* or to *Society*? How might the speaker have insured that you'd have a high level of credibility for this publication?

How effective was the story of Melody Gavigan?

How effective is this transition?

How effectively are the three underlying factors stated? How might they have been stated differently?

the American Medical Association has repeatedly cited hypnosis as the critical underlying factor in current cases of False Memory Syndrome. Though hypnosis can be effective for a variety of needs, memory recall is not one of them. Dr. George Ganway explains in the May 17, 1993, *New Yorker* that memories recovered in hypnosis are more likely to contain a mixture of fact and fantasy.

By convincing patients that they were abused and should prosecute, the therapist is creating a source of income for years to come. *Newsweek* of December 13, 1993, reported that therapists justify legal action as a legitimate way to pay for the cost of therapy. Dr. Michael Yapko, a psychologist and expert of suggestive therapies, claims, "in essence, therapists create the problem they have to treat."

Finally, the third institution that fuels the production of false memories is our current legal system. Two recent legal trends in the United States are responsible for false memories entering the courtroom. First, according to *Society* of March/April, 1993, within the last two years, 15 states have decided to allow therapy-induced memories to serve as actual evidence in childhood sexual abuse cases. What we must understand is that under current law, once we are accused, we have virtually no way of defending ourselves against the testimony of the alleged victim and his or her therapist. The memories, whether real or false, can serve as grounds to convict us. Additionally, states the *Minneapolis Star and Tribune* of October 10, 1993, 23 states have enacted laws extending the statute of limitations for sexual abuse cases from three to nine years after the memory is recalled. This opens the door for more therapy patients to act on the suggestions of their therapists, filling our courtrooms with cases that consist of no more than fabricated evidence.

With the precedent toward hypnosis, combined with a legal system that drives therapists' profits, the stage is set for intense victimization of families. In order to end the needless destruction of American families, three steps need to be taken. Eleanor Goldstein in her 1992 book, *Confabulations,* argues that the first step to ending the injustice is through legislation. The *New York Times* of March 27, 1994, reported that Illinois has recently introduced a bill "to protect people from lawsuits based on psychological quackery." This bill will reduce the statute of limitations for sexual abuse cases based on therapy-induced

How effectively does the speaker establish the profit motive as one of the factors underlying false memory syndrome? What else might the speaker have said?

How effectively does the speaker establish that the current laws are a factor in false memory syndrome?

What additional information would you have liked to have included in the speech?

How effective is this internal summary and transition? Would you have preferred to have a brief preview of the three steps? Would this have helped you follow the remainder of the speech?

memories. Furthermore, the 15 states that currently allow therapy-induced memories to serve as evidence need to rescind their laws. The remaining states that have no legislation dealing with these issues need to pass laws that do not allow therapy-induced memories into the courtroom. Therefore, the only way we can protect ourselves from being wrongly accused or even imprisoned is by insisting that these laws are changed in each of our own states.

Second, the psychiatric community needs regulations regarding the use of hypnosis as a treatment for sexual abuse. As a model for our own personal advocacy, we can turn to the state of Ohio. According to the June 20, 1993, issue of the Athens, Ohio, *Messenger,* a citizen group asked the State Board of Psychology to establish guidelines pertaining to therapy for patients who may have been abused or molested. We must confront our own State Boards of Psychology and demand that rigorous regulations be placed on counselors and therapists, declaring hypnosis and memory-induced therapies unethical.

Third, and most importantly, we must be willing to take the time to protect ourselves. Before seeing a therapist of any kind for any reason, there are two things you need to ask your potential therapist: first, ask what percentage of the therapist's patients have been diagnosed as victims of childhood sexual abuse. If the number is unusually high and makes you uncomfortable, ask a second question. Find out what types of therapy the therapist tends to rely on. If the answer is hypnosis or suggestive therapy, seek out another therapist. Only by questioning our potential therapists can we ensure that our problems are accurately and fairly diagnosed.

By better understanding the problems created by False Memory Syndrome, how and why false memories are created and how we can protect ourselves, it is clear that reliance on memory is far from foolproof. As more of us turn to the aid of therapy to understand our problems, it is essential that the advice we receive is accurate and, ultimately, healing. By allowing false memories to be created, we undermine the very point of mental health. Our alarm must produce change. Change that will protect not only the legitimate victims of abuse, but more importantly, the truly innocent.

Speech given by Cindy Weisenbeck, a student at the University Eau Claire, Wisconsin. Reprinted from *Winning Orations of the Interstate Oratorical Association*, Larry G. Schnoor, ed. (1994). Reprinted by permission.

Did the speaker effectively make the case for "ending the injustice through legislation"? What else might have been included?

Are you convinced that the psychiatric community needs to be regulated in its use of hypnosis in treating sexual abuse cases?

What do you think of the speaker's recommendations for taking charge of our own lives when, for example, seeking a therapist?

What percentage of patients diagnosed as victims of childhood sexual abuse would you consider high? 10, 25, 40, 55, 70, or 85 percent? How would you have handled this if you were the speaker?

Are you ready to rule out hypnosis as a viable therapeutic procedure for childhood sexual abuse?

Was the type of evidence appropriate to the speech and topic? How effectively did the speaker integrate the research?

Assuming your class as your audience, how would you have titled the speech?

What effect did the speech have on you? Did it inform? Did it strengthen or change your attitudes and beliefs about false memory syndrome? Will it move you to any specific action (perhaps at a later date)?

SUMMARY

This unit focused on the informative speech, its types, and its principles.

1. Informative speeches are more likely to be effective when they follow these principles of informative speaking: Limit the amount of information you communicate, adjust the level of complexity, stress the relevance and the usefulness of the information to your audience, relate new information to old, and vary the levels of abstraction.

2. Speeches of description describe a process or procedure, an event, an object, or a person.
3. Speeches of definition define a term, system or theory, or similarities and/or differences among terms.
4. Speeches of demonstration show how to do something or how something operates.

KEY TERMS

informative speaking (p. 361)

imiting the amount of information (p. 361)

adjusting the level of complexity (p. 361)

stressing relevance and usefulness (p. 361)

relating new information to old (p. 362)

vary the levels of abstraction (p. 363)

speeches of description (p. 363)

speeches of definition (p. 366)

speeches of demonstration (p. 369)

 ## THINKING CRITICALLY ABOUT
Informative Speeches

1. You want to give an informative speech on virtual reality simulation but most of your audience members have never experienced it. How would you communicate this concept and this experience to your audience?

2. You're planning to give an informative speech on the history of doctor-assisted suicides and are considering the strategies that you might use. What organizational pattern would be appropriate? What types of presentation aids might you use? How would you define "doctor-assisted suicide"? How would you introduce your speech?

3. You're scheduled to be the third speaker in a series of six presentations today. Unfortunately, the first speaker presented a really excellent speech on the same topic you're speaking on—how the Internet works. What should you do?

4. Select an advertisement (television or print) and examine how closely it follows the principles of informative speaking identified here. In what ways does an advertisement differ from a speech?

5. Visit the Web site of the Society for Technical Communication at http://www.stc-va.org/ for guides for writing and speaking on technical matters.

6. Visit the Hypertext Webster Interface at http://c.gp.cs.cmu.edu:5103/prog/webster/ for an unusual dictionary that provides hypertext definitions so that you can get definitions of the words in the definition itself.

7. Prepare and deliver a two-minute speech in which you
   - describe some common object in the classroom
   - define one of the following terms: love, friendship, power, pride, jealousy, truth, freedom, honesty, or faithfulness (use at least two different types of definitions)
   - demonstrate—without the aid of the object—how to tie a shoe lace, use a blender, make a phone call, sew on a button, open a door with a credit card, move a bloc of text on a computer, print out a computer file, or use a template
   - explain one of the principles of informative speaking using a variety of examples
   - explain how one or more of the principles of informative speaking are used or violated in one of your textbooks

UNIT 19

The Persuasive Speech

UNIT OUTLINE

Facts, Values, and Policies

Principles of Persuasion

The Speech to Strengthen or Change
Attitudes or Beliefs

The Speech to Stimulate Action

A Sample Persuasive Speech

UNIT GOALS

After completing this unit, you should be able to:

define and distinguish among
questions of fact, value, and policy

explain the principles of persuasion:
selective exposure, cultural difference,
audience participation, inoculation,
magnitude of change, identification,
consistency, logos, pathos, and ethos.

define and explain the strategies for
developing the speech to strengthen
or change attitudes or beliefs.

define and explain the strategies
for developing the speech to
stimulate action.

analyze a speech according to the
principles of persuasion

Most of the speeches you hear are persuasive. The speeches of politicians, advertisers, and religious leaders are clear examples. In most of your own speeches, you too will aim at persuasion. You will try to change your listeners' attitudes and beliefs or perhaps get them to do something. In school you might try to persuade others to (or not to) expand the core curriculum, use a plus–minus or a pass–fail grading system, disband the basketball team, allocate increased student funds for the school newspaper, establish competitive majors, or eliminate fraternity initiation rituals. On your job you may be called upon to speak in favor of (or against) having a union, a wage increase proposal, a health benefit package, or the election of a new shop steward.

In this unit we look at facts, values, and policies, the principles of persuasion, and the types of persuasive speeches. For example, you might want to strengthen or change the attitudes or beliefs of your listeners or you might want to get them to do something; that is, you might want to influence their behavior.

Recall from Unit 15, in our discussion of the audience, that the beliefs, attitudes, and values of your listeners are important in persuasion because people's behavior—which is what you ultimately want to influence—depends on their attitudes, beliefs, and values. So, if you can change their beliefs about, say, abortion, you might get them to vote one way or another or contribute to a particular abortion position. If you can change the values that people have toward animals and animal experimentation, you might get them to boycott cosmetics companies that use animals in their testing.

Further, the audience members' beliefs, attitudes, and values will influence how they respond to your thesis, your propositions, your arguments, your evidence, and just about everything else you do in your speech. For example, if you were going to give a speech defending doctor-assisted suicide, it would be crucial for you to know the beliefs, attitudes, and values that your audience has before you frame and support your propositions. You would have to prepare very different speeches for an audience that believes that suicide of any kind is morally wrong and an audience whose concern centers on how doctor-assisted suicides can be monitored to prevent violating the patients' wishes. So, in constructing your persuasive speeches and in using the 10 principles

of persuasion discussed later in this unit, be sure to take into consideration the beliefs, attitudes, and values of the audience as these relate to *anything* you'll say in your speech—but particularly your thesis, main propositions, and main supports.

FACTS, VALUES, AND POLICIES

A useful way to look at the issues you'll be dealing with in your persuasive speeches (whether as your thesis or a particular proposition) is to view them as questions of facts, values, or policies.

Questions of Fact

Questions of fact concern what is or is not true, what does or does not exist, what did or did not happen. In 1998 the media of the entire country were focused on what did or did not take place between the president and a White House intern and whether or not what was said constituted perjury—questions of fact. Sometimes a speaker will formulate a thesis around a questions of fact such as:

- Iraq is hiding (not hiding) chemical weapons.
- This company has (doesn't have) a glass ceiling for women.
- Wellington was (wasn't) slandered (or libeled or defamed).
- Ali's death was (wasn't) a case of doctor-assisted suicide.
- Marijuana does (not) lead to hard drugs.
- Gay men and lesbians make (do not make) competent military personnel.
- Television violence leads (doesn't lead) to violent behavior in viewers.

At other times, you may want to establish a question of fact as one of your major propositions. So, for example, let's say you're giving a speech on a military policy in which gay men and lesbians are given full equality. In this case, one of your propositions might focus on a question of fact and here you might seek to establish that gay men and lesbians make competent military personnel. Once that is established, you might then be in a better position to argue for equality in military policy.

Questions of Value

A question of value concerns what a person considers good or bad, moral or immoral, just or unjust.

MEDIA WATCH

MEDIA CREDIBILITY

Among many people, the media enjoy enormous credibility. People generally believe what they hear on television or read in the newspapers. In part they believe the media because they believe the media spokespersons, Dan Rather, Ted Koppel, or Connie Chung. Many believe what Oprah Winfrey says about relationships and self-esteem, what Geraldo Rivera says about politics, and what Montel Williams says about dealing with problem teenagers. The belief seems to come in part because these personalities are so impressive and because they are on TV.

In a similar way, we believe what we read. We believe our newspapers and magazines. Unless it's marked "editorial" or "advertisement," we assume that what appears in a newspaper or news magazine is accurate and objective. The News Credibility Scale presented here provides an interesting way to look at the credibility of a newspaper. It is also an interesting way to think about the factors you take into consideration when you make your judgments of believability.

How Credible is Your Newspaper?

Select a specific newspaper and circle the number for each pair of phrases that best represents your feelings about this newspaper.

Is fair	5 4 3 2 1	Is unfair
Is unbiased	5 4 3 2 1	Is biased
Tells the whole story	5 4 3 2 1	Doesn't tell the whole story
Is accurate	5 4 3 2 1	Is inaccurate
Respects people's privacy	5 4 3 2 1	Invades people's privacy
Does watch after readers' interesets	5 4 3 2 1	Does not watch after readers' interests

Is concerned about the community's well-being	5 4 3 2 1	Is not concerned abut the community's well being
Does separate fact and opinion	5 4 3 2 1	Does not separate fact and opinion
Can be trusted	5 4 3 2 1	Cannot be trusted
Is concerned about the public interest	5 4 3 2 1	Is concerned about making profits
Is factual	5 4 3 2 1	Is opinionated
Has well-trained reporters	5 4 3 2 1	Has poorly trained reporters

To compute your score, simply add up the circled numbers. The higher the score, the greater degree of credibility you perceive this newspaper to have and, more important, the more likely you are to believe this newspaper. The highest possible score would be 60, the lowest 12, and the midpoint 36. You might wish to try completing this scale for several different newspapers and see if the scores on the test correspond to the degree with which you believe the newspaper.

This scale, although designed for newspapers, can easily be extended to all news media—television, magazines, radio, and the various computerized information sources—and across media, for example, how does the credibility of your local paper compare to CNN news?

From "Media Watch: Media Credibility" from "Measuring the Concept of Credibility," by C. Gaziano and K. McGrath, *Journalism Quarterly,* 63, 1986, pp. 451–462. Reprinted by permission Association for Education in Journalism and Mass Communication.

Theses devoted to questions of value might look something like this:

- IQ tests are biased.
- Bullfighting is inhumane.
- Doctor-assisted suicide is humane.
- The death penalty is morally unjustifiable.

And, in the same way you might relate a proposition to a question of fact, you might have a proposition devoted to a question of value. For example, you might want to establish that IQ tests are biased as one of your propositions, with your thesis being that IQ tests should be discontinued at our school. Or you might want to show that bullfighting in inhumane in a speech with the thesis that bullfighting should be declared illegal throughout the world.

Questions of Policy

Questions of policy concern exactly that—policy—and focus on what should be done, what policy should be adopted, what law should be changed, what practice should be followed, and so on. Frequently, persuasive speech theses revolve around questions of policy, for example:

- What should the college's sexual harassment policy be?
- What should our drug policy be?
- What immigration policy should we adopt?
- What alcohol level should be used to establish "drunk driving"?
- What should our laws say about doctor-assisted suicide?
- What should our position be on affirmative action?

Generally, you find questions of policy used more often as theses than as major propositions. Still, in many instances, you might phrase a major proposition around a policy issue. For example, you might want to argue that the alcohol level that is used to establish "drunk driving" should be much higher than it currently is in a speech designed to get your client off a driving-while-intoxicated charge.

As noted previously, any of these questions can be used to help you conceptualize a thesis statement or frame a major proposition. A single speech, of course, may involve questions of fact, value, and policy. For example, you might argue, first, that home-lessness is growing (question of fact) and, second, that everyone is responsible for the less fortunate (question of value) and then conclude with your thesis that legislation must be enacted to reduce homelessness (question of policy).

PRINCIPLES OF PERSUASION

Your success in strengthening or changing attitudes or beliefs and in moving your listeners to action will depend on your use of the principles of persuasion.

Persuasive Strategies and Ethics

As you consider the persuasive strategies you'll use in your speech (and, actually, in any form of communication), keep in mind that ethical considerations must be a part of your overall persuasive plan. To get you started thinking about the ethics of persuasive strategies, here's a list of eight persuasive techniques that are generally considered unethical but in wide use in public speeches and in the appeals of advertisers (Lee & Lee 1972, 1995; Pratkanis & Aronson 1991).

Name-calling. Here the speaker gives an idea, a group of people, or a political philosophy a bad name ("atheist," "Neo-Nazi") to try to get you to condemn the idea without analyzing the argument and evidence. The opposite of name-calling is **glittering generality**, in which the speaker tries to make you accept some idea by associating it with things you value highly ("democracy," "free speech," "academic freedom"). By using *virtue words*, the speaker tries to get you to ignore the evidence and simply approve of the idea.

Transfer. Here the speaker associates her or his idea with something you respect (to gain your approval) or with something you detest (to gain your rejection). For example, a proposal for condom distribution in schools may be characterized as a means for "saving our children from AIDS" (to encourage acceptance) or as a means for "promoting sexual promiscuity" (to encourage disapproval). Sports car manufacturers try to get you to buy their cars by associating them with high status and sex appeal. Exercise clubs and diet plans try to get you to buy their services by associating them with health, self-confidence, and interpersonal appeal.

Testimonial. This device involves using the image associated with some person to gain your approval

Using the classification of fact, value, and policy, how would you classify the majority of speeches given by politicians to potential voters? Speeches given by religious leaders to their followers? Speeches within a business organization?

(if you respect the person) or your rejection (if you don't respect the person). This is the technique of advertisers who use people dressed up to look like doctors or plumbers or chefs to sell their products. Sometimes this technique takes the form of using only vague and general "authorities," for example, "experts agree," "scientists say," "good cooks know," or "dentists advise."

Plain folks. Using this device, the speaker identifies himself or herself with the audience. The speaker is good—the reasoning goes—because he or she is one of the people, just "plain folks" like everyone else.

Card-stacking. The speaker here selects only the evidence and arguments that support the case, and might even falsify evidence and distort the facts to better fit the case. Despite these misrepresentations, the speaker presents the supporting materials as "fair" and "impartial."

Bandwagon. Using this method, the speaker persuades the audience to accept or reject an idea or proposal because "everybody's doing it" or because the "right" people are doing it. The speaker persuades you to jump on this large and popular bandwagon. This is a popular technique in political elections where results of polls are used to get undecided voters to jump on the bandwagon with the candidate leading in the polls. After all, you don't want to vote for a loser.

Agenda-setting. A speaker might argue that XYZ is the issue and that all others are unimportant and insignificant. This appeal is heard frequently: Balancing the budget is the key to the city's survival. There's only one issue confronting elementary education in our largest cities and that is violence. In almost all situations, however, there are many issues and many sides to each issue. Often the person proclaiming X is the issue really means "I'll be able to persuade you if you focus solely on X and ignore the other issues."

Attack. This method involves accusing another person (usually an opponent) of some serious wrongdoing so that the issue under discussion never gets examined. Arguments such as "How can we support a candidate who has been unfaithful (smoked pot, avoided the military)?" are often heard in political discussions. When personal attack is used to draw attention away from other issues, it becomes unethical.

Selective Exposure

Your listeners (in fact, all audiences) follow the "law of selective exposure." It has at least two parts:

1. Listeners actively seek out information that supports their opinions, beliefs, values, decisions, and behaviors.
2. Listeners actively avoid information that contradicts their existing opinions, beliefs, attitudes, values, and behaviors.

Of course, if you're very sure that your opinions and attitudes are logical and valid, then you might not bother to seek out supporting information. And you may not actively avoid nonsupportive messages. People exercise selective exposure most often when their confidence in their opinions and beliefs is weak.

This principle of selective exposure suggests a number of implications. For example, if you want to persuade an audience that holds very different attitudes from your own, anticipate selective exposure operating and proceed inductively; that is, hold back on your thesis until you have presented your evidence and made your argument. Only then should you relate the evidence and argument to your initially contrary thesis.

If you were to present the people in the audience with your thesis first, they might tune you out without giving your position a fair hearing. So, become thoroughly familiar with the attitudes of your audience if you want to succeed in making these necessary adjustments and adaptations.

Let's say you're giving a speech on the need to reduce spending on college athletic programs. If your audience were composed of listeners who agreed with you and wanted to cut athletic spending, you might lead with your thesis. Your introduction might go something like this:

> Our college athletic program is absorbing money that we can more profitably use for the library, science labs, and language labs. Let me explain how the money now going to unnecessary athletic programs could be better spent in these other areas.

On the other hand, let's say that you were addressing alumni who strongly favored the existing athletic programs. In this case, you might want to lead with your evidence and hold off stating your thesis until the end of your speech.

Cultural Differences

Members of different cultures respond very differently to persuasive attempts (Lustig & Koester 1999; Dodd 1995). In some cultures, for example, credibility is extremely influential in persuasion. If the religious leader says something, it's taken as true and therefore believed. In other cultures, the religious leader's credibility would be assessed individually—not all religious leaders are equally believable. In still other cultures, the religious leader's credibility would be assessed negatively.

The schools in the United States teach students to demand logical and reliable evidence before believing something. The critical thinking emphasis throughout contemporary education and in this text are good examples of this concern with logic, argument, and evidence. Other cultures give much less importance to these forms of persuasion.

Some audiences favor a deductive pattern of reasoning. They expect to hear the general principle first and the evidence, examples, and argument second. Other audiences favor a more inductive pattern (Asian audiences are often cited as examples) in which the examples and illustrations are given first and the general principle or conclusion is given second.

Still other cultures expect a very clear statement of the speaker's conclusion. Low-context cultures (the United States, Germany, and Sweden, for example) generally expect an explicit statement of the speaker's position and an explicit statement of what he or she wants the audience to do. Low-context cultures prefer to leave as little unspoken as possible. High-context cultures (Japanese, Chinese, and Arabic, for example) prefer a less explicit statement and prefer to be led indirectly to the speaker's conclusion. An explicit statement ("Vote for Smith" or "Buy Viterall") may be interpreted as too direct and even insulting.

Audience Participation

Persuasion is greatest when the audience participates actively in your presentation. In experimental tests the same speech is delivered to different audiences. The attitudes of each audience are measured before and after the speech. The difference between their attitudes before and after the speech is taken as a measure of the speech's effectiveness. For one audience the sequence consists of (1) pretest of attitudes, (2) presentation of the persuasive speech, and (3) post-test of attitudes. For another audience the sequence consists of (1) pretest of attitudes, (2) presentation of the persuasive speech, (3) audience paraphrases or summarizes the speech, and (4) post-test of attitudes. Researchers consistently find that those listeners who participated actively (as in paraphrasing or summarizing) are more persuaded than those who received the message passively. Demagogues and propagandists who succeed in arousing huge

Going Online

Propaganda Web site

Visit this Web site focusing on propaganda. What additional principles of persuasion can you learn from this Web site?

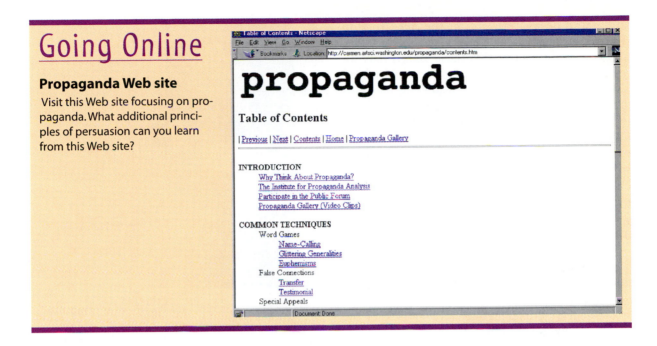

crowds often have the crowds chant slogans, repeat catch phrases, and otherwise participate actively in the persuasive experience.

The implication here is simple: persuasion is a transactional process. It involves both speaker and listeners. You will be more effective if you can get the audience to participate actively in the process.

Inoculation

The principle of inoculation can be explained with the biological analogy on which it's based (McGuire 1964). Suppose that you lived in a germ-free environment. Upon leaving this germ-free environment and upon exposure to germs, you would be particularly susceptible to infection because your body had not built up an immunity—it had no resistance. Resistance, the ability to fight off germs, might be achieved by the body, if not naturally, then through some form of inoculation. You could, for example, be injected with a weakened dose of the germ so that your body could begin to fight the germ by building up antibodies that create an "immunity" to this type of infection. Your body, because of the antibodies it produced, would be able to fight off even powerful doses of this germ.

The situation in persuasion is similar to this biological process. Some of your attitudes and beliefs have existed in a "germ-free" environment, that is, they have never been attacked or challenged. For example, many of us have lived in an environment in which the values of a democratic form of government, the importance of education, and the traditional family structure have not been challenged. Consequently, we have not been "immunized" against attacks on these values and beliefs. We have no counter-arguments (antibodies) prepared to fight off these attacks on our beliefs, so if someone were to come along with strong arguments against these beliefs, we might be easily persuaded.

Contrast these "germ-free" beliefs with issues that have been attacked and for which we have a ready arsenal of counter-arguments. Our attitudes on the draft, nuclear weapons, college athletics, and thousands of other issues have been challenged in the press, on television, and in our interpersonal interactions. As a result of this exposure, we have counter-arguments ready for any attacks on our beliefs concerning these issues. We have been inoculated and immunized against attacks should someone attempt to change our attitudes or beliefs.

If you're addressing an inoculated audience, take into consideration the fact that people in this audience have a ready arsenal of counter-arguments to fight your persuasive assault. For example, if you're addressing heavy smokers on the need to stop smoking or alcoholics on the need to stop drinking, you might assume that these people have already heard your arguments and that they have already inoculated themselves against the major arguments. In such situations, be prepared, therefore, to achieve only small gains. Don't try to reverse totally the beliefs of a well-inoculated audience. For example, it would be asking too much to get the smokers or the alcoholics to quit their present behaviors as a result of one speech. But, it might not be too much to ask to get them—at least some of them—to attend a meeting of a smoking clinic or Alcoholics Anonymous.

If you're trying to persuade an uninoculated audience, your task is often much simpler since you do not have to penetrate a fully developed immunization shield. For example, it might be relatively easy to persuade a group of high school seniors about the values of a college core curriculum since they probably have not thought much about the issue and probably do not have arguments against the core curriculum at their ready disposal.

Do recognize, however, that even when an audience has not immunized itself, members of this audience often take certain beliefs to be self-evident. As a result they may well tune out attacks on cherished beliefs or values. This might be the case, for example, if you try to persuade an audience of communists to support capitalist policies. Although they may not have counter-arguments ready, they may accept their communist beliefs as so fundamental that they simply will not listen to attacks on such beliefs. Again, proceed slowly and be content with small gains. Further, an inductive approach would suit your purposes better here. Attacking cherished beliefs directly creates impenetrable resistance. Instead, build your case by first presenting your arguments and evidence and gradually work up to your conclusion.

If you try to strengthen an audience's belief, give it the "antibodies" it will need if ever under attack. Consider raising counter-arguments to this belief and then demolishing them. Much as the injection of a small amount of a germ will enable the body to build an immunization response, presenting counter-arguments and then refuting them will enable your listeners to immunize themselves against future attacks on these values and beliefs. This pro-

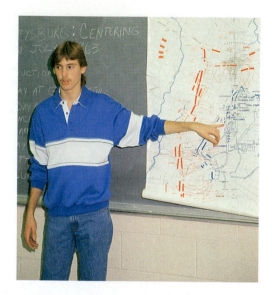

How would you describe your class in terms of inoculation for the following topics: (1) Abortion is a woman's right; (2) suicide is an individual's right; and (3) access to free needles is a drug user's right?

cedure results in greater and longer-lasting resistance to strong attacks than merely providing the audience with an arsenal of supporting arguments.

Magnitude of Change

The greater and more important the change you want to produce in your audience, the more difficult your task will be. The reason is simple: we normally demand a greater number of reasons and lots more evidence before we make important decisions—career changes, moving our families to another state, or investing our life savings in certain stocks.

On the other hand, we may be more easily persuaded (and demand less evidence) on relatively minor issues—whether to take a course in "Small Group Communication" rather than "Persuasion," or to give to the United Heart Fund instead of the American Heart Fund.

People change gradually, in small degrees over a long period of time. And although there are cases of sudden conversions, this general principle holds true more often than not. Persuasion, therefore, is most effective when it strives for small changes and works over a considerable period of time. For example, a persuasive speech stands a better chance when it tries to get the alcoholic to attend just one AA meeting rather than to give up alcohol for life. If you try to convince members of your audience to change their attitudes radically or to engage in behaviors to which they're initially opposed, your attempts may backfire. In this type of situation, the audience may tune you out, closing its ears to even the best and most logical arguments.

When you have the opportunity to try to persuade your audience on several occasions (rather than simply delivering one speech), two strategies will prove relevant: the foot-in-the-door and the door-in-the-face techniques.

Foot-in-the-Door Technique

As its name implies, this technique involves getting your foot in the door first. That is, you first request something small, something that your audience will easily comply with. Once this compliance has been achieved, you then make your real request (Freedman & Fraser 1966; Dejong 1979; Cialdini 1984; 403 & Aronson 1991). Research shows that people are more apt to comply with a large request after they have complied with a similar but much smaller request. For example, in one study the objective was to get people to put a "Drive Carefully" sign on their lawn (a large request). When this (large) request was made first, only about 17 percent of the people were willing to comply. However, when this request was preceded by a much smaller request (to sign a petition), between 50 and 76 percent granted permission to install the sign. The smaller request and its compliance paved the way for the larger request and put the audience into an agreement mode.

In using this strategy, be sure that your first request is small enough to gain compliance. If it isn't, then you miss the chance ever to gain compliance with your desired and larger request.

Door-in-the-Face Technique

This technique is the opposite of foot-in-the-door (Cialdini & Ascani 1976; Cialdini 1984). In this strategy you first make a large request that you know will be refused (for example, "We're asking most people to donate $100 for new school computers"). Later, you make a more moderate request, the one you really want your listeners to comply with (for example, "Might you be willing to contribute $10?").

In changing from the large to the more moderate request, you demonstrate your willingness to compromise and your sensitivity to your listeners. The general idea here is that your listeners will feel that since you have made concessions, they will also make concessions and at least contribute something. Listeners will probably also feel that $10 is actually quite little, considering the initial request and, research shows, are more likely to comply and will donate the $10.

In using this technique, be sure that your first request is significantly larger than your desired request but not so large as to seem absurd and be rejected out of hand.

Identification

If you can show your listeners that you and they share important attitudes, beliefs, and values, you'll clearly advance your persuasive goal. Other similarities are also important. For example, in some cases similarity of cultural, educational, or social background may help you identify yourself with your audience. Be aware, however, that insincere or dishonest identification is likely to backfire and create problems for the speaker. So, avoid even implying similarities between yourself and your audience that don't exist.

Consistency

People strive for consistency among their attitudes, beliefs, values, and behaviors. We expect there to be logical relationships among them and when those relationships exist we feel comfortable. When they contradict each other, we feel uncomfortable and we seek change—usually just enough to restore balance and comfort.

Consistency is the more common case and you can probably see lots of examples in your own thoughts and behaviors. For example, if you have positive attitudes toward, say, animal rights, then you probably believe that animals do in fact have rights that have to be recognized and that, were you in a position to do something for animal rights, you would do it.

Inconsistency or dissonance occurs when, say, attitudes contradict behavior. For example, if you have positive attitudes toward helping the homeless but don't actually do anything about it, you're probably in a state of dissonance or discomfort—not always, but just when you think about the homeless and particularly when you bring to consciousness this discrepancy between attitude and behavior. And, when dissonance occurs, you'll try to do something to reduce it. For example, if your dissonance becomes too uncomfortable, you might decide to give money to the homeless shelter or to buy coffee for the homeless man who sits by your apartment building.

Generally, direct your propositions at increasing the audience's sense of consistency. Show them that by accepting your thesis their attitudes and behaviors will be consistent and in harmony. For example, you might remind your listeners of their positive attitude toward helping those less fortunate and then show them that by doing as you advise, their behavior will be consistent with their attitude. In a very different circumstance, the salesperson uses this technique regularly: "You want status, you want performance, you want luxury; a BMW, it's your only choice." In this case, buying the BMW brings your behavior into consistency with your attitudes and values.

If the audience is experiencing dissonance, try to connect your thesis or your propositions to its reduction. For example, let's say you're giving a speech to persuade the neighborhood merchants to recycle more carefully. Although they believe in recycling, they aren't following the rules because, they say, it takes too much time. Here is a situation in which the audience is experiencing dissonance—their belief in the value of recycling is contradicted by their nonrecycling behavior. As a speaker, your task would be to show the merchants how they can reduce dissonance by, for example, following a few simple rules or by using color-coded trash cans. If you can show them how they can easily change their behavior to be consistent with their attitudes, you'll have a favorably disposed audience.

Logos: Logical Appeals

The logical aspect of public communication consists basically of arguments, which in turn consist of evidence (for example, facts) and a conclusion. Evidence together with the conclusion (that the evidence supports) equal an argument. *Reasoning* is the process you go through in forming conclusions on the basis of evidence. For example, you might reason that since college graduates earn more money than nongraduates (evidence), Jack and Jill should go to college if they wish to earn more money (conclusion).

The same principles of logic will prove useful to the speaker in constructing the speech, to the listener in receiving and responding to the speech, and to the critic in evaluating the speech. A poorly reasoned argument, inadequate evidence, and stereotypical thinking, for example, should be avoided by the speaker, recognized and responded to by the listener, and negatively evaluated by the critic. Three general tests of evidence and argument are especially important: recency, corroboration, and fairness.

Recency

We live in a world of rapid change. Economic strategies that worked for your parents will not work for you. Political strategies in place 10 years ago are now considered inappropriate. As the world changes, so must the strategies for coping with it. Therefore, it is important that supporting materials be as recent as possible. Recency alone, obviously, does not make an effective argument. Yet, other things being equal, the more recent the evidence and support, the better.

Corroboration

In drawing a conclusion (or in supporting a thesis) gather evidence and arguments from numerous and diverse sources. When all or most of the evidence points in the same direction, you are on pretty firm ground. If some evidence points to yes and some evidence points to no, then perhaps your conclusion needs to be reevaluated. Just as you would be convinced by evidence all pointing in the same direction, so will your listeners.

Fairness

Each person sees the world through his or her individual filters. You see the world, not objectively, but through your prejudices, biases, preconceptions, and stereotypes. Others see the world through their own filters. No one is totally objective. Consequently, in evaluating evidence, establish how fair or biased the sources are and in what direction they may be biased. A report on the connection between smoking and lung cancer from a tobacco company and an impartial medical research institute should be treated very differently. Question research conducted and disseminated by any special interest group. It is always legitimate to ask: To what extent might this source be biased? Might this source have a special interest that leads her or him to offer this evidence or this conclusion?

Pathos: Emotional (Motivational) Appeals

When you use emotional (or motivational) appeals you direct your appeals to your listeners' needs and desires. Although psychological appeals are never totally separate from logical appeals, we consider them separately here. We are concerned here with motives, with those forces that energize or move or motivate a person to develop, change, or strengthen particular attitudes or ways of behaving. For example, one motive might be the desire for status. This desire might motivate you to develop certain attitudes about what occupation to enter, the importance of saving and investing money, and so on. It may move you to behave in certain ways—to buy Gucci shoes, a Rolex watch, or a Tiffany diamond. As these examples illustrate, appeals to status (or to any motive) may motivate different persons in different ways. Thus, the status motive may lead one person to enter the poorly paid but respected occupation of social work. It may influence another to enter the well-paid but often disparaged real estate or diamond business.

Motive Hierarchy

One of the most useful analyses of motives is Abraham Maslow's five-fold classification, reproduced in Figure 19.1. One of the assumptions here is that you would seek to fulfill the need at the lowest level first and only then the need at the next higher level. Thus, for example, you would not concern yourself with the need for security or freedom from fear if you were starving (that is, if your need for food had not been fulfilled). Similarly, you would not be concerned with friendship or affectional relationships if your need for protection and security had not been fulfilled.

In this system certain needs have to be satisfied before other needs can motivate behavior. Thus, you need to determine what needs of the audience have been satisfied and, therefore, what needs might be used to motivate it. In most college classrooms, for example, you may assume that the two lowest levels—physiological needs and safety needs—have been reasonably fulfilled. For many students, however, the third level (love needs) is not fulfilled, and propositions may be linked to these with great effectiveness. Thus, to assure your listeners that what you are saying will enable them to achieve more productive interpersonal relationships or greater peer acceptance will go a long way toward securing their attention and receptiveness.

Motive Appeals

Think about the ways in which appeals may be addressed to specific motives. Each audience, of course, is different, and motives that are appropriately appealed to in one situation might be inappropriate or ineffective in another. Here are some of the motives speakers (and advertisers) appeal to. As you read through the list, you may find it interesting to recall a recent print or television advertisement that makes use of each of these motive appeals.

- **Altruism.** People want to do what they consider the right thing—to help others, contribute to worthy causes, help the weak, feed the hungry, and cure the sick.
- **Fear.** People are motivated in great part by a desire to avoid fear, fear of the loss of those things desired, for example, money, family, friends, love, attractiveness, health, job, and just about everything now possessed and valued. People also fear punishment, rejection, failure, the unknown, the uncertain, and the unpredictable.
- **Individuality and conformity.** People want to stand out from the crowd and may fear being lost in the crowd, being indistinguishable from everyone else. Yet many also want to conform, to be one of the crowd, to be "in."
- **Power, control, and influence.** People want power, control, and influence over themselves and over their own destinies. People also want control over other persons, to be influential, and to be opinion leaders.
- **Self-esteem and approval.** People want to see themselves as self-confident, as worthy and contributing human beings. Because of this need, inspirational speeches, speeches of the "you are the greatest" type, never seem to lack receptive and suggestive audiences.

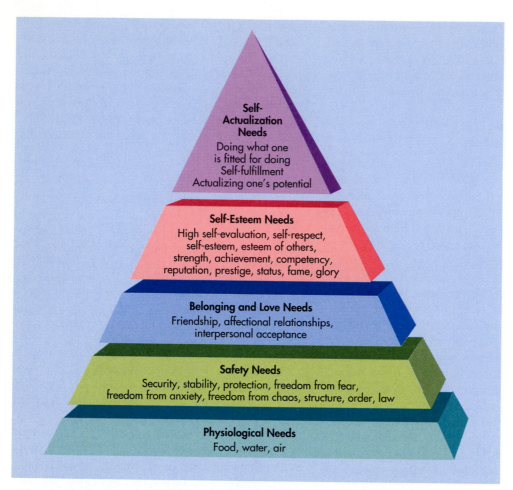

Figure 19.1 **Maslow's Hierarchy of Needs.**   According to Maslow, satisfied needs do not motivate. For example, if the safety need of an individual is satisfied, that individual will not be motivated to seek further safety. Therefore, appeals to satisfied needs will not be persuasive for this listener. The insights of Maslow—as well as of various other theorists—underlie the principles of motivation discussed in this section.

Data from Abraham Maslow, *Motivation and Personality*. 1970 HarperCollins, New York, NY.

- **Love and affiliation.** People are strongly motivated to love and be loved, to be assured that someone (preferably lots of people) loves them and at the same time to be assured they are capable of loving in return.
- **Achievement.** People want to achieve in whatever they do. You want to be a successful student. You want to achieve as friends, as parents, as lovers. This is why you read books and listen to speeches that purport to tell you how to be better achievers.
- **Financial gain.** Most people seem motivated by the desire for financial gain—for what it can

buy, for what it can do. Advertisers know this motive well and frequently get us interested in their messages by using such keywords as "sale," "50 percent off," "save now," and the like. All of these are appeals to the desire for money.
- **Status.** In our society our status is measured by our occupation and wealth, but also by competence on the athletic field, excelling in the classroom, or superiority on the dance floor.
- **Self-actualization.** According to Maslow, the self-actualization motive only influences attitudes and behaviors after all other needs are satisfied. Yet we all have in some part a desire

to self-actualize, to become what we feel we are fit for. If we see ourselves as poets, we must write poetry.

Emotional Appeals and Ethics

Emotional appeals are all around. Persons who want to censor the Internet might appeal to the audience's fear of children accessing pornographic materials; those who want to restrict the media's portrayal of violence may appeal to the audience's fear of increased violence in their community. Similarly, the real estate broker appealing to your desire for status, the friend who wants a favor appealing to your desire for social approval, and the salesperson appealing to your desire for sexual rewards are familiar examples. The question we need to ask about these appeals is, are they ethical? Here are just a few questions to get you thinking about the ethical aspects involved in the use of emotional appeals in persuasion:

- Is it ethical for parents to use fear appeals to dissuade their teenage children from engaging in sexual relationships? From interacting with teens of other races? Are the parents' motives relevant in deciding whether such appeals are ethical or unethical?
- Is it ethical to use fear appeals in public speeches or in advertisements to prevent sexually transmitted diseases? Is it ethical to use the same appeals if the motive is to sell condoms?
- Is it ethical for religious organizations to use fear appeals to get people to live their lives as the religion holds?

Ethos: Credibility Appeals

Think about how believable you are as a speaker. How believable are you apart from any evidence or argument you might advance? What is there about you as a person that makes others believe or not believe you? These are questions of credibility or believability.

You have probably made judgments on many occasions of speakers apart from any arguments, evidence, or motivational appeals they offered. Often you believe or disbelieve a speaker because of who the speaker is, not because of anything the speaker says. You may, for example, believe certain informa-

tion or take certain action solely by virtue of Lee Iacocca's or Shirley MacLaine's reputation, personality, or character. Alexander Pope put it more poetically in his "Essay on Criticism":

> Some judge of author's names, not works, and then
> Nor praise nor blame the writings, but the men.

Credibility is not something the speaker has or does not have in any objective sense. Rather, it is a quality that a listener attributes to the speaker; it's a quality that the listener thinks the speaker possesses. In reality the speaker may be a stupid, immoral person. But, if the audience perceives the speaker as intelligent and moral, then that speaker has high credibility. Further, research tells us, the audience will believe this speaker. The Thinking about Theory and Research box "How Do You Form Credibility Impressions?" explains how credibility impressions are formed.

Everyone seems interested in credibility. Advertisers, for example, are interested because it relates directly to the effectiveness of their ad campaigns. Is Michael Jordan an effective spokesperson for Haynes underwear? Is Susan Lucci an effective spokesperson for Ford? Is Jerry Seinfeld an effective spokesperson for American Express? Politicians are interested in credibility because it determines in great part how people vote. Educators are interested in it because students' perceptions of teacher credibility determine the degree of influence the teacher has on a class. There seems to be no communication situation that credibility does not influence.

Before reading about the specific characteristics of credibility, you may wish to take the self-test, "How Credible Are You?"

SELF-TEST

How Credible Are You?

Respond to each of the following phrases as you think members of this class (your audience) see you when you deliver a public speech. Use the following scale: 7 = very true; 6 = quite true; 5 = fairly true; 4 = neither true nor untrue; 3 = fairly untrue; 2 = quite untrue; and 1 = very untrue.

_____ 1. Knowledgeable about the subject matter
_____ 2. Experienced

_____ 3. Confident
_____ 4. Informed about the subject matter
_____ 5. Fair in the presentation of material (evidence and argument)
_____ 6. Concerned with the audiences' needs
_____ 7. Consistent over time on the issues addressed in the speech
_____ 8. Similar to the audience in attitudes and values
_____ 9. Positive rather than negative
_____ 10. Assertive in personal style
_____ 11. Enthusiastic about the topic and in general
_____ 12. Active rather than passive

This test focuses on the three qualities of credibility: competence, character, and charisma, and is based on a large body of research (for example, McCroskey 1997; Riggio 1987). Items 1 through 4 refer to your perceived **competence**: How competent or capable does the audience see you when you give a public speech? Items 5 through 8 refer to your perceived **character**: Does the audience see you as a person of good and moral character? Items 9 through 12 refer to your perceived **charisma**: Does the audience see you as dynamic and active rather than as static and passive? You may wish to consider what specific steps you can take to change any audience perception with which you may be unhappy.

We can identify three major qualities of credibility: competence, character, and charisma. Competence refers to the knowledge and expertise the audience thinks the speaker has. Character refers to the intentions and concern of the speaker for the audience. Charisma refers to the personality and dynamism of the speaker.

Generally, in the United States, speakers are advised to stress their credibility and make their audience know that they are competent, of good character, and dynamic or charismatic. In some cultures, however, to stress your own competence or that of your corporation may be taken to mean that your audience members are inferior or that their corporations are not as good as yours. As with any principle of communication, it helps to know something of the culture of your listeners.

Competence

Competence refers to the knowledge and expertise a speaker is thought to have. The more knowledge and expertise the audience perceives the speaker as having, the more likely the audience will be to believe the speaker. For example, we believe a teacher to the extent that we think he or she is knowledgeable on the subject.

Competence is logically subject-specific. Usually, it is limited to one specific field. A person may be competent in one subject and totally incompetent in another. Your political science instructor, for example, may be quite competent in politics but quite incompetent in mathematics or economics.

Often, however, we do not make the distinction between areas of competence and incompetence. Thus, we may see a person who we think competent in politics as competent in general. We will, therefore, perceive this person as credible in many fields. We refer to this as the **halo effect**—when listeners generalize their perception of competence to all areas. Listeners see the speaker's competence as a general trait of the individual.

This halo effect also has a counterpart—the reverse halo effect. Here the person, seen as incompetent in, say, mathematics, is perceived to be similarly incompetent in most other areas as well. As a critic of public communication, be particularly sensitive to competence being subject-specific. Be sensitive to both halo and reverse halo effects.

Character

We perceive a speaker as credible if we perceive that speaker as having high moral character. Here our concern is with the individual's honesty and basic nature. We want to know if we can trust that person. We believe a speaker we can trust. An individual's motives or intentions are particularly important in judging character. When the audience perceives your intentions as good for them (rather than for your personal gain), they will think you credible. And they will believe you.

Charisma

Charisma is a combination of the speaker's personality and dynamism as seen by the audience. We perceive as credible or believable speakers we like rather than speakers we do not like. We perceive speakers as credible if they are friendly and pleasant rather

UNDERSTANDING
Theory and Research

HOW DO YOU FORM CREDIBILITY IMPRESSIONS?

We form a credibility impression of a speaker on the basis of two sources of information (Figure 19.2). First, we assess the reputation of the speaker as we know it. This is initial or what theorists call "extrinsic credibility." Second, we evaluate how that reputation is confirmed or refuted by what the speaker says and does during the speech. This is derived or "intrinsic credibility." In other words, we combine what we know about the speaker's reputation with the more immediate information we get from present interactions and form a collective final assessment of credibility.

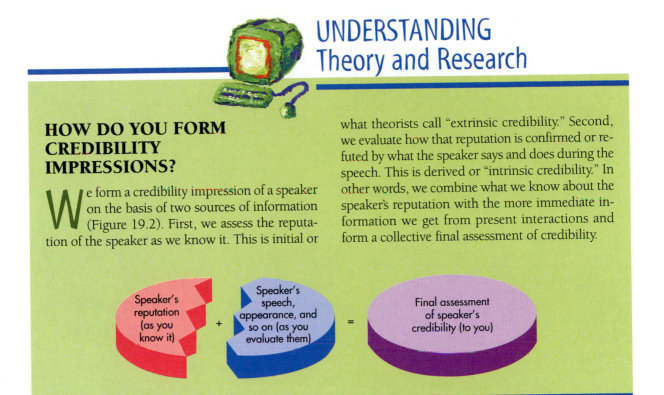

Speaker's reputation (as you know it) + Speaker's speech, appearance, and so on (as you evaluate them) = Final assessment of speaker's credibility (to you)

than aloof and reserved. Similarly, we favor the dynamic over the hesitant, nonassertive speaker. We perceive the shy, introverted, soft-spoken individual as less credible than the extroverted and forceful individual. The great leaders in history have been dynamic people. Perhaps we feel that the dynamic speaker is open and honest in presenting herself or himself. The shy, introverted individual may be seen as hiding something. As speakers, there is much that we can do to increase our charisma and hence our perceived credibility.

Credibility and Ethics

Triple academy award winner Ingrid Bergman once said, "It's not whether you really cry. It's whether the audience thinks you are crying." Now, you'd probably agree that there's nothing unethical about actors fooling you by faking their emotions or presenting themselves to be people they aren't. As an audience member you go to the movies prepared and expecting to be fooled. But what about public speaking? Communication theorists tell us that, like acting, what makes for effective persuasion is not whether you really are competent or moral but whether the audience thinks you are. Unlike the movies, however, the public speaking audience does not expect to be fooled; they expect the speaker to honestly present himself or herself.

At what point does following the principles for increasing credibility, such as those covered in this unit, raise ethical issues? Is it unethical for speakers to make the audience see them as more competent than they really are? Would it be ethical for a lawyer to make himself or herself appear competent (though really not competent) to effectively represent a client? Would it be ethical for the lawyer to do otherwise?

THE SPEECH TO STRENGTHEN OR CHANGE ATTITUDES, BELIEFS, OR VALUES

Many speeches seek to strengthen existing attitudes, beliefs, or values. Much religious and political

BUILDING
Communication Skills

HOW CAN YOU DEVELOP PERSUASIVE STRATEGIES?

The objective of this exercise is to stimulate the discussion of persuasive strategies on a variety of contemporary cultural situations and may be completed individually, in small groups, or with the entire class.

What persuasive strategies would you use to convince your class of the validity of either side in any of these points of view? For example, what persuasive strategies would you use to persuade your class members that interracial adoption should be encouraged or discouraged? Do realize that these points of view are simplified for purposes of this exercise and should not be taken to suggest that the viewpoints given here are complete descriptions of these complex issues.

Point of View: Interracial Adoption. Those in favor of interracial adoption argue that the welfare of the child—who might not get adopted if not by someone of another race—must be considered first. Adoption (regardless of race) is good for the child and therefore is a positive social process. Those opposed to interracial adoption argue that children need to be raised by those of the same race if the child is to develop self-esteem and become a functioning member of his or her own race. Interracial adoption is therefore a negative social process.

Point of View: Gays and Lesbians and the Military. Regardless of the status of the current law, a large group within the United States military is opposed to gay men and lesbians in the military. The gay and lesbian communities argue that gay men and lesbians should be accorded exactly the same rights and privileges as heterosexuals—no more, no less. Those opposed argue that gay men and lesbians will undermine the image of the military and will make heterosexuals uncomfortable.

Point of View: Affirmative Action. Those in favor of affirmative action argue that because of the injustices in the way certain groups (racial, national, gender) were treated, they should now be given preferential treatment to correct the imbalance caused by the social injustices. Those opposed to affirmative action argue that merit must be the sole criterion for promotion, jobs, entrance to graduate schools, etc., and that affirmative action is just reverse racism; one form of injustice cannot correct another form of injustice.

speaking, for example, tries to strengthen beliefs and values. People who listen to religious speeches usually are already believers, so these speeches strive to strengthen the beliefs and values the people already hold. Here the audience is already favorable to the speaker's purpose and is willing to listen. Speeches designed to change attitudes or beliefs are more difficult to construct. Most people resist change. When you try to get people to change their beliefs or attitudes you're fighting an uphill (but not impossible) battle.

Speeches designed to strengthen or change attitudes or beliefs come in many forms. Depending on the initial position of the audience, you can view the following examples as topics for speeches to strengthen or change attitudes or beliefs.

- Marijuana should be legalized.
- General education requirements should be abolished.
- Expand college athletic programs.
- History is a useless study.

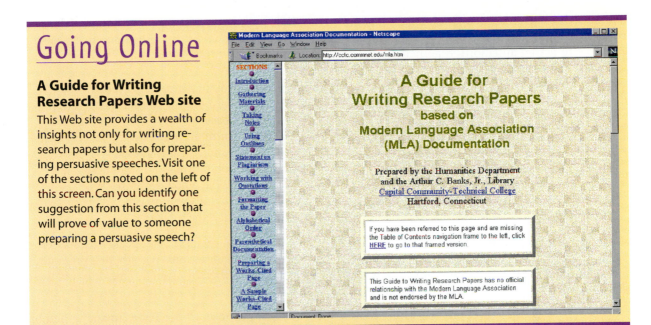

Going Online

A Guide for Writing Research Papers Web site

This Web site provides a wealth of insights not only for writing research papers but also for preparing persuasive speeches. Visit one of the sections noted on the left of this screen. Can you identify one suggestion from this section that will prove of value to someone preparing a persuasive speech?

- Television shows are mindless.
- CDs and tapes should be rated for excessive sex and violence.
- Puerto Rico should become the fifty-first state.

Strategies for Strengthening or Changing Attitudes, Beliefs, and Values

When you attempt to strengthen or change your listeners' attitudes, beliefs, and values, consider the following principles.

Estimate Listeners' Attitudes, Beliefs, and Values

Carefully estimate—as best you can—the current state of your listeners' attitudes, beliefs, and values. If your goal is to strengthen these, then you can state your thesis and your objectives as early in your speech as you wish. Since your listeners are in basic agreement with you, your statement of your thesis will enable you to create a bond of agreement between you. You might say, for example:

> Like you, I am deeply committed to the fight against abortion. Tonight, I'd like to explain some new evidence that has recently come to light that we must know if we are to be effective in our fight against legalized abortion.

If, however, you're in basic disagreement and you wish to change their attitudes, then reserve your statement of your thesis until you have provided them with your evidence and argument. Get listeners on your side first by stressing as many similarities between you and your audience members as you can. Only after this should you try to change their attitudes and beliefs. Continuing with the abortion example (but this time with an audience that is opposed to your antiabortion stance), you might say:

> We're all concerned with protecting the rights of the individual. No one wants to infringe on the rights of anyone. And it is from this point of view—from the point of view of the inalienable rights of the individual—that I want to examine the abortion issue.

In this way, you stress your similarity with the audience before you state your antiabortion position to this pro-abortion audience.

Seek Small Changes

When addressing an audience that is opposed to your position and your goal is to change their attitudes and beliefs, seek change in small increments. Let's say, for example, that your ultimate goal is to get an antiabortion group to favor abortion on demand. Obviously, this goal is too great to achieve in one speech. Therefore, strive for small changes. Here, for example, is an excerpt in which the speaker attempts to get an antiabortion audience to agree that some abortions should be legalized. The speaker begins as follows:

> One of the great lessons I learned in college was that most extreme positions are wrong. Most of the important truths lie somewhere between the extreme opposites. And today I want to talk with you about one of these truths. I want to talk with you about rape and the problems faced by the mother carrying a child conceived in this most violent of all the violent crimes we can imagine.

Notice that the speaker does not state a totally proabortion position but instead focuses on one area of abortion and attempts to get the audience to agree that in some cases abortion should be legalized.

Demonstrate Your Credibility
Show your listeners that you are knowledgeable about the topic, have their own best interests at heart, and are willing and ready to speak out in favor of these important concerns.

Give Listeners Good Reasons
Give the members of your audience good reasons for believing what you want them to believe. Give them hard evidence and arguments. Show them how such attitudes and beliefs relate directly to their goals, their motives.

Developing the Speech to Strengthen or Change Attitudes, Beliefs, and Values

Here are some examples to clarify the nature of this type of persuasive speech. These examples present the specific purpose, the thesis, and the question asked of the thesis to help identify the major propositions of the speech.

This first example deals with birth control and uses a topical organizational pattern.

General purpose: to persuade (to strengthen or change attitudes, beliefs, and values)

Specific purpose: to persuade my audience that advertisements for birth control devices should be allowed in all media

Thesis: media advertising of birth control devices is desirable (Why is media advertising desirable?)

I. Birth control information is needed.
   A. Birth control information is needed to prevent disease.
   B. Birth control information is needed to prevent unwanted pregnancies.
II. Birth control information is not available to the very people who need it most.
III. Birth control information can best be disseminated through the media.

In this second example, the speaker uses a problem–solution organizational pattern, first presenting the problems created by cigarette smoking, and then the solution.

General purpose: to persuade (to strengthen or change attitudes, beliefs, and values)

Specific purpose: to persuade my audience that cigarette advertising should be banned from all media

Thesis: cigarette advertising should be abolished (Why should it be abolished?)

I. Cigarette smoking is a national problem.
   A. Cigarette smoking causes lung cancer.
   B. Cigarette smoking pollutes the air.
   C. Cigarette smoking raises the cost of health care.
II. Cigarette smoking will be lessened if advertisements are prohibited.
III. Fewer people would start to smoke.
IV. Smokers would smoke less.

In delivering such a speech a speaker might begin like this:

> I think we all realize that cigarette smoking is a national problem that affects each and every one of us. No one escapes the problems caused by cigarette smoking—not the smoker and not the nonsmoker. Cigarette smoking causes lung cancer. Cigarette smoking pollutes the air. And cigarette smoking raises the cost of health care for everyone.

> Let's look first at the most publicized of all smoking problems: lung cancer. There can be no doubt—the scientific evidence is overwhelming—that cigarette

UNDERSTANDING
Theory and Research

HOW MACHIAVELLIAN ARE YOU?

Before reading about this fascinating concept, take the accompanying self-test, "How Machiavellian Are You?" It focuses on your beliefs about how easily you think people can be manipulated.

 SELF-TEST

How Machiavellian Are You?*

For each statement record the number on the following scale which most closely represents your attitude: 1 = disagree a lot; 2 = disagree a little; 3 = neutral; 4 = agree a bit; and 5 = agree a lot.

____ The best way to handle people is to tell them what they want to hear.

____ When you ask someone to do something for you, it is best to give the real reasons rather than giving reasons that might carry more weight.

____ Anyone who completely trusts anyone else is asking for trouble.

____ It is hard to get ahead without cutting corners here and there.

____ It is safest to assume that all people have a vicious streak and it will come out when they are given a chance.

____ One should take action only when sure it is morally right.

____ Most people are basically good and kind.

____ There is no excuse for lying to someone.

____ Most people forget more easily the death of their parents than the loss of their property.

____ Generally speaking, people won't work hard unless they're forced to.

To compute your Mach score follow these steps:

Reverse the scores on items 2, 6, 7, and 8 according to the following scale:

If you responded with	Change it to
5	1
4	2
3	3
2	4
1	5

Add all 10 scores, being sure to use the reversed numbers for 2, 6, 7, and 8.

Your Mach score is a measure of the degree to which you believe that people in general are manipulable and not necessarily that you would or do manipulate others. If you scored somewhere between 35 and 50 you would be considered a high Mach; if you scored between 10 and 15 you would be considered a low Mach. Most of us would score in between these extremes.

The concept of Machiavellianism comes from Niccolo Machiavelli (1469–1527), a political philosopher and advisor who wrote his theory of political control in *The Prince*. In greatly simplified form, the book takes the position that the prince must do whatever is necessary to rule the people; the ends justified the means. The ruler is in fact obligated to use power to gain more power and thus better achieve the desired goals (Steinfatt 1987). The term *Machiavellian* has thus come to refer to the techniques or tactics one person uses to control another.

Research finds significant differences between those who score high and those who score low on the Mach scale. Low Machs are more easily susceptible to social influence; they're more easily persuaded. High Machs are more resistant to persuasion. Low Machs are more empathic while high Machs are more logical. Low Machs are more interpersonally oriented and involved with other

(continued on next page)

Understanding Theory and Research *(continued)*

people; high Machs are more assertive and more controlling. Business students (especially marketing students) score higher in Machiavellianism than do nonbusiness majors (McLean & Jones 1992).

Machiavellianism seems in part at least to be culturally conditioned. Individualist orientation, which favors competition and being Number One, seems more conducive to the development of Machiavellianism. Collectivist orientation, which favors cooperation and being one of a group, seems a less friendly environment for the development of Machiavellianism in its members. Some evidence of this comes from research showing that Chinese students attending a traditional Chinese (Confucian) school rated lower in Machiavellianism than similar Chinese students attending a Western-style school (Christie 1970).

Your own level of Machiavellianism will influence the communication choices you make. For example, high Machs are more strategic and manipulative in their self-disclosures than are low Machs; that is, high Machs will self-disclose to in-

fluence the attitudes and behaviors of listeners (Steinfatt 1987). Machiavellianism influences the way you seek to gain the compliance of others. High Machs are more likely to be manipulative in their conflict-resolving behavior than are low Machs. High Machs are generally more effective in just about all aspects studied (they even earn higher grades in communication courses that involve face-to-face interaction; see Burgoon 1971). Low-Mach women, however, are preferred as dating partners by both high- and low-Mach men (Steinfatt 1987).

You've probably noted a similarity between this concept and self-monitoring (discussed in Unit 9, "Conversation"). Both high self-monitors and high Machs try to manipulate others and get their own way. The difference is that self-monitors change their own behaviors as a way of pleasing and manipulating others; Machiavellians try to change the behaviors of others to get what they want.

*Reprinted with permission from *Psychology Today* magazine, Copyright© 1970 Sussex Publishers, Inc.

---

smoking is a direct cause of lung cancer. Research conducted by the American Cancer Institute and by research institutes throughout the world all come to the same conclusion: cigarette smoking causes lung cancer. Consider some of the specific evidence. A recent study—reported in the November 1998 issue of the . . . .

- Give money to the American Cancer Society.
- Buy a ticket to the football game.
- Watch "20/20."
- Major in economics.
- Take a course in computer science.
- Buy a Pontiac.

THE SPEECH TO STIMULATE ACTION

Speeches designed to stimulate the audience to action or to engage in some specific behavior are referred to as speeches to actuate. The persuasive speech addressed to motivating a specific behavior may focus on just about any behavior imaginable. Here are some possible topics:

- Vote in the next election.
- Vote for Smith.
- Do not vote for Smith.

Strategies for Stimulating Listeners to Action

When designing a speech to get listeners to do something, keep the following principles in mind.

Be Realistic

Set reasonable goals for what you want the audience to do. Remember you have only 10 or 15 minutes and in that time you cannot move the proverbial mountain. So, ask for small, easily performed behaviors—to sign a petition, to vote in the next election, to donate a small amount of money.

Demonstrate Your Own Compliance

As a general rule, never ask the audience to do what you have not done yourself. So, demonstrate your own willingness to do what you want the audience to do. If you don't, your listeners will rightfully ask, "Why haven't you done it?" In addition to your having done what you want them to do, show them that you're pleased to have done so. Tell them of the satisfaction you derived from donating blood or from reading to blind students.

Stress Specific Advantages

Stress the specific advantages of these behaviors to your specific audience. Don't ask your audience to engage in behaviors solely for abstract reasons. Give them concrete, specific reasons why they will benefit from the actions you want them to engage in. Instead of telling your listeners that they should devote time to reading to blind students because it's the right thing to do, show them how much they will enjoy the experience and how much they will personally benefit from it.

Developing the Speech to Stimulate Action

Here are a few examples of the speech to actuate. First is a speech on devoting time to helping people with disabilities. Here the speaker asks for a change in the way most people spend their leisure time. It utilizes a topical organizational pattern; each of the subtopics is treated about equally.

General purpose: to persuade (to stimulate action)

Specific purpose: to persuade members of my audience to devote some of their leisure time to helping people with disabilities.

Thesis: leisure time can be well used in helping people with disabilities (How can leisure time be spent helping people with disabilities? or What can we do to help people with disabilities?)

I. Read for the blind.
   A. Read to a blind student.
   B. Make a recording of a textbook for blind students.

II. Run errands for students confined to wheelchairs.
III. Type for students who can't use their hands.

In this second example the speaker tries to persuade the audience of parents and teachers to see the advantages of the new multicultural curriculum at the town's high school and stresses two major issues.

General purpose: to persuade (to strengthen and change attitudes)

Specific purpose: to persuade my audience to believe that the multicultural curriculum should be adopted

Thesis: the multicultural curriculum is beneficial (Why is the multicultural curriculum beneficial?)

I. The multicultural curriculum will teach tolerance.
II. The multicultural curriculum will raise all students' self-esteem.

In delivering the speech, the speaker might say:

We've all heard about the new multicultural curriculum proposed for the high schools in our county. After years of research I can tell you what we know about the effects of multicultural education on students. And what we know is that multicultural education— such as presented in the curriculum before you— teaches tolerance for all people and all groups and, equally important, raises the self-esteem of all our sons and daughters. Let me explain how this curriculum teaches tolerance.

A SAMPLE PERSUASIVE SPEECH

This speech is presented as a summary of our discussion of the persuasive speech. As with the informative speech in the previous unit, read the speech without looking at the critical thinking questions. Then reread the speech, this time responding to the questions. This speech was given by William E. Franklin, President of Franklin International, LTD, to the Graduate School of Business of Columbia University at the Japan Business Association & International Business Society, New York City, April 8, 1998.

I have been asked to lead a discussion today about careers in international business. I am honored and pleased to do so. Thank you for coming. There is a Japanese proverb that says "Rongo yomi no rongo shirazu"…just because you read Confucious does not necessarily mean you understand what he says. Just because I have worked and studied in Asia the past 25 years does not mean I understand everything about Asia. In fact, I spend more time studying about Asia today than when I first moved to Tokyo in 1973. So I would like to have this be a dialogue, more than a lecture, a sharing of experiences and ideas.

Notice the mixture of expertise (he has worked and studied in Asia for 25 years) and modesty (he doesn't understand everything about Asia and wants to dialogue rather than lecture) in this first paragraph. How appropriate and effective do you think this introduction was?

After I accepted your invitation I read the report on rankings of business schools and learned Columbia was awarded an overall ranking of 99%. And also, not unimportant, you rank number one in placement success with a median starting salary of $88,000…a higher starting salary than graduates of any other business school in the world. With that kind of success perhaps you should be leading the discussion, with me in the audience. I really do want to hear your ideas, your questions…your comments, business questions, personal questions…anything that is on your mind.

What function does this paragraph serve? If you were in the audience, would this make you receptive to the speech?

I recently saw some demographic information which may help to bring perspective to your opportunities and responsibilities, some perspective on your place or role in the world.

If we shrink the world's 5.7 billion population to a village of 100 people…with all existing human ratios remaining the same, here is the resulting profile.

Of these 100 people 57 are Asian, 21 European, 14 from North and South America and eight from Africa.

51 female, 49 male
80 live in sub-standard housing
70 cannot read
half suffer from malnutrition
75 have never made a phone call
less than one is on the Internet
Half the entire villages wealth would be in the hands of six people
Only one of the hundred have a college education

Here's an excellent example of statistics that are made meaningful to an audience that will hear the figures just once. Do these figures gain and maintain your attention? Do they effectively support the speaker's point?

You are in a very elite group of only 1% who have a college education. But you are even more elite and distinctive because you will soon graduate from what many consider to be the number one Graduate School of Business. The dictionary definition of elite is "the choice part"…"a powerful minority group."

How does the speaker achieve a speaker-audience-topic relationship?

Whether you realize it or not the fact is that you are the choice part...and you have the power of education and knowledge.

Of course that does not guarantee you a good life...having that degree does not guarantee you anything. Your graduation will merely be the beginning of a new phase of learning in your life. I personally think the most valuable thing you can learn in any university is to develop your own personal method of learning so you can be a good student the rest of your life.

But being part of this very elite group does give you the potential for power and wealth...probably much more than you now realize. Many of you will be important global leaders...some of you will be important governmental leaders. You will have far more power than you now realize...power to enhance the quality of your personal life...power to help others in the world who are less fortunate than yourself. It's not too early to begin thinking seriously about your personal value...and how you will use your power.

How would members of your class respond to this paragraph if they were Franklin's Audience?

Now why do I talk about all that? Well, you don't have very much uncertainty about finding a job and I would imagine most of you have given a lot of thought to selecting a challenging career.

Your larger question will be "how will you create a rich and rewarding and balanced life?" There are two things to aim for in life. One, to get what you want in life and two to enjoy it. Only the wisest of women and men achieve the second.

In what ways does the speaker orient the audience?

I will share with you 5 ideas or principles about careers, and about life because it is difficult to have a full decision about your lifetime career without talking about your total life.

FIRST IDEA...Learn from other cultures. Let me read a quote from a speech by an American...see if you can guess who said this, "we have a favorable balance of trade. But if you think you can maintain that balance just by sending salesmen to Japan and China as you would to Montana or Chicago, you are mistaken. You must send people to live there to learn the culture, to learn the language, to learn the way of doing business there." John Wheeler said that in his inaugural speech as the first President of the United States Chamber of Commerce in 1912.

What do you think of this technique to involve the audience? How might you use this basic idea in your next speech?

Sometimes we are very diligent in learning about other cultures...but to be good leaders we want to learn from other cultures. The other day I was looking at some speeches I made 8 or 9 years ago...

attempting to persuade skeptical American audiences that American business and American ideas were not finished...and that Asia was not going to take over the world. You may remember how pessimistic everyone was about America then.

Now in 1998, with America's current up cycle and Asia's economic problems, there is a temptation to totally flip-flop and say, only the American way is the right way...and reject all Asian values.

As future global leaders, I ask you to think about the possibility that a more rewarding approach is to learn from each other...and try to adopt and adapt the best from each culture.

Iris Berlin said "the great human delusion is monism...the proposition that there is a single, final solution...the ultimate over-arching truth." Sometimes Americans are so passionate about our ideals that we want the whole world to accept our ideals... and we feel some obligation to have all countries adopt our form of democracy...now. To accept our concept of human rights...now. To accept our rule of law...now. I think most Americans do this out of a sense of good purpose...but when we think that our ideals and institutions are the one best way for all cultures we automatically forgo the possibility of learning that other social and economic systems may have equal validity.

On my first trip to China almost 20 years ago, as part of a government delegation, I had the opportunity to meet Mr. Deng Xiao Peng. After the official government discussions he turned to me and said "I understand your company has expertise in tree growing and in utlization of the forest resource. Our country needs to improve both...Will you help us?" We then met with the Minister of Forestry and that led to us becoming the principal forestry advisor to the PRC during the early 1980s. Mr. Deng said "it does not matter whether the cat is black or white as long as it helps to improve our country"...he was open to ideas from other cultures.

One time my friend, Mogi-san, was attempting to explain Japanese business philosophy to us. He said, "you Americans always talk about fairness, arms length business transactions, objectivity, no favor to friends...very detailed contracts" all words that are pleasing to the ears of most American business women and men. He went on to say, "if we think that is a very cold way to do business we wouldn't want to do business that way. We want to do business with friends."

The speaker uses a wide variety of personal examples throughout the speech. What do you think of the personal examples used in the discussion of this first idea, that we need to learn from (not just about) other cultures? Did the speaker convince you of the importance of this first idea?

How does the speaker demonstrate that he himself follows the first idea?

And later many American companies learned that in order to have a total quality system we needed to adopt some Japanese ideas with respect to customer and supplier relationsips. Which, by the way, many Japanese tell me they learned a lot about from Dr. Frederic Demming. We learned from each other.

There is a Zen saying…"in a beginner's mind there are many possibilities, in the experts mind, there are none." I have observed in myself that I am a much better leader when I think of myself as the student of Asia than when I think of myself as an expert on Asia.

To be a good international leader it is not enough to just study other cultures. We need to learn from other cultures.

SECOND POINT. And closely related to the first point. This may sound contradictory to the first point, but it is not. We need to be very conscious of our personal values…personal values as defined by our behavior…not just what we say…but how we spend our time each day. Write them down so you can look at them…and update as you get new insights. Be aware you are forming habits today, good habits and bad habits, that you may have the rest of your life.

Do these signpoints—First Idea, Second Point— help you follow the speech?

When you are selecting a company to join do some research to see if the companies values are consistent with your personal values. This is important. You will not do your best work with an organzation and people whose values are incompatible with your values.

The call to uphold our personal values in our actions is a relatively abstract principle that is often difficult to make clear to an audience. How effectively does the speaker handle this?

When I was at another university recently a student asked me "what's the biggest mistake you ever made?" My first response was that I had made so many that it would be difficult to say which is the biggest. But later, after I had an opportunity to reflect, I said to this student, "the biggest mistake I ever made was anytime I compromised my personal values."

And it usually does not happen in big ways with big issues…my values get compromised in small ways for small gains or no gains. One time I was offered a bribe of $1,000,000 on a project in southeast Asia. That was a no brainer; it is easy for anyone to decide what to do in a circumstance that is that black and white. But on a daily basis the choices are always in the gray areas where it is not so clear and the decision may seem so unimportant. But the cost for small compromises in your values is cumulative…and it can be a big cost to your effectiveness as a leader…a big cost to your total being. One needs to be vigilant every moment to see that doesn't happen.

Would you have liked to hear an example of "gray areas"? Would it have clarified this idea?

I heard John Wayne say once, "…perversion and corruption masquerade as ambiguity. I don't like ambiguity. I don't trust ambiguity." I don't like ambiguity either, but ambiguity is part of reality for an international leader. Your day to day life will not be so black and white as we like to see in John Wayne's movies. Always seek clarity, but learn to live with complexity and ambiguity.

And it is my observation that individuals who have strong personal values have the most freedom and ability and perspective to learn from other cultures. This is even more important in Asia. There is a generalization that Japanese business leaders are selected based on their character, American business leaders are selected for their competence. I believe that is changing…the integrity and character of an American business leader is more important than it may have been at one time…and Japanese are giving more weight to competence.

When I moved back to my home country last year I saw a survey that says a majority of Americans think a businessman will do anything for money. A politician will do anything for a vote. A journalist will do anything for a story. That simply is not true.

Be true to your personal values. That will be your greatest strength.

THIRD POINT. Leadership. Take any opportunity to experience leadership. It is helpful to study leadership, and study other great leaders. But you only learn leadership by experiencing leadership. You only learn leadership by being a leader. You learn leadership by leading a study project, by being a secretary of the camera club, by having a part time job by introducing a speaker.

There will always be temporary shortages of certain technical skills but the law of supply and demand will correct that imbalance. But I have never been in any organization that had enough proven leadership.

Some say leaders are made. Some say leaders are born. It is really not too important whether leaders are made or born…because all of us have leadership potential that is never discovered…or discovered late in life. I'm talking about leaders who bring about win–win solutions. It's been my experience whether it be trade negotiations or internal corporate competition, only win–win solutions last.

The opening of the Japan building products market is an example of a win–win outcome. I will relate

What effects do you suppose this John Wayne example has on the audience?

Does the speaker help you to see yourself as a leader? If so, what specifically does he say that achieves this? If not, what could he have done?

it to you briefly because it has some applicability to trade negotiations in general.

Twenty years ago Japan's residential building codes included many restrictive materials based specifications. Wood was excluded from many uses. Working cooperatively, the North American and Japanese industry and government groups asked the Japanese regulatory agencies to consider using scientific tests to move from materials-based specifications to performance-based specifications. Wood would be required to pass the same fire and earthquake tests as steel, concrete or any other building material...but not be prohibited just because it is wood.

After a very long process the regulations were modified to be more performance based. Because leaders in Japan and North America took a win–win approach there is true win–win outcome. Japanese producers have more business. Foreign suppliers have more business. Wood housing boomed in Japan.

And, most important, the Japanese people are the big winners with high quality, lower cost, safe wood homes. During the Kobe earthquake 2x4 wood frame homes proved to be the safest of all. In the 21st century effective leaders will be win–win leaders.

When you have different job opportunities ask yourself which job will give me the best opportunity to experience leadership. When you are starting out with your career many times the worst place to work is the corporate headquarters...because a young person has so little opportunity to experience leadership. You are usually better off to take any job in the field where you have measurable accountability for the results of an operation, no matter how small.

Don't confuse being close to leaders at the corporate headquarters with leading. Don't confuse having proximity to power with actually having power. Experience leadership.

FOURTH POINT. Persevere. Johann Goethe, the German philosopher said "in the realm of ideas everything depends on enthusiasm...in the real world all rests on perseverance." I heard Paul Newman being interviewed recently. He was asked what makes the difference..."why do some actors become very successful and some do not...is it luck, is it timing, is it connections...or, in the end, doesn't talent rule out?" His response "no...the most important element for an actor to succeed is tenacity."

Nothing will be more important to your getting what you want than perseverance...many times making that one final effort when you feel mentally

The principle that leadership can only be learned by actually leading is a good one. What types of supporting materials does the speaker use in explaining this principle?

Has Franklin convinced you that if you want to become a leader you must experience leadership?

and physically exhausted will be just enough to put you across the finish line.

When you join your new organization you will see many things that need to be changed. I don't know about univerisities but in corporations you are going to find many people are opposed to change, they will persuasively deny it's necessary. There's a line in a Grateful Dead song, "Denial ain't just a river in Egypt."

Many years ago I heard Jack Welsh being quizzed about how he was bringing about change at GE. He said "change has no constituency." Don't confuse what I said about win–win solutions with waiting until you get consensus before implementing needed changes…it will be a long wait. Don't expect applause for making change at least not while you are doing it. Expect failure, rejection and humiliation sometimes.

I keep something on my desk that says "growth involves confusion and pain, moving from the comfortable known to the uncomfortable unknown." Most of us don not welcome confusion and pain …even when it is necessary and beneficial for us. You will need perseverance to bring about change.

There is a Zen saying "before enlightenment chop wood, carry water…after enlightenment…chop wood, carry water." An effective international leader does a lot of choping wood and carrying water.

Perseverance.

And finally Network. Network. Network. If the U.S. is characterized as a market economy then Japan might be called a network system. And that is true to some degree in many Asian countries. In any culture that is influenced more by rule of man rather than rule of law, networking is not a optional part of doing business…it's a requirement for successful business. In many Asian countries it is more customary to do business with friends. And traditional Chinese take it even one step further…the business is most often a family business.

Many of us talk about when China adopts the rule of law…as if that is inevitable and imminent. Many Chinese do not feel the rule of law is a necessary aspect of the human condition. Confucius said laws are too inflexible to handle all the diversity of human experiences. Chinese say they prefer to trust people, not laws.

Akio Morita, the co-founder of Sony, a fine man and a global thinker long before most of us…was being questioned at a dinner one day about the closed Japan market. Finally Morita-san said "well, technically the Japan market is open, it's just that sometimes

Do you find the juxtaposition of the great philosopher Goethe, the highly successful actor and entrepreneur Newman, and the lyrics from the Grateful Dead an effective persuasive device?

The speaker draws on an amazingly wide range of materials. *In what ways does this help establish the speaker's credibility?*

the door is so small that it is hard for you big going to get in." His good humor got him off the hook that day but there was as much truth as humor in what he said. The system is designed to do business the Japanese way. Networking is not something you do in your spare time, it's an essential part of business.

To summarize.

FIRST IDEA. Learn from other cultures.

SECOND. Be true to your personal vlaues. You will learn that success, on the whole, success depends more on character than either intellect or luck.

THIRD IDEA. Take any opportunity to experience leadership. Leadership must be experienced to be learned.

FOURTH. In the realm of ideas everything depends on enthusiasm, in the real world all rests on perseverance.

AND FINALLY. Network. Network. Network.

Baron Charles Montesquie said a couple hundred years ago, "Commerce is the best cure for prejudice, peace is the natural effect of trade." If that was true in the 18th century it will be even more true in the 21st century. Trade and investment bring more than just money and goods, they bring ideas. As 21st century leaders you have great opportunity to help us all to overcome prejudice and bring about understanding and peace for all people. I have great confidence that is what you will do.

Did the speaker succeed in convincing you of the importance of networking to your own professional success?

What type of organizational pattern did the speaker use? Was this an effective pattern? What other patterns might have also worked with this topic?

What functions does the speaker's conclusion serve? Can you identify a summary, a motivation, and a closing statement?

From William E. Franklin, "Careers in International Business" in *Vital Speeches of the Day,* September 15, 1988, 64:23. Copyright © 1988 City News Publishing Co., Mount Pleasant, SC.

SUMMARY

This unit focused on persuasive speeches, the principles by which people are persuaded and the ways to develop the speech to strengthen or change attitude and belief and to motivate to action.

1. An attitude is a tendency to behave in a particular way.
2. A belief is a conviction in the existence or nonexistence of some person, object, or event, for example, a belief in the existence of God or a belief in the usefulness of communication.
3. A value is the measure of goodness or badness that you attribute to something, for example, you positively value democracy or you negatively value sexual discrimination.
4. Behavior is an observable action.
5. Persuasive speeches can often be classified as revolving around three types of questions: (1) Questions of fact focus on what is or is not, (2) questions of value focus on what is good or bad, and (3) questions of policy focus on what the policy should be.
6. Among the principles of persuasion are selective exposure, cultural difference, audience participation, inoculation, magnitude of change, identification, consistency and dissonance, logos, pathos, and ethos.
7. In seeking to strengthen or change an audience's attitudes and beliefs, follow these general principles: Estimate the current status of your listeners' attitudes, beliefs, and values; seek change in small increments; demonstrate your credibility; and give your listeners logical and motivational reasons.
8. In moving an audience to action, consider these general guidelines: Be realistic in what you ask listeners to do, ask for small, easily performed behaviors, demonstrate your own willingness to do what you're asking your listeners to do, and stress the specific (rather than the general).

KEY TERMS

question of fact (p. 378)

question of value (p. 378)

question of policy (p. 380)

selective exposure principle (p. 381)

cultural differences principle (p. 382)

audience participation principle (p. 382)

inoculation principle (p. 383)

magnitude of change principle (p. 384)

foot-in-the-door technique (p. 385)

door-in-the-face technique (p. 385)

identification (p. 385)

consistency (p. 385)

logos (p. 386)

pathos (p. 387)

ethos (p. 389)

credibility (p. 389)

speeches to strengthen or change attitudes or beliefs (p. 391)

speeches to stimulate action (p. 396)

 ## THINKING CRITICALLY ABOUT
Persuasive Speaking

1. You're planning to give a speech persuading your audience to be more conscientious in recycling to two very different audiences. One audience is composed solely of women and the other audience solely of men. Otherwise the audience members are similar: around 30 years old, college educated, professionals. In what ways would the two speeches differ? What general principles or assumptions about gender are you making as you differentiate these two speeches?

2. You want to get your listeners to contribute one hour a week to the college's program of helping high school students prepare for college. You're considering using the foot-in-the-door or the door-in-the-face technique. How would you develop each of these strategies? Which would you eventually use?

3. Read a persuasive speech, focusing on the principles of persuasion noted in this unit. Does the speaker make use of any of these principles? What persuasive principles can you identify from reading this speech?

4. Examine a speech for questions of fact, value, and policy. How are these issues used in the speech?

5. Visit the National Press Club Web site for complete texts of the speeches from the National Press Club's luncheons at http://npc.press.org/. Read one of the speeches and evaluate it in terms of the principles of persuasion discussed in this unit. This is also an excellent research Web site; it provides guides that will prove useful for just about any topic.

6. Visit "The Speaker's Companion" Web site at http://www.lm.com/~chipp/spkrhome.htm. How would you compare the principles discussed in this unit with the principles used in this program?

7. Prepare and deliver a two-minute speech in which you
   - explain an interesting attitude, belief, or value that you have come across
   - explain how a speech strengthened or changed one of your attitudes or beliefs
   - explain an advertisement in terms of the principles of persuasion
   - explain cultural differences in popularly held beliefs regarding such concepts as God, life, death, family, happiness, education, law, or men and women

GLOSSARY OF HUMAN COMMUNICATION CONCEPTS AND SKILLS

A word is dead
When it is said
Some say
I say it just begins to live.

—*Emily Dickinson*

Listed here are definitions of the technical terms of human communication—the words that are peculiar or unique to this discipline—and, where appropriate, the corresponding skills. These definitions and statements of skills should make new or difficult terms a bit easier to understand and should help to place the skill in context. The statements of skills appear in italics. All boldface terms within the definitions appear as separate entries in the glossary.

abstraction A general concept derived from a class of objects; a part representation of some whole.

abstraction process The process by which a general concept is derived from specifics; the process by which some (never all) characteristics of an object, person, or event are perceived by the senses or included in some term, phrase, or sentence.

accent The stress or emphasis placed on a syllable when pronounced.

acculturation The processes by which a person's culture is modified or changed through contact with or exposure to another culture.

active listening A process of putting together into some meaningful whole the listener's understanding of the speaker's total message—the verbal and the nonverbal, the content and the feelings. *Listen actively by paraphrasing the speaker's meanings, expressing an understanding of the speaker's feelings, and asking questions to check the accuracy of your understanding of the speaker.*

adaptors Nonverbal behaviors that satisfy some personal need and usually occur without awareness, for example, scratching to relieve an itch or moistening your lips to relieve the dry feeling. Three types of adaptors are often distinguished: **self-adaptors**, **alter-adaptors**, and **object-adaptors**. *Generally, avoid adaptors (especially self-adaptors); they interfere with effective communication and may be taken as a sign of your discomfort or anxiety.*

adjustment (principle of) The principle of verbal interaction that claims that communication takes place only to the extent that the parties communicating share the same system of signals. *Expand the common areas between you and significant others; learn each other's system of communication signals and meanings in order to increase understanding and interpersonal communication effectiveness.*

affect displays Movements of the facial area that convey emotional meaning—for example, anger, fear, and surprise.

affinity-seeking strategies Behaviors designed to increase our interpersonal attractiveness. *Use the various affinity-seeking strategies (for example, listening, openness, and dynamism), as appropriate to the interpersonal relationship and the situation, to increase your own interpersonal attractiveness.*

affirmation. The communication of support and approval. *Use affirmation to express your supportiveness and to raise esteem.*

agenda A list of the items that a small group must deal with in the order in which they should be covered.

agenda-setting A persuasive technique in which the speaker argues that XYZ is the issue and that all others are unimportant.

aggressiveness See *Verbal aggressiveness.*

allness The assumption that all can be known or is known about a given person, issue, object, or event. *End statements with an implicit "etc." ("et cetera") to indicate that more could be known and said; avoid allness terms and statements.*

alter-adaptors Body movements you make in response to your current interactions, for example, crossing your arms over your chest when someone unpleasant approaches or moving closer to someone you like.

altercasting Placing the listener in a specific role for a specific purpose and asking that the listener approach the question or problem from the perspective of this specific role.

ambiguity The condition in which a message may be interpreted as having more than one meaning.

analogy, reasoning from A type of reasoning in which you compare like things and conclude that since they are alike in so many respects then they are also alike in some previously unknown respect.

apology A type of excuse in which you acknowledge responsibility for the behavior, generally ask forgiveness, and claim that the behavior will not happen again.

appraisal interview A type of **interview** in which the interviewee's performance is assessed by management or by more experienced colleagues.

apprehension See **communication apprehension**.

arbitrariness The feature of human language that reflects the absence of a real or inherent relationship between the form of a word and its meaning. If we do not know anything of a particular language, we cannot examine the form of a word and thereby discover its meaning.

argot The language (largely **cant** and **jargon**) of a particular class, generally an underworld or criminal class, which is difficult and sometimes impossible for outsiders to understand.

argument Evidence (for example, facts or statistics) and a conclusion drawn from the evidence.

argumentativeness A willingness to argue for a point of view, to speak one's mind. *Cultivate your argumentativeness, your willingness to argue for what you believe by, for example, treating disagreements as objectively as possible, reaffirming the other, stressing equality, expressing interest in the other's position, and allowing the other person to save face.* Distinguished from **verbal aggressiveness**.

artifactual communication Communication that takes place through the wearing and arrangement of various artifacts—for example, clothing, jewelry, buttons, or the furniture in your house and its arrangement.

assertiveness A willingness to stand up for one's rights but with a respect for the rights of others. *Increase assertiveness (if desired) by analyzing the assertive and nonassertive behaviors of others, analyzing your own behaviors in terms of assertiveness, recording your behaviors, rehearsing assertive behaviors, and acting assertively in appropriate situations. Secure feedback from others for further guidance in increasing assertiveness.*

assimilation A process of message distortion in which messages are reworked to conform to our own attitudes, prejudices, needs, and values.

attack A persuasive technique that involves accusing another person (usually an opponent) of some serious wrongdoing so that the issue under discussion never gets examined.

attention The process of responding to a stimulus or stimuli; usually some consciousness of responding is implied.

attitude A predisposition to respond for or against an object, person, or position.

attraction The state or process by which one individual is drawn to another, by having a highly positive evaluation of that other person.

attraction theory A theory holding that we form relationships on the basis of our attraction for another person.

attractiveness The degree to which a person is perceived to be physically attractive and to possess a pleasing personality.

attribution A process through which we attempt to understand the behaviors of others (as well as our own), particularly the reasons or motivations for these behaviors.

attribution theory A theory concerned with the processes involved in attributing causation or motivation to a person's behavior. *In attempting to identify the motivation for behaviors, examine consensus, consistency, distinctiveness, and controllability. Generally, low consensus, high consistency, low distinctiveness, and high controllability identify internally motivated behavior; high consensus, low consistency, high distinctiveness, and low controllability identify externally motivated behavior.*

audience participation principle A principle of persuasion stating that persuasion is achieved more effectively when the audience participates actively.

authoritarian leader A group leader who determines the group policies or makes decisions without consulting or securing agreement from group members.

avoidance An unproductive **conflict** strategy in which a person takes mental or physical flight from the actual conflict.

back-channeling cues Listener responses to a speaker which do not ask for the speaking role. *Respond to back-channeling cues as appropriate to the con-*

versation. Use back-channeling cues to let the speaker know you are listening.

bandwagon A persuasive technique by which the speaker tries to gain compliance by saying that "everyone is doing it" and urges you to jump on the bandwagon.

barriers to communication Those factors (physical or psychological) that prevent or hinder effective communication. *Applying the skills of human communication covered throughout this text will help reduce the existing barriers and prevent others from arising.*

behavioral synchrony The similarity in the behavior, usually nonverbal, of two persons. Generally, it is taken as an index of mutual liking.

belief Confidence in the existence or truth of something; conviction. *Weigh both verbal and nonverbal messages before making believability judgments; increase your own sensitivity to nonverbal (and verbal) deception cues—for example, too little movement, long pauses, slow speech, increased speech errors, mouth guard, nose touching, eye rubbing, or the use of few words, especially monosyllabic answers. Use such cues to formulate hypotheses rather than conclusions concerning deception.*

beltlining An unproductive **conflict** strategy in which one hits at the level at which the other person cannot withstand the blow. *Avoid it.*

blame An unproductive **conflict** strategy in which we attribute the cause of the conflict to the other person or devote our energies to discovering who is the cause and avoid talking about the issues causing the conflict. *Avoid using blame to win an argument, especially with those with whom you're in close relationships.*

boundary marker A marker that sets boundaries that divide one person's territory from another's—for example, a fence.

brainstorming A technique for generating ideas either alone or, more usually, in a small group. *In brainstorming avoid evaluating contributions, strive for quantity, combine and extend your own or the ideas of others, and try really wild ideas.*

breadth The number of topics about which individuals in a relationship communicate.

cant The conversational language of a special group (usually, a lower-social-class group), generally understood only by members of that group.

card stacking A persuasive technique in which the speaker selects only the evidence and arguments that build a case and omits or distorts any contradictory evidence.

causes and effects, reasoning from A form of reasoning in which you reason that certain effects are due to specific causes or that specific causes produce certain effects.

censorship Legal restriction imposed on one's right to produce, distribute, or receive various communications.

central marker A marker or item that is placed in a territory to reserve it for a specific person—for example, the sweater thrown over a library chair to signal that the chair is taken.

certainty An attitude of closed-mindedness that creates a defensiveness among communication participants; opposed to **provisionalism.**

channel The vehicle or medium through which signals are sent.

character One of the qualities of **credibility**; the individual's honesty and basic nature; moral qualities. *In establishing character stress your fairness, your concern for enduring values, and your similarity with the audience.*

charisma One of the qualities of **credibility**; the individual's dynamism or forcefulness. *In establishing charisma demonstrate positiveness, act assertively, and express enthusiasm.*

cherishing behaviors Small behaviors we enjoy receiving from others, especially from our relational partner—for example, a kiss, a smile, or being given flowers.

chronemics The study of the communicative nature of time—the way you treat time and use it to communicate. Two general areas of chronemics are cultural and psychological time.

civil inattention Polite ignoring of others so as not to invade their privacy.

cliché An overused expression that has lost its novelty and part of its meaning, and that calls attention to itself because of its overuse; "tall, dark, and handsome" as a description of a man is a cliché. *Avoid clichés in all forms of communication.*

closed-mindedness An unwillingness to receive certain communication messages.

code A set of symbols used to translate a message from one form to another.

coercive power Power dependent upon one's ability to punish or to remove rewards from another person.

cognitive restructuring A theory for substituting logical and realistic beliefs for unrealistic ones and used in reducing communication apprehension and in raising self-esteem.

cohesiveness The property of togetherness. Applied to group communication situations, it refers to the mutual attractiveness among members; a measure of the extent to which individual members of a group work together as a group.

collectivist culture A culture in which the group's goals rather than the individual's are given greater importance and where, for example, benevolence, tradition, and conformity are given special emphasis. Opposed to **individualistic culture**.

color communication The meanings that different cultures communicate. *Use colors (in clothing and in room décor, for example) to convey desired meanings and recognize the cultural meanings that different colors have.*

communication (1) The process or act of communicating; (2) the actual message or messages sent and received; (3) the study of the processes involved in the sending and receiving of messages. (The term **communicology** is suggested for the third definition.)

communication accommodation theory The theory holding that speakers adjust their speaking style to their listeners to gain social approval and achieve greater communication effectiveness.

communication apprehension Fear or anxiety over communicating and may be "trait apprehension"—a fear of communication generally, regardless of the specific situation,—or state apprehension—a fear that is specific to a given communication situation. *Manage your own communication apprehension by reversing the potential causes of apprehension, trying performance visualization, systematically desensitize yourself, and use the skills and techniques for dealing with apprehension.*

communication competence A knowledge of the rules and skills of communication and is often used to refer to the qualities that make for effectiveness in communication.

communication network The pathways of messages; the organizational structure through which messages are sent and received.

communicology The study of communication, particularly the subsection concerned with human communication.

competence One of the qualities of **credibility** which encompasses a person's ability and knowledge. *In establishing your competence tell your listeners of your special experience or training, cite a variety of research sources, and stress the particular competencies of your sources.*

complementarity A principle of **attraction** holding that one is attracted by qualities one does not possess or one wishes to possess and to people who are opposite or different from oneself; opposed to **similarity**.

Identify the characteristics that you do not find in yourself but admire in others and that therefore might be important in influencing your perception of another person.

complementary relationship A relationship in which the behavior of one person serves as the stimulus for the complementary behavior of the other; in complementary relationships, behavioral differences are maximized.

compliance-gaining strategies Behaviors that are directed toward gaining the agreement of others; behaviors designed to persuade others to do as we wish. *Use the various compliance-gaining strategies to increase your own persuasive power.*

compliance-resisting strategies Behaviors directed at resisting the persuasive attempts of others. *Use such strategies as identity management, nonnegotiation, negotiation, and justification as appropriate in resisting compliance.*

confidence A quality of interpersonal effectiveness; a comfortable, at-ease feeling in interpersonal communication situations. *Communicate a feeling of being comfortable and at ease with the interaction through appropriate verbal and nonverbal signals.*

confirmation A communication pattern that acknowledges another person's presence and also indicates an acceptance of this person, this person's definition of self, and the relationship as defined or viewed by this other person; opposed to **disconfirmation**. *Avoid those verbal and nonverbal behaviors that disconfirm another person. Substitute confirming behaviors, behaviors that acknowledge the presence and the contributions of the other person.*

conflict An extreme form of competition in which a person attempts to bring a rival to surrender; a situation in which one person's behaviors are directed at preventing something or at interfering with or harming another individual. *See also* **interpersonal conflict**.

congruence A condition in which both verbal and nonverbal behaviors reinforce each other.

connotation The feeling or emotional aspect of meaning, generally viewed as consisting of the evaluative (for example, good-bad), potency (strong-weak), and activity (fast-slow) dimensions; the associations of a term. *see also* **denotation**.

consensus A principle of attribution through which we attempt to establish whether other people react or behave in the same way as the person on whom we are now focusing. If the person is acting in accordance with the general consensus, then we seek reasons for the behavior outside the individual; if the person is not acting in accordance with the general consensus, then we seek reasons that are internal to the individual.

consistency A perceptual process that influences us to maintain balance among our perceptions; a process that makes us tend to see what we expect to see and to be uncomfortable when our perceptions run contrary to our expectations. *Recognize the human tendency to seek and to see consistency even where it does not exist—to see our friends as all positive and our enemies as all negative, for example.*

contact The first stage of an interpersonal relationship in which perceptual and interactional contact occurs.

contamination A form of territorial encroachment that renders another's territory impure.

content and relationship dimensions A principle of communication which suggests that messages refer both to content (the world external to both speaker and listener) and to the relationship existing between the individuals who are interacting.

context of communication The physical, psychological, social, and temporal environment in which communication takes place. *Assess the context in which messages are communicated and interpret that communication behavior accordingly; avoid seeing messages as independent of context.*

controllability One of the factors considered in judging whether or not a person is responsible for his or her behavior. If the person was in control, then you judge that he or she was responsible. See **attribution theory**.

conversation Two-person communication usually possessing an opening, feedforward, a business stage, feedback, and a closing.

conversational management The ways in which a conversation is conducted. *Respond to conversational turn cues from the other person, and use conversational cues to signal your own desire to exchange (or maintain) speaker or listener roles.*

conversational maxims Principles that are followed in conversation to ensure that the goal of the conversation is achieved. *Discover, try not to violate, and, if appropriate, follow the conversational maxims of the culture in which you are communicating.*

conversational turns The process of exchanging the speaker and listener roles during conversation. *Become sensitive to and respond appropriately to conversational turn cues, such as turn-maintaining, turn-yielding, turn-requesting, and turn-denying cues.*

cooperation An interpersonal process by which individuals work together for a common end; the pooling of efforts to produce a mutually desired outcome.

cooperation (principle of) An implicit agreement between speaker and listener to cooperate in trying to understand what each is communicating.

counseling interview A type of **interview** in which the interviewer tries to learn about the interviewee in an attempt to provide some form of guidance, advice, or insight.

credibility The degree to which a receiver perceives the speaker to be believable; **competence**, **character**, and **charisma** (dynamism) are its major dimensions.

critical thinking The process of logically evaluating reasons and evidence and reaching a judgment on the basis of this analysis.

critical thinking-hats technique A technique developed by Edward deBono in which a problem or issue is viewed from six distinct perspectives.

criticism The reasoned judgment of some work; although often equated with faultfinding, criticism can involve both positive and negative evaluations.

cultural display Signs that communicate one's cultural identification, for example, clothing or religious jewelry.

cultural rules Rules that are specific to a given cultural group. *Respond to messages according to the cultural rules of the sender; avoid interpreting the messages of others exclusively through the perspective of your own culture in order to prevent misinterpretation of the intended meanings.*

cultural time The meanings given to time communication by a particular culture.

culture The relatively specialized life-style of a group of people—consisting of their values, beliefs, artifacts, ways of behaving, and ways of communicating—that is passed on from one generation to the next.

culture shock The psychological reaction one experiences at being placed in a culture very different from one's own or from what one is used to.

date An **extensional device** used to emphasize the notion of constant change and symbolized by a subscript: for example, John Smith$_{1986}$ is not John Smith$_{1996}$.

deception cues Verbal or nonverbal cues that reveal the person is lying.

decoder Something that takes a message in one form (for example, sound waves) and translates it into another form (for example, nerve impulses) from which meaning can be formulated (for example, in vocal-auditory communication). In human communication, the decoder is the auditory mechanism; in electronic communication, the decoder is, for example, the telephone earpiece. Decoding is the process of extracting a message from a code—for example, translating speech sounds into nerve impulses. *See also* **encoder.**

decoding The process of extracting a message from a code—for example, translating speech sounds into nerve impulses. *See also* **encoding**.

defensiveness An attitude of an individual or an atmosphere in a group characterized by threats, fear, and domination; messages evidencing evaluation, control, strategy, neutrality, superiority, and certainty are assumed to lead to defensiveness; opposed to **supportiveness.**

delayed reactions Reactions that are consciously delayed while a situation is analyzed.

Delphi method A type of problem-solving group in which questionnaires are used to poll members (who don't interact among themselves) on several occasions so as to arrive at a group decision on, say, the most important problems a company faces or activities a group might undertake.

democratic leader A group leader who stimulates self-direction and self-actualization of the group members.

denial One of the obstacles to the expression of emotion; the process by which we deny our emotions to ourselves or to others.

denotation Referential meaning; the objective or descriptive meaning of a word. *See also* **connotation.**

depenetration A reversal of penetration; a condition in which the **breadth** and **depth** of a relationship decrease. See **social penetration theory**.

depth The degree to which the inner personality—the inner core of an individual—is penetrated in interpersonal interaction.

deterioration A stage in an interpersonal relationship in which the bonds holding the individuals together are weakened.

determinism (principle of) The principle of verbal interaction that holds that all verbalizations are to some extent purposeful, that there is a reason for every verbalization.

dialogue A form of **communication** in which each person is both speaker and listener; communication characterized by involvement, concern, and respect for the other person; opposed to **monologue.**

direct speech Speech in which the speaker's intentions are stated clearly and directly. *Use direct speech, for example, in making requests or in responding to others (1) to encourage compromise, (2) to acknowledge responsibility for your own feelings and desires, and (3) to state your own desires honestly so as to encourage honesty, openness, and supportiveness in others.*

disclaimer Statement that asks the listener to receive what the speaker says as intended without its reflecting negatively on the image of the speaker. *Avoid using disclaimers that may not be accepted by your listeners; they may raise the very doubts you wish to put to rest. But, consider using disclaimers when you think your future messages might offend your listeners.*

disconfirmation The process by which one ignores or denies the right of the individual even to define himself or herself; opposed to **confirmation.**

dissolution The breaking of the bonds holding an interpersonal relationship together. *In dealing with the end of a relationship consider: (1) breaking the loneliness-depression cycle, (2) taking time out to get to know yourself as an individual, (3) bolstering your self-esteem, (4) removing or avoiding uncomfortable symbols that may remind you of your past relationship and may make you uncomfortable, (5) seeking the support of friends and relatives, and (6) avoiding the repetition of negative patterns.*

dyadic communication Two-person communication.

dyadic consciousness An awareness of an interpersonal relationship or pairing of two individuals; distinguished from situations in which two individuals are together but do not perceive themselves as being a unit or twosome.

dyadic effect The process by which one person in a dyad imitates the behavior of the other person, usually used to refer to the tendency of one person's self-disclosures to prompt the other to self-disclose also. *Be responsive to the dyadic effect; if it is not operating, consider why.*

ear marker A marker that identifies an item as belonging to a specific person—for example, a nameplate on a desk or initials on an attaché case.

effect The outcome or consequence of an action or behavior; communication is always assumed to have some effect.

emblems Nonverbal behaviors that directly translate words or phrases—for example, the signs for "OK" and "peace."

emotion The feelings we have—for example, our feelings of guilt, anger, or sorrow.

empathy The feeling of another person's feeling; feeling or perceiving something as does another person. *Increase empathic understanding by sharing experiences, role-playing, and seeing the world from his or her perspective. Express this empathic understanding verbally and nonverbally.*

employment interview A type of **interview** in which the interviewee is questioned to ascertain his or her suitability for a particular job. *In interviewing for a job: prepare yourself, prepare answers and questions, make an effective presentation of self, acknowledge cultural rules and customs, demonstrate effective interpersonal communication, and follow up the interview.*

encoder Something that takes a message in one form (for example, nerve impulses) and translates it into another form (for example, sound waves). In human communication, the encoder is the speaking mechanism; in electronic communication, the encoder is, for example, the telephone mouthpiece. Encoding is the process of putting a message into a code—for example, translating nerve impulses into speech sounds. *See also* **decoder.**

encoding The process of putting a message into a code—for example, translating nerve impulses into speech sounds. *See also* **decoding.**

enculturation The process by which culture is transmitted from one generation to another.

E-prime A form of the language that omits the verb "to be" except when used as an auxiliary or in statements of existence. Designed to eliminate the tendency toward **projection.**

equality An attitude that recognizes that each individual in a communication interaction is equal, that no one is superior to any other. It encourages supportiveness and is opposed to **superiority.** *Talk neither down nor up to others but communicate as an equal to increase interpersonal satisfaction and efficiency; share the speaking and the listening; recognize that all parties in communication have something to contribute.*

equilibrium theory A theory of proxemics holding that intimacy and physical closeness are positively related; as relationship becomes more intimate, the indiviudals will use shorter distances between them.

equity theory A theory claiming that we experience relational satisfaction when there is an equal distribution of rewards and costs between the two persons in the relationship.

etc. (et cetera) An **extensional device** used to emphasize the notion of infinite complexity; because one can never know all about anything, any statement about the world or an event must end with an explicit or implicit "etc." *Use the implicit or explicit etc. to remind yourself and others that there is more to be known, more to be said.*

ethics The branch of philosophy that deals with the rightness or wrongness of actions; the study of moral values.

ethnocentrism The tendency to see others and their behaviors through our own cultural filters, often as distortions of our own behaviors; the tendency to evaluate the values and beliefs of one's own culture more positively than those of another culture.

euphemism A polite word or phrase used to substitute for some taboo or otherwise offensive term.

excluding talk Talk about a subject in a vocabulary that only certain people understand, often in the presence of someone who does not belong to this group and therefore does not understand; use of terms unique to a specific culture as if they were universal.

excuse An explanation designed to lessen the negative consequences of something done or said. *Avoid excessive excuse making. Too many excuses may backfire and create image problems for the excuse maker.*

exit interview A type of **interview** in which employees and management discuss the reasons for the employee's leaving the corporation.

expectancy violations theory A theory of proxemics holding that people have a certain expectancy for space relationships. When that is violated (say, a person stands too close to you or a romantic partner maintains abnormally large distances from you), the relationship comes into clearer focus and you wonder why this "normal distance" is being violated.

experiential limitation The limit of an individual's ability to communicate, as set by the nature and extent of that individual's experiences.

expert power Power dependent on a person's expertise or knowledge; knowledge gives an individual expert power.

expressiveness A quality of interpersonal effectiveness; genuine involvement in speaking and listening, conveyed verbally and nonverbally. *Communicate involvement and interest by providing appropriate feedback, assuming responsibility for your thoughts and feelings and your role as speaker and listener, and using variety and flexibility in voice and bodily action.*

extemporaneous speech A speech that is thoroughly prepared and organized in detail and in which certain aspects of style are predetermined.

extensional devices Linguistic devices proposed by Alfred Korzybski to keep language a more accurate means for talking about the world. The extensional devices include **etc., date,** and **index** (the working devices) and the **hyphen** and **quotes** (the safety devices).

extensional orientation A point of view in which the primary consideration is given to the world of experience and only secondary consideration is given to labels. *Opposed to* **intensional orientation.**

face saving Maintaining a positive public self-image in the minds of others.

facial feedback hypothesis The hypothesis or theory that your facial expressions can produce physiological and emotional effects.

facial management techniques Techniques used to mask certain emotions and to emphasize others, for example, intensifying your expression of happiness to make a friend feel good about a promotion.

fact-inference confusion A misevaluation in which one makes an inference, regards it as a fact, and acts upon it as if it were a fact. *Distinguish facts from inferences; respond to inferences as inferences and not as facts.*

factual statement A statement made by the observer after observation and limited to what is observed. *See also* **inferential statement.**

family A group of people who consider themselves related and connected to one another and where the actions of one have consequences for others.

fear appeal The appeal to fear to persuade an individual or group of individuals to believe or to act in a certain way.

feedback Information that is given back to the source. Feedback may come from the source's own messages (as when we hear what we are saying) or from the receiver(s) in the form of applause, yawning, puzzled looks, questions, letters to the editor of a newspaper, increased or decreased subscriptions to a magazine, and so forth. *Give clear feedback to others, and respond to others' feedback, either through corrective measures or by continuing current performance, to increase communication efficiency and satisfaction. See also* **negative feedback, positive feedback.**

feedforward Information that is sent prior to the regular messages telling the listener something about what is to follow. *When appropriate, preface your messages in order to open the channels of communication, to preview the messages to be sent, to disclaim, and to altercast. In your use of feedforward, be brief, use feedforward sparingly, and follow through on your feedforward promises. Also, be sure to respond to the feedforward as well as the content messages of others.*

field of experience The sum total of an individual's experiences, which influences his or her ability to communicate. In some views of communication, two people can communicate only to the extent that their fields of experience overlap.

flexibility The ability to adjust communication strategies on the basis of the unique situation. *Apply the principles of interpersonal communication with flexibility; remember that each situation calls for somewhat different skills.*

focus group A group designed to explore the feelings and attitudes of its individuals and which usually follows a question and answer format.

force An unproductive **conflict** strategy in which one attempts to win an argument by physical force or threats of force. *Avoid it.*

forum A small group format in which members of the group answer questions from the audience; often follows a symposium.

free information Information that is revealed implicitly and that may be used as a basis for opening or pursuing conversations.

friendship An interpersonal relationship between two persons that is mutually productive, established and maintained through perceived mutual free choice, and characterized by mutual positive regard. *Adjust your verbal and nonverbal communication as appropriate to the stages of your various friendships. Learn the rules that govern your friendships; follow them or risk damaging the relationship.*

fundamental attribution error The tendency to attribute a person's behavior to the kind of person he or she is (to the person's personality, say) and to not give sufficient importance to the situation the person is in.

game A simulation of some situation with rules governing the behaviors of the participants and with some payoff for winning; in transactional analysis, "game" refers to a series of ulterior transactions that lead to a payoff; the term also refers to a basically dishonest kind of transaction in which participants hide their true feelings.

General Semantics The study of the relationships among language, thought, and behavior.

glittering generality (the opposite of **name calling**) occurs when the speaker tries to gain your acceptance of an idea by associating it with things you value highly.

gossip Communication about someone not present, some third party, usually about matters that are private to this third party. *Avoid gossip that breaches confidentiality, is known to be false, and is unnecessarily invasive.*

grapevine The informal lines through which messages in an organization may travel; these informal lines resemble the physical grapevine, with its unpredictable pattern of branches.

group A collection of individuals related to each other with some common purpose and with some structure among them.

group norm Rules or expectations of appropriate behavior for a member of the group.

groupthink A tendency observed in some groups in which agreement among members becomes more important than the exploration of the issues at hand.

gunnysacking An unproductive **conflict** strategy of storing up grievances—as if in a gunnysack—and holding them in readiness to dump on the person with whom one is in conflict. *Avoid it.*

halo effect The tendency to generalize an individual's virtue or expertise from one area to another.

haptics Technical term for the study of touch communication.

heterosexist language Language that assumes all people are heterosexual and thereby denigrates lesbians and gay men. *Avoid it.*

high-context culture A culture in which much of the information in communication is in the context or in the person rather than explicitly coded in the verbal messages. **Collectivist cultures** are generally high context. Opposed to **low-context culture.**

home field advantage The increased power that comes from being in your own territory.

home territories Territories for which individuals have a sense of intimacy and over which they exercise control—for example, a professor's office.

hyphen An **extensional device** used to illustrate that what may be separated verbally may not be separable on the event level or on the nonverbal level; although one may talk about body and mind as if they were separable, in reality they are better referred to as body-mind.

idea-generation group A group whose purpose is to generate ideas; see **brainstorming.**

illustrators Nonverbal behaviors that accompany and literally illustrate the verbal messages—for example, upward movements that accompany the verbalization "It's up there."

I-messages Messages in which the speaker accepts responsibility for personal thoughts and behaviors; messages in which the speaker's point of view is stated explicitly; *opposed to* **you-messages** *Use I-messages to take responsibility for your thoughts and behaviors.*

immediacy A quality of interpersonal effectiveness; a sense of contact and togetherness; a feeling of interest and liking for the other person. *Communicate immediacy through appropriate word choice, feedback, eye contact, body posture, and physical closeness.*

implicit personality theory A theory of personality that each individual maintains, complete with rules or systems, through which others are perceived. *Be conscious of your implicit personality theories; avoid drawing firm conclusions about other people on the basis of these theories.*

impromptu speech A speech given without any explicit prior preparation.

inclusion principle In verbal interaction, the principle that all members should be a part of (included in) the interaction. *Include everyone present in the interaction (both verbally and nonverbally) so you do not exclude or offend others or fail to profit from their contributions.*

inclusive talk Communication which includes all people; communication which does not exclude certain groups, for example, women, lesbians and gays, or members of certain races or nationalities.

index An **extensional device** used to emphasize the notion of nonidentity (no two things are the same) and symbolized by a subscript—for example, $politician_1$ is not $politician_2$.

indirect speech Speech that may hide the speaker's true intentions or which may be used to make requests and observations indirectly. *Use indirect speech, for example, (1) to express a desire without insulting or offending anyone, (2) to ask for compliments in a socially acceptable manner, and (3) to disagree without being disagreeable.*

indiscrimination A misevaluation caused by categorizing people, events, or objects into a particular class and responding to them only as members of the class; a failure to recognize that each individual is unique; a failure to apply the **index.** *Index your terms and statements to emphasize that each person and event is unique; avoid treating all individuals the same way because they are covered by the same label or term.*

individualist culture A culture in which the individual's rather than the group's goals and preferences are given greater importance. Opposed to **collectivist cultures.**

inevitability A principle of communication holding that communication cannot be avoided; all behavior in an interactional setting is communication. *Because all behavior in an interactional situation communicates, seek out nonobvious messages and meanings.*

inferential statement A statement that can be made by anyone, is not limited to what is observed, and can be made at any time. See also **factual statement.**

informal time terms Terms that describe approximate rather than exact time, for example, "soon," "early," and "in a while." *Recognize that informal-time terms are often the cause of interpersonal difficulties. When misunderstanding is likely, use more precise terms.*

information That which reduces uncertainty.

information overload A condition in which the amount of information is too great to be dealt with effectively or the number or complexity of messages is so great that the individual or organization is not able to deal with them.

information power Power dependent on one's information and one's ability to communicate logically and persuasively. Also called "persuasion power."

informative interview A type of **interview** in which the interviewer asks the interviewee, usually a person of some reputation and accomplishment, questions designed to elicit his or her views, predictions, and perspectives on specific topics. *In interviewing for information: secure an appointment, prepare your questions, establish rapport with the interviewer, ask permission to tape the interview, and close and follow up the interview.*

inoculation principle A principle of persuasion stating that persuasion will be more difficult to achieve when beliefs and attitudes that have already been challenged are attacked, because the individual has built up defenses against such attacks in a manner similar to inoculation. *In persuading an audience inoculated against your position, be content with small gains; trying to reverse an inoculated audience in one speech is probably unrealistic.*

insulation A reaction to **territorial encroachment** in which you erect some sort of barrier between yourself and the invaders.

intensional orientation A point of view in which primary consideration is given to the way things are labeled and only secondary consideration (if any) to the world of experience. *Respond first to things; avoid responding to labels as if they were things; do not let labels distort your perception of the world. Opposed to **extensional orientation.***

interaction management A quality of interpersonal effectiveness; the control of interaction to the satisfaction of both parties; managing conversational turns, fluency, and message consistency. *Manage the interaction to the satisfaction of both parties by sharing the roles of speaker and listener, avoiding long and awkward silences, and being consistent in your verbal and nonverbal messages.*

interaction process analysis A content analysis method that classifies messages into four general categories: social emotional positive, social emotional negative, attempted answers, and questions.

intercultural communication Communication that takes place between persons of different cultures or persons who have different cultural beliefs, values, or ways of behaving.

interpersonal communication Communication between two persons or among a small group of persons and distinguished from public or mass communication; communication of a personal nature and distinguished from impersonal communication; communication between or among intimates or those involved in a close relationship; often, intrapersonal, dyadic, and small group communication in general.

interpersonal conflict A conflict or disagreement between two persons. *To fight more productively: look for win-win strategies, fight actively, use talk instead of force, focus on the present rather than gunnysacking, use face-enhancing instead of face-detracting strategies, express acceptance instead of attacking the other person, and use your skills in argumentation, not in verbal aggressiveness.*

interpersonal perception The perception of people; the processes through which we interpret and evaluate people and their behavior. *Increase the accuracy of your interpersonal perceptions by checking your perceptions, subjecting your perceptions to critical thinking, reducing uncertainty, and becoming aware of cultural differences and influences on perception.*

interview A particular form of interpersonal communication in which two persons interact largely by question-and-answer format for the purpose of achieving specific goals. Also see the specific types of interviews: **appraisal interview, counseling interview, employment interview, exit interview, information interview,** and **persuasion interview.**

intimacy The closest interpersonal relationship; usually used to denote a close primary relationship.

intimacy claims Obligations incurred by virtue of being in a close and intimate relationship. *Reduce the intensity of intimacy claims when things get rough; give each other space as appropriate.*

intimate distance The closest proxemic distance, ranging from touching to 18 inches. *See also* **proxemics.**

intrapersonal communication Communication with oneself.

invasion The unwarranted entrance into another's territory that changes the meaning of the territory. See **territorial encroachment.**

involvement stage That stage in an interpersonal relationship that normally follows contact in which the individuals get to know each other better and explore the potential for greater intimacy.

irreversibility A principle of communication holding that communication cannot be reversed; once something has been communicated, it cannot be uncommunicated. *Avoid saying things (for example, in anger) or making commitments that you may wish to retract (but will not be able to) in order to prevent resentment and ill feeling.*

jargon The technical language of any specialized group, often a professional class, which is unintelligible to individuals not belonging to the group; "shop talk."

johari window A diagram of the four selves (**open, blind, hidden,** and **unknown**) which illustrates the different kinds of information in each self.

kinesics The study of the communicative dimensions of facial and bodily movements.

laissez-faire leader A group leader who allows the group to develop and progress or make mistakes on its own.

lateral communication Communication among equals—for example, manager to manager, worker to worker.

leadership That quality by which one individual directs or influences the thoughts and/or the behaviors of others. *See* **laissez-faire leader, democratic leader,** and **authoritarian leader**.

leave-taking cues Verbal and nonverbal cues that indicate a desire to terminate a conversation. *Increase your sensitivity to leave-taking cues; pick up on the leave-taking cues of others, and communicate such cues tactfully so as not to insult or offend others.*

legitimate power Power dependent on the belief that a person has a right, by virtue of position, to influence or control another's behavior.

leveling A process of message distortion in which a message is repeated but the number of details is reduced, some details are omitted entirely, and some details lose their complexity.

level of abstraction The relative distance of a term or statement from the actual perception; a low-order abstraction would be a description of the perception, whereas a high-order abstraction would consist of inferences about inferences about descriptions of a perception.

listening An active process of receiving messages sent orally; this process consists of five stages: receiving, understanding, remembering, evaluating, and responding. *Adjust your listening perspective, as the situation warrants, between judgmental and nonjudgmental, surface and depth, and empathic and objective listening. Listen actively when appropriate.*

logic The science of reasoning; the study of the principles governing the analysis of inference making.

looking-glass self The self-concept that results from the image of yourself that others reveal to you.

loving An interpersonal process in which one feels a closeness, a caring, a warmth, and an excitement for another person.

low-context culture A culture in which most of the information in communication is explicitly stated in the verbal messages. **Individualistic cultures** are usually low-context cultures. Opposed to **high-context culture**.

magnitude of change principle A principle of persuasion stating that the greater and more important the change desired by the speaker, the more difficult its achievement will be.

maintenance A stage of relationship stability at which the relationship does not progress or deteriorate significantly; a continuation as opposed to a dissolution of a relationship.

maintenance strategies Specific behaviors designed to preserve an interpersonal relationship. *Use appropriate maintenance strategies (for example, openness, sharing joint activities, and acting positively) to preserve a valued relationship. See also* **repair strategies.**

manipulation An unproductive **conflict** strategy that avoids open conflict; instead, attempts are made to divert the conflict by being especially charming and getting the other person into a noncombative frame of mind. *Avoid it.*

manuscript speech A speech designed to be read verbatim from a script.

markers Devices that signify that a certain territory belongs to a particular person. Become sensitive to the markers (central, boundary, and ear) of others, and learn to use these markers to define your own territories and to communicate the desired impression. *See also* **boundary marker, central marker,** and **ear marker.**

mass communication Communication addressed to an extremely large audience, mediated by audio and/or visual transmitters, and processed by gatekeepers before transmission.

matching hypothesis An assumption that we date and mate with people who are similar to ourselves—who match us—in physical attractiveness.

meaningfulness A perception principle that refers to your assumption that people's behavior is sensible, stems from some logical antecedent, and is consequently meaningful rather than meaningless.

mere exposure hypothesis The theory that repeated or prolonged exposure to a stimulus may result in a change in attitude toward the stimulus object, generally in the direction of increased positiveness.

message Any signal or combination of signals that serves as a **stimulus** for a receiver.

metacommunication Communication about communication. *Metacommunicate to ensure understanding of the other person's thoughts and feelings: give clear feedforward, explain feelings as well as thoughts, paraphrase your own complex thoughts, and ask questions.*

metalanguage Language used to talk about language.

metamessage A message that makes reference to another message, for example, the statements "Did I make myself clear?" or "That's a lie" refer to other messages and are therefore considered metamessages. *Use metamessages to clarify your understanding of what another thinks and feels.*

metaskills Skills for regulating more specific skills, for example, the skills of interpersonal communication such as openness and empathy must be regulated by the metaskills of flexibility, mindfulness, and metacommunication.

mindfulness and mindlessness States of relative awareness. In a mindful state, we are aware of the logic and rationality of our behaviors and the logical connections existing among elements. In a mindless state, we are unaware of this logic and rationality. *Apply the principles of interpersonal communication mindfully rather than mindlessly. Increase mindfulness by creating and re-creating categories, being open to new*

information and points of view, and being careful of relying too heavily on first impressions.

mixed message A message that contradicts itself; a message that asks for two different (often incompatible) responses. Avoid emitting mixed messages by focusing clearly on your purposes when communicating and by increasing conscious control over your verbal and nonverbal behaviors. *Detect mixed messages in other people's communications and respond to them as appropriate. Avoid sending mixed messages; they make you appear unsure and unfocused.*

model A representation of an object or process.

monochronic time orientation A view of time in which things are done sequentially; one thing is scheduled at a time. Opposed to **polychronic time orientation**.

monologue A form of **communication** in which one person speaks and the other listens; there is no real interaction among participants. *Avoid it, at least generally.* Opposed to **dialogue.**

motivated sequence An organizational pattern for arranging the information in a discourse to motivate an audience to respond positively to one's purpose.

name calling A persuasive technique in which the speaker gives an idea a derogatory name.

negative feedback Feedback that serves a corrective function by informing the source that his or her message is not being received in the way intended. Negative feedback serves to redirect the source's behavior. Looks of boredom, shouts of disagreement, letters critical of newspaper policy, and teachers' instructions on how better to approach a problem would be examples of negative feedback. See **positive feedback.**

neutrality A response pattern lacking in personal involvement; encourages defensiveness; opposed to **empathy.**

noise Anything that interferes with a person's receiving a message as the source intended the message to be received. Noise is present in a communication system to the extent that the message received is not the message sent. *Combat the effects of physical, semantic, and psychological noise by eliminating or lessening the sources of physical noise, securing agreement on meanings, and interacting with an open mind in order to increase communication accuracy.*

nominal group A collection of individuals who record their thoughts and opinions which are then distributed to others. Without direct interaction, the thoughts and opinions are gradually pared down until a manageable list (of solutions or decisions) is produced. When this occurs the nominal group (a group in name only) may restructure itself into a problem-solving group that analyzes the final list.

nonallness   An attitude or point of view in which it is recognized that one can never know all about anything and that what we know, say, or hear is only a part of what there is to know, say, or hear.

nondirective language   Language that does not direct or focus our attention on certain aspects; neutral language. *Use nondirective language when you wish to encourage others to talk without moving them in any specific direction.*

nonnegotiation   An unproductive **conflict** strategy in which the individual refuses to discuss the conflict or to listen to the other person.

nonverbal communication   Communication without words; communication by means of space, gestures, facial expressions, touching, vocal variation, and silence, for example.

nonverbal dominance   Nonverbal behavior that allows one person to achieve psychological dominance over another. *Resist (as sender and receiver) nonverbal expressions of dominance when they are inappropriate—for example, when they are sexist.*

norm   See **group norm**.

object-adaptors   Movements that involve your manipulation of some object, for example, punching holes in or drawing on the styrofoam coffee cup, clicking a ball point pen, or chewing on a pencil. *Avoid them; they generally communicate discomfort and a lack of control over the communication situation.*

object language   Language used to communicate about objects, events, and relations in the world; the structure of the object language is described in a **metalanguage**; the display of physical objects—for example, flower arranging and the colors of the clothes we wear.

olfactory communication   Communication by smell.

openness   A quality of interpersonal effectiveness encompassing (1) a willingness to interact openly with others, to self-disclose as appropriate; (2) a willingness to react honestly to incoming stimuli; and (3) a willingness to own one's feelings and thoughts.

oral style   The style of spoken discourse that, when compared with written style, consists of shorter, simpler, and more familiar words; more qualification, self-reference terms, allness terms, verbs and adverbs; and more concrete terms and terms indicative of consciousness of projection—for example, "as I see it."

other talk   Talk about the listener or some third party.

other-orientation   A quality of interpersonal effectiveness involving attentiveness, interest, and concern for the other person. *Convey concern for and interest in the other person by means of empathic responses, appropriate feedback, and attentive listening responses.*

owning feelings   The process by which you take responsibility for your own feelings instead of attributing them to others. *Use I-messages to express ownership and to acknowledge responsibility for your own thoughts and feelings.*

packaging   See **reinforcement**.

panel or round table   A small group format in which participants are arranged in a circular pattern and speak without any set pattern.

paralanguage   The vocal (but nonverbal) aspect of speech. Paralanguage consists of voice qualities (for example, pitch range, resonance, tempo), vocal characterizers (laughing or crying, yelling or whispering), vocal qualifiers (intensity, pitch height), and vocal segregates ("uh-uh," meaning "no," or "sh" meaning "silence"). *Vary paralinguistic elements, such as rate, volume, and stress, to add variety and emphasis to your communications, and be responsive to the meanings communicated by others' paralanguage.*

parasocial relationship   Relationships between a real and an imagined or fictional character, usually used to refer to relationships between a viewer and a fictional character in a television show.

pauses   Silent periods in the normally fluent stream of speech. Pauses are of two major types: filled pauses (interruptions in speech that are filled with such vocalizations as "er" or "um") and unfilled pauses (silences of unusually long duration).

perception   The process of becoming aware of objects and events from the senses. See **interpersonal perception**.

perception checking   The process of verifying your understanding of some message or situation or feeling to reduce uncertainty. *Use perception checking to get more information about your impressions: (1) describe what you see or hear and what you think is happening, and (2) ask whether this is correct or in error.*

perceptual accentuation   A process that leads you to see what you expect to see and what you want to see—for example, seeing people you like as better looking and smarter than people you do not like. *Be aware of the influence your own needs, wants, and expectations have on your perceptions. Recognize that what* *you perceive is a function both of what exists in reality and what is going on inside your own head.*

personal distance The second-closest proxemic distance, ranging from 18 inches to 4 feet. *See also* **proxemics.**

personal rejection An unproductive conflict strategy in which the individual withholds love and affection, and seeks to win the argument by getting the other person to break down under this withdrawal.

persuasion The process of influencing attitudes and behavior.

persuasive interview A type of **interview** in which the interviewer attempts to change the interviewee's attitudes or behavior.

phatic communication Communication that is primarily social; communication designed to open the channels of communication rather than to communicate something about the external world; "Hello" and "How are you?" in everyday interaction are examples.

pitch The highness or lowness of the vocal tone.

plain folks A persuasive strategy in which the speaker identifies himself or herself and the proposal with the audience.

polarization A form of fallacious reasoning by which only two extremes are considered; also referred to as "black-or-white" and "either-or" thinking or two-valued orientation. *Use middle terms and qualifiers when describing the world; avoid talking in terms of polar opposites (black and white, good and bad) in order to describe reality more accurately.*

polychronic time orientation A view of time in which several things may be scheduled or engaged in at the same time. Opposed to **monochronic time orientation.**

positive feedback Feedback that supports or reinforces the continuation of behavior along the same lines in which it is already proceeding—for example, applause during a speech.

positiveness A characteristic of effective communication involving positive attitudes toward oneself and toward the interpersonal interaction. Also used to refer to complimenting another and expressing acceptance and approval. *Verbally and nonverbally communicate a positive attitude toward yourself, others, and the situation with smiles, positive facial expressions, attentive gestures, positive verbal expressions, and the elimination or reduction of negative appraisals.*

power The ability to control the behaviors of others.

power communication Communicate power through forceful speech, avoidance of weak modifiers and excessive body movement, and demonstration of your knowledge, preparation, and organization in the matters at hand.

power play A consistent pattern of behavior in which one person tries to control the behavior of another. *Identify the power plays people use on you and respond to these power plays so as to stop them. Use an effective management strategy such as "cooperation," by, for example, expressing your feelings, describing the behavior you object to, and stating a cooperative response.*

pragmatic implication An assumption that seems logical but is not necessarily true. *Identify your own pragmatic implications, and distinguish these from logical implications (those that are necessarily true) and recognize that memory often confuses the two. In recalling situations and events, ask yourself whether your conclusions are based on pragmatic or logical implications.*

premature self-disclosures Disclosures that are made before the relationship has developed sufficiently. *Resist too intimate or too negative self-disclosures early in the development of a relationship.*

primacy effect The condition by which what comes first exerts greater influence than what comes later. *See also* **recency effect.**

primacy and recency Primacy refers to giving more credence to that which occurs first; recency refers to giving more credence to that which occurs last (that is, most recently). *Resist the normal tendency for first impressions to leave lasting impressions and to color both what we see later and the conclusions we draw. Take the time and effort to revise your impressions of others on the basis of new information Be at your very best in first encounters because others may well be operating with a primacy bias.*

primary relationship The relationship between two people that they consider their most (or one of their most) important, for example, the relationship between spouses or domestic partners.

primary territory Areas that one can consider one's exclusive preserve—for example, one's room or office.

problem-solving group A group whose primary task is to solve a problem, but more often to reach a decision.

problem-solving sequence A logical step-by-step process for solving a problem frequently used by groups and consisting of defining and analyzing the problem, establishing criteria for evaluating solutions, identifying possible solutions, evaluating solutions, selecting the best solution, and testing the selected solutions.

process Ongoing activity; communication is referred to as a process to emphasize that it is always changing, always in motion.

productivity The feature of language that makes possible the creation and understanding of novel utterances. With human language we can talk about matters that have never been talked about before, and we can understand utterances we have never heard before. Also referred to as **openness**.

progressive differentiation A relational problem caused by the exaggeration or intensification of differences or similarities between individuals.

projection A psychological process whereby we attribute characteristics or feelings of our own to others; often used to refer to the process whereby we attribute our own faults to others.

pronunciation The production of syllables or words according to some accepted standard, as presented, for example, in a dictionary.

protection theory A theory of proxemics holding that people establish a body-buffer zone to protect themselves from unwanted closeness, touching, or attack.

provisionalism An attitude of open-mindedness that leads to the creation of supportiveness; opposed to **certainty.**

proxemic distances The spatial distances that are maintained in communication and social interaction. *Adjust spatial (proxemic) distances as appropriate to the specific interaction; avoid distances that are too far, too close, or otherwise inappropriate, as they might falsely convey, for example, aloofness or aggression.*

proxemics The study of the communicative function of space; the study of how people unconsciously structure their space—the distance between people in their interactions, the organization of space in homes and offices, and even the design of cities.

proximity As a principle of perception, the tendency to perceive people or events that are physically close as belonging together or representing some unit; physical closeness; one of the qualities influencing **interpersonal attraction.** *Use physical proximity to increase interpersonal attractiveness.*

psychological time The importance you place on past, present, or future time. *Recognize the significance of your own time orientation to your ultimate success, and make whatever adjustments you think desirable.*

public communication Communication in which the source is one person and the receiver is an audience of many persons.

public distance The longest proxemic distance, ranging from 12 to over 25 feet.

public territory Areas that are open to all people—for example, restaurants or parks.

punctuation of communication The breaking up of continuous communication sequences into short sequences with identifiable beginnings and endings or stimuli and responses. *To increase empathy and mutual understanding, see the sequence of events punctuated from perspectives other than your own.*

punishment Noxious or aversive stimulation.

pupillometrics The study of communication through changes in the size of the pupils of the eyes. *Detect pupil dilation and constriction, and formulate hypotheses (not conclusions) concerning their possible meanings.*

quotes An **extensional device** to emphasize that a word or phrase is being used in a special sense and should therefore be given special attention.

racist language Language that denigrates or is derogatory toward members of a particular race. *Avoid racist language so as not to offend or alienate others or reinforce stereotypes.*

rate The speed with which you speak, generally measured in words per minute.

receiver Any person or thing that takes in messages. Receivers may be individuals listening to or reading a message, a group of persons hearing a speech, a scattered television audience, or machines that store information.

recency effect The condition in which what comes last (that is, most recently) exerts greater influence than what comes first. *See also* **primacy effect.**

redundancy The quality of a message that makes it totally predictable and therefore lacking in information. A message of zero redundancy would be completely unpredictable; a message of 100 percent redundancy would be completely predictable. All human languages contain some degree of built-in redundancy, generally estimated to be about 50 percent.

referent power Power dependent on one's desire to identify with or be like another person.

reflexiveness The feature of human language that makes it possible for that language to be used to refer to itself; that is, we can talk about our talk and create a **metalanguage**, a language for talking about language.

regulators Nonverbal behaviors that regulate, monitor, or control the communications of another person.

reinforcement theory A theory of behavior that when applied to relationships would hold (essentially) that relationships develop because they are rewarding and end because they are punishing. *Reinforce others as a way to increase interpersonal attractiveness and general interpersonal satisfaction.*

rejection A response to an individual that rejects or denies the validity of that individual's self-view.

relational communication Communication between or among intimates or those in close relationships; used by some theorists as synonymous with interpersonal communication.

relationship deterioration The stage of a relationship during which the connecting bonds between the partners weaken and the partners begin drifting apart.

relationship development The stages of relationships during which you move closer to intimacy; in the model of relationships presented here, relationship development includes the contact and the involvement stages.

relationship dialectics theory A theory that describes relationships along a series of opposites representing competing desires or motivations, such as the desire for autonomy and the desire to belong to someone, for novelty and predictability, and for closedness and openness.

relationship maintenance The processes by which you attempt to keep the relationship stable.

relationship messages Messages that comment on the relationship between the speakers rather than on matters external to them. *Recognize and respond to relationship as well as content messages in order to ensure a more complete understanding of the messages intended.*

relationship repair Attempts to reverse the process of relationship deterioration. *To repair a relationship: recognize the problem, engage in productive conflict resolution, pose possible solutions, affirm each other, integrate solutions into normal behavior, and take risks.*

response Any bit of overt or covert behavior.

reward power Power dependent upon one's ability to reward another person.

rigid complementarity The inability to break away from the complementary type of relationship that was once appropriate and now is no longer.

role The part an individual plays in a group; an individual's function or expected behavior.

rules theory A theory that describes relationships as interactions governed by a series of rules that a couple agrees to follow. When the rules are followed, the relationship is maintained and when they are broken, the relationship experiences difficulty.

secondary territory Areas that do not belong to a particular person but have been occupied by that person and are therefore associated with her or him—for example, the seat you normally take in class.

selective exposure (principle of) A principle of persuasion that states that listeners actively seek out information that supports their opinions and actively avoid information that contradicts their existing opinions, beliefs, attitudes, and values.

self-acceptance Being satisfied with ourselves, our virtues and vices, and our abilities and limitations.

self-adaptors Movements that usually satisfy a physical need, especially to make you more comfortable, for example, scratching your head to relieve an itch, moistening your lips because they feel dry, or pushing your hair out of your eyes. *Because these often communicate your nervousness or discomfort, they are best avoided.*

self-attribution A process through which we seek to account for and understand the reasons and motivations for our own behaviors.

self-awareness The degree to which a person knows himself or herself. *Increase self-awareness by asking yourself about yourself and listening to others; actively seek information about yourself from others by carefully observing their interactions with you and by asking relevant questions. See yourself from different perspectives (see your different selves), and increase your open self.*

self-concept An individual's self-evaluation; an individual's self-appraisal.

self-disclosure The process of revealing something about ourselves to another, usually used to refer to information that would normally be kept hidden. *Self-disclose when the motivation is to improve the relationship, when the context and the relationship are appropriate for the self-disclosure, when there is an opportunity for open and honest responses, when the self-disclosures will be clear and direct, when there are appropriate reciprocal disclosures, and when you have examined and are willing to risk the possible burdens that self-disclosure might entail. Self-disclose selectively; regulate your self-disclosures as appropriate to the context, topic, audience, and potential rewards and risks to secure the maximum advantage and reduce the possibility of negative effects. In responding to the disclosures of others, demonstrate the skills of effective listening, express support for the discloser (but resist evaluation), reinforce the disclosing behavior, keep the disclosures confidential, and avoid using the disclosures against the person.*

self-esteem The value you place on yourself; your self-evaluation; usually used to refer to the positive value placed on oneself. *Increase your self-esteem by* *attacking self-destructive statements and engage in self-affirmation.*

self-fulfilling prophecy The situation in which we make a prediction or prophecy and fulfill it ourselves—for example, expecting a class to be boring and then fulfilling this expectation by perceiving it as boring. *Avoid fulfilling your own negative prophecies and seeing only what you want to see. Be especially careful to examine your perceptions when they conform too closely to your expectations; check to make sure that you are seeing what exists in real life, not just in your expectations or predictions.*

self-monitoring The manipulation of the image one presents to others in interpersonal interactions so as to give the most favorable impression of oneself. *Monitor your verbal and nonverbal behavior as appropriate to communicate the desired impression.*

self-serving bias A bias that operates in the self-attribution process and leads us to take credit for the positive consequences and to deny responsibility for the negative consequences of our behaviors. *In examining the causes of your own behavior, beware of the tendency to attribute negative behaviors to external factors and positive behaviors to internal factors. In self-examinations, ask whether and how the self-serving bias might be operating.*

self-talk Talk about oneself. *Balance talk about yourself with talk about the other; avoid excessive self-talk or extreme avoidance of self-talk to encourage equal sharing and interpersonal satisfaction.*

semantics The area of language study concerned with meaning.

sexist language Language derogatory to one sex, usually women. *Whether man or woman, avoid sexist language—for example, terms that presume maleness as the norm ("policeman" or "mailman") or terms that may be considered insulting or demeaning.*

sexual harassment Unsolicited and unwanted sexual messages. *If confronted with sexual harassment, consider talking to the harasser, collecting evidence, using appropriate channels within the organization, or filing a complaint. Avoid any indication of sexual harassment by beginning with the assumption that others at work are not interested in sexual advances and stories; listen for negative reactions to any sexually explicit discussions, and avoid behaviors you think might prove offensive.*

shyness The condition of discomfort and uneasiness in interpersonal situations.

sign, reasoning from A form of reasoning in which the presence of certain signs (clues) are interpreted as leading to a particular conclusion.

signal and noise (relativity of) The principle of verbal interaction that holds that what is signal (meaningful) and what is noise (interference) is relative to the communication analyst, the participants, and the context.

signal reaction A conditioned response to a signal; a response to some signal that is immediate rather than delayed.

silence The absence of vocal communication; often misunderstood to refer to the absence of any and all communication. Silence is often used to communicate feelings or to prevent communication about certain topics. *Interpret silences of others through their culturally determined rules rather than your own.*

similarity A principle of **attraction** holding that one is attracted to qualities similar to those possessed by oneself and to people who are similar to oneself; opposed to **complementarity.**

slang The language used by special groups that is not considered proper by the general society; language made up of the **argot, cant,** and **jargon** of various groups and known by the general public.

small group communication Communication among a collection of individuals, small enough in number that all members may interact with relative ease as both senders and receivers, the members being related to each other by some common purpose and with some degree of organization or structure.

snarl words Highly negative words that express the feelings of the speaker rather than refer to any objective reality; opposite to purr words.

social comparison processes The processes by which you compare yourself (for example, your abilities, opinions, and values) with others and then assess and evaluate yourself; one of the sources of **self-concept.**

social distance The third **proxemic** distance, ranging from 4 to 12 feet; the distance at which business is usually conducted.

social exchange theory A theory hypothesizing that we develop relationships in which our rewards or profits will be greater than our costs and that we avoid or terminate relationships in which the costs exceed the rewards.

social penetration theory A theory concerned with relationship development from the superficial to the intimate levels and from few to many areas of interpersonal interaction.

source Any person or thing that creates messages. A source may be an individual speaking, writing, or gesturing or a computer sending an error message.

spatial distance Use spatial distance to signal the type of relationship you are in: intimate, personal, social, or public. Let your spatial relationships reflect your interpersonal relationships.

specific instances, reasoning from A form of reasoning in which several specific instances are examined and then a conclusion about the whole is formed.

speech Messages utilizing a vocal-auditory channel.

speech rate Use variations in rate to increase communication efficiency and persuasiveness as appropriate.

spontaneity The communication pattern in which one verbalizes what one is thinking without attempting to develop strategies for control; encourages **supportiveness;** opposed to **strategy.**

stability The principle of perception that refers to the fact that our perceptions of things and of people are relatively consistent with our previous perceptions.

static evaluation An orientation that fails to recognize that the world is characterized by constant change; an attitude that sees people and events as fixed rather than as constantly changing. *Date your statements to emphasize constant change; avoid the tendency to think of and describe things as static and unchanging.*

status The relative level one occupies in a hierarchy; status always involves a comparison, and thus one's status is only relative to the status of another.

stereotype In communication, a fixed impression of a group of people through which we then perceive specific individuals; stereotypes are most often negative but may also be positive. *Avoid stereotyping others; instead, see and respond to each individual as a unique individual.*

stimulus Any external or internal change that impinges on or arouses an organism.

stimulus-response models of communication Models of communication that assume that the process of communication is linear, beginning with a stimulus that then leads to a response.

subjectivity The principle of perception that refers to the fact that one's perceptions are not objective but are influenced by one's wants and needs and one's expectations and predictions.

supportiveness An attitude of an individual or an atmosphere in a group that is characterized by openness, absence of fear, and a genuine feeling of equality. *Exhibit supportiveness to others by being descriptive*

rather than evaluative, spontaneous rather than strategic, and provisional rather than certain.

symmetrical relationship A relation between two or more persons in which one person's behavior serves as a stimulus for the same type of behavior in the other person(s). Examples of such relationships include those in which anger in one person encourages or serves as a stimulus for anger in another person or in which a critical comment by the person leads the other person to respond in a like manner.

symposium A small group format in which each member of the group delivers a relatively prepared talk on some aspect of the topic. Often combined with a **forum.**

systematic desensitization A theory and technique for dealing with a variety of fears (such as communication apprehension) in which you gradually desensitize yourself to behaviors you wish to eliminate.

taboo Forbidden; culturally censored. Taboo language is language that is frowned upon by "polite society." Topics and specific words may be considered taboo—for example, death, sex, certain forms of illness, and various words denoting sexual activities and excretory functions. *Avoid taboo expressions so that others do not make negative evaluations; substitute more socially acceptable expressions or euphemisms where and when appropriate.*

territoriality A possessive or ownership reaction to an area of space or to particular objects. *Establish and maintain territory nonverbally by marking or otherwise indicating temporary or permanent ownership. Become sensitive to the territorial behavior of others.*

testimonial A persuasive technique in which the speaker uses the authority or image of some positively evaluated person to gain your approval or of some negatively evaluated person to gain your rejection.

theory A general statement or principle applicable to a number of related phenomena.

thesis The main assertion of a message—for example, the theme of a public speech.

temporal communication The messages that one's time orientation and treatment of time communicates.

touch avoidance The tendency to avoid touching and being touched by others. *Recognize that some people may prefer to avoid touching and being touched. Avoid drawing too many conclusions about people from the way they treat interpersonal touching.*

touch communication Communication through tactile means. *Use touch when appropriate to express positive effect, playfulness, control, and ritualistic meanings* *and to serve task-related functions. Avoid touching that is unwelcomed or that may be considered inappropriate.*

transactional Characterizing the relationship among elements whereby each influences and is influenced by each other element; communication is a transactional process because no element is independent of any other element.

transfer A persuasive technique in which a speaker associates an idea with something you respect to gain your approval or with something you dislike to gain your rejection.

uncertainty reduction strategies Passive, active, and interactive ways of increasing your accuracy in interpersonal perception. *Use all three as ways of reducing your uncertainty about others.*

uncertainty reduction theory The theory holding that as relationships develop, uncertainty is reduced; relationship development is seen as a process of reducing uncertainty about one another.

universal of interpersonal communication A feature of communication common to all interpersonal communication acts.

unknown self That part of the self that contains information about the self that is unknown to oneself and to others, but that is inferred to exist on the basis of various projective tests, slips of the tongue, dream analyses, and the like.

upward communication Communication in which the messages originate from the lower levels of an organization or hierarchy and are sent to upper levels—for example, line worker to management.

value Relative worth of an object; a quality that makes something desirable or undesirable; ideals or customs about which we have emotional responses, whether positive or negative.

verbal aggressiveness A method of winning an argument by attacking the other person's **self-concept.** *Avoid inflicting psychological pain on the other person to win an argument.* Often considered opposed to **argumentativeness.**

violation Unwarranted use of another's territory. See **territorial encroachment.**

visual dominance The use of your eyes to maintain a superior or dominant position, for example, when making an especially important point, you might look intently at the other person. *Use visual dominance behavior when you wish to emphasize certain messages.*

voice qualities Aspects of **paralanguage**—specifically, pitch range, vocal lip control, glottis control, pitch control, articulation control, rhythm control, resonance, and tempo.

volume The relative loudness of the voice.

withdrawal (1) A reaction to territorial encroachment in which we leave the territory. (2) A tendency to close oneself off from conflicts rather than confront the issues.

you-messages Messages in which the speaker denies responsibility for his or her own thoughts and behaviors; messages that attribute the speaker's perception to another person; messages of blame; *opposed to* **I-messages.**

Adler, Ronald B. (1977). *Confidence in Communication: A Guide to Assertive and Social Skills*. New York: Holt, Rinehart and Winston.

Agee, Warren K., Phillip H. Ault, and Edwin Emery (1997). *Introduction to Mass Communications*, 12th ed. New York: HarperCollins.

Akinnaso, F. Niyi (1982). On the Differences between Spoken and Written Language. *Language and Speech* 25 (Part 2):97–125.

Albas, Daniel C., Ken W. McCluskey, and Cheryl A. Albas (1976). Perception of the Emotional Content of Speech: A Comparison of Two Canadian Groups. *Journal of Cross Cultural Psychology* 7 (Dec.):481–490.

Albert, Rosita and Gayle L. Nelson (1993). Hispanic/Anglo American Differences in Attributions to Paralinguistic Behavior. *International Journal of Intercultural Relations* 17 (Winter):19–40.

Alessandra, Tony (1986). *How to Listen Effectively, Speaking of Success* (Video Tape Series). San Diego, CA: Levitz Sommer Productions.

Altman, Irwin (1975). *The Environment and Social Behavior*. Monterey, CA: Brooks/Cole.

Altman, Irwin and Dalmas Taylor (1973). *Social Penetration: The Development of Interpersonal Relationships*. New York: Holt, Rinehart and Winston.

Andersen, Peter (1991). Explaining Intercultural Differences in Nonverbal Communication. In Larry A. Samovar and Richard E. Porter, eds., *Intercultural Communication: A Reader*, 6th ed. (pp. 286–296). Belmont, CA: Wadsworth.

Andersen, Peter A. and Ken Leibowitz (1978). The Development and Nature of the Construct Touch Avoidance. *Environmental Psychology and Nonverbal Behavior* 3:89–106. Reprinted in DeVito and Hecht (1990).

Angier, Natalie (1995). Scientists Mull Role of Empathy in Man and Beast. *New York Times* (May 9): C1, C6.

Argyle, Michael (1986). Rules for Social Relationships in Four Cultures. *Australian Journal of Psychology* 38 (December):309–318.

Argyle, Michael (1988). *Bodily Communication*, 2nd ed. New York: Methuen and Co.

Argyle, Michael and Monika Henderson (1984). The Rules of Friendship. *Journal of Social and Personal Relationships* 1 (June):211–237.

Argyle, Michael and Monika Henderson (1985). *The Anatomy of Relationships: And the Rules and Skills Needed to Manage Them Successfully*. London: Heinemann.

Arliss, Laurie P. (1991). *Gender Communication*. Englewood Cliffs, NJ: Prentice-Hall.

Armstrong, Cameron B. and Alan M. Rubin (1989). Talk Radio as Interpersonal Communication. *Journal of Communication* 39 (Spring):84–94.

Arnold, Carroll C. and John Waite Bowers, eds. (1984). *Handbook of Rhetorical and Communication Theory*. Boston MA: Allyn and Bacon.

Aronson, Elliot, Timothy D. Wilson, and Robin M. Akert (1994). *Social Psychology: The Heart and the Mind*. New York: HarperCollins.

Asante, Molefi (1987). *The Afrocentric Idea*. Philadelphia, PA: Temple University Press.

Asch, Solomon (1946). Forming Impressions of Personality. *Journal of Abnormal and Social Psychology* 41:258–290.

Aune, R. Kelly and Toshiyuki Kikuchi (1993). Effects of Language Intensity Similarity on Perceptions of Credibility, Relational Attributions, and Persuasion. *Journal of Language and Social Psychology* 12 (Septembr):224–238.

Auter, Philip J. and Roy L. Moore (1993). Buying from a Friend: A Content Analysis of Two Teleshopping Programs. *Journalism Quarterly* (Summer): 425–436.

Axtell, Roger E. (1990). *Do's and Taboos of Hosting International Visitors*. New York: Wiley.

Axtell, Roger E. (1992). *Do's and Taboos of Public Speaking: How to Get Those Butterflies Flying in Formation*. New York: Wiley.

Axtell, Roger E. (1993). *Do's and Taboos Around the World,* 3rd ed. New York: Wiley.

Ayres, J. (1983). Strategies to Maintain Relationships: Their Identification and Perceived Usage. *Communication Quarterly* 31:62–67.

Ayres, Joe (1986). Perceptions of Speaking Ability: An Explanation for Stage Fright. *Communication Education* 35:275–287.

Ayres, Joe and Tim S. Hopf (1992). Visualization: Reducing Speech Anxiety and Enhancing Performance. *Communication Reports* 5:1–10.

Ayres, Joe and Tim Hopf (1993). *Coping with Speech Anxiety*. Norwood, NJ: Ablex Publishing Company.

Ayres, Joe and Janice Miller (1994). *Effective Public Speaking*, 5th ed. Dubuque, IA: Wm. C. Brown.

Ayres, Joe, Tim Hopf, and Debbie M. Ayres (1994). An Examination of Whether Imaging Ability Enhances the Effectiveness of an Intervention Designed to Reduce Speech Anxiety. *Communication Education* 43 (July):252–258.

Ayres, Joe, Tim Hopf, and Debbie Ayres (1997). Visualization and Performance Visualization: Applications, Evidence, and Speculation. In Daly, John A., James C. McCroskey, Joe Ayres, Tim Hopf, and Debbie M. Ayres (1997). *Avoiding Communication: Shyness, Reticence, and Communication Apprehension*, 2nd ed. (pp. 401–419). Cresskill, NJ: Hampton Press, Inc.

Bales, Robert F. (1950). *Interaction Process Analysis: A Method for the Study of Small Groups*. Cambridge, MA: Addison-Wesley.

Banks, Jack (1995). *MTV as Gatekeeper and Censor: A Survey of the Program Service's Attempts to Impose Its Standards on U.S. Popular Music*. Paper presented at the Eastern Communication Association Convention (Pittsburgh, April 27–30).

Barbato, Camle A. and Elizabeth M. Perse (1992). Interpersonal Communication Motives and the Life Position of Elders. *Communication Research* 19:516–531.

Barge, J. Kevin (1994). *Leadership: Communication Skills for Organizations and Groups*. New York: St. Martin's Press.

Barker, Larry L. (1990). *Communication*, 5th ed. Englewood Cliffs, NJ: Prentice-Hall.

Barker, Larry, R. Edwards, C. Gaines, K. Gladney, and F. Holley (1980). An Investigation of Proportional Time Spent in Various Communication Activities by College Students. *Journal of Applied Communication Research* 8:101–109.

Barna, LaRay M. (1985). Stumbling Blocks in Intercultural Communication. In Larry A. Samovar and Richard E. Porter, eds., *Intercultural Communication: A Reader*, 4th ed. (pp. 330–338). Belmont, CA: Wadsworth.

Barnlund, Dean C. (1970). A Transactional Model of Communication, *Language Behavior: A Book of Readings in Communication*, comp. J. Akin, A. Goldberg, G. Myers, and J. Stewart. The Hague: Mouton.

Barnlund, Dean C. (1975). Communicative Styles in Two Cultures: Japan and the United States. In A. Kendon, R. M. Harris, and M. R. Key, eds., *Organization of Behavior in Face-to-Face Interaction*. The Hague: Mouton.

Barnlund, Dean (1989). *Communicative Styles of Japanese and Americans: Images and Realities*. Belmont, CA: Wadsworth.

Baron, Robert A. and Donn Byrne (1984). *Social Pscyhology: Understanding Human Interaction*, 4th ed. Boston, MA: Allyn and Bacon.

Barrett, Lennard and T. Godfrey (1988). Listening. *Person Centered Review* 3 (November):410–425.

Barron, James (1995). It's Time to Mind Your E-Manners. *New York Times* (January 11): C1.

Basso, K. H. (1972). To Give Up on Words: Silence in Apache Culture. In Pier Paolo Giglioli, ed., *Language and Social Context*. New York: Penguin.

Baxter, Leslie A. (1983). Relationship Disengagement: An Examination of the Reversal Hypothesis. *Western Journal of Speech Communication* 47:85–98.

Baxter, Leslie A. (1986). Gender Differences in the Heterosexual Relationship Rules Embedded in Break-up Accounts. *Journal of Social and Personal Relationships* 3:289–306.

Baxter, Leslie A. (1988). A Dialectical Perspective on Communication Strategies in Relationship Development. In Steve Duck, ed., *Handbook of Personal Relationships*. New York: Wiley.

Baxter, Leslie A. (1990). Dialectical Contradictions in Relationship Development. *Journal of Social and Personal Relationships* 7 (February): 69–88.

Baxter, Leslie A. and Eric P. Simon (1993). Relationship Maintenance Strategies and Dialectical Contradictions in Personal Relationships. *Journal of Social and Personal Relationships* 10 (May):225–242.

Baxter, Leslie A. and William W. Wilmot (1984). 'Secret Tests': Social Strategies for Acquiring Information about the State of the Relationship. *Human Communication Research* 11: 171–201.

Beach, Wayne A. (1990–1991). Avoiding Ownership for Alledged Wrongdoings. *Research on Language and Social Interaction* 24:1–36.

Beall, Anne E. and Robert J. Sternberg (1995). The Social Construction of Love. *Journal of Social and Personal Relationships* 12 (August):417–438.

Beatty, Michael J. (1988). Situational and Predispositional Correlates of Public Speaking Anxiety. *Communication Education* 37:28–39.

Beck, A. T. (1988). *Love Is Never Enough*. New York: Harper and Row.

Becker, Samuel L. and Churchill L. Roberts (1992). *Discovering Mass Communication*, 3rd ed. New York: HarperCollins.

Beebe, Steven A. and John T. Masterson (1997). *Communicating in Small Groups: Principles and Practices*, 5th ed. New York: Longman.

Behzadi, Kavous G. (1994). Interpersonal Conflict and Emotions in an Iranian Cultural Practice: QAHR and ASHTI. *Culture, Medicine, and Psychiatry* 18 (September): 321–359.

Beier, Ernst (1974). How We Send Emotional Messages. *Psychology Today* 8 (October):53–56.

Bell, Robert A. and John A. Daly (1984). The Affinity-Seeking Function of Communication. *Communication Monographs* 51:91–115.

Benne, Kenneth D. and Paul Sheats (1948). Functional Roles of Group Members. *Journal of Social Issues* 4:41–49.

Bennett, Mark (1990). Children's Understanding of the Mitigating Function of Disclaimers. *Journal of Social Psychology* 130 (February):29–37.

Bennis, Warren and Burt Nanus (1985). *Leaders: The Strategies for Taking Charge*. New York: Harper and Row.

Berg, John H. and Richard L. Archer (1983). The Disclosure-Liking Relationship. *Human Communication Research* 10:269–281.

Berger, Charles R. and James J. Bradac (1982). *Language and Social Knowlege: Uncertainty in Interpersonal Relations*. London: Edward Arnold.

Berman, John J., Virginia Murphy-Berman, and Purnima Singh (1985). Cross-Cultural Similarities and Differences in Perceptions of Fairness. *Journal of Cross Cultural Psychology* 16 (March):55–67.

Bernstein, W. M., W. G. Stephan, and M. H. Davis (1979). Explaining Attributions for Achievement: A Path Analytic Approach. *Journal of Personality and Social Psychology* 37:1810–1821.

Berry, John W., Ype H. Poortinga, Marshall H. Segall, and Pierre R. Dasen (1992). *Cross-Cultural Psychology: Research and Applications*. Cambridge, MA: Cambridge University Press.

Blieszner, Rosemary and Rebecca G. Adams (1992). *Adult Friendship*. Thousand Oaks, CA: Sage.

Blumstein, Philip and Pepper Schwartz (1983). *American Couples: Money, Work, Sex*. New York: Morrow.

Bochner, Arthur (1978). On Taking Ourselves Seriously: An Analysis of Some Persistent Problems and Promising Directions in Interpersonal Research. *Human Communication Research* 4:179–191.

Bochner, Arthur (1984). The Functions of Human Communication in Interpersonal Bonding. In Carroll C. Arnold and John Waite Bowers, eds., *Handbook of Rhetorical and Communication Theory* (pp. 544–621). Boston, MA: Allyn and Bacon.

Bochner, Arthur and Clifford Kelly (1974). Interpersonal Competence: Rationale, Philosophy, and Implementation of a Conceptual Framework. *Communication Education* 23:279–301.

Bochner, Arthur P. and Janet Yerby (1977). Factors Affecting Instruction in Interpersonal Competence. *Communication Education* 26:91–103.

Bochner, Stephen and Beryl Hesketh (1994). Power, Distance, Individualism/Collectivism, and Job-Related Attitudes in a Culturally Diverse Work Group. *Journal of Cross Cultural Psychology* 25 (June): 233–257.

Bok, Sissela (1978). *Lying: Moral Choice in Public and Private Life*. New York: Pantheon.

Bok, Sissela (1983). *Secrets*. New York: Vintage Books.

Borden, George (1991). *Cultural Orientation: An Approach to Understanding Intercultural Communication*. Englewood Cliffs, NY: Prentice-Hall.

Bourland, D. D., Jr. (1965–66). A Linguistic Note: Writing in E-prime. *General Semantics Bulletin* 32–33:111–114.

Bremner, John B. (1980). *Words on Words: A Dictionary for Writers and Others Who Care About Words*. New York: Columbia University Press.

Brennan, Maire (1991). Mismanagement and Quality Circles: How Middle Managers Influence Direct Participation. *Employee Relations* 13:22–32.

Brody, Jane E. (1994). Notions of Beauty Transcend Culture, New Study Suggests. *New York Times* (March 21): A14.

Brody, Jane F. (1991, April 28). How to Foster Self-Esteem. *New York Times Magazine* 26–27.

Brown, Jane D. and Laurie Schulze (1990). The Effects of Race, Gender, and Fandom on Audience Interpretations of Madonna's Music Videos. *Journal of Communication* 40 (Spring):88–102.

Brown, P. and S. C. Levinson (1987). *Politeness: Some Universals of Language Usage*. Cambridge, MA: Cambridge University Press.

Brown, Penelope (1980). How and Why Are Women More Polite: Some Evidence from a Mayan Community. In Sally McConnell-Ginet, Ruth Borker, and Mellie Furman, eds., *Women and Language in Literature and Society* (pp. 111–136). New York: Praeger.

Brownell, Judi (1987). Listening: The Toughest Management Skill. *Cornell Hotel and Restaurant Administration Quarterly* 27:64–71.

Bruneau, Tom (1985). The Time Dimension in Intercultural Communication. In Larry A. Samovar and Richard E. Porter, eds., *Intercultural Communication: A Reader*, 4th ed. (pp. 280–289). Belmont, CA: Wadsworth.

Bruneau, Tom (1990). Chronemics: The Study of Time in Human Interaction. In Joseph A. DeVito and Michael L. Hecht, eds., *The Nonverbal Communication Reader* (pp. 301–311). Prospect Heights, IL: Waveland Press.

Bugental, J. and S. Zelen (1950). Investigations into the 'Self-Concept,' I. The W-A-Y Technique. *Journal of Personality* 18:483–498.

Buller, David B. and R. Kelly Aune (1992). The Effects of Speech Rate Similarity on Compliance: Application of Communication Accommodation

Theory. *Western Journal of Communication* 56 (winter):37–53.

Buller, David B., Beth A. LePoire, Kelly Aune, and Sylvie Eloy (1992). Social Perceptions as Mediators of the Effect of Speech Rate Similarity on Compliance. *Human Communication Research* 19 (December):286–311.

Burgoon, Judee K. (1978). A Communication Model of Personal Space Violations: Explication and an Initial Test. *Human Communication Research* 4:129–142.

Burgoon, Judee K. (1991). Relational Message Interpretations of Touch, Conversational Distance, and Posture. *Journal of Nonverbal Behavior* 15 (Winter):233–259.

Burgoon, Judee K., David B. Buller, Amy S. Ebesu, and Patricia Rockwell (1994). Interpersonal Deception: V. Accuracy in Deception Detection. *Communication Monographs* 61 (December):303–325.

Burgoon, Judee K., David B. Buller, and W. Gill Woodall 95). *Nonverbal Communication: The Unspoken Dialogue*, 2nd ed. New York: McGraw-Hill.

Burgoon, Michael (1971). The Relationship between Willingness to Manipulate Others and Success in Two Different Types of Basic Speech Communication Courses. *Communication Education* 20: 178–183.

Burke, N. Denise (1993). Restricting Gang Clothing in the Public Schools. *West's Education Law Quarterly* 2 (July):391–404.

Burleson, Brandt R., W. Samter, and A. E. Luccetti (1992). Similarity in Communication Values as a Predictor of Friendship Choices: Studies of Friends and Best Friends. *Southern Communication Journal* 57:260–276.

Burleson, Brant R., Adrianne W. Kunkel, and Jennifer D. Birch (1994). Thoughts about Talk in Romantic Realtionships: Similarity Makes for Attraction (and Happiness, Too). *Communication Quarterly* 42 (Summer):259–273.

Busse, Wilfried, M. and Janice M. Birk (1993). The Effects of Self-Disclosure and Competitiveness on Friendship for Male Graduate Students Over 35. *Journal of College Student Development* 34 (May):169–174.

Butler, Pamela E. (1981). *Talking to Yourself: Learning the Language of Self-Support*. New York: Harper and Row.

Callahan, Victor J. (1993). Subordinate-Manager Communication in Different Sex Dyads: Consequences of Job Satisfaction. *Journal of Occupational and Organizational Psychology* 66 (March):13–27.

Camden, Carl, Michael T. Motley, and Ann Wilson (1984). White Lies in Interpersonal Communica-tion: A Taxonomy and Preliminary Investigation of Social Motivations. *Western Journal of Speech Communication* 48:309–325.

Canary, Daniel J. and Laura Stafford (1994a). *Communication and Relational Maintenance*. Orlando, FL: Academic Press.

Canary, Daniel J. and Laura Stafford (1994b). Maintaining Relationships Through Strategic and Routine Interaction. In D.J. Canary and Laura Stafford, eds., *Communication and Relational Maintenance*. New York: Academic Press.

Canary, Daniel J., Laura Stafford, Kimberly S. Hause, and Lisa A. Wallace (1993). An Inductive Analysis of Relational Maintenance Strategies: Comparisons Among Lovers, Relatives, Friends, and Others. *Communication Research Reports* 10 (June): 5–14.

Canary, Daniel, William R. Cupach, and Susan J. Messman (1995). *Relationship Conflict*. Thousand Oaks, CA: Sage.

Capella, Joseph N. (1993). The Facial Feedback Hypothesis in Human Interaction: Review and Speculation. *Journal of Language and Social Psychology* 12 (March-June):13–29.

Carducci, Bernardo J. with Philip G. Zimbardo (1995). Are You Shy? *Psychology Today* 28 (November/December):34–41, 64–70, 78–82.

Care, R, J. Henton, J. Koval, R. Christopher, and S. Lloyd (1982). Premarital Abuse: A Social Psychological Perspective. *Journal of Family Issues* 3:79–90.

Carle, Gilda (1995). 10 Reasons Why Talk Shows Are Good for You. *All Talk* (Spring):27.

Cathcart, Dolores and Robert Cathcart (1985). Japanese Social Experience and Concept of Groups. In Larry A. Samovar and Richard E. Porter, eds., *Intercultural Communication: A Reader,* 4th ed. (pp. 190–197). Belmont, CA: Wadsworth.

Cegala, Donald J., Grant T. Savage, Claire C. Brunner, and Anne B. Conrad (1982). An Elaboration of the Meaning of Interaction Involvement. *Communication Monographs* 49:229–248.

Chadwick-Jones, J. K. (1976). *Social Exchange Theory: Its Structure and Influence in Social Psychology*. New York: Academic.

Chaney, Robert H., Carolyne A. Givens, Melanie F. Aoki, and Michael L. Gombiner (1989). Pupillary Responses in Recognizing Awareness in Persons with Profound Mental Retardation. *Perceptual and Motor Skills* 69 (October):523–528.

Chang, Hui-Ching and G. Richard Holt (1996). The Changing Chinese Interpersonal World: Popular Themes in Interpersonal Communication Books in Modern Taiwan. *Communication Quarterly* 44 (Winter): 85–106.

Chanowitz, B. and Ellen Langer (1981). Premature Cognitive Commitment. *Journal of Personality and Social Psychology* 41:1051–1063.

Chen, Guo-Ming (1990). Intercultural Communication Competence: Some Perspectives of Research. *The Howard Journal of Communication* 2 (Summer):243–261.

Chen, Guo Ming (1992). Differences in Self-Disclosure Patterns Among Americans versus Chinese: A Comparative Study. Paper presented at the annual meeting of the Eastern Communication Association (Portland, ME).

Christie, Richard (1970). Scale Construction. In R. Christie and F.L. Geis, eds., *Studies in Machiavellianism* (pp. 35–52). New York: Academic Press.

Cialdini, Robert T. (1984). *Influence: How and Why People Agree to Things.* New York: Morrow.

Cialdini, Robert T. and K. Ascani (1976). Test of a Concession Procedure for Inducing Verbal, Behavioral, and Further Compliance with a Request to Give Blood. *Journal of Applied Psychology* 61:295–300.

Coalition Commentary, a Publication of the Illinois Coalition against Sexual Assault (1990) Urbana, IL (Spring): 1–7.

Coates, Jennifer (1986). *Women, Men and Language.* New York: Longman.

Cohen, C. E. (1983). Inferring the Characteristics of Other People: Categories and Attribute Accessibility. *Journal of Personality and Social Psychology* 44:34–44.

Collier, Mary Jane (1991). Conflict Competence Within African, Mexican, and Anglo American Friendships. In Stella Ting-Toomey and Felipe Korzenny, eds., *Cross-Cultural Interpersonal Communication* (pp. 132–154). Thousand Oaks, CA: Sage.

Collins, Caroline L. and Odette N. Gould (1994). Getting to Know You: How Own Age and Other's Age Relate to Self-Disclosure. *International Journal of Aging and Human Development* 39:55–66.

Comadena, Mark E. (1984). Brainstorming Groups: Ambiguity Tolerance, Communication Apprehension, Task Attraction, and Individual Productivity. *Small Group Behavior* 15:251–254.

Cook, Mark (1971). *Interpersonal Perception.* Baltimore, MD: Penguin.

Cooley, Charles Horton (1922). *Human Nature and the Social Order,* rev. ed. New York: Scribner's.

Copeland, Lennie and Lewis Griggs (1985). *Going International: How to Make Friends and Deal Effectively in the Global Marketplace.* New York: Random House.

Cragan, John F. and David W. Wright (1990). Small Group Communication Research of the 1980's: A Synthesis and Critique. *Communication Studies* 41 (Fall):212–236.

Crohn, Joel (1995). *Mixed Matches.* New York: Fawcett.

Dainton, M., and Laura Stafford (1993). Routine Maintenance Behaviors: A Comparison of Relationship Type, Partner Similarity, and Sex Differences. *Journal of Social and Personal Relationships* 10:255–272.

Daly, John A., James C. McCroskey, Joe Ayres, Tim Hopf, and Debbie M. Ayres (1997). *Avoiding Communication: Shyness, Reticence, and Communication Apprehension,* 2nd ed. Cresskill, NJ: Hampton Press, Inc.

Davis, Murray S. (1973). *Intimate Relations.* New York: Free Press.

Davitz, Joel R., ed. (1964). *The Communication of Emotional Meaning.* New York: McGraw-Hill.

Deal, James E. and Karen Smith Wampler (1986). Dating Violence: The Primacy of Previous Experience. *Journal of Social and Personal Relationships* 3:457–471.

deBono, Edward (1976). *Teaching Thinking.* New York: Penguin.

deBono, Edward (1987). *The Six Thinking Hats.* New York: Penguin.

DeFrancisco, Victoria (1991). The Sound of Silence: How Men Silence Women in Marital Relations. *Discourse and Society* 2:413–423.

DeJong, W. (1979). An Examination of Self Perception Mediation of the Foot-in-the Door Effect. *Journal of Personality and Social Psychology* 37:2221–2239.

Delia, Jesse G., Barbara J. O'Keefe, and Daniel J. O'Keefe (1982). The Constructivist Approach to Communication. In Frank E. X. Dance, ed., *Human Communication Theory: Comparative Essays* (pp. 147–191). New York: Harper and Row.

Derlega, V. J., B. A. Winstead, P. T. P. Wong, and S. Hunter (1985). Gender Effects in an Initial Encounter: A Case Where Men Exceed Women in Disclosure. *Journal of Social and Personal Relationships* 2:25–44.

Derlega, Valerian J., Barbara A. Winstead, Paul T. P. Wong, and Michael Greenspan (1987). Self-Disclosure and Relationship Development: An Attributional Analysis. In Michael E. Roloff and Gerald R. Miller, eds., *Interpersonal Processes: New Directions in Communication Research* (pp. 172–187). Thousand Oaks, CA: Sage.

DeStephen, R. and R. Hirokawa (1988). Small Group Consensus: Stability of Group Support of the Decision, Task Process, and Group Relationships. *Small Group Behavior* 19:227–239.

DeTurck, Mark A. (1987). When Communication Fails: Physical Aggression as a Compliance-Gaining Strategy. *Communication Monographs* 54:106–112.

DeVito, J. A. (1970). *The Psychology of Speech and Language: An Introduction to the Study of Psycholinguistics.* New York: Random House.

DeVito, Joseph A. (1974). *General Semantics: Guide and Workbook,* rev. ed. DeLand, FL: Everett/Edwards.

DeVito, Joseph A. (1986). *The Communication Handbook: A Dictionary.* New York: Harper and Row.

DeVito, Joseph A. (1989). *The Nonverbal Communication Workbook.* Prospect Heights, IL: Waveland Press.

DeVito, Joseph A. (1996). *Brainstorms: How to Think More Creatively about Communication (or About Anything Else).* New York: Longman.

DeVito, Joseph A. (1999). *Messages: Building Interpersonal Communication Skills,* 4th ed. New York: Longman.

DeVito, Joseph A. (2000). *The Elements of Public Speaking,* 7th ed. New York: Longman.

DeVito, Joseph A. and Michael L. Hecht, eds. (1990). *The Nonverbal Communication Reader.* Prospect Heights, IL: Waveland Press.

Dewey, John (1910). *How We Think.* Boston, MA: Heath.

Dindia, Kathryn and Mary Anne Fitzpatrick (1985). Marital Communication: Three Approaches Compared. In Steve Duck and Daniel Perlman, eds., *Understanding Personal Relationships: An Interdisciplinary Approach* (pp. 137–158). Thousand Oaks, CA: Sage.

Dindia, Kathryn, and Leslie A. Baxter (1987). Strategies for Maintaining and Repairing Marital Relationships. *Journal of Social and Personal Relationships* 4:143–158.

Dodd, Carley H. (1995). *Dynamics of Intercultural Communication,* 4th ed. Dubuque, IA: Wm. C. Brown.

Dolgin, Kim G., Leslie Meyer, and Janet Schwartz (1991). Effects of Gender, Target's Gender, Topic, and Self-Esteem on Disclosure to Best and Middling Friends. *Sex Roles* 25:311–329.

Donohue, William A. with Robert Kolt (1992). *Managing Interpersonal Conflict.* Thousand Oaks, CA: Sage.

Dreyfuss, Henry (1971). *Symbol Sourcebook.* New York: McGraw-Hill.

Driskell, James, Beckett Olmstead, and Eduardo Salas (1993). Task Cues, Dominance Cues, and Influence in Task Groups. *Journal of Applied Psychology* 78 (February): 51–60.

Drucker, Susan J. and Gary Gumpert (1991). Public Space and Communication: The Zoning of Public Interaction. *Communication Theory* 1 (November):294–310.

Duncan, S. D., Jr. (1972). Some Signals and Rules for Taking Speaking Turns in Conversation. *Journal of Personality and Social Psychology* 23:283–292.

Duran, Robert L. and L. Kelly (1988). The Influence of Communicative Competence on Perceived Task, Social, and Physical Attractiveness. *Communication Quarterly* 36:41–49.

Eakins, Barbara and R. Gene Eakins (1978). *Sex Differences in Communication.* Boston, MA: Houghton Mifflin.

Eastbrook, Noel (1997). *Teach Yourself the Internet in 24 Hours.* Indianapolis, IN: SamsNet.

Edelstein, Alex S. (1993). Thinking About the Criterion Variable in Agenda-Setting Research. *Journal of Communication* 43:85–99.

Eden, Dov (1992). Leadership and Expectations: Pygmalion Effects and Other Self-Fulfilling Prophecies in Organizations. *Leadership Quarterly* 3 (Winter):271–305.

Ehrenhaus, Peter (1988). Silence and Symbolic Expression. *Communication Monographs* 55 (March): 41–57.

Ekman, Paul (1985). *Telling Lies: Clues to Deceit in the Marketplace, Politics, and Marriage.* New York: W. W. Norton.

Ekman, Paul and W. V. Friesen (1969). The Repertoire of Nonverbal Behavior: Categories, Origins, Usage, and Coding. *Semiotica* 1:49–98.

Ekman, Paul, Wallace V. Friesen, and Phoebe Ellsworth (1972). *Emotion in the Human Face: Guidelines for Research and an Integration of Findings.* New York: Pergamon Press.

Epstein, N., J.L. Pretzer, and B. Fleming (1987). The Role of Cognitive Appraisal in Self-Reports of Marital Communication. *Behavior Therapy* 18:51–69.

Esten, Geri and Lynn Willmott (1993). Double-Bind Messages: The Effects of Attitude Towards Disability on Therapy. *Women and Therapy* 14:29–41.

Exline, R. V., S. L. Ellyson, and B. Long (1975). Visual Behavior as an Aspect of Power Role Relationships. In P. Pliner, L. Krames, and T. Alloway, eds., *Nonverbal Communication of Aggression.* New York: Plenum.

Festinger, Leon (1954). A Theory of Social Comparison Processes. *Human Relations* 7:117–140.

Field, R. H. G. (1989). The Self-Fulfilling Prophecy Leader: Achieving the Metharme Effect. *Journal of Management Studies* 26 (March):151–175.

Fiske, Susan T. and Shelley E. Taylor (1984). *Social Cognition.* Reading, MA: Addison-Wesley.

Fitzpatrick, Mary Anne (1983). Predicting Couples' Communication from Couples' Self-Reports. In R.N. Bostrom, ed., *Communication Yearbook 7 (pp. 49–82).* Thousand Oaks, CA: Sage.

Fitzpatrick, M. A. (1988). *Between Husbands and Wives: Communication in Marriage.* Thousand Oaks, CA: Sage.

Floyd, James J. (1985). *Listening: A Practical Approach.* Glenview, IL: Scott, Foresman.

Foddy, Margaret and Ian Crundall (1993). A Field Study of Social Comparison Processes in Ability Evaluation. *British Journal of Social Psychology* 32 (December):287–305.

Folger, Joseph P., Marshall Scott Poole, and Randall K. Stutman (1997). *Working Through Conflict: A Communication Perspective,* 3rd ed. New York: Longman.

Foss, Sonja K. (1996). *Rhetorical Criticism: Exploration and Practice,* 2nd ed. Prospect Heights, IL: Waveland Press.

Fraser, Bruce (1990). Perspectives on Politeness. *Journal of Pragmatics* 14 (April):219–236.

Freedman, J. and S. Fraser (1966). Compliance Without Pressure: The Foot-in-the Door Technique. *Journal of Personality and Social Psychology* 4: 195–202.

French, J. R. P., Jr. and B. Raven (1968). The Bases of Social Power. In Dorwin Cartwright and Alvin Zander, eds., *Group Dynamics: Research and Theory,* 3d ed. (pp. 259–269). New York: Harper and Row.

Frentz, Thomas (1976). A General Approach to Episodic Structure. Paper presented at the Western Speech Association Convention. San Francisco, CA. Cited in Reardon (1987).

Frey, Kurt J. and Alice H. Eagly (1993). Vividness Can Undermine the Persuasiveness of Messages. *Journal of Personality and Social Psychology* 65 (July): 32–44.

Frymier, Anne B. and Catherine A. Thompson (1992). Perceived Teacher Affinity-Seeking in Relation to Perceived Teacher Credibility. *Communication Education* 41 (October):388–399.

Frymier, Ann B. and Gary M. Schulman (1995). "What's In It For Me?": Increasing Content Relevance to Enhance Students' Motivation. *Communication Education* 44 (January): 40–50.

Furlow, F. Bryant (1996). The Smell of Love. *Psychology Today* (March/April): 38–45.

Furnham, Adrian and Nadine Bitar (1993). The Stereotyped Portrayal of Men and Women in British Televison Advertisements. *Sex Roles* 29 (August):297–310.

Furnham, Adrian and Stephen Bochner (1986). *Culture Shock: Psychological Reactions to Unfamiliar Environments.* New York: Methuen.

Gao, Ge (1991). Stability of Romantic Relationsihps in China and the United States. In Stella Ting-Toomey and Felipe Korzenny, eds., *Cross-Cultural Interpersonal Communication* (pp. 99–115). Thousand Oaks, CA: Sage.

Garner, Alan (1981). *Conversationally Speaking.* New York: McGraw-Hill.

Gaziano, C. and K. McGrath (1986). Measuring the Concept of Credibility. *Journalism Quarterly* 63:451–462.

Gelles, R. and C. Coarnell (1985). *Intimate Violence in Families.* Thousand Oaks, CA: Sage.

Gerbner, George, L. P. Gross, M. Morgan, and N. Signorielli (1980). The 'Mainstreaming' of America: Violence Profile No. 11. *Journal of Communication* 30:10–29.

Gergen, K. J., M.S. Greenberg, and R.H. Willis (1980). *Social Exchange: Advances in Theory and Research.* New York: Plenum Press.

Gibb, Jack (1961). Defensive Communication. *Journal of Communication* 11:141–148.

Giles, Howard, Anthony Mulac, James J. Bradac, and Patricia Johnson (1987). Speech Accommodation Theory: The First Decade and Beyond. In Margaret L. McLaughlin, ed., *Communication Yearbook 10* (pp. 13–48). Thousand Oaks, CA: Sage.

Giordano, Joseph (1989). *Telecommuting and Organizational Culture: A Study of Corporate Consciousness and Identification.* Unpublished doctoral dissertation, University of Massachusetts. Amherst, MA.

Glucksberg, Sam and Joseph H. Danks(1975). *Experimental Psycholinguistics: An Introduction.* Hillsdale, NJ: Lawrence Erlbaum.

Goffman, Erving (1967). *Interaction Ritual: Essays on Face-to-Face Behavior.* New York: Pantheon.

Goffman, Erving (1971). *Relations in Public: Microstudies of the Public Order.* New York: Harper Collins.

Goleman, Daniel (1995). *Emotional Intelligence.* New York: Bantam.

Goleman, Daniel (1995). For Man and Beast, Language of Love Shares Many Traits. *New York Times* (February 14): C1, C9.

Gonzalez, Alexander and Philip G. Zimbardo (1985). Time in Perspective. *Psychology Today*

19:20–26. Reprinted in Guerrero, DeVito, and Hecht (1999), pp. 227–236.

Gorden, William I. And Randi J. Nevins (1993). *We Mean Business: Building Communication Competence in Business and Professions.* New York: Longman.

Goss, Blaine, M. Thompson, and S. Olds (1978). Behavioral Support for Systematic Desensitization for Communication Apprehension. *Human Communication Research* 4:158–163.

Gottman, John M. and S. Carrere (1994). Why Can't Men and Women Get Along? Developmental Roots and Marital Inequities. In D.J. Canary and Laura Stafford, eds., *Communication and Relational Maintenance* (pp. 203–229). San Diego, CA: Academic Press.

Gould, Stephen Jay (1995). No More 'Wretched Refuse'. *New York Times* (June 7, 1995):A27.

Gouran, Dennis S. and Randy Y. Hirokawa (1986). Counteractive Functions of Communication in Effective Group Decision-Making. In Randy Y. Hirokawa and M. S. Poole, eds., *Communication and Group Decision-Making* (pp. 81–90). Thousand Oaks, CA: Sage.

Graham, E. E. (1994). Interpersonal Communication Motives Scale. In R. B. Rubin, P. Palmgreen, and H. E. Sypher, eds., *Communication Research Measures: A Sourcebook* (pp. 211–216). New York: Guilford.

Graham, E. E., Carole A. Barbato, and E. M. Perse (1993). The Interpersonal Communication Motives Model. *Communication Quarterly* 41:172–186.

Graham, Jean Ann and Michael Argyle (1975). The Effects of Different Patterns of Gaze Combined with Different Facial Expressions, on Impression Formation. *Journal of Movement Studies* 1 (December):178–182.

Graham, Jean Ann, Pio Ricci Bitti, and Michael Argyle (1975). A Cross-Cultural Study of the Communication of Emotion by Facial and Gestural Cues. *Journal of Human Movement Studies* 1 (June):68–77.

Grant, August E., K. Kendall Guthrie, Sandra J. Ball-Rokeach (1991). Television Shopping: A Media System Dependency Perspective. *Communication Research* 18 (December):773–798.

Grice, H. P. (1975). Logic and Conversation. In Cole and J.L. Morgan, eds., *Syntax and Semantics*, V. 3: Speech Acts (pp. 41–58). New York: Seminar Press.

Griffin, Em (1991). *A First Look at Communication Theory.* New York: McGraw-Hill.

Gronbeck, Bruce E., Raymie E. McKerrow, Douglas Ehninger, and Alan H. Monroe (1997). *Principles and Types of Speech Communication*, 13th ed. New York: Longman.

Gross, Larry (1991). The Contested Closet: The Ethics and Politics of Outing. *Critical Studies in Mass Communication* 8 (September):352–388.

Gross, Ronald (1991). *Peak Learning.* Los Angeles: Jeremy P. Tarcher.

Gross, T., E. Turner, and L. Cederholm (1987). Building Teams for Global Operation. *Management Review* (June):32–36.

Grossin, William (1987). Monochronic Time, Polychronic Time and Policies for Development. *Studi di Sociologia* 25 (January-March):18–25.

Gudykunst, William B., ed. (1983). *Intercultural communication theory: Current perspectives.* Thousand Oaks, CA: Sage.

Gudykunst, William B. (1989). Culture and the Development of Interpersonal Relationships. In J. A. Anderson, ed., *Communication Yearbook/12* (pp. 315–354). Thousand Oaks, CA: Sage.

Gudykunst, William B. (1994). *Bridging Differences: Effective Intergroup Communication*, 2nd ed. Thousand Oaks, CA: Sage.

Gudykunst, William B. and Y. Y. Kim, eds. (1992). *Readings on Communication with Strangers: An Approach to Intercultural Communication.* New York: McGraw-Hill.

Gudykunst, William B. and Young Yun Kim (1992). *Communicating with Strangers: An Approach to Intercultural Communication*, 2nd ed. New York: Random House.

Guerrero, L. K., S. V. Eloy, and A. I. Wabnik (1993). Linking Maintenance Strategies to Relationship Development and Disengagement: A Reconceptualization. *Journal of Social and Personal Relationships* 10:273–282.

Guerrero, Laura K. and Peter A. Andersen (1994). Patterns of Matching and Initiation: Touch Behavior and Touch Avoidance Across Romantic Relationship Stages. *Journal of Nonverbal Behavior* 18(Summer):137–153.

Guerrero, Laura K., Joseph A. DeVito, and Michael L. Hecht, eds., (1999). *The Nonverbal Communication Reader: Class and Contemporary Readings*, 2nd ed. Prospect Heights, IL: Waveland Press.

Gumpert, Gary and Susan J. Drucker (1995). Place as Medium: Exegesis of the Cafe Drinking Coffee, The Art of Watching Others, Civil Conversation—with Excursions into the Effects of Architecture and Interior Design. *The Speech Communication Annual* 9 (Spring):7–32.

Guo-Ming, Chen and William J. Starosta (1995). Intercultural Communication Competence: A Synthesis. In Brant R. Burleson, ed., *Communication Yearbook/19.* Thousand Oaks, CA: Sage.

Gupta, U., and P. Singh (1982). Exploratory Studies in Love and Liking and Types of Marriages. *Indian Journal of Applied Psychology* 19:92–97.

Hackman, Michael Z. and Craig E. Johnson (1991). *Leadership: A Communication Perspective.* Prospect Heights, IL: Waveland Press.

Haferkamp, Claudia J. (1991–92). Orientations to Conflict: Gender, Attributions, Resolution Strategies, and Self-Monitoring. *Current Psychology Research and Reviews* 10 (Winter):227–240.

Hall, Edward T. (1959). *The Silent Language.* Garden City, NY: Doubleday.

Hall, Edward T. (1963). A System for the Notation of Proxemic Behavior. *American Anthropologist* 65:1003–1026.

Hall, Edward T. (1976). *Beyond culture.* Garden City, NY: Anchor Press.

Hall, Edward T. and Mildred Reed Hall (1987). *Hidden Differences: Doing Business with the Japanese.* New York: Doubleday [Anchor Books].

Hall, Joan Kelly (1993). Tengo una Bomba: The Paralinguistic and Linguistic Conventions of the Oral Practice Chismeando. *Research on Language and Social Interaction* 26:55–83.

Hall, Judith A. (1984). *Nonverbal Sex Differences.* Baltimore, MD: Johns Hopkins University Press.

Hambrick, Ralph S. (1991). *The Management Skills Builder: Self-Directed Learning Strategies for Career Development.* New York: Praeger.

Haney, William (1973). *Communication and Organizational Behavior: Text and Cases,* 3rd ed. Homewood IL: Irwin.

Harnack, Andrew and Eugene Kleppinger (1997). *Online! The Internet Guide for Students and Writers.* New York: St. Martin's Griffin.

Hatfield, Elaine and Richard L. Rapson (1996). *Love and Sex: Cross Cultural Perspectives.* Boston, MA: Allyn and Bacon.

Hayakawa, S. I. and A.R. Hayakawa (1989) *Language in Thought and Action,* 5th ed. New York: Harcourt Brace Jovanovich.

Hays, Robert B. (1989). The Day-to-Day Functioning of Close Versus Casual Friendships. *Journal of Social and Personal Relationships* 6: 21–37.

Heap, James L. (1992). Seeing Snubs: An Introduction to Sequential Analysis of Classroom Interaction. *Journal of Classroom Interaction* 27:23–28.

Heasley, John B., Charles E. Babbitt, and Harold J. Burbach (1995). Gender Differences in College Students' Perceptions of 'Fighting Words.' *Sociological Viewpoints* 11 (Fall): 30–40.

Hecht, Michael (1978a). The Conceptualization and Measurement of Interpersonal Communication Satisfaction. *Human Communication Research* 4:253–264.

Hecht, Michael (1978b). Toward a Conceptualization of Communication Satisfaction. *Quarterly Journal of Speech* 64: 47–62.

Hecht, Michael and Sidney Ribeau (1984). Ethnic Communication: A Comparative Analysis of Satisfying Communication. *International Journal of Intercultural Relations* 8:135–151.

Hecht, Michael L., Mary Jane Collier, and Sidney Ribeau (1993). *African American Communication: Ethnic Identity and Cultural Interpretation.* Thousand Oaks, CA: Sage.

Heenehan, Meg (1997). *Networking.* New York: Random House.

Heiskell, Thomas L. and Joseph F. Rychiak (1986). The Therapeutic Relationship: Inexperienced Therapists' Affective Preference and Empathic Communication. *Journal of Social and Personal Relationships* 3:267–274.

Hendrick, Clyde, and Susan Hendrick (1990). A Relationship–Specific Version of the Love Attitudes Scale. In *Handbook of Replication Research in the Behavioral and Social Sciences* [Special Issue], J. W. Heulip, ed., *Journal of Social Behavior and Personality* 5: 239–254.

Hersey, Paul and Ken Blanchard (1988). *Management of Organizational Behavior: Utilizing Human Resources.* Englewood Cliffs, NJ: Prentice-Hall.

Herzog, Thomas (1996). *Research Methods and Data Analysis in the Social Sciences.* New York: Longman.

Hess, Eckhard H. (1975). *The Tell-Tale Eye.* New York: Van Nostrand Reinhold.

Hess, Ursula, Arvid Kappas, Gregory J. McHugo, John T. Lanzetta, et al (1992). The Facilitative Effect of Facial Expression on the Self-Generation of Emotion. *International Journal of Psychophysiology* 12 (May):251–265.

Hewitt, John and Randall Stokes (1975). Disclaimers. *American Sociological Review* 40:1–11.

Hofstede, Geert (1984). *Culture's Consequences: International Differences in Work-Related Values.* Thousand Oaks, CA: Sage.

Hofstede, Geert (1997). *Cultures and Organizations: Software of the Mind.* New York: McGraw-Hill.

Hofstetter, C. Richard and Christopher L. Gianos (1997). Political Talk Radio: Actions Speak Louder than Words. *Journal of Broadcasting and Electronic Media* 41 (Fall): 501–515.

Hoft, Nancy L. (1995). *International Technical Communication: How to Export Information about High Technology.* New York: Wiley.

Holden, Janice M. (1991). The Most Frequent Personality Priority Pairings in Marriage and Marriage Counseling. *Individual Psychology Journal of Adlerian Theory, Research, and Practice* 47(September):392–398.

Hollander, Barry A. (1996). Talk Radio: Predictors of Use and Effects on Attitudes about Government. *Journalism and Mass Communication Quarterly* 73 (Spring): 102–113.

Holmes, Janet (1986). Compliments and Compliment Responses in New Zealand English. *Anthropological Linguistics* 28:485–508.

Holmes, Janet (1995). *Women, Men and Politeness*. New York: Longman.

Hosman, Lawrence A. (1989). The Evaluative Consequences of Hedges, Hesitations, and Intensifiers: Powerful and Powerless Speech Styles. *Human Communication Research* 15:383–406.

Iizuka, Yuichi (1993). Regulators in Japanese Conversation. *Psychological Reports* 72 (February):203–209.

Imahori, T. Todd and William R. Cupach (1994). A Cross-Cultural Comparison of the Interpretation and Management of Face: US American and Japanese Responses to Embarrassing Predicaments. *International Journal of Intercultural Relations* 18 (Spring):193–219.

Infante, Dominic A. (1988). *Arguing Constructively*. Prospect Heights, IL: Waveland Press.

Infante, Dominic A. and Andrew S. Rancer (1982). A Conceptualization and Measure of Argumentativeness. *Journal of Personality Assessment* 46:72–80.

Infante, Dominic A. and Andrew S. Rancer (1995). Argumentativeness and Verbal Aggressiveness: A Review of Recent Theory and Research. In Brant R. Burleson, ed., *Communication Yearbook/19*. Thousand Oaks, CA: Sage.

Infante, Dominic A. and C. J. Wigley (1986). Verbal Aggressiveness: An Interpersonal Model and Measure. *Communication Monographs* 53:61–69.

Infante, Dominic A., Andrew S. Rancer, and Deanna F. Womack (1993). *Building Communication Theory*, 2nd ed. Prospect Heights, IL: Waveland Press.

Insel, Paul M. and Lenore F. Jacobson, eds. (1975). *What Do You Expect? An Inquiry into Self-Fulfilling Prophecies*. Menlo Park, CA: Cummings.

Jablin, Fred M. (1981). Cultivating Imagination: Factors that Enhance and Inhibit Creativity in Brainstorming Groups. *Human Communication Research* 7:245–258.

Jacobs, A. J. (1995). Talkin' Trash. *Entertainment Weekly*, No. 304 (December 8):42–43.

Jaffe, Clella (1998). *Public Speaking: Concepts and Skills for a Diverse Society*, 2nd ed. Belmont, CA: Wadsworth.

Jaksa, James A. and Michael S. Pritchard (1994). *Communication Ethics: Methods of Analysis*, 2nd ed. Belmont, CA: Wadsworth.

James, Phil and Jan Weingarten (1995). *Internet Guide for Windows 95*. Research Triangle Park, NC: Ventana.

James-Catalano, Cynthia N. (1996). *Researching on the World Wide Web*. Rocklin, CA: Prima.

Jamieson, Kathleen Hall and Karlyn Kohrs Campbell (1992). *The Interplay of Influence*, 3rd ed. Belmont, CA: Wadsworth.

Jandt, Fred E. (1999). *Intercultural Communication*, 2nd ed. Thousand Oaks, CA: Sage.

Jandt, Fred E. and Mary B. Nemnich (1995). *Using the Internet in Your Job Search*. Indianapolis, IN: Jist Works, Inc.

Janis, Irving (1983). *Victims of Group Thinking: A Psychological Study of Foreign Policy Decisions and Fiascoes*, 2nd ed., rev. Boston, MA: Houghton Mifflin.

Jaworski, Adam (1993). *The Power of Silence: Social and Pragmatic Perspectives*. Thousand Oaks, CA: Sage.

Jecker, Jon and David Landy (1969). Liking a Person as a Function of Doing Him a Favor. *Human Relations* 22: 371–378.

Jensen, J. Vernon (1985). Perspectives on Nonverbal Intercultural Communication. In Larry Samovar and Richard E. Porter, eds., *Intercultural Communication: A Reader*, 4th ed. (pp. 256–272). Belmont, CA.: Wadsworth.

Johannesen, Richard L. (1974). The Functions of Silence: A Plea for Communication Research. *Western Speech* 38 (Winter):25–35.

Johannesen, Richard L. (1994). *Ethics in Human Communication*, 5th ed. Prospect Heights, IL: Waveland Press.

Johansson, Warren and William A. Percy (1994). *Outing: Shattering the Conspiracy of Silence*. New York: Harrington Park Press.

Johnson, Kirk (1998). Self Image is Suffering From Lack of Esteem. *New York Times* (May 5): F7.

Johnson, M. P. (1973). Commitment: A Conceptual Structure and Empirical Application. *Sociological Quarterly* 14:395–406.

Johnson, M. P. (1982). Social and Cognitive Features of the Dissolution of Commitment to Relationships. In Steve Duck, ed., *Personal Relationships 4: Dissolving Personal Relationships* (pp. 51–73). New York: Academic Press.

Johnson, M. P. (1991). Commitment to Personal Relationships. In W.H. Jones and D. Perlman, eds.,

Advances in Personal Relationships, vol. 3 (pp. 117–143). London: Jessica Kingsley.

Johnson, Scott, A. (1993). *When "I Love You" Turns Violent: Emotional and Physical Abuse in Dating Relationships*. Far Hills, NJ: New Horizon Press.

Jones, E. E. and K. E. Davis (1965). From Acts to Dispositions: The Attribution Process in Person Perception. In L. Berkowitz, ed., *Advances in Experimental Social Psychology*, vol. 2 (pp. 219–266). New York: Academic Press.

Jones, Stanley (1986). Sex Differences in Touch Communication. *Western Journal of Speech Communication* 50:227–241.

Jones, Stanley and A. Elaine Yarbrough (1985). A Naturalistic Study of the Meanings of Touch. *Communication Monographs* 52:19–56. A version of this paper appears in DeVito and Hecht (1990).

Jourard, Sidney M. (1968). *Disclosing Man to Himself*. New York: Van Nostrand Reinhold.

Jourard, Sidney M. (1971a). *Self-Disclosure*. New York: Wiley.

Jourard, Sidney M. (1971b). *The Transparent Self*, rev. ed. New York: Van Nostrand Reinhold.

Joyner, Russell (1993). An Auto-Interview on the Need for E-prime. *Etc.: A Review of General Semantics* 50 (Fall):317–325.

Kanner, Bernice (1989). Color Schemes. *New York Magazine* (April 3):22–23.

Kanter, Arnold B. (1995). *The Essential Book of Inteviewing: Everything You Need to Know from Both Sides of the Table*. New York: Random House [Times Books].

Kapoor, Suraj, Arnold Wolfe, and Janet Blue (1995). Universal Values Structure and Individualism-Collectivism: A U.S. Test. *Communication Research Reports* 12 (Spring):112–123.

Kearney, P., T.G. Plax, V.P. Richmond, and J.C. Mc-Croskey (1984). Power in the Classroom IV: Alternatives to Discipline. In Robert B. Bostrom, ed., *Communication Yearbook* 8th ed. (pp. 724–746). Thousand Oaks, CA: Sage.

Kelley, H. H. (1979). *Personal Relationships: Their Structures and Processes*. Hillsdale, NJ: Erlbaum.

Kelly, Lynne (1997). Skills Training as a Treatment for Communication Problems. In Daly, John A., James C. McCroskey, Joe Ayres, Tim Hopf, and Debbie M. Ayres (1997). *Avoiding Communication: Shyness, Reticence, and Communication Apprehension*, 2nd ed. (pp. 331–365). Cresskill, NJ: Hampton Press, Inc.

Kelly, P. Keith (1994). *Team Decision-Making Techniques*. Irvine, CA: Richard Chang Associates.

Kennedy, C. W. and C. T. Camden (1988). A New Look at Interruptions. *Western Journal of Speech Communication* 47:45–58.

Kim, Hyun J. (1991). Influence of Language and Similarity on Initial Intercultural Attraction. In Stella Ting-Toomey and Felipe Korzenny, eds., *Cross-Cultural Interpersonal Communication* (pp. 213–229). Thousand Oaks, CA: Sage.

Kim, Min-Sun and William F. Sharkey (1995). Independent and Interdependent Contruals of Self: Explaining Cultural Patterns of Interpersonal Communication in Multi-Cultural Organizational Settings. *Communication Quarterly* 43 (Winter):20–38.

Kim, Sung Hee and Richard H. Smith (1993). Revenge and Conflict Escalation. *Negotiation Journal* 9 (January):37–43.

Kim, Young Yun (1988). Communication and Acculturation. In In Larry A. Samovar and Richard E. Porter, eds., *Intercultural Communication: A Reader*, 4th ed. (pp. 344–354).

Kindler, Herbert S. (1996). *Managing Disagreement Constructively*, rev. ed. Menlo Park, CA: Crisp Publications.

King, Robert and Eleanor DiMichael (1992). *Voice and Diction*. Prospect Heights, IL: Waveland Press.

Klein, Jeremy, ed. (1992). Special Issue: The E-Prime Controversy: A Symposium. *Etc.: A Review of General Semantics* 49, No. 2.

Kleinfield, N. R. (1992). The Smell of Money. *New York Times* (October 25): 9:1, 8.

Kleinke, Chris L. (1986). *Meeting and Understanding People*. New York: W. H. Freeman.

Klineberg, O. and W. F. Hull (1979). *At a Foreign University: An International Study of Adaptation and Coping*. New York: Praeger.

Klopf, Donald W. (1997). Cross-Cultural Apprehension Research: Procedures and Comparsions. In Daly, John A., James C. McCroskey, Joe Ayres, Tim Hopf, and Debbie M. Ayres (1997). *Avoiding Communication: Shyness, Reticence, and Communication Apprehension*, 2nd ed. (pp. 269–284). Cresskill, NJ: Hampton Press, Inc.

Knapp, Mark and Judith Hall (1992). *Nonverbal Behavior in Human Interaction*, 3rd ed. New York: Holt, Rinehart and Winston.

Knapp, Mark L. and Gerald R. Miller, eds. (1995). *Handbook of Interpersonal Communication*, 2nd ed. Thousand Oaks, CA: Sage.

Knapp, Mark L. and Eric H. Taylor (1995). Commitment and Its Communication in Romantic Relationships. In Ann L. Weber and John H. Harvey, eds., *Perspectives on Close Relationships* (pp. 153–175). Boston, MA: Allyn and Bacon.

Knapp, Mark L. and Anita L. Vangelisti (1992). *Interpersonal Communication and Human Relationships,* 2nd ed. Boston, MA: Allyn and Bacon.

Kochman, Thomas (1981). *Black and White: Styles in Conflict.* Chicago, IL: University of Chicago Press.

Kohn, Alfie (1989). Do Religious People Help More? Not So You'd Notice. *Psychology Today* (December): 66–68.

Korzybski, A. (1933). *Science and Sanity.* Lakeville, CN: The International Non-Aristotelian Library.

Kramarae, Cheris (1981). *Women and Men Speaking.* Rowley, MA: Newbury House.

Krivonos, P. D. and M. L. Knapp (1975). Initiating Communication: What Do You Say When You Say Hello? *Central States Speech Journal* 26:115–125.

Kurdek, Lawrence A. (1994). Areas of Conflict for Gay, Lesbian, and Heterosexual Couples: What Couples Argue About Influences Relationship Satisfaction. *Journal of Marriage and the Family* 56 (November):923–934.

Kurdek, Lawrence A. (1995). Developmental Changes in Relationship Quality in Gay and Lesbian Cohabiting Couples. *Developmental Psychology* 31 (January):86–93.

Laing, Milli (1993). Gossip: Does It Play a Role in the Socialization of Nurses? *Journal of Nursing Scholarship* 25 (Spring):37–43.

Laing, Ronald D., H. Phillipson, and A. Russell Lee (1966). *Interpersonal Perception.* New York: Springer.

Lamm, Kathryn (1998). *10,000 Ideas for Term Papers, Projects, Reports, and Speeches,* 5th ed. New York: Macmillan [Arco].

Langer, Ellen J. (1989). *Mindfulness.* Reading, MA: Addison-Wesley.

Lanzetta, J. T., J. Cartwright-Smith, and R. E. Kleck (1976). Effects of Nonverbal Dissimulations on Emotional Experience and Autonomic Arousal. *Journal of Personality and Social Psychology* 33:354–370.

Larsen, Randy J., Margaret Kasimatis, and Kurt Frey (1992). Facilitating the Furrowed Brow: An Unobtrusive Test of the Facial Feedback Hyopothesis Applied to Unpleasant Affect. *Cognition and Emotion* 6 (September):321–338.

Lawlor, Julia (1998). Videoconferencing: From Stage Fright to Stage Presence. *New York Times* (August 27): G6.

Leathers, Dale G. (1986). *Successful Nonverbal Communication: Principles and Applications.* New York: Macmillan.

Lederer, William J. (1984). *Creating a Good Relationship.* New York: Norton.

Lederman, Linda (1990). Assessing Educational Effectiveness: The Focus Group Interview as a Technique for Data Collection. *Communication Education* 39:117–127.

Lee, Alfred McClung and Elizabeth Briant Lee (1972). *The Fine Art of Propaganda.* San Francisco, CA: International Society for General Semantics.

Lee, Alfred McClung and Elizabeth Briant Lee (1995). The Iconography of Propaganda Analysis. *ETC.: A Review of General Semantics* 52 (Spring):13–17.

Lee, John Alan (1973). Styles of Loving. *Psychology Today* 8:43–51.

Lee, John Alan (1976). *The Colors of Love.* New York: Bantam.

Lee, Raymond L. M. (1984). Malaysian Queue Culture: An Ethnography of Urban Public Behavior. *Southeast Asian Journal of Social Science* 12:36–50.

Leung, K. (1987). Some Determinants of Reactions to Procedural Models for Conflict Resolution: A Cross-National Study. *Journal of Personality and Social Psychology* 53:898–908.

Leung, Kwok (1988). Some Determinants of Conflict Avoidance. *Journal of Cross Cultural Psychology* 19 (March):125–136.

Levenger, George (1983). The Embrace of Lives: Changing and Unchanging. In George Levenger and Harold L. Raush, eds., *Close Relationships: Perspectives on the Meaning of Intimacy* (pp. 1–16). Amherst, MA: University of Massachusetts Press.

Lever, Janet (1995). The 1995 Advocate Survey of Sexuality and Relationships: The Women, Lesbian Sex Survey. *The Advocate* 687/688 (August 22):22–30.

Lewin, Kurt (1947). *Human Relations.* New York: Harper and Row.

Lewis, David (1989). *The Secret Language of Success.* New York: Carroll and Graf.

Lewis, Peter H. (1995). The New Internet Gatekeepers. *New York Times* (November 13): D1, D6.

Lindeman, Marjaana, Tuija Harakka, and Liisa Keltikangas-Jarvinen (1997). Age and Gender Differences in Adolescents' Reactions to Conflict Situations: Aggression, Prosociality, and Withdrawal. *Journal of Youth and Adolescence* 26 (June): 339–351.

Littlejohn, Stephen W. (1996). *Theories of Human Communication.* 5th ed. Belmont, CA: Wadsworth.

Loftus, Elizabeth F. (1979). *Eyewitness Testimony.* Cambridge, MA: Harvard University Press.

Lu, Shuming (1998). *Critical Reflections on Phatic Communication Research: Schematizations, Limitations and Alternatives.* Paper delivered at the New York State Speech Communication Association (October 9). Monticello, New York.

Luft, Joseph (1969). *Of Human Interaction*, 3rd ed. Palo Alto, CA: Mayfield Publishing Co.

Luft, Joseph (1984). *Group Processes: An Introduction to Group Dynamics*, 3rd ed. Palo Alto, CA: Mayfield Publishing.

Lumsden, Gay and Donald Lumsden (1996). *Communicating in Groups and Teams*, 2nd ed. Belmont, CA: Wadsworth.

Lustig, Myron W. and Jolene Koester (1999). *Intercultural Competence: Interpersonal Communication Across Cultures*, 3rd ed. New York: Longman.

Ma, Ringo (1992). The Role of Unofficial Intermediaries in Interpersonal Conflicts in the Chinese Culture. *Communication Quarterly* 40 (Summer): 269–278.

MacLachlan, John (1979). What People Really Think of Fast Talkers. *Psychology Today* 13 (November):113–117.

Main, Frank and Ronald Oliver (1988). Complementary, Symmetrical, and Parallel Personality Priorities as Indicators of Marital Adjustment. *Individual Psychology Journal of Adlerian Theory, Research, and Practice* 44 (September):324–332.

Malandro, Loretta A., Larry Barker, and Deborah Ann Barker (1989). *Nonverbal Communication*, 2nd ed. New York: Random House.

Malinowski, Bronislaw (1923). The Problem of Meaning in Primitive Languages. In C. K. Ogden and I. A. Richards, *The Meaning of Meaning* (pp. 296–336). New York: Harcourt Brace Jovanovich.

Manes, Joan and Nessa Wolfson (1981). The Compliment Formula. In Florian Coulmas, ed., *Conversational Routines* (pp. 115–132). The Hague: Mouton.

Mao, LuMing Robert (1994). Beyond Politeness Theory: 'Face' Revisited and Renewed. *Journal of Pragmatics* 21 (May):451–486.

Marien, Michael (1992). *Vital Speeches of the Day* (March 15): 340–344.

Markman, Howard J., Louise Silvern, Mari Clements, and Shelley Kraft-Hanak (1993). Men and Women Dealing with Conflict in Heterosexual Relationships. *Journal of Social Issues* 49 (Fall):107–125.

Marsh, Peter (1988). *Eye to Eye: How People Interact*. Topside, MA: Salem House.

Marshall, Evan (1983). *Eye Language: Understanding the Eloquent Eye*. New York: New Trend.

Marshall, Linda L. and Patricia Rose (1987). Gender, Stress, and Violence in the Adult Relationships of a Sample of College Students. *Journal of Social and Personal Relationships* 4:299–316.

Martin, Matthew M. and Carolyn M. Anderson (1995). Roommate Similarity: Are Roommates Who Are Similar in Their Communication Traits More Satisfied? *Communication Research Reports* 12 (Spring):46–52.

Martin, Scott L. and Richard J. Klimoski (1990). Use of Verbal Protocols to Trace Cognitions Associated with Self- and Supervisor Evaluations of Performance. *Organizational Behavior and Human Decision Processes* 46:135–154.

Matsumoto, David (1991). Cultural Influences on Facial Expressions of Emotion. *Southern Communication Journal* 56 (Winter):128–137.

Matsumoto, David (1994). *People: Psychology from a Cultural Perspective*. Pacific Grove, CA: Brooks/Cole.

McCombs, Maxwell E. and Donald L. Shaw (1972). The Agenda-Setting Function of Mass Media. *Public Opinion Quarterly* 36:176–185.

McCombs, Maxwell E. and Donald L. Shaw (1993). The Evolution of Agenda-Setting Research: Twenty-five Years in the Marketplace of Ideas. *Journal of Communication* 43:58–67.

McCroskey, James C. (1997). *Introduction to Rhetorical Communication*, 7th ed. Englewood Cliffs, NJ: Prentice-Hall.

McCroskey, James C. and Virginia P. Richmond (1995). Correlates of Compulsive Communication: Quantitative and Qualitative Characteristics. *Communication Quarterly* 43 (Winter):39–52.

McCroskey, James C., and Michael J. Beatty (1998). Communication Apprehension. In McCroskey, James C., John A. Daly, Matthew M. Martin, and Michael J. Beatty, , eds. (1998). *Communication and Personality: Trait Perspectives* (pp. 215–231). Cresskill, NJ: Hampton Press, Inc.

McGill, Michael E. (1985). *The McGill Report on Male Intimacy*. New York: Harper and Row.

McGuire, William J. (1964). Inducing Resistance to Persuasion: Some Contemporary Approaches. In Leonard Berkowitz, ed., *Advances in Experimental Social Psychology*, vol. 1 (pp. 191–229). New York: Academic Press.

McLaughlin, Margaret L. (1984). *Conversation: How Talk Is Organized*. Thousand Oaks, CA: Sage.

McLean, Paula A. and Brian D. Jones (1992). Machiavellianism and Business Education. *Psychological Reports* 71 (August): 57–58.

McLoyd, Vonnie and Leon Wilson (1992). Telling Them Like It Is: The Role of Economic and Environmental Factors in Single Mothers' Discussions with Their Children. *American Journal of Community Psychology* 20 (August):419–444.

Mehrabian, Albert (1976). *Public Places and Private Spaces*. New York: Basic Books.

Merton, Robert K. (1957). *Social Theory and Social Structure*. New York: Free Press.

Mesick, R. M. and K.S. Cook, eds. (1983). *Equity Theory: Psychological and Sociological Perspectives*. New York: Praeger.

Meyer, Janet R. (1994). Effect of Situational Features on the Likelihood of Addressing Face Needs in Requests. *Southern Communication Journal* 59 (Spring):240–254.

Millar, Frank E. and L. E. Rogers (1987). Relational Dimensions of Interpersonal Dynamics. In Michael E. Roloff and Gerald Miller, eds., *Interpersonal Processes: New Directions in Communication Research* (pp. 117–139). Thousand Oaks: Sage.

Miller, Dale T., William Turnbull, and Cathy McFarland (1988). Particularistic and Universalistic Evaluation in the Social Comparison Process. *Journal of Personality and Social Psychology* 55 (December):908–917.

Miller, Gerald R. (1978). The Current State of Theory and Research in Interpersonal Communication. *Human Communication Research* 4:164–178.

Miller, Gerald R. and Malcolm R. Parks (1982). Communication in Dissolving Relationships. In Steve Duck, ed., *Personal Relationships. 4: Dissolving Personal Relationships*. New York: Academic Press.

Miller, Gerald R. and Judee Burgoon (1990). Factors Affecting Assessments of Witness Credibility. In Joseph A. DeVito and Michael L. Hechts, eds., *The Nonverbal Communication Reader* (pp. 340–357). Prospect Heights, IL: Waveland Press.

Miller, J. G. (1984). Culture and the Development of Everyday Social Explanation. *Journal of Personality and Social Psychology* 46:961–978.

Moghaddam, Fathali M., Donald M. Taylor, and Stephen C. Wright (1993). *Social Psychology in Cross-Cultural Perspective*. New York: W. H. Freeman.

Molloy, J. (1981). *Molloy's Live for Success*. New York: Bantam.

Molloy, John (1975). *Dress for Success*. New York: P. H. Wyden.

Molloy, John (1977). *The Women's Dress for Success Book*. Chicago, IL: Foilet.

Mongeau, Paul A., Jerold L. Hale, and Marmy Alles (1994). An Experimental Investigation of Accounts and Attributions Following Sexual Infidelity. *Communication Monographs* 61 (December):326–344.

Montagu, Ashley (1971). *Touching: The Human Significance of the Skin*. New York: Harper and Row.

Moon, Dreama G. (1966). Concepts of 'Culture': Implications for Intercultural Communication Research. *Communication Quarterly* 44 (Winter): 70–84.

Moore, Q. L. (1993/1994). A "Whole New World" of Diversity. *Journal of Intergroup Relations* 20 (4): 28–40.

Morales, Jorge (1995). London: Death by Outing. *The Advocate* 680 (May 2):20–22.

Morris, Desmond (1977). *Manwatching: A Field Guide to Human Behavior*. New York: Abrams.

Muller, Brian, Edwardo Salas, and James Driskell (1989). Salience, Motivation, and Artifact as Contributions to the Relation Between Participation Rate and Leadership. *Journal of Experimental Social Psychology* 25 (November): 545–559.

Muller, Brian, Anthony Tara, Eduardo Salas, and James E. Driskell (1994). Group Cohesiveness and Quality of Decision Making: An Integration of Tests of the Groupthink Hypothesis. *Small Group Research* 25 (May):189–204.

Murata, Kumiko (1994). Intrusive or Co-operative? A Cross-Cultural Study of Interruption. *Journal of Pragmatics* 21 (April):385–400.

Naifeh, Steven and Gregory White Smith (1984). *Why Can't Men Open Up? Overcoming Men's Fear of Intimacy*. New York: Clarkson N. Potter.

Naisbitt, John (1984). *Megatrends: Ten New Directions Tranforming Our Lives*. New York: Warner.

Nakanishi, Masayuki (1986). Perceptions of Self-Disclosure in Initial Interaction: A Japanese Sample. *Human Communication Research* 13 (Winter): 167–190.

Napier, Rodney W. and Matti K. Gershenfeld (1992). *Groups: Theory and Experience*, 5th ed. Boston, MA: Houghton Mifflin.

Nash, Nathaniel C. (1995). Advertising. *The New York Times* (July 7):D6.

Neugarten, Bernice (1979). Time, Age, and the Life Cycle. *American Journal of Psychiatry* 136:887–894.

Nichols, Ralph (1961). Do We Know How to Listen? Practical Helps in a Modern Age. *Communication Education* 10: 118–124.

Nicotera, Anne Maydan and Andrew S. Rancer (1994). The Influence of Sex on Self-Perceptions and Social Stereotyping of Aggressive Communication Predispositions. *Western Journal of Communication* 58 (Fall):283–307.

Noelle-Neumann, Elisabeth (1973). Return to the concept of Powerful Mass Media. In H. Eguchi and K. Sata, eds., *Studies in Broadcasting: An International Annual of Broadcasting Science* (pp. 67–112). Tokyo: Nippon Hoso Kyokai.

Noelle-Neumann, Elisabeth (1980). Mass Media and Social Change in Developed Societies. In G. C. Wilhoit and H. de Bock, eds., *Mass Communication*

Review Yearbook, vol. 1 (pp. 657–678). Thousand Oaks, CA: Sage.

Noelle-Neumann, Elisabeth (1991). The Theory of Public Opinion: The Concept of the Spiral of Silence. In James A. Anderson, ed., *Communication Yearbook/14* (pp. 256–287). Thousand Oaks, CA: Sage.

Noller, Patricia (1993). Gender and Emotional Communication in Marriage: Different Cultures or Differential Social Power? Special Issue: Emotional Communication, Culture, and Power. *Journal of Language and Social Psychology* 12 (March-June):132–152.

Noller, Patricia and Mary Anne Fitzpatrick (1993). *Communication in Family Relationships*. Englewood Cliffs, NJ: Prentice Hall.

Northouse, Peter G. (1997). *Leadership: Theory and Practice*. Thousand Oaks, CA: Sage.

Norton, Robert and Barbara Warnick (1976). Assertiveness as a Communication Construct. *Human Communication Research* 3:62–66.

Oberg, Kalervo (1960). Cultural Shock: Adjustment to New Cultural Environments. *Practical Anthropology* 7:177–182.

Oggins, Jean, Joseph Veroff, and Douglas Leber (1993). Perceptions of Marital Interaction Among Black and White Newlyweds. *Journal of Personality and Social Psychology* 65 (September):494–511.

O'Hair, D., M.J. Cody, B. Goss, and K.J. Krayer (1988). The Effect of Gender, Deceit Orientation and Communicator Style on Macro-Assessments of Honesty. *Communication Quarterly* 36: 77–93.

Olday, David and Beverly Wesley (1990). Intimate Relationship Violence Among Divorcees. *Free Inquiry in Creative Sociology* 18 (May):63–71.

Osborn, Alex (1957). *Applied Imagination*, rev. ed. New York: Scribners.

Osborn, Michael and Suzanne Osborn (2000). *Speaking in Public*, 5th ed. Boston, MA: Houghton Mifflin.

Page, Richard A. and Joseph L. Balloun (1978). The Effect of Voice Volume on the Perception of Personality. *Journal of Social Psychology* 105: 65–72.

Patton, Bobby R., Kim Giffin, and Eleanor Nyquist Patton (1989). *Decision-Making Group Interaction*, 3rd ed. New York: HarperCollins.

Pearson, Judy C. (1980). Sex Roles and Self Disclosure. *Psychological Reports* 47:640.

Pearson, Judy C. and B. H. Spitzberg (1990). *Interpersonal Communication: Concepts, Components, and Contexts*, 2nd ed. Dubuque, IA: Wm. C. Brown.

Pearson, Judy C., Richard West, and Lynn H. Turner (1995). *Gender and Communication*, 3rd. ed. Dubuque, IA: Wm. C. Brown.

Peck, Janice (1995). TV Talk Shows as Therapeutic Discourse: The Ideological Labor of the Televised Talking Cure. *Communication Theory* 5 (February):58–81.

Pennebacker, James W. (1991). *Opening Up: The Healing Power of Confiding in Others*. New York: Avon.

Peters, Roger (1987). *Practical Intelligence: Working Smarter in Business and the Professions*. New York: HarperCollins.

Peterson, Candida C. (1996). The Ticking of the Social Clock: Adults' Beliefs about the Timing of Transition Events. *International Journal of Aging and Human Development* 42: 189–203.

Peterson, Russell W. (1985). *Vital Speeches of the Day* (July): 549.

Petronio, Sandra and Charles Bantz (1991). Controlling the Ramifications of Disclosure: "Don't Tell Anybody But . . ." *Journal of Language and Social Psychology* 10:263–269.

Phillips, Pamela A. and Lyle R. Smith (1992). The Effect of Teacher Dress on Student Perceptions. ERIC Document No. ED347151.

Philogene, Gina (1994). "African American" as a New Social Representation. *Journal of the Theory of Social Behaviour* 24 (June):89–109.

Pilkington, Constance J. and Deborah R. Richardson (1988). Perceptions of Risk in Intimacy. *Journal of Social and Personal Relationships* 5:503–508.

Piot, Charles D. (1993). Secrecy, Ambiguity, and the Everyday in Kabre Culture. *American Anthropologist* 95 (June):353–370.

Pittenger, R.E., C.F. Hockett, and J.J. Danehy (1960). *The First Five Minutes*. Ithaca, NY: Paul Martineau.

Place, Karen S. and Judith A. Becker (1991). The Influence of Pragmatic Competence on the Likeability of Grade School Children. *Discourse Processes* 14 (April-June):227–41.

Pollack, Andrew (1995). A Cyberspace Front in a Multicultural War. *New York Times* (August 7):D1, D4.

Porter, J. R. and R. E. Washington (1993). Minority Identity and Self-Esteem. *Annual Review of Sociology* 19:139–161.

Porter, R. H. and J. D. Moore (1981). Human Kin Recognition by Olfactory Cues. *Physiology and Behavior* 27:493–495.

Postman, Neil and Steve Powers (1992). *How to Watch TV News*. New York: Penguin.

Potter, Ellen F., and Sue V. Rosser (1992). Factors in Life Science Textbooks That May Deter Girls' Interest in Science. *Journal of Research in Science Teaching* 29 (September):669–686.

Potter, W. James (1986). Perceived Reality and the Cultivation Hypothesis. *Journal of Broadcasting and Electronic Media* 30:159–174.

Potter, W. James and Ik Chin Chang (1990). Television Exposure Measures and the Cultivation Hypothesis. *Journal of Broadcasting and Electronic Media* 34:313–333.

Pratkanis, Anthony and Elliot Aronson (1991). *Age of Propaganda: The Everyday Use and Abuse of Persuasion.* New York: W. H. Freeman.

Prisbell, Marshall (1994). Students' Perceptions of Teachers' Use of Affinity-Seeking and Its Relationship to Teachers' Competence. *Perceptual and Motor Skills* 78 (April):641–642.

Prosky, Phoebe S. (1992). Complementary and Symmetrical Couples. *Family Therapy* 19:215–221.

Prusank, Diane T., Robert L. Duran, and Dena A. DeLillo (1993). Interpersonal Relationships in Women's Magazines: Dating and Relating in the 1970s and 1980s. *Journal of Social and Personal Relationships* 10 (August):307–320.

Qubein, Nido R. (1986). *Get the Best from Yourself.* New York: Berkley.

Rabinowitz, Fredric E. (1991). The Male-to-Male Embrace: Breaking the Touch Taboo in a Men's Therapy Group. *Journal of Counseling and Development* 69 (July-August):574–576.

Radford, Marie L. (1998). Approach or Avoidance? The Role of Nonverbal Communication in the Academic Library User's Decision to Initiate a Reference Ecounter. *Library Trends* 46 (Spring): 699–717.

Ramsey, S. J. (1981). The Kinesics of Femininity in Japanese Women. *Language Sciences* 3:104–123.

Rancer, Andrew S. (1998). Argumentativeness. In McCroskey, James C., John A. Daly, Matthew M. Martin, and Michael J. Beatty, eds. (1998). *Communication and Personality: Trait Perspectives* (pp. 149–170). Cresskill, NJ: Hampton Press, Inc.

Rancer, Andrew S., Roberta L. Kosberg, and Robert A. Baukus (1992). Beliefs about Arguing as Predictors of Trait Argumentativeness: Implications for Training in Argument and Conflict Management. *Communication Education* 41 (October): 375–387.

Rankin, Paul (1929). Listening Ability. *Proceedings of the Ohio State Educational Conference's Ninth Annual Session.*

Raven, R., C. Centers, and A. Rodrigues (1975). The Bases of Conjugal Power. In R. E. Cromwell and D. H. Olson, eds., *Power in Families* (pp. 217–234). New York: Halsted Press.

Rawlins, William K. (1989). A Dialectical Analysis of the Tensions, Functions, and Strategic Challenges of Communication in Young Adult Friendships. In James A. Andersen, ed., *Communication Yearbook/12* (pp. 157–189). Thousand Oaks, CA: Sage.

Rawlins, William K. (1992). *Friendship Matters: Communication, Dialectics, and the Life Course.* Hawthorne, NY: Aldine DeGruyter.

Reardon, Kathleen K. (1987). *Where Minds Meet: Interpersonal Communication.* Belmont, CA.: Wadsworth.

Reynolds, Christina L. and Larry G. Schnoor, eds. (1991). *1989 Championship Debates and Speeches.* Normal, IL: American Forensic Association.

Richards, I. A. (1951). Communication Between Men: The Meaning of Language. In Heinz von Foerster, ed., *Cybernetics, Transactions of the Eighth Conference.*

Richmond, Virginia P. and James C. McCroskey (1998). *Communication: Apprehension, Avoidance, and Effectiveness,* 5th ed. Scottsdale, AZ: Gorsuch Scarisbrick.

Roach, David K. (1991). The Influence and Effects of Gender and Status on University Instructor Affinity-Seeking Behavior. *Southern Communication Journal* 57 (Fall):73–80.

Roberts, Wes (1987). *Leadership Secrets of Attila the Hun.* New York: Warner.

Robinson, Janet and Leslie Zebrowitz McArthur (1982). Impact of Salient Vocal Qualities on Casual Attribution for a Speaker's Behavior. *Journal of Personality and Social Psychology* 43: 236–247.

Robinson, W. Peter (1993). Lying in the Public Domain. *American Behavioral Scientist* 36 (January):359–382.

Rogers, Carl (1970). *Carl Rogers on Encounter Groups.* New York: Harrow Books.

Rogers, L. E., and R. V. Farace (1975). Analysis of Relational Communication in Dyads: New Measurement Procedures. *Human Communication Research* 1:222–239.

Rogers-Millar, Edna and Frank E. Millar (1979). Domineeringness and Dominance: A Transactional View. *Human Communication Research* (Spring):238–246.

Rosenbaum, M.E. (1986). The Repulsion Hypothesis. On the Nondevelopment of Relationships. *Journal of Personality and Social Psychology* 51: 1156–1166.

Rosenfeld, Lawrence (1979). Self-Disclosure Avoidance: Why I Am Afraid to Tell You Who I Am? *Communication Monographs* 46 (1979):63–74.

Rosenfeld, Lawrence B. and Gary L. Bowen (1991). Marital Disclosure and Marital Satisfaction: Direct-Effect versus Interaction-Effect Models. *Western Journal of Speech Communication* 55 (Winter):69–84.

Rosenthal, Robert and B. M. DePaulo (1979). Sex Differences in Accommodation in Nonverbal Communication. In Robert Rosenthal, ed., *Skill in Nonverbal Communication: Individual Differences* (pp. 68–103). Cambridge, MA: Oelgeschlager, Gunn and Hain.

Rosenthal, Robert and L. Jacobson (1968). *Pygmalion in the Classroom*. New York: Holt, Rinehart and Winston.

Rotello, Gabriel (1995). The Inning of Outing. *The Advocate* 679 (April 18):80.

Rothwell, J. Dan (1992). *In Mixed Company: Small Group Communication*. Fort Worth, TX: Harcourt Brace Jovanovich.

Ruben, Brent D. (1985). Human Communication and Cross-Cultural Effectiveness. In Larry A. Samovar and Richard E. Porter, eds., *Intercultural Communication: A Reader*, 4th ed. (pp. 338–356). Belmont, CA: Wadsworth.

Rubenstein, Carin and Philip Shaver (1982). *In Search of Intimacy*. New York: Delacorte.

Rubin, Alan M. (1994). News Credibility Scale. In R. B. Rubin, P. Palmgreen, and H. E. Sypher, eds., *Communication Research Measures: A Source Book*. New York: Guilford Press.

Rubin, Alan, Elizabeth Pearse, and Robert Powell (1985). Loneliness, Parasocial Interaction, and Local Television News Viewing. *Human Communication Research* 12:155–180

Rubin, Rebecca and Michael McHugh (1987). Development of Parasocial Interaction Relationships. *Journal of Broadcasting and Electronic Media* 31:279–292.

Rubin, Rebecca B. (1982). Assessing Speaking and Listening Competence at the College Level: The Communication Competency Assessment Instrument. *Communication Education* 31 (January):19–32.

Rubin, Rebecca B. (1985). The Validity of the Communication Competency Assessment Instrument. *Communication Monographs* 52:173–185.

Rubin, Rebecca B. and Alan M. Rubin (1992). Antecedents of Interpersonal Communication Motivation. *Communication Quarterly* 40:3–5–317.

Rubin, Rebecca B., and M. M. Martin (1994). Development of a Measure of Interpersonal Communication Competence. *Communication Research Reports* 11:33–44.

Rubin, Rebecca B., and Matthew M. Martin (1998). Interpersonal Communication Motives. In Mc-Croskey, James C., John A. Daly, Matthew M. Martin, and Michael J. Beatty, eds. (1998). *Communication and Personality: Trait Perspectives* (pp. 287–307). Cresskill, NJ: Hampton Press, Inc.

Rubin, Rebecca B., C. Fernandez-Collado, and R. Hernandez-Sampieri (1992). A Cross-Cultural Examination of Interpersonal Communication Motives in Mexico and the United States. *International Journal of Intercultural Relations* 16:145–157.

Rubin, Rebecca B., Elizabeth M. Perse, and Carole A. Barbato (1988). Conceptualization and Measurement of Interpersonal Communication Motives. *Human Communication Research* 14:602–628.

Rubin, Zick (1973). *Liking and Loving: An Invitation to Social Psychology*. New York: Holt.

Rubin, Zick and Elton B. McNeil (1985). *Psychology: Being Human*, 4th ed. New York: Harper and Row.

Rundquist, Suellen (1992). Indirectness: A Gender Study of Fluting Grice's Maxims. *Journal of Pragmatics* 18 (November):431–449.

Rusbult, Caryl E. and Bram P. Buunk (1993). Commitment Processes in Close Relationships: An Interdependence Analysis. *Journal of Social and Personal Relationships* 10 (May):175–204.

Sabatelli, Ronald M. and John Pearce (1986). Exploring Marital Expectations. *Journal of Social and Personal Relationships* 3:307–321.

Samovar, Larry A. and Richard E. Porter (1995). *Communication Between Cultures*, 2nd ed. Belmont, CA: Wadsworth.

Sanders, Judith A, Richard L. Wiseman, and S. Irene Matz (1991). Uncertainty Reduction in Acquaintance Relationships in Ghana and the United States. In Stella Ting-Toomey and Felipe Korzenny, eds., *Cross-Cultural Interpersonal Communication* (pp. 79–98) . Thousand Oaks, CA: Sage.

Sayre, Shay (1992). T-shirt Messages: Fortune or Folly for Advertisers? In Sammy R. Danna, ed., *Advertising and Popular Culture* (pp. 73–82). Bowling Green, OH: Bowling Green State University Popular Press.

Schaap, C., B. Buunk, and A. Kerkstra (1988). Marital Conflict Resolution. In Patricia Noller and Mary Anne Fitzpatrick, eds., *Perspectives on Marital Interaction* (pp. 203–244). Philadelphia, PA: Multilingual Matters.

Scherer, K. R. (1986). Vocal Affect Expression. *Psychological Bulletin* 99: 143–165.

Schmidley, Dianne and Herman A. Alvarado (1997). *The Foreign-Born Population in the United States: March 1997* (Update). Washington, DC: US Bureau of the Census.

Schramm, Wilbur (1988). *The Story of Human Communication: Cave Painting to Microchip*. New York: Harper and Row.

Schramm, Wilbur and William E. Porter (1982). *Men, Women, Messages and Media: Understanding Human Communication*. New York: Harper and Row.

Schultz, Beatrice G. (1996). *Communicating in the Small Group: Theory and Practice*, 2nd ed. New York: HarperCollins.

Schwartz, Marilyn and the Task Force on Bias-Free Language of the Association of American University Presses (1995). *Guidelines for Bias-Free Writing*. Bloomington, IN: Indiana University Press.

Scott, Dini Graham (1994). *The Truth about Lying*. Petaluma, CA: Smart Publications.

Seidman, I. E. (1991). *Interviewing as Qualitative Research: A Guide for Researchers* in *Education and the Social Sciences*. New York: Teachers College, Columbia University.

Severin, Werner J. with James W. Tankard, Jr. (1988). *Communication Theories*, 2nd ed. New York: Longman.

Shaffer, David R., Linda J. Pegalis, and David P. Cornell (1992). Gender and Self-Disclosure Revisited: Personal and Contextual Variations in Self-Disclosure to Same-Sex Acquaintants. *Journal of Social Psychology* 132 (June):307–315.

Shannon, J. (1987). Don't Smile When You Say That. *Executive Female* 10:33, 43. Reprinted in DeVito and Hecht (1990), 115–117.

Shaw, Marvin E. and Dennis S. Gouran (1990). Group Dynamics and Communication. In Gordon al. Dahnke and Glen W. Clatterbuck, eds., *Human Communication: Theory and Research*. Belmont, CA: Wadsworth.

Shea, Virginia (1994). *Netiquette*. Albion Books.

Shimanoff, Susan (1980). *Communication Rules: Theory and Research*. Thousand Oaks, CA: Sage.

Shimanoff, Susan B. (1985). Rules Governing the Verbal Expression of Emotions Between Married Couples. *Western Journal of Speech Communication* 49 (Summer):147–165.

Shuter, Robert (1990). The Centrality of Culture. *Southern Communication Journal* 55 (Spring): 237–249.

Siegert, John R. and Glen H. Stamp (1994). 'Our First Big Fight' as a Milestone in the Development of Close Relationships. *Communication Monographs* 61 (December):345–360.

Signorielli, Nancy and Margaret Lears (1992). Children, Television, and Concepts about Chores: Attitudes and Behaviors. *Sex Roles* 27 (August): 157–170.

Signorile, Michelangelo (1993). *Queer in America: Sex, the Media, and the Closets of Power*. New York: Random House.

Sincoff, Michael Z. and Robert S. Goyer (1984). *Interviewing*. New York: Macmillan.

Skopec, Eric William. *Situational Interviewing*. Prospect Heights, IL: Waveland Press, 1986.

Slade, Margot (1995). We Forgot to Write a Headline. But It's Not Our Fault. *New York Times* (February 19):5.

Snyder, C. R. (1984). Excuses, Excuses. *Psychology Today* 18:50–55.

Snyder, C. R., Raymond L. Higgins, and Rita J. Stucky (1983). *Excuses: Masquerades in Search of Grace*. New York: Wiley.

Snyder, Mark (1987). *Public Appearances, Private Realities*. New York: W. H. Freeman.

Snyder, Maryhelen (1992). A Gender-Informed Model of Couple and Family Therapy: Relationship Enhancement Therapy. *Contemporary Family Therapy: An International Journal* 14 (February):15–31.

Sommer, Robert (1969). *Personal Space: The Behavioral Basis of Design*. Englewood Cliffs, NJ: Prentice-Hall [Spectrum].

Sorenson, Paula S., Katherine Hawkins, and Ritch L. Sorenson (1995). Gender, Psychological Type and Conflict Style Preferences. *Management Communication Quarterly* 9 (August): 115–126.

Spitzberg, Brian H. (1991). Intercultural Communication Competence. In Larry A. Samovar and Richard E. Porter, eds., *Intercultural Communication: A Reader* (pp. 353–365). Belmont, CA: Wadsworth.

Spitzberg, Brian H. and William R. Cupach (1984). *Interpersonal Communication Competence*. Beverly Hills, CA: Sage.

Spitzberg, Brian H. and William R. Cupach (1989). *Handbook of Interpersonal Competence Research*. New York: Springer-Verlag.

Spitzberg, Brian H. and Michael L. Hecht (1984). A Component Model of Relational Competence. *Human Communication Research* 10:575–599.

Sprecher, Susan and Sandra Metts (1989). Development of the "Romantic Beliefs Scale" and Examination of the Effects of Gender and Gender-Role Orientation. *Journal of Social and Personal Relationships* 6: 387–411.

Staines, Graham L., Kathleen J. Pottick, and Deborah A. Fudge (1986). Wives' Employment and Husbands' Attitudes Toward Work and Life. *Journal of Applied Psychology* 71:118–128.

Steil, Lyman K., Larry L. Barker, Kittie W. Watson (1983). *Effective Listening: Key to Your Success*. Reading, MA: Addison-Wesley.

Steinfatt, Thomas M. (1987). Personality and Communication: Classic Approaches. In James C. McCroskey and John A. Daly, eds., *Personality and Interpersonal Communication* (pp. 42–126). Thousand Oaks, CA: Sage.

Stephan, Walter G. and Cookie White Stephan (1985). Intergroup Anxiety. *Journal of Social Issues* 41:157–175.

Stephan, Walter G., Cookie White Stephan, Brenda Wenzel, and Jeffrey Cornelius (1991). Intergroup Interaction and Self-Disclosure. *Journal of Applied Social Psychology* 21 (August):1370–1378.

Stewart, Charles J. and William B. Cash, Jr. (1988). *Interviewing: Principles and Practices*, 4th ed. Dubuque, IA: Wm. C. Brown.

Stillings, Neil A., et al. (1987). *Cognitive Science: An Introduction*. Cambridge, MA: MIT Press.

Strecker, Ivo (1993). Cultural Variations in the Concept of 'Face.' *Multilingua* 12:119–141.

Swan, W. B., Jr. (1987). Identity Negotiation: Where Two Roads Meet. *Journal of Personality and Social Psychology* 53:1038–1051.

Swensen, C. H. (1973). *Introduction to Interpersonal Relations*. Glenview, IL: Scott, Foresman.

Swets, Paul W. (1983). *The Art of Talking so that People Will Listen*. Englewood Cliffs, NJ: Prentice-Hall/Spectrum.

Tannen, Deborah (1990). *You Just Don't Understand: Women and Men in Conversation*. New York: William Morrow.

Tannen, Deborah (1994a). *Gender and Discourse*. New York: Oxford University Press.

Tannen, Deborah (1994b). *Talking from 9 to 5: How Women's and Men's Conversational Styles Affect Who Gets Heard, Who Gets Credit, and What Gets Done at Work*. New York: William Morrow.

Thibaut, John W. and Harold H. Kelley (1986). *The Social Psychology of Groups*. New Brunswick, NJ: Transaction Books.

Thorne, Barrie, Cheris Kramarae, and Nancy Henley, eds. (1983). *Language, Gender and Society*. Rowley, MA: Newbury House Publishers.

Tichenor, P. J., G. A. Donohue, and C. N. Olien (1970). Mass Media Flow and Differential Growth in Knowledge. *Public Opinion Quarterly* 34:159–170.

Ting-Toomey, Stella (1985). Toward a Theory of Conflict and Culture. *International and Intercultural Communication Annual* 9:71–86.

Ting-Toomey, Stella (1986). Conflict Communication Styles in Black and White Subjective Cultures. In Young Yun Kim, ed. *Interethnic Communication: Current Research* (pp. 75–88). Thousand Oaks, CA: Sage.

Torbiorn, I. (1982). *Living Abroad*. New York: Wiley.

Trager, George L. (1958). Paralangauge: A First Approximation. *Studies in Linguistics* 13:1–12.

Trower, P. (1981). Social Skill Disorder. In S. Duck and R. Gilmour, eds., *Personal Relationships* 3 (pp. 97–110). New York: Academic Press.

Tschann, J. M. (1988). Self-Disclosure in Adult Friendship: Gender and Marital Status Differences. *Journal of Social and Personal Relationships* 5: 65–81.

Ueleke, William, et al. (1983). Inequity Resolving Behavior as a Response to Inequity in a Hypothetical Marital Relationship. *A Quarterly Journal of Human Behavior* 20:4–8.

UNESCO [United Nations Education, Scientific, and Cultural Organization] (1993). *World Education Report*. Paris, France: UNESCO Publishing.

Valenti, Jack (1982). *Speaking Up with Confidence: How to Prepare, Learn, and Deliver Effective Speeches*. New York: William Morrow.

Verderber, Rudolph (2000). *The Challenge of Effective Speaking*, 11th ed. Belmont, CA: Wadsworth.

Vernon, JoEtta A., J. Allen Williams, Terri Phillips, and Janet Wilson (1990). Media Stereotyping: A Comparison of the Way Elderly Women and Men Are Portrayed on Prime-Time Television. *Journal of Women and Aging* 4:55–68.

Victor, David (1992). *International Business Communication*. New York: Harper Collins.

Viswanath, K. and John R. Finnegan, Jr. (1995). The Knowledge-Gap Hypothesis: Twenty-Five Years Later. In Brant R. Burleson, ed., *Communication Yearbook/19*. Thousand Oaks, CA: Sage.

Walster, E., G. W. Walster, and E. Berscheid (1978). *Equity: Theory and Research*. Boston, MA: Allyn and Bacon.

Watson, Arden K. and Cadey H. Dodd (1984). Alleviating Communication Apprehension through Rational Emotive Therapy: A Comparative Evaluation. *Communication Education* 33:257–266.

Watzlawick, Paul (1977). *How Real Is Real? Confusion, Disinformation, Communication: An Anecdotal Introduction to Communications Theory*. New York: Vintage Books.

Watzlawick, Paul (1978). *The Language of Change: Elements of Therapeutic Communication*. New York: Basic Books.

Watzlawick, Paul, Janet Helmick Beavin, and Don D. Jackson (1967). *Pragmatics of Human Communi-

cation: A Study of Interactional Patterns, Pathologies, and Paradoxes. New York: Norton.

Weinstein, Eugene A. and Paul Deutschberger (1963). Some Dimensions of Altercasting. *Sociometry* 26:454–466.

Weinstein, Fannie (1995). Professionally Speaking. *Profiles: The Magazine of Continental Airlines* 8 (April): 50–55.

Werner, Elyse K. (1975). *A Study of Communication Time.* M. A. Thesis, University of Maryland, College Park. Cited in Wolvin and Coakley (1982).

West, Daniel V. (1995). *Further Validity Assessment of the News Credibility Scale.* Paper presented at the Eastern Communication Association Convention (Pittsburgh, April 27–30).

Westwood, R. I., F. F. Tang, and P. S. Kirkbride (1992). Chinese Conflict Behavior: Cultural Antecedents and Behavioral Consequences. *Organizational Development Journal* 10 (Summer): 13–19.

Wetzel, Patricia J. (1988). Are 'Powerless' Communication Strategies the Japanese Norm? *Language in Society* 17:555–564.

Wheeless, Lawrence R. and Janis Grotz (1977). The Measurement of Trust and Its Relationship to Self-Disclosure. *Human Communication Research* 3:250–257.

Wigley, Charles J., III (1998). Verbal Aggressiveness. In McCroskey, James C., John A. Daly, Matthew M. Martin, and Michael J. Beatty, eds. (1998). *Communication and Personality: Trait Perspectives* (pp. 191–214). Cresskill, NJ: Hampton Press, Inc.

Wilmot, William W. (1987). *Dyadic Communication,* 3rd ed. New York: Random House.

Wilson, A. P. and Thomas G. Bishard (1994). Here's the Dirt on Gossip. *American School Board Journal* 181 (December):27–29.

Wilson, R. A. (1989). Toward Understanding E-prime. *Etc.: A Review of General Semantics* 46:316–319.

Winhahl, Sven and Benno Signitzer with Jean T. Olson (1992). *Using Communication Theory: An Introduction to Planned Communication.* Thousand Oaks, CA: Sage.

Wolfson, Nessa (1988). The Bulge: A Theory of Speech Behaviour and Social Distance. In J. Fine, ed., *Second Language Discourse: A Textbook of Current Research* (pp. 21–38). Norwood, NJ: Ablex.

Wolpe, Joseph (1958). *Psychotherapy by Reciprocal Inhibition.* Stanford, CA: Stanford University Press.

Wolvin, Andrew D. and Carolyn Gwynn Coakley (1982). *Listening.* Dubuque, IA: Wm. C. Brown.

Won-Doornink, Myong-Jin (1985). Self-Disclosure and Reciprocity in Conversation: A Cross-National Study. *Social Psychology Quarterly* 48:97–107.

Won-Doornink, Myong Jin (1991). Self-Disclosure and Reciprocity in South Korean and U.S. Male Dyads. In Stella Ting-Toomey and Felipe Korzenny, eds., *Cross-Cultural Interpersonal Communication* (pp. 116–131). Thousand Oaks, CA: Sage.

Woodward, Kenneth L. (1998). Religion: Using the Bully Pulpit? *Time* (June 22): 69.

Zima, Joseph P. (1983). *Interviewing: Key to Effective Management.* Chicago, IL: Science Research Associations, Inc.

Zincoff, M. Z. and Robert S. Goyer (1984). *Interviewing.* New York: Macmillan.

Zuckerman, M., R. Klorman, D. T. Larrance, and N. H. Spiegel (1981). Facial, Autonomic, and Subjective Components of Emotion: The Facial Feedback Hypothesis Versus the Externalizer-Internalizer Distinction. *Journal of Personality and Social Psychology* 41:929–944.

CREDITS

PHOTOS

Chapter 1 Page 1: © Bob Daemmrich/The Image Works; 8: © Mary Kate Denny/Photo Edit; 12: © David R. Frazier

Chapter 2 Page 20: © Michael Newman/Photo Edit; 23: © Grunnitus Studios/Monkmeyer; 31: © Sotographs/Liaison International

Chapter 3 Page 37: © The Kobal Collection; 46: © Art Montes de Oca/FPG International; 48: © Robert Brenner/Photo Edit

Chapter 4 Page 56: © Hazel Hankin/Stock Boston; 65: © Joseph Nettis/Tony Stone Images; 70: © Jon Riley/Tony Stone Images

Chapter 5 Page 73: © Bob Daemmrich/Stock Boston; 79: © AP/Wide World Photos; 81: © Jim Whitmer

Chapter 6 Page 89: © Chuck Savage/The Stock Market; 97: © Roger Tully/Tony Stone Images; 100: © Jon Riley/Tony Stone Images

Chapter 7 Page 107: © Hugh Scott/Liaison International; 112: © Felicia Martinez/Photo Edit; 124: © Timothy Shonnard/Tony Stone Images

Chapter 8 Page 129: © Bob Daemmrich/Stock Boston; 137: © Globe Photos, Inc.; 141: © Myrleen Ferguson/Photo Edit; 149: © Jim Whitmer;

Chapter 9 Page 152: © OkoniewskiThe Image Works; 154: © John Coletti/Stock Boston; 171: © Yellow Dog Productions/The Image Bank

Chapter 10 Page 174: © Jim Whitmer; 192: © David Harry Stewart/Tony Stone Images; 198: © David Joel/Tony Stone Images

Chapter 11 Page 200: © Jim Whitmer; 206: © John Nordell/The Image Works; 209: © Billy Barnes/Photo Edit

Chapter 12 Page 219: © Bob Daemmrich/The Image Works; 221: © Yvette Vega/Rose Communications; 235: © Chuck Savage/The Stock Market

Chapter 13 Page 238: © Jean-Marc Giboux/Liaison International; 241: © Steve Niedorf/The Image Bank; 250: © Charles Gupton/Stock Boston

Chapter 14 Page 260: © Dan Bosler/Tony Stone Images; 270: © Walter Hodges/Tony Stone Images; 276: © Bob Daemmrich/Stock Boston

Chapter 15 Page 279: © Michael Newman/Photo Edit; 291: © Bob Daemmrich/Stock Boston; 298: © B.W. Hoffmann/Unicorn Stock Photos

Chapter 16 Page 307: © 1999 ABC, Inc.; 325: © Carl J. Single/The Image Works

Chapter 17 Page 334: © Joe Gaffney/Retna Limited, USA; 362: Walter hodges/Tony Stone Images; 349: © M. Schwarz/The Image Works

Chapter 18 Page 362: © Walter Hodges/Tony Stone Images; 365: © McLaughlin/The Image Works; 371: © Richard Hutchings/Photo Edit

Chapter 19 Page 379: © Tom Stewart/The Stock Market; 383: © Bob Daemmrich/Stock Boston; 386: © Rich Baker/Unicorn Stock Photos;

WEB SITES

Chapter 1 Page 13: © National Communication Association. Used by permission.

Chapter 2 Page 30: © International Communication Association. Reprinted by permission.

Chapter 3 Page 51: Reprinted by permission of Steven Morgan Friedman. All rights reserved.

Chapter 4 Page 63: © International Listening Association. Reprinted by permission.

Chapter 5 Page 87: Reprinted by permission of Self Improvement Online, Inc. http://www.selfgrowth.com

Chapter 6 Page 92: Copyright © Worldbiz.com. Reprinted by permission.

Chapter 7 Page 117: Copyright © International Linguistics Center, Dallas.

Chapter 8 Page 147: Copyright © Go2Net, Inc. Reprinted by permission.

Chapter 9 Page 163: © Addison-Wesley Longman

Chapter 10 Page 195: © Nando Times. Reprinted by permission.

Chapter 11 Page 210: © Family Violence Prevention Fund. Reprinted by permission.

Chapter 12 Page 227: © Monster.com. Reprinted by permission.

Chapter 13 Page 244: © NeoSoft Inc. Reprinted by permission.

Chapter 14 Page 265: Reprinted by permission of CASAA Publications.

Chapter 15 Page 297: © Liszt. Reprinted by permission.
Page 303: Reprinted by permission of College and Research Library news.

Chapter 16 Page 314: Courtesy of FedStats.

Chapter 17 Page 350: Reprinted by permission of Douglas Archives of American Public Address. All rights reserved.

Chapter 18 Page 369: © Addison-Wesley Longman
Page 370: Courtesy of Liz Linton, Sweet Briar College.

Chapter 19 Page 385: Reprinted by permission of the author. Note sources: *Propaganda Analysis, 1938, Institute for Propaganda Analysis, Columbia University Press; The Fine Art of Propaganda, 1939, Institute for Propaganda Analysis*, Harcourt, Brace, and Company. See other references listed on the web site.
Page 395: © Humanities Department and the Arthur C. Banks, Jr., Library, Capital Community Technical College, Hartford, CT. Reprinted by permission.

INDEX